POSTBRIDGE

THE HEART OF DARTMOOR

REG BELLAMY

I drew my breath first on this moor;
There my forefathers dwelled;
Its hills and dales I've traversed o'er,
Its desert parts beheld.
Jonas Coaker

DEVON BOOKS

First published in Great Britain in 1998

British Library Cataloguing-in-Publication Data
A CIP record for this title is available from the British Library

ISBN 1 8522 645 6

DEVON BOOKS
OFFICIAL PUBLISHER TO DEVON COUNTY COUNCIL

in association with

HALSGROVE
PUBLISHING, MEDIA AND DISTRIBUTION

Halsgrove House
Lower Moor Way
Tiverton, Devon EX16 6SS
Tel: 01884 243242
Fax: 01884 243325

DEDICATION

My Father and Mother, Jack and Elsie Bellamy,
and my wife to whom I owe so much.

Printed and bound in Great Britain by Bookcraft Ltd, Midsomer Norton

Contents

Acknowledgements

My thanks go to Mr Robert (deceased), and Mrs Arrowsmith-Brown (history of Archerton with photographs and Postbridge Church), Mr and Mrs Fisher (Lakehead), Mr and Mrs David Cooper (Bridge Cottage and the Warne family), Mr and Mrs Farrow (Dart Cottage-sight of plans relating to Admiral Sturdee's conversion of the property), Mr McMurtree (Penlee, details of its history and sight of original plans), Lt-Com. Leadgate (Redgate/Durnford Cottage history). Mr and Mrs Tom Webb and Mrs Emmie Webb (Stannon Lodges, The Church and Village Hall), Mr M.L.J.(Bob) White (papers relating to Lower Merripit, field names and permission to quote from Miss Annie Sleep's articles in *Parish Pump*), Miss Jennie White (Higher Merripit - photographs), Mr and Mrs Bishop (Hartyland), Mr and Mrs Adaway (Dury - details of its history including sight of relevant papers), Mr James Martin (Bellever Youth Hostel and Postbridge Village Hall), Miss Lily Toms (deceased) - (sight of papers relating to the land at Pencroft), Mrs Dorothy Williams and Mrs Eileen Exell (Higher Lydgate - photographs and details of the Dawe family), Mrs Anthea Johnson (Details of the Chudleigh family), Mr Dave Brewer (history and maps of Headland),

Dr Tom and Elizabeth Greeves (photographs, mining information and encouragement), Mr and Mrs B. Klamman (Soussans photographs), Mr Stephen Arrowsmith-Brown (Vaglas and Soussans), Mr Jack Irish (deceased) - (information about Challacombe and the Irish family), Mr Philip Coaker (Runnage and Walna), Mrs B.Brooks (Torview - information about Caroline and the Hannaford's of Headland), Miss C.Belam (Coaker family history), Miss Jill Money (The Williamson family history and East Dart and Dartfordleigh), Mrs Eva Webb (deceased) - (Ferndale, the mines, Postbridge Home Guard, Capt James Webb family history), Michael Lockton FRPS. (Dartmoor postal history), Mr John Marchant and Mr Bob Hudson (British Trust for Ornithology). Particular thanks are due to Lady Sylvia Sayer for the photographs from her Grandfather, Robert Burnard.

The archivists at the Devon Record Office and the Public Record Office at Kew and Chancery Lane. The archivist at the Duchy of Cornwall Office, London, and Mr Colin Sturmer at the Duchy of Cornwall Office, Princetown. The Archivists at the Telecom Technology Showcase and at the Post Office Archives. The librarians at Poppleton for their efforts in obtaining out of print Westcountry books. The librarian of York Minster Library for help in tracing the rectors, vicars and curates of the Lydford, Princetown and Postbridge Churches. Mr Jan Kaluski for drawing the field maps from my draft copies.

Finally my long suffering wife for all her help with research and the correction of drafts. Wherever feasible I have tried to check verbal information against documents but this has not always been possible, because old documents are not easy to read, and spellings of surnames and place names are not always consistent; variations occur throughout the book.

FOREWORD

Dartmoor is fascinating because it is a landscape which, largely due to its climate and terrain, has absorbed and retained successive evidence of human occupation over thousands of years. Here, lying side-by-side, can be seen the 3000 year-old dwellings of our ancestors, alongside medieval wayside crosses, overlooking mine workings where tin and copper were wrested from the ground well within living memory. Add to this scene the patterns laid down by successive generations of farmers and we are left with a unique landscape spanning almost six thousand years of human settlement.

It is hardly surprising that such a landscape has inspired and intrigued writers over the last two or three hundred years, culminating in a veritable deluge of books in the years running up to the end of the present century. Many of these works add greatly to our understanding of the past, and help towards the management and conservation of this complex environment. But what is so often missing from such books is the personal element which reveals to us the detail of everyday life on Dartmoor in the past – or at least as far back as memory and photography can take us. In this sense alone we should set a great value on the work of authors such as Reg Bellamy, who has recorded here so much of that 'real' history of Postbridge. Without his determination to collect together memories, photographs and memorabilia of his birthplace, this important facet of our past would be irretrievably lost.

John Weir
Communications Officer
Dartmoor National Park Authority
Parke – 1998.

Postbridge clapper bridge, April 1889. (R. Burnard)

INTRODUCTION

Strictly speaking the name Postbridge applies to a 'cyclopean' pack-horse bridge over the River East Dart. The derivation of the name is obscure, and when the bridge was built is not known. The reason for building it, who the builders were, and where the stones came from is also open to conjecture.

Gradually cottages and Inns were built close by. These and the local Ancient Tenements formed a village which took its name from the bridge. Later still the name became associated with a postal area and included many more properties. This book is, in the main, a history of these properties and of the people who lived in them. For as long as I can remember I have loved the village, after all, my roots are there.

Its history has fascinated me and I loved to talk about it to my family and to the old villagers, most of whom have passed on. They never begrudged the time spent talking to me and since I started writing this book I have received courtesy and help from everyone I approached and for this I am most grateful.

Distant view of Postbridge, 1889. Note the ruins at Barracks in the foreground. (R. Burnard)

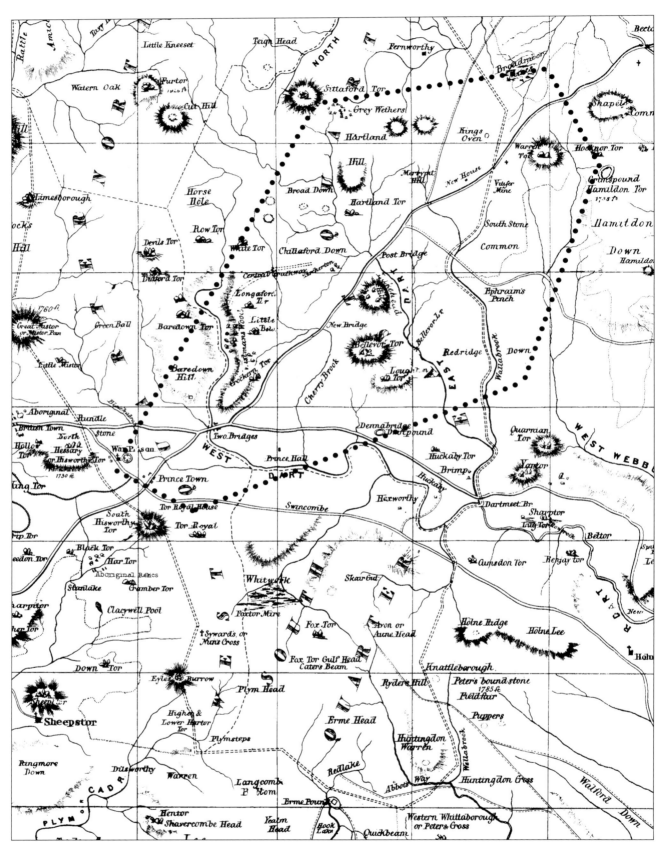

Central Dartmoor from Samuel Rowe's map first published in 1848, The dotted line shows the approximate area covered in this book.

Chapter 1 - The Bridges

EARLY OCCUPATION

With the exception of the Ancient Tenements the village as it is seen today is modern with only a few houses dating back to the end of the eighteenth century. There is however plenty of evidence of early occupation dating back to about 3500BC. Around Postbridge quantities of worked flints and flint chips have been found on the surface and, close to the Post Office, a cache of flints was found some 4 to 5ft under the surface in a 'clitter' of rocks.

Within easy walking distance there are rings and hut circles and, from a later date, evidence of stream-working for tin in Greyhound Marsh. It is there that the remains of a tinner's hut which had been built into a bank may be found, unfortunately over the years the site has suffered some damage from the tipping of rubbish.

There is still much to be learned about the occupation of the area and it is interesting to note that the severe gales which damaged Archerton Ring uncovered the sites of some ancient dwellings.

Cache of flints found between 4–5 feet in a clitter of rocks at Postbridge Post Office. (Author)

THE CLAPPER BRIDGE.

Many centuries ago the site of the bridge would have been covered by a lake as evidenced by the finds of ball clay and china clay in Archerton Marsh, around the bridge and in the 'Straps' (see the map on page 20). Eventually the waters of the lake broke through at Jester Hole and the area was drained towards Bellever, probably following the existing course of the East Dart.

It was across this river that the clapper bridge was built. The best description of the bridge is undoubtedly William Crossing's. In his *Guide to Dartmoor* he wrote:

It is the finest example of these interesting objects on the moor. It is 42ft.-8ins.long and consists of three openings and the buttresses and piers are formed of large blocks of granite carefully fitted and dry laid. The upper ends of the piers are roughly pointed in order to offer as little resistance as possible to the rush of water during a freshet. These,which are rather more that 2ft. thick project about 18 ins on each side of the roadway. The latter is formed of four immense slabs, one being laid over the western opening, one over the eastern opening, while two span the centre water-way. The two former are 15ft-2ins in length, one being 6ft-9ins in width and the other 6ft-5ins. The two centre slabs are smaller but each is over 12ft long. They vary in thickness from about 8ins to 1ft. The height of the bridge from the bed of the river to the top of the centre stones is 8ft-6ins; the ends a little lower, as the roadway is slightly arched.

Most writers suggest that it was built during the middle ages, possibly between the twelfth and fifteenth centuries. If this is so then the most likely builders were the occupiers of the Ancient Tenements e.g. Merripit, Pizwell, and Bellever.

The construction of the bridge must have caused considerable problems for the builders. It might have been possible to find the granite blocks locally, but the slabs would most probably have had to be transported from further afield. Mr Jack Warne, who had expert knowledge of working granite, suggested they came from Lower

A watercolour painting c.1859, looking south, showing the clapper bridge with the middle span lying in the river. Beyond is the house at Barracks. (Devon Record Office)

White Tor, but an article in the *Western Morning News*, dated 16 May 1930, stated that 'The late Mr George French had located on the south side of Bellever Tor the actual spot from which the stones of the old bridge were taken'.

The river is easily fordable for cattle and horses for most of the year. There were few occasions that my father was unable to ride across the river and bring back his cattle. People on foot would

The clapper bridge showing chains which hold up the horizontal cattle barriers. This explains the drill holes and metal fittings that can be seen in the bridge today. The photograph, c.1900, also shows the gravel bank which provided sand a gravel for building purposes. (Author)

have difficulty, but it seems strange that such a structure was necessary for their convenience.

The earliest mention of a name for the bridge that I have been able to find was in 1655, when it is mentioned in a lease between William French and Walter and John French relating to Higher Merripit. (A date of 1555 is usually attributed to this lease a mistake that probably came about because the front of the document had been wrongly annotated.).

The Ogilby map of 1675 shows 'a stone bridg of 3 arches called Post-bridg'. These roads, especially in the West Country, shown on maps by Ogilby and others, were not all post roads. Some were of course, but I have not found any evidence that the post was carried on the one over the moor until a much later date. So it is unlikely that the derivation of the name came from the carrying of the post.

There has also been a suggestion that it derived from 'pawsts', relating to the granite slabs.

Postbridge is also mentioned c.1697, in the Parish Constable's Accounts of Marytavy, pertaining to bridge repairs.

The bridge was vandalized c.1820 when one of the centre slabs was tipped into the river. There is a painting in the Devon Record Office which shows the missing stone c.1857 and some photographs at a later date, by Frith, were probably

Two views of the flood of 1938, taken when the river level had started to fall. On the left the top of the clapper bridge can just been seen, on the right, the scene is shown looking upriver to the north, taken from the road bridge. (Author)

taken just before it was replaced by Messrs Duke, of Tor Granite Quarries, Merrivale. In 1879 Mr Lough of Chagford wrote to Lord Portman about the stone being off the bridge. He in turn wrote to the Duchy who instigated the replacement by Messrs Duke. Lord Portman paid £4.8s - the cost of the restoration.

The bridge has certainly stood the test of time. During a flood on 17 July 1890 the waters just overtopped the lowest of the imposts, and after a severe thunder storm in August 1938 the waters lapped the underside of the slabs. By the time I was allowed on the road bridge to photograph the river had started to fall.

The whole area around the bridge has radically changed over the years. The stone retaining banks between the clapper and the road bridge are relatively new and were made up from stones removed from the bed of the river. The buttressing at both ends is new and was necessary as some of the pier stones were slipping out of place.

At some time the right bank, downriver, had been reinforced by a stone retaining wall. The foundations can still be seen in some places.

On the Princetown side a granite path now leads to the bridge and a retaining kerb has been laid between the road and the grassed-over space between the two bridges. Much of the work has been necessary because of erosion and pedestrian wear.

The clapper bridge c. 1880, showing one of the centre stones missing, possible just visible lying in the river on the near side of the bridge. (Frith photo - Author)

A later photo, c.1910, showing the central stone replaced. (Chapman photo - Author)

Two views of the clapper bridge, c.1890. On the left the view is looking towards the north-west and the figure is the Revd J.B. Shattock, curate of Postbridge and Dartmeet 1883, and the view on the right is looking north-east, with the road bridge seen on the left. (Robert Burnard)

THE ROAD BRIDGE.

The road from Tavistock to Moretonhampstead was turnpiked by two Acts of 1772, and constructed during the 1790s by a man called Carter, who lived at Rundlestone, assisted by his two sons. The bridge was built of granite c.1792 possibly at the site of the old fording place. It was 85ft in length with two arches 12ft-2in. wide and one of 16ft-2in. The roadway was 12ft-6in. wide and the bridge opened out to 19ft-9in. at the northern end and to 19ft at the southern end.

Originally the hump was quite pronounced and with the increasing speeds of vehicles it has been necessary to build up the approaches on both sides of the bridge.

During the late 1940s the bridge was severely damaged when two army lorries, one towing the other, knocked down parts of the wall on both sides of the bridge. Generally however it has needed very little repair, mainly repointing and mortar injection.

Devon County Council was, and still is, responsible for the repairs to the approach roads and for the bridge itself. Two stones engraved with a capital 'C', one opposite 'Greyhound' and the other opposite 'Dart Cottage' mark the original limits of that responsibility.

Nowadays the bridge is heavily trafficked, a count of two-way traffic at Easter 1988 showed about 800 vehicles an hour using the bridge around midday.

The road bridge, with Dart Cottage in the background. (Author)

Chapter 2 - A Place to Live

ARCHERTON

Sometime around 1780 John and Thomas Hullett took over a lease of 3000 acres on Dartmoor which had been granted to Mr Patterson. After John died Thomas relinquished the Dartmoor holdings. In 1805 a new 99-year lease, which included many acres of moorland and properties such as Greyhound, the Lodges, Middle Merripit and Stannon, was granted to Revd Vollans. This lease was eventually purchased by Mr J.N. Bennett of Plymouth. He built the original house and cottages; the house costing about £600.

J.W. Page writing in his *An exploration of Dartmoor and its Antiquities*, 1889 (Page 166), described part of the estate and house:

From Lakehead circle we look down upon the scattered cottages of Postbridge, while immediately opposite are the enclosed grounds and plantations of Archerton, a picturesque dwelling with a high pitched roof of thatch the residence of Mr Bennett.

It seems that Mr Bennett was not always in residence as, in 1851, John and Grace Coaker lived there, John being the bailiff; (they were my great-great-grandparents). In 1861 John was farming 150 acres, and the two cottages were occupied by Ann French and Mary Hamlyn respectively. After John left, the farming was carried on by Richard Arscott, and in 1891 by his son William. The cottages had several different occupiers during this time, including John and Richard French, James and Ellen Robbins, and Jane James, a seamstress.

Mr Bennett died in September 1899 and the lease passed to Mr Ellery Bennett. William Crossing wrote in his *One Hundred Years on Dartmoor*, 1901 (Page 58):

Another has but recently passed away – Mr John Bennett of Archerton who was long resident on the Moor. He was 17 years old at the death of George III, and had some recollections of events which took place in those days.

In 1903 the estate, plus Rowtor Newtake, was about 636 acres, and in 1904 a new 21-year lease

Archerton prior to the fire of 1917. (Chapman photo. Author)

was obtained and a bathroom added to the house. About this time some of the village properties were retained by the Duchy and let by them as annual tenancies.

In 1915 Ellery assigned the lease to Sir Courtenay Walter Bennett, the son of John Bennett. He was born on the 11 May 1855 and married Edith Russell Leay, who died in 1931. They had two sons and a daughter. From 1876 onwards he was engaged in Consular duties in Panama, Guatemala, Rio Grande du Sul, Reunion and Bilbao before being employed in Paris concerning Indian immigration. From 1901 he was Consul General in San Francisco and in New York from 1907–15. He was awarded the CIE in 1900, the Coronation Medal in 1911, and knighted in 1914.

They were in residence when the house was burned down in January 1917, due to a smouldering wooden beam in the drawing room chimney. The house was being thatched at the time, with North Devon reed, and my father recalled the event saying 'I was helping to remove the thatch, burning on one side of my body and freezing on the other as the men sprayed me with water.'

In 1923 a 99-year lease was obtained and a new house, designed in the colonial style by Albert Richardson, was built by John Halfyard of Princetown. Water was brought in from Chittaford Down for household purposes and a decision was made to use water power for generating electricity.

Archerton - return to the new house. (Author)

The cost was considerable. Gilbert Gilkes of Kendal quoted £450 for a 3hp turbine, rising to £800 for one of 33hp. Added to this was about £1000 for cleaning out the old Powdermills Leat. There was a head of about 125 feet, producing 12.9 kilowatts at 220 volts DC. The water was returned to the East Dart river via Gawlor Brook.

Sometime in the past, probably soon after the cottages were built, a path led from Archerton to Greyhound Farm. A bridge was built over Gawlor Brook and a rough paving was laid from the bridge to a hunting gate in Drift Lane. Close to this gate was a notice 'NO THOROUGHFARE'. There was a similar notice at the end of the drive-way. The pathway was closed for one day a year,

certainly during Sir Courtenay's time, as I well remember the postman, William French, complaining it meant a longer journey for him as he lived in one of the cottages at Archerton.

Sir Courtenay died on 15 December 1937, and Miss Edith Bennett continued to reside there until she moved to Ringhill. Miss Edith published a booklet *Dartmoor By-Ways* by 'Gipsy', and in the last paragraph of the preface wrote:

Go forth little book in full hope that you may give pleasure to lovers of Dartmoor, and ask all to remember in passing over these tracks, to save the moormen much trouble and, in some cases, loss of stock, by closing all gates, and also to leave all clean and fair with no litter of papers etc. to spoil the pleasure of those who may follow.

The house, comprising 3 reception rooms, 7–8 bedrooms, 2 bathrooms, with a good water supply, electric light, central heating, cottage garage and stables etc., with approximately 600 acres, was advertised in *The Times* on 3 August 1938, by Harrods, for quick sale.

The property was bought by Mr and Mrs John Henley who resided there until Mr Henley's death. It was then bought by Mrs A. Arrowsmith-Brown and after she left it passed to her son Robert. He was a JP and chairman of the magistrates for many years, a prison visitor and was the chair-man of the Dartmoor Commoners Assoc-iation. His widow Jill, who has done much for the Anglican Church in the dis-trict, kept on the house after his death.

In recent years the house has benefited from mains electrici-ty and a bore hole, sunk to a depth of about 200 feet, for a water supply.

Storm damage at Archerton 1987. (Author)

LAKEHEAD COTTAGE

Miss Mabel Chudleigh applied for a Duchy of Cornwall lease of 99 years in 1914. In July 1914 plans were prepared and submitted by F.D. Parker, architects of Newton Abbot, for a house to be built on Lakehead Newtake from which enclosure the property took its name.

Miss Mabel was the daughter of John and Grace Reed Chudleigh (née Linscott). John was an amateur archaeologist with a passion for Dartmoor and was known by the family as 'Dartmoor Chudleigh'. He was born at Newton Abbot on 20 April 1847, the son of John Adolphus and Susan Chudleigh (née Tozer), of Howden, Moretonhampstead).

John Chudleigh was an architect, builder and surveyor in Newton Abbot and was responsible for the design of Newton Abbot Market (1870), and the Starcross asylum for children (demolished in 1980).

Chudleigh was a member of Newton Abbot Town Council at the end of the nineteenth century and died in 1907. He wrote *An Exploration of Dartmoor Antiquities* in 1892, reprinted in 1893, and a facsimile edition was published in 1987.

Miss Mabel had in her garden a summer house in which, as a youngster, I played games and took tea with her nephew and niece, Tony and Elizabeth Baskett. Their mother was Mabel's sister Gwyneth. I have been told, but have been unable to verify, that Miss Mabel delivered the post on horseback during the First World War.

Other occupiers were Mrs Sparkes, who often rode my fathers horse, Dandy. Mr and Mrs Williamson (Mr Williamson was a judge in the Sudan for many years), Mr and Mrs Roberts, Mr and Mrs Woolley, Mr Dunbar, and the present occupiers Mr and Mrs Fisher.

During the Second World War the property, then occupied by the Williamsons, was used as the Civil Defence headquarters, and also as the headquarters for the Home Guard platoon, commanded by Lt. F.G. Harrison and his 2I/C Sgt. Robinson. The rateable value c.1950 was £14.

Above: *Mrs Sparkes, of Lakehead Cottage, on Dandy.*

Above right: *Open moor on which Lakehead was built, showing the leat to Barracks.* (Valentine photo - Author)

Right: *Lakehead, newly built, c.1916* (Author)

The Dartmoor National Park Authority Information Centre, converted from Bill Withycombe's workshop, with stonework by Tom Webb. (Author)

WHISTLE WIND

This cottage, standing at SX 6457 7875, is shown on an early map, dated 26 May 1809, and the tenement is listed in the tithe records as 'No.246 Cot house and garden 2 rood 3 perches near Postbridge'.

The garden enclosure, which is now part of Whistle Wind can still be seen but there is no visible evidence of the cottage foundations. I can remember potatoes being grown in the enclosure and the ploughing may have disturbed any sign of the building. I have not, as yet, found any record of who lived there or when the cot was demolished.

DUCHY OF CORNWALL WORKSHOP DARTMOOR NATIONAL PARK CENTRE

The workshop was built by the Duchy as a centre for its building operations in Postbridge. The ground floor of the building was of earth, with a rack for storing timber on one side and a bench and fireplace on the other. There were double doors on the Greyhound side and a single door facing Drift Lane. This bottom floor was used, in miserable conditions, for a short time, by a family who had difficulty in finding accommodation locally.

A wooden staircase against the Drift Lane wall led to the first floor which had a long carpenter's bench along its centre. For many years William Withycombe worked there making gates, meat safes and windows. His work was of excellent quality and such was the demand for his gates that he purchased a mortice machine to speed up production. Harold White from Sunnymead often helped in their making.

After Mr Withycombe gave up the tenancy the building was used by my father, at a rental of £20 per annum, for the storage of hay and farm machinery, before being converted to the National Park Centre. The Centre has an information desk and sells a wide range of books and maps. On the first floor is a video display and occasionally lectures are given there. Toilet facilities were made available in this building after the toilets in the car park were demolished. The granite stonework was completed by Mr Tom Webb and is a fine example of the art.

BEEHIVE

This cot had the typical two-room layout which occurred elsewhere in the village. On the north side was another building, the foundations of which were clearly visible in the 1920s. Exactly when Beehive was built is not known but George and Elizabeth French along with their grandson George F. Rowse were certainly living there in 1881 and possibly George and Mary French as early as 1861.

In later years the cot was used for housing cattle, especially calves and pigs. A wooden and corrugated iron structure was erected on the foundations to the north, as a hay shed, and an area in front of the cot was totally enclosed. The whole was demolished to make way for the car park, although some of the, foundations can still be seen. It was unfortunate that a tinner's mould, formerly used in the building, was buried in the foundations of a large cattle shed which has since been demolished.

GREYHOUND
INN, COTTAGE AND FIRST POST OFFICE

It seems that Greyhound was built in the later half of the eighteenth century. In 1806 the Hulletts' leaseholds were assigned to Revd Vollans and the Greyhound Inn and its lands became part of his estate. The first recorded innkeeper was Robert Valling who was licenced in 1809. He was followed by James Davis in 1816, John Lower in 1818 and John Davis again in 1819. (The assize records are often incomplete and this may have come about when the same innkeeper was licenced year after year.).

By 1839 the inn and its lands were let by Vollans to Joseph Warne and comprised:

	a	r	p
Plot 1 adjoining Inn		2	3
Inn. outhouses,			
court and garden		1	14
Plot 2 adjoining plot 1		3	18
Plot adjoining Turnpike house		1	3
Moor	4	2	21
Moor	2	3	10
Moor	18	2	6
Meadow adjoining The Lodge	21	0	24
Meadow	3	2	4
	52	2	14

Joseph Warne eventually left to become landlord of the New Inn (Warren Inn), and William Connabear became the tenant.

In 1841 part of the Vollans estate, which included the inn and its lands, were leased to John Nicholas Bennett of Plymouth, who built Archerton. During the 1850s John and Emma Harvey (1851) and George and Mary French kept house there and by 1861 Simon and Elizabeth Martin were the tenants. Simon was also a miller by trade, working at Powdermills, where he eventually went to live.

In 1877 William Worth was the tenant and on 14 January 1878 the Duchy wrote to J.N. Bennett about the surrender of some of the leaseholds and asked that Greyhound should be put into good repair.

By 1881 George and Jane Ann French were the new tenants and during the ensuing years George became a well known local character, being a leading Methodist, local councillor, and Justice of the Peace. He was born in 1852 and married Jane Ann Arscott, of Archerton, in 1878. For many years he repaired the road from Two Bridges through Postbridge and beyond. Along with Robert Burnard he re-erected many of the prehistoric stones in the area, including the two large circles at Grey Wethers. For this purpose he carted some 26 cartloads of stone to help trig up the stones they erected.

George French JP, Greyhound Farm, c. 1890. First sub-postmaster at Postbridge (Author)

Elsie Bellamy (nee Coaker), for many years at Postbridge Post Office, she was the wife of sub-postmaster, John Bellamy, who delivered his post by pony. (Author)

He once told the Revd Hugh Breton that he built the long stone wall which runs from Archerton, along the back of Arch Tor and on to the Cherrybrook.

On 28 October 1895 a Rural Sub-Post Office was opened with George as the sub-postmaster. In 1899 a telegraph was installed for receiving and sending telegraph messages.

When Robert Burnard photographed 'Greyhound Cot', as it was then called, the photograph (Sayer collection) shows the house, much as it was, when originally built. Inside were open granite hearths (these were found a few years ago and opened up by Malcolm Waite). The upstairs floors were of plain oak boards (later a deal floor was laid over them). At the east end was an outdoor open hearth, possibly used for smoke curing, or some such purpose – there was no evidence of a building ever being attached to that end of the house.

Drinking water had to be fetched from a spring in Drift Lane and pot-water came from the overflow from the duck pond, which in turn was fed by a leat from Gawlor Brook, or from the East Dart river. The leat had originally led to Barracks but had been diverted.

From Lady Day 1906 the rent for the farm, of about 39 acres, was £21.10s. and sometime between then and 1910 considerable improvements were made to the house. This entailed

The Greyhound Inn, c.1895. (Robert Burnard)

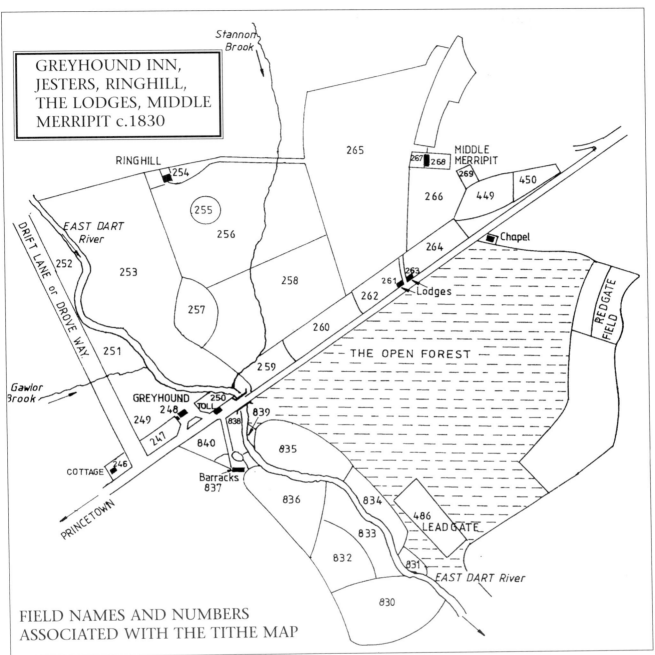

GREYHOUND INN,
JESTERS, RINGHILL,
THE LODGES, MIDDLE
MERRIPIT c.1830

FIELD NAMES AND NUMBERS
ASSOCIATED WITH THE TITHE MAP

GREYHOUND INN
247 Plot adjoining Inn.
248 Inn outhouses court and
garden.
249 Plot adjoining 247.
250 Plot adjoining Turnpike House.
251 Moor.
252 Moor.
253 Moor.
265 Meadow near Lodges.
266 Meadow.
BARRACKS
837 House outhouses court
and Garden.
838 Meadow.

839 Coarse.
840 Arable.
THE LODGES
261 Lodge and garden. (Lower)
262 Plot and Plantation.
263 Lodge and garden. (Higher)
264 Plot and plantation.
267 Plantation.
JESTERS
830 Arable.
831 Coarse.
832 Arable.
833 Hilly Piece.
834 Moor.
835 Moor.

836 Arable.
RINGHILL
254 House court and
Garden.
255 Little Ring
256 Ring Hill.
257 Great Ring.
258 Great Marsh and Plantation.
259 Lower Road Marsh and
Plantation.
260 Higher Road Marsh
and Plantation.
MIDDLE MERRIPIT
268 House and garden.
269 Plot.

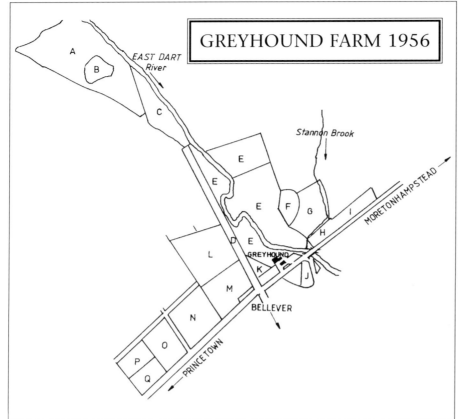

GREYHOUND FARM 1956

KEY

A ROUNDY PARK
B LITTLE ROUNDY PARK
C LONGAMEADS
D DRIFT LANE (DROVEWAY)
E GREYHOUND MOOR
F THE RING
G RINGHILL MOOR
H LOWER STRAPS
I HIGHER STRAPS
J BARRACK PLATS
K BEEHIVE PLATS
L THE MASH
M WHISTLEWIND or
    DROVEWAY MEADOW
N ARCHERTON GATE FIELD
O FURTHER FIELD GATE
P LOWER MEADOW
Q HIGHER MEADOW

Another of Burnard's photographs of the Greyhound, taken c.1890. Note the lack of porch compared to the later photos, opposite, and the very rudimentary lean-to on the left of the building. (Robert Burnard)

removing the thatch, raising the roof level and covering the roof with slate. Later a piped water supply was brought in from Webb's moor.

Around 1923 Richardson and Gill drew up plans for an extension to the premises. These incorporated a room at the front for the Post Office and a small shop, a second room downstairs, and a dairy. Upstairs were two additional bedrooms and a box room.

When the extensions were completed the property consisted of the rooms in the extension, five other bedrooms, kitchen, scullery, sitting room and downstairs bathroom. I think it was about this time that the new farm buildings were built. They consisted of a calves house, stalls for cows, a hay store and stabling. A water supply for them was connected to a tank supplied by the Gawlor leat.

George died in February 1925 and his widow Jane Ann and their daughter, Dorothy, carried on the Post Office and shop. The farm was sub-let to my father for a few years until Jack Withycombe from Soussons became the tenant. During 1930 the Post Office was transferred to Bridge Cottage (Western Cottage), and after Jack Withycombe died during October 1947 the farm was let to his daughter Winifred and her husband Ernest Webb. They remained at Greyhound until 1954, the last of the 'French' descendants to live there.

I took over the tenancy that year and lived in the farmhouse whilst my father farmed the land.

In 1966 I moved to Plymouth and he and mother moved to Greyhound where they farmed until father died in 1973.

The farm was then let to Malcolm Waite, with considerable tracts of land added. A large farm building was put up (later removed) and, after Malcolm left, the farm was taken over by Gerald Watson. About this time the farmhouse was divided into two and the west end let as a residence for a National Park Warden.

The tenants in 1995 are Mr and Mrs Ken Watson who farmed Middle Merripit Farm for many years.

Greyhound Farm and Post Office c.1910. Note the telegraph pole on the left. (Chapman photo - Author)

Postbridge Post Office c.1926. (Chapman photo - Author)

WESTERN AND EASTERN COTTAGES, BRIDGE COTTAGES and IVY COTTAGES

The original cottages were built on a plot of land adjoining the East Dart river and are possibly those mentioned by the Revd John Swete in 1797. Western Cottage comprised 2 rooms and a lean-to shed, whilst Eastern Cottage had 3 rooms and a shed. For some reason Postbridge School records shows them as Ivy Cottages.

They were semi-detached, built of stone and had a thatched roof. Drinking water was fetched from a spring at Barracks, whilst river water was used for all other purposes. Each house had an earth closet for sanitation. So far it has not been possible to find out exactly who lived in the houses during the early years.

An early drawing in the Devon Record Office shows a blacksmith's shop attached to Eastern Cottage. I think John Herring was the blacksmith in 1827. He was married to Ann, and their son John was baptised at Princetown on 17 June 1827. John Senior is listed as a blacksmith at Postbridge.

The plot had been part of the Hullett estate which passed to the Revd Vollans and then to John Bennett of Archerton. The annual rent early this century was £5.10s. for Eastern Cottage, and £4.10s. for Western Cottage.

The cottages reverted to the Duchy in 1906 and, although the roof had been slated, by about 1910 they had deteriorated and were very damp. The Duchy were approached by my grandfather, John James Coaker, who lived in Western Cottage, and also by Mr Warne who occupied Eastern Cottage, requesting urgent repairs, but it was decided that new cottages should be built on the site where Bridge Cottage and the Post Office now stand. These were built by John Halfyard of Princetown, both were identical.

Water was piped from a spring in Webb's Moor (SX648 792) and outdoor flush toilets were installed, draining to a cess pit. It was not until the 1930s that bathrooms and hot water systems were installed. I can well remember being bathed in front of the kitchen range in a hip bath by the light of a single burner paraffin lamp. The water had been heated in the 'copper' and carried to the bath in large enamelled jugs. One advantage was the warmth from the cooking range and the hot towels which it provided.

Each cottage had some land attached. Western Bridge Cottage had Ringhill Moor and Eastern Bridge Cottage the 'Straps', which eventually became part of Greyhound Farm.

The original tenancy agreement for the new Western Cottage, which became known as Bridge Cottage (except to the Duchy), was in the name of my grandmother, but eventually it was a shared agreement with mother and father. Rent in 1937 was £15.10s. per annum.

This photograph shows the old cottages (at the left of the picture) which were replaced by Western and Eastern Cottages. These were known as Ivy Cottages. (Chapman photo - Author)

Western and Eastern Cottages, later known as Bridge Cottages. (Author)

Father had two corrugated iron buildings erected on the west side of the house and these were used as a shippen and for stabling. He also kept poultry in a hen house in Ringhill Moor and the stepping stones at the back of the house were used to reach them. He also rented Longameads and Roundaparks from the Duchy for £2.15s. and £3 per annum, respectively (see Hartyland). The same year, 1935, he also rented Lakehead Hill for £10 per annum.

Mr Warne had a turf house to the east of his cottage and each year filled it with turf from Gawlor Bottom. The turf was carried by horse and cart, usually on a shared basis; he would help to cut and see to the drying whilst someone else, usually Matthew White, would provide the horse and cart.

Mr Warne also kept poultry, but they were housed over in Jesters. He was an excellent gardener and invariably had a magnificent show of dahlias and lupins, along with a very productive vegetable garden. His grandson David Cooper and wife Margaret now live in the property, maintaining an unbroken family tenancy lasting for the best part of a hundred years.

THE VILLAGE SHOP

Miss Sleep writing in *Parish Pump* relates how Granny Sleep kept a shop in the village in the early 1890s. She sold raspberry drops and pear drops for a penny a quarter-pound, and at Christmas time as a special treat, oranges and nuts. In the 1920s Francis Redstone ran a shop from a hut at the side of the cottage at Lower Merripit.

I also seem to remember that George Endacott sold a few items of ironmongery at Dart Cottage.

Customers knocked at a stable-type door (about where the kitchen window facing Lydgate Lane is now) and were served from there.

After Greyhound had been extended the French's also had a shop along with the Post Office. They sold cigarettes and tobacco, sweets, postcards (a few local views were published by Dorothy French), stationery, pens and pencils. In 1930 the Post Office and telephone exchange were transferred to Bridge Cottage (Western Cottage) and my father became the sub-postmaster at an annual remuneration of £79.5s.6d. This was reduced to £56.10s. when the automatic telephone became operational, and was only £375 per annum when the Post Office was given up in 1966.

Sub-postmasters' remuneration depended on whether the Post Office had a telephone exchange, handled telegraph, money orders and Savings Bank business, sorted mail and supervised postmen. If so each of these duties was allocated units which were added to those relating to the value of stamps and postal orders sold, the number of pension transactions and licences issued etc. These were totalled and the annual salary calculated.

As the Post Office pay was not a living wage father worked a small holding and ran a small riding stables, whilst mother became the shopkeeper. She was helped in this by the representatives of various firms: Mr Davis from Brown Wills & Nicholson, Plymouth (groceries); Mr Rule of Walter Weighell, Launceston (stationery, haberdashery and toys); Frederick Wright Newton Abbot (tobacco, cigarettes, sweets and chocolate); and Mr Chapman of Dawlish (postcards). Mr Rule used to arrive after closing time bringing along several large parcels and suitcases, each containing samples of his wares. He seemed to have everything, collar studs, hairpins, hair slides, pins and needles, wrappings and bags, writing paper and envelopes, playing cards, pens, pencils and rubbers, cottons and darning wools, buttons, elastic, toys and much more – each parcel and case had something different, and had to be displayed. This took until late evening and afterwards he joined the family for supper.

Over the years he and many of the other 'travellers' became our friends. Mr Davis came on a Friday for the orders and the groceries etc. were delivered by lorry the following Tuesday, and had to be unpacked that evening. Cheese came wrapped in muslin and had to be 'skinned', dried fruit arrived in boxes and had to be weighed and all the other items put away.

At one time mother sold dried cod, 'toe-rag' to the uninitiated – I can smell it now. Nevertheless it made an excellent meal when cooked.

Cigarettes and tobacco were much in demand, twopenny packets of 5 woodbines and 20 Players for 11½d. Wills' Shag in its tube-like packet was a popular tobacco, as was Pigtail and Plug. Pigtail was wrapped in cloth and sliced to requirement, whilst Plug was in a long solid strip from which 'plugs' of about an ounce were cut. Plug was mainly bought for chewing.

Sweets came in large glass jars or tins, and rows of these made a delightful display. Chocolate bars, liquorice allsorts and dolly mixtures seemed far less exciting in their cardboard boxes.

Jocelyn Haines writing in the August 1973 *Devon Life* 'Childhood Summers on Dartmoor', wrote of my mother and father:

Our cousins always rented Ringhill and we met them each morning at the Post Office. Our pennies in our hands, the six of us dithered over Mrs Bellamy's large glass jars of sweets. She stocked the world's biggest bull's-eyes. The Bellamy's were rosy-cheeked and ageless. We loved Mrs Bellamy for her gentle face and endless patience, and secretly admired her husband's jodh-pured bow legs (he ran the riding stables). I used to think that he had been born straight on to the back of a pony.

Mother always welcomed a visit from Mr Chapman and I have reason to be grateful to him as he printed several old views from his glass plates which started my collection.

London newspapers were not stocked until Dr Rendel and Sir Courtenay Bennett, amongst others, approached the publishers. As a result *The Times, Morning Post, News Chronicle, Daily Sketch, Daily Mirror, Daily Telegraph, Daily Express,* and *Daily Mail,* were forwarded daily by rail from London to Yelverton and thence to Postbridge by carrier. It could never have paid the publishers to do this. The *Western Morning News* was sent by post in a parcel to the shop and individually to other addresses.

Slowly the range of stock increased, for example Ferguson's of Plymouth delivered their mineral waters in marble-stoppered bottles, and the range of postcards was extended by purchasing from publishers such as E.A. Sweetman, Frith and Jarrold. With the increase of business it soon became apparent that the sitting room, which had become the Post Office and shop, would not be large enough, and an approach was made to the Duchy for an extension. As a result a single room was added to the west end of the building.

Disaster nearly struck on an August morning in 1938. For days radio programmes had been interrupted by crackling and during the previous night a vicious thunderstorm centered over the moor. It seemed to be locked in the hills, going around and around, with torrential rain. By morning the river was well out over its banks and eventually it broke through and came in the back door and out the front. Fortunately some scouts had taken shelter in one of the outbuildings and when they saw what was happening they came in and helped to put the stock, which was threatened by the water, out of harms way.

A year later came the war and for several years rationing was the order of the day. Mother always seemed to manage – from somewhere or other she invariably found a little extra of this and that for which her customers were very thankful. Many of them loyally supported her until she retired. One of the jobs in which she took a great delight was weighing up the ration of sweets for the boys of Pinewood School. She considered that the one or two extra that went into each packet was no one else's business.

It was after the war that the shop started to flourish. In 1942 the turnover amounted to £717 and this had risen to £14,250 by 1966.

The winter of 1947 was a problem, but mother had been brought up to prepare for bad winters. She was born at Vitifer Mine and her mother had always stocked up for the winter months, so she carried on the tradition. Despite the difficulties of rationing and the interruption of supplies she did not run out of stocks, and kept open throughout. Soon after this a double garage was built on the west side of the property. Its design had to be similar to that of the Post Office and shop. It was built by Stone's of Chagford at a cost of £351, a considerable sum for those days.

In 1950 planning permission was granted for the installation of a petrol pump and a 500-gallon storage tank. The pump was a hand-operated Gilbarco with a swing arm attachment which permitted car tanks to be filled some distance from the pump. The initial digging for the hole for the tank was fairly easy but then Dartmoor granite got in the way. I was doing the excavation, so called on Jack Warne (Uncle Jack) for help:

'Well my buckie I'll provide the hammer, drills and feathers and tears and I'll show you what to do. You drill here, and here, and here (there were an awful lot of 'heres'), and then you use the feathers and tears and a sledge hammer. You had better call me when you've drilled all the holes.' I can still remember those blisters but, sure enough, when the granite broke away it left a straight edge near enough where I wanted it.

The shop and many other houses still used paraffin for lighting, heating and to a lesser extent cooking; to provide for this a 200-gallon paraffin tank was installed, along with another of the same capacity for tractor vapourising oil. As the number of motor cars and visitors increased so did the takings and, in 1960, a Lister diesel generator was bought for the purpose of providing electricity for the Post Office and Greyhound Farm, where I was living. With electricity to work the pumps, planning permission was obtained to install two more pumps and an additional 2000-gallon compartment tank, thus allowing three grades of petrol to be dispensed.

The excavation of the hole was a major undertaking some 12 feet long, 8 feet wide and 9 feet deep. During the dig, at between 4 and 5 feet, we came across a number of rocks and amongst them a cache containing a several of flints (see photo page 9). Lower still there were deposits of grey clay and, at about 9 feet, river sand.

Petrol was available from about 5.30am until midnight and, during the summer, early morning sales were brisk with holidaymakers travelling to Cornwall. Many of them had travelled overnight, stopping at the bridge for refreshment, and calling in before driving on. In order to work the pumps the electricity supply had to be switched from the houses to avoid overloading. All was well unless father or I stopped to talk and forgot to switch it back, especially if someone was hoovering or watching television.

After repeated requests for ice-cream, Walls were asked for a supply. Their representative was very sceptical and it was very difficult to convince him of the viability of the project. He eventually agreed but would only install a small cabinet. Within two days it was empty and a week later a large conservator arrived.

The 1963 winter was by far the worst ever encountered during the time mother kept the shop. Supplies which did arrive came by helicopter which landed in the field by the river. Most times it was met by my wife who helped to unload. Father often told people that 'all that was left on the shelves when the thaw came were pins and pickles!'

In 1964 mains electricity came to Postbridge and it was possible to connect the pumps and other items to it, and to install a frozen food cabinet.

Over the years mother depended on the help of the family, everyone was expected to pull their weight. Eventually however it became necessary to employ an assistant, and for many years Mrs Chalmers from Bellever helped out.

In 1966 mother and father decided to retire and they went to Greyhound to live. Father carried on farming, some retirement!

The shop and Post Office (with the agreement of the Post Office authorities) was sold to Mr and Mrs Maye who improved the access to the petrol pumps. There have been a number of occupiers since.

During the occupation of Mr and Mrs Savva the property was considerably extended, the work being done by Fred Ballamy, a builder then living in the converted chapel.

With the construction of the car park and the designation of Postbridge as 'Honey Pot' area, the shop has become very busy. Mr and Mrs Beer now run it and have extended the range of goods and services. I think my parents were fortunate that firms in their day delivered to the door, many have now stopped deliveries and this means fetching from 'Cash and Carry', leading to longer days and added costs.

TELEGRAPHS AND TELEPHONES.

In 1898 Miss Langley asked the Lydford Parish for help in obtaining telephonic communication for the village. The Council wrote to the Post Master General who agreed to provide a service on condition that a contribution was made towards the running costs.

Local residents promised to subscribe £13.18s.6d for 7 years if needed, the Duchy contributing £5 per annum. The telegraph between Postbridge and Princetown was installed at Greyhound Post Office sometime during 1899, followed by an announcement in the *Post Office Guide* that Postbridge had a telegraph office.

In 1900 there was a shortfall of £6.13s.0d in connection with the working of the telegraph, for which amount the Post Master General demanded immediate payment. Further shortfalls were recorded between then and 1904 of £8.10s.5d, £7.19s.8d, and £6.17s.5d.

The telegraph continued in use until 9 September 1925 when a telephone call office came into use at Greyhound, connected to the Princetown exchange. It is surprising this had not been done before as a telephone line had for some time (c.1919–20) connected the AA Box near the Warren Inn to Princetown (Princetown 13).

The Postbridge telephone exchange using non-multiple central battery signalling (CBS2) equipment was installed at the same address and opened on 27 May 1927. The telephone directory of April 1927 (Vol. 2 at the British Telecom Resource Centre), lists the following subscribers and their numbers: No.1 Postbridge Rural Call Office, Greyhound P.O; No.2 Alex Shaw, Farm Manager, Bellever Farm; No.3 Postbridge Private Hotel Boarding Establishment (Dartfordleigh): No.4 Sir Courtenay Bennett; No.5 Miss A.WS. Festing, Vaglas; No.6 Miss Janet Lind, The Brake; No.7 Dr A.B. Pendel, Penlee; No.8 Warren Inn Parties catered for Postbridge; No.9 Mrs E. Warne (Boarding Establishment), Lydgate.

There were also two junctions connected to the Princetown exchange through which calls could be routed to all parts of the country.

The installation was in four parts – a battery system using Leclanché cells, a distribution panel and fuse board, the exchange console and a night service switching unit. A call indicator was allocated to each subscriber and junction, and the operator transferred a call by means of plugs and a hand-operated generator. There were further indicators which showed that the subscriber had finished talking and put down the handset. The operator would then remove the plugs.

A typical conversation for connecting a call would be like this:

Postbridge operator – 'Number please.'
Subscriber – 'Plymouth 4301.'
Postbridge operator would select outgoing
    Princetown junction.
Princetown operator – Princetown
Postbridge operator – Plymouth
Princetown operator would select outgoing
    Plymouth junction.
Plymouth operator – 'Plymouth.'
Postbridge operator – '4301.'

When the Plymouth number answered the Postbridge operator would say 'You're through'. The operator would listen in to ensure that the call was properly connected and a ticket would be completed recording details of the subscriber's number, the number called, date, time and cost. These tickets would be sent to head office for processing. An extra charge was made for night service and subscribers paying for this had their lines routed through the night service switching unit to Princetown.

Once the exchange had been installed anyone could use the call box at the Post Office by asking the operator to obtain the number and by paying for it over the counter. In 1930 the telephone exchange along with the Post Office counter and call box were transferred and installed in the sitting room at Western Cottage (Bridge Cottage).

Jack Bellamy and riders outside the Post Office at Western Cottage in the 1930s. A posting box can be seen in the wall, the public telephone was inside, and the battery shed (to power the exchange) can be seen behind the horse in the centre. (Author)

It was decided that my mother should be the exchange operator and she was sent to Princetown to gain experience. This was followed by a period of supervision by a Plymouth exchange supervisor who came to Postbridge for this purpose.

There were one or two embarrassing moments when wrong plugs were pulled out or wrong connections made. On one occasion she was accused of listening in to what was said to be particularly private calls. Full details of the complaint were sent and an urgent reply requested. When the family read it, we all started to laugh, as at the time the calls were being made the subscriber was on night service and listening-in would have been impossible.

The exchange could also be a friendly place with 'Elsie my dear I am going over to — would you put any calls through there.' Or 'Elsie has the butcher been yet? Oh good ask him to call there's a dear'.

Thunderstorms could be a nuisance as the lightning would cause indicators to fall, while pole and line strikes would cut off communications. When the distribution pole outside the house was struck there was a mighty bang and all the protective devices blew. So complete was the damage that the cable was more or less a molten mass of copper and lead, which had to be renewed quickly as the whole village was cut off. In the early 1930s it was decided that an automatic exchange should be installed to provide more line capacity. A new building was erected just beyond Dart Cottage in Lydgate Lane and during 1936–37 a new automatic exchange 12 (UAX12) was installed there. This had its drawbacks however, as the batteries had to be charged by a petrol generator.

During the heavy snowfalls of 1963 two telephone technicians from Tavistock had to walk through the snow from Princetown in order to start the generator. They were so exhausted that when they reached Cherrybrook Farm one remained there whilst the other continued on in atrocious conditions until he reached our house. He refused even a cup of tea before attending to the generator as the batteries were so low, and with the telephone being the only lifeline to the village, Postbridge was virtually cut off.

When he had attended to the generator he came back to us had a meal and stayed the night. He was joined next morning by his colleague in time for breakfast and, after checking all was well at the exchange, they started the walk back to Tavistock.

I can vouch for the difficulties they encountered coming out as I accompanied them back to Tavistock in much better weather conditions and that was difficult enough.

This reminded me of an incident many years before when father, riding back from Two Bridges, where he worked, found an exhausted telephone engineer who had been trying to repair lines brought down by snow and ice. He helped him to our home where he too stayed the night.

Lines were frequently brought down by snow and ice, particularly the Dartmoor 'ammil' (that thin coating of ice which covers every projecting object). The weight would often snap the poles as well and eventually the Post Office decided that many of the lines should go underground.

Finally, on 1 August 1973 at 1pm, a new Unit 13 exchange (UAX13) was brought into service, and Postbridge subscribers were allocated Tavistock numbers. This exchange is in a new building between the East Dart Hotel and Dartfordleigh.

Prior to the installation of the telephone system communications were by letter and telegram. Messengers from Plymouth originally delivered telegrams to Princetown and Postbridge addresses, their wages being agreed in 1872. Later Postbridge telegrams were delivered from Princetown and, after 1901, from the Postbridge Rural Sub-Office. Telegrams remained an important means of communication, especially when so few houses had telephones. During the summer months delivering them to visitors could be lucrative for a telegram boy (one of my holiday occupations!).

Pay was on a sliding scale from 6d for local deliveries to 2/6 for riding out to such places as Dunnabridge or Headland Warren - the recipient in these places having to contribute 6d porterage, and in theory the telegram should not have been handed over until this had been paid. The messenger would bring back replies if the telegram had been reply paid. It could be somewhat frustrating however having arrived back from Dunnabridge to find another telegram waiting – for that address.

Sometimes a word to the sender could help solve delivery problems. Mr Spiller of Chagford had the habit of sending a telegram late in the day to Smith Hill Farm saying he would be out next day. One of these arrived after dark on a winter's evening with a gale blowing and torrential rain. Father decided enough was enough and the next time he saw Mr Spiller explained the problem to him. He immediately replied 'Good Lord, Jack, I never thought about that, in future I'll get them off first thing in the morning'. He always did.

The messenger would often know the contents of the telegram before he set out and it was not always an easy task, especially if the message was a sad one.

1896

POSTAL SERVICES

During the seventeenth century the Post Roads to Plymouth and Falmouth went south around Dartmoor via Exeter, Chudleigh, Ashburton and Plymouth. A Bye Post went to Barnstaple. During 1704–05 the post to Cornwall was conveyed through Crockernwell, Okehampton and Launceston. The post to Tavistock came from Plymouth. In 1722 a Cross Post was established from Okehampton to Tavistock, Callington and Liskeard. It can be seen therefore that the post routes during the eighteenth century avoided the unhospitable heights of Dartmoor.

The establishment of the Turnpike between Moretonhampstead and Tavistock during the later part of the eighteenth century was to be an important event in the history of Postbridge. Probably the first Post Office on Dartmoor was at Moretonhampstead, where John Treleaven was Postmaster. Mr Brewer's article in the *Dartmoor Magazine* (Issue No.38, Spring 1995) establishes the existence of a private postal service, set up after a meeting in the White Hart Inn at Moretonhampstead, on 16 July 1792. This arranged for the collection and delivery of mail to Crockernwell on the Post Road. It seems probable that letters addressed to the Warren Inn, the tin mines, Challacombe, Headland Warren and Soussons, in the 'Forest of Dartmoor', would have passed through Moretonhampstead which was a centre of commerce for the inhabitants of properties on that side of the Moor. This predates the official Exeter Penny Post of 1812 which used Moretonhampstead as a Receiving House (Receiving House No. 1).

Letters to various other properties in the Postbridge area would have been serviced by Tavistock. The postmark (a mileage mark) for Tavistock in 1808 was 'TAVISTOCK', with the boxed figures 233 underneath, indicating the mileage from London as 233 miles. Such mail would have first been sent to Plymouth (mileage 218) and then on to Tavistock.

A new mileage mark for Tavistock, indicating a mileage of 209 miles, is recorded from 1816–1828, indicating the reduction in mileage via Moretonhampstead, across Dartmoor, and thence to Tavistock. This obviously occurred after Dartmoor Prison opened at Princetown in 1809, with mail there very busy until 1815. The horse-drawn railway from Plymouth to Princetown opened in 1826 but it does not seem to have been used for the conveyance of mail until a much later date.

The Tavistock Penny Post was established in 1828 and Princetown was allocated Receiving House No.2. This number is often mistakenly allocated to Exeter but that is because mail posted at Princetown received a boxed No.2 postmark and then was carried by Post to Exeter where it received an 'Exeter/Penny Post' mark. In 1847 Princetown received a Postmark comprising 'PRINCETOWN', with an undated double arc.

Prior to 1855 the post had been carried by mounted messenger between Tavistock and Princetown but, on 15 August 1855, a tender from Mr Martin Foot of £52 per annum was accepted for a cart to carry the mails. The Postmaster at Princetown was paid an allowance of £4 for the delivery of letters, work previously done by the Messenger. The following year the driver of the cart was dismissed for being convicted and fined for intoxication. Two years later another driver was dismissed for carrying passengers.

The journey time to Princetown was extended from 75 minutes to 90 minutes, but the return journey remained at 65 minutes. The service was re-advertised and, on 20 October 1856, Mr Joseph Long was appointed, with an allowance of £63.1s.0d.

1847

A single-circle date stamp was sent to Princetown via Tavistock in 1859 and a Rural Sub-Office was set up there in 1863. In 1866 Joseph Gilbert was the Receiver of letters from Horrabridge, arriving at 8.45am with despatches at 4.45pm.

Burnard's photograph of the Princetown train in a snowdrift, March 1891, is a reminder of just how treacherous the Dartmoor weather can be. The train left Princetown on 9 March at 6.34pm with six passengers who were stranded until the morning of 11th. Dartmoor postmen were often faced with the decision of whether or not to venture out when bad weather threatened. (Robert Burnard)

On 16 December 1863 an oval B98 canceller was sent there and is recorded in use from 30 January 1873 to 26 November 1874.

In 1872 the Plymouth, Princetown and Postbridge Messengers' wages were agreed, so it would seem that some letters were being taken to Postbridge, although at some time official post to Postbridge had been ruled out because of the trifling amount of mail. Tavistock was the Head Office but by 1885 this had been transferred to Plymouth.

1863

In 1878 an upright oval B98 canceller was sent from the GPO but is not recorded as being used. Two types of squared-circle date stamps were forwarded to Princetown and are recorded in use from 8 December 1880. It seems that the Horrabridge Cart was for the morning mail as, in 1883, the night mail was sent to Horrabridge by rail. The Princetown delivery seems to have been well established as, in 1881, it was extended to Dartmeet. This would have been via Two Bridges

where Jack Warne, in conversation with Wilfred Pickles, the well known broadcaster, in 1950, recalled: 'I collected letters from Two Bridges for three and a half pence a day. I was 10.'(1876).

Letters were carried by a Rural Auxilliary Postman on foot from Princetown to Postbridge and in 1894 his wages were reviewed. A year later the delivery was officially established and extended. Letters arrived at 9am and were despatched at 2pm. Wall letter boxes were cleared at 2pm in winter and 3pm in summer.

The same year the Post Master General was approached asking that regular postal deliveries should be made to Bellever Farm, Warren Inn, Bawden's Bungalow, Birch Tor Mine, Cape Horn Cottage, Stannon Farm, Hartyland, Ringhill Farm, Higher and Middle Merripit. The PMG replied:

That from enquiries made the Postbridge Rural Postman did not walk more than 16 miles a day and that the weight he carried was not excessive, also that arrangements had been sanctioned for the delivery of letters to the places named with the exception of Bellever Farm; the cost of which would be out of proportion to the revenue available for the purpose.

In 1895 the Postbridge Rural Sub-Office, with George French as sub-postmaster, was established at Greyhound Farm. On 22 May 1896 a single ring rubber datestamp 'POSTBRIDGE/PLYMOUTH' was forwarded from head office. In 1896 the Postbridge delivery was extended to Warren Inn and to Lydgate, and in 1897 the Princetown/Dunnabridge post was extended to Laughter Hole. A bi-weekly delivery was established to Bellever Farm in 1898.

That year there were heavy snow storms and it was suggested that gratuities be paid to sub-postmasters, postmen and contractors, on a sliding scale of ten shillings downwards, for getting the mail through from Yelverton and Princetown. An allowance for a shelter for a postman at Postbridge was refused in 1899. The same year his wages were raised. On 7 July a single ring date stamp was received at Postbridge but does not seem to have been used as a canceller until a later date. (I have a postcard with the stamp cancelled with a Princetown squared-circle date stamp of 1904, which also has a Postbridge mark towards the bottom of the address.).

The Warren Inn delivery was increased in frequency in 1903, and in 1905 it was extended to Golden Dagger Mine. Deliveries to Bellever were increased to 3 days a week in 1907.

In 1909 the Yelverton/Princetown mail cart service was extended to Postbridge and I think it must have been about this time that mail was sorted at Postbridge, with two Auxillary postmen employed on deliveries, for in 1911 arrangements were made for deliveries to Laughter Farm and House. They were: April-October daily delivery; November March 3-days a week, on Mondays, Wednesdays and Fridays. In 1917 the Yelverton/Postbridge cart service was discontinued and the mail transferred by rail to Princetown.

1880

For many years the mail for Postbridge was sorted at Princetown and delivered to Postbridge where it was again sorted into two rounds or walks. All addresses in the village were Postbridge/Princetown. Outgoing mail was bagged in the morning and again in the afternoon. A double-circle date stamp, with one pair of thick arcs broken by PRINCETOWN DEVON, would be used.

A selection of postmarks appear on these pages, along with their dates. Above is a scarce serpentine postmark from mail dated 22 February 1808. Only two other copies are known. (Author)

A letter 'A' above the date denoted morning mail, a letter 'B' denoting afternoon mail. Originally the mails arrived at 6.20am and the postmens' deliveries were completed by about noon. William French and William Withycombe were the postmen for many years. Their rounds were:

William French
Archerton; Lakehead; Greyhound; Bridge Cottage; Dart Cottage; East Dart Hotel; Dartfordleigh Hotel; Lydgate Hotel; Higher Lydgate; Penlee; Furzimeads; Hermitage; Redgate; Smallwaters; Sunnymead; Lower Merripit; Guiting; Reads Bungalow; Pencroft; Runnage; Pizwell; Laughter Hole; Bellever.

William Withycombe
Craigs; Parsonage; Lodges; Church Cottage; Beechwood; Chapel Cottage; Higher Merripit; Middle Merripit; Ringhill; Hartland; Stannon; Torview; Vaglas; The Brake; Fairholm; Warren Inn; Headland Warren; Challacombe; Soussons.

Above and below left are photographs of Jack Bellamy - the 'Postman on a Pony'. (Devon News Service)

Mail could be very heavy at times. During the summer visitors would send away scores of pounds of cream. This was placed in a bag marked 'perishable'. Likewise, at Christmas, there would be several bags of parcel mail, mainly containing poultry.

Eventually Postbridge addresses were changed to POSTBRIDGE/YELVERTON DEVON, and Yelverton became the sorting office. A new date stamp was sent to Postbridge. The *Western Morning News* was sent in bulk to Postbridge Post Office, unless the recipients wanted it to be delivered by post, in which case the postman always had to call at that particular address. As he also carried postage stamps, the postman could be used to take mail back for posting.

After the two Williams retired, the rounds were completed by Mr Archibald Adams and Jack Bellamy. Jack was well known as the 'Postman on a Pony' riding one or other of his three ponies, Smokey, Tinker, and Tosca. He was featured in several newspapers and appeared on television. One newspaper photograph was syndicated overseas and he received letters from as far afield as Canada and Australia. Another local postman was Mr M.L.J. (Bob) White.

Eventually the two rounds were taken over by Yelverton. Deliveries to all addresses are now made by mail van and the boxes are cleared by the van driver. Sorting is no longer done at Postbridge.

TELEVISION COMES TO POSTBRIDGE.

From a letter written by my wife to *Farmers Weekly* and published on 17 April 1959.

When you live in a small isolated village in the middle of Dartmoor, you hardly expect your living room to be suddenly turned into a television studio, but that is exactly what happened to me one morning not long ago when two men knocked on the front door and announced that they were from the BBC Television, and could they shelter in my porch as they had valuable equipment which they did not want ruined by the weather. Of course I said they could.

After a good deal of preparation in the porch and a cup of tea with us. the two men went to work on filming father-in-law, who does a postal round. riding up our drive on Tinker, complete with parcels bulging out of his two postbags. Not many minutes passed before the door opened and a dejected cameraman came in and said.

'It is no good, the weather is too bad. We will have to do it it inside. Can we do it in here?' I goggled slightly, but took them into the sitting room. 'We will have to have light,' they said. So I trotted off obediently to turn on the engine and produce our home made electricity.

The cameraman looked at our solitary ceiling light dubiously and decided that the light was not good enough. It was better in the living room he said, as I do have a reading lamp on a table by my fireside chair, as well as the central light.

Some mothers may be very well organized, but I am not. In the mornings my room is far from tidy. So you can imagine my horror when the men started setting up their apparatus and said they were going ahead. When I protested they said. 'We want it to look lived in.'

'Lived in be blowed!' I exploded. If you are going to use my room it is going to be tidy. I'll have you know I have friends with television and what would they think?' So saying, I swept the lot up and dumped it into the middle of the dining table. At last all was ready. The cameraman sang out: 'Scene 1 Act 1. Take! Silence!'

Father-in-law was good. He did not even clear his throat or start with the inevitable word 'Well' when the interview started. After he had explained his reasons for doing the post round on horseback, and told how he had been riding across the moor in all winds and weather since he was five years old, it was finished.

'I am sorry,' said the cameraman to the interviewer. 'Your head was in the way, we will have to do it again.' With a resigned glance at the clock, father-in-law went through it all again. I think they did it four times in all before it was perfect.

At last father-in-law was set free to deliver his post amid congratulations all round for doing his part so well. The men packed up their equipment and departed. They promised to phone and let me know when this epic was to be shown and we had a call from Bristol one Tuesday saying it was being shown that night.

My husband drove us all to a friend's house as pre-arranged and I sat there idly wondering what the 'magic eye' of television would make of my contemporary wall paper.

The film was good. It showed father-in-law riding over the bridge and across the open moor. Then the camera focused on Tinker's legs wading through part of the river; the reeds stood up stiffly from their soggy beds and the mist swirled all around. It was full of atmosphere. Then the cameras took us to a scene in Canterbury Cathedral. Perhaps our lighting was not good enough after all!

Chapter 3 - Around the Village

TURNPIKE COTTAGE

The Moretonhampstead–Tavistock turnpike was completed between 1772 and 1790. Sometime during this period a turnpike house was built on the western side of the bridge. Its location can be seen in the painting c.1859 by an unknown artist, in the possession of the Devon Record Office, and shown below.

The names of some of the toll house keepers are known: Joseph and Jane James 1834; Francis Coaker 1836; Jane Coaker 1841; and William Bickell 1851. According to Jonas Coaker (1801-1890) a cross which once stood on Merripit Hill was removed for use as a gatepost at the turnpike. This may have been the 'Stone called Merry Pitt' referred to by Ogilby.

The house was still there in 1880 as it was offered to the Duchy by the Turnpike Trustees for £20. It was very dilapidated and repairs would then have cost about £5. As it is also mentioned in the 1881 Census returns, demolition must have occurred after that date. The gates were due to have been removed by 1 November 1880, and Mr Bickell was approached to remove them, but they were still in situ on 25 November in that year. There is a gatepost let into the wall in Lydgate lane, opposite Dart Cottage, which may have been one of the posts. Some credence for this is the fact that one of the hangings is screw threaded so that a nut could be fitted to prevent unhanging of the gate, thus avoiding payment of the toll.

THE BARRACKS

In 1763 the Duchy records show William Warren in possession of a newtake at Postbridge. William Simpson wrote of Warren in his survey of Dartmoor dated 1786:

One of these gentlemen has already built a smelting house and is now building tenant houses for his tinners labourers etc. at a place called Postbridge upon the east quarter for which quarter he solicits he has a lease.

A watercolour of Postbridge showing the toll house and old cottages, c.1859. (Devon Record Office)

The mines which he is now working (and which were begun many years ago) belong to Lord Courtenay. They are on the edge of the Forest and the lodes shoot into it (vide the plan).

The smelting house is built upon a newtake which he purchased from Mr William Norris the Reeve for which he gave 12 guineas. The newtake is about 100 acres.

He says that his partner is going to bring down a great many thousand people out of Yorkshire with a view to establishing a woollen manufactory, that he may be better enabled to fulfil his contracts with the Government for blankets etc. and for which purpose an architect has orders to build an Inn and a village at Postbridge which are to be succeeded by a capital mansion house etc.

However this may be Postbridge may easily be made as convenient a place for such a purpose as can be desired.

On 11 November 1797, the Revd John Swete wrote in the fifteenth volume of his *Sketches of Devon*:

Two or three gunshots lower down the river appeared the front shell of a large house which I found out from some labourers who lived in a tenement behind, had been erected to the height of the first storey about 12 or 15 years ago by a Mr Warren who had been the conductor of the mines in the neighbourhood. Contiguous to these a smelting house and other necessary buildings had been raised.

It seems from Swete's further writings that he had a poor opinion of Warren's efforts in the area.

The smelting house soon fell into disrepair after the lands and other buildings had been taken over by Robert Kilminster. However, the house itself was kept in repair, for c.1839 it was tenanted by Sussanna Rowse and Jane Coaker.

A watercolour (see page 10) by an unknown artist, painted about the middle of the nineteenth century, shows a large building on the site, while photographs at the end of the century show the ruins of a building of some size (see page 7 and below).

Left: *A Chapman photograph of the clapper bridge c.1909, with the Barrack ruins beyond. (Author)*

Below: *The ruins of the house at Barracks c.1916 (foreground) where a horse and cart can be seen carrying gravel from the gravel pit. Note the built-up walls and the tinners' mould stone (arrowed). (Chapman via Author)*

The original leat which brought water to Barracks came from a point in Gawlor Brook SX 644788. It was later diverted to provide water in Whistlewind, the Beehive Plats, the duckpond, and buildings at Greyhound Farm.

Worth lists two mould stones each measuring 23.5 x 14 inches at the top, 16.25 x 8.5 inches at the base and 8 inches in depth at the site. I can remember him leading a party of people to see them after they had been uncovered. At the time of writing I can only find one. There was at that time a cattle shelter with a galvanized roof which Worth lists as a pigsty.

Behind the ruins was a gravel quarry, the stone being used in road building. In the centre of the quarry was the entrance to an adit (Barracks Hole). This adit was reputed to have curved towards Jesters. As a boy I often played there and was fascinated by a moss which glowed green. At the top of the quarry was a huge rock which became unsafe and had to be dislodged by local workmen. It can still be seen on the floor of the old quarry. For many years the quarry was used as a nesting site for sandmartins.

The trackway to Barracks had stone walls on both sides. The one nearest the river fell into disrepair and many of the stones were 'cracked' for road building.

There was a fine spring at SX 469788 now somewhat difficult to locate as it has been filled in by sand washed down through the forestry drainage systems. Theo Brown in *A Dartmoor Village* tells of a man by the name of Shadrack who gave lessons there. I have heard it said that these were for older people who had a desire to read and write. The small plats, which were included in the 1840 tithes, were eventually incorporated into Greyhound Farm. For many years they were used as a camping site. A Mr Orpen from Kent first camped there in 1910 and, except for the war years, continued to do so until about 1972. These plats have now been let to the Dartmoor National Park Authority and are used for recreational purposes.

JESTER HOLE

These enclosures have been known locally for many years as Jesters but the correct name is Jester Hole. The addition of 'Hole' has the same connotation as in Laughter Hole – a narrowing or a valley. They have had several different names in the past such as Jeastar Hole (1684), Foster Hole (incorrect interpretation of Court Roll 1738), Jester Hall (Duchy letters 1862 and 1868):

On 2 July 1684 Jacob Newcombe surrendered into the hands of our Lord the King one Newtake called Jeastar Hole and Walter French was admitted tenant. The steward was John Northmore and Thomas Hammet the Reeve. Also present were John Crossman, William French and William Wilcocks Homagers.

On 22 May 1783 Mary Willcocks being the lawful heir to John French was admitted tenant to Foster Hole. John Fortescue was the steward, William Norris Reeve. Also present were Thomas Leaman the elder, Thomas Leaman the younger, Andrew Leaman, Joseph Cleave, William Norris the younger and John Beard Homagers.

Around 1840 the Revd John White held the land and sublet it to Robert Hannaford (Leadgate). and John Cleave. C. Barrington's report to the Duchy dated 4 January 1862 mentions a proposal for a lease of Jester Hall (22 acres) of 50 years at 2d per acre. This lease was granted to Samuel White.

In 1868 William Bickell was granted a lease of part of the lands which were held on lease by Kilminster and Benjamin, or in the lease of Jester Hall which had been granted to Samuel White. From about 1900 onwards Jesters was let to the leaseholders of Lydgate. Virtually all the land has only been fit for grazing, although a small part of it was improved during the Second World War by William Warne, and has been cut for hay.

DART COTTAGE

In 1865 William Bickell a stonemason applied to the Duchy for a lease of land on which to build a house. The lease was finally granted on 21 August 1868 for a piece of land 2 rods and 23 perches in area (about .872 acres, O.S.1429), for a period of 60 years. This land was part of property held on lease by Kilminster and Benjamin, or in the lease of Jester Hall which had been granted to Samuel White. It was reported to the Duchy that the house was being built in November 1869.

Soon after the house was completed the Bickells' started to 'take in' people and one of their first guests was Miss Wakeford, the local school mistress. In 1881 William's wife Ann was shown as a 'Boarding House Keeper' and on 3 April 1881 the census return shows six undergraduates from Oxford staying there. The Frith photograph, probably taken around 1885, shows the house very much as it was originally built.

Early in the 1900s the Endacott family who were now in residence added a porch and some extra rooms (see Chapman photo).

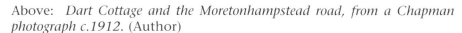

Top: *Frith's photograph of the clapper bridge and Dart Cottage, taken c.1885.* (Author)

Above: *Dart Cottage and the Moretonhampstead road, from a Chapman photograph c.1912.* (Author)

Lucy Endacott (née Bickell) at Dart Cottage – a Chapman portrait (Author).

The Endacott's continued taking in boarders and in the 1930s George Endacott decided to install an electricity plant. This comprised a gas engine and dynamo which charged a bank of batteries. Before the gas engine could be started it was necessary .to heat a metal plug with a blowlamp. When this plug was red hot the flywheel was cranked over and, hopefully, the engine would start. The success of this procedure could be often judged by the comments overheard by passers by!

In 1945 Francis Barker, Chartered Architect of Upton Cottage, Chagford, drew up plans for improvements to the cottage for Rear Admiral Sir Lionel Doveton Sturdee Bt. (1884–1970). He was the 2nd Baronet and son of Admiral of the Fleet Sir Doveton Sturdee, of Falklands fame. Sir Lionel married Dorothy Mary Mowbray Sayer in 1910, she died in 1966. He was chief telecommunications censor 1940–45, and in 1926 he published, for private circulation, *Their Majesties' Ships Defiance*. The frontispiece, a drawing of a ship's figurehead was by Lady Sylvia Sayer.

The house was for many years the residence of Mrs Pamela Gill, before she later moved to Tavistock.

NEW INN
WEBB'S TEMPERANCE HOTEL

In 1861 John Webb, a tin miner who also farmed 20 acres at Ringhill, applied for a lease of two acres of unenclosed land for the purpose of building a house. He later changed his mind and asked that he should be allowed to build an inn. The inn was built c.1862 and on 26 August 1863 an application was made to Tavistock Brewster Sessions for a licence in respect of New Inn, Postbridge (it seems that each new inn in the area used this name at some time or other). John's wife, Charlotte, died, I think in 1870 or 1871, and Selina, his daughter, who had married Solomon Warne, was his housekeeper. John Webb Senior died on 10 February 1878 and the lease passed to his son, another John Webb.

It seems that there were three cottages attached to the inn. According to the census return of 1881, one was unoccupied and the other two were occupied by Solomon and Selina Warne, and Grace Coaker respectively. This is borne out by the rating books c.1910 which also lists three cottages.

It was during John Webb junior's tenure that the inn became a Temperance house and was renamed Webb's Temperance Hotel. This came about, so it is said, that after attending a chapel meeting where the evils of drink were roundly condemned, John came home and poured the barrels of ale into the gutter and vowed never to sell intoxicating liquor again.

Temperance House seems to have been unoccupied in 1891. Two cottages were occupied, one by Solomon Warne, Selina and their family, William Charlotte, John, Henry, Frederick, Solomon, Richard, Rebecca and Frank. The other was the home of Edwin Hyde, a licensed hawker, and his wife.

At this time Postbridge had become very popular and many visitors stayed at 'The Temperance'. They were met at either Moretonhampstead or Princetown railway stations and transported with their luggage in wagonettes belonging either to the hotel or to George French of Greyhound. Others availed themselves of a coach and four which, during the summer months, ran daily from Moretonhampstead to Princetown. It arrived at Postbridge just after 12 noon from Moreton and just after four o'clock from Princetown, announcing its arrival by a postilion blowing his posthorn. After John died the lease passed to his wife Elizabeth A. Webb, then to Mr David Japp, and in 1909 to Solomon Warne.

The property then consisted of twelve rooms. The cottages had been converted into a single building, occupied by Henry Warne. At that time Solomon was the tenant of Elizabeth Webb and the annual rent for the hotel, cottages and 5 acres

Temperance Hotel (now the East Dart) c.1900. (Author)

A view at the back of the Temperance Hotel, from a Chapman photograph c.1912. (Author)

of land was £27.10s. Henry Warne paid £2.15s rent for the cottage.

As with many older dwellings the hotel eventually required modernization and, in 1926, it was closed and Solomon purchased the lease of Dartfordleigh from Miss Carey.

EAST DART AND DARTFORDLEIGH

Plans were drawn up for a new hotel by Richardson and Gill and this was built, c.1930, on the site of the old Temperance Hotel. The new hotel was named East Dart and with Solomon Warne as the leaseholder he was able to run both properties as hotels. He then decided to apply to the Brewster Sessions for a full licence but there was considerable opposition to its being granted by the local 'Gentry'. He was somewhat disappointed when a table licence was granted instead.

Mr Warne decided to do away with the acetylene gas plant and installed an electric light plant at East Dart which would light both premises. In order to cope with the laundry from both hotels an electric washing machine and electric ironing board was set up in the old coach house. The loft over the coach house was converted into bedrooms for staff use.

At East Dart a hand operated Shell petrol pump was installed. The petrol cost about 1s.4d a gallon and was measured by pumping it up into glass containers and then transferring it to the car tank by moving a lever, which also recorded the amount transferred.

The next holders of the leases were Mrs Edmunds, who ran East Dart, and Mrs Williamson who ran Dartfordleigh. This arrangement lasted until 1941 when both premises were occupied by Pinewood School whose pupils had been evacuated. Soon after they arrived Mr Cecil Ranger, the headmaster died. A friend wrote:

The news of the death of Cecil Ranger, Headmaster of Pinewood School, will come as a shock to all who knew him. He was at the height of his success as a schoolmaster. Having built up the school for a number of years at Farnborough in Hampshire, he had transferred it shortly before the war began to Melchet Court near Romsey. More recently he had moved temporarily to a quiet and beautiful part of the country near Postbridge in Devon where he died suddenly on Saturday last. He looked forward to a time of useful work there while the war lasted, then to a happy return to Melchet, on which his heart was set.

For himself this was not to be. Perhaps the thought of this would not have saddened him overmuch if he could have been certain that all would be well with his boys. For Cecil Ranger was a signal example of the kind of educationalist with which this country is richly endowed: he gave himself day and night, in term time and in the holidays, for the school which he loved.

Unmarried and without other absorbing claims on his time and energy, he was free to devote himself unstintingly to his work. Nothing was unimportant if it affected the well-being of the school; nothing was too much trouble if the boys were to gain from it. The school gave no hint of luxury.

Dartfordleigh Hotel. (Author)

At the same time care and thought and imagination lay behind every arrangement. Nothing was haphazard, nothing left to chance. The atmosphere was that of a well-disciplined home. Ranger's life was in his school and his work there is and will be the monument which he leaves behind him. He had no desire for impressive scholarship lists, though scholarships came to the school. Untouched by self-interest, he made it his aim to train the children entrusted to him to the highest which each was capable. He built for the future. A generation of boys and their parents have reason to bless his name.

Cecil Ranger is buried in Postbridge Cemetery.

In 1946 Pinewood School left the village and the two properties reverted to hotels. Eventually they became separate entities, each changing occupiers several times. During the early 1950s Mr Bracken obtained a full licence for the East Dart and in recent years the Dartfordleigh has become a Nursing Home. The old coach house is now a house. Further extensions have been made.

DARTFORDLEIGH – DURYMEAD

Miss B.M. Langley was granted a 60 year lease in 1892 of 2 to 3 rods of land, then tenanted by Mr Webb of the Temperance Hotel in order to build a house. The plans were drawn up by J.W. Rowell & Sons, architects of Newton Abbot, and building was in progress in 1893.

The house had 4 sitting rooms, 5 bedrooms, dressing rooms, W.C. etc, kitchen and offices. Outside there was stabling for three horses, a coach house and loft, grounds and tennis court. An early postcard shows a windpump for pumping water. In 1896 Miss Langley pressed for the road to Lydgate to be made up and become the responsibility of the Council, but it was only made up as far as Dartfordleigh. The house was lit by acetylene gas.

The lease was assigned to Miss Penn-Gaskell and then, in 1924, to Miss Carey who changed the name of the house to Durymead.

In 1926 the lease was transferred to Solomon Warne who in 1929 extended the premises and built a long bungalow-type building adjacent to

Postbridge from a Chapman photograph c. 1907. Dart Cottage can be seen on the left and next to it the Temperance Hotel. Moor Cottage is centre distance and Dartfordleigh (Durymead) is the large house centre right. The windpump can be seen rising above the roofline. Far right is the parsonage. (Author)

the tennis court (this was to allow fishermen who came back late from fishing for sea trout to enter their rooms without disturbing guests in the main hotel). The name of the house once again reverted to Dartfordleigh.

LEADGATE
LYDGATE

It has been said that if a man could fence a piece of ground and build a house with roof and chimney and have a fire burning in the hearth between sunrise and sunset, he established a right to live there undisturbed. Richard Hannaford is alleged to have done just this at Leadgate and after living there for a while, sold his very small cot to another man who enlarged it.

This may have been the Robert Hannaford who lived there with Mary and Arthur Hannaford in 1841. Robert was then about 80 and, by 1851, Mary and Arthur were there farming 5 acres. Arthur was granted a 50 year lease by the Duchy in 1855, but by 1864 the house was in a very dilapidated condition, and by 1871 was unoccupied.

Sometime after 1871 the property passed to James Robbins, a tin miner, and his wife Ellen. I think it was Ellen who ran a Dame School there when the village school closed for a short time between 1876 and 1880. The pool on the corner below the house is known as Dame's Pool to this day. It seems that Arthur's lease must have been

surrendered as, in 1885, the Robbins were granted a lease of a cot and lands. They continued to live at Leadgate until 1893 when the lease was assigned to Alfred and S. Balkwill for upwards of £1000.

In 1894 the name was changed to Lydgate and, as Mr Balkwill intended to spend quite an amount on improvements, a new 50 year lease was granted which included about 12.5 acres of land.

The old house was burnt down in 1899 and a new house with five downstairs and six upstairs rooms, plus bath and WC, was built.

Balkwill was granted permission in 1902 to abstract water from the East Dart river to work a 3-foot water wheel for the purpose of pumping water to the house, with the proviso that the water used for pumping had to be returned to the river.

In order to obtain the water a wooden launder was erected further up the river, diverting water to a leat and on to the pumping house. The pumping house can still be seen today and has given its name Wheel Pool to the pool nearby. Below Wheel Pool there is an island which was used as a bridging point across the river, as the Lydgate lands lay on both sides of the East Dart. This bridge was eventually removed downriver where it still stands. This bridge is locally called Lydgate Clam and the metalwork is reputed to have come from the tin mines.

Mr Balkwill was a chemist from Plymouth and when he was not in residence the house was

Above: *Lydgate, with higher Lydgate, from a Chapman photograph c.1913.* (courtesy L. Germon).

Right: *Preparations for hay-making at Lydgate: William Warne; Jack Bellamy and a visitor.* (Author)

looked after by William and Elizabeth Warne. Eventually they took over the house and started to take in people. The house became Lydgate House Hotel and, after William was killed in an accident, Elizabeth carried on helped by her sons, William and Solomon. William married and he and his wife Nellie improved the hotel with the addition of an electric light plant and other internal improvements.

They kept cattle and supplied the hotel with milk and cream using their land for grazing. My father used to cut hay there with a mowing machine drawn by horses. He used our own carthorse, Stella, and another belonging to Mr Warne.

Mr Warne installed a petrol pump which was the only one in operation in the village during the war. He improved land on the other side of the river adjacent to Lakehead Hill by ripping up the gorse and re-seeding.

There have been several occupiers since the Warnes left. The house has been re-roofed and a bore hole sunk for the supply of water.

HIGHER LYDGATE.

In 1871 Samuel Stanbury was granted a lease of seven acres of land on which to build a house. The house was small and had low ceilings. He sold the remnants of the lease to Zacharias Stephens who, in 1896, submitted plans to the Duchy to enlarge the house. As a result of these proposals he was granted a new 40 year lease.

In 1906, John Dawe, who had been a farm bailiff at Prince Hall, bought the lease. He worked the stamps at Vitifer Mine, working two shifts, 7am–5pm and 7pm–5am. He looked older than he really was because of premature grey hair caused by rheumatic fever while a young man. I well remember him riding his grey horse whilst driving his cattle to graze on Lakehead Hill. He rented an Archerton field adjacent to Drift Lane, The field has a large boulder in the middle of it and is still spoken of as Dawe's field.

Around 1910 Higher Lydgate was a small five-roomed cottage with about eight acres of land comprising OS 1453, 1455, 1456, 1457.

Above: *Mary Dawe at Higher Lydgate c.1940.* (courtesy Mrs Exell)

Left: *John and Mary Dawe with Eileen Willcocks, Higher Lydgate.* (courtesy Mrs Exell)

I used to visit the cottage to meet the young people there. I am not too sure Mary, John's wife, approved, as she was heard to say 'Tell that boy to go home, what's he hanging about for?'

After John died his son Frederick took over the smallholding, helped by his wife. Margery Cooper writing in *Parish Pump* (July 1968) said:

They came to Postbridge in 1937 when Freddie's father died at the age of 88, to live with his mother. They lived together for several years and then the old lady became bedridden. She was in bed for three years, attended to night and day by Mrs Freddie. She died at the ripe old age of 96. Freddie was always very active. Before he came to Postbridge he was head stable man to Mr Woodman and Mr Mitchell of Yelverton, racehorse trainers. He has run a small farm since living in Postbridge. At one time, he told me, he had 13 cows to look after, but he just loves it and now, at the age of 86, he still carries on. Not only on the farm, but also he looks after his wife who, unfortunately had a stroke five years ago and has been bedridden ever since. They are a wonderful couple, and in spite of her handicap she is always so cheerful.

After Fred's death Higher Lydgate passed to William Waite who had previously been the landlord of East Dart Hotel. He improved the house and built a large shed on land opposite.

A few years ago the house was further extended by Mr Greatorex. The trackway for Lydgate Lane to the cemetery is a permitted path.

PENLEE

The Rendel family were regular visitors to Postbridge around the turn of the century and they eventually decided to live there. Initially they considered the possibility of rebuilding Higher Lydgate to suit their needs but decided against this and, in 1909, Dr Rendel bought a number of fields from Mrs Lucy Beare, the wife of Henry Beare of Newton Abbot, and Harriet Thomas, also of Newton Abbot, for £527.10s.

All these fields (with the exception of Pt. Tithe No.487 which became the local football field) were enclosed from a large enclosure (Tithe No.594) which in 1840 belonged one-third to M. Germon and two thirds to John E. Nosworthy, both of Pizwell.

In 1932 The Prince of Wales transferred to Dr Rendel a field of about 5 acres for £75 and this field, together with those previously mentioned, now comprise the property known as Penlee Farm.

In 1910 Dr Rendel instructed Halsey Ricardo, his brother-in-law, to design a house which not only provided his family with a home but which also had accommodation for patients suffering from tuberculosis. This plan was not entirely successful as, during the first winter, snow covered patients were sleeping on the open verandah.

The house was built in 1911 by Stones of Chagford at a cost of £1737 and, because of its importance as an example of Halsey Ricardo's design, and the modern use of local building traditions and materials, it eventually became a

Grade II listed building, in 1987. The plans and drawings are preserved inside the house.

Dr and Mrs Rendel had one son, Terence Blair Rendel, and two daughters, Cecilia Margaret Grant and Katherine Sarah Wedgwood.

In 1911 Walter Beard from Winkleigh was a coachman at Penlee and, for many years, Mary and Sidney French worked there as cook–house keeper and chauffeur–groom respectively. Miss Ruth James was also employed there and she walked to and fro from Chapel Cottage daily.

After the French's left in 1937 Mr and Mrs Archibald Adams, who at one time lived at Pizwell Cottage (now demolished), were employed in their place.

In 1936 a tenancy agreement was drawn up between Dr Rendel and John Bellamy relating to certain fields or closes of land and certain out-buildings at Penlee at a yearly rental of £14 per annum. This tenancy lasted until 1948.

The fields and closes referred to were :

Ordnance No.	Description	Acreage
1493	Pasture	6.191
1494	Pasture	3.837
1509	Rough Pasture	1.269
1519Pt.	ditto	2.475 Est.
1495	ditto	2.864
1496	ditto	6.969
1459Pt.		3.400 Est.

This was a total of 27.005 acres. The buildings comprised Sheds in OS No.1493 and Pt.1459 and outbuildings at Penlee consisting of Open Shed, Piggery and Hay Shed.

Mr Bellamy supplied milk to Pinewood School from 1941 to 1946 and much of it was carried in churns from Penlee to the Post Office using a path to a hunting gate in Dawe's Lane, then to a stile opposite Higher Lydgate, along a path to steps leading to Lydgate lane and thence to the Post Office.

After the Rendel's left Penlee Mr Bellamy gave up the tenancy and Mr and Mrs Adams continued to live there, farming the land and providing for paying guests.

Dr Rendel died on 17 March 1948 at Richmond in Surrey and left his entire estate to his widow Elizabeth Cecilia Rendel. He once told me that he had no intention of being buried in Postbridge cemetery as 'it was far too cold a place' as far as he was concerned.

Mrs Rendel died on 24 September 1954 and bequeathed Penlee to her granddaughter Pamela Margaret Rawden of Plainville, Connecticut, USA,

the second daughter of Terence Blair Rendel.

She offered the property to Mr and Mrs Adams for £4000 but the offer was not taken up and they remained as tenants until Mr Adams died in 1960. In 1961 it was let on a yearly tenancy to Mr Geoffrey Day at a commencing rent of £250, and in 1966 Mr Day bought the property from Mrs Rawden.

Then followed three more owners: 1976 Mr and Mrs W.H. Thomas, 1978 Mr B.J. Turner, and in 1987 Mr and Mrs Peter McMurtrie.

Dr and Mrs Rendel often made the music room available for parties and dances for the local inhabitants. Mrs Rendel took a great delight in dancing the polka, whirling around the room much to the consternation of her partner.

Dr Rendel could always be called in an emergency and I can vaguely remember him sitting with me for hours when in crisis owing to suppressed measles and pneumonia. He was also very interested in swimming and had permission to construct a weir in order to create a pool on the Dart just below the house. He encouraged local youngsters to swim and rewarded them with 10 shillings when they could do this to his satisfaction.

Mrs Rendel kept poultry which were penned in a field near the house. She was bothered by crows taking feedstuffs and attacking young chickens. The local youths, on hearing she would pay for each crow that was shot, decided to shoot rooks instead – she was not deceived!

She also delighted in weaving and wove some curtains for the local church altar. Into the seam she sewed a note thanking the Lord 'for her husband's recovery from illness'. Unfortunately the curtains were later destroyed.

The walled vegetable garden was very productive and the flower garden, tended by Mrs Rendel, was a delight in the cottage style. She did not approve of some of the pathways which rather resembled a swastika and these had to be relaid.

MOOR COTTAGE
(CRAGG'S COTTAGE, CRAIGS)

This cottage was originally built by Philip Crossman c.1865. The Duchy had granted a 60 year lease of unenclosed forest for the purposes of land improvement. The original name was Moor Cottage.

Crossman's daughter, Sarah, married Thomas Coaker c.1867 and they lived there with him and his wife Elizabeth c.1871, before the lease was assigned to Mrs E.H. Pethybridge in 1878. In 1886

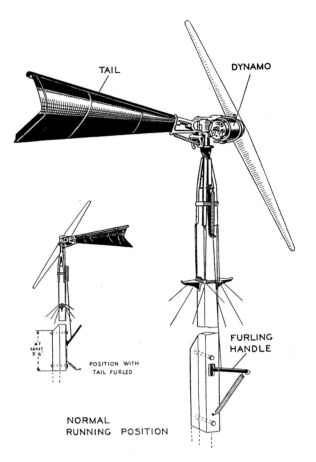

TAIL

DYNAMO

POSITION WITH
TAIL FURLED

AT
LEAST
2' 6"

FURLING
HANDLE

NORMAL
RUNNING POSITION

Detailed drawings of the wind generator installation at Craigs Cottage.

the property was in the possession of William Craggs and was known as Cragg's cottage. It seems that its present name, Craigs, is a corruption of Cragg's. The same year the cottage was assigned to Miss Freestone. In 1891 it was occupied by James and Ann Sleep and later by their relatives, Harriet and Ernest Willcocks.

I can remember George Warne and his family living there, because of an incident when one of his sons lost his way in fog, when returning from digging china clay to the north-west of Postbridge.

The property was improved in 1922 and again since. Various trades have been carried on there, one family making boot polish and candles.

In 1932 Charlie and Hilda Rowlands came to live at Craigs and remained there until Charlie died in 1967, aged 75. Charlie had left home in Plymouth at the age of 14 to work for Mr and Mrs Jack Withycombe at Soussons. He became great friends with the Warne brothers and was made 'at home' by old Mrs Warne who treated him as a son.

At various times he worked at Vitifer and Hexworthy mines and at the clay works previously mentioned. He also worked for the Forestry Commission, and as a gardener for the Henley's at Archerton. While Charlie was out working, Hilda ran Craigs as a boarding house and also provided cream teas for residents. In some ways they were ahead of their time. Charlie installed a 'Freelight' wind-driven lighting plant, later to be replaced by a diesel generating plant. They were also early possessors of a television set and a motor car.

At the time of writing, the occupier is Mrs Phyllis Parish.

THE VILLAGE HALL

One evening Mrs Webb, the church caretaker who lived at the Lodge, was seeing to the stove in the church by the light of a lantern when she heard a noise by the church door. Looking up she saw an elderly white-bearded gentleman dressed in black standing just inside the door. She told me she was somewhat taken aback until he spoke. 'I am the Bishop of Exeter and I am on my way to see Mrs Pethybridge about the consecration of the church, perhaps you can help me? If I consecrate the church is there anywhere else that the villagers could use as a hall?'

'Nowhere' said Mrs Webb.

'Then I shall tell Mrs Pethybridge that I will consecrate the church when a hall has been provided for the village.'

Thus, on 5 April 1933 an account was opened with Lloyds Bank Plymouth and subscriptions towards building the Hall commenced, with Miss Edith M Bennett as treasurer. A deed of conveyance of one rood of land (part of Close 1367 on the OS Map of the Parish of Lydford, 1905 edition) was executed on 23 August 1933 between HRH The Prince of Wales, and Sir Walter Courtenay Bennett of Archerton, Robert Paley Kitcat of Vaglas, and Mrs Elsie Douglas Pethybridge of Hartyland (called the first trustees).

The deed stipulated that a Village Hall, surrounded by substantial fences, should be erected within six months. A first schedule to the conveyance provided for the setting up of a Council of Management and listed the rules and method by which the Hall should be managed. A second schedule named the first Council of Management:

Permanent Trustees ex officio for the first year only: Sir C W Bennett; Mr R.P. Kitcat; Mrs E D Pethybridge.

Elected by village general meeting: Mr William Warne; Miss Janet Lind; Mr Sidney French

Also:
Mr Archibald Adams	Church of England
Mrs Ethel White	Wesleyan Methodist Church
Mr Jack Bellamy	Lydford Parish Council
Mrs Elsie Rendel	Nursing Association
Mr Solomon Warne	British Legion
Miss Edith M Bennett	Parochial Church Council
Mr Harold White	Football Club

The conveyance was enrolled in the Duchy of Cornwall Office on 27 September 1933. By the 20 October 1933 subscriptions amounted to £439.11s.9d., including a loan of £145 from the National Council for Social Services and a donation of £200 from Mrs Pethybridge. In November 1933 the Carnegie United Kingdom Trust donated £75, and further contributions continued to be received. During this period Stones of Chagford, using plans provided free by the architect of the National Council for Social Services, were paid £537.5s.3d. for their building work.

Many local people gave their services free, building walls and laying drains etc.

Major McCormick, Secretary to the Duchy, opened the hall on 12 December 1933. Sir Courtenay Bennett proposed a vote of thanks which was followed by a whist drive and dance. Entry tickets for the opening night were 1s.6d.

The Church Committee gave a piano against which Turner & Phillips of Plymouth allowed £10 for a secondhand one in excellent condition, costing £35. The Committee also handed over the china and cupboard from the vestry along with the school gramophone.

The County Library agreed to lend fifty volumes for a library, changeable every 4 months. Mrs Chudleigh (Lakehead) agreed to open the library every Friday from 7pm–8pm. As a village library it was quite successful and by 1936 there were 60 members on the roll with an average attendance of 25. Other librarians through the years were Miss Grant and Mrs Hibbert.

The initial charges for the use of the Committee room and the hall ranged from 1–3 shillings depending on the time of day and whether or not lighting was used.

The first concert given in the hall was by the Chagford Concert Party and during the first four months there were 13 whist drives, 2 dances (one of which was a hunt ball), 14 dancing classes, 2 concerts, 2 social gatherings, 1 private hire, 1 jumble sale, 2 Church Committee meetings, a reception following consecration of the Church, and 4 Lantern services.

This in itself showed there was a need for a hall and that it could be run satisfactorily by the villagers. It had been especially remarked by visitors that there was an exceptionally friendly spirit shown by everyone.

During the year ending 8th April 1935 there were 23 whist drives, 3 concerts, 4 dances, 1 hunt ball, 1 jumble sale, a Village Fete which raised £40 for hall funds, and 3 private lettings. A women's guild had been formed and had used the hall on 4 occasions. A dramatic society had also been formed.

To mark the Silver Jubilee celebrations Mrs James had provided a high tea in the hall at 8pm and this was followed by a bonfire.

In the following year the hall saw similar use, including service as a polling station. The local Member of Parliament, Mark Kirkpatrick, had made two visits.

During the war the building was used by the Home Guard and as a First Aid Point, along with its usual use as a place for entertainment. The boys of Pinewood School gave a number of concerts there and, when they left the village, the school was presented with a painting of a Dartmoor scene which Mr Wakeham the headmaster said had been hung in the dining room of their new school.

In 1945 a committee was set up to plan a welcome home fund. It was decided to give every ex-service man and woman from the village a sum of money in an inscribed wallet. There were seventeen recipients. In 1947 a fund was started in order to purchase an electric light plant or to pay for a public supply if it came to the village. In the event a plant was purchased as a public supply was not available until 1966.

Over the years, like most village halls, this one has had its ups and downs. There have been disagreements which have led to resignations among committee members and at one time it seemed doubtful if the hall would continue. Recently however, mainly thanks to the efforts of Jimmy Martin, who ran the YHA at Bellever for many years, many thousands of pounds were raised and the roof has been renewed, a new floor laid, double-glazed windows fitted, the kitchen and toilets refurbished, new furniture purchased and the hall completely redecorated. New curtains to the stage and controlled stage lighting has meant that concerts such as 'Phil's Follies' have been arranged with considerable success.

St Gabriel's Church, formerly Postbridge Church of England School. (Author)

Chapter 4 – St Gabriel's Church

The church was built c.1868 by Stone's of Chagford to a design which was originally for a school and a schoolmaster's house (see chapter on Education). It seems that it was the Revd Morris Fuller's idea that the building should be used as a church and a church school. It was built on open moorland which had a quarry pit where Dury Head Cottage now stands. This quarry was filled in with the earth and rock taken out for the church foundations.

On Monday 19 May 1869 the Bishop of Exeter granted a licence for services to be held in St Gabriel's Church. A copy of the official document was framed and hung in the church to mark the centenary of the grant. It reads:

To all to whom these Presents shall come Henry by Divine permission Bishop of Exeter Greeting. Whereas it has been represented unto us by Petition of the Reverend Morris Joseph Fuller, Rector of the Rectory Parish of Lydford in the County of Devon and our Diocese and the church wardens and those whose names were subscribed inhabitants of the said Parish that for the spiritual benefit of those of the Parishioners of the Parish of Lydford who are resident in the Hamlet of Postbridge and neighbourhood at a distance of eighteen miles from the Parish Church a building intended for Chapel for the performance of Divine Service in conformity with the rites and ceremonies of the Church of England had been built in Postbridge aforesaid. That the Chapel was fitted up and provided with all things necessary for the performance therein of Divine Service. Wherefore the petitioners prayed that we would be pleased to grant our Licence for the performance of Divine Service in the said Chapel by the vicar of the said Parish of Lydford or his licenced curate until the same shall be consecrated from me the said Bishop do by these Presents so far as in us lies and by law we can give and grant our licence and authority for the performance of Divine Service in the said Chapel according to the rites and ceremonies of the United Church of England and Ireland by the vicar of the said parish or his curate duly licenced reserving to us and our successors power at all times to revoke the licence hereby granted or to take any other order in this behalf.

Given under our hand and Episcopal Seal this nineteenth day of May in the year of our Lord one thousand eight hundred and sixty nine and in the thirty ninth year of our Consecration.
Henry Exeter.

The licencing of the church should have been followed by its consecration but owing to Bishop Phillpott's illness this was never done. In fact the church was not consecrated until 1934. The reasons for the delay are obscure and may have been due to the forgetfulness by the clergy and parishioners or for some other reason. We shall probably never know.

In 1870 the Education Act was passed and the Educational Commissioners probably added to the muddle as, at a later date, the nave/schoolroom was used as a meeting place for lectures, recreation etc. The first churchwarden was Richard Coaker of Runnage, and members of the Sleep family were caretakers, vergers and sidesmen.

Originally a Chapel of Ease in the Parish of Lydford the church later became part of the Parish of Princetown. It continued as a combined church and school until 1931 when the school closed. In 1934 a new bell was hung, the cost was defrayed in full by a private donation.

On 17 March 1934 the church was consecrated by the Bishop of Exeter. He was assisted in the service by Sir Courtenay Bennett who presented the parishioners petition. Mr Henry W. Michelmore, Commissary to the Chancellor and Deputy Registrar of the Consistory Court of Exeter; the Archdeacon of Plymouth the Ven. F. Whitfield-Daukes; the Rural Dean of Tavistock and Rector of Milton Abbot Revd W.D. Henry; and Revd Stanhope Lovell, vicar of Princetown.

Other clergy present were the Revd G. Thorpe vicar of Lydford; Revd Kenneth Lake Exeter; Revd R.C. Burnett, rector of Alphington; Revd Owen Davies, vicar of Brentor; Revd W.T. Wood vicar of Widecombe, and Revd E.F. Hall rector of Leusdon.

In 1936 Mrs Pethybridge of Hartyland made over the sum of £1250 for the restoration of St Gabriel's and a petition listed the following improvements: 1. To erect an east window of stained glass. 2. To erect an oak rerodos and

Interior of Postbridge Church prior to the fitting of the new pews, c.1932. Schoolchildren were taught in the area on the left where the chairs stand. A Chapman photograph. (Author)

The Lychgate at Postbridge Church, dedicated to the memory of Mrs Janet Lind, and Stannon Lodges. (Author)

panelling in the chancel. 3. To concrete the floor levels of the sanctuary and enlarge it. Then refloor in granite and slate the whole of the flooring in the chancel and sanctuary. 4. To put in new oak altar rails. 5. To cut down the existing screen to transom level and to slightly alter the position of three tablets to accommodate the panelling.

The plans were drawn up by Cowell Drewitt and Wheatley, architects of Truro, and the east window was designed by Donald B. Taunton of Picadilly, London. He wrote that the two rolls at the foot of the right hand light represents the scrolls for the old testament while the chalice in the corresponding light represents the new law.

The pews are dedicated as follows: on the left hand side of the church: 1. Walter Ley Pethbridge MD and Barbara and Elsie Douglas. 2. Silas Samuel Sleep, Harriet Sleep, James Sleep. 3. Kate Douglas James. 4. Courtenay Walter Bennett Kt., Edith M Bennett. Behind these pews is an oak bookcase designed and made by John S. Bellamy in memory of Marjorie Cooper and her brothers Leonard, Fernley and Stanley Warne. On the right hand side of the church: 1. Thomas Webb and his sister Rebecca, Thomas Redvers Webb, William John Webb, Evelyn Webb, James Webb, Doris Webb. 2. Coronation pew to commemorate the coronation of Queen Elizabeth II 2 June 1953. 3. Elsie Rendel. 4. William and Elizabeth Warne and their son Solomon and son William. 5. Richard

Coaker and Fanny Coaker. 6. Katherine Corisande Smyth FDS.FCSEng. Helen Mary Blundell b.1893–d.1970. Charlotte Mary Strickland b.1959–d. 1968. 6. Ila Hooper, Bertram Hooper. 7. John Henley, Olive Henley. 8. Pinewood School. 9. Pinewood School gratefully remembers 1941–1946. The carvings on the Pinewood pews represent some of the natural history subjects which interested the boys.

The carvings in the church were executed by the Misses Pinwell. In the porch is a notice board in memory of Jack and Elsie Bellamy who served the village for over 50 years. It was also made by John S. Bellamy, their grandson. On the South Wall is a clock in memory of Joan Martin a Beloved Pilgrim.

Of the three tablets mentioned in the petition of 1936 only one remains, and this is in memory of John Webb killed in action in France with the Devonshire Regiment 21 August 1916, aged 39, and his wife Elizabeth Jane who died 18 August 1956, aged 78.

The original large silver chalice and two patens were stored for safekeeping, but I know not where. A smaller chalice, given in memory of Miss Janet Lind, and a paten, were stolen a few years ago but these have been replaced, with similar inscriptions. The lych gate was also erected in memory of Miss Lind.

The following rectors, vicars, and curates were licenced to officiate at St Gabriel's:

Postbridge Church outing, early 1930s. Adults l-r: Mr Kitcat; Mrs Pethybridge; Miss Grant; unknown.

RECTORS OF LYDFORD

1867 M.J. Fuller
1879 J.H. Bennett
1891 R. Turner
1895 W.A. Badger
1901 G.S. Thorpe

VICARS OF PRINCETOWN

1916 J.H. Scott
1919 H.R. Cooke
1925 A.W.J. Murphey
1932 G.W.L.S. Lovell
1935 G.S. Lodge
1936 B.P.H. Ball (With Postbridge and Huccaby from 1944)
1948 L.L. Rees
1956 C.V.A. Longden
1959 D.V.G. Brock
1963 C. Johns

STIPENDARY ASSISTANT CURATES

1869 G.C. Caffin (Parish Church of Lydford and Chapels of Dartmeet and Postbridge).
1873 D.C. McKenzie (Parish of Lydford for service in Princetown Chapel and to reside in Princetown).
1875 W.F. Adey (Parish of Lydford for service of Princetown Church and Mission Chapels of Postbridge and Dartmeet).
1878 J.C. Dunn (Parish of Lydford for service of Mission Chapels of St Raphael Dartmeet and St Gabriel Postbridge and to reside at Huccaby).
1881 E. Harris (Parish of Lydford for service in the licenced Chapels of Postbridge and Huccaby and to reside at Huccaby).
1882 J. Henry (Parish of Lydford for service at Princetown and to reside in the Parsonage House).
1883 J.B. Shattock (Parish of Lydford and for service of the Chapels of Postbridge and Dartmeet and to reside at Postbridge).
1886 C.W.H. Reynolds (Parish of Lydford and Princetown).
1891 H.W. Macklin (Parish of Lydford with Princetown).
1892 A.C. Denman (Parish of Lydford with Princetown).
1893 C.L.M. Fenn (Parish of Lydford and the Chapel of Ease at Princetown and the Chapels of Postbridge and Dartmeet and to reside at Postbridge).
1894 W.A. Badger (Parish of Lydford and St Michael's and All Angels Princetown and to reside at Princetown Parsonage).

In memoriam card John Bellett Shattock, curate of Postbridge and Dartmeet 1883. (Author)

1895 C.H. Gill (Parish of Lydford and the Chapel of Ease at Princetown and in the Chapels of Postbridge and Dartmeet).
1896 A. Bowman (Parish of Lydford and to reside at Postbridge distant from the Parish Church of Lydford not more than 20 miles).
1897 A. Baring-Gould (Parish of Lydford and Princetown and to reside at Princetown).
1899 T.E. Fox (Parish of Lydford and to reside at Postbridge).
1902 W.D. Williams (Parish of Lydford and to reside at the Parsonage Postbridge).
1903 H. Knowles (Parish of Lydford and to reside at Princetown).
1903 H.St John E. Wrenford (Parish of Lydford and to reside at Postbridge).
1903 J. Chapman (Parish of Lydford and to reside at Postbridge Parsonage).
1906 C.M. Hawker (Parish of Lydford and to reside at Princetown Parsonage).
1907 J.L. Coles (Parish of Lydford and to reside at Postbridge Parsonage).
1907 Heathcote Smith (Parish of Lydford and to reside at Princetown Parsonage).
1909 M.A. Reading (Parish of Lydford and to reside at Princetown Parsonage).
1910 F.W. Botterill (Parish of Lydford and to reside at Postbridge Parsonage).
1912 H.C. Pratt (Parish of Lydford and for service of the Chapels of St Gabriel's Postbridge and St Raphael's Huccaby and to reside at Postbridge Parsonage).
1916 W.H.C. Lane (Parish of Lydford and to reside at Postbridge Parsonage).
1916 G.M.H. Hughes (Parish of Lydford and to reside at Postbridge Parsonage. He probably stayed there until about 1925; the last curate in residence).

POSTBRIDGE - THE HEART OF DARTMOOR

BURIALS AND A NEW CEMETERY

Prior to 1260 the dead were carried along the lychways for burial at Lydford, a place which was said to be 8 miles distant in fair weather and 15 miles in foul.

Et quod loca predicta a matrice ealisia de Lideford sereino tempore per octo et tempestabis exortis in circuitu per quindecem distant miliaria.

Thus Bishop Brontescombe decided in 1260 to partially transfer two small settlements named Balbery (Babeny) and Pushyll (Pizwell) from the parish of Lydford to the parish of Widecombe. By this arrangement the inhabitants were to worship at Widecombe and could also bury their dead there. They were to make offerings three times a year with the tithe of lambs, and send other tithes to Lydford.

The other tenements which are of interest in this study were not mentioned until some years later. Warner 1301–2, Runnage 1304–05, Dury 1344, Lower Merripit 1344, Lake 1347–48, Bellever 1355 and Hartiland 1521. It seems possible that the inhabitants of these tenements followed the example of those who lived at Babeny and Pizwell and used Widecombe both for worship and burials. This seems to have some credence for in 1612–13 the Vicar of Lydford alleged;

The parish of Lydford extends far into the said Moor, and that 50 of his parishioners do dwell over 12 miles from Lydford Church, and that the church, town of Lydford, and Forest of Dartmoor, is within the jurisdiction of Vendfield, and the tenants do yearly suit and service, and do pay and ever have paid a yearly rent unto the Lord Prince and his noble progenitors, and yet nevertheless do pay and ever have paid all manner of tithes to the complainant and his predecessors, saving the tithe of lambs and offerings of the said 50 dwellers in the said Forest of Dartmoor, which tithe lambs are allowed to the Vicar of Withicombe-in-the- Moor by an ancient composition for that the said remote parishioners of Lydford do resort to the parish church of Withicombe aforesaid for their better use and conveniency...

The problems of carrying the dead from Postbridge to Lydford prior to 1260 must have been considerable. Imagine if you can a lonely procession, heads down into the wind, the rain beating down as they stumbled over the moor.

Path or no path, uphill and downhill for fifteen miles, it must have seemed endless as cold wet and weary they reached their destination.

Carrying the dead to Widecombe must have eased their task, even more so after the building of the Church of St Michael's and All Angels at Princetown, and the granting of a faculty on 1 November 1815 for the interment of the dead in the 'Dartmoor Chapel and Burying Ground'.

A description of the funeral of Jonas Coaker on 16 February 1890 was sent to my father by Martin Spiller of Eaglehurst, Chagford in 1969:

It was Sunday the 16 February 1890 the day of the burial of Jonas Coaker at Widecombe. The sun was shining, the sky was bright and clear with a cold wind. Snow was still laying about the ground in great white patches dotted about the moor.
All the rustic population of Postbridge, and all the Dartmoor tin miners from the East and West Vitifer, Birch Tor and Golden Dagger Mines, also from the Great Henroost Mine which is far out beyond the back of the great hill at Hexworthy.
All had assembled at Ringhill, donned in their Sunday 'black' to pay their last tribute to Jonas. They carried him 'uphill and downdale' across the Wallabrook, over Soussons Common to the Webbern, thence ascending Hillhead and over the scarp of Hambledon. Here the great funeral procession of the people, who had known and loved him, heard the music of the ringing of the bells, for the afternoon service. Whence from here they left the Moor behind, to enter the enclosures, footpaths and lanes, to carry him down the hill to his last resting place, in the churchyard at the Cathedral of the Moor.

By this time there was considerable disquiet about the lack of a cemetery at Postbridge. 'Clapper Bridge' in a letter to a local newspaper headed 'Church matters in the Parish of Lydford' wrote;

There is no burial ground for the Moor district. The dead of Postbridge and Huccaby have to be carried at least six miles across the Moor to Princetown or Widecombe for interment in all weathers, times and seasons. It may be in summer under most oppressive heat and dangerous conditions or in wintry storms. To instance any case would be pathetic! To describe several cases known to the writer would touch the hearts of all those who have never witnessed the services incident to Moor funerals!

In 1902 the Revd G.S. Thorpe the vicar of Lydford sent a petition to the Lydford Parish Council asking for a burial ground at Postbridge. The Council set up a committee to enquire into the matter. In 1903 the committee reported that the inhabitants of Postbridge and district numbered about 300. The cost of providing the burial ground would be about £60 and it was thought that this would cover all expenses – site, fencing, gates and posts, levelling, drainage, planting and consecrating. Fees for interments and tombstones would meet the cost of maintenance and the council recommended acceptance of the Burial Act.

Two sites were looked at, one occupied by Mr Rowse and the other by Mr Cleave. Money was to be raised by public subscription and it was hoped that the Duchy would provide land free of charge. Unfortunately the Duchy were unable to do this, but offered to sell land for £10. Mr Balkwill of Lydgate agreed to pay £10 plus £3.3s for registering the assignment on certain conditions:

The cemetery to be divided into two equal parts. One part being free and the other subject to the rules of the Church of England.

The free part to be open for the free use of the inhabitants of Postbridge and their relatives, and also for strangers using any religious ceremony the friends of the deceased may wish, so long as such ceremony may not interfere with the free grounds for the burials of others.

After a Parish Meeting in 1904 the Burial Act was adopted and the Duchy were asked to transfer the land. The parishioners collected £63 towards a total expenditure of between £90 and £100.

In 1905 Mr Barrington laid out the site previously tenanted by Mr Rowse, who waived his claim for compensation for loss of occupation. Messrs Rice & Sons tendered for the erection of the walls at 5s.4d. per perch which was accepted. Mr Barrington agreed that stone could be cut from Merripit Hill or Stannon for the purpose. Mr Silas Sleep was appointed as the first grave digger/caretaker and the council agreed a scale of fees. The first burial was that of Henry Endacott aged 58 who died on 1 January 1906.

In December 1907 the left hand side of the cemetery (looking from the gate) was consecrated by the Bishop of Exeter. Other clergy present were Revd G.S. Thorpe, Revd Heathcote Smith, Revd Lister Coles, (Curate at Postbridge), Revd H.G. Pigot (Chaplain Dartmoor Prison) and Mr A.G. Mackay (Diocesan Registrar).

Prior to this ceremony there had been a service at the church and when the procession reached the cemetery Mr George French was presented with a silver key bearing the inscription 'Presented to Mr G. French on the occasion of the opening of Postbridge cemetery December 1907' which he used to open the gates.

The cemetery is a lonely place and to stand there on a winter's day, the ground covered with snow, the ammil tinkling as the wind soughs through the trees is unforgettable. There was such a day when Ernest Willcocks of Higher Merripit was laid to rest.

Digging the grave had been difficult enough with the frosted ground as 'hard as iron' – even more difficult had been clearing the snowdrifts in Penlee Lane. All the able-bodied men arrived at his home and the procession left for the church. The coffin was carried in the time-honoured fashion by six men, with another six walking on ahead to a 'knock out' point selected by the 'knocker out' where the changeover took place. (for a long-distance carry several groups of six would share the burden). After about 1950 it became virtually impossible to continue with the 'carry' and a hearse was used for most funerals. Some of the older families did ask however that their loved ones were carried from the chapel or church to their last resting place.

There are two military graves maintained by the War Graves Commission. There were others but these were exhumed. Another exhumation was of Walton Howard whose body had been found by John Bailey in Archerton Newtake. The mystery of how or why he came to Dartmoor and died there is the subject of Beatrice Chase's *The Corpse on the Moor.*

THE PARSONAGE

In 1894 the Rector of Lydford, the Revd Richard Turner, applied to the Duchy of Cornwall for a grant of land on which to build a Parsonage to be used by a local curate who would assist at the Postbridge and Huccaby Chapels of Ease.

The original suggestion by the Duchy was for a plot of land somewhere near Lakehead. They said that if this offer was accepted building stones could be removed from Barracks free of charge. This did not suit the local parishoners and their objections were summed up by a letter from 'Clapper Bridge'.

The site and the materials are almost valueless. The site is a swamp and the stone worthless for building purposes. A worst position for the Parsonage could hardly be found. It is a long way from the school where the Services are held and if the house is built upon this site, the curate in charge would probably at times during each year have to wade knee deep through water to get to the school from his house.

The parishioners therefore petitioned the Duchy asking that land behind the school, then tenanted by Mr Sleep, should be used instead. He agreed to relinquish the land on payment of £100 and in due course the Duchy made the grant.

In February 1895 a public meeting was held at Princetown to discuss the proposed Parsonage. It was resolved that efforts should be made to raise £600 and that a committee should be formed and that Revd Turner, Mr Powell and Mr R. Coaker (Sherberton) should be treasurers.

Many letters were read supporting the scheme, including those from the Bishop of Exeter, the Archdeacon of Totnes, Mr R. Mallock MP, Messrs Burnard, Bennett and others. At the meeting £60 was promised in subscriptions. Eventually a tender of £1172.10s. was accepted and building went ahead.

Prior to its completion licenced curates, who had to reside in Postbridge, lived with local people. The names of those who lived in the Parsonage are listed earlier in this chapter.

On 1 May 1924 the Parsonage was conveyed by Revd Thorpe, the Ecclesiastical Commissioners, and His Royal Highness the Prince of Wales, to the Parochial Church Council of Princetown and the Diocesan Board of Finance, to be used as a residence for an assistant curate or other ecclesiastical purposes.

If the Parsonage was ever sold provision was made for how the monies raised should be used. At some time charitable status was obtained. For many years there was no assistant curate residing in Postbridge and the premises were used as a guest house by Mr and Mrs Richard Warne and later by Mrs and Miss Loveys.

In July 1960 the Charity Commissioners authorized its sale for not less that £1750, the sale to be completed in one year. The proceeds after the payment of expenses to be applied in accordance with the provisions of the conveyance dated 1 May 1924. Thereafter the Parsonage became a private residence.

Postbridge seen from the top of Merripit Hill, showing Ferndale and the Chapel. (Author)

Chapter 5 – Chapel

POSTBRIDGE METHODIST CHAPEL

The Tavistock Circuit minutes of Local Preachers Meetings from 26 December 1814–31December 1850 show that, as early as 1814, local Methodist preachers were preaching at locations on Dartmoor on a fortnightly basis. Some of these preachers included messrs Mitchel, King, Pengelly and Williams.

Postbridge is first mentioned on 4 September 1819 at the Calstock meeting when it was resolved to preach there. These meetings would have taken place in private houses and I have heard it said that it was something of an honour to provide for the meeting and to look after the preacher. Best of everything was the order of the day. It appears that these meetings were a success because at the Horrabridge meeting on 27 December 1819 it was agreed to keep Postbridge on the plan. The number of chapel members was small and on 15 August 1833 only seven members were recorded on Dartmoor, but despite this the meetings at Postbridge continued and, on 30 March 1835, it was decided to preach there once a fortnight at 3pm. However later that year, on 22 December, it was resolved to give up preaching there because no society had been formed, and also because of the distance involved in travelling out to the meeting places.

Whether Postbridge was actually given up is not clear but in any case, on 3 October 1836, a meeting at Tavistock agreed that preaching should take place there once a fortnight in the afternoon at 2.30pm. Postbridge members certainly contributed to local preachers' funds as, during a collection in July 1837, they collected 3s.3d.

It was about this time that steps were taken to build a chapel at Postbridge, at the end of the Ancient Tenement lane (Chapel Lane in modern times), and close to the metalled road from Moretonhampstead to Princetown. Mr Windeatt granted a lease dated 10 October 1837 to Mr Brian and others and this lease was assigned to Mr Kent and others on 4 June 1838.

Building was completed around 1838 and much of the work would have been done by local labour and the total cost is not known.

On 2 January 1838 the Local Preachers' meeting at Tavistock decided that Postbridge should have weekly meetings at 2.30pm and Princetown weekly meeting at 6pm. This would probably have meant the preachers riding out to Postbridge in time for Sunday dinner, taking the service, and riding to Princetown in time for tea, and later that evening riding home. This must have been a very much a labour of love when the vagaries of Dartmoor weather are taken into account.

At a meeting on 30 March 1840 Brother Joseph James of Postbridge was received as an 'Exhorter'. This term reminded me of Sunday afternoons in the chapel. It brought back memories of one or two old 'fire and brimstone' preachers who, by their ranting and thumping of the bible, sent me home somewhat frightened and with a desire never to return. In any case playing by the river would have been much more fun. Undoubtedly this description is unfair to those 'Exhorters' who, by definition, were not fully qualified local preachers but who Sunday after Sunday gave their time so that services could be held both in their local chapel and further afield. The service times seemed to have been changed fairly frequently as 11am, 2pm. 2.30pm and 3pm all appear from time to time.

During the 1840s many local preachers left for America but, with mining fully established in the district, Tavistock in 1844 had 54 local preachers with three more on trial.

In 1844 Alderman George Frean of Plymouth commenced building the Powdermills in the Cherry Brook valley and around about this time a Methodist chapel was brought into use there for the benefit of the workers and their families. This chapel was often referred to as Cherry Brook Chapel but can be seen listed on some old plans as Powdermills. On the l January 1850 a Local Preachers' meeting resolved that Cherry Brook Chapel should be attended to in connection with Postbridge and on 1 July of that year it was decided to hold morning and evening services there.

In 1853–54 the Local Preachers' plan covered a wide area around Tavistock. Some of the places listed were: Tavistock, Horrabridge, Mary Tavy, Beer Alston, Calstock, Gunnislake, Albaston, Latchley, Chilsworthy, Morwellham, Cotts,

Horndon, Diperton & Cholwell, Walkhampton, Moortown, Milton Abbot, Ogbear, Lamerton, Lumburn, Peter Tavy, Milton Buckland, Princehall, Postbridge & Powdermills, Princetown and Tavistock Union.

Unfortunately records for the next 20 years are missing but in the 1950s, during renovations to Beechwood, my father-in-law, Bernard Springate, found a Postbridge Wesleyan Chapel Memorandum Book, dated 1874, in the roof of the old stables.

The book was in a very poor condition but much useful information comes from it. It shows a record of seat rent collections, chapel accounts, anniversary and Harvest Festival accounts, and the names of those who contributed in raising money for the School Room and the accounts for building that room.

In 1874 the seat rent was 6d. per person per quarter, due on Lady Day, Midsummer. Michaelmas and Christmas. The monies collected were used to pay the quarterly circuit contribution and for chapel expenses.

During that year the villagers listed as paying seat rents were: Mr M Rowse, Mr G. French, Mrs E. Stacey, Mrs L. White, Mr J. Robbins, Mr G. French; Mrs Worth, Mr Wm White, Mrs Robbins, Mr G. Hannaford, Mr W. Worth, Mr and Mrs Bailey (2), Mr Thomas Rowse, Mr Jos. Coaker, Mrs White Snr, Mr Wm James Jnr, Mrs M. Rowse, Mr G. Coaker, Mr White Snr, Mrs M.A. James, Mr J. Hannaford, Mr Jory and Family(4), Mr M. White, Mr J. Webb, Mrs Hannaford, Mr Thomas Hambley, Mr Jonas Coaker Snr, Mr Hannaford, Mr S. Hambley, Mr R. Stephens, Mrs Arscott, Mr W. Hambley, Mrs J. French, Mr Arscott, Mrs Tanner, Mr R. French, Mr Wm Arscott, Mrs Hawke, Mr J. Coaker Jnr, Miss Mares, Mrs Hamlyn.

THE SCHOOL ROOM

The School Room, or as it was later known, the Reading Room, was erected in 1880 as an extension to the chapel. The money to pay for it £68.15s.2d. was raised by public subscription, a list of those who subscribed being shown opposite. The amounts subscribed ranged from 6d. to £3.10s. and the account for the cost of building are shown overleaf.

The room had its own fireplace for heating, and a side room with a copper (boiler), heated by a coal and wood fire, to provide hot water for teas and washing up.

Early on it provided a room for the Sunday School, a meeting place and reading room for the young men of the village, and a library. Two accounts tell about its use, the first by Matthew Rowse describes a Christmas Eve Meeting in 1903:

It was very interesting to see 23 young men of the village gathered together in the Reading Room on the evening of Christmas Eve partaking of a nice supper toward which they had contributed a shilling each. There were present also Messrs A.P. Balkwill, M. Rowse, Geo. French and J. Webb, together with Mrs Rowse, Mrs Balkwill and Mrs Webb. It is right to say that the services of the ladies already named were invaluable.
After supper a very pleasant time was spent in singing and addresses, thus a very enjoyable and we hope profitable evening was spent saving our young men also from the temptations and snares of the public house.

Miss S.A. Sleep (Annie) wrote in the June 1968 edition of *Parish Pump*:

The young men and boys had their reading room, built by public money, adjoining the Chapel. No girls or women were allowed in. The boys met there every evening to read or play games: chess, draughts, or any quiet games.
They had a party every Christmas with a lovely supper of cold ham and beef, apple tarts, plum puddings with cream, cooked for them by the people at the Hotel (again no women or girls were allowed). After midnight they would go carol singing around the village.

The fact that no women or girls were allowed in was very much resented. No doubt the reason, yet again, was to save the young men from temptation.

The room was also used for educational purposes, especially to help young men to read and write. I understood from my grandmother that Mr Balkwill and Matthew Rowse gave their time for this purpose.

ANNIVERSARY AND HARVEST FESTIVAL SERVICES

The Anniversary and Harvest Festival Services were generally a two-day affair with the Sunday Services followed by a Monday tea and Service. The following is an account of the Harvest Festival Services which took place on 23 and 24 September 1906, recorded by Matthew Rowse. The occasion also marked Mr and Mrs Rowse's Silver Wedding Anniversary:

SUBSCRIBERS TO THE METHODIST CHAPEL SCHOOL ROOM

Mr Isaac Foot
Mr Matthew Rowse
Mr Thomas Rowse
Mr George French
Mr John Stacey
Miss Hunt
Mr W. Sercombe
Mrs Loveys
Mrs Crossfield
Mr S. Stidstone
J.W. Smith Esq
Mr William King
Mr James Robbins
D. Radford Esq
Mr R. Arscott
Miss E.H. Pethybridge
Mr W Lyddon
Mr R. Thorne
Miss Robertson
Mr William Eva
J.R. Evans
Miss Congdon
Miss Hoste
Mrs Rushdon
Admiral Coode
Edward James & Sons
Mr Johns
Dr Hingston
Mr J.E. Dawe
The Misses Langdon
Mr J. Lyddon
Mr J. Jeffery
Mrs Carr
Revd J.A. Bewes
Mr N.H. Spooner
Mr N. Stephens
Miss Windeatt
Mr J. Windeatt
Mr M Rowse
Mr J.T.F. Pearce
Mr F. Prideaux
I. and A. Symons
Miss J. Coombes
Mr Homer
J.D.
Mrs Gibson
Miss B. Bennett
Miss Bennett
Miss Warrington
Mr and Mrs Thinner
Mrs and Mrs Hamlyn
Miss J. Webber
Miss Midgley
Mrs Harvey
Mrs S. White Snr
Mr W. Coaker

Mrs Hinde
Miss M.J. Clampitt
Mr Thomas
Miss M. Rowse
Mr Bowden
Mr Gidley
Mr T.N. Bennett
Mr E.J. Bennett
Mr E. Bennett
Mr G. French Snr
Mr J. French
Mr H. White
Mrs Robertson
Mr T. Goard
Miss S. Eliott
Mrs Lyne
Mr J.R. Donovan
Mr R.C. Serpell
Mrs Halliburton
Miss Gumbledon
Mr J. Brimblecombe
Mr Smith
Mr Hunt
Mr Baker
Mr J. White
Mr Redaway
Mr S. Arscott
Mrs H.A. Waldron
Miss Meese
Mrs Tregillis
Mr J. Moon
Mrs Knight
Mr Westlake
Mr Pedrick
Mr G. Harvey
Mr W. Stone
Mrs Hooper
Grant from Sunday School
Mr H. Hannaford
Mr T. Nosworthy
Mr Beard
General Income Grant
Mr Robert French
Mr Mackinnon
Mr and Mrs S. Wells
Mr Allen
Mrs A.E. Spooner
Mr R.R. Fox
Miss Burnell
Miss E. Picken
Miss Stawell
Mr C Prideaux
Mrs Fox
Mr J Price

There was an amount for items which had been sold and ten anonymous donations.

Pages from the account book relating to the cost of building the School Room, 1880. (Author)

On the Sunday two sermons were preached by Revd E. Jessop Winter. On the Monday a public tea was given by Mr and Mrs Matthew Rowse in honour of their Silver Wedding and they were much pleased by a good attendance on the occasion. After tea a public meeting was held when suitable addresses were given by Circuit Ministers and Mr Geo. French. The meeting was presided over by Mr S. Earl of Plymouth. During the evening Mr and Mrs Rowse were presented with a travelling clock bearing the following inscription 'Presented to Mr and Mrs Matthew Rowse on the occasion of their Silver Wedding September 20th 1906 by past and present members of the Sunday School and Friends'.

The present came as a very pleasant surprise. Mr Geo. French's remarks on the occasion were most appropriate and both Mr and Mrs Rowse very gratefully acknowledged the receipt of the same saying they would always appreciate prize the present for its beauty and its value but most all because of the motive that prompted the donors.

My own recollections of the Services were of the teas held in the Reading Room; trestle tables end to end down the length of the-room covered in pristine white cloths, blue and white plates emblazoned with the chapel name, full of split tuffs covered with thick cream and a 'dob' of strawberry jam, slices of fruit cake full of dried fruit, and seed cake, and buns of all descriptions. There were thin slices of bread spread thick with farmhouse butter, and bowls of strawberry and raspberry jelly. Later, after the children had gone out to play, sandwiches, some filled with home-cured ham, would be added to the food already on the table for the benefit of the adults. As youngsters we had learnt at an early age to appreciate good cream and surreptitious enquiries by those whose mothers were spreading the tuffs soon elicited which plate had Aunt So-and-So's cream – this information being quickly passed on to favourite cronies. Squabbles about who should sit next to whom were soon settled, either by gentle persuasion or a less gentle smack on the leg.

POST BRIDGE

WESLEYAN TEA.

———◆———

ONE SHILLING.

Prior to the Harvest Festival there had been the fun of collecting and decorating the chapel. There was always a hunt for jars for flowers and a need for someone to collect moss. The decorated chapel always looked beautiful and even those who didn't attend regularly put in an appearance. It was all too soon over, the produce was auctioned and the profits were credited to chapel funds. Normality reigned for another year.

THE SUNDAY SCHOOL

The Sunday School was very much a Wesleyan tradition and no doubt the children of the village had been attending the school prior to 1880 when the School Room had been built. In 1893 the rules to be followed by the officers, teachers and scholars at Postbridge were:

1. The Superintendent shall be responsible for the opening of the Sunday School with, singing and prayer.

2. The time for opening the School 10.30am subject to alteration.

3. Each teacher is expected to take his or her class or let the Superintendent know a day or two before.

4. That teachers are to be marked late if not in before prayer.

5. Resolved also that a monthly prayer meeting shall be held among the scholars when short and suitable addresses shall be given.

6. That the scholars have a mark for early attendance which is to be given before prayer, also a mark for good behaviour and one or more according to the number of scripture verses or hymns learnt.

The officers in 1896 were Matthew Rowse Superintendent and Treasurer, and George French Secretary, who also taught the young men in the Bible Class. Also there were Mr S. Rowse, 1st Bible Class; John Webb, 2nd Boy's and Girl's Class; and Edward Dower 3rd Boy's and Girl's Class. By 1900 the teachers were Mr M. Rowse, Mrs M.S. Rowse, John Webb and Mr A.P. Balkwill. In 1904 John Webb was no longer listed as a teacher, and by 1915 Mr M. Rowse and Mrs Rowse had again been joined by George French, along with his daughter Dorothy.

In 1896 43 scholars attended the Sunday School. These children came from a very wide area, either on foot, on horse back or in a pony and trap. Many, probably the majority, would stay on with families and friends for Sunday lunch prior to going to the afternoon service. Some even remained for the evening service so, in reality, Sunday became one long day of worship.

Further records of numbers attending the Sunday School are as follows: 1897(36); 1898(35); 1899(29); 1900(34); 1901(32); 1902(28); 1903(27); 1904(30); 1905(26); 1906(22); 1907, 1908, 1909 the records are missing, 1910 (18); 1911(13); 1912(20); 1913(20); 1914(21); 1915(18); 1916(17); 1917(14); 1918(16); 1919(18); 1920(14); 1921(13); 1922(15).

When I attended the school in the late 1920s and early 1930s the service was at 3pm and was conducted by a local preacher who stayed on for the 6 o'clock service. He was always invited to someone's home for tea where he was made most welcome.

Each child would have a favourite preacher; some were interesting, some were frightening and others comical in their efforts to talk down to them. I have often been reminded by older friends that my behaviour on occasion left much to be desired. Standing on the seat, stamping the foot, making faces at those sitting behind and whispering was undoubtedly disruptive. Nevertheless promises of retribution to come, or the ultimate indignity of being taken out, had a corrective effect.

I was always fond of music and singing except perhaps 'Jesus Wants Me For a Sunbeam', but the Walter John Mathus hymn 'Jesus Friend of Little Children', especially the last verse, has remained with me because of its simple message:

Never leave me or forsake me
Ever be my friend
For I need thee from life's dawning
To its end.

Likewise William Henry Parker's Hymn 'Tell me the Story of Jesus' will always in my mind be associated with Sunday School. The tempo of the

CHILDREN ATTENDING SUNDAY SCHOOL IN 1896

Francis White	Richard Warne
Edith French	Lillie Coaker
Jessie French	Sidney French
Louise Leaman	Fanny White
Harry French	William Leaman
Jessie White	Mary Stephens
George Endacott	William Withycombe
Rebecca Warne	Frank Warne
Blagdon French	George Coaker
Florrie Withycombe	John Potter
Mary Withycombe	Mary French
May French	Herbert Leaman
John Withycombe	Mabel Cleave
Emma Stephens	John Hamlyn
Sidney French (Merripit)	Rosina Coaker
Charles French	Richard French
Fred Warne	John Warne
Solomon Warne	William French
Bertie White	Alberta Coaker
Emma French	Frederick White
Joseph Warne	John Webb
Mary Warne	

tune 'Stories of Jesus' by F.A. Challinor has a lilt which appealed to the young and was regularly accompanied by movements in time with the music, accentuating the mood of enjoyment.

The Sunday School kept its own accounts and besides running its own affairs contributed to the chapel funds. For example, the balance of the Sunday School account for 1882, by sanction of the teachers, was appropriated for the purchase and installation of a furnace for use in the chapel.

As with the chapel anniversary and Harvest Festival celebrations, the Sunday School anniversary was also held over two days and there was the inevitable tea. The children provided much of the entertainment with singing, recitations and suitable plays. In order that the performers could be seen by the whole congregation a stage was built near the pulpit by fixing a platform on trestles. To accommodate this some of the seats had to be removed.

THE SUNDAY SCHOOL OUTING

The Sunday School outing was the highlight of the year. A charabanc was hired and all the arrangements made. Mothers, grandmothers and children planned with much excitement how to dress and what to put in the picnic basket. There would be rivalry about who was going to sit with the driver and who was going to sit in the back

seat. An early photograph c.1928 shows the party aboard their charabanc somewhere on their journey (note the speed limit of 12mph and the absence of the menfolk).

On one of our trips to Paignton we travelled via Dartmouth and this meant we had to use the ferry to cross the Dart. My grandmother insisted that she did not come to go on the sea and wasn't going on the sea. It took some time to convince her that it was only a river crossing.

There was considerable excitement when an enclosed coach was hired for the first time, as in the early charabancs fine weather was essential.

One memorable outing was to Bigbury. The Devon General Omnibus Company had sent their very latest coach with the driver in a separate compartment. I remember a slight accident on the way when the side of the coach touched the wall of a building and part of the window was broken. There were one or two minor injuries.

Most of the children were content to play on the beach and generally eat, drink and be merry. Paddling too was of course part of the fun and we thought the sight of our mothers and grandmothers holding up their skirts, and their capering to avoid getting wet, hilarious.

Long before motorised transport was available the children and other members of their families enjoyed trips to the seaside. Locally owned wagonettes would take them either to Princetown

Postbridge Methodist Chapel Sunday School outing c.1928. (Author)

or Moretonhampstead where they would continue their journeys by rail. On occasion the Postbridge people would join those from Princetown and then travel to Plymouth for a boat trip on the Tamar.

A DECLINING CONGREGATION

The Methodist tradition in the Postbridge area came about because of the influx of miners to the tin mines. Followers of Wesley had come from the working classes and, with the closure of the mines and later with the demise of the the old families who remained in the village, the congregation declined and eventually the chapel closed.

Through the later half of the nineteenth century and into the early part of the twentieth century the chapel flourished and played an important part in the life of the village. Pew rents however had declined by nearly a half over some thirty years.

In letters home during the First World War my uncle often referred to the chapel and it was obvious that he had retained great respect for its traditions. One paragraph refers to his refusal to take part in sports on a Sunday: 'Fancy sports on a Sunday!'

Through the 1920s and 1930s there was still a good congregation as evidenced by the £61.l0s.7d. raised in 1922 by the sale of needle-

work and from profits of a tea, which was used to pay off repairs to the chapel. After the Second World War it declined despite an increase in attendance by the forestry workers, but there came a time when, in order to swell the congregations of both the chapel and the church, several parishioners attended both denomination services on a Sunday, regardless of their religious preferences.

Despite the problems of poor attendance, the stewards maintained a healthy bank balance until 1961 when a bill for £75 for repairs put the accounts in the red.

The last service to be held at the chapel was the funeral service of John Stansford Perrett during August 1966. He had attended the chapel for many years and although it had been officially closed it was specially re-opened for this service.

A history of Postbridge Chapel would not be complete without a tribute to Mrs Ethel White (née Jory). She was born at Birch Tor in 1882 and at the age of 13 started playing the organ in the chapel. This she continued to do for about 45 years. Her husband, Herbert White, was killed in a motor accident in 1928, and although she had two sons to bring up, she was still able to devote time as an organist and steward at the chapel.

After she moved to Northam she was the organist at Northam Methodist Chapel for 10 years and after retiring from this she continued to play the piano for Northam Over 60s Club until she was aged over 90. She died aged 92, the last survivor of a family of eight children.

I shall always remember how over the years many of us gathered around her piano at Sunnymead for a sing-song after Sunday evening service. It was a tradition which had been much loved by the Jory family.

EXTRACTS FROM THE CHAPEL MEMORANDUM BOOK

In 1876 it was agreed to give E. Worth and Bessie Stacey 2d. per week for brushing and dusting the chapel. A further 9d., plus the cost of soap, was paid for washing out the chapel. They started their duties in the last week in January and up to 2 September of that year were paid 5s.5d.

In each year's accounts a sum was set aside to pay for the hire of the preacher's horse (the horse hire fund). Payments were also met for stabling the horse, e.g. John James was paid 6d. for attending to the minister's horse and 2d. for hay.

The cost of the preacher's dinners were also met from chapel funds. Mrs James was paid 2s, 1s. and 1s.6d. at various times for this service.

In 1880 Mr Brimblecombe was paid 7s. for two days' work painting the chapel. He used 10lbs. of paint which cost 5s., and 2lbs of putty at 3d. A total of 12s.3d.

In 1882 Mr Stone carried out repairs and was paid 7s.1d. for one man for one day and 8 hours, 6s. for four pecks of cement (a peck was formerly a measure for dry goods, two gallons, or one-fourth of a bushel. My grandmother often said 'You have to eat a peck of dirt before you die'). Stone was also paid 1s.6d. for three slates 20 inches x 10 inches, and three slates 22 inches x 11 inches. A total cost of 14s.7d. Ground rent for the chapel held on lease was one shilling each quarter and the insurance for the same period was 3 shillings.

On 15 July 1884 £1.19s.0d. was paid for forming a new trust deed from the Charity Commissioners.

Other entries give an indication of everyday items: 1 cwt. coal is 3d., 1 quart paraffin 4d., 1 yard of lamp wick 3d., lamp glass 4d. and chimney pot 3s. A new stove cost £1.11s.6d. plus 3s.9d. carriage and 6d. toll; 5 mould candles cost 4d., and Brunswick Black 6d.

One new lamp, guide and brackets, one lamp glass, 1 dozen screws, one knot of cord and two brackets and one winder came to 5s.7d.

THE CHAPEL – A LAST VISIT

It was late evening when I opened the porch door and walked slowly up to and through the red baize-covered door into the chapel proper. The last rays of the setting sun shone through the west windows highlighting the damp twisted covers of the hymn books. There was a mustiness in the air and the damp patches on the wall and ceiling seemed more pronounced than ever. Over the pulpit the two messages 'GOD IS LOVE' and 'WORSHIP THE LORD IN THE BEAUTY OF HOLINESS' stood out as if to remind the visitor that this was still a holy place, full of memories. The memorial plaques to George French and the Rowse family bore witness to those whose work had meant so much.

Looking around I remembered those occasions when many years before I had stood in the pulpit and preached to 'the few gathered together in the Lord's name'. On other occasions I had acted as organist and it was to the organ that, as always, I was drawn. As I selected the stops I decided to play a harvest hymn, as of all the festivals it was the harvest which held a special place in my heart.

As the notes of G.J. Elvey's great hymn 'Come Ye Thankful People Come' to the tune of St George's Windsor flooded out over the chapel, I was no longer alone. Every pew was full, the partitions at the back were down and there was standing room only.

The windowsills, aisles and tables were covered with flowers, fruit, huge vegetable marrows, washed turnips, bags of potatoes, pots of jam and cream, sheaves of corn, bundles of hay and, pride of place, the harvest loaf, baked especially for the occasion.

The fading light seemed to mirror the flickering of oil lamps and I thought I could catch the odour of paraffin and smeech. I sang out loud and the whole building seemed to reverberate with the sound of the organ and voices until at last with 'Come with all thine angels come, raise the song of harvest home', all became silent.

It was nearly dark and a quietness had settled over all. The shabby old chapel seemed more shabby than ever. I closed the organ and walked slowly down the aisle past the family pew where the Jory's, Coaker's and Bellamy's had worshipped, and as I passed through the porch door into the evening, I clearly heard 'The busy world is hushed, the fever of life over and our day's work done'.

I never went back.

CHAPEL COTTAGES

So far I have been unable to ascertain which were the earliest buildings on the site, the chapel or the cottages. It seems, however, that of the two cottages the one adjacent to the chapel was the first to be built and the other added at a later date. There was evidence of this when the two cottages were converted into one after 1988. The cottage nearest to the chapel had four rooms and the other had two.

Early occupiers were:

Cottage No.1
1861 Thomas and Mary Hext
1871 Jane Doney
1881 William James Jnr.
1891 William Lance

Cottage No.2
1861 James and Mary Ann James
1871 James and Mary Ann James
1881 Mary Ann James
1891 Edward and Mary Ann Dower

In 1907, George James, who was Edward Dower's stepson, was granted a 25 year lease of the cottages by the Windeatt estate. One was let to Freddy Warne while Mrs Dower continued to live in the other.

Miss Ruth James, Aunt Ruth as she was affectionately known in the village, lived in one of the cottages for many years. She worked at Penlee and regularly attended the chapel services. She always helped with the preparations for the Harvest Festival and Anniversary Services.

I can remember some other families living there, the Summerfields, in the late 1920s, James and Phyllis Warne, and Donald Rowse, who ran a chicken hatchery in the field opposite.

Drinking water was from a well on the opposite side of the road.

Mrs Mary Ann Dower at Chapel Cottage c.1890.
(Courtesy Mrs Exell and Mrs Williams)

Postbridge School c.1915. (Author)

Chapter 6 – Education

The first definite record of organized children's education in the area is to be found in the account book of the Dartmoor and Widecombe Charity Schools, 1796-1875. This organization set up small schools originally in cottages. The rules of the charity were:

1. That no child be admitted to this charity whose parents can afford to pay for instruction. 2. That none be admitted under the age of four years. 3. That each child be entitled to three years instruction. 4. That each child at his or her dismission from school shall be presented with a bible and some religious work. 5. That the children after their dismission if within convenient distance shall attend the Sunday School and be examined from time to time by the Minister. 6. That this Charity be extended to all poor children resident in the Withycombe parish or in the Forest of Dartmoor whether belonging to the parish or not. 7. That there shall be a meeting of farmers and any other person who chose to attend in the Parish Chamber on someday every year between the 1st of March and Easter when the annual account of the Charity for the year past shall be exhibited. 8. And that this account be afterwards shewn to each subscriber and then deposited in the Parish Chest.

The first school at Postbridge was at Lower Merripit and the teacher was Elizabeth French. She collected pence from the children and forwarded these small amounts to the charity. The charity in turn, out of donations and other income, provided psalters, primers, teaching materials and paid the teacher a wage.

The school seems to have been in existence before 1796 as some pupils are shown as having been admitted in 1794.

The pupils listed in 1796 with their dates of admission were.

Amy French 1794
Charity Browning
Martha French 1795
William Browning 1796
Maria Hannaford
James (Ivy) French 1796
Robert Hannaford 1795
Jonas Waldron
Susanna French 1796
Jane Coaker
John French
Mary Hannaford
Arthur Hannaford
Joshua Waldon 1794
Mary Coaker

From March to June 1796 the teacher forwarded 6s.6d. for six children to the charity. Elizabeth French moved from Merripit at Christmas 1797 and it seems that the school may have lapsed, until 1800, when Jane Coaker was appointed teacher, and she taught at Merripit until 1803. After this date there is no record of the school until 1821 when Susanna Rowse is shown as the teacher at Postbridge School – a post she held until 1845.

Whether or not there had been another gap in the provision of a school between 1803 and 1821 is not certain, as the account book records in 1821 that 3 Psalters, 6 Primers and 3 books *Reading made Easy* were provided for 'The School now to be established at Postbridge'.

In 1847 Susan Hawke was appointed teacher with 16 pupils. She was the wife of a tin miner and after she moved to Ringhill in 1851 Mary Ann Tanner, who lived a Merripit, took over. The 1851 census shows Mary Ann Tanner as a school mistress. Her appointment lasted until 1852 when Elizabeth Warne became the teacher. She taught at Lower Merripit, until, 1853 when the school there closed. The reason for the closure was the withdrawal of mine support. The children did not go without education for very long as 'At the special solicitation of the parents' the Dame School, Postbridge, was re-opened in November, with Elizabeth Warne in charge. She held the post she until 1858.

The location of the Dame's school is not known but may have been at Lydgate (Leadgate) as, to this day, the corner pool below Lydgate House Hotel is known as Dame's Pond. In 1858 Elizabeth Rowse became the last recorded mistress of the Charity School which finally closed in 1868 with the opening of the Church of England School.

The architect's drawings of the proposed school and master's house at Postbridge, 1868. The master's house was never built.

Two other schools were opened in the area, one at Cator in 1824, and the other at Challacombe in 1858.

In 1861 Elizabeth Westington is recorded as a schoolmistress living at South Sands (Soussons), but it is not known where she taught.

Many children started work at an early age, for example Robert Hext, from Stamp Cottage, was a tin dresser at the age of 12, and Betsy Gilbert was a house servant at South Challacombe at the same age (1861).

In 1868 the Duchy of Cornwall (under the authority of 26th and 27th Victoria Cap. 49, the Duchy of Cornwall Management Act 1863, and for the purposes of the Acts of the 5th and 8th year of the reign of her Majesty for affording facilities for the conveyance and endowment of sites for schools), conveyed to the Rector and Church Wardens of the Parish of Lydford one acre of land situated on the south-eastern side of the Moretonhampstead–Two Bridges road (the present site of St Gabriel's Church).

This land was to be used for 'the erection of premises and buildings to be for ever hereafter used as and for the education of children and adults or children only, of the labouring, manufacturing and other poorer classes in the Parish of Lydford and for no other purposes.' The deed was enrolled in the office of the Duchy of Cornwall on the 18 June 1869 before I.V. Bateman, Keeper of the Records.

Plans were drawn up and dated 24 June 1868 by R. Medley-Fulford, an architect of Woodbury, Exeter, for a schoolroom and masters house. For some reason the master's house was never built, instead a chancel was added to the north end of the building, divided from the schoolroom by a removable partition. Although this allowed for a place of religious worship no one seems to have realized how this would affect the recruitment and retention of teachers later on.

In 1876 the school was in an unsettled state due to being handed over to a School Board and consequently it closed for a time. It was re-opened with support from the Duchy and, in 1880, a meeting was held in order to get agreement to transfer the school to the Education Department of the Privy Council.

Some accounts exist for the period 1882–1888. The account for 1882 shows:

Receipts	£	s	d
Mr Bawden		10	0
Mr Gregg		10	0
Mr E Palmer		5	0
Mr W Waterfall		5	0
School pence and stationery	7	19	0
Government Grant	25	2	6
Share of subscriptions to			
Postbridge & Huccaby schools	34	18	5
Total	69	9	11

Payments

Teachers Salary	40	0	0
Ditto 1/4 grant	7	10	9
Clock		5	0
Mr & Mrs Sleep for cleaning	2	9	6
Ironmonger		4	0
Materials for needlework		8	1
Stationery	2	15	9
Stone Builder	9	0	4
Lime	1	7	0
Coal	1	7	10
Flue		4	6
Hauling Coal		12	0
Postage		7	6
Donation to Mr Rowse		5	0
Balance	2	12	8
Total	69	9	11

Another Account for 1888 shows:

Receipts	£	s	d
Balance B/F	24	0	0
Duchy of Cornwall	10	0	0
D Radford	2	2	0
Pt. Voluntary Rate*	11	0	0
School pence etc	7	1	4

Government Grant	31	8	8
Mrs Davies		17	9
Total	86	9	9

Payments

Teachers Salary	45	0	0
Books, apparatus & stationery	3	15	10
Fuel & cleaning	5	9	0
Repairs	2	12	8
Collector's salary*	1	11	6
Balance	28	0	9
Total	86	9	9

*In 1886 notice was given of a voluntary 4d. rate in support of local schools.

A complete register exists dating from 1 May 1885 until the school finally closed in 1931. The register gives the following details: 1. Date of admission to the school. 2. Surname and Christian names of the pupil. 3. Residence. 4. Date of birth. 5. Progress through the school. 6. Leaving particulars. 7. Name and occupation of parent or guardian. 8. Whether exemption of the child from religious instruction is claimed (Yes or No).

BOARD OF EDUCATION.
Form 146a. (1).

SCHEDULE III.

Local Education Authority *Devon County*

LABOUR CERTIFICATE, No. 1 (a) (for total exemption after 13 years of age).

AGE AND EMPLOYMENT.

I certify that *Thomas Redvers Webb* residing at *Postbridge* was on the 20th day of *May* 19 14, not less than **thirteen** years of age, having been born on the 9th day of *May* 1914, as appears by the Registrar's Certificate [or the Statutory Declaration] now produced to me, and has been shown, to the satisfaction of the local education authority for this district to be beneficially employed.

(Signed) *Baldwin*
For
(1) Clerk to the Local Education Authority.

PREVIOUS ATTENDANCE.

I certify that *Thomas Redvers Webb* residing at *Postbridge*, has made 350 attendances in not more than two schools during each year for five preceding years, whether consecutive or not, as shown by the (2) certificate furnished by the Principal Teacher of the (3) *Postbridge* School.

(Signed) *Baldwin*
For
(1) Clerk to the Local Education Authority.

Dated the 9th day of *May* 1914.

(2) For this certificate see Schedule VI.
(3) Here name School or Schools in which the attendances have been made.
(1) or other officer.

Board of Education certificate exempting Thomas Redvers Webb from school on the grounds that, aged thirteen, he is gainfully employed. Note the Registrar's mistake – the date of birth should read 9 May 1901.

Some of the children started school when they were as young as three or four years old. Only a few parents claimed exemption from religious instruction for their children. My grandfather, a staunch Methodist, claimed exemption for my mother, aunt and uncle, as did another well-known dissenter, for his daughter. I suspect this may have had more to do with differences with the local incumbent rather than religious intolerance.

Some children only attended the school for a very short time, either because they were visiting the area, or just passing through. One relates to the step-children of a steamroller driver who lived in a caravan, and the other to four children of a hawker who lived in a tent.

Children came from miles around, from Lakeland, Vitifer and Golden Dagger Mines, Challacombe, Soussons, Cator Court, Pizwell, Dury and Bellever, the majority had to walk, even the little four- and five-year-olds. In wintertime it would be dark when they left home and dark when they arrived home. The teacher often had the task of drying their wet clothes and stockings.

Many of the children brought their own dinners and Mrs Sleep and Miss Webb, who lived close by, would provide hot drinks of tea or cocoa in the dinner hour. The first teachers, according to Miss Sleep, were Miss Back and Mrs Bickell. Details of other teachers, although not complete as to dates of appointment were:

Miss Emilie Wakeford – 1871
E.J. Geddes – 4 April 1880–1 July 1881
A. Rider – 4 July 1881–18 August 1881
H.G. Newton – 12 Sept 1881–28 Oct 1881
H Isaac – 30 Oct 1881–Christmas 1881
J.A. Farrell – 9 Jan 1882–March 1884
S. Drew – June 1884

After S.Drew gave up the appointment there followed three teachers: Case, Earl and Gould.

Miss B. Horrell – 1891
Miss Westcott – 1 Oct 1906–31March 1915
Miss Jackson – 1 Sept 1915
A.M. Lewis – 7 Oct 1919
Mrs E.A. Ladd – 1919 (temporary charge)
Miss Snell – 1920
Miss E.A. Stanton – Sept 1920–July 1922
A.G. England – Sept 1922 (temporary charge)
M. Palmer – 9 April 1923
M. Ford – 2 Sept 1924 – 19 Dec 1924
Mrs E.A. Ladd – 1925–1931 (closed)

The lack of a schoolhouse undoubtedly contributed to the frequent change of teachers as renting accommodation always proved difficult, and lodgings were not always satisfactory. For example Miss Stanton resigned in 1922 because she could not get suitable accommodation. The appointment of mistresses seemed to have caused some concern as Mr Balkwill wrote to the Lydford Parish Council in 1895 suggesting that a master should be appointed. I have also been told that the curate had at times to be called in to administer appropriate punishments. Throughout the years monitoress/teachers were appointed to assist the headmistress. Some of these are known: Miss Nellie Sleep, Miss Winnie Durrant and Miss Ruby Bailey.

Pupils attendance was generally very good but sometimes the school did close for the day, or occasionally longer. Princetown Fair day usually saw most of the children accompanying their parents and friends to the fair. The few that did attend would be sent home.

In bad weather, such as heavy snow, the school closed as it would not have been safe for those who had to walk from the outlying homesteads to even try to set out. A whooping cough epidemic in 1922 also led to closure.

The weather could disrupt lessons even if there was a good attendance. On 12 February 1924 the teacher recorded 'It is a very dark morning and the children cannot see to read or write, have given handwork instead of ordinary lessons'.

In 1924 the Physical Training Organizer at Exeter sent one football, one skipping rope and two rubber balls for the use of the children, and in 1925 the school received books from George Nympton School South Molton: *Piers Plowman* Books IV & V – 4 of each; *Man on Earth* – 11 of each, and *Nature Knowledge Readers* – 10 of each.

Many of us who went to the school during Mrs Ladd's time remember her with awe and affection. A fine teacher, strict to a degree, I can still see her sitting at her high desk dressed in tweed skirt, knitted red jumper, hair swept tightly back and with her pince-nez at the end of her nose. She rarely missed any sign of misbehaviour and kept us hard at it with 'times tables', mental arithmetic, writing and spelling.

Early on we used cardboard slates and chalk for our writing exercises but as we grew older we used pens, dipping them into inkwells and writing on paper. Lower case and capital letters had to be properly and correctly formed. She ensured we had good religious instruction, that we knew our manners and kept our hands clean.

Boys and girls were rigorously separated each having separate access to their respective play grounds and toilets. The boys and girls toilets were of the 'bucket and chuckit' variety, with the boys also having a separate urinal. The buckets were removed through a side door, which never seemed to close properly, resulting in a certain amount of horseplay using stinging nettles. Decency forbids I say any more!

Some entries in the school diary pay tribute to Mrs Ladd's abilities.

May 17th 1926. Report of Instruction by Revd E.F. Hall Diocesan Inspector.
14 scholars on books 13 present.
'The childrens work showed signs of careful and thorough preparation, the result of consistent teaching.
Knowledge of detail was good and the practical application of the lessons has been kept well to the foreground.
The children are making steady progress."

July 21st 1927. Report of H.M.I. Mr J. Leicester. Postbridge Church of England School No. 294 Reg. No. E9/294/3
'The Head mistress controls the school in a capable manner. She is doing sound work by getting the scholars to take an interest in the study of plant and animal life. Systematic observing and recording have been done.
In English a satisfactory standard is reached. More and better reading books are required and with a wider selection especially poetry, the subject might be made more attractive.
In arithmetic systematic and useful work has been done. The exercises are carefully supervised and corrected.
The Head Mistress has used singing and drama in an interesting manner. A larger selection of good songs should be learned and further attention paid to voice training.
In drawing there are some good chalk exercises. Painting if introduced would allow of more detail.

Also in 1927 the school was entered in the essay competition held for all the schools throughout England and Wales, organized by the Health Week Committee of London, and approved by the regional Education Committees. Nationally there were 1523 essays submitted and, following judging, two awards were made to individual Postbridge pupils, whilst the school received a Certificate of Merit in recognition of the excellence of the submissions.

In 1928 all the scholars who sat the Bishop Phillpott's Prayer Book examination in Set A were successful. One passed with 2nd Class Honours and three others with 3rd Class Honours.

In 1929 Mrs Ladd decided to purchase an His Master's Voice portable gramophone, complete with records and two storage cupboards. £20.11.4d. was collected for this purpose and music took on a new meaning.

Later that year in order to provide more reading material a collection was again made and £5.12s.0d. was raised. One new book *Flags of the World Past and Present* was purchased for 6s.9d. and the rest of the money deposited in the bank. The reason for this was that Revd Murphy had obtained a large number of secondhand books which were given to the school.

Mrs Ladd also had considerable success with scholars who wanted to sit the Grammar School entrance exams. Three boys were awarded County Scholarships with full board to attend Ashburton Grammar School. One of these boys came second in the County list.

Four girls also passed entrance exams, two with scholarships with full board. Three girls attended Crediton and the other Okehampton Grammar School. A board was set up on the school wall by the school managers to mark these successes.

By 1930 rumours about closure and the 'bussing' of children to Princetown were circulating and, despite the efforts of many individuals and objections by the Parish Council, a decision was made to close the school. One of the last visitors to the school was County Councillor and JP Mr E. Darke-Bennett. Like many before him he was strongly impressed by the keenness of the scholars and the good work being quietly and effectively done by the mistress in charge. On leaving he left a sum of money to be divided amongst the pupils.

The eventual closure came on 22 December 1931, and after the Christmas holidays the children were taught at Princetown. Some were fortunate enough to gain County Scholarships whilst the others finished their education there. Looking back, it was with sadness that we moved on but personally I believe that being able to mix with other children, who had come from all over the country, with their Prison Officer fathers, certainly helped when I moved on to Grammar School.

The juniors are still taught at Princetown where my father was a school manager for many years and where there is a memorial cup in his name. Seniors now transfer to Tavistock Comprehensive.

Boarders at Ashburton Grammar School, c.1935. Third row, second from left, the author. Sitting, second row, third from right Gordon Hambley (Challacombe); third row, fifth from right, Reginald White (Sunnymead).

A PERSONAL NOTE

In the spring of 1933 I sat the Special Place Examination for entry into Ashburton Grammar School. The examination was at Tavistock, following extra coaching by Mr Burton the headmaster of Princetown Primary School, where I attended after the closure of Postbridge Church of England School. At first I was not particularly happy at Princetown probably because my parents had strongly opposed the Postbridge closure and some of their objections had rubbed off on me. The examination was taken and eventually the result came on Form H24 signed by R.E. Tucker MA, Clerk to the Governors and R.A. Evans Prosser, Headmaster of Ashburton Grammar School, saying that I had been successful.

Eventually my parents were sent a long list of the items a boy would need when going to a boarding school for the first time. Looking back, how on earth they afforded them I know not, but off we went to Plymouth driven by Mr Warne from Lydgate in his Austin 16 to make the purchases. He always parked at Andrews Garage, and in those days it was possible to have your shopping delivered there in time for your departure. The list seemed endless as we wandered in and out of Dingle's, Yeo's, Coster's, and innumerable shoe shops, for even the slippers had to be of a special type of elastic-sided slip-ons. First we purchased a trunk and tuck box and arranged for the initials R.B. to be painted on, then a black coat and waistcoat and grey flannels for everyday wear, another black coat, waistcoat and black pinstripe trousers for Sundays. Next came several white

shirts with Eton collars, underwear, socks, football kit, cricket kit, towels, overcoat, macintosh, cap, boater, and so on, even down to toilet bag and contents, serviettes and serviette ring. My parents gave me an initialled silver serviette ring of unusual design which is still in daily use. At last it was finished, except for the name tapes. These had to be ordered and mother and grandmother spent many an evening sewing them on.

Although I looked forward to a new school the thought of leaving home was not a pleasant one, but at last the great day came and I can still remember the apprehension as we drove up the driveway to the boarding house. I had one advantage over the other new boys because my cousin Reg White from Sunnymead and Gordon Hambley from Challacombe were already at the school. I shall always be grateful for the opportunity of a boarding school education, but there were times when I was unhappy. I well remember looking wistfully towards Postbridge during a walk to Buckland Beacon; but these troubles were far outweighed by everything I gained.

Recently I visited St Lawrence Chapel and was delighted to see that it was being refurbished. As I stood there I could not help regretting that the County, in 1938, had found it necessary after 600 years to close such a fine school. I can only hope that St Lawrence Chapel will forever remain a memorial to all the Governors, Headmasters, Masters and Pupils who were associated with it over all those years. A history of Ashburton Grammar School *The Story Of Six Hundred Years* by W.S. Graf MA, was published by S.T. Elson of Ashburton in 1938.

Chapter 7 – More Farms and Cottages

STANNON LODGES

These two houses opposite the Church were built by the Hullett brothers, towards the end of the eighteenth century, as lodges on an approach road to their house at Stannon. After the Hulletts gave up their leases the rents were paid firstly to the Revd Vollans and then to J.N. Bennett of Archerton. They reverted to the Duchy around 1906. They were generally known as Lower and Higher Lodge.

It is somewhat difficult to sort out exactly who lived in which cottage but some of the names and dates are:

1814 Robert and Joan Cleave
1816 John and Elizabeth Hannaford (Lower Lodge)
1820 Harriet Hannaford (Lower Lodge)
1825 Robert Hannaford (Lower Lodge)
1825 Anne Cleave
1827 Peter and Mary Hannaford
1828 Arthur and Mary Hannaford
1829 William and Susanna Leaman
1831 Robert and Elizabeth Nankivells

1832 Peter Hannaford
1833 Solomon and Eliza Warne
1841 Thomas and Elizabeth Webb (Lower Lodge)
1851 ditto
1861 Thomas and Mary Rowse (Higher Lodge)
1861 Elizabeth Webb (Lower Lodge)
1871 ditto
1871 John Martin (Higher Lodge)
1881 Elizabeth Webb (Lower Lodge), farming 10 acres)
1881 John Stacey (Higher Lodge), tin miner
1891 Thomas and Elizabeth Webb (Lower Lodge), farming
1891 Silas and Harriet Sleep (Higher Lodge) powdermaker
1906 William Mogridge (Higher Lodge) rent £6.6s.6d. for 2 acres,10 rods, 3 perches
1906 Mrs Thomas Webb farming 20 acres at Lower Lodge, rent £12.10s.
1916 Frederick & Elizabeth Warne (Higher Lodge)

I can remember Thomas and Rebecca Webb at Lower Lodge. They were affectionately known in

The Avenue, Postbridge, with Stannon Lodges on the left. Note the unmade road surface at the time Chapman took this photograph, c.1916. (Author)

the village as Uncle Tom and Aunt Bec. Lower Lodge fell into disrepair after the death of Thomas and Rebecca Webb but it has been rebuilt in the past few years by his grandson, Thomas, who now lives there with his wife Sheila. Much of the rebuilding has been in granite. The Webb family have lived in one or other of the Lodges for the past 160 years.

Both cottages originally had the usual plats for keeping a cow, a pig and poultry, and for many years Lower Lodge had extra land. One field had been part of Greyhound in 1840, but this field is now incorporated into Middle Merripit.

Many of the Webbs had been tin miners and this included William. I remember him as a rabbit trapper and an expert at rick-making and thatching. He was also an excellent fisherman and naturalist. His wife, known to us all as Emmie, came from the north of England. After William died Emmie continued to live at Higher Lodge.

A Thomas Webb kept an account book between 1840 and 1843 (quoted in Theo Brown's book *A Dartmoor Village*, which lists the cost of food and clothes during those years).

STANNON

Stannon Newtake was mentioned in the 1702 depositions (Dartmoor 1890). A likely derivation is 'Stone Hill'.

Stannon House was built at the end of the eighteenth century by John and Thomas Hullett, after they decided to build a starch factory in the area. When John died Thomas gave up the lease-holds acquired from Patterson. Stannon's lease passed first to Revd Vollans, then to J.N. Bennett, and the property was let on a rental basis. On 13 January 1830 Elizabeth Warn, aged 7 months, who had died there, was buried at Widecombe.

The 1839 tithe return records a farmhouse, garden, meadow and another small plot, it was then in the hands of Richard Horsham. Abraham and Elizabeth Harvey and another family, Joseph and Jane James, were residing there in 1841. They moved out to be replaced by Richard and Prudence Tawden. The three men were tin miners, Richard came from Cornwall.

The James family returned to Stannon after Jane, then a widow, had married William Davey. They were accompanied by Robert James, aged 16, a tin miner, and a younger son Richard James. Jane's eldest son, another Joseph, had married Sarah Tanner and they too lived at Stannon, accompanied by Elizabeth James, a nurse.

Later the Stephens family were in occupation and they stayed there until the early 1890s when they moved to Higher Lydgate.

In 1910 the Duchy let the property to William Hambley. The house was re-roofed and repaired, in 1913, at a cost of about £50. It was described as being stone built with a kitchen, dairy and parlour, with a further two rooms on the first floor. There was an earth closet but no other drainage. Water came from a spring,

There is a leat from a point near the house which passes the old 'Sheep Dip' on its way to Higher Merripit and beyond.

For many years Ernest and Harriet Willcocks were the tenants. Harriet was Annie Sleep's sister. She was a great walker and could be seen most days somewhere in the village. I remember her coming into the shop and giving me a halfpenny. I asked her why and she commented 'You gave me a halfpenny change too much, I wouldn't cheat you just as I wouldn't expect to be cheated.'

After they moved to Higher Merripit the house was unoccupied for a time. I remember a young man called Jonathan living there, and also a member of the Rolling Stones. He installed electricity and added a music room with a gallery.

In 1995 the Duchy sold the lease at auction.

HARTYLAND

An Ancient Tenement, first mentioned in 1521 and variously known as Harterland (1608), Hastiland (1702), Hasterland (1786), Hartland (1801), and Hearty Land (1809). Richard Cabell and Thomas Langworthie paid 6s.9d. copyhold rent for Harterland in 1608.

In 1702 'Hastiland' was in the possession of Sir Thomas Leare Bt., and in 1733 by Samuel Pugsley, who is listed in the Dunnabridge Pound account as a Moorman. The Duchy Survey of 1786 mentions that William Tapper paid 6s.9d. copyhold rent for Hasterland.

A Dartmoor longhouse existed on the site and it was there that Jonas Coaker, 'the Dartmoor Poet', was born on 23 February 1801. At some-time a small cottage was attached to the long-house. Other occupiers were Francis and Ann Le Chevalier (1814), James Conybere, a yeoman, and his wife Catherine (1835), and John and Julia Williams (1837). The 1841 census mentions two families at Hartland: John Widecombe, an agri-cultural labourer, and his wife Maria, and Thomas Rowse, a tin miner, and his wife Mary.

The tithe maps list Hartyland, with an acreage of 94 acres, 3rods and 4 perches, as being in the

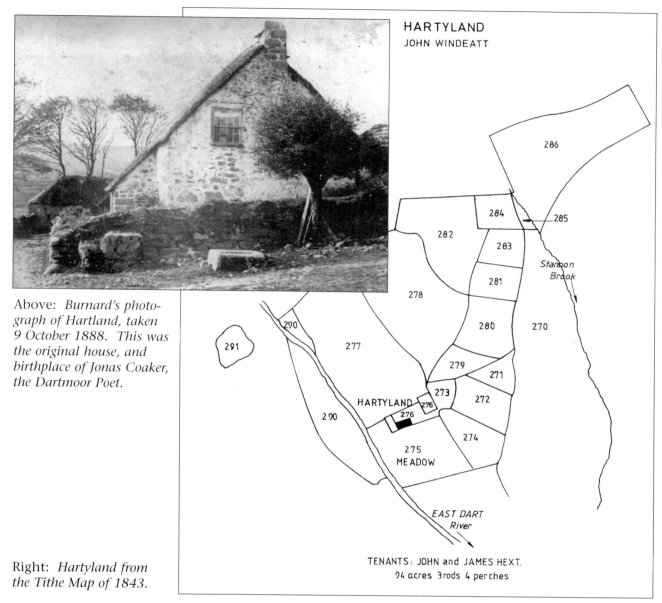

Above: *Burnard's photograph of Hartland, taken 9 October 1888. This was the original house, and birthplace of Jonas Coaker, the Dartmoor Poet.*

HARTYLAND

JOHN WINDEATT

Stannon Brook

HARTYLAND

MEADOW

EAST DART River

TENANTS: JOHN and JAMES HEXT.
94 acres 3rods 4 perches

Right: *Hartyland from the Tithe Map of 1843.*

possession of John Windeatt, and let to John and James Hext. James and his wife, Ann, occupied the longhouse for many years, whilst for a time, John and Elizabeth Kernick, lived in the cottage (1847). Philip Crossman, a Mine Captain, and his wife, Elizabeth, were occupiers in 1851.

In 1859 E.H. Windeatt paid a copyhold rent of 8s.3d., and in 1861 James Hext was a hind at Hartyland.

At about this time the Duchy bought the copyholds and, in 1864, granted a 60 year lease to J.C.S. Windeatt of the farm and newtakes, a total acreage of 276 acres, 1 rood and 27 perches, at an annual rent of £40 per annum. These lands were tenanted by George French.

In 1864 two other newtakes adjacent to Hartyland were purchased by the Duchy. One known as Long Mead, or Long-a-Meade, of 6 acres from James Cleave for £20, and the other Roundapark, or Little Roundypark as it is now known, of 1 acre 3 rods and 15 perches, for £5 from Mary Cleave. (Long-a-Meade is mentioned in an indenture, first written in 1715, between William Meardon and John Hamatt, when it changed hands for £3.10s. The witnesses were J. Hogg, Philip Oxenham, Vincent Andrew and Henry Tozer. The land changed hands again in 1728 when a John Coaker was involved).

Other families who either lived in the farmhouse or the cottage were John Hamlyn and his wife, Sarah (1871), and William Symons (1880).

The Potter family farmed there for many years from c.1883. About 1910 the house was reported to be very old and thatched. It had two rooms

Left: *View of Old Hartland Farm and Hartland Tor from just below Still Pool. A Chapman photograph c.1912.* (Author)

Right: *View of Old Hartland Farm and Hartland Tor from Bathing Pool on the East Dart. A Chapman photograph c.1912.* (Author)

upstairs and two downstairs, there was no closet or drainage. Pot-water was leated from Stannon Brook and its outlet to a stone trough can still be seen in the driveway. Drinking water came from a spring. An outbuilding which was formerly thatched now had a galvanized roof.

After John Potter relinquished his tenancy Mrs Pethybridge was granted a 99 year lease in the 1930s. The old house was torn down and the present property, designed by Martin Bazeley of Plymouth, was built by Stone's of Chagford. Granite was used extensively in the construction and the original thatched roof has now been replaced by tiles.

Water was piped in from Roundypark and the house was lit using a Kohler generator. There is a considerable amount of panelling and a feature fireplace, with decorative tiles by the famous potter, Bernard Leach, is in the hall. The tiles represent features of local interest.

The Dartmoor garden with its leat, pools, clapper bridges and granite steps was largely constructed by Jack Warne, Freddy Warne and Sidney French. The granite was brought from Hartland Tor on sledges and then fitted into place. It took many years to complete.

A large vegetable garden was laid out to the east of the property and a wide bridlepath was constructed between the house and the garden. This was to maintain a bridleway already in existence. Eventually this bridleway was diverted to enter the gate by a little wood east of Hartland, and thence to Hartland Tor. The present route, via the river, did not exist, and was certainly not entered on to the right of way map compiled by my father and myself. The original roadway to Hartland was through the courtyard of Ringhill and can still be seen. The present road, paid for by Mrs Pethybridge, starts just above Mucks Hole bridge at the end of the county road.

Prior to the completion of the present house Mrs Pethybridge had a caravan sited above the quarry at Mucks Hole. The present occupiers are Mr and Mrs Bishop who use this delightful house with its magnificent views for the provision of bed and breakfast accommodation.

SHEEPFOLD

Several opinions have been suggested as to the use of this site. Theo Brown in *Tales of a Dartmoor Village* mentions that it was originally associated with a starch factory, an enterprise of the Hullett brothers. Crossing in his *One Hundred years on Dartmoor* (1901) states: 'It was built by a Scotchman who engaged extensively in sheep farming on the Moor and was admirably adapted to its purpose'.

In the past it has certainly been used as a sheep-fold, but when I was young some of the old villagers favoured the starch factory as its original purpose. The construction of its walls is markedly similar to those enclosing some derelict fields in the valley between Stannon and Merripit. Perhaps it was here that the potatoes were to be grown for use in making the starch.

There is a similarity in the window construction of the house which stood at the eastern end of the enclosure, and was burnt down, with the windows in Stannon House. This would seem to suggest an association between the two buildings.

Two families are known to have lived there, both in 1833. They were Samuel and Mary Thomas, and Samuel and Thirza Gifford, mining families.

Stone was readily available all over the area and evidence can be seen of stone cutting for gateposts and lintels. It is interesting to note the different methods of drilling the granite.

In 1864 a local builder applied to the Duchy for permission to cut gateposts and hearthstones on Stannon Tor. In 1871 there is a report of a builder apologising for taking stone from Sheepfold. In 1995 some repairs to the walls were carried out and part of the old house was demolished.

Left: *Ruins of the cottage, Stannon Sheepfold c.1938.* (Author)

Below: *Stannon Sheepfold, 1938.* (Author)

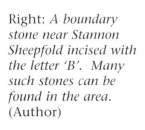

Right: *A boundary stone near Stannon Sheepfold incised with the letter 'B'. Many such stones can be found in the area.* (Author)

THREE CHIMNEYS SX 655801

Sometime in the past a house stood on this site but the dates are unknown. The name has been used locally for 'donkey's years' and is still used today. The site, because of its magnificent views, was frequently used by my father and John Bailey as a view point for watching the hounds after a meet in the village.

RINGHILL

The cottage was built at the end of the eighteenth century on land leased to the Hullett Brothers. This land was firstly assigned to Revd Vollans and later to J.N. Bennett of Archerton. One of the earliest occupiers was John Penrose.

The cottage took its name from the ring situated on a low hill nearby. Baring Gould writing in *Dartmoor Idylls* tells us:

The ring enclosed an old walled village and the stones from the primeval bee-hive huts were removed and utilised for the construction of the farmstead. The courtyard was paved with great slabs of granite and the sheds were buttressed with long posts of the same material laid at an incline to prop up the mortarless walls.

The name was also applied to a 16-acre enclosure surrounding the ring.

In 1839 the property was sub-let to George Tanner by Francis Le Chevalier who in 1814 lived at Hartland. The lands at that time comprised:

	a	r	p
Dwelling house, court and garden		1	22
Little Ring		1	20
Ring Hill	16	2	30
Great Ring	2	0	34
Great Marsh	11	3	29
Great Marsh Plantation			29
Lower Road Marsh		3	32
Lower Road Marsh Plantation		1	2
Higher Road Marsh	2	1	21
Higher Road Marsh Plantation		3	9
Total	36	0	28

By 1851 the property was occupied by Francis Hawke, a tin miner, and in 1861 by John Webb, a tin miner who farmed 20 acres. By 1871 Mary Hawke, a miner's widow, was in residence but it is not clear whether she farmed any of the land at that time, although by 1881 it is known she was farming 12 acres, and Jonas Coaker (the Dartmoor Poet) shared her home. In 1878 the cottage seems to have been in need of repair as J.N. Bennett was asked to put it in order.

The next family to live there were the Sleeps. Silas Sleep paid £12.10s. rent to the Duchy for the cottage and 23 acres 3 rods of land. Previous tenants would have paid rent to the leaseholders.

The cottage comprised kitchen, back kitchen. dairy and three bedrooms. Water was drawn from a stream and there was no drainage.

Originally thatched, the house was re-roofed in 1911 at a cost of £150, and a water closet was added in 1912.

In 1922 a new house was built to the north of the old one by John Halfyard of Princetown. This was occupied early on by W.J. Hale, a forester for the Duchy of Cornwall. He later moved to Bellever.

For many years the house was used as a holiday home by Dr Dancey and his family. Other occupiers were Miss Edith Bennett (daughter of Sir Courtenay Bennett of Archerton) Mr and Mrs F.R. Dunne, who were school teachers, and the present occupiers Mr and Mrs Allanson.

Remains of the original old house can still be seen.

Mucks Hole Bridge c. 1938, with Thomas and Jack Webb, and Reg White on the cycle. (Author)

MUCKS HOLE BRIDGE

In 1895 the Lydford Parish Council agreed that Tavistock Rural District Council should be asked to provide a bridge over Stannon Brook on the trackway from Middle Merripit to Hartyland. The Rural District Council agreed to do so if one half of the cost was contributed by persons residing in the area and that the land owners would give any land required for the purpose. Originally the Parish Council had proposed to pay for the bridge out of the rates but this was deemed illegal.

The Duchy of Cornwall contributed £4 and a free gift of the necessary stone. They also waived any other charges for the land. Mr Windeatt contributed £2 and J.N. Bennett £1. A tender of £10.10s. was accepted from John French and, in December 1896, the surveyor passed the construction and agreed a final cost of £12.

LOWER MERRIPIT

MERIPUT 1344. MIRAPYT 1347. MYRAPYTTE. MYRYPYTTE 1417. MIRAPYT 1481. MEREPIT 1585. ('Pleasant Hollow' - from *The Place Names of Devon*. English Place Names Society). Hemery in *High Dartmoor* suggests 'Miry Pit or Bottom'. In 1344 William de Meriput is recorded as holding ferlings of land on Dartmoor. Merepit is mentioned in the Court Roll of 21 September 1584 when it was surrendered at that Court.

The Duchy records lists Thomas Knapman as a tenant of Merripit in 1608 paying 6s.9d. rent.

On the 5 July 1654 John French took possession of 8 acres of waste ground called Furzameads Corner:

bounded from the corner of a tenement called Higher Furzameade, in the tenure of John Crossman in the East, and one tenement in the West called Smeetha, being in the tenure of William French, lying along the river Dart, saving twenty yards thereof or thereabouts lying on the wester side of the said river, in the name of a new-take. Rent twelve pence yearly.

On 10 May 1655 William French granted a 99 year lease to Walter and John French (see Higher Merripit). On 2 July 1684 Jacob Newcombe surrendered Furzameade Corner lying within the Forest:

bounded by the corner of a certain tenement called Higher Furzameade, now in the possession of the said Jacob Newcombe, on the East side and a tenement on the West called Smeetha, now in the tenure of Walter French, adjoining to a certain river called Dart to Walter French.

Lower Merripit, taken by Burnard in 1889. (R. Burnard)

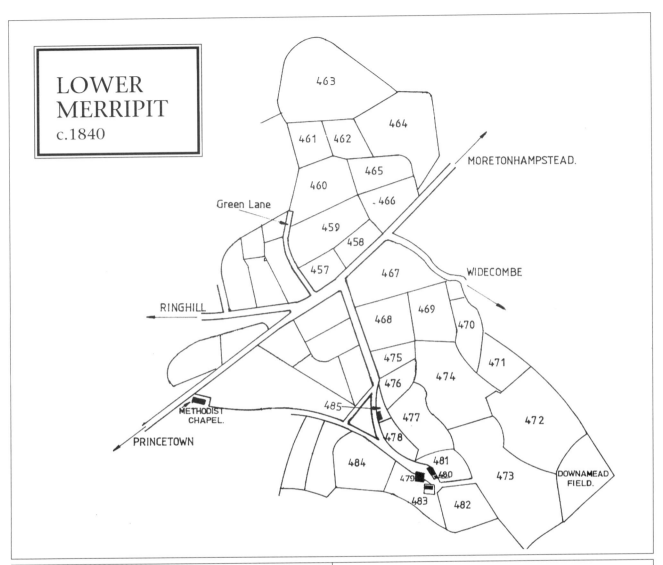

ROBERT HANNAFORD: TENANT		JAMES CLEAVE: TENANT	
		459	Lower Western Park
457	Leany Park	460	Higher Western Park
458	ditto	463	Higher Coarsefield
461	Squarefields	464	Lower Coarsefield
462	ditto	467	Soakfield
465	Higher Roundepark	468	Squarefield
466	Lower Roundepark	469	Higher Moors
470	Vaglas	472	The Brake
471	ditto	473	Lower Moor
475	Higher Meadpark	474	Higher Moors
476	Lower Meadpark	480	Dwelling House etc.
477	Big Meadow	481	Little Meadow
478	Higher Little Meadow	482	Uncle Bill's Meadow
479	Dwelling House etc.	483	Lower Barnspark
		484	Higher Barnspark

Mary French of Merripit appointed John French of Peswell as her attorney on the 5 November 1691. On 25 March 1732 there is a 99 year lease between

Warwick Hawkey of Trevego in the Parish of St Winnow in the County of Cornwall and Peter Willcocks of Withycomb for the tenement lying and being in the village of Merripit, which was late in the possession of Walter French, deceased, commonly called Merrypitt also Mary Mans tenement or Mary Mans Parke.

Consideration for the lease was £38 and the annual rent was £1. There was also a herryott (heriot) of 7s.6d. to be paid on the death of each, Peter Willcocks, Mary his wife, and Mary their daughter.

John Crossman is also mentioned in connection with another tenement at Lower Merripit.

On 21 May 1738 certain newtakes namely Foster Hole (Jesters), Furzameade Corner, and Smythay in the possession of Peter Willcocks, yeoman, and John Cleave the elder, passed to Mary Willcocks, the next heir of John French, yeoman of Merrypitt.

Warwick Hawkey of Trevego appointed 'John Bennett of St Nyott' as his attorney on 20 September 1740. The Court Roll mentions that two tenements at Merripit are in the 'tenure possesssion', or occupation, of Peter Willcocks and Gilbert Babbacombe, and that these persons have contracted to purchase the said tenements.

On 18 May 1741, Warwick Hawkey, as tenant in fee, through his attorney, surrendered Merripit or Lower Merripit to Gilbert Babbacombe of Moretonhampstead. On 9 October 1753 Merripits, or Lower Merripit, came into the possession of Elias Babbacombe on the death of his father, Gilbert Babbacombe, late of Moretonhampstead. The tenement at that time was in the possession of John French.

Simpson's survey of 1786 lists Peter Willcocks paying 6s.9d. for Lower Merripit. This was the same amount of rent which Knapman paid in 1608. At an earlier date, c.1763, John Willcocks was paying three shillings for three newtakes associated with the tenement.

The premises were used as a school c.1796 when Elizabeth French was the teacher. Jane Coaker taught there c.1797–1800. Before the church was built, c.1868, Anglican services were also held there.

The Court Roll of 18 October 1813 shows that Susanna Germon held two-thirds of Lower Merripit which she and her husband surrendered at that Court.

Grace Hamlyn of Lower Merripit was buried at Widecombe in 1818. In 1825 James House, the son of Joseph and Elizabeth House, from the same address, was baptised at Princetown. John White of Woodlands, clerk, was admitted to two-thirds of Merripitt, or Lower Merripit, on 31 October 1819, and on the 2 December 1846 he and Matthew White were admitted to the other one third.

The tithe apportionments of c.1840 show Robert Hannaford farming about 18 acres, and James Cleave farming about 56 acres. By 1841 Robert Hannaford had been replaced by Richard Cleave.

The two Cleave families were still there in 1851, but by 1861 they had been replaced by Philip Crossman, farming 20 acres. He also worked at the tin mines, and Samuel White, Samuel White senior, and his wife Eliza, were farming there in 1871. Their son Samuel Henry, a cooper, and their other two sons, William aged 21, and Matthew aged 17, were living with them.

Two other families are listed: Susan Hutchings and her family, and Walter and Mary Bailey and their children. After Walter died his widow married Robert Cleave from Pizwell and they moved to Higher Merripit.

Samuel White senior died on 6 February 1879, and on 8 July 1879 his will was proved by his wife Eliza. The will provided annuities for his wife and his daughter, Mary Ann Reed, 'his lands at Langworthy and Blackmoor and Merripitts, all other real estate and leaseholds, if any belonging, equally between his three sons Samuel, William and Matthew'.

William and Matthew were admitted to one-third of Lower Merripit and two-thirds of Merripitts, or Lower Merripit, at a Court Baron held on 31 October 1879.

On the 4 February 1880 an indenture between Samuel White and others provided that William and Matthew 'should hold in severalty the hereditaments called Merripits'. Samuel was to hold North and South Langworthy, and Blackmoor situate in Widecombe. The same year William and Matthew agreed to divide Merripits. William built a house and outbuildings for his own use.

In 1891 Matthew, his wife Mary, and their family, and William, his wife Lucy, and their family, were still occupying the tenements. Their children attended Postbridge School. James Hext, a farm labourer, was also living there. Later on two of Matthew's children married into the Jory

Cutting turf (peat) at Gawlor Bottom c.1925.

family. Bessie married William Jory and Herbert married Ethel Jory.

In 1903 tithes 457. 458. 459. 460. 461. 462. 463. 464. 465 and 466 were let to S.S. Sleep by Messrs Conran at an annual rental of £25. The only building on this part of the holding was an iron and wooden shed. Eventually Mr Sleep bought the land for £600.

Matthew sold some land in the bend of the road between Moreton and Widecombe main roads to J.H. Bailey in 1907 for £150. Over the years other parcels of land were sold off and Tor View, Vaglas, The Brake, Pencroft, Read's Bungalow, and Hoddinott's bungalow, were built on them.

Lewis White became the tenant of Lower Merripit in 1922. His wife was Nellie Sleep and she often reminded me that we were related. My family pooh-poohed the idea, but in fact it was true, although it was far removed, dating back to my great-great-grandfather.

The old house is a Grade II listed Devon Longhouse which was still thatched up to 1931. I can still smell the smoke from the vags and peat fire and remember Matthew carting the turf from the Gawlor turf ties. He also used his horse and cart in connection with his work of repairing roads.

Lower Merripit was eventually left to M.L.J. (Bob) White and at a later date was advertised for sale by public auction. The cottage was also sold and both have been extensively renovated.

At some time Francis Redstone had a small shop alongside the cottage. I can just remember it.

There was a tin mine here, Wheal Merripit, and the promoter was Mr Edward Mogridge from Moretonhampstead who was granted annual licences from 6 April 1887 and 6 April 1888. John Webb was his agent. It seems the mine was busy in April 1888 but by November there was 'every probability it would be abandoned'. A clock was presented to Capt John Webb bearing the inscription:

Presented to Capt John Webb on the opening of Wheal Merripit Mine as a memento of the promoters appreciation of his Zeal and Energy, 21st May 1888.

HIGHER MERRIPIT

This tenement is of interest because of its age, without being one of the Ancient Tenements. An early document, dated 10 May 1655 (not 1555 as usually recorded), relates to a 99 year lease

Higher Merripit from a Burnard photograph dated October 1888. (R. Burnard)

between William French the elder of Withecomb(e), and Walter French and John French in which William:

demised granted and farme letten one close or parcell of with the appartenances called outter nutake scituate lying and being between postbridge and a nutake of on Richard Leeres within the Forrest of Dartmore etc.

The rent was to be one penny. At this time 'farm' could denote land let on a lease instead of the general meaning it has today.

The newtake had obviously been enclosed before this date and the use of 'appartenances' probably indicates a dwelling. 'Merry Pitt' appears on Ogilby's *Brittania Depicted*, published in 1675, and Hemery writes in *High Dartmoor* that 'Eyre Merrypit' is mentioned in Revd Thomas Berraford's Bill in the Exchequer dated 1702.

Barrington's report to the Duchy, dated 4 January 1862, reports that a tenant was admitted to Higher Merripit in 1766. However Simpson's survey of 1786 only mentions that a house had been built on the 39 acre newtake.

John Swete, writing in 1797 (Volume 15 of *Sketches of Devon*) describes 'skirting Higher and Lower Merripit where the grass had not been mowed and the oats were perfectly green'.

We have some idea of occupation early in the nineteenth century as William Cleave, Harriet Stancombe and Ann Horsham, all of Higher Merripit, were buried at Widecombe in 1824, 1829 and 1837 respectively.

The Tithe Maps and associated documents show that the tenement was held by John Windeatt and let to Richard Horsham (c.1840).

Billing's directory of 1857 lists a certain Hannaford farming there. I think this was John Hannaford who was farming 20 acres with his wife Elizabeth and family in 1861, and who remained a tenant after the Duchy had granted J.C. Windeatt a 60 year lease in 1864. John, now a widower, was still in residence in 1671.

The next tenant was John Rowe (*White's Directory* 1878–79), and in 1881 John and Avis Rowe were farming 40 acres. By 1883 Robert Cleave and his wife had taken over. Robert had lived at Lower Pizwell and married Mrs Bailey, a widow with four children.

One of his stepsons, John H. Bailey, was to take over Higher Merripit and farm it until 1946 when it was purchased by Miss Annie Sleep. It had been offered to my father when John and his house-keeper, Mrs Annie Bellamy, moved to Beechwood, but father never took up the offer.

On 3 January 1907 a disastrous fire destroyed the house. The house had combined living

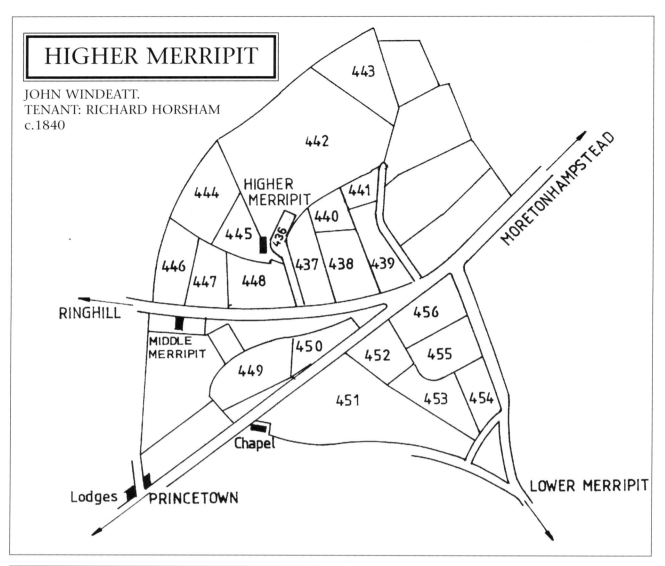

HIGHER MERRIPIT

JOHN WINDEATT.
TENANT: RICHARD HORSHAM
c.1840

KEY TO THE MAP

436 House, outhouses, court and garden
437 Homer Park
438 Middle Close
439 Green Lane Field
440 Middle Close
441 ditto
442 The Brake
443 ditto
444 Outer Stonymead
445 Little Stonymead
446 Outer Little Meadow
447 Little Meadow
448 Big Meadow
449 Moory Meadow
453 Brake

Mrs and Mrs Cleave at Higher Merripit, 4 August 1892. The child is probably their daughter, Ruby. (R. Burnard)

The new farmhouse at Middle Merripit, c.1923, which replaced the old cottages. (Author)

rooms, offices and cowsheds, all under one roof. There was a common entrance, human occupants turning to the right and the cattle to the left. Two photographs were published in the *Western Morning News* – one before the fire was by Helen Langley and the other after the fire by J.B. Windeatt.

The house was put into some sort of repair and John and his wife brought up their three children Ronald, Ruby and George, at Higher Merripit. George was a great friend of mine who sadly died in his early twenties.

Eventually the Duchy sold part of the holding to John Bailey, but retained some of the enclosures on the south side.

MIDDLE MERRIPIT

At the time of writing Middle Merripit is one of the largest farms in the district. It has been farmed for many years by Mr and Mrs Watson and now by their eldest son. It has not always been a farm, and around 1840 it comprised a small cottage, garden and plot, in all about 66 perches.

This cottage was probably built by the Hulletts and the earliest names that I have been able to find of people living there were Sam and Mary Thomas in 1829. It is difficult to determine when the other two cottages were eventually built on the site. The census of 1861 shows three families: No.1 Middle Merripit – Thomas and Susanna Gilbert, No.2 Middle Merripit – John and Ann Brown, and No.3 Merripit (it does not specify Middle) – Samuel and May Stanbury.

Samuel and May Stanbury certainly lived there in 1871 as did a widow Elizabeth Rowse.

It appears that by 1881 21 acres were being farmed by John and Susanna French, whilst William and Mary Knott lived in one of the cottages, the third cottage having been turned into a stable. Rents were paid to the Revd Vollans and then to J.N. Bennett, until 1906, when the lands reverted to the Duchy.

It was then tenanted by John French who paid a rental of £21.5s. per annum for Stannon Hill, a cot and outbuildings. George Warne and his family lived there about this time but from Michaelmas 1908 the cottage was let to Richard Coaker at a rental of £4 per annum.

The cottages were thatched in 1912 and repairs were made to the thatch in 1917. In the early 1920s a new farmhouse was built to replace the old cottages, which were turned into farm buildings, and the lands, which now incorporated much of the Ringhill and Hartyland enclosures, were farmed for many years by Sidney French. He was born at Middle Merripit in 1889 and died at Newton Abbot in 1976. He served in the Army during the First World War and, besides farming, he had been a tin miner and a contractor for repairing roads.

He married two of my great aunts, firstly Hilda Jory and, after her death, Alberta Coaker. Like many men of his time he depended very much on his wife to look after his finances (especially Hilda). I can vouch for this because, after she died, I helped in sorting them out, as he had little idea of his worth.

PRICED CATALOGUE OF THE FURNITURE AND EFFECTS AT BEECHWOOD, POSTBRIDGE, THE PROPERTY OF MR J. BELLAMY, SOLD ON 9TH DAY OF JUNE 1936, BY MESSERS COE AND AMERY, AUCTIONEERS AND VALUERS CHAGFORD DEVON

Item	£	s	d	Item	£	s	d
				Lamp		2	6
Iron fender and guard		6	6	Ditto		1	6
Brass fire irons		7	6	Wooden box		2	6
Oak coal box		3	0	3 chairs		3	0
Mirror and two clocks		5	0	Bucket and water can		1	6
Mirror		5	0	2 zinc pails		3	6
Plant stand etc		2	0	Chair and stool		1	0
Five walnut framed chairs		17	6	2 meat safes		1	6
Arm chair		5	0	Kitchen table		3	0
Glazed cabinet		7	6	China		4	0
Ornaments		3	6	Washstand		1	0
Walnut sideboard	1	2	6	Cooking Unensils		1	6
4 writing boxes		1	6	Scales,box etc		1	0
Bamboo table		3	0	2 oil drums		5	0
Sofa		4	6	2 rolls lino		4	0
Eiderdown and 5 cushions		3	6	2 ditto, folding stand and tray		6	0
Bookshelves and books		4	6	Lamps etc		2	6
Sofa		2	0	Meat dishes		2	0
Pair of plush curtains		4	6	Flask etc		1	0
5 plants and pots		1	0	Teapot etc		3	0
4 tablecloths		1	6	Lap table		2	6
Easy chair		11	0	Carpet sweeper		1	6
Extending table		15	0	4 brushes and mop		3	0
Quantity linen		2	0	Brushes etc		1	0
Ditto and curtains etc		2	0	Heating lamp		2	6
Linen		1	0	Iron bed and spring	1	8	0
Carpet		14	0	Mattress and 2 pillows		14	0
2 pairs prints		10	0	Bath			6
6 pictures		1	0	2 towel rails		3	6
4 Ditto		10	0	Washstand and ware		1	6
6 Ditto		3	0	Chest of drawers		7	0
8 Ditto		2	6	China		3	0
2 pairs curtains and rods		1	6	Single iron bed and spring		18	0
Chair, mirror etc		1	6	Feather bed		2	0
Camp bed and mattress		9	0	Matting		9	0
Trays,rack,rug etc		2	0	Ditto		7	0
Toilet glass		6	0	Stair carpet		7	0
Ditto		3	0	Stair rods		1	0
Bookshelves and pictures		1	0	Odd carpet		3	6
2 fenders and brass fire irons		5	6	Blue carpet		4	6
Quantity pictures		1	6	Mahogany washstand		4	6
Folding chair		5	0	Scales etc			6
4 cane seat chairs		6	0	Mahogany washstand		10	0
2 chairs		1	6	Ditto toilet glass		6	0
2 walnut framed ditto		4	0	Ditto		4	0
2 ditto		3	0	Occasional table		1	6
Chest of drawers		7	0	Oak folding chair		11	0
Toilet glass		1	6	6 Saucepans etc		1	6
Bolster and pillow		3	0	3 ditto and kettle		4	0
Mattress		7	0	Cake tins etc		2	0
Mahogany chest of drawers		7	0	Carpet		1	6
Quantity plates		2	6	2 ditto		6	0
Mahogany chest of drawers	2	10	0	Linoleum			6
Ditto frame toilet glass		14	0	Umbrella stand		2	0
Washstand and ware		5	0	Oak coal box		4	6
Ditto		3	6	4 lamp shades		1	0
Mahogany chest of drawers	1	7	6	5 coco mats		2	6
Iron bed and spring		2	0	Bread pan		5	6
Chest of drawers		3	0	2 trunks		2	0
Sundries		1	6	8 fowls	1	0	0
Washstand and cupboard		1	6	---------------			
Towel rail and stand		3	6				
Washstand and ware		4	0	TOTAL SALE	31	18	0

Chapter 8 – Farther Afield

BEECHWOOD

In 1871 The Duchy of Cornwall granted Thomas Rowse a 60 year lease in order to build a house on waste ground in the Forest. Two houses were eventually built on part of the land, one having 7 rooms and the other 4. Thomas and his wife Mary were living there in 1881 and, by 1891, Matthew and Maria Rowse were in Beechwood House whilst Mary was living in the cottage.

By 1900 the lease had been assigned to Matthew Rowse and after his death, to John Donovan Rowse who held it until 1931 when the lease expired. It was renewed for 31 years from 25 March 1931, and in 1936 Mr Rowse assigned it to William Henry Worth.

In the same year Mr Worth assigned it to Mr Bellamy for £100. Mr Bellamy also bought the contents for £20. These were later auctioned and realized £31.18s. The complete list of items sold is printed opposite and is interesting as an indication of the type of content and furnishing, and their worth, to be found in a modest rural house in the 1930s.

The two houses had various tenants through the years and eventually was in need of modernization and repair. In 1955 this work was put in hand by Mr Springate who with his wife were tenants in the lower house by the road. In 1962 the lease was again renewed for 31 years, and in 1972 it was assigned to Mr and Mrs Maye who converted the two houses into one. During the conversion they found three open hearths which were returned to their former state.

For many years the fields had been cut for hay, with the rick being built in the middle field. During the war one field had been ploughed and tilled with corn.

Along with the fields there was an area of ground known as the 'rough piece,' from which the cemetery was enclosed, and the Hermitage field, were held on annual tenancy. The Hermitage field is now part of Greyhound Farm and is managed as a traditional hay meadow by virtue of an agreement between the Duchy of Cornwall, the Dartmoor National Park Authority and the tenant. As a result public access to the field is restricted.

Beechwood, c.1923, from a Chapman postcard. (Author)

Beechwood, 1995. (Author)

DURY HEAD/CHURCH COTTAGE.

James Sleep was granted a 60 year lease of 2 acres 28 perches of land adjacent to the Church, from midsummer 1870, at a rent of £1 per annum. Part of the land had been a quarry which was filled in with earth and stone dug out when the church foundations were excavated.

A small house with 5 rooms was built of stone with a slate roof on the site. It has been extended from time to time since. It may have been here that Granny Sleep kept a shop, as in the 1881 census James Sleep is shown as a grocer.

A further lease of 10 acres 1 rood 35 perches of land was granted in 1880 at an annual rent of £2.10s. Part of this land was released by Mr Sleep on payment of £100 so that a parsonage could be built close to the church. For many years the lease was held by Major McAlpine who built the wooden garage and workshop in which he installed an electric lighting plant. He was associated with Kelvin Bottomley & Baird of Basingstoke, and lived at Hook. His son Alan was a pupil at Postbridge School for a short time during 1922.

Later the lease passed to Mrs Blundell and Miss Smyth. Their memorial pew is in Postbridge Church.

THE BUNGALOW/FAIRWATER

In 1910 an iron-clad bungalow with 5 rooms and a kitchen, matchboarded inside, stood on this site. The holding, sometimes referred to as Dury Head, also included a field of about two and a quarter acres which was part of the lease granted to Joseph James in 1870. It was owned by Miss B.M. Langley and let to Mrs Aitken at a rent of £7 per annum.

I always understood that Miss Lind purchased the bungalow c.1914 and lived there prior to the The Brake being built. The bungalow was taken down and removed to Fairholm by Mr Bill Miners of Widecombe. The foundations can still be seen and I understand there is a well beneath them.

At a later date two small wooden huts were erected on the site and, in the 1930s, Mrs Pettitt paid the rates for these. The name was then changed to The Perfumed Garden. Mr Pryor used to site a holiday caravan there but was refused planning permission for a permanent dwelling.

THE HERMITAGE/PRIMROSE COTTAGE

In 1870 Joseph James applied to the Duchy for a piece of land on which to build a house. A 60 year lease was granted of about two acres of land at Dury Head. The house was built about 1871 and was occupied by Joseph, his wife Sarah, and their four children Elizabeth, Joseph, George and Charles.

In 1881 Thomas and Elizabeth Webb and their five children James, Elizabeth, Richard, Rebecca and John were living there. Thomas and James were tin miners. It was then called Primrose Cottage.

It seems to have been unoccupied in 1891, but there is a mention of a 'South View' in the Census Return which might have been this property. At some time Matthew Rowse must have purchased the lease as, in 1895, he sold it to Colonel Edmund S. Walcott, who in 1899 sold it to the Misses E.A and B.M Langley. H. Vigars Harris was the owner in 1910 when Hermitage was described as having two rooms, kitchen, scullery, and with a small iron bungalow adjacent.

At some time the lease passed to Mrs M.P. Beare who paid the rates in the 1930s.

After their marriage Harold and Queenie White rented the property, and they were followed by Mr and Mrs Freddy Bellamy.

For many years Chris Hill and his wife lived there, accompanied for a time by his mother-in-law. Chris was well known as he had bought rabbits from the warreners. He was an excellent salmon and sea trout fisherman. His daughter, her husband and family now live there.

BROADUN (BROAD DOWN)

This is one of the few new houses to be completed in the village in recent years. It was built by Mr A.W. Bracken who, at one time, was the licensee of the East Dart Hotel. He bought the land which was part of Furzimeads from Mr and Mrs Ernest Webb. This parcel of land may have been part of a newtake called Furzamead Corner, mentioned in the Court Roll of 22 May 1738.

After Mr and Mrs Bracken left the village the property was occupied by Mr and Mrs John Skittery. John was the Chief Constable of Plymouth and he and his wife resided there, both during his term of office and after his retirement. Mr and Mrs Bracken, and John and his wife, are all buried in Postbridge cemetery.

REDGATE/DURNFORD COTTAGE

In 1910 Herbert James Roberts bought about half an acre of freehold land (OS 6025), which was part of the Pizwell/Yellowmeads/Furzimeads customary heriditaments, from Mrs Lucy Beare for £65. The land (tithe 490) had been enclosed before 1840 and was known as Redgate field at that time. The house which was subsequently built was also named Redgate. There was a covenant which provided for access by a narrow lane to the rest of the field and beyond.

In 1919 the property was sold to William Henry Wakeford Bickell for £750. Successive owners were W. Chaplin-Bennett, a chemist from Totnes; Miss F.L. Brook; Rt. Hon Sir Henry Slesser; Mr and Mrs Chinn (who changed the name to Durnford Cottage); and the present owners Lt-Commander and Mrs Leadgate (1997).

For several years Colonel and Mrs Hibbert, and later Mr Wilfred Barratt and his wife, Dolly, occupied the premises.

Redgate when newly built c.1912. From a Chapman photograph. (Author)

A view from the Widecombe road showing Lower Merripit, Sunnymead and Redgate. A Chapman photograph. (Courtesy Mr and Mrs Reg White)

SMALLWATERS

So far I have been unable to find out exactly when the old Smallwaters were built, but judging from the lists of known occupiers, it seems as if there were two properties on or adjacent to the site. The only property shown on the Tithe Map c.1840 was a cottage (Tithe 485) which was burnt down in June 1881.

We know that Celia Pasco from 'Smallwaters' died and was buried at Princetown in the 1850s and that the Pasco's were living with John and Maria Widecombe in 1851. Certainly John and Maria (now spelt Withycombe) were there in 1861. John senior and his son John were working at the Powdermills, whilst their other two sons William and George were tin miners.

Another cottage, Watersmeet, probably built after the Tithe Maps were drawn, and which at sometime became a tavern The Good Intent, was occupied by Richard and Susan Hannaford, their son George an agricultural labourer, and Thomas Daw, aged 12, a tin miner.

Ten years later Richard and Susan were still there, aged 76, but the Withycombe's had moved to Pizwell, all except William, now a farmer, and his wife Elizabeth who remained. George and Eliza Withycombe replaced William and his wife but their house was the one which burnt down in June 1881. George and Susan Rowse were in the other house and George was farming 20 acres.

Susan was highly respected in the village. My grandmother told me 'Her was at the comings and goings of lots of us yer.' They were still at Smallwaters c.1910. The cottage was very dilapidated and by then had 9 acres attached to it. The rent was £1.5s. He also rented 8 acres of grazing from Mr Balkwill. The other cottage does not seem to have been replaced after 1881.

A Chapman postcard of the cottage shows a gutter which was fed by the overflow from a pipe where spring water was collected. Maybe Smallwaters took its name from this water supply.

In 1914 George and Ivy Harvey attended Postbridge School from there. They had previously lived at Pizwell.

Around 1918 two new bungalows were built by Mr Halfyard of Princetown, leaving the old ruin of Rowse's cottage to be seen to this day. These bungalows were occupied by Freddy and Elizabeth Warne and John (Jack) and Fanny Hamlyn.

Freddy worked as a tin miner, built walls, laboured on farms, and worked for the Forestry Commission. He helped create the garden at Hartyland for Mrs Pethybridge. He could 'sink a pint' and often met his brother at Warren Inn.

He liked my grandfather John James Coaker and once told me 'If you grow up to be as good a man as your grandfather you will be a credit to your family.'

Above: *Burnard's superb photograph of The Good Intent, taken August 1895. He describes it as 'Watersmeet, formerly a public, "The Good Intent", Postbridge'.* (R. Burnard)

Left and below: *Ruins of the Good Intent.* (Author)

Jack Hamlyn was born in 1883 and died in 1985. His wife pre-deceased him in 1963 and was buried in Postbridge cemetery during the 1963 blizzard. She was a White from Lower Merripit. Jack's son, Matthew John, was born in 1916 and after attending Postbridge School obtained a full boarding scholarship to attend Ashburton Grammar School. He then went to Seale Hayne College and Reading University.

Harry and Fanny White lived in the cottage vacated by the Warne's and after they and the Hamlyn's left the two bungalows were converted into one by Messrs Brandon and Gomm.

SUNNYMEAD

A wooden bungalow, originally of three rooms, built on copyhold land belonging to Lower Merripit by Mr William Herbert (Bert) White. He married Ethel Jory one of Richard Jory's daughters. They had two sons, Harold and Reginald.

Ethel was the organist and trustee of the Wesleyan Chapel for many years. Bert was tragically killed in 1928. He was working with his father Matthew White doing road repairs. On the way home he jumped off the horse and cart into the path of a motor car and died instantly.

Ethel eventually left the village and went to live in Northam, near Bideford where she continued to play the organ in the Methodist Chapel.

FERNDALE

Ferndale was built for Mr and Mrs T.R. Webb by Stones of Chagford to a design by Harold Settle.

The land had been part of the Lower Merripit Estate which had been sold to John Bailey of Higher Merripit in 1907 for about £150. It was later bought by the Webb's of Tor View.

Thomas Redvers Webb, the son of James Webb, worked at the mines for many years and afterwards with the Forestry Commission at Bellever. He regularly rode an ancient Triumph motorcycle which was kept in pristine condition.

He used to store dynamite in the house which he used for blasting tree trunks and sinking wells. After his death some was found which had started to 'weep', fortunately it was found in time or the house could have been destroyed. The property has been much improved over recent years by the present owner.

FAIRHOLM

The first bungalow to be erected on the land, which was part of the Lower Merripit Estate, had originally been built on land at Fairwater, a site in Chapel Lane.

As previously stated, the bungalow was taken down and rebuilt adjacent to Merripit Hill by William (Bill) Miners of Widecombe-in-the-Moor on behalf of the Sleep family.

In 1953 it was burnt down and Miss Annie Sleep had the present bungalow built by Stones of Chagford. The property comprises a kitchen-diner, sitting room, two bedrooms and bathroom. It has magnificent views.

Annie was a great character with a wonderful memory. She wrote many interesting articles for Postbridge *Parish Pump* magazine.

Above: *Annie Sleep's Aunt's 100th birthday party at Fairholm, l-r: Kate Webb (née Coaker); Annie Sleep; Annie's Aunt; unknown; Nellie White (née Sleep); Harriet Willcocks (née Sleep).* Top left: *The old bungalow at Fairholm.* Left: *Harriet, Annie and Nellie Sleep.* Far left: *The new bungalow at Fairholm.* (Photos courtesy Jenny White)

TORVIEW

A wooden bungalow with iron roof built in 1907 by James Webb, a Mine Captain, on land purchased from Mr White of Lower Merripit. He paid £40 for the freehold and the right to graze one horse on the Forest free of charge.

The building cost about £117 to erect and comprised four rooms and closet. There was a quarter acre of garden.

In the 1920s a two-storied building was built on part of the garden using granite. This was originally used as a workshop and storage space. Later it was converted into a house.

VAGLAS

Built in 1923 by building contractors from Totnes for Miss Festing. She had purchased the freehold land from Mr White of Lower Merripit. The design is said to be one that was shown at an Ideal Home Exhibition.

Miss Festing was a Roman Catholic and a small area of the house was set aside as a chapel. The name of the house derives from the name of a field meaning 'rough grass'. 'Vag' is a local term for the top piece of turf or scad containing grass roots etc.

THE BRAKE

Built in 1907 for Miss Janet Lind by the same builders from Totnes on freehold land purchased from Mr White of Lower Merripit. The builders lodged in Postbridge for three weeks at a time.

Miss Lind was a trained nurse and was much loved by the villagers. It was a great shock when she was killed in a car accident. Her ashes were scattered in 'Happy Valley' and the Church lych gate was erected in her memory.

Sir Henry and Lady Slesser lived there for several years. Sir Henry was born in 1883 and died in 1970. He married Margaret Grant who predeceased him in 1969. He was a Lord Justice of Appeal from 1929 to 1940, and a Privy Councillor. For several years he was a Devon JP, Chairman of the Dartmoor National Park Committee, and was elected an Alderman. He published several books including *Middle Ages in the West* (1949) and *The Anglian Dilemma* (1952).

The house took its name from Merripit Brake – a thicket.

READ'S BUNGALOW

A wooden holiday bungalow built on land purchased from the Whites of Lower Merripit. It was originally listed in the ratings list as being owned by F.G. Read. After Mr Read died, Mrs Read and her two daughters continued to visit the village for many years. They had a great love of Dartmoor and spent many happy hours walking on the moor and picking whortleberries during the summer. Nan, the youngest daughter spent many years in Africa as a teacher.

The bungalow was demolished in 1995 and replaced by a house.

GUITING/KIT LODGE

Guiting was originally a wooden holiday hut built by Mr Hoddinott, a veterinary surgeon from Plymouth, on land purchased from the White's of Lower Merripit.

One of the occupiers, Rex Hardinge. was a co-author of the Sexton Blake novels. He also wrote under the pseudonym of Vivian Charles. He presented a copy of *The Hard Way*, published in 1963, by Ward Lock, to my wife. At the time he was living at Bachelor Hall, Princetown.

The wooden building was demolished and replaced by a house and renamed Kit Lodge.

PENCROFT

Mr William Dingle bought the freehold land from Mr White of Lower Merripit in 1923. He erected a small hut and dug a well and for several years camped on the site.

The present bungalow was built in 1954 by Blackmore's of Moretonhampstead. For many years it was the home of Miss Lily Toms who was the organist at Postbridge Church until she became the victim of severe arthritis.

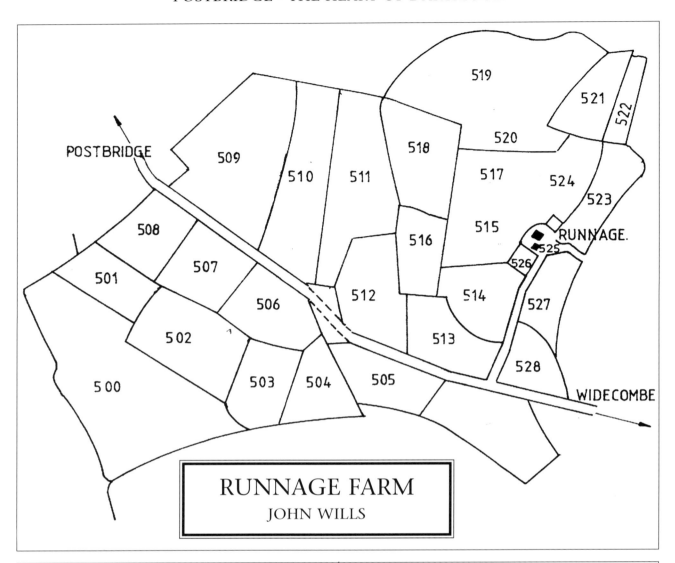

RUNNAGE FARM

JOHN WILLS

500	Moor	516	Colly Park
501	Furze Brake	517	Higher Barn Park
502	ditto	518	Summer Barn Park
503	ditto	519	Heath
504	Moor	520	Lex Close
505	Sullett	521	Yonder Barn Park
506	Homer Park	522	Higher Mead
507	Middle Park	523	Homer Mead
508	Yonder Park	524	Barn Park
509	Yonder Down Mead	525	House, Court, Garden etc.
510	Middle Down Mead	526	Plot
511	Homer Down Mead	527	Pitts Meadow
512	Yonder South Hay	528	ditto
513	Middle South Hay		
514	Homer South Hay		
515	Hill Park	Total	92 acres, 2rods, 35 perches

Chapter 9 – Outlying Settlements

RUNNAGE AND WARNER

There are many names associated with Runnage. Those listed in *The Place Names of Devon* (English Place Names Society) are: Renewych 1317; Renewith 1365 and 1379; Renewich 1386; Renyneche 1452; Rynnweche 1474 and 1477; Renwige 1608; Ranage 1666; Rennidge 1702.

The possible derivation is from a personal name Raegna. In *Dartmoor – A New Study* it states that Warner was first mentioned in 1301–2 and Runnage in 1304–5. Warner has at various times been documented as Walland and Walna. They were both Ancient Tenements and, early in the eighteenth century were in the possession of Richard Braker. In 1733 John Rogers was the tenant.

The 1786 survey of Dartmoor by William Simpson lists Richard Wills as having possession of the two tenements, Rennidge and Walland, and that he paid an annual sum of 9s.10d. to the Duchy.

On Monday 6 March 1797, between the hours of nine and ten o'clock in the evening, John aged 13, the son of John Stook, was murdered here by shooting. He was buried at Widecombe on 8 March.

On 20 December 1813 John Wills was admitted tenant for the rest of his life. In 1841 Richard, Nancy, and George French were living there. Richard was a farm labourer. Both tenements were tenanted by Richard Coaker in 1843 and in 1851 he was farming about 110 acres and employing four labourers.

An extract of the Court Roll of the 8 October 1851 shows that John Wills of 'Hooks' in the Parish of Ashburton requested that the two tenements should be merged. This was agreed and he was granted seizin. (He was the son and heir of the John Wills mentioned in 1813.).

It seems that Richard died early in 1851 as Ann is mentioned as a widow in the Court Roll. In 1861 she was farming 70 acres and employing William Westington as a hind. She continued farming for many years, helped by her sons William, John, Edward and Richard.

In 1868 the old house was burnt down and it was replaced by one built of stone with 3 rooms downstairs, 5 small bedrooms on the first floor, a dairy and a turf house. The water supply was from a spring but there was no drainage.

It was Richard who eventually became the tenant and Moorman, renting the North Quarter. He was affectionately known as 'Farmer Dicky' and my father gained his intimate knowledge of the moor from him.

Father went to work at Runnage at the age of 13 and attended Postbridge School by day. He always loved riding and frequently accompanied Farmer Dicky 'up over', checking on the cattle summer grazing on the moor. He also rode Mr Coaker's ponies at Huccaby races. I know he rode 'Active' but I do not know whether he rode 'Flying Fox' which was so successful over the years.

The cattle were brought out from collecting points as far away as Denbury Green. They were driven out in large numbers and the drovers at the back rarely saw the front of the herd.

There was another fire at Runnage in 1913 when a cart shed with a loft over was destroyed.

The next Coaker family at Runnage was Adolphus, his wife Lilian, and their two children Richard and Margaret. Adolphus died in tragic circumstances which shocked the whole village.

I always held the family in high regard. I went to school with Richard and I recall with pleasure driving with them to check the cattle on land they owned in the Ashburton area. Richard and his mother carried on with the farm until eventually Richard became the tenant and Moorman. Richard died in 1978 and his wife Alice and their young son, Philip, continued farming until Philip took over the farm. The Coaker family have been tenants at Runnage for over 150 years.

PIZWELL
YELLOWMEADS/FURZIMEADS

The Place Names of Devon gives Pushylle 1206; Pusshill 1260; Pishull 1305 and 1347; Pushull 1355; Pyshill 1417; Pysehyll 1443; Pushill 1452; Peselford and Peselsmyth 1521; Pesehill 1578; 'The hill where peas are grown'.

Pusshill is mentioned in 1260 in the Bishop's Register of Exeter which gave permission to the

Parishioners living in the villages of Balbeny and Pusshill to resort to the Church at Widecomb(e) instead of Lydford and contribute their offering there, together with a tithe of lambs.

In the account of John de Tresympel, Edward I (1300–1301), the accounts show 3s.4d. for repairs of the chamber of Pishull, and in 1305 the accounts for an extra 71/2d. for one clawe of land (8 acres) at Pishull rented to John Renewith, and that it should be manured the following year.

Thomas de Shirigge, in his accounts for 1313–1316 mentions an expense of 13s.4d. for the repair of the King's house at Pushull.

John Frensse (John French) was charged 4d in 1354–1355 for an enclosure he made at Pishull. This was one of the early enclosures, which with many others through the years, extended the boundaries of Pizwell to the Moretonhampstead Turnpike.

John French was mentioned again in 1368–1369 relating to the enclosure payment of 1354–1355.

Four tenements, properly three, are listed in the Duchy Records of 1608. The occupants and their rents are: 1. William Baron and Richard French. Rent 7s.3d. 2. Joan Horsham. Rent 6s.21/4d. 3. Thomas Langworthy and Peter Smerdon. Rent 7s.3d.

In 1635 William French of Pizwell complained to the Duchy about unfair tithing demands by the Parson of Lydford (see Hemery, *High Dartmoor* Page 519). I think this was the same William French who in 1627 filed a Bill in the Exchequer against William Barber, the parson of Lydford, respecting tithes on Dartmoor.

The Duchy records for 1672 show only one tenement paying rent and this was in the names of John Howe and William Hext paying 6s.21/4d.

In 1676 Mary the daughter of Mary Hext of Pieswell was baptised at Widecombe.

The tenements were listed in 1702 as being in the possession of Mary Cock, John Eales. Pancras Horsham and Barbary Cock. Andrew Horsham, the son of Pancras Horsham, along with John Northman, both from Pizwell, took part in the Duchy Drift of 1733. (Hemery, *High Dartmoor* Page 519). In 1745 Jacob Ellis:

was admitted to a newtake lying and being near Dury Head, bounded on the East corner with Dury Head and from there to a small water stile. On the north with Hornhill adjoining Magey Cross, leading by Plymouth road so far as long stone by Postbridge (except where such quantity of ground as Peter Willcock's claims).

Crossing in *Ancient Crosses of Dartmoor*, 1887, places the cross close to the gate of Stannon Lodge, where Mr Coaker (Jonas) recollected a cross standing, and that it was known as 'Maggie Cross'.

Rents paid for newtakes in 1763 were: Jacob Eales – two newtakes 2s; Robert Nosworth(y) – two newtakes 2s; John French two-thirds newtake 8d. Newtakes held at later dates were:

1774 John French and Christian Gilbert.
1778 John Tonkin.
1781 Edward Bray (own right). Edward Bray and Elias Babbacombe in right of his two-thirds of a newtake in the tenement known as Lower Merripit.
1781 Edward Bray on surrender of Jacob Ellis who held the newtake by right of his Pizwell tenement.

Simpson's survey of 1786 reported the tenements held by: Andrew Elliott, one tenement – rent 2s.9d; Jacob Elliot one tenement – rent 7s.3d; Robert Nosworthy, one tenement – rent 6s.21/2d; John French, one tenement – rent 4s.11/2d.

Early in the nineteenth century Joseph Warne was at Lower Pizwell. John Ellis Nosworthy at Middle Pizwell and John French at Higher Pizwell. Higher Pizwell was later referred to as French's Pizwell.

The tithe apportionments c.1840 list John French and John French Jnr. one tenement; John Ellis Nosworthy two – one of which was Yellowmeads (let to Joseph Warne); and Richard Medland Germon one (also let to Joseph Warne).

The census returns are not particularly helpful. In 1841 the only farmer shown is John French, aged 60, and apparently his son, John, who was to take over the farm at a later date, was then living with him. There is also another John French, a farm labourer, and Solomon Warne, a farm labourer living in the other properties.

By 1851 John Jnr and his wife Mary are farming French's Pizwell. John the farm labourer and his wife, Ann, along with Peter Hannaford a farm labourer, and his wife Susan, and Thomas Gilbert a tin miner, and his wife Susan, are listed as being at Pizwell.

The Duchy surveyed French's Pizwell in 1860 and reported:

The stables are quite in ruins and would require to be rebuilt if the whole of the estate was in the occupation of an improving tenant. The fences are constructed of turf and bank and at present in a

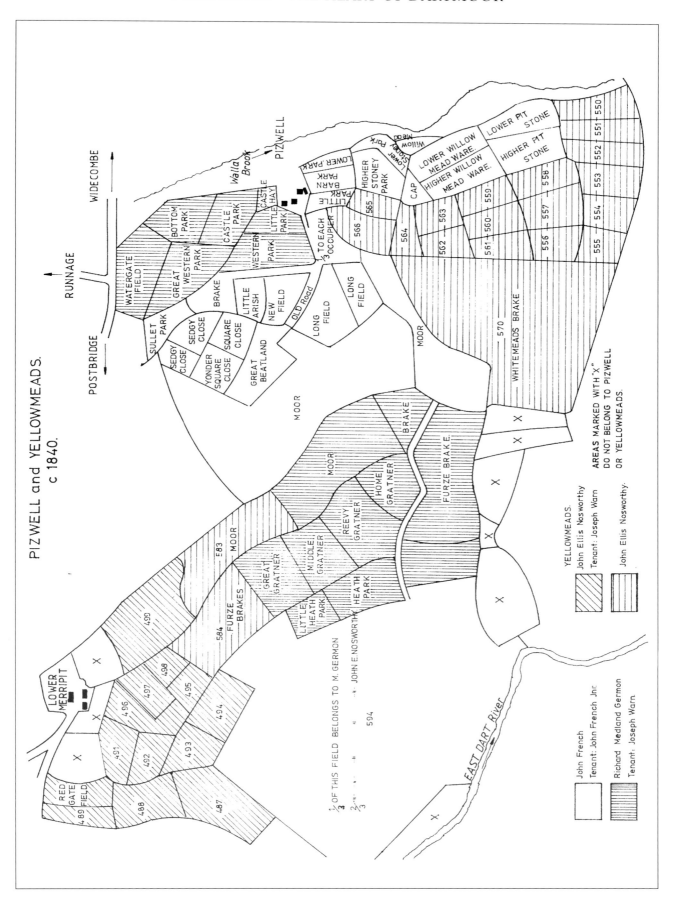

PIZWELL and YELLOWMEADS.
c 1840.

Burnard's photograph of 'The Middle House at Pizwell', which he took in August 1892. (R. Burnard)

very dilapidated condition – and there is scarcely a gate or gatepost on the farm.

The land appears to be much exhausted from bad farming. Some of the land may be improved from drainage etc. but I do not apprehend that the value of the property can be materially enhanced without a large outlay for improvements. Interest on outlay for immediate repairs upon dwelling house. shippen and the erection of gates and gate posts £2.10s. Out goings at that time were:

Tithe rent charge	*£2.1s.7d.*
Land tax	*£0.18s.9d.*
Rates	*£4.19s.8d.*
Copyhold rent	*£0.4s.11/2d*

Miss Annie Sleep writing in *Parish Pump* told how her old aunt loved to tell how her grandmother, Mary, eloped with a servant lad Richard Cleave, who worked at both Natsworthy and Pizwell. They were married at Tavistock Registry Office and it was some time before the French's found out. As she put it 'They were not cut off with a shilling' but were given a sum of money, a cow, and set up at Babeny. Many years later they moved to Lower Pizwell and farmed there. In 1861 Richard and Mary, now 60 and 64 respectively, were farming 40 acres at Pizwell, and Mary Hawke was farming a further 20 acres. The Duchy bought French's Pizwell in 1863 paying £553.4s.6d. of which the French's received £146.15s.6d.

A decade later Richard and Mary were still farming. The other properties were occupied by John Withycombe, a farm labourer, his wife Maria, and John Westington, a farmer, and his wife Betsy.

Germon's Pizwell was sold in 1877 to a Mr Thomas who already owned one of the other Pizwells. He paid £1070. The acreage was a little over 84 acres.

Furzimeads (Yellowmeads) was confirmed as copyhold in 1878. Barrington's report of 1862 had queried whether this tenement was in fact copyhold.

Richard and Mary lived to a good age and continued to live at Pizwell. Their son Richard, who was living with them, took over the farm and was farming 63 acres in 1881. Maria Withycombe was farming another 50 acres. William Leaman was working there as a farm labourer in 1886 and George Withycombe, from Smallwaters, started farming there about the same time.

In 1891 the three farms were tenanted by Richard and Mary Cleave, George and Mary Gidley, George and Eliza Withycombe, and their families (George Gidley was in occupancy from about 1890). Later tenants were William Westington c.1892–1898, and John Potter Jnr. c.1899, who came from Ringhill.

From 1900 to 1930 there were a number of farm labourers at Pizwell: John Lethbridge, Robert Cole, Jonas Coaker, Ernest Wakeham, Charles Vincent, Thomas Grattan, and Albert Brooks, all of whose children attended Postbridge School.

A Chapman postcard, known to be the interior at Pizwell, c.1900. The fireplace, where all the cooking would be done, is typical of a Dartmoor farm of the period, complete with pothooks, andirons, trivets and the huge kettle. Note also the high-backed settle on the right.

At some time Yellowmeads/Furzimeads and the two Pizwells belonging to Mr Thomas, which he bought in 1877, were divided between Mrs Lucy Beare, S.F. Thomas, and J.R. Thomas, along the lines of the Tithe map for Nosworthy's Yellowmeads, Germon's Pizwell, and Nosworthy's Pizwell, except that Mrs Beare retained the whole of Tithe 594.

Parts of Yellowmeads/Furzimeads were sold to Dr Rendel in 1908, and half an acre of Tithe 490 (Redgate) to H.J. Roberts in 1910.

The field books compiled following the Finance Act 1910, show Middle Pizwell tenanted by George Withycombe paying £34 annual rent to J.R. Thomas. The fences were in good repair and the buildings had been renovated. The house comprised kitchen, parlour, downstairs closet, and four bedrooms.

Higher Pizwell was let to Richard Coaker by S.F. Thomas at an annual rent of £34. The field books note that the buildings were very old. Yellowmeads/Furzimeads was also let to Coaker by Mrs Beare at an annual rent of £34.10s.

There is also a mention of Pizwell Cottage, occupied by G.W. Withycombe, and that the buildings were old and badly kept. I can only think this was the cottage, close to Pizwell Bridge on the Bellever to Cator road, mentioned in Crossing's *Guide to Dartmoor* (page 471). If so I know Sam Withycombe and his family lived there at one time and that Archibald Adams and his wife were possibly the last to live there prior to leaving to work at Penlee.

In 1922 the Sleep family moved to French's Pizwell where a new farmhouse had been built by the Duchy, remaining there until 1936. Annie tells of a ruin called The Castle where her mother used to play: obviously the field named Castle Park is associated with this ruin. Was it a house at some time or was it to do with tin mining?

The two remaining Pizwells were auctioned on 21 September 1927 and bought by the Duchy. Prior to the sale they had been occupied by the executors of the late Richard Coaker and Nancy and Thomas Coaker. There was also a close of land 3 rods 28 poles which it was suggested would form an excellent camping site.

Yellowmeads/Furzimeads was eventually sold to Jack Withycombe of Greyhound complete with a stone built and slated linhay. Jack left it to his daughter Winifred and her husband Ernest Webb who had the present bungalow built. Pieces of land were sold off on which the Woodward Hut and Broadun were built.

Later it was bought by Robert Arrowsmith-Brown and is now farmed by his son Stephen. For a time it was the home of Mr and Mrs Cornelius Pascoe. The bungalow is now used for holiday accommodation.

The Hoopers followed the Sleeps at Pizwell. The rateable value then was £11.

Middle Pizwell was rented to J.F. Skittery who was the Chief Constable of Plymouth. The rateable value was £8 and the cottage (Lower Pizwell) was rented to R. Coaker & Sons where the rateable value was £3.

Postwar Mr and Mrs John Martin were Duchy tenants and after John left the tenancy was taken over by one of his sons.

WOODWARD HUT

This small hut was built on land belonging to Furzimeads. Commander Woodward bought the land from Ernest and Winifred Webb who had inherited it on the death of Jack Withycombe of Greyhound. Entrance to the hut is from Love Lane which runs from the cemetery to the Hermitage.

Commander Woodward was a well known figure in the village as for many years he had lived at Riddon Brake and regularly walked from there to shop at the Post Office.

When he died he requested that my father should scatter his ashes on a level piece of the moor to the north of Postbridge. Father never told anyone exactly where he scattered the ashes. He had been a friend of the Commander for many years and felt this is what he would have wanted.

DURY FARM

Dury is an Ancient Tenement first mentioned in 1344, along with the name of Richard Dury, or Drury, (a common surname which occurs in 1838, and later at Drury Head). There are many documents extant dealing with mortgages, admissions and surrenders listed in at the end of this section, together with the names of some of the owners and tenants).

In 1476 another Richard Drury paid the Bailiff of the Manor 3d. for enclosing 2 acres of waste land. John Tickell of Exeter, clerk aged 64, held Dury on lease from the French family in 1689 (possibly a French from French's Pizwell).

A marriage settlement document dated 9 May 1700 between William Woodley and John Crispin relates to the Dury Estate. Some 200 years later, in 1900, Simon Leaman rented the farm from Edward Scott-James who had bought it from J.H. Foaden in 1898 for about £1200. By 1907 the Leamans had become a Limited Company and were paying £75 per annum for the farmhouse, buildings and land. They also rented a 153 acre newtake from M. Foaden for £4.10s.

The farmhouse, probably built on the site of an old longhouse was then in fair condition and comprised a kitchen, parlour, 5 bedrooms, dairy and offices. It had a water closet which was drained by irrigation. At sometime, probably later, a water wheel pumped water up to the house. In 1926 the Leamans purchased Lakehead Mead, Bullock Ware and Willow Piece (sometimes called Willow Place Ware) from Walter Irish of Bellever and added these enclosures to Dury.

The Duchy Rent Lists of 1928 show Louise, William George, Robert and Samuel Herbert shared rent of 3s.5½d. for Dury.

The Leamans lived and farmed at Cator and the house at Dury fell into disrepair. It was eventually restored by Stone's of Chagford (builders) and the Leamans left Cator and took up residence.

I knew Annie and Herbert very well and went with them when they bought a new home at Buckfastleigh. Prior to this move the Leaman family (sometimes spelt Leman) had lived and farmed on the moor for several generations. I remember Herb as a tall man with huge hands and as a friend of my father and fellow Mason he regularly called at our home.

The field names are still used today and certainly date back over 150 years. A new bungalow was built near the farmhouse.

EVENTS RECORDED IN THE HISTORY OF DURY

9 May 1700	Marriage Settlement
2 October 1758	Surrender from Edward Whitefield and admission of John Woodley.
11 March 1811	Surrender from John Woodley Jnr. to use of Robert Abraham
8 May 1816	Surrender from John Woodley to Revd John White
22 May 1868	Surrender from Matthew White to John White and mortgagees
8 December 1971	Admission of Elizabeth White
20 December 1880	Surrender from Hardinge de Fontblanque Cox to J.H. Foaden

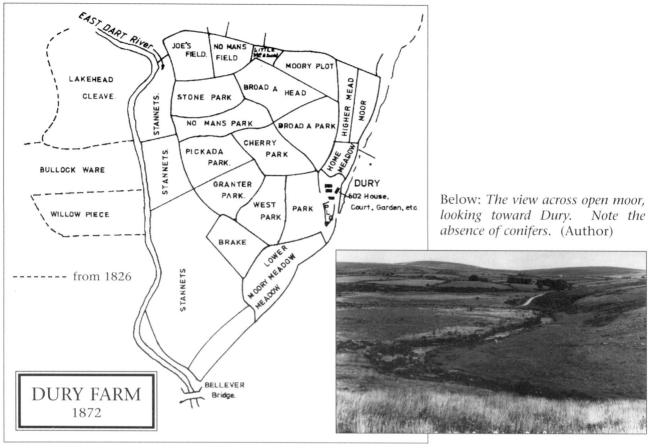

EAST DART River

LAKEHEAD CLEAVE.

JOE'S FIELD.

NO MANS FIELD

LITTLE MEADOW

MOORY PLOT

STONE PARK

BROAD A HEAD

STANNETS.

NO MANS PARK

BROAD A PARK

HIGHER MEAD

MOOR

BULLOCK WARE

STANNETS.

PICKADA PARK.

CHERRY PARK

HOME MEADOW

DURY
602 House, Court, Garden, etc

GRANTER PARK.

WILLOW PIECE

WEST PARK

PARK

BRAKE

STANNETS

------- from 1826

LOWER MOORY MEADOW

MEADOW

BELLEVER Bridge.

DURY FARM
1872

Below: *The view across open moor, looking toward Dury. Note the absence of conifers.* (Author)

1883	Admission of William White.
1898	Surrender from J.H.Foaden to Edward Scott-James.
1911	Admission of Mrs Louise Leaman and others from Edward Scott-James.
1926	Sale to Leamans of Bellever enclosures.

TENANTS AND OWNERS.

1841	William Philip (Philips in the Widecombe register, Philp in 1851).
1851	Matthew White.
1851	William Philp (Farming 59 acres).
1861	William Withycombe (Agricultural Labourer.)
1871	William Westington (Farmer)
1881	William Westington (Hind)
1900	Simon Leaman
	C.M.Gardener
	N. Arrowsmith-Brown
	L. Russell
	W.Hutchings
	Mr & Mrs D. Adaway (Present owners)

BELLEVER/SOUTH BELLEVER/LAKE

The Place Names of Devon gives the following variations: WELFORD 1355; WELLFORD 1477 AND 1481; WELLAFORD MYLLS 1579; BELL(A)BOUR 1608– 09; BELLAFORD 1663 AND 1702; BELLE-FOR 1736. The tenements at Bellever have been dated as Lake 1347, and the others 1355.

Wellford is mentioned in the unpublished Court Rolls of 1477 and 1481 in the possession of the Dean and Chapter of Exeter Cathedral.

In 1608 William Leaman and his wife, Thomasine, paid 3s.4d. rent for one tenement, Thomas Stephens the same for another, and Pancras lodge 6s.01/2d for Lakehead.

On 6 July 1609 Torrent de Beltabur Combe (Bellavur Combe Lake) is mentioned in the Court Roll. Lake in this context refers to a stream which ran through the Combe to a point near Dart Cleave Ford on the East Dart River.

Thomas Row and Robert Mann are mentioned in connection with Lakehead in 1689.

Evidence given in the 1702 lawsuit by the Rector of Lydford mentions three ancient Bellever tenements: 1. One tenement, Bellever, in the possession of William Northmore. Gent. 2. Two called Bellaford – one lying in Bellaford and the

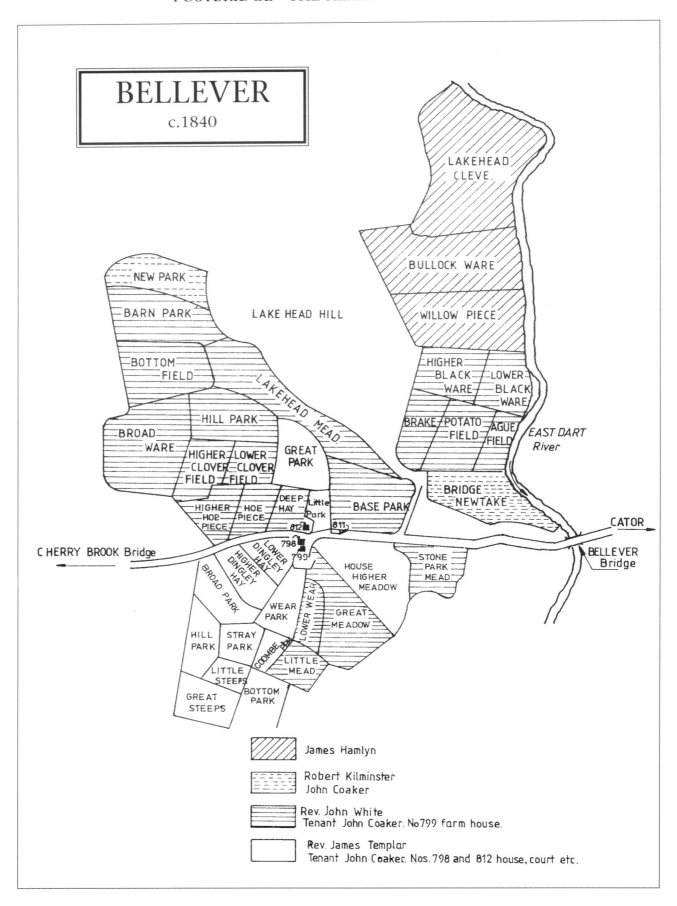

BELLEVER
c.1840

LAKEHEAD CLEVE.

BULLOCK WARE

WILLOW PIECE

NEW PARK

BARN PARK

LAKE HEAD HILL

HIGHER
BLACK
WARE

LOWER
BLACK
WARE

BOTTOM
FIELD

LAKEHEAD MEAD.

BRAKE

POTATO
FIELD

AGUE
FIELD

EAST DART
River

HILL PARK

BROAD
WARE

HIGHER
CLOVER
FIELD

LOWER
CLOVER
FIELD

GREAT
PARK

DEEP
HAY

Little
Park

BASE PARK

BRIDGE
NEWTAKE

CATOR

HIGHER
HOE
PIECE

HOE
PIECE

812

811

798

799

CHERRY BROOK Bridge

LOWER
DINGLEY
HAY

HIGHER
DINGLEY
HAY

HOUSE
HIGHER
MEADOW

STONE
PARK
MEAD.

BELLEVER
Bridge

BROAD PARK

WEAR
PARK

LOWER WEAR

GREAT
MEADOW

HILL
PARK

STRAY
PARK

COOMBE

LITTLE
MEAD

LITTLE
STEEPS

GREAT
STEEPS

BOTTOM
PARK

James Hamlyn

Robert Kilminster
John Coaker

Rev. John White
Tenant John Coaker. No799 farm house.

Rev. James Templar
Tenant John Coaker. Nos. 798 and 812 house, court etc.

Robert Burnard's photo of 'Old Bellever Farm' c.1890 (R. Burnard)

other called Lake, in the possession of Mr Gardner or his tenants.

Tenants associated with Bellever after 1702 were: Dorothy Gardner 1704; Andrew Horsham 1738; John Rowe 1786 (paying 6s.101/2d. for two tenements – Simpson's Survey); Judge Buller (Paying 3s.4d. for one tenement – Simpson's Survey); James Hamlyn (paying 2s.6d. for part of a tenement named Lakehead – Simpson's survey); Dorothy Rowe and John Hussey 1791 (a tenement leased at that time to Walter Whittaker and George Carey). John Hussey was admitted to copyhold in 1796; John Brown and Edmund Clutterbuck 1814, the same year James Davis paid £1500 for tenements. John White 1820; Matthew White 1846; Edward Cox 1873, and the same year William, Walter and George Irish. Capt and Mrs Edwards 1874; Ada Rosalind Edwards; Edward Bainbridge Cox and James Powell 1880.

In 1881 The Duchy of Cornwall purchased Tithe 792. 793. 799. 800. 802. 805. 806. 807. 808. 810. 814. 815. 816. 817. 818. 820. 821. 822. 823 and 825 from Hardinge de Fontblanque Cox and others.

Judge Buller bought one of the tenements in 1785 and it was later owned by Revd James Templer.

The Coaker family probably started living at Bellever in the eighteenth century. They were there in 1813 when Martha, the daughter of William and Elizabeth Coaker, was baptised at Widecombe, and in 1819 when John Coaker, aged 57, was buried at Widecombe.

The Coaker entourage was a large one in 1841. John and his wife, Ann, had several children. lodgers and servants. John Elms, a lodger, was a hairdresser. The Coakers were then farming the whole of Bellever, including Higher Park and Bridge Newtake which belonged to Robert Kilminster, but not the enclosures belonging to John Hamlyn.

In separate accommodation was John and Ann Smerdon. John was still farming Bellever in 1851 when two of his farm labourers were James Coneybear and John Saturley.

Billings Directory of 1857 lists John Coaker as a farmer at Bellever. John retired soon after, for in 1859 Richard Coaker was paying the copyhold rent of 3s.4d. John Hamlyn was paying 2s.6d. for Lakehead. In 1861 Richard was employing two men and two boys. One of the men was Amos Tuckett, a carter, and the two boys were Richard Tuckett and Samuel Rowse.

Richard and Avis continued farming about 88 acres until 1873 when, on 23 March of that year, William, Walter and Thomas Irish obtained a lease of Bellever and South Bellever which reduced the Coaker's holding.

The cottage was occupied in 1861 by John and Martha Osborne. They had a lodger, John Campion, a stone mason. In 1871 it was occupied by William and Jane Ferris.

Bellever clapper bridge, from a Chapman postcard c.1912. Note the complete absence of conifers, which in recent times so dominate the landscape. (Author)

Without the screen of conifers, Bellever Tor (c.1907) takes on a quite different aspect. This land was part of Great Bellever Newtake, granted to the Revd John Templer, and shown on the 1809 map on page 104. (Author)

Bellever Tor from Cherrybrook Bridge, c.1912. (Author)

In 1881 The Duchy of Cornwall bought part of Bellever. That year William and Elizabeth Irish were farming about 65 acres and, after the Duchy had bought Lakehead in 1882, this was increased to about 500 acres.

John Hamlyn, a shepherd, and his wife Sarah were then living at Bellever.

It seems that the Coakers had left but had retained an interest in one of the tenements as the Field Book of 1910 lists Bellever No.1 as copyhold, in the possession of John Coaker. It recorded the long house as being built of granite, thatched and very old. It had been renovated in parts. There was a kitchen, back kitchen, closet in the garden, and two bedrooms. The cow shippen was under the same roof and there was a slated barn.

William Irish is listed under Bellever and Lakehead, farming about 550 acres. He was renting from the Duchy at a yearly rental of £71.

In 1886 Walter, Laura and Maud Irish attended Postbridge School. Two years later Blanche Irish and Louise Leaman were attending. Louise's father William, a shepherd, and his wife, were then at Bellever.

The Irishes and the Leamans were still there in 1891 and Sidney Irish, listed as a farmer's son, was eventually to take over at Bellever. Some of his children attended Postbridge School. Walter Wilfred and Constance Cynthia in 1911. Gertrude in 1912 and Austin 1913.

Zacharius Stephens and his family were at Bellever in 1909, when Frances attended Postbridge School. They were still there in 1917 when Richard George, Mabel Jane, and Gladys May, also attended the school. George Caunter, an agricultural labourer, was also working there at the same time.

In 1917 a bungalow was transported from Cornwall by W.H. Rothery of Saltash and rebuilt on a site above the old longhouse. Eventually the longhouses were demolished.

The Duchy which had purchased most of Bellever, except Bullock Ware, Lakehead Cleave and Willow Piece, which were sold to the Leamans of Dury by the Irishes in 1926, started a stock farm for a herd of Aberdeen Angus. They built a large house for the farm bailiff, farm buildings, and two semi-detached cottages. One of their farm bailiffs was Alex Shaw. Some of the fields used for crops were:

Higher Clover Field – Swedes 1914 – Potato and Cabbage 1915 – Oats and Seeds 1916.

Lower Clover Field – Swedes 1913 – Oats and Seeds 1915.
Great Park – Swedes 1912 – Oats and Seeds 1914. Bridge Newtake – Oats 1912 – Turnips 1913 – Oats and Swedes 1914.

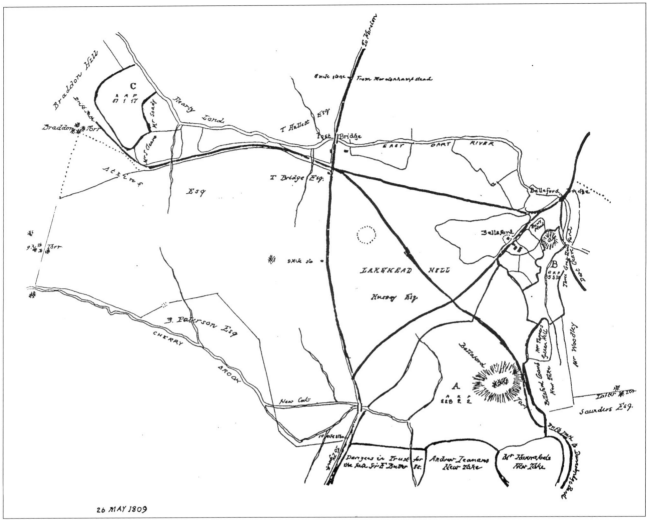

Part of the map detailing the lease of parcels of land to Revd John Templer from the Duchy, May 1809.

The Duchy bought a thresher and an oil engine in 1917 from Clayton and Shuttleworth. There also exists an inventory and valuation of live and dead stock dated 13 December 1920.

Charles Francis Williams and his wife who had lived at Laughter, moved to Bellever Bungalow c.1921. Several of their children attended Postbridge School. Those who attended from Bellever were: Glendor Charles, Theodore, Joan, Sidney, William Eric George, and Redford Alexander James.

Bertram Hooper and his wife lived in the bungalow in 1931 when their children Muriel, John and Derek also attended the school. In recent years the old bungalow has been replaced by a more permanent structure.

On 29 September 1931 the Duchy of Cornwall conveyed Bellever to the Forestry Commission and some of the first trees were planted by Harry Trude.

Mr W.J. Hale, who had been a forester for the Duchy, became the first forester for the Forestry Commission. He had once lived at Ringhill. Mr H.J. Wallington was the forester in 1938, and Mr Williams post war. Initially only the central area of Lakehead Hill (naked as far as the locals were concerned) was planted.

In the early 1930s a road was cut from the Postbridge–Moretonhampstead road to Bellever. I remember there was a large granite boulder which had to be dynamited and all the Bellever children had to leave early. We all stood just below the School to watch the explosion.

My father was offered the grazing rights of two areas: one of 88 acres, marked 'A' on the map and 132 acres, marked 'B' on the map. This was in 1935 and the rights cost £10 per 364 days. The 132 acres were reduced to 90 acres in 1938.

One of the conditions was 'That the white gate marked Private Road (New Road) should not be

Above: *The new farmhouse, farmbuildings and cottages built by the Duchy of Cornwall, c.1923. From a Chapman postcard.* (Author)

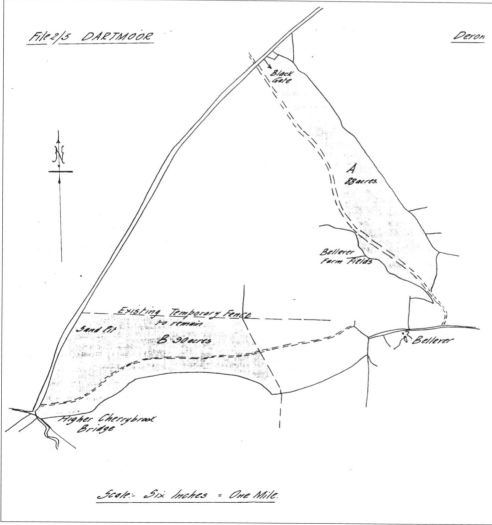

Left: *The map of Lakehead Hill, showing the areas let for grazing, offered to the author's father in 1938.* (Author)

used for the ingress and egress of cattle to and from the area'. A black gate which had to be used (long since gone) was erected adjacent to the wall surrounding Lakehead Cottage. In 1932 part of the farm buildings was let to the Youth Hostel Association. One of the first wardens was Mrs Joe Whiteway who lived in a cottage on the Green. Mr and Mrs Hugh Bray lived in the other. Another was Mrs Shillabeer, who with her husband and son, have farmed Bellever for several years. Mr Jim Martin was another of the wardens.

When the Hostel became run down and in financial trouble in the 1950s the Dartmoor Rambling Club formed a group 'The Friends of Bellever'. As a result of their efforts the Hostel was modernized with showers, washrooms, kitchen and cooking facilities. The whole ambience was changed.

My family looked forward each year to the annual carol singing in the barn at the Youth Hostel. The seats were bales of straw, the lighting by hurricane lamps, and the heating supplied by well wrapped up human bodies sitting close together. The breathing and movement of the cows in adjacent stalls added to the atmosphere. All the old familiar carols were sung and sometimes we had a fiddler to accompany them.

At the end of the singing there was an extra air of excitement as the children eagerly awaited the arrival of Father Christmas who then opened his sack and handed out a present to every child in the village. For those unfortunate not to be there. gifts were handed to friends to pass on, so no one was left out. Then out into the cold Dartmoor night and a walk back to the village.

In 1949 ten houses were built for the forestry workers. Most of them, including the cottages on the Green, have been sold off by the Forestry Commission, when its work was hived off to private contractors.

Large areas of the forest have now been harvested and roads cut into the forest to facilitate this work. Fortunately when Bellever Tor Newtake was planted, the planting stopped well short of the summit.

LAKEHEAD

The Place Names of Devon give this as LAKE-HEVEDE 1347 – 'stream head'. I can only surmise that the name comes from the stream which rises about SX 651781 and flows through the Hamlyn's Ground Plantation to join the East Dart River at Forestry Pool. Forestry Pool (a recent name) was scoured out in 1938 by the effects of the flooded

river and a torrential flood from the stream. 'Lake' is rarely mentioned in connection with the Tenements, however 'Lakehead' seems to be associated with the Tenements and Lakehead Hill, for example in 1702 there is reference to two tenements called Bellaford, one lying in Bellaford and the other called Lake. Other references are as follows:

1786 Lakehead no house on this part of the tenement.
1880 Three parts in four of the ancient tenement called Lakehead, conveyed by Ada Rosalind Edwards to Edward Bainbridge Cox and James Powell. This comprised the same enclosures. called Bellever/South Bellever/Lakehead which the Duchy of Cornwall purchased from Hardinge de Fontblanque Cox in 1881.
1881 William and Elizabeth Irish were farming 65 acres at Bellever.
1882 Duchy of Cornwall bought Lakehead (Hill).
1883 Irish's Bellever with Lakehead about 500 acres.

BELLEVER NEWTAKES

Some of the newtakes and their occupiers were:

No.1. 1717 William Northmore.

1733 James Tuckett.

1781 Elias Tuckett.

1785 Judge Buller.

1787 James Templer.

No.2.1781 Elias Tuckett.

1785 Judge Buller.

1787 James Templer.

No.3.1781 Elias Tuckett and James Templer.

1785 Judge Buller.

1787 James Templer.

Elias Tuckett was the heir to Thomas Tuckett. We also know that Newtake No.1. was about 350 acres.

Bellever prior to the construction of the Forestry Houses - a Chapman photograph c.1934. (Author)

The same scene showing the Forestry Houses, built in 1949. Note the plantation on the left, absent from the earlier photo. Note also the two cars parked by the side of the road close to the bridge, heralding the growth in tourist traffic which now so plagues the moor. A Chapman photograph. (Author)

An early example of trick photography to please the tourists. Chapman took this picture of Bellever Tor around 1912, and superimposed the photograph of the ponies on to it. They can be seen in another Chapman postcard standing by a gate! (Author)

The 1809 map mentions two newtakes leased to John Templer. They are Bellaford Great Newtake and Brown Hill Newtake. It also shows Mr (John) Hussey holding Lakehead Hill and Mr Tapper holding Green Hill. Green Hill was later held by Mr Sawdye who offered it for sale in 1862.

On 1 December 1869 Bellever Combe Newtake was surrendered by Messrs J.C. Sawdye and Windeatt and Andrew Sawdye Windeatt. This was part of a lease granted in 1865. There was also a small newtake called Bridge Newtake which belonged to Robert Kilminster.

In 1811 Hullett left certain lands to Frances Le Chevalier. In 1826 Frances Le Chevalier conveyed lands on Dartmoor to Kilminster and Benjamin.

LAUGHTER HOLE HOUSE

The house and stables was built in 1912 by John Halfyard of Princetown to a design by J.D. Coleridge, architect, of 10 Davies Street, Berkley Square, London. It was built for Sir Raleigh Phillpotts who was the brother of Frank Phillpotts, pioneer of the peat passes on the moor.

It was enlarged at a later date and there was a small swimming pool, fed by a natural spring, to the south of the house.

The property passed to Mrs Boger and then to Mr and Mrs Arrowsmith-Brown and their family. They spent many of their holidays there, riding horses on the moor, hired from livery stables in Tavistock. During their occupation an accidental fire destroyed trees in the adjoining forestry.

Some other occupiers were Mrs Briscoe and Dr Bailey. There is a bridle path nearby to Venford which father and I often used when out riding. The grounds of the house are private.

LAUGHTER HOLE FARM

There are many names associated with the area around Laughter Hole. Those listed in The Place Names of Devon are: Laddretorre 1362 and 1417; Ladretorcomb 1379; Laddertorcomb 1416; Laddercombe 1475; Ladderton and Laddercomb 1476; Ladercomb 1555; Lethertorrehall 1557; Loterhall 1616; Latercombfoote 1606; Laster Hall and Laughter Combe 1702. It is thought that the name may derive from the Celtic *Llethr*, a slope, cliff, or declivity).

An early name associated with Laddretorre in 1362 was John Northway (Dartmoor 1890). Later names were John French, Laster Hall, and Quintin Brown, Laughter Combe, both in 1702.

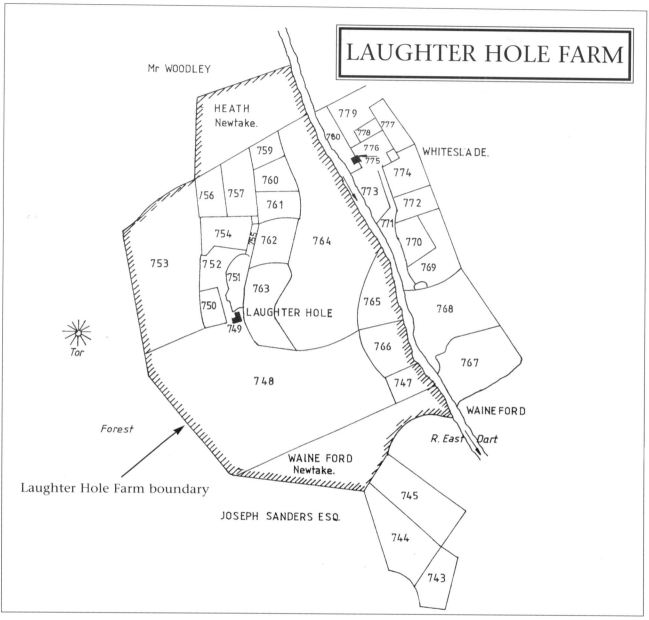

LAUGHTER HOLE FARM

Mr WOODLEY

HEATH
Newtake.

WHITESLADE.

LAUGHTER HOLE

Tor

Forest

Laughter Hole Farm boundary

WAINE FORD

WAINE FORD
Newtake.

R. East Dart

JOSEPH SANDERS ESQ.

HENRY BROWSE C.1839
Tenant: William Hayward

747 Wind Ford (Little Brake)
748 Heath Close (Waine Ford Steps)
749 Dwelling house etc.
750 Plantation
751 Barn Park (Great Hays)
752 Waste (Stone Park)
753 White Mead (Whiteways Mead)
754 Homer Stile Park (Long Park)
755 Garden

756 Higher Field (Hill Park)
757 Stile Park (Stile Close)
758
759 Little Field (Little Park)
760 George's Field (Middle Park)
761 Plantation
762 Bottom Close (Mead Park)
763 Meadow (Great & Little Meadow)
764 Hamlyn's Close
765 Watery Moor (Marsh)
766 Windford Moor (Great Brake)

View from Laughter Hole House, c.1932. A Chapman photograph. (Author)

Laughter Hole House c.1932, showing the new conifer plantation at Whiteslade (Snails House). A Chapman photograph. (Author)

Laughter Hole Farm, c.1932, showing the new bungalow and old farmhouse and new farm buildings. (Author)

The earliest documents I have seen are:

1728 Transfer from George Hamworthy to Elizabeth Leaman.
1740–41 Transfer from R. Caunter to G. French.
1742 Transfer from George French to George Browse.
1786 Simpson's survey lists Mr Brown (no initial) having one and a half newtakes at Laughter Hall paying 1s 6d. rent. He noted there was a house built on the newtake.
1798 A lease was granted to Samuel Hannaford and Richard Hamlyn.
1832 (27 July). A lease was granted to Thomas Heywood.
c.1839 A field map showing the owner as Henry Browse and William Hayward as the tenant. The acreage was a little over 78 acres and the rent £25.5s.6d., Tithe £2.00.

In 1851 Mrs Browse wrote to the Duchy saying that 'She would make over all deeds and writings and relinquish all right, title and intent in the estate and also the right of common on the Forest, which the family have held for above 100 years.'

Barrington's report of 1863 confirmed the purchase of Laughter Hole by the Duchy. In 1851 the farm was let to James Coneybear (Conabeare)

who at first farmed 15 acres which had increased to 101 acres by 1872.

On 1 June 1872 the Duchy advertised 'Lafter Hole' to be let by private contract from Michaelmas next. The new tenant was Joseph Holmes who remained there for many years. The house was known to have been dilapidated in 1860 so presumably some repairs must have been done. It was not until 1897 that tenders were asked for the building of a bungalow and other buildings to replace the old existing ones. The architect was Richard Merson of Yelverton. The bungalow seems to have been built after 1909 during the tenancy of William Irish who had held it from Michaelmas 1900 at a rent of £21 per annum.

In 1910 an estimate was made for a road from Dunnabridge Pound to Laughter. It was to be 14 feet wide with culverts as necessary, coated with stone and good hard rubble at a suggested price of 8 shillings per perch of 16.5 feet. George French tendered 10 shillings but withdrew. The road was built by George Coaker for 10s.6d. per perch. In 1912 the road was extended to Bellever at a cost of 14 shillings per perch but only 10 feet wide.

Other tenants have been Francis Williams whose children Beatrice, Cuthbert, Francis and Kenneth went to Postbridge School. Zacharius

Stephens who moved there from Bellever, Bertram Hooper, Mr and Mrs C Wilkinson, and Mr and Mrs Donovan.

On the early field map of 1839, Plantation Field is marked but it was not until the 1930s that the area was overplanted.

WHITE'S SLADE - WHITESLADE
SNAILY HOUSE - SNAILS HOUSE - SLADE

The name means a little valley or dell – a piece of low moist ground, from the Old English *slaed* – a dell. As a Dartmoor yarn the famous story of the spinsters of Whiteslade (who were said to live on a diet of snails) is an interesting one. Could it be true, or was it just a nickname which arose when someone living there seemed to have no visible means of support?

I can just hear a Dartmoor wag saying 'I reckon they be livin' on snails', so the name stuck. Similarly Lakehead Hill became Naked Hill when another wag stated 'Its as naked as a bird's arse'.

An old friend of mine left a note in S. Baring-Gould's *Dartmoor Idylls* (1896) stating 'I don't go much on his version of Snaily House. A pity he had to draw on his imagination and garnish with twins'. Perhaps this raises the question of how much more garnish has been added to a simple story over the years.

Just when the house at Whiteslade was built I have been unable to ascertain, although the history of the enclosures can be traced (see *Dartmoor Forest Farms* by Elizabeth Stanbrook, pages 106-113 'Whiteslade'). Simpson's survey of the Forest of Dartmoor at the end of the eighteenth century does not mention a dwelling. We know that William and Mary Stook were in residence in 1813 as their son, George, was baptised from there on 22 August 1813. They were followed by William and Elizabeth Pooke whose daughter was baptised at Princetown on 20 July 1819.

Eric Hemery in *High Dartmoor* writes that the house had two ground floor rooms, one with a fine fireplace and cupboard recesses. There are also ruined outhouses against the north and east walls. In about 1840 the property was owned by the Revd John White. In 1841 it was tenanted by Ernest Caunter and Elizabeth Kivell. They were followed by the Frenches and, in 1851, Thomas and Martha Isaac were living there. Martha was the daughter of William and Elizabeth Coaker (née Warren), and the sister of my great-great-grandfather, John Coaker. Betsy Stancombe died at Whiteslade and was buried at Princetown on 13

July 1851(?). *Billing's Directory* of 1857 lists William Widdicombe farming Whiteslade. Four years later Elizabeth Coaker, three sons and a lodger, John Matthews, had taken over.

In Barrington's report to the Duchy 'Dartmoor Newtakes', dated 4 January 1863, he lists a grant of a 50 year lease of Whiteslade (24 acres) and also a 50 year lease of Laughter Heath to Matthew White, both at 2d. per acre. These leases passed to Mr Cox in 1882, and the same year to Mr Foaden and Mr Irish.

Around 1910 it is listed in the field books as being copyhold in the possession of E. Irish and tenanted by W.H. White at a rental of £6.6s.

Eventually it was taken over by the Forestry Commission and overplanted, which obscured the field outlines. In the early 1990s a new road and a bridge were constructed in order that the timber could be harvested. The field patterns are now visible and I understand that it will not be replanted. I think the main approach would have been via Babeny, with the river crossings at Venford and Dart Cleave Ford also being used. Dart Cleave Ford was near the three grey stones at Bellever (1809 map).

BAWDEN'S BUNGALOW
KINGS OVEN BUNGALOW

Moses Bawden was granted a 60 year lease of land on 20 September 1875 and it seems likely that the bungalow was built about that time. It was a wooden building with four rooms and closet, and water was obtained from a spring close by. Some stabling was provided behind the bungalow.

Moses regularly stayed there when visiting the mines and was well known by my family. When John James Coaker died he wrote to his wife and a copy of the letter is included in the section concerning the mines.

The alternative name of King's Oven Bungalow came from the nearby site of 'Furnum Regis' an ancient smelting house first mentioned in the 1240 perambulation of Dartmoor.

At one time it was owned by a Miss R.C. Kendells, and for a few years it was the home of the Winterburn family. Lt Winterburn RNVR Retd, later moved to South Tawton and died in 1975. The bungalow was demolished in 1976.

NEW INN – MORETON INN – NEW HOUSE –
WARREN INN – WARREN HOUSE INN

The first inn was built on the opposite side of the road from the present one. It stood on land

Bawden's Bungalow, or King's Oven Bungalow, demolished June 1976. (Dr Tom Greeves)

belonging to the ancient tenement of Walna or Warner. It was probably built in the mid eighteenth century as a cider house as, in 1797, the Revd John Swete wrote of 'Meads Warren'. It was not until 1800 that John Newton was licensed as an alehouse keeper. From quite early on it was named New Inn.

John remained as licensee until 1813 when, in the same year, on 20 December, John Wills, a farmer from Ashburton, was admitted as tenant of Walna (which included the inn) for the term of his life.

There are no records for the years 1814 and 1815, but in 1816 the inn was recorded as being the Moreton Inn and the inn keeper as Robert Browning. Robert was licensed until 1823 and he was followed by John Jenkin, who may have continued as 'mine host' until the licence was taken over by Jonas Coaker who kept house there in 1839.

According to S. Baring-Gould in *Dartmoor Idylls* the old inn was burnt down. If so, he probably obtained his information from Jonas.

A plaque above the entrance to the present property reads I WILLS SEPTR 18TH 1845. This building was of stone, with a slate roof, and had a sitting room, tap room, cellar, kitchen, four bedrooms and closet in the back yard.

The 1851 census records that Joseph Warne, aged about 45, his wife Elizabeth, aged 40, their five children and two lodgers, were living at New House (a name often used to this day by people of my generation).

The same year John Wills, of Hooks in the parish of Ashburton, farmer, eldest son of John Wills, deceased, was granted seizin of the Ancient Tenement called Walna comprising 'two small plots of arable land and the site of an ancient dwelling, now destroyed, heretofore called New House adjoining the Moreton Turnpike Road and of a tract of land enclosed with a wall and used as a rabbit warren in the occupation of Joseph Warne'.

Billing's Directory lists a W.M. Jinnings as a victualler at the Moreton Inn near Princetown in 1857. William R Maddock was the inn keeper and warrener in 1861, he also worked in the mines, and the inn's name was changed to The Warren Inn.

Sometime after this date Joseph Warne returned as landlord. He was there in 1871 and 1881 by which time he was about 77 years of age. Thomas Hext became the next innkeeper and warrener. He seems to have been a well remembered character, often mentioned by writers because of his stature and long beard. He remained there for many years until the inn was taken over by William Toop Stephens. It was a great shock to the villagers when they learnt that William had taken his own life in March 1929.

Arthur (Daddy) Hurn was the next licensee. He had been head groom at the Prince of Wales Stud,

Left: *A previously unpublished photograph of the Warren House Inn c.1910. The sign over the door reads 'Thomas Hext, licensed to sell Wines, Spirits, Berr, Cider and Tobacco'. The long-bearded figure in the doorway is undoubtedly the landlord.*

Below: *A hay cart and a four-wheeled waggon passing the Warren House c.1912.*

The Warren House Inn c. 1925. Compare this with the first two pictures on the opposite page. Here the road is unmade, and the buildings on the left of the inn are fairly makeshift, with the porch unchanged from that shown in the pictures above. This is the age of popular motoring and the sign advertises Pratts petrol. (Author)

Although the road is still unmetalled, the Warren House (c.1935) is beginning to show signs of the increasing popularity of Dartmoor for tourists. A motorcycle and sidecar stands outside the garage on the left shows which signs of recent renovation, as does the 'shopfront' immediately next to the inn. On the opposite side of the road are the tea rooms, no longer in existence. (Author)

The cars suggest this photo was taken in the mid 1940s. The scene reveals a new prosperity around the inn with a new porch on the 'shop' and with the road now tarmac. Arthur Hurn was landlord at this time. (Author)

HOPKINS & SONS' Blue Moorland Cars

MOTOR COACH TOUR

Across Dartmoor

TO

Princetown & Dartmeet

Leaving Dawlish 2.15 p.m.   Due Back 6·45 p.m.   Fare 8/-

ITINERARY

This is one of the longest and most beautiful of the many afternoon Tours undertaken by the **Blue Moorland Cars,** embracing the very heart of Dartmoor.   Truly a journey through some of the most picturesque country in the British Isles. To know Dartmoor is to love it, and as Sir Walter Besant says, " Those love it most who know it best." Dartmoor belongs to the Duchy of Cornwall, and is the property of each successive Prince of Wales, or otherwise reverts temporarily to the Crown.   Formerly managed from Lydford, Princetown is now the centre of the Duchy.

The Clapper Bridge at POSTBRIDGE

Leaving Dawlish at 2.15 p.m. we follow the main road to Teignmouth and Kingsteignton, passing over the Stover Canal amidst the China Claypits. But to press on.   About three miles further we come to Bovey Tracey, now noted for its pottery, but historically associated with the Traceys, who

Above: *The interior of the Warren House Inn from a postcard by Charles Worcester & Co, based on a painting by R.J. Dymond (Chic Series).* Opposite: *The front page of a brochure promoting coach trips across the moor from Dawlish - cost 8 shillings.* (Author)

Tor Royal, before moving to New House with his wife, two sons and a daughter. It was during his tenancy that trade increased considerably as more and more vehicles used the road across Dartmoor. During the summer months coach after coach stopped for refreshment – and to see the peat fire which, it was said, had been burning continually for a hundred years.

Coffee and tea was served in a wooden building on the opposite side of the road and beer etc. in the pub itself.

Petrol in cans and lubricating oils were also available and AA members who required assistance could telephone from an AA box nearby.

On 7 March 1946 Hurn and his wife had the unhappy experience of finding themselves locked upstairs. Some Borstal boys, who had escaped from Dartmoor Prison, had locked the door at the bottom of the stairs, ransacked the sitting room, stolen some money, cheque books and clothes, and made good their escape. Entry had been made through the sitting room window but Mr and Mrs Hurn had heard nothing.

For many years Brian Sillem was the landlord. He was a great friend of Commander C.R. Brent who visited Postbridge annually over many years.

There have been several stories about the old inn. Those told many times over include the salting in of 'father' (deceased) because the weather had been too bad for a funeral; the tale of Jonas Coaker playing peek-abo after some drunken miners had taken over his pub; and the famous sale of some 'grey wethers' to an unsuspecting farmer.

WEST COTTAGES – WEST BUNGALOW
– CAPE HORN – WEST NEW HOUSE.

The exact date when these cottages were built for miners is uncertain but in 1871 it was occupied by Samuel Aldridge, a miner, his wife and five children. They had two lodgers, John Begam and John Hall, who were also miners.

The building had four rooms and was constructed of iron, stone and brick with a mixture of slate and iron roofs. There were no drains and drinking water had to be fetched from a spring at King's Oven.

Moses Bawden was granted a 60 year lease in 1875 which also included Wheal Caroline.

Several of my family lived there. My great grandfather, John Coaker, and his wife, Mary Ann, lived there in 1881. John, his wife and

West Bungalow, or Cape Horn, from a Chapman postcard c.1912.

family of eight children were still there in 1891. They also had a lodger called Tom Phillips (where on earth did they all sleep?).

Other tenants at various times were my grandfather, John James Coaker, and his wife, Mary. Also Frank Hellier, Silas Sleep, James Webb and Jack Warne My other great-grandfather, Richard Jory, and his wife, Anna, were tenants there on a 7 year lease from Moses Bawden, commencing on Lady day 1905. All that now remains is the outline of the foundations.

Chapter 10 – The Mines

THE MINES.

My great-grandfather, Richard Jory, and my grandfather, John James Coaker, were both Captains at Vitifer and Golden Dagger Mines.

Richard Jory (1842–1915) was the son of a Cornish couple William and Mary Jory. He married Anna Maria Bickell (1846–1922) from Dart Cottage and they had five daughters and three sons (one died in infancy).

He is listed in the census returns as a Mine Agent and I came across the following report about part of Great Week Mine near Chagford:

Birch Tor Mine
May 11th 1888

Dear Sir,
At your request I have inspected West Consol Tin Mine situated in the Parish of Chagford in the County of Devon. The property is very extensive being over 400 fms in length, being commanded by good roads and three miles from Moretonhampstead Railway Station.
The property contains 7 tin lodes, 5 junctions and very considerable working has been done on the backs of the lodes by the ancients, which shows very clearly that large quantities of tin have been raised from the lodes.
The granite and elvan about the lodes are of a good description for the production of large quantities of tin ore, and on examination of the old miners workings I saw several branches or feeders, all containing tin ore dropping into the lodes which cannot fail to enrich the lodes in depth.
The situation of footaway property lays well for the erection of machinery and laying out the floor for dressing the tin for market, also for sinking the shafts and developing the adjoining property.
I would strongly recommend a shaft to be sunk 12 fms. below the old miners workings on the Western portion of the footaway property so as to command the Western junction and the adjoining lodes west, and at the same time drive East on the lode to intersect the No.2 junction. This would lay open a very large extent of tin ground which could be profitably worked.
When the work is accomplished I would also recommend a shaft to be sunk in the Eastern portion of footaway property and drive west on the junction lode and effect a communication with the Western shaft, this would give good ventilation and at the same time lay open the lode upwards of 115fms in length which would with a certainty considerably increase the returns of tin.
When your Western shaft is proceeded with I should advise the machinery to be erected for pumping, winding and stamping the tin ores so as to make returns quickly. There is a small stream of water running through the property which could be stored and utilized for dressing purposes.
I have enclosed a portion of the tin ore for your inspection. This tin is from one of the many stones which I took up, laying at the surface and is rich in quality. It will make a produce of 141/2 in 20. Realizing it would command a good price in the market, I feel confident that if the work is carried out which I have recommended in a very short time you would have a good paying mine. When the lodes are laid open I should be very pleased to report on the size, character and value of the lode. I should be able to take samples and assay them and give the value of the lode per ton. I should be prepared to do so if my services should be required.

I remain.
Yours respectfully,
Rd. Jory, Resident Agent,
Birch Tor and Golden Dagger Tin Mine.

W.P. St. Leonard Chubb Esq,
29 Lincolns Inn Field
London WC.

An old friend of the author, Commander C.R. Brent tried to get more information about Mr Chubb. It appears that he was admitted a solicitor in December 1880 and practised at the above address until 1889. He was adjudicated bankrupt on 15 August 1889 (*London Gazette* 20 August 1889).

Richard's eldest daughter, Mary Elizabeth Maria (1872-1958), was born at Birch Tor and like all the children from there attended school and Chapel Services in Postbridge village. Most of the time they had to walk to and fro and perhaps it was

Old mine workings at Vitifer Mine, Postbridge, c.1912. These spoil heaps once littered the river valleys of Dartmoor, wherever ore bearing rock or alluvial ore was to be found. Many are still visible today. A Chapman photograph. (Author)

The dressing floor at Vitifer Mine c.1905. Here the finely crushed ore was mixed with water in the huge tubs or 'kieves', and stirred in order to release the various qualities of tin, 'tailings', 'middles', and 'heads'. Dr Tom Greeves identifies the boy as Sidney French, and the man with the moustache as Tommy Webb of Postbridge. The white-bearded man in the centre, wearing a bowler hat, is the Mine Captain, Richard Jory, the author's great-grandfather. (Author)

Mine Captain Richard Jory and his wife, Anna (née Bickell). (Author)

this and the lack of other transport which made them such great walkers. She married John James Coaker (1873-1913) in 1894 at North Bovey Parish Church and lived at the mines.

It was from here that she would leave on foot early in the morning for Moretonhampstead, complete her shopping and sometimes walk on to Chagford before returning home. Occasionally grandfather would go to meet her with his pony and trap. Halfway through the week when he worked at Owlacombe Mine near Ashburton, she would walk and meet him at Cold East Cross with a fresh bake of pasties and cake.

They really were the 'long and short of it'. She was a little over 5ft, and he was 6ft 4ins or more. She had a quick temper and on one occasion threw a carving knife at him, which fortunately missed. It knocked a prized cup and saucer off the shelf and, although he was renowned for being placid, he picked her up and smacked her on her nether regions.

She was an excellent manager and was able to save £8 during the first year of her marriage, which was deposited with Dingley, Pethybridge, White and Dingley's Bank at Tavistock. This Bank

John James Coaker, Mine Captain at Golden Dagger. (Author)

Tin miners outside the adit at Golden Dagger Mine c.1912. Dr Greeves identifies the men as follows l-r: Frank Rensfield; Johnny Wills of Ashburton; Bill Crout of Buckfast; William Jory, son of Captain Richard Jory; Harry Earling; George Coaker, brother of John James; Charlie Rowlands of Postbridge; unknown; George Coaker, son of Jonas; Sam Withycombe of Postbridge; John James Coaker, Mine Captain. (Author)

Underground at Golden Dagger c.1912. (Author)

became the National Provincial and Union Bank of England Ltd, and later the National Provincial Bank Ltd, and finally the National Westminster Bank plc. She was also a good provider in the home and prepared for winter by ensuring there were adequate stocks to see them through. She had four children and they were well clothed. Her mother helped in this as she was a dressmaker.

I have a small note book in which grandfather recorded the number of days of pony work from 1900–1906. In 1900 they totalled 88 days, but decreased to 10 days in 1906.

On 6 July 1908 he recorded some measurements pertaining to underground workings: 'East 7ft 8ins West 7ft 3ins and length 43ft 4ins'. Another entry shows that on the 17 March the draft mark was 20ft, and on the 31 March was 31 feet. He also lists the amount of dynamite, caps, fuse and candles used over a 7 week period. They amounted to 9 packets of dynamite, 2 boxes of caps, 9 coils of fuse, and 19lbs of candles.

Besides his work at the mines he kept poultry, a pig, milking cows, young cattle and Dartmoor ponies, as evidenced by entries in the note book.

Gran used to tell the story about Marjorie Hayward, the violinist, who used to stay in the

Right and below: *A bank statement and cheque of John James and Mary Elizabeth Coaker, 1913.* Centre below and bottom: *The tape and compass used by John James at Golden Dagger, and the brass nameplate from the company offices.* Below right: *the bronze palstave found at Golden Dagger Mine.* (Author)

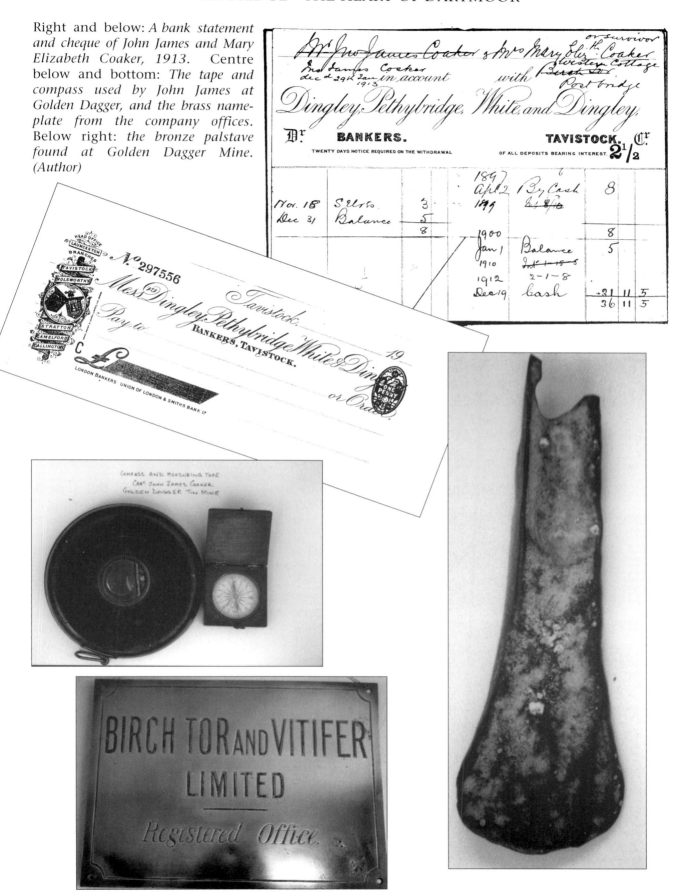

The waterwheel at Golden Dagger Mine c.1912. It had a diameter of 22.5 feet and was used to drive the sixteen head of stamps located in the adjacent shed. (Author)

area, and how the men would stop and listen as the sound of her music drifted down over the mines from the direction of Warren Inn. They would have loved that, as many of the miners were Cornishmen and in particular the Jory family were very musical. All the girls sang and two played the piano and harmonium, often giving concerts in the Methodist Chapel.

The history and the names of many of the people who lived and worked at the mines are recorded in Dr Tom Greeves' book *Tin Mines and Miners of Dartmoor*.

In 1841 John and Elizabeth Truscott, Jane Doidge, Richard Sowden, James Goldsmith and Walter and Mary Sampson lived at Vitifer. Richard and Jane Dunstan (was Dunstan's shaft named after him?), William Harris, Joseph and Mary Gilbert, Edward Westlake, Thomas (blacksmith) and Pamela Jackman were there in 1851.

Joseph and Elizabeth Gilburn and Sophia Merritt lived at Stamps Cottages in 1841. Mary Gilbert and her son Edward, and Thomas and Mary Angvil, were there in 1851. One cottage was unoccupied at that time.

In 1861 John (tin mine agent) and Sarah Symons, Matthew and Ann Rowse, Mary Thomas and her son, William, John Manley (master black-

smith), Richard Manley (journeyman blacksmith), Joseph Manley and William Hellier were at Vitifer, whilst at Stamps Cottages were Richard and Mary Lee, John and Eliza Snell, and Dinah Hext and her sons, John, William and Robert (aged 12 – a tin dresser).

In 1871 Dinah and Robert Hext were still at Stamps Cottage. Two other cottages were now occupied, one by John and Elizabeth Jackson and their family, and the other by Mary, William and James Thomas. James, aged 11, was a tin miner.

At Vitifer Richard Trevarthen (a tin mine agent) and his wife Elizabeth May shared their home with William Skewes (manager and purser), and his wife Margaret. Two cottages were occupied, one by Elias and Avis Tucker, and their lodger, a young Richard Jory, who had come up from St Agnes. The other cottage was occupied by William and Mary Routley and their family. Jacob Wright was listed as living at Bennets Cross.

Over the next 20 years there was a steady decline in the occupation of the cottages. We know from school records that William Slade was a caretaker at both Vitifer and Golden Dagger, Harold Wilcocks, a mine secretary, and that various members of the Warne and Webb families resided there.

The Cornish stamps at Golden Dagger Mine c.1912. This huge machine, driven by the waterwheel shown opposite, was used to crush the ore-bearing rock. (Author)

After crushing, the ore was washed across these sloping buddles from which the heavier ore could then be separated from the waste rock. Dr Greeves identifies the three buddle boys as Reginald Coaker, Sidney Warne (from King's Oven), and John Withycombe of Postbridge. (Author)

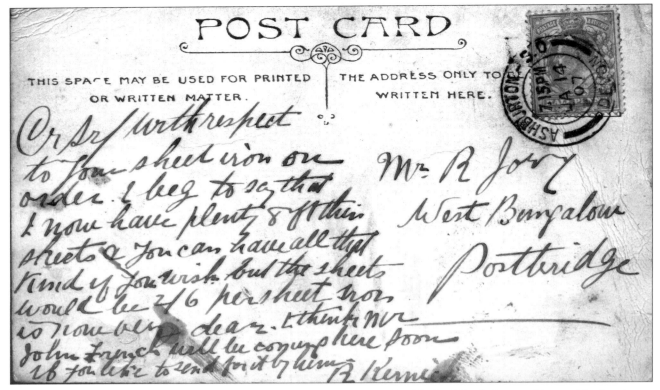

Postcard from R. Kernick of Widecombe, to Richard Jory, quoting 2s.6d. for 8ft of sheets of iron. (Author)

Richard and Anna Jory remained as the longest residents. They eventually moved to Cape Horn, unlike John and Mary Coaker, who moved to the village (Western Cottage). After John died in 1913 my grandmother received a most sympathetic letter from Moses Bawden who had owned the mines.

> Tamar View
> Tavistock
> 8th Febry 1913

Dear Mrs Coaker,
In a letter from your father this morning I received the first intimation of the severe loss that you have sustained in the death of your dear husband. You and your dear children have my deepest sympathy. We cannot see why such things are permitted to happen but we must trust to a Providence that watches over us to lessen your grief.
My daughter Amy who is the only one at home with me just now joins with me in sympathy.
With kind regards,
Yours very truly

Moses Bawden

One of the last families to live at Vitifer was Henry Warne and his wife. When delivering telegrams to Headland I could always rely on a glass of lemonade from Mrs Warne.

Two items from the mines were given to me many years ago. One was the brass nameplate from the Birch Tor and Vitifer Registered Office. The second was a palstave (a type of bronze axe used in the Middle Bronze Age), found at Golden Dagger.

WHEAL CAROLINE

It seems that as the mine was not mentioned in *Mining Records* it was of little importance. There are two assignments, however, dated 14 May 1825 and 25 May 1825, which give details of the bounds. They are:

On the first side of the North East by an old tin work leading to Waters Down. On the second side of the North East by the side of Waters Down by a path. On the third side by the top of Waters Down. On the first side of the South by Waters Down leading to Landlakes. On the first side of the South West by the head of Landlakes, the tail bound by the lower end of Landlakes.

The assignment of the 14 May for a consideration of £228 was from:

Mine Captain James Webb and wife Kate (née Coaker), and (l-r) his sons Redvers, James and Leslie. (Author)

1. James Jenkin Miner Lydford.
2. James Jenkin Junior Miner Lydford.
3. James Jeffery Miner South Bovey.
4. William Pinsent Tailor Chagford.
5. John Frost Wheelwright Moreton.
6. John Frost Publican Okehampton.
7. William Leaman Miner Lydford.
8. Sarah Browning Widow Lydford (Sarah was the widow of Robert Browning.)

The assignment was to Samuel and Thomas Honichurch and others. The assignment of 25 May was also to Samuel and Thomas Honichurch from: (consideration in brackets).

1. John Hext Yeoman North Bovey (£8)
2, William Roberts Manaton   (£3)
3. William Snow Butcher Moreton (£3)

Mining ended in the late 1830s for, in 1839, John Paull was the lessee and Henry Jenkin tenant of 'a cot house and potato garden'. The 1841 census return shows two entries for Wheal Caroline: Richard Nancarron, his wife Ann and three children, and John Hamblyn, his wife Mary, and seven children. In 1850 Captain Carpenter wanted to work Wheal Caroline but this came to nothing.

The 1851 return again lists two families: John French, his wife Piff and two children, also William Lance, his wife Margaret, and two children. William had come up from Cornwall to work in the mines.

William Pounsay requested a tin sett there for mining operations in 1858 but this too did not materialize and by 1861 John Hamblyn had returned to Wheal Caroline. His daughter Agnes was the local dressmaker.

Agnes Hamblyn married Edward Caunter and in 1871 they were the tenants, along with Matthew Rowse and his family.

In 1875 a 60 year lease of the property was granted to Moses Bawden and, although it was unoccupied in 1881, two other families are known to have lived there. One was Harry Warne who married Mary Elizabeth Caunter (their daughter, Mrs Beatrice Brooks, lives at Tor View), and James Webb who built Tor View in 1907.

After Moses Bawden's lease expired James Webb and his wife took on the tenancy.

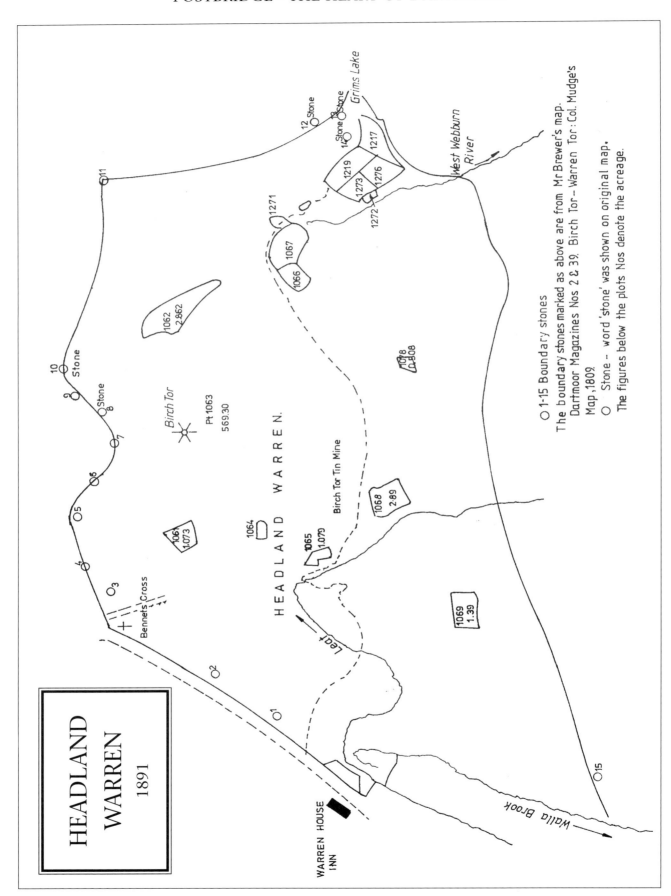

HEADLAND WARREN
1891

WARREN HOUSE INN

HEADLAND WARREN.

Birch Tor

Birch Tor Tin Mine

Bennets Cross

Grims Lake

West Webburn River

Walla Brook

Leat

Pt 1063
569.30

1062
2.862

1066
1067
1271
1219
1273
1217
1276
1272

12 Stone
13 Stone
14 Stone
11
10 Stone
9
8 Stone
7
6
5
4
3
2
1
15

1061
1.073

1064

1065
1.079

1068
2.89

1078
0.808

1069
1.39

O 1-15 Boundary stones
The boundary stones marked as above are from Mr Brewer's map.
Dartmoor Magazines Nos 2 & 39. Birch Tor-Warren Tor:Col. Mudge's
Map,1809.
O Stone - word 'stone' was shown on original map.
The figures below the plots Nos denote the acreage.

Chapter 11 – Moorland Settlements

HEADLAND WARREN

The 1780 Land Tax lists William Roberts as the warrener, and by 1818 his son and daughter-in-law, Thomas and Elizabeth, had succeeded him (Hemery *High Dartmoor*, page 643). Elizabeth died and was buried at Widecombe on 15 December 1837, and the 1841 census return lists Thomas as a Publican living there with four children James, Nancy, David and Mary.

In 1851 Thomas was listed as a victualler, and David and a daughter lived with him. There were three lodgers Jacob German (tin miner), John Rowden (woodwarden), and William Roberts (hatter). I think that it was during this period when Thomas was a publican/victualler that Headland was known as Birch Tor Inn and it seems probable that the following 'sign' was seen there at that time:

Jan Roberts lives here,
Sells cider and beer,
Your hearts for to cheer:

And if you want meat,
To make up a treat,
Here be rabbits to eat.

J.L.W. Page, writing in *An Exploration of Dartmoor* (page 169) places the well-known sign at Warren Inn (New House), and gives the following legend:

Jan Roberts lives here,
Sells brandy and beer.,
Your spirits to cheer:

And should you want meat,
To make up a treat,
There be rabbits to eat.

He also tells us that 'John was a celebrated character, a wag as well as a poet, and notorious for his readiness to join in meetings of a convivial nature'. Mrs Bray's journal, *The Borders of the Tamar and Tavy*, contains an extract from her husbands journal of 27 July 1831, which says the sign

Headland Warren c.1916. A Chapman photograph. (Author)

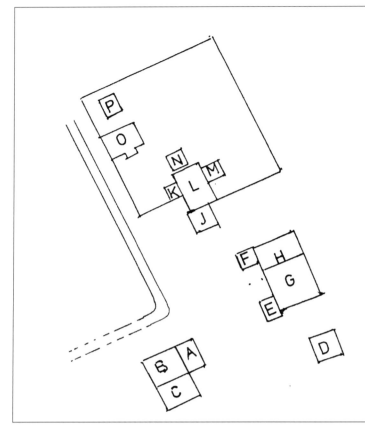

HEADLAND
A PLAN OF THE SETTLEMENT

KEY

A   Trap House - stone
B   Loose Box
C   Store
D   2 stall stable. tallet over - stone walls, iron roof
E   Pigs house
F   Fowls house
G   Cow house for 3 and one calf's house. Loft over
H   Peat House
J   Store - stone walls, slate over
K   As J.
L   Farm house built of stone, thatched roof, kitchen and store, two beds
M   Dairy
N   Earth closet
O   Bungalow - 1 floor, 1 bed and 1 sitting room. Wood and gal. iron outside.
P   Earth closet

(CROWN COPYRIGHT)

was at New House, and that he had probably seen it when young. Crossing in his *Guide to Dartmoor* contradicts this but he too seems to have known John as 'a noted character. But who was John? Thomas maybe, or has something been missed out in the telling.

David Roberts, farmer and warrener, had succeeded his father by 1861, and John Hext, a tin mine labourer, was living in the cottage.

The warren in 1871 covered about 591 acres, and David was still the warrener. The cottage was then occupied by Ann Hambley and her family. Three of her boys, Thomas 15, William 13, and Stephen 11, were tin miners.

After David Roberts left, Headland was taken over by the Hannafords, and James was farming 8 acres in 1881. Ten years later James, then aged 70, and his wife Mary, aged 65, were still farming, accompanied by their son, John, and his wife Henrietta, a niece Mary E. Caunter, and Annie Palmer, a granddaughter. Annie attended Postbridge School (1889–1895).

Although the Hannafords were listed as farmers they were also warreners.

The 1891 map showed only a few of the marker stones ('stone' on the map). The other markers are taken from the late Dave Brewer's article in the *Dartmoor Magazine*, Summer 1995. He also

mentions an estate map, inscribed Plan XVII, which was prepared for the Courtenay family. It is centered on Shapley Common, and Headland Warren in particular.

The Field Book c.1910 shows the approximate position of the buildings at Headland Warren and notes their uses. They were then old and in poor condition. Water came mainly from springs. The acreage was then about 593 acres (mainly a rabbit warren). G.H. Hext was listed as tenanting the warren from W.S.H. Beever of Yewden Estate.

On the warren were a number of enclosures known as 'Jan Reynolds Cards'. The land was said to have been won in a card game and the shape of the enclosure walls were built to look like the four suits in a pack of cards – a permanent reminder to their erstwhile owner. My grandmother always referred to them as 'The Dartmoor pack of cards', which was something of a misnomer. Jim Collins was the last of the warreners.

I can remember some of the later occupants. I used to deliver telegrams to Major Pearce, and John Fosbery, a stamp dealer, often called into the Post Office. There was also Mrs Graham, who was mentioned in an article by 'Bon Viveur' in the *Daily Telegraph*, when she happened to call at Headland and was provided with a Devonshire Cream Tea for 2s.9d.

Left: *One of Dartmoor's great worthies, George French of Postbridge, here at the outer wall of Grimspound during restoration and exploration by Revd S. Baring-Gould, Burnard and others, May 1894.* (R. Burnard)

Below: *Hut circle at Grimspound, c.1930.* (Author)

Below: *The north end stone of the stone row at Headland Warren. L-r: Revd S. Baring-Gould, Revd. Gordon Gray, Dr Rowse and Mr Wilder. c.1890.* (R. Burnard)

CHALLACOMBE

The Place Names of Devon gives CHALVECOMB(E) 1481, 1505 and 1481, relating to Challacombe Common, meaning 'calves valley'.

The settlement dates back for many centuries being mentioned in the Domesday Book (1086), 'Testa de Nevil' c.1244, and again in 1303, when it was said to have one messuage, one mill and three ferlings of land. (see Hemery's *High Dartmoor*, page 639). There was a mill at Challacombe for several hundred of years.

In 1505 the Forester's Account for the East Bailiwick includes 'Villat de Chalnecombe in parochia de Manaton vjd'. A survey for the Earl of Devon in 1787 shows Joan Burnal holding about 67 acres at North Challacombe and that a right of common upon Coombe, West Down and Hameldown belonged to this estate (*Transactions of the Devonshire Association* Vol 102, 1970, page 68).

An Act of 5th and 6th Victoria (C24, 26 June 1841, and 19 June 1843) authorized the Trustees of the will of the Earl of Devon to raise money on mortgage, and extended power to grant leases.

Challacombe comprised North Challacombe, South Middle Challacombe, East Challacombe, South and North Middle Challacombe, West Down and Challacombe Commons.

In 1841 John Hext was listed in the census return as a farmer at Challacombe. Three other families who were also living there were Samuel (agricultural labourer), and Elizabeth Warren; Ernest (labourer), and Elizabeth Waldron; Robert (tin miner), and Elizabeth Browning. These last named had seven children, one of whom, James, aged 15, was a tin miner.

Occupiers of North Challacombe in 1851 were: James (tin miner), and Mary Browning; Jane Browning (a widow), her son Robert, a tin miner, and two other children. She also had two lodgers: John Hext (agricultural labourer), and John Franklyn (jeweller). Jane was the widow of and James the son of Robert Browning who was listed in the 1841 census.

At some time William Heywood was farming 38 acres at North Challacombe.

East Challacombe was occupied by John Nosworthy in 1842. In 1851 Robert Hext (tin miner), and his wife, Dinah, were farming about 10 acres there, accompanied by their 8 children.

In 1858 a school was opened and Ann Hambley taught there. James Wilcocks farmed 20 acres at East Challacombe in 1861, and by 1881 had increased his holding to 50 acres. Four cottages were associated with East Challacombe in 1861 and they were occupied by

1. Hannah May (washerwoman), and two of her sons, Isaac and William (tin miners). She also had a lodger, David Germon.

2. John May (tin miner) and his wife Harriet (dressmaker).

3. William Gilbert (tin dresser), his wife Jane, their daughter Cecilia, and a lodger Edwin Caunter (tin miner).

4. Richard Hambley (tin miner), his wife Ann, five children, and mother-in-law, Mary Hamlin (char-woman).

In 1863 the Revd Mr Jenkins asked for assistance from the Duchy of Cornwall in order that a Church could be built at Challacombe. None was built, but there was a Methodist Chapel there at one time, as Jack Irish told me that his grandfather used to be carried out of the house so that he could listen to the services and the singing.

The Gilberts remained in the cottage for the next 20 years, and although Ann Hambley moved to Headland for a period, she returned to Challacombe in 1881. Her son, Thomas, was then employed as a groom, whilst another son was a copper miner. Other cottagers were Elias and Grace Warne and John and Eliza Snell (1871).

South Challacombe was occupied in 1851 by Betsy and Charlotte Pethybridge, who were probably related to William Pethybridge who kept a Cider House and at one time farmed South Middle Challacombe. At the same time John and Mary Hamlyn, whose son Samuel, aged 14, was a tin miner, and Thomas and Ann Southcombe, lived there. The Southcombe's had a lodger, Thomas Kernel, a tin miner, who had come up from Cornwall.

John and Ann Nosworthy farmed 25 acres there in 1861. Their mother-in-law and three children lived with them. They had two servants, John Leaman aged 16, a farm servant, and Betsy Gilbert aged 12, a house servant.

Ten years later John and Mary Irish and their family were farming 65 acres but ten years after that the acreage was 500, mostly unenclosed.

In 1874 a road, always called 'New Road' by my family, was cut through from the Princetown–Moretonhampstead road to link up with Cator, Grendon and Challacombe.

There is a covenant dated 6 December 1876

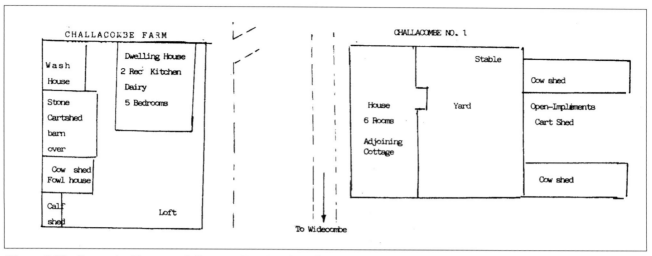

Plan of Challacombe Farm and Cottage No.1, taken from the Field Books of 1910. (Crown copyright)

between the Earl of Devon and others and John Durden. On the 7 December there is an agreement between Cookson and Durden, and the same year there is a schedule of Title Deeds all relating to Challacombe.

On 25 March 1880, and again on 25 March 1881, W.J. Cookson and John Irish signed an agreement concerning the letting of Challacombe Farm.

In 1851, 24 acres at North Middle Challacombe was farmed by John and Mary Hamlyn. Their granddaughter, Susanna Datson, and grandson, John Hamlyn, were living with them. They had three lodgers Jacob, Arthur and John Williams (tin miners), and Thomas Coleman (agricultural labourer).

South Middle Challacombe was farmed by William Pethybridge at some time, and 24 acres were farmed by Elias and Mary Hamlin in 1861. They had a domestic servant, Susanna Dodson.

South and North Middle Challacombe was farmed by Robert Nosworthy, and Daniel Hext rented Broad Park, Broad Park Moor and Langey Moor from him.

Challacombe and Soussons were purchased by Moses Bawden for £13 000 in 1881. Soussons, formerly South and North Soussons, was about 597 acres.

John and Ann Withycombe, who had been living at Soussons, moved to Challacombe and, in 1891, John was the rabbit warrener. Alfred Martin, a tin miner, lodged with them. George and Mary Warren also resided there at that time. Eventually Challacombe passed to Sir H.T. Eve (Squire Eve as he was known to my family).

On 12 September 1905 The South Devon Hunt met at Challacombe. Washington Singer, the son of I.M. Singer, the founder of the American sewing machine business which became a household name, was the joint master with R. Vicary. The pack met at 7am with Mr Rendell as huntsman. Next day the thoroughbred, Challacombe, named after this very place, won the St Leger at odds of 100–6.

The Field Books c.1910 confirm Squire Eve as the owner. Henry Ball occupied a farmhouse (Challacombe No.1) and Mr Willcocks Challacombe Farm. The cottage was unoccupied. There is a note 'No details of Challacombe House, forms not returned'.

The cottage adjoining Challacombe No.1 is described as a labourer's cottage, stone built, slate roof, in poor repair. The tenant paid rent to Challacombe Farm. George Warne, a tin miner, lived there in 1911 when his daughter Florence and son James attended Postbridge School. Although he left for a short while, he returned in 1912, and another son, Horace Frazer, attended the same school. Squire Eve granted a yearly lease of about 180 acres to Norman Hambley and, in 1917, the Duchy of Cornwall bought the estate.

Norman, and his wife Jessie, continued with the farm and in 1919, their son, William Gordon, was born. After attending Postbridge School he obtained a boarding scholarship in 1930 to Ashburton Grammar School. Upon leaving school he returned to the farm which he eventually took over. After he gave up farming, the farm was let to Mr Peter Cullen.

Much has been written about the strip lynchets in the Challacombe area and no doubt the present day fields have their origins in the underlying early patterns (see Jeremy Butler, *Dartmoor Atlas of Antiquities* Vols 1 and 5).

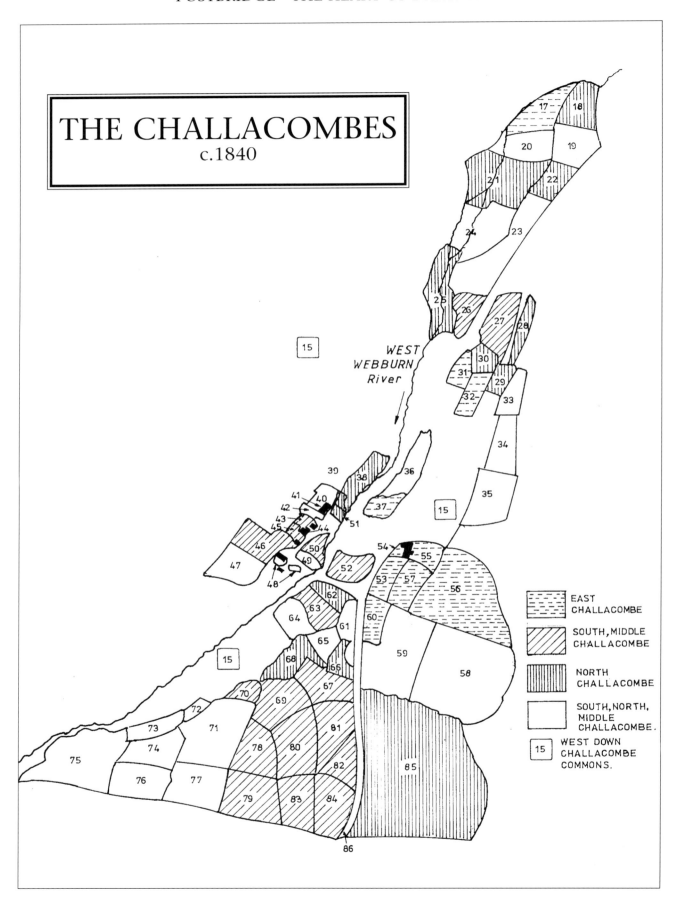

THE CHALLACOMBES
c.1840

WEST
WEBBURN
River

EAST
CHALLACOMBE

SOUTH, MIDDLE
CHALLACOMBE

NORTH
CHALLACOMBE

SOUTH, NORTH,
MIDDLE
CHALLACOMBE.

15 WEST DOWN
CHALLACOMBE
COMMONS.

CHALLACOMBE FIELD NAMES FROM TITHE MAP

SOUTH AND NORTH MIDDLE CHALLACOMBE

19 Broad Park. (1787)

20 Broad Park Moor. (1787)

23 Langey Park Moor.

24 Langey Park Moor.

33 Hamilton Park.

34 Fight Over.

35 Hamilton Park.

36 Moory Meadow.

42 Haye Meadow.

45 Little Plot.

47 Croft.

48 House Barton Etc.

49 Stoney.

58 Great Close Ware.

59 Little Close Ware.

61 Dippin Mead.

64 Moor.

65 Moorey.

71 Brake.

72 Smithy Mead.

73 Long Smithy Mead.

74 Middle Street.

75 Lower Street.

76 Middle Street.

77 Higher Street.

15 West Down and Challacombe Common.

40 Garden.

41 House etc.

SOUTH MIDDLE CHALLACOMBE.

26 Lower Cross Gate.

27 Higher Cross Gate.

43 Garden.

44 House Barton etc.

50 Stony Meadow.

52 Brook Meadow.

63 Homer Park.

67 Broad Meadow.

69 Lower Steat.

76 Costilost.

79 Higher Steat.

80 Broad Park.

81 Yonder Moor.

82 Clover Close.

83 Higher Close.

84 Lower Footland.

70 Catchet.

EAST CHALLACOMBE.

17 North Mead.

31 Round Park.

32 Fight Over.

37 Challow Mead.

53 Sandy Meadow.

54 House Barton and Garden.

55 Homer Park.

56 Close Ware.

57 Parks.

58 Barley Eadish. (Eddish)

NORTH CHALLACOMBE.

18 North First Field.

21 Coarse Marsh.

22 Roberts Field.

35 Common Field.

28 Long Close.

29 Middle Close.

30 Pound Close.

38 Cot Meadow.

39 Waste in Cot Meadow and Garden.

51 Garden.

62 Cot Meadow.

66 Berry. (1787)

68 Berry Moor.

85 Moors Hogs. (Moor Soggs) (1787)

86 Road by Moors Hogs (Moor Soggs) & Waste.

SOUTHSANDS – SOUSSONS

The Place Names of Devon gives SOUESTON; NORTH SOUESTON 1771; SOUTHSTONE FARM 1809. The name possibly derives from 'at the seven stones'. Some of the early occupiers are mentioned by Hemery in *High Dartmoor*: William Cominge (1664); George Lamond at East South Sands; and Joan Withecombe at West South Sands (c.1764).

An early indenture relating to the property between Edmund Bastard, his wife, and Edmund Poliflex Bastard and Richard Temple is dated 1805. In 1815 William Roberts, a blacksmith, and his wife Elizabeth lived there, and they were followed by John and May Hamlyn in 1819.

The importance of the holding was as a rabbit warren and William Washington paid tithes for it c.1841.

On 17 May 1844 there is a release and surrender of charge etc. between Sir Francis Bastard and others to J.P.P .Bastard. On the 18 May 1844 a deed of covenant, relating to the production of title to tenements called North and South Soussons, was made between Richard Durant and W.P.P. Bastard.

On the 1 January 1851 J.P.P. Bastard granted a lease, from 23 March 1851, to Messrs Joseph Elliot and John Bailey:

...of metals and metallic ores within the Forest of Dartmoor and the Commons of Devon bounded on the north by a straight line drawn from at stone post BV1 little gate near Assacombe to BV2 near Bennett's Cross. A straight line through Warren to BV3 placed where a small rivulet falls into West Webbern river.
On west by a straight line from BV1 to BV6 placed at the entrance to a lane on road leading from the turn-pike road at Merripit towards Runnage.
On the south by a straight line drawn from BV6 to a stone post marked BV5 placed by the western bank of the Wallabrook at the southern extremity of Mr Wills newtake and thence by a straight line from BV5 to a stone post BV4 placed by a small rivulet which

flows from Vitifer Mine and continued in the same direction to the west bank of the Webbern river. On the east by the west Webbern aforesaid.

The same year William Westington, a warrener, and his wife, Millicent, lived there, as did John and Betsy Westington. By 1861 John and Betsy were farming 50 acres as well as trapping rabbits. Their daughter Elizabeth was a schoolmistress.

On 7 February 1866 Soussons was conveyed from J.P.P. Bastard to Charles Millar. On 8 April 1868 Soussons Common was released to Charles Millar by His Royal Highness the Prince of Wales, and on the 9 April 1868 Charles Millar conveyed Soussons to John T. Dobson.

Sometime between then and 1875 it seems that Soussons passed to Gabriel Samuel Brandon and Horatio Brandon who, on 29 October of that year, conveyed the property to Francis Ommanney who, a few days later, conveyed it to Joseph Durden. On 21 December 1875 there was a transfer of mortgage and further charge on Soussons from Cuthbert Raymond and William J. Cookson, and the same day an agreement between Joseph Durden and William Cookson.

There is an abstract of documents relating to Soussons concerning mortgages etc. dated 1877. In 1881 the Challacombe and Soussons estates were purchased from Isaac Cookson of Worksop by Moses Bawden. Soussons, formerly known as North and South Soussons, was then about 597 acres. The same year John and Anne Withycombe lived there. John was a farm bailiff, and the lands were listed as being mainly unenclosed.

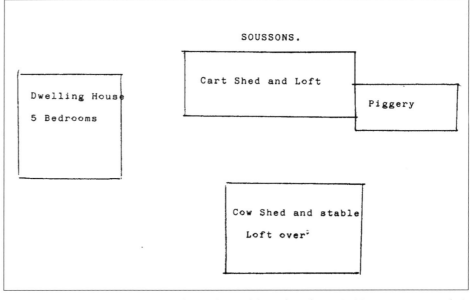

Plan of Soussons Farm, taken from the Field Books of 1910. (Crown copyright)

The stone circle at Soussons Common, near Ephraim's Pinch, c.1911 Note the absence of conifers. (Author)

An old farmhouse at Soussons, now a barn (note the chimney breast on the right-hand end). (Author)

Above and below left: *Soussons Farmhouse, 1995.* (Author)

By 1890 William and Elizabeth Hambley resided there with their two children, Norman and Anne, who attended Postbridge School.

Later it was owned by Sir H.T. Eve. The 1910 Field books show him as the owner, with J. Withycombe as tenant. The buildings were listed as being all of stone with slate roofs, rough fittings and in a poor state of repair. The house, with five rooms, was very damp. The Duchy bought the property in 1917.

The Duchy granted a 999 year lease to the Forestry Commission in 1945 and most of the land was overplanted. A gap was left for the stone ring adjacent to the Postbridge—Widecombe road near Ephraim's Pinch. Close by is a stone marked CB which was unearthed by Post Office Engineers laying a cable. They enquired of my father what to do with it and he suggested placing it upright as near as possible to where they had found it.

The old longhouse can still be seen in the yard. At one time it had threshing machinery, and local farmers brought their harvest there for threshing.

The newer house, standing on a higher level, is notable for its large granite quoins, or corner stones. In later years it was occupied at various times by Jack Withycombe (who moved to Greyhound), Blagdon French, Mr Newton and Bernard Klamman.

Recently, when the Forestry wanted to dispose of the property, it had firstly to be offered back to the Duchy. In 1995 the remainder of the lease was auctioned and purchased by Stephen Arrowsmith-Brown who now lives there with his family (1997).

Chapter 11 – Postbridge at War

During the First World War many of the young men of Postbridge were called up. Most of them returned safely but my uncle, Reginald Coaker, lost his life and was buried in the Villiers–Brettonneux Military Cemetery, France.

Richard A. French, the eldest son of George French of Greyhound, died of wounds and was buried in Postbridge cemetery, and John Webb, the youngest son of Thomas and Elizabeth Webb, was killed in action in France in 1916. A memorial to John can be seen in Postbridge church). These are the men I know about, but there may be others, of whom I have no information.

Reginald James Coaker (1898-1918, killed in France. The photograph was probably taken when serving in the Cycle Battalion, North Devon. (Author)

Likewise, during the Second World War, several young men and women from the village served in the three services. This time Leslie Webb RN, the eldest son of James and Kate Webb, lost his life when his ship was sunk by enemy action.

At the end of the war all those who served were presented with a wallet and sum of money collected by the villagers. The wallet was inscribed with their initials and 'Postbridge Thanks You 1939–46'.

Postbridge also had its Home Guard, originally Platoon 22, affiliated to the Devonshire Regiment, but in 1944 it is recorded as 'C' Company 23rd Battalion Devon Home Guard. Officers and NCOs were:

Btln Commander – Col. H.G. Thompson DSO.
Company Commander – Maj. A.F. Hoile.
2 i/c – Capt Trask.
Platoon Commander – Lt F .O. Harrison.
2 i/c – Sgt Robinson.
Section Leaders – Cpl Gratton.
                 Cpl Withycombe.
                 Cpl Warne (Medical).

Sidney Oswald French, served in Mesopotamia and India. Miner, roadbuilder and farmer at Middle Merripit. (Author)

Remains of the searchlight unit, Archerton. (Author)

There were several subjects which they could take to qualify for efficiency badges. These were, (depending on their location): General knowledge (all candidates); rifle; 36M grenade; other weapons e.g. sten; signalling; battlecraft; coast artillery; heavy A.A. battery work; 'Z' A.A. battery work; bomb disposal; watermanship; motor transport; map reading; fieldwork and first aid.

The following are details of a local Home Guard Exercise:

I am trying to arrange to bring 3 casualties from Princetown on Saturday and shall call for them about 1.50pm and return them to Princetown about 3.30pm.

Propose following incidents which you have to assume you hear and see as they happen. Reports to Tavistock 451 should be made as usual, whenever necessary, calling for ambulance etc. (it will not be sent) and messages should be prefixed 'Postbridge Home Guard Exercise'.

14.00 At stand to stations.

14.05 Several planes fly over. You hear machine gunning. several small explosions (caused by 4lb anti-personnel bombs) and A.A. fire. One 4lb anti-personnel bomb lands on the side of the road 20 yards below Lakehead Cottage Gate unexploded (I hope to put a tin down there).

14.15 Several planes fly over dropping H.E. bombs and incendiaries, more heavy gun fire. Dart Cottage (Endicotts) hit by H.E., clouds of dust, main road practically blocked by crater and rubble. 4 casualties of which one is dead. Greyhound Farm House and ricks on fire. Many H.Es. and incendiaries in surrounding fields. Much damage to glass doors and roofs on main road houses including First Aid point and main road covered in rubble, three or four inches thick in places. Air filled with dust particles for the next 20 minutes, much reduced visibility.

One enemy plane down between Merripit Hill and Warren Inn (to be reported by Hurn at 14.20), plane burning fiercely. Two seen to bail out.

While investigating later, Hurn discovers another anti-personnel bomb 100 yards from his house, close to the road. This he should know how to deal with.

15.30 Stand down.

The exercise may be reminiscent of 'Dads Army' but the bomb at Dart Cottage would have been only too real if the stick of bombs which fell between Stannon and Ringhill had been released a second or so before they were.

Postbridge also had its own Civil Defence network:

Wartime RAF Radio Direction Finding station on Merripit Hill. These stations sent and received radio signals to aid the navigation of aircraft. (Gilbert Warne).

Civil Defence H.Q – Mr Williamson – Lakehead
Cottage First Aid Post – Mrs Pethybridge – Village Hall
Hospital – Tavistock
Medical Officer – Maj Roper – Dartmoor Prison
Decontamination Centres
    Mrs Hibbert – Hermitage

Lady Slesser – The Brake
Mrs Rendel – Penlee
Miss Bennett – Ringhill
N.F.S. Unit – Yelverton
Police – P.C.Pike – Princetown
        Sp/Sgt Bellamy – Postbridge P.O.
Military Units with Telephone Systems
    RAF Radio Location Merripit Hill
    Searchlight Station Archerton
    Searchlight Station Dunnabridge

The Army personnel were billeted on site but RAF personnel were billeted in the village.

Much of the land around the village was requisitioned by the War Department to be used by the Military for manoeuvres and the firing of live ammunition. 'Fox holes', shell and mortar craters could be found over a wide area. Units from the Allied Forces, including the U.S. Army, all made use of the area.

A War Department Land Agent (Capt. Carter) was stationed at Princetown and when the land was requisitioned a map and schedule of condition of boundaries and internal divisions was provided, for example:

Part Ringhill walls between 0.S.1358,1431 and 1359. Low sod wall 1ft to 2ft high and 4ft thick - average. Ditch on 1358 and 1431 side of wall. Wall rough and uneven. Ditch clear.

Early in the war an RAF aircraft crashed near Lower White Tor. Fortunately the crew escaped with their lives. Had the aircraft been any lower I doubt if they would have been so lucky. They made their way to Powdermills Farm and I think it was about 30 years later that one of the crew called at my mother's home to know if the Stephens family still lived at the farm.

World War Two bomb crater, between Ringhill and Stannon. (Author)

Powder Mills and Cherrybrook Bridge.

In past centuries, travellers on Dartmoor were confined to trackways, some marked by wayside crosses. The top photograph, showing the trackway from Bellever where it meets the road between Powdermills and Cherrybrook Bridge, gives some idea of the difficulties of getting from one place to another. The lower picture, taken around 1930, shows an improvement in the roads at that time, but many of Dartmoor's lanes remained unmetalled. The motorcyclist is climbing Nine Mile Hill, site of the famous 'Hairy Hands' story, and on the left is the area used for cracking stones for roadmaking. (Author)

Chapter 12 – Travelling Tradesmen

BOLT'S OF PRINCETOWN

A highly respected family who, besides running two shops in Princetown, delivered bread, groceries, coal and coke, and other essentials around the local district. Ewart drove the van and Wesley delivered the bread and cakes etc., collecting orders on Tuesdays which were delivered on Fridays.

Meanwhile Miss Louie ran the shop in Princetown Square and Dingley ran the top shop. Miss Louie was a much loved Methodist local preacher who was well received wherever she went. In the shop she was almost an embarrassment to us children with her 'Have a pastie or cream cake dear,' free of course. Aunt Amy Warne once told me that 'Many local people would have been in difficulties during the depression, but the Bolt's never let them down, delivering their orders, sometimes without much hope of payment.'

The coal deliveries were made by Mr Ballamy (nicknamed Twister, but I don't know why), driving a Model-T Ford lorry.

BUTCHER SAMPSON – PRINCETOWN

A large man with huge hands who with his son, Headley, delivered meat around the village. I shall always remember him as he sat in the van with his left leg outside the door, the foot resting on the running board. It really must have been a problem in wet weather.

When mother chided him about a piece of meat having too much bone, he replied 'It grows there chiel. I can't alter that'.

BUTCHER CHOWEN – COCKINGFORD

He delivered meat mainly in the Bellever area.

ROBERT (BOBBY) WALLACE

He and his son Harold delivered greengroceries, paraffin and a small selection of crockery. They had a large covered lorry and usually called on Tuesdays. Bobby would tap on the door, open it and call out 'Yes um, Please um'. He also did a bit of cattle dealing on the side.

Approaching Princetown from Postbridge – from a postcard by Valentines c.1920. (Author)

Tavistock Road, Princetown, c. 1920. The large building on the left, originally the Princetown and District Co-operative Society premises, housed Bolt's 'top shop'. On the far left can be seen the wooden hut housing W.H. Smith, newsagents. (Author)

Princetown c. 1910. On the right is the Imperial Hotel, site of the Post Office, sorting office and telephone exchange. Further down the road is Princetown Primary School. (Author)

POSTBRIDGE - THE HEART OF DARTMOOR

FINCH'S – PRINCETOWN

Besides their two shops in Princetown they also had the contract for conveying the children from Postbridge to Princetown School.

FREDDY WEBBER – CHAGFORD

Freddy had an ironmongery shop in Chagford and took orders for wireless sets, batteries, oil lamps etc. The sets in those days required two or three batteries: a rechargable accumulator, high tension and grid bias batteries. Sometimes the high tension and grid bias were combined.

My mother bought two 'Pye' portables from him. Today describing these as 'portables' would be a misnomer.

CHARLIE HILL – CHAGFORD

He used to deliver bread and cakes to the surrounding area including Postbridge.

BOWDEN'S – CHAGFORD

Peter Smith used to deliver Calor Gas and other ironmongery items. On one occasion he rescued me when I was stranded by snow, and his family very kindly gave me a bed for the night.

DAVID MACMASTER – TAVISTOCK

He came out from Tavistock carrying his wares, consisting of linens etc. in a bundle wrapped in oil cloth. Well known, he often had lifts, otherwise he walked the distance, some twelve miles each way.

He was considered 'long-headed' and would be asked to witness documents or give other advice.

SKEWES – PLYMOUTH

Mr Skewes, and later his traveller, Mr Dower, were travelling tailors. They took orders for everything from suits, breeches, shirts and so on. These would, in the main, be sent by post, as would any orders posted or phoned through to them. Payment would be made when next they called.

DASHWOOD – YELVERTON

Mr Dashwood delivered fresh fish in the area.

CHARD'S – CHAGFORD

Billy Chard was a greengrocer who sold his fruit and vegetables mainly in the Bellever area.

Robert Burnard's photographs, taken after the blizzard, 14 March 1891. The top photograph shows the Princetown train, now largely dug out of the snowdrift, although the depth of the original drift on the weather-side of the train is apparent. The lower photograph shows the depth of the snow on the road near Roborough. Burnard records 'the drift here was about 14 feet deep, and the road was quite impassable.' As Roborough lies several miles from Postbridge, and at a lower altitude, the spectacular effects of this blizzard on the high moor can only be imagined. (R. Burnard)

Chapter 13 – Bleak Midwinter

In recent times the blizzard of 1963 will always be remembered by those who experienced it, but blizzard conditions are not unknown on Dartmoor. In 1853 three soldiers returning to Princetown lost their lives, an event commemorated by a plaque in Princetown churchyard. In 1881 Dartmoor suffered from a severe blizzard and roads were completely blocked.

The 1891 blizzard brought about huge losses of sheep buried in large drifts. The Princetown train was snowed up and passengers stranded. According to the Revd Hugh Breton it was always known amongst the Dartmoor inhabitants as 'The Blizzard'. The antiquarian and photographer Robert Burnard recorded the scene in a series of memorable photographs.

In 1901, 1907, 1908, 1916 and 1917 there were heavy snowfalls with deep drifts but it was in 1927 that the 'Great Blizzard' was recorded by Revd Hugh Breton in his book *The Great Blizzard of Christmas 1927*. At Postbridge Mr Warne recorded drifts of 6 feet and more, and at the Warren Inn enormous drifts 12 feet high were said to exist. Several ponies died.

Ice on the East Dart at Postbridge during the severe winter of 1963. (Author)

This was followed in 1928 by further snow-storms with heavy drifting.

In 1939 the Warren Inn was cut off for six days and the event was recorded in some detail, with photographs appearing in the *Western Morning News*.

I well remember the blizzard of 1947. I had just been demobbed from the RAF and Postbridge was cut off for several days. The East Dart river was partially frozen over and there was a notable occurrence of 'ammil' (described in the section on the cemetery).

In 1963 I was due to go back to work after the Christmas and New Year holidays. Thinking the road from Princetown to Yelverton was bound to be kept open I went that way instead of towards Moreton. Unfortunately the snow-clearing lorry became separated from the snow plough and I had to abandon my car between Princetown and Dousland. I returned to Postbridge and it was several days before I could go to work by walking to Princetown and getting a lift to Tavistock.

Let my wife take up the story:

After Reg eventually got off the moor I did not see him again for over six weeks. It was sometime after our eldest daughter's eighth birthday, which is on the 9 February. Luckily he was able to stay with a colleague of his and we talked on the telephone every day.

My parents lived with me in the wing at Greyhound that winter, which was a great help. Mother took over the cooking and Pop helped me out of doors.

We had no water as the pipe which fed the Post Office and Greyhound came through the East Dart river, and as the river was low at the start of the bad weather, the pipe was exposed, and froze. Pop and I tried thawing the pipe by covering it with sacking and then applying short bursts from a blow lamp, he took one end and I took the other until we met in the middle. Paddling with wellies in the river, with a ground blizzard cutting like needles into my face and any other exposed part, was not my idea of fun. I think we may have got a trickle through before it froze again.

We then tried melting snow in galvanized washing tubs on the Rayburn, one heaped tub

The effects of the storm in Roborough plantation following the blizzard of 1891. Compare this with the photograph of Archerton on page 14. (R. Burnard)

would yield very little water in the bottom and leave a rim of black grease around the sides. It was a wonder to me how such beautiful white, newly fallen snow could be so filthy. It just shows how much dirt there is in the atmosphere!

Finally we took buckets up to Lakehead Cottage and pumped up water from Mrs Wooley's well, which luckily did not freeze or dry up. We also drew water for the Post Office, as Jack was busy on the farm with his cattle.

At the height of the snow the passage between the house and the coal shed was completely filled in. It was a good thing that Pop was thin as he had to get in through an opening at the back where some of the stones were loose. At that time it was impossible to walk up our drive, where the gate is now which leads out by the entrance to the present day car park.

The car park then was our vegetable garden, where in summer, the cats used to lie under the runner beans out of the sun.

It was a good thing my mother-in-law kept a well stocked shop as, by the end of the freeze, there was very little in the way of food on the shelves.

Helicopters were our lifeline, my father and I used to go out into the field opposite the Post

Office and receive the sacks which were let down. We received mail, bread, potatoes and cattle food in this way.

When the Forestry Commission men managed to get out in their Land Rovers, they went to Chagford for the men's wages, and the late Dr Purves sent out a box of assorted medicines for use in emergencies.

The doctors held surgery once a week at Greyhound, and Wednesday afternoons were quite a little social gathering. If anyone fell sick they phoned the doctor who in turn phoned me and asked me to give them the appropriate number on the list, which I would then strike off and enter the patient's name. It worked well and at the end of the winter there was some medication left over, which shows how well we all kept.

There were two occasions when the helicopters had to take people into hospital, one was a lady with diabetes and the other an expectant mother. The first was before Reg left, we were told the estimated time of arrival, which was early in the morning, and we were asked to make some sort of cross on the ground where the helicopter could land, so we carried up buckets of ashes and made a marker with them.

The children had only two weeks schooling between Christmas and Easter because the school bus could not get through. I think they had one whole week and the rest was made up of odd days. It was somewhat wearing on a mother's nerves. having waved them off in the morning, wondering if they were going to get snowbound on the way home. Luckily the Headmaster arranged for them to come home as soon as fresh snow started to fall.

The children enjoyed the snow and the unusual conditions under which we were living, but even they got tired of it before it was over, not being able to have a bath and conserving every drop of water soon began to pall.

John was seven at the time, and as tough as a Dartmoor boy should be. Pop made him a wooden sledge and Jimmy Martin from the Youth Hostel used to take John with him when he took paraffin to the old folks who could not get out. We had signs of water coming through our ceiling at one time and Jim climbed into the loft and found there was a snowdrift up there which had blown in and was slowly melting, so he helped to clear it out.

The telephone was our real link with the outside world and the situation would have been very serious, had not the telephone engineers walked out to service the exchange (as described earlier in this book).

We were a tight-knit community under severe conditions and the old war-time spirit of helping each other prevailed.

The gateway at Barracks during the floods of 1938. (Author)

Cranmere Pool – a favourite Dartmoor destination for walkers, particularly in the Victorian period when James Perrott, the Dartmoor guide, began taking parties out to Cranmere where he built the small cairn (see here) in which he placed a bottle to act as a repository for visiting cards. He also provided a book in which people signed their names. Later postcards would be left to be posted on by the next visitant, or stamped with the Cranmere 'postmark', as evidence of reaching this remote spot. – as with the postcard below. (Author)

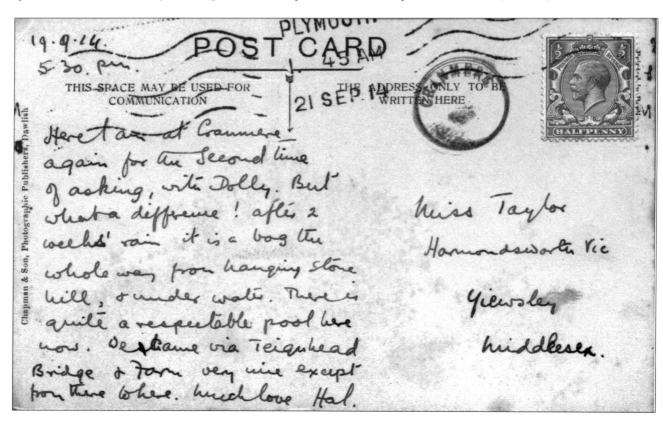

Chapter 14 – Traditional Pastimes

THE RIVER

Postbridge has always been a good centre for fishing. There are trout and occasional sea trout and salmon in the East Dart, and the same fish can be caught in the West Dart where the sea trout and salmon are more plentiful. Besides the main rivers there are several tributaries worth fishing especially if the 'Water is right'.

For many years fishermen stayed in the local hotels and farmhouses, many for weeks at a time, and fishing tackle was sold at the Parsonage by Richard Warne, and later at the Post Office.

There was a requirement for two licenses, one from the Duchy of Cornwall and another from the Dart District Fishery Board. The latter, in 1902, cost: Salmon – season £1.00, week 7s.6d, day 2s.6d. Trout – season 10 shillings, week 5 shillings, day 2 shillings. There was a gradual increase in these fees until eventually the River Boards were taken over by the National River Authority and more recently by the Environment Agency. Their licence covers English and Welsh Rivers and, in 1996, a salmon and sea trout licence, which also covered brown trout, cost £55 or £27.50 (concession) for the season. A Duchy of Cornwall permit for the same species, fishing their waters for a season was £100, £50 a week and £15 a day.

In 1902 the Water Bailiff was Mr Gregory, and in 1903 Mr Silas Sleep and Mr Frederick Coaker were engaged for eight weeks to help Mr Gregory during the spawning season. For many years bailiffs from lower down the river came up to the higher reaches to help out in the spawning season.

In 1914 father was appointed as a bailiff and when he enlisted, Mr Nolton and Mr Frederick Warne carried out his duties. In 1915 the bailiffs were authorized to examine Duchy permits. Father was reappointed in 1916 but resigned in 1918. His place was taken by Harold Jory who became well known for being very conscientious. He lodged at Dunnabridge and, after breakfast, would walk up to the head of the West Dart, cross over to the East Dart, and be at Postbridge in time for lunch. He would then follow the river to Dartmeet and back up to Dunnabridge.

Along with fishing, the river provides endless opportunities for fun. Here visitors are using the 'bathing pool' on the East Dart c.1939. (Author)

The Duchy paid part of his wages and after the spawning was over, his old diaries show that he spent many hours clearing the river banks of obstructions for the benefit of anglers. Unfortunately this is not now being done and many pools are virtually unfishable.

Eventually he bought a motorcycle in order to cover more of the fishery and the Duchy provided him with a pair of binoculars.

The River Boards in the early part of the century had to deal with complaints about pollution from the mines. In 1903 Capt Jory wrote saying that he would do 'all he could to prevent solids from entering the stream but could not prevent discolouration'. There were further complaints in 1905.

In 1911 there was a complaint about the increase in the number of herons at the Archerton heronry, but neither Mr Bennett nor the Duchy were prepared to reduce the numbers. Following a complaint in 1913 about the scarcity of trout in the East Dart, and that the bailiff was rarely seen on the river banks, the River Board Committee decided to appoint a supervisor of bailiffs and also to rearrange their districts.

Over the years there had been pressure. mainly from visitors to ban any bait except artificial fly

Right up to its closure in 1956, the Princetown railway remaining a great attraction for tourists and brought visitors right into the heart of Dartmoor. Today, the same visitors arrive by car in order to pursue their leisure interests. (Author)

for fishing for salmon. This applied mainly to the West Dart but in later years was extended to all fishing in the Duchy of Cornwall waters on Dartmoor.

This was resented by local anglers as worming for trout in a flood could provide good catches of large trout many of which were 'cannibals'. By removing these it helped maintain a healthy stock of good sized fish.

After Harold Jory retired he was replaced by Fernley (Swifty) Warne. I remember him asking a visiting angler, dressed for the occasion, if he had had any luck.

'No not yet,' was the reply.

'Well try this fly,' said Swifty handing him his speckled hen speciality. The angler, no doubt remembering his beautifully tied artificial flies, was visibly taken aback, but obviously did not want to be rude. He tied on the fly and with his second cast hooked and landed a beautiful trout well over a pound in weight. Yes, it was on Swifty's fly, and I shall never forget the look on the angler's face.

Time has passed so quickly since I caught my first trout weighing about three-quarters of a pound. I showed it to Uncle Jack Warne and he slapped me across the face with its tail and said 'Now you will make a fisherman'. I like to think I did, as I have now fished the East and West Dart rivers for 66 seasons (I missed out one season during the war).

Perhaps it is too easy to recall the great fishing days of the past and to forget the blank days. Somehow it does seem that the fishing has deteriorated. Who or what do we blame? Is it the catching of salmon on the high seas, or has trout fishing worsened because of acid rain?

I was interested to see the bailiffs electro-fishing Stannon Brook a few years ago and was surprised at the number of parr they caught in a short stretch above the bridge. Perhaps this was a good omen for the future.

BIRDWATCHING

The whole district, with its wide ranging habitat, is excellent for this pastime. People have the opportunity of walking over a large area enjoying their own company, or they may join a party led by knowledgeable and enthusiastic guides approved by the Dartmoor National Park Authority.

I was taught when very young to cultivate countryman's eyes, and my family have all learnt the value of keen observation and now take a great delight in pointing out something I have missed. A necessary aid is a good pair of binoculars, preferably not too heavy, although I would not want to change my old Swift Audubons for a lighter pair.

In the preface to Carrington's *Dartmoor* there is a list of birds which could be found on Dartmoor about 170 years ago. Since this list was printed there have been many changes in habitat, especially afforestation, which in turn has led to an increase in the variety of birdlife. Some species have suffered from disturbance, in particular the common sandpiper hasn't been seen for some time, bobbing its head and tail when perched and then flying low over the river with its curious flight and call. It once regularly nested in Drift Lane.

DEVONSHIRE CREAM

My mother used this method for making cream until 1972. She and father used a separator for a short time but soon went back to the old ways.

The fresh milk, straight from the cow, was strained into a large enamelled pan and allowed to stand overnight. By morning the cream 'ream', as she called it, had risen to the top, and the pan was placed over some form of heat such as a Florence oilstove or a Rayburn.

The gentle heat allowed a 'scud' to form, which would be spoilt if the milk underneath boiled. The art was in knowing when to remove the pan from the heat and a good guide was when very small bubbles appeared in the 'scud'. After cooling the cream was removed from the milk using a 'reamer'.

This implement could be of several different shapes, each having a number of small holes allowing the milk to drain away. Each piece of cream was placed in a bowl, one on top of the other, until it was several inches thick. This is a sure way for identifying genuine Devonshire scalded cream. Over the years my mother must have made many hundredweights of cream using the scalded method. Much of what she made was posted all over the country.

A more efficient way of separating out cream was by using a mechanical separator. We used two types, a Diabolo and a Lister. The Diabolo was bench-mounted and hand-operated. It was essential to turn the handle at the correct speed, and for this purpose it was fitted with a bell indicating whether or not the speed was correct. The Lister was bench-mounted and could be hand-operated or driven by an electric motor.

The milk was placed in a large bowl on top of the machine and allowed to flow into the separator which had two outlets, one for the cream and the other for the milk. The milk was taken away and fed either to the calves or the pigs.

The raw cream was heated over water until it was 'cooked' and a crust had formed. The set and texture depended to some extent on the weather, remaining 'runny' if it was warm.

There has been much controversy about whether or not the cream or the jam should be spread on the bread first. In my home the cream was always spread on first followed by the jam, to do otherwise was thought of as heresy.

Cream was often used in the first snack of the day with the morning cup of tea. One farmer's family always started the day with a thick slice of bread, spread thickly with cream and sprinkled with brown sugar. An uncle of mine (as my wife can testify) spread cream on a thick slice of fruit cake and served it with the morning cup of tea.

Bibliography and Sources

Baring-Gould S. *A book of Dartmoor*, 1923. Metheun & Co., London.

Baring-Gould S. *Dartmoor Idylls*, 1896. Metheun & Co., London.

Bray Mrs Anna Eliza. *A Description of the Part of Devonshire Bordering on the Tamar and Tavy*, 1836. John Murray, London.

Breton Rev H. Hugh. *The Great Blizzard of Christmas 1927*. Hayter & Cole, Plymouth.

Breton Rev H. Hugh. *The Heart of Dartmoor*, 1926. Hayter & Cole Plymouth.

Carrington N.T. *Dartmoor: A descriptive Poem*, 1826. Hatchard & Co. London.

Chudleigh John. *Devonshire Antiquities. Illustrated*. 2nd Edition 1903. Henry S. Eland Exeter.

Cornelius D.B. *Devon and Cornwall. A Postal Survey*, 1973. The Postal History Society.

Crossing William. *Guide to Dartmoor*, 1912 Edition. Reprinted By David & Charles Newton Abbot 1965.

Crossing William. *One Hundred Years on Dartmoor*, 1901. *Western Morning News*, Plymouth.

Crossing William. *Gems in a Granite Setting, 1905*. Western Morning News, Plymouth.

Crossing William. *Ancient Crosses of Dartmoor*, 1897. James G. Commin Exeter and C. Elkin Matthews London.

Gill Crispin (Editor) *Dartmoor: A New Study*, 1970. David & Charles, Newton Abbot).

Gower J.E.B. Mawar A., and Stenton S.M. *The Place Names of Devon*. English Place Names Society.

Graf W.S. *Ashburton Grammar School 1314–1938*, 1938. S.T.Elson Ashburton.

Greeves Tom. *Tin Mines and Miners of Dartmoor*, 1986. Devon Books.

Hemery Eric. *High Dartmoor*, 1983 Robert Hale Ltd, London.

Moore Stuart A. *A Short History of The Rights of Common upon the Forest of Dartmoor and the Commons of Devon*, 1890. The Dartmoor Preservation Association.

Morris John. (General Editor) *History from the Sources. Domesday Book, Devon, Parts 1 and 2*, 1985 Phillimore, Chichester.

Page John Lloyd Warden. *An Exploration of Dartmoor and its Antiquities*, 1889. Seeley & Co. London.

Pettit Paul. *Prehistoric Dartmoor*, 1974. David & Charles, Newton Abbot.

Richardson, John. *The Local Historian's Encyclopedia*, 1974, reprinted 1989. Historical Publications Ltd New Barnet, Herts.

Risdon Tristram. *The Chronographical Description or Survey of the County of Devon*, 1714, new Edition 1811. Rees & Curtis Plymouth.

Stanbrook Elisabeth. Editor. *Dartmoor Magazine* Vols. 2, 38 and 39. Quay Publications, Brixham.

Transactions of the Devonshire Association Vol 82 (1950), Vol 102 (1970), Vol 103 (1971). The Devonshire Association, Exeter.

Worth Richard Hansford. *Worth's Dartmoor* 1967 edition with introduction by G.M. Spooner. First published 1953, reprinted David & Charles Newton Abbot.

SOURCES OF INFORMATION

DUCHY OF CORNWALL OFFICE LONDON

Box R2/3 Laughter Hole Title Deeds and purchase from Mrs Browse and another.

Box R2/4 Purchases from John Hannaford.

Box R2/5 Challacornbe and Soussons Estates.

Box R2/6 Bellever and Lakehead Estate. Leases and purchases.

Box R2/7 Further papers relating to the Challacombe and Soussons Estates.

Box R3/1 Plans for the rebuilding of cottages etc.

Box R3/4 Papers relating to Merripits and Dury. Further papers relating to Lakehead and Bellever.

Box R3/13 Ancient Tenement documents.

Box R3/16 Papers relating to Dury Head and Conveyance of

School to Rector and Churchwardens.

Box R4/8 Leases and Assigns 1840—1850.

Box R4/10 Leases and Assigns for Laughter Heath, Lakehead, Higher Lydgate and Jester Hall (Jesters), 1860s. 1870s, 1880s.

Box R4/13 Various extracts from Court Rolls.

Box 21 Jester Hall (Jesters) 1863 on.

Box 26 Lower Merripit cottage and land Tithe 485 and Assigns to William White 1861.

Box 39 Toll House Gate 1863—1880.

Box 53 Vollans Leasehold.

Miscellaneous correspondence prior to 1896.

DUCHY OF CORNWALL OFFICE PRINCETOWN

Miscellaneous correspondence prior to 1896.

1809 Map of Bellever Newtake Leases.

Early Map of Laughter Hole (Date uncertain).

DEVON COUNTY RECORD OFFICE

Postbridge School. Original material in the form of log books, Minute books, Register etc.

2632/10/19 Postbridge School Building Plan.

2276D/115-116 Postbridge Chapel account books.

2276D/117 Postbridge Chapel Sunday School account book.

2276D/11/14/29/32/52/74 Tavistock Methodist Circuit minutes.

2955A/PF1-3 Dartmoor Widecombe Charity Schools.

Postbridge Paintings (Photographic Copies). c1857

QS 90/132 Clapper Bridge, Toll House etc.

Q5 90/133 Looking down river towards Barracks.

90M/761-774 Soussons Assigns 1765–1805.

924B/B8/30-31 Wheal Caroline Mine boundaries etc.

Sketches of Devon by John Swete Volume 15 November 11th, 1797 (Extract).

Dart District Fishery Board Minute Books 1900-1924.

PUBLIC RECORD OFFICES KEW AND CHANCERY LANE

The following items are Crown Copyright and are published with the permission of the Controller of her Majesty's Stationery Office.

TITHE MAPS AND APPORTIONMENTS

PRO 29/9/271

PRO 30/9/271

PRO 29/9/148

PRO 30/9/148

FIELD BOOKS COMPILED FOLLOWING THE FINANCE (1909-1910) ACT 1910 (10 EDW VII C8)

1R58/835/94—95

1R58/830/13

1R58/662/ 60/61/62/63.

CENSUS RETURNS

For the years 1841,1851,1861,1871.1881,1891.

TELEPHONE TECHNOLOGY SHOWCASE

Telephone Directories 1927 on.

Telephone Exchanges and locations.

Total numbers of subscribers 1927-1958 and 1961-1989.

POST OFFICE ARCHIVES

Postmaster General's Minute Books.

Vol 160/310

Vol 168/89

Vol 194/434

Vol 196/163

Vol 82/492

Date stamp record books – various impressions.

Post Office Guides 1900 on.

SHELL UK LTD

Petrol pumps (Photographs and slides)

Petrol prices.

LUCAS INDUSTRIES

Lucas Freelight (Craigs).

ALSO

Private papers belonging to my Grandmother, Father, Mother and the author (letters, bankbooks, accounts, leases and agreements).

Subscribers

Mr and Mrs S.J. Alcock, Abergavenny
Gwyneth Amery, Chagford, Devon
Hugh Aplin, Exeter, Devon
Stephen and Tessa Arrowsmith-Brown,
    Postbridge, Devon
Anthony M. Ash, Dartmouth, Devon
John A. Baker, Exeter, Devon
Mr Ronald Baker, Exeter, Devon
Peter L. Balkwill, South Australia
Mr R. N. Barber, St Neot
Grace and Eric Barrass, Tunbridge Wells, Kent
Chris Barrett, Barby, Rugby
Maureen J. Bartle (née Hamlyn), Australia
Paul R. Bartlett, Drewsteignton, Devon
D. Batehup, Haywards Heath, Sussex
The Revd P.L. and Mrs Baycock, Chagford,
    Newton Abbot, Devon
Anthony E. Beard, Widecome-in-the-Moor,
    Devon
A C W Beard, Chudleigh, Newton Abbot, Devon
Paul and Mary Beckers, Rawreth, Wickford, Essex
N.L. Beere, Postbridge, Devon
Caroline F. Belam, Holne, Newton Abbot, Devon
Anne M.J. Belam (née Coaker), Holne, Newton
    Abbot, Devon
John and Hazel Bell, Kingsnympton,
    Umberleigh, Devon
John, Clare, Sarah and Laura Bellamy, Whitton,
    Middlesex
Mrs Margaret Belt, Purton, Swindon, Wiltshire
Mr Peter Benjamin, Cheriton Bishop, Devon
Courtenay R. Bennett, Archerton and Ringhill,
    1928–1945
Mrs Joyce E. Bennett, Petts Wood, Kent
Mr J.D. Bewsher, Paignton, Devon
Mr B. Bewsher and Ms L. Orton, Buckfastleigh,
    Devon.
Raymond J. Bishop, Tonbridge, Kent
Ralph Bond, Brixham, Devon
Nicholas Borissow, Cupar, Fife
Gordon Bray, Burwash, Sussex
Kath Brewer, Torquay, Devon
Miss H, Brickel, Caln, Wilts.
Sandra T. Bright, Ashford, Kent
Mrs B. Brooks, Postbridge
Mrs L.F. Brown, Taunton, Somerset
Mary Brunt-Rolfe, The Netherlands
Michele and Brian Brusey, Postbridge, Devon

Mr R.J.Burnett, Flackwell Heath, Bucks.
K.J. Burrow, Bucks Cross, Bideford
Keith J. Butler, Newton Abbot, Devon
Marian P. Butler, Bovey Tracey, Devon
Ann and Simon Butler, Manaton, Devon
Anita Carney, Yelverton, Devon
Betty W. Carter, Taunton, Somerset
Sir John and Lady Chilcot, Postbridge, Devon
Estelle Clarke, Somerset
P.R. Coaker, Runnage, Postbridge, Devon
Mr and Mrs A. Cook Plymouth, Devon
Lt. Col. (Rtd) and Mrs R.K. Cooley, York
B.A. Coombes, Kingskerswell, Newton Abbot,
    Devon
Mr and Mrs David Cooper, Postbridge
Brian Cosford, Chagford, Newton Abbot, Devon
J.S. and N. M. Cotton, Cerne Abbas, Dorset
Mr Sean A. Dart, Bovey Tracey, Devon
Dartmoor National Park Authority
Heather David (née Bellamy), Hensall, Nr Goole,
    Yorks.
Andrew Davies, Thaxted, Dunmow, Essex
Pat Day, Boscastle, Cornwall
Mrs D. Drake, Plymouth, Devon
Joan C. Drwiega, Northallerton, Yorks.
Lyndall Dunne, Tavistock, Devon
Jean and Michael Dunning, Potters Bar, Herts.
John Earle, Widecombe-in-the-Moor, Devon
Hugh Farrer, Maidstone, Kent
Marilyn and Chris Farrow, Postbridge, Devon
Richard and Oliver Field, Plymouth, Devon
David Fisher, Postbridge, Devon
Mrs M.J. Flowerday, Orpington, Kent
Paul Flowerday, Croydon, Surrey
Mr And Mrs W. Foster, Tavistock, Devon
Audrey J. Frampton, Morchard Bishop, Devon
Mr and Mrs French, Yorks
Doreen Frismodt (née Withycombe), Haderslev,
    Denmark
Luigi, Annalice and Chiara Fulgoni, Osterley,
    Middlesex
Ghislaine, Ian and Samuel Gaitley, Petersfield,
    Hants.
David German, Mullion, Cornwall
Miss Jemma German, Princetown, Devon
Michael T. Giles, Elham, Kent
Mr and Mrs G.W. Gilliam, Tavistock, Devon
Ron and Sheila Goodgame, Tonbridge, Kent

Mrs S.M. Goodgame, Tonbridge, Kent
Rosemary and David Goodwin, Terrington, York
Mr and Mrs Greatrex, Postbridge, Devon
Evelyn Green, Huntington, York
Dr Tom and Mrs Elisabeth Greeves, Tavistock
Mr and Mrs Grigg, Plymouth, Devon
Gavin Grimsey, Bovey Tracey, Devon
Stella Grimsey, Overton, Hants.
Albert Hall, Devon
Elizabeth Hallett, South Brent, Devon
Mr P. Hamilton Legatt Bsc, Tavistock, Devon
Eleanor Hamlyn, Auckland, New Zealand
Alf Hamlyn, New Zealand
M.J. Hamlyn, Nantwich, Cheshire
Glenn M. Hannigan, Tavistock, Devon
Joan A. Harrington (née Sams), (now of) Colchester, Essex
Adrian F.C. Harris, London
Shirley D.M. Harris, Paignton, Devon
Mr and Mrs Harris, Okehampton, Devon
Bruce and Diana Harris 'Cobblers Cottage', Ipplepen, Devon
June F.E. Harris (née Heath), Surrey
David J. Heaton, Carterton, Oxon
Jane Hewitt, Manaton, Newton Abbot, Devon
Winifred H. Hibbert (formerly of Postbridge)
Mawgan, Diane, James and Helen Higgins, Hampton, Middlesex
David and Hazel Hill, Kington, Herefordshire
Sarah Hill, Postbridge, Devon
Peter Hirst, Dartmeet, Yelverton, Devon
David and Janet Hopton, Nether Poppleton, York.
Keith Chudleigh Hortop, North Bovey, Devon
Dennis S. Hounsell, Plymouth, Devon
Norman Humphreys, Bellever, Postbridge, Devon
Robin Humphreys, St Neots, Cambs.
Alistair B. Jeffery, Chandlers Ford, Hants
Peter John Jeffs, Gunnislake, Cornwall
Mrs J. Loveys Jervoise, Rowden
Anthony Loveys Jervoise, Rowden
Elizabeth Jewitt, York
Anthea Johnson, Ponsanooth, Truro, Cornwall
Mrs D. Jones, Dousland, Yelverton, Devon
Graham Joyce, Exeter, Devon
Kath Judd, Cupar, Fife
David Judd, Ladybank, Fife
Mr and Mrs J. Kaluski, Upper Poppleton, York
Paul and Joan Kent, West Charleton, Kingsbridge, Devon
Colin Kilvington, Stoke, Plymouth, Devon
T.J. Lakey, Derriford, Plymouth, Devon
Lillian J. Lambert (née Sams), West Mersea, Essex
D.G. Lavington-Evans, Blackawton, Totnes, Devon

Petrina Lawrie-Brown, Canada
Brian Le Messurier, Exeter
Miss J. Lee, Tavistock, Devon
E. Lee, South London
Jean and Jimmy Legate, Postbridge, Devon
J.A. Lieurance, Poundsgate, Newton Abbot, Devon
Pamela B. Lind, Bovey Tracey, Newton Abbot, Devon
Dr Christine Linfield, Barnecourt, Moretonhampstead, Devon
Michael Loly, Oslo, Norway
Mr E.W. Luscombe, Plymouth, Devon
Bet Mabin, Torquay, Devon
Mrs Dot Maddock, Princetown, Devon
Paul Marsh, Caterham, Surrey
Douglas B. Marsh, Chagford, Devon
Frank Martin, Postbridge, Devon
William John Martin, Postbridge, Devon
Jim Martin, (warden Bellever Y.H. 1960-1990)
Mr E.A. Martin, Leicester
T.E. Mason, Exeter, Devon
M.P .McElheron, Kingskerswell, Devon
Gordon and Anne, Medd, Nether Poppleton, York
Mr S.B. Millgate, Maidstone, Kent
W.L. Mole, Newport, South Wales
R. Montgomery, Waterlooville, Hants
David George Moore, Plymouth, Devon
R.P. Mouat, Horrabridge, Devon
Sam and Rose Mulligan, Newton Abbot, Devon
B. and A. J. Murphy, Bellever
Mary Osborn, Yelverton, Devon
Mr N.J. Osborne, Westbury
Mr and Mrs K. Owen, Tavistock, Devon
Mr and Mrs Joe Pacynski, Toledo, Ohio, U.S.A.
Jack and Ann Palmer, Lords of Princetown, Devon
Peter Parsons, Postbridge, Devon
Andrew Passmore, Exeter, Devon
Mike and Jane Passmore, Exeter, Devon
Margaret Pearce, Yeovil, Somerset
Mr and Mrs M. Pearce, Postbridge, Devon
Peter Pearson, Shaldon, Teignmouth, Devon
Revd Michael J. Pearson, Barnstaple, Devon
Mr and Mrs R. M. Perry, Plymouth, Devon
T.C. Pilkington, Tavistock, Devon
Keith Potter, Harrowbarrow, Devon
Miss Doris Potter, Milton Abbot, Tavistock, Devon
Audrey Prizeman, Plymouth, Devon
Sheila M. Pugh, Rowley Regis, West Midlands
Mr and Mrs D.W. Puttick, Eastbourne
Anthony and Patricia Quinsee, Huntington, York
W. Radcliffe, Teddington, Middlesex

Professor Nicholas Rawlins, Oxford
Sir John Rawlins, Holne, Newton Abbot, Devon
Ann C. Reed, London
Mr Paul Rendell, Okehampton, Devon
Amanda Reynolds, Tavistock, Devon
John and Susan Reynolds, Tavistock, Devon
Ken Rickard, Lydford, Devon
Mr and Mrs Rolfe, St Ann's Chapel
Jane Rolfe, Mary Tavy, Tavistock, Devon
John H. Rolfe, Newcastle
Mr and Mrs Rolfe, Tamerton Foliot, Plymouth, Devon
Serina L. Rouse, Gidleigh, Devon
Monica E. Royle, Plympton, Plymouth, Devon
Mrs Jenny Sanders, Tavistock, Devon
Tim Sandles, Denbury
Peter Saunders, Ringwood, Hants.
J. Norton Scorer, Modbury, Ivybridge, Devon
Sir David Serpell, Dartmouth, Devon
Belinda Sharp, The Mint House, Hurstpierpoint, Sussex
Celia M. Short, Worthing, Sussex
Mrs M.E. Silver, Sand Hutton, York
Robin W. Skinner, Worthing, Sussex
Gerald Chaffe Smerdon, Bellever/Postbridge, Devon
John E. Smith, Turnchapel, Plymouth, Devon
Mary Stanbrook, Brixham, Devon
Heather E. Stanley, Princetown, Devon
Robert Steemson, Postbridge, Devon
Les Stephens, Princetown, Devon
Brian E. Sturt, Hither Green, London, SE13
Brian and Wendy Sugg, Ashbourne, Derbyshire
David and Sandra Swetman, Amersham Common, Bucks.
Captain (Rtd) R.S. Trude, Plymouth, Devon
Mr and Mrs Stuart Tucker, Tiverton, Devon
A.R. Tulley, Wembury, Plymouth, Devon
Joe Turner, Pinhoe, Exeter, Devon

Sylvia Tyler, Plympton, Plymouth, Devon
Miss Edith Urch, Plymouth, Devon
Mrs N.K. Van Der Kiste, South Brent, Devon
Mr and Mrs R.A. Vane, Lincoln
Lt Col. P.G.H. Varwell, South Zeal, Okehampton, Devon
Dr. Denys J. Voaden, College Park (md), U.S.A.
Mr G. Waldron, Plymouth, Devon
Patricia M. Wallace MVO (formerly of Postbridge)
Richard Waller, Chagford, Devon
John F.W. Walling, Newton Abbot, Devon
Mrs Walters, Denbury, Newton Abbot, Devon
Richard W. Warne, Kingsteignton, Newton Abbot, Devon
Alex and Barbara Warne, Postbridge, Devon
Mr and Mrs F.G. Warne, Princetown, Devon
Alan Watson, Exeter, Devon
Mr and Mrs Tom Webb, Postbridge
Mrs E. Webb, Postbridge
John and Margaret Weir, Meacombe, Devon
Richard Wells, Camberley, Surrey
Ginny Westacott, Bellever, Postbridge, Devon
Marnie Wheeler, Chagford, Devon
Lorna M. Whitaker, Hitchin, Herts.
Miss A.E. White, Newton Abbot, Devon
Mrs R.R. White, Westward Ho! Devon
Mrs Q. White, Stoke Fleming
Freda Wilkinson, Poundsgate, Newton Abbot, Devon
Mr and Mrs J.G. Willcox, Chapel Cottage, Postbridge, Devon
Mrs M.M. Williams, Plymouth, Devon
C.N. Williams, Horabridge, Yelverton, Devon
Dorothy Williams (née James), Hexworthy, Yelverton, Devon
Stephen Woods, Portchester, Hants.
Phoebe Wortley-Talbot, 'Shotts', Haytor, Newton Abbot, Devon

I deulu'r gorffennol, y presennol
... a'r dyfodol

....

For the family; past, present ...
and future

BLAS

TASTE

Cyhoeddwyd yn 2016 gan
Wasg Gomer, Llandysul, Ceredigion SA44 4JL

ISBN 978-1-78562-174-1

Dymuna'r cyhoeddwyr gydnabod
cymorth ariannol Cyngor Llyfrau Cymru.

Argraffwyd a rhwymwyd yng Nghymru gan
Wasg Gomer, Llandysul, Ceredigion

Gyda chefnogaeth Bwydydd Castell Howell

Published in 2016 by
Gomer Press, Llandysul, Ceredigion SA44 4JL

ISBN 978-1-78562-174-1

The publishers wish to acknowledge the
financial support of the Welsh Books Council

Printed and bound in Wales at
Gomer Press, Llandysul, Ceredigion

With the support of Castell Howell Foods

lisa@thepumpkinpatch.org.uk   www.thepumpkinpatch.org.uk

The Pumpkin Patch Kitchen & Garden   lisaannefearn   @thepumkinpatch

Blas Taste

Dathlu bwyd a theulu

A celebration of food and family

LISA FEARN

To Jean

Happy Christmas

Lisa xx 2018.

Gomer

Sut ddechreuodd y cyfan?

Mae'n ddiddorol gweld i ble mae bywyd yn eich tywys. Feddyliais i erioed y byswn i'n rhan o'r byd bwyd. Roeddwn i'n mwynhau bwyd ac yn bendant roeddwn i'n gwerthfawrogi bwyd da ac yn dwlu ar goginio. Ond lwc ac amgylchiadau teuluol ddenodd fi at goginio ac at ddysgu ac agor Ysgol Goginio a Garddio The Pumpkin Patch yn Felin-wen, Sir Gâr.

Ar ôl i'n pumed plentyn a'n cyw melyn ola gyrraedd, fe symudon ni i Gaerfyrddin, lle ces i fy magu. Fe brynon ni le bach a magu ein teulu ifanc i werthfawrogi'r wlad o'u cwmpas. Fe gawson ni ieir a hwyaid, gwyddau, geifr a moch, adnewyddu ein ffermdy a dysgu am ffyrdd y wlad.

Rwy'n dwlu ar y byd tu fas ac ar arddio a choginio. Felly, pan ddechreuodd y cyw melyn ola yn yr ysgol, cymerais stoc o'r hyn roeddwn i'n gyfarwydd ag e. Ac felly y daeth The Pumpkin Patch i fodolaeth – ysgol goginio a garddio i blant, yn eu dysgu sut i dyfu a choginio'u bwyd eu hunain. O fewn misoedd, roedd yr ysgol yn llawn, a dechreuais rannu ein ryseitiau teulu-gyfeillgar â phobl eraill.

Mae *Blas • Taste* yn llawn o'n hoff ryseitiau ni yn Fferm Allt y Gog. Dyma'r ryseitiau rwy'n gobeithio y bydd fy mhlant yn eu defnyddio pan fyddan nhw'n gadael y nyth – ffefrynnau Mam. Dim ffws; prydau a byrbrydau hawdd sy'n rhoi blas ar bob dim yn ei dymor ac yn ddathliad o flwyddyn gron gyda'r teulu a ffrindiau. Rhowch wahoddiad i bawb ddod draw i gael blas ar bethau!

How did it all start?

Well, it's interesting to see where life takes you. Never ever did I plan on getting caught up in the world of food. I enjoyed food and I certainly appreciated good food and loved to cook. But it was mere fluke and family circumstances that drew me to cooking and teaching and opening up The Pumpkin Patch Cookery and Gardening School in Felin-wen, Carmarthenshire.

Following the arrival of our fifth and final child, we relocated to Carmarthen, my home-town. We bought ourselves a smallholding and raised our young family with an appreciation of the countryside around us. We dabbled in chickens and ducks, geese, goats and pigs, renovated our farmhouse and learnt the country ways.

I love the outdoors, gardening and cooking. So, when our youngest reached school age, I took stock of what I knew and The Pumpkin Patch became a reality – a children's cookery and gardening school teaching them how to grow and cook their own food. Within months the school was fully booked, and I started sharing our family-friendly recipes with people.

Blas • Taste is full of our favourite 'go to' recipes at Allt y Gog Farm. They are the recipes that I hope my children will use when they leave home – Mum's favourites. No fuss; easy meals and snacks that flavour the seasons and the year's celebrations with the family. So invite everybody round to taste!

Cynnwys

Contents

Cynnwys

LL = LLYSIEUOL **DG** = DIGLWTEN

Contents

V = VEGETARIAN   GF = GLUTEN FREE

Y flwyddyn newydd

1

The new year

Croeso i ddechrau'r flwyddyn fel hyn. Shwd y'ch chi'n teimlo? Lluddedig? Yn llawn egni? Yn barod i ddechrau eto?

Mae dechrau blwyddyn yn gychwyn newydd; mae'n amser i ni edrych yn ôl ond mae'n gyfle hefyd i ni fwrw'n golygon tua'r dyfodol. Mae'n amser pan fydd y byd yn llonyddu ac yn amser i arafu a phwyso a mesur.

Rwy'n synnu bob blwyddyn pa mor gyflym mae'r dyddiau'n ymestyn ym mis Ionawr. Yn fuan wedi cau pen y mwdwl ar y Nadolig, mae'r ieir yn dychwelyd i ddodwy ac yn raddol mae'r dyddiau'n hirach; mae'r plant yn dychwelyd o'r ysgol ac awr arall o olau dydd yn eu disgwyl. Mae bywyd yn bwrw yn ei flaen i bwrpas ac nid dim ond goroesi i gwblhau'n tasgau angenrheidiol yn ddygn mewn glaw, oerfel neu dywyllwch, ry'n ni mwyach.

Fy nghyngor i yw; bwriwch i mewn i'r flwyddyn newydd yn llawn gobeithion ac archwaeth am fwyd da ac am gwmni da. Mae eleni am fod yn flwyddyn ardderchog!

Welcome to the beginning of the year. How do you feel? Tired? Energised? Ready to start again?

The beginning of any year is a new start; it's a time for looking back but also a chance to look towards the future. It's a time when the world becomes still, a time to slow down and take stock.

Each year I am astounded how soon the day lengthens in January. Once is Christmas is done and dusted, the chickens often return to lay and gradually the days are longer, and the children return from school to an extra hour of daylight. Life seems to take on more purpose, no longer a mere existence, completing necessary tasks and coping doggedly with chores in either rain, cold or darkness.

My advice is to throw yourself into the new year full of hopes and an appetite for good food and good company. This year's going to be great!

DECHRAU YN
Y DECHRAU'N DEG

A CLEAN START

14

⭐ Os bu amser addas erioed i feddwl am fwyta'n iach ond hefyd i fwynhau bwyd cysurlon, yr amser yma o'r flwyddyn yw hwnnw – ar ôl y Nadolig – yn nhrymder gaeaf. Wedi eithafion yr ŵyl, mae angen i chi gadw corff ac enaid ynghyd, a pha ffordd well o fwynhau tywydd oer y gaeaf na chyda phowlennaid iachus a sylweddol o gawl cartref a bara da, ffres.

Mae sawl cawl ymysg fy ffefrynnau, a fedra i ddim enwi dim ond un. Os ydw i'n hollol onest, rydw i'n hoffi fy nghawl â darnau mawr o lysiau ynddo, wedi'i weini mewn powlen fas gyda chwlffyn mawr o fara gwyn, ffres a digon o fenyn. A fydda i byth yn gwrthod caws, yng nghlydwch fy nghartref fy hun yn aml fe welwch chi fi'n malu briwision caws mewn i gawl sydd ar fin berwi er mwyn creu llond powlen o wychder toddedig yn barod i'w fopio a'i fwynhau gyda'r bara.

⭐ If there was ever a good time in the year to be eating healthily whilst also enjoying comfort food, it's now – post-Christmas – in the depths of winter. After the excesses of the festive season, you still need to keep body and soul nourished and what better way to enjoy the cold winter weather than with a warming, wholesome, hearty bowl of homemade soup and some crusty bread.

I have several favourite soups, and I really can't name just one. If I'm totally honest, I like my soup chunky; I like it served in a shallow bowl and with large chunks of fresh white bread with plenty of butter. I'll never pass on the cheese and, in the privacy of my own home, will even be found crumbling it into the near-boiling soup to create a bowlful of molten loveliness ready to be mopped up with the bread.

CAWL

Un o'r pethau gwych am gawl yw pa mor gyflym mae modd gwneud peth a'i weini. O'r dechrau i'r diwedd, gall gymryd cyn lleied â 15 munud, neu tua 25 munud o ran amser os ydych chi'n fwy hamddenol am bethau. Mae'n hawdd gwneud cyflenwad mawr, digon i'r teulu, ychydig brydau canol dydd neu er mwyn llenwi'ch rhewgell â phrydau ar gyfer y dyfodol.

SYLFEINI CADARN

Gellir gwneud sylfaen cawl ardderchog drwy greu stoc syml gan ddefnyddio winwnsyn, seleri a moronen. Enw'r Ffrancwyr ar hyn yw mirepoix, a dyma'r sylfaen ar gyfer amrywiaeth mawr o gawl o flasau hyfryd gwahanol. I wneud y stoc: torrwch winwnsyn, dwy foronen ac un coesyn o seleri yn fân a'u ffrio mewn ychydig o olew. Yna ychwanegwch ychydig o ddŵr a'i fudferwi hyd nes bod y llysiau'n feddal. Ychwanegwch fymryn o halen a phupur at y stoc.

Felly, ar gyfer cawl cennin a thatws, gwnewch y stoc sylfaenol fel rydw i'n esbonio uchod, ychwanegwch dair cenhinen a thaten fawr wedi'u torri a'u mudferwi hyd nes bydd y daten yn feddal. Malwch y cymysgedd yn drylwyr gyda chymysgydd bwyd i wneud cawl llyfn neu defnyddiwch stwnsiwr tatws i greu cawl o ansawdd mwy lympiog. Ychwanegwch ddiferyn o hufen ar y diwedd. Am gawl hynod flasus sy'n fwy o stiw nag o gawl, ond peidiwch â gofyn i fi am ddiffiniad o'r naill na'r llall, ewch i weld fy rysáit am gawl sgwash cnau menyn a chnau coco. Mae hwn yn ffefryn pendant yn ein teulu ni, ac wrth i'r tywydd oeri alla i ddim dychmygu unrhyw beth gwell na phalu mewn i lond powlennaid (neu ail bowlennaid)

o'r pryd cynnes, blasus, hwn. Cadwch y cawl yn yr oergell a'i gynhesu'n barod ar gyfer y plant pan ddôn' nhw adre o'r ysgol. Bydd yn eu cynhesu nhw ac yn llenwi'u boliau ddigon i'w cadw'n bell oddi wrth y tun bisgedi.

Rhowch gynnig ar wneud cawl newydd bob wythnos. Gan fod llawer o'r ryseitiau yma heb gig ynddyn nhw, maen nhw'n ffordd hynod ddarbodus o fwydo'r teulu ac yn addas ar gyfer llysieuwyr a figaniaid, wrth reswm. Unwaith y byddwch wedi meistroli'r sylfaen, ewch yn wyllt a rhowch gynnig ar gyfuniadau gwallgo.

BABANOD A PHLANTOS

Os oes gennych chi fabanod neu blant bach yn y tŷ, fe fyddwch chi'n deall yn iawn bod cawl yn fwyd i bawb. Peidiwch â defnyddio cymaint o halen wrth wneud y bwyd neu cadwch y bwyd i'r babanod a'r plant bach ar wahân cyn i chi'n ychwanegu halen a phupur a bydd gennych chi fwyd cartref hynod iach i fabis. Storiwch brydau unigol yn yr oergell neu'r rhewgell yn barod i'w defnyddio rywbryd eto. Mae'n bosib rhewi ychydig bach o gawl mewn blwch ciwbiau iâ ac yna arllwys y ciwbiau bwyd sydd wedi'u rewi i fag y mae modd ei selio. Tynnwch rai o'r ciwbiau o'r rhewgell cyn gadael y tŷ a bydd bwyd y babi wedi dadmer erbyn amser cinio, ond bydd yn dal i fod yn oer, felly ailgynheswch y bwyd yn drylwyr a'i oeri i'r tymheredd cywir i'w ddefnyddio. Does dim i guro cawl cartref.

Iawn 'te, dyma ni, fy neg ucha ym myd cawl ... ond dydyn nhw ddim mewn trefn benodol.

Cawl sgwash cnau menyn a chnau coco – cawl hollol anhygoel sy'n llenwi
Cawl berwr dŵr – cawl glanhaol
Cawl pupur rhost a thomato – ychwanegwch at basta
Cawl tomato a basil – ysgafn a hafaidd
Cawl dynad poethion – glanhaol a blasus
Cawl cennin a thatws – llenwol a chysurlon
Cawl seleriac ac afal – syndod o flasus
Cawl ham Cymreig – ysgafnach na'r cawl cig oen cyfatebol
Cawl winwns Ffrengig – blas cryf, hyfryd
Cawl corgimychiaid Gwlad Thai a nwdls – cynhesol a chynhaliol gyda'r tsili a'r sinsir

10

SOUP

One of the great things about a soup is the speed in which it can be made and served. From start to finish can take as little as 15 minutes, or around likely around 25 minutes at a more relaxed pace. It's easy to make up large batches, enough for the family, a few lunches or to feed the freezer for future meals.

BASE CAMP

A great soup base can be made by making a simple stock with an onion, celery and carrot; known to the French as a mirepoix, this makes the base for many lovely soups. To make the stock: dice an onion, two carrots and a stick of celery, and fry in a little oil. Finally, add a little water and simmer until the vegetables are soft. Season the stock with salt and pepper.

So, for a leek and potato soup, make the basic stock as above, add three chopped leeks and a large potato; then simmer until the potato is soft. Blitz to make a smooth soup or use a potato masher for a more textured soup. Add a splash of cream to finish. For a really delicious soup which is more of a stew than a soup, though please don't ask me for the definition of either, see my butternut squash and coconut soup. This is a firm family favourite of ours, and as the weather gets colder I can't imagine anything better than tucking into a bowlful (or two) of this highly flavoured warming dish. Store the soup in the fridge,

and warm it up ready for the kids when they arrive home from school. It'll soon warm them up, fill them up and keep them out of the biscuit tin.

Try making a new soup each week. As many of the soups I've listed are meat free, they really are a very economical way to feed the family, and obviously suitable for vegetarians and vegans. Once you've mastered the basics ... go crazy and try some whacky combinations.

BABIES AND TODDLERS

If you have babies or toddlers in the house, you'll totally understand that soup really does feed all. Ease up on the salt or keep the baby portion separate before seasoning with salt and pepper, and you have some super healthy, homemade baby food. Store individual portions in the fridge or freezer, ready for future use. It's possible to freeze small quantities in an ice cube tray, then tip out the frozen cubes into a sealed bag. Remove a few cubes from the freezer before leaving home, and baby's food will be thawed by lunch time but still be chilled, so reheat thoroughly and cool to the right temperature before using. Nothing quite beats a homemade soup.

Okay, here we go, my top ten in the world of soups ... but in no particular order.

Butternut squash and coconut soup – truly incredible and filling

Watercress soup – a detox soup

Roast pepper and tomato soup – add to pasta

Tomato and basil soup – light and summery

Stinger soup (nettle) – a tasty detox

Leek and potato soup – filling and comforting

Celeriac and apple soup – surprisingly good

Welsh ham cawl – lighter than the lamb equivalent

French onion soup – strong-flavoured and wonderful

Thai prawn and noodle soup – warming and nutritious, with chilli and ginger

CAWL CORGIMYCHIAID GWLAD THAI

Dyma gawl braster isel hynod flasus a iachus, ac mae mor hawdd i'w wneud.

Corgimychiaid mawr heb eu cregyn,
heb eu coginio
1 litr stoc llysieuol
3 llwy fwrdd o saws soi
2cm o sinsir ffres, wedi'i dorri'n denau
1 tsili coch wedi tynnu'r hadau a'i dorri
1 coesyn o lemonwellt, wedi'i gleisio â chyllell
5 shibwnsyn
100g nwdls reis
Madarch y coed neu wystrys
Llond llaw o goriander wedi'i dorri'n fân i addurno
Dewisol:
Ychydig o mangetout, tun bach o India corn,
unrhyw llysiau yn eu tymor

Rhowch 1 litr o stoc llysieuol mewn sosban fawr. Ychwanegwch 3 llwy fwrdd o saws soy.

Ychwanegwch y 2cm o sinsir wedi'i dorri'n denau, y tsili coch (cymaint ag y mentrwch), y lemonwellt wedi'i gleisio a'r shibwns.

Dewch ag ef i'r berw, yna gostyngwch y gwres ac ychwanegu'r madarch, y mangetout, y nwdls reis ac unrhyw gynhwysion eraill y dewisoch eu cynnwys, e.e. yr India corn.

Yn olaf, ychwanegwch y corgimychiaid a mudferwi'r cyfan am tua 4–5 munud hyd nes bod y corgimychiaid wedi'u coginio.

 Tip: gallwch ddefnyddio brest cyw iâr wedi'i thorri'n giwbiau neu ddarnau o gyw iâr dros ben o bryd arall ar gyfer fersiwn gwahanol o'r pryd bwyd blasus hwn.

Diglwten – defnyddiwch saws soi Tamari, sydd i'w gael yn y rhan fwyaf o siopau bwyd, defnyddiwch nwdls diglwten hefyd.

THAI STYLE PRAWN SOUP

This is a really tasty, healthy, low-fat soup and so easy to make.

Peeled large prawns, uncooked
1 litre vegetable stock
3 tbsp soy sauce
2cm piece of fresh ginger, finely chopped
1 red chilli deseeded and chopped
1 stalk of lemongrass, bruised with a knife
5 spring onions
100g rice noodles
Shitake or oyster mushrooms
A handful of coriander, chopped to garnish
Optional:
A few mangetout, a small tin of corn, any seasonal vegetables

Place 1 litre of vegetable stock in a large saucepan. Add 3 tablespoons of soy sauce.

Add 2cm fresh ginger, thinly sliced, some red chilli (as much as you dare), the bruised lemongrass and the spring onions.

Bring to the boil, then turn down the heat and add the mushrooms, mangetout, the rice noodles and any other ingredients you choose, e.g. sweetcorn.

Finally, add the prawns and simmer gently for about 4–5 minutes until the prawns are cooked.

 Tip: use diced chicken breast or even shredded leftover chicken for an alternative take on this tasty dish.

Gluten-free – use Tamari soy sauce, found in most food shops; use gluten-free noodles as well.

CAWL BERWR DŴR

Rwy'n dwlu ar y ffaith bod y cawl yma, sydd â blas puprog hyfryd, hefyd mor llesol i'r corff.

1 llwy de o fenyn
1 winwnsyn mawr
1 daten fawr
1 bag o ferwr dŵr
400ml stoc cyw iâr neu stoc llysieuol
300ml llaeth
Diferyn o hufen crème fraîche i'w weini

Paratowch yr holl lysiau – golchwch a thorri'r winwnsyn, pliciwch a thorri'r daten.

Toddwch ychydig o fenyn mewn sosban, ychwanegwch yr olew a chwyswch neu ffrio'r winswnsyn yn ysgafn am ychydig funudau hyd nes ei fod yn feddal ond heb frownio. Ychwanegwch y daten a'r stoc, ychydig o halen a digon o bupur, a berwi'r cyfan.

Coginiwch y daten am tua 10 munud hyd nes ei bod hi'n feddal, yna ychwanegwch y bag o ferwr dŵr i'r sosban. Tynnwch y cyfan oddi ar y gwres a gadael iddo oeri ryw ychydig cyn ei gymysgu.

Pan fydd y cymysgedd yn llyfn, ychwanegwch ychydig o laeth i'w wneud yn hufennog. Blaswch, yna ychwanegwch ychydig halen a phupur du wedi'i falu os oes angen.

Gallwch ychwanegu chwyrlïad o hufen neu crème fraîche i'r cawl yn y bowlen. Fe synnwch chi pa mor flasus yw'r cawl hwn.

WATERCRESS SOUP

I love the fact that this soup with its wonderful peppery taste is so beneficial for the body.

1 tsp butter
1 large onion
1 large potato
1 bag of watercress
400ml of chicken or vegetable stock
300ml milk
A drop of crème fraîche cream to serve

Prepare all the vegetables – wash and chop the onion, peel and chop the potato.

Melt a little butter in a pan, add the oil and sweat or gently fry the onion for a few minutes until soft but not browned. Add the potato and the stock, season with salt and plenty of pepper and bring to the boil.

Cook the potato for about 10 minutes until soft, then add the bag of watercress to the pan. Remove from the heat and allow to cool a little before blending.

Once the mixture is smooth, add a little milk to form a creamy consistency. Taste to check the seasoning, add salt and ground black pepper if needed.

You can add a swirl of cream or crème fraîche to the soup in the bowl. You will be amazed how delicious this soup is.

CAWL MINESTRONE

Dyma bryd cyflawn a chynhesol – rwy'n teimlo 'mod i wedi cael pryd da ar ôl bwyta llond powlen o minestrone.

100g stribedi cig moch mwg
2 foronen, wedi'u torri'n fras
2 goesyn seleri, wedi'u sleisio
1 winwnsyn, wedi'i dorri'n fras
2 ewin garlleg, wedi'u malu
2 sbrigyn o rosmari ffres
1 llwy de o deim, wedi'i sychu
1 llwy fwrdd o biwrê tomato
Tun 400g o domatos, wedi'u malu
1 litr o stoc cyw iâr
Tun 400g o ffa cannellini, wedi'u golchi a'u draenio
50g sbageti o hyd byrrach neu basta arall
Halen a phupur du, wedi'i falu
25g caws Parmesan neu gaws caled tebyg, wedi'i gratio

Rhowch ffrimpan mawr ar wres isel, ychwanegu'r cig moch a'i goginio am 10 munud hyd nes ei fod yn grimp ac yn euraid. Trosglwyddwch i blât.

Arllwyswch y moron, y seleri a'r winwns i fraster y cig moch a'u ffrio am ddwy funud cyn ychwanegu'r garlleg a'r perlysiau a'r piwrê tomato.

Coginiwch am funud, ychwanegwch y tomatos o'r tun a'r rhan fwyaf o'r stoc. Dewch â'r cyfan i'r berw. Gorchuddiwch â chlawr a'i goginio hyd nes bod y llysiau'n feddal.

Cymysgwch y ffa a'r pasta i mewn i'r cawl, gan ychwanegu gweddill y stoc os yw'n edrych yn rhy drwchus. Coginiwch am 20 munud hyd nes bydd y pasta'n feddal.

Blaswch ac ychwanegu halen yn ôl y galw, a phupur du wedi'i falu hefyd. Yna rhowch mewn powlenni a'i weini gyda digonedd o gaws Parmesan.

MINESTRONE SOUP

This is a lovely all-round warmer, I always feel well fed after eating a bowlful of minestrone.

100g smoked lardons or bacon pieces
2 carrots, roughly chopped
2 sticks celery, sliced
1 onion, roughly chopped
2 garlic cloves, crushed
2 sprigs fresh rosemary
1 tsp dried thyme
1 tbsp tomato purée
400g can chopped plum tomatoes
1 litre chicken stock
400g can cannellini beans, rinsed and drained
50g spaghetti in short lengths or other pasta
Salt and freshly ground black pepper
25g Parmesan or similar hard cheese, grated

Put a large frying pan over a low heat, add the bacon and cook for 10 minutes until crisp and golden. Transfer onto a plate.

Tip the carrots, celery and onion into the bacon fat and fry for two minutes before adding the garlic, herbs and tomato purée.

Cook for a minute, add the tomatoes and most of the stock. Bring to the boil. Cover with the lid, then cook until the vegetables are tender.

Stir the beans and pasta into the soup, adding the rest of the stock if it looks too thick. Cook for 20 minutes until the pasta is tender.

Season to taste with salt and freshly ground black pepper, then serve in bowls with plenty of Parmesan.

Mae'r cawl hwn mor ffres ac adfywiol.

Such a fresh and revitalising soup.

 LL

CAWL MORON A CHORIANDER

1 llwy fwrdd o olew llysiau
25g menyn
1 winwnsyn, wedi'i dorri
1 daten fawr, wedi'i thorri
500g moron (tua 5) wedi'u plicio a'u torri
1.2 litr o stoc llysiau neu stoc cyw iâr
1 llond llaw o goriander
Halen a phupur du, wedi'i falu
1 llwy fwrdd o iogwrt naturiol neu crème fraîche

Cynheswch yr olew a'r menyn mewn sosban fawr. Ychwanegwch y winwnsyn a'i ffrio am 5 munud hyd nes ei fod wedi meddalu, ond peidiwch â gadael iddo frownio a newid ei liw.

Ychwanegwch y daten, yna'r moron a'r stoc, a dod â'r cyfan i'r berw. Ychwanegwch binsiaid da o halen.

Wedi iddo ferwi, gostyngwch y gwres a rhoi clawr ar y sosban; coginiwch am 20 munud hyd nes bod y moron yn feddal.

Arllwyswch y cyfan i bowlen fawr ac ychwanegu'r coriander, a chan ddefnyddio cymysgydd llaw, cymysgwch y cawl nes ei fod yn llyfn (efallai bydd yn rhaid i chi wneud hyn mewn dwy ran). Rhowch y cyfan yn ôl yn y sosban, blaswch, ac ychwanegu halen a phupur. Yna ailgynheswch a'i weini.

 V

CARROT AND CORIANDER SOUP

1 tbsp vegetable oil
25g butter
1 onion, chopped
1 large potato, chopped
500g carrots (about 5), peeled and chopped
1.2 litres vegetable or chicken stock
1 handful coriander
Salt and ground black pepper
1 tbsp natural yoghurt or crème fraîche

Heat the oil and butter in a large pan, add the onion and fry for 5 minutes until softened, but do not allow to brown and colour.

Add the potato, then the carrots and stock, and bring to the boil. Add a good pinch of salt.

Once boiling, reduce the heat and cover; cook for 20 minutes until the carrots are tender.

Pour into a large bowl, add the coriander, and using a hand blender, blitz the soup until smooth (you may need to do this in two batches). Return the soup to the pan, taste, add salt and pepper. Then reheat to serve.

BARA

Does dim i guro bara syml, da; mae torth gartref yn medru bod yn bryd ynddi ei hun. Dyw gwneud bara ddim yn anodd o gwbl ac os nad ydych chi wedi gwneud hynny erioed, mae'n bryd i chi roi cynnig arni. Os ydych chi'n eitha profiadol gyda thoes ond heb wneud torth ers tro, mae'n bryd i chi estyn am eich powlen gymysgu eto.

I wneud torth syml, dim ond pum cynhwysyn sydd eu hangen arnoch

dŵr ★ blawd bara cryf gwyn ★ burum ★ halen ★ diferyn o olew olewydd neu fenyn

Dyw hi ddim yn rhestr hir, a dyw torth ddim yn beth drud i'w gwneud. Dilynwch y camau syml yn rysáit y bara pot Cymreig ar dudalen 48 a defnyddiwch y toes i wneud unrhyw beth o focaccia fflat o Fôr y Canoldir, gyda rhosmari a halen môr, i roliau bara neu blethen fara.

Does dim esgusodion mewn gwirionedd, ac wedi i chi feistroli cymysgu'r toes, ei dylino a gadael iddo godi, fydd dim i'ch rhwsytro rhag dod yn feistr ar y pobi.

BREAD

Nothing beats a good basic bread; a homemade loaf can be a meal in itself. Making bread really isn't difficult and if you've never tried, give it a go. If you're quite competent in the dough department, but haven't made a loaf in a while, then it's time to get the mixing bowl out again!

For a basic loaf you really only need five ingredients:

water ★ strong white bread flour ★ yeast ★ salt ★ a drop of olive oil or butter

So, not a long list and it's certainly not expensive. Follow the simple steps listed in the Welsh pot bread recipe on page 48 and use the dough to make anything from a flat Mediterranean focaccia, topped with rosemary and sea salt, to bread rolls and plaits.

There really are no excuses, and once you've mastered the mixing and kneading, proving and baking, there really won't be anything to stop you becoming a master baker.

TEISEN DIFERION LEMWN

Mae lemwn yn flas mor lân a bywiol, mae'n deisen berffaith ar gyfer dechrau'r flwyddyn.

225g menyn, wedi'i feddalu
225g siwgwr mân
275g blawd codi
1 llwy de o bowdwr pobi
4 wy
Diferyn o laeth
Croen 2 lemwn (neu oren), wedi'i gratio'n fân
175g siwgwr
Sudd 2 lemwn

Cynheswch y ffwrn i 160°C / 325°F / Nwy 3

Leiniwch dun pobi teisen sgwâr neu dun torth draddodiadol â phapur gwrthsaim. Gwthiwch y papur i'r corneli'n gymen; bydd hyn yn gwneud i'r deisen orffenedig edrych yn daclus.

Hufennwch y menyn a'r siwgwr ynghyd. Ychwanegwch yr wyau fesul un.

Mewn powlen ar wahân, cymysgwch y blawd, y powdwr codi, yr halen a'r croen lemwn.

Cyfunwch y cynhwysion gwlyb â'r rhai sych fesul traean, gan gymysgu'n dda bob tro. Ychwanegwch y llaeth, ac yna trowch y cyfan nes ei fod wedi'i gymysgu'n dda.

Arllwyswch y cymysgedd i mewn i'r tun, gan wneud yn siŵr bod y cyfan yn wastad.

Pobwch yng nghanol y ffwrn am tua 35–40 munud neu hyd nes bod y deisen yn weddol solet yn y canol ac yn bownsio 'nôl o'i gwasgu'n ysgafn â'ch bys.

Ar ôl iddi goginio, gadewch i'r deisen oeri yn y tun am rai munudau, ac yna codwch hi allan o'r tun yn y papur gwrthsaim. Tynnwch y papur a rhowch y deisen ar resel wifrau wedi'i gosod dros hambwrdd, er mwyn dal diferion y topin.

I wneud y topin crensiog, cymysgwch y sudd lemwn a'r siwgwr i greu cymysgedd o ansawdd rhedegog. Taenwch y sudd dros y deisen tra mae hi'n dal i fod yn gynnes. Yna torrwch y deisen yn ddarnau a'i mwynhau.

LEMON DRIZZLE CAKE

Lemon is such a clean and life-giving taste, it's perfect as a zesty cake for the start of the year.

225g butter, softened
225g caster sugar
275g self-raising flour
1 tsp baking powder
4 eggs
A drop of milk
Finely grated rind of 2 lemons (or oranges)
175g granulated sugar
Juice of 2 lemons

Preheat the oven to 160°C / 325°F / Gas 3

Line a tray bake tin or traditional loaf tin with greaseproof paper. Push it neatly into the corners of the tin; this will make the cooked cake look neat.

Cream the butter and sugar together. Add the eggs one by one.

In a separate bowl, mix the flour, baking powder, salt, and lemon zest.

Add the dry ingredients to the wet ingredients in thirds, mixing well each time. Add the milk, then stir until it's completely mixed in.

Pour the mixture into a tin and level the top just a little.

Bake in the middle of the preheated oven for about 35–40 minutes or until the cake is firm in the middle and springs back when pressed lightly with a finger.

Once cooked, allow to cool in the tin for a few minutes, then lift it out of the tin still in the lining paper. Remove the paper and put the cake onto a wire rack placed over a tray, to catch drips of the topping.

To make the crunchy topping, simply mix the lemon juice and granulated sugar in a small bowl to give a runny consistency. Spoon this over the cake whilst it is still just warm, then cut the cake and enjoy.

* Gwnewch fersiwn myffins o'r rysáit yma. Coginiwch am tua 25–30 munud ac ychwanegwch lond lwy de o hadau pabi i'r cymysgedd i wneud teisennau bach brith pert.

* Make a muffin version, cook for about 25–30 minutes and add a tablespoon of poppy seeds to the mixture for pretty little speckled cakes.

CWTSH BACH I'R ENAID

⭐ Mae'n bosib ystyried yr adeg hon o'r flwyddyn fel amser 'rhamantus', gyda dyddiau Santes Dwynwen a San Ffolant i'r cariadon. Ond peidiwch â chael eich twyllo, mae hefyd yn adeg i fod yn ofalus gan y gall yr adeg yma deimlo'n llwm a diflas ac ymddangos fel pe bai am bara am byth. Gall misoedd cyntaf, anwadal y flwyddyn ein harwain i gredu'n obeithiol o ffôl bod y gwanwyn ar gyrraedd ac yna, ein gollwng yn ddisymwyth yn ôl i ganol trymder gaeaf.

Ar ôl plymio i ganol y deiet ym mis Ionawr er mwyn dadebru yn dilyn y gor-wneud ym mis Rhagfyr, mae'n amser i ni fod yn garedig, mwynhau cysur y tân, cymryd pwyll a thretio'n hunain i fwydydd llesol a chynhesol, ac wrth gwrs, i deisennau a phwdinau. Bydd carthenni a blancedi cynnes yn help yn sicr i gwtsho wrth danllwyth o dân, a bydd mwynhau diodydd cynnes a phrydau cartrefol gyda theulu a ffrindiau yn ffordd bleserus iawn o helpu'r gaeaf i droi'n wanwyn. Cyn bo hir, daw'r nosweithiau'n fwy golau wrth i'r ddaear barhau i droi ar ei hechel o gwmpas yr haul a daw ein gaeaf gogleddol i'w derfyn. Hyd nes bydd hynny'n digwydd, mwynhewch wres y tŷ a chynnyrch y bwrdd bwyd.

SOUL FOOD

⭐ This time of year could be seen as a 'romantic' time, what with Santes Dwynwen and Valentine's Day. But don't be fooled, it's also a time to be wary as it can often be bleak and uninteresting and feel like it's going to last forever. Very rarely does winter just leave us quietly and the first unsettled months of the year can often lead us into a hopeful, false sense of spring's arrival and then can just as easily plunge us straight back into the depths of winter.

Having plunged into the diet in January to recover from December's indulgences, now is the time to be kind, to enjoy the comfort of the fire, to ease up a little and treat ourselves to some soul food – richer, nourishing winter warmers, and cakes and puddings of course. Warm throws and blankets will certainly help us snuggle up by the fire, steaming hot drinks and cosy evening meals with family and friends also help the winter pass pleasurably into spring. Soon, the evenings will be lighter as the earth continues in its orbit around the sun, and our northern winter comes to an end. Until then, enjoy the warmth indoors and the contents of the table.

MORNAY CREGYN BYLCHOG A CHORGIMYCHIAID

Os byddwch am nodi achlysur arbennig rywbryd neu os byddwch chi am gael trît, paratowch gregyn blychog blasus yn eu cregyn deniadol.

8 cragen fylchog, wedi'u glanhau
8 corgimwch mawr
300ml llaeth cyflawn
4 shibwnsyn, wedi'u sleisio
30g menyn
½ llwy fwrdd o flawd corn
1½ llwy de o fwstard
3 llwy fwrdd o win gwyn
3 llwy fwrdd o hufen dwbl
Halen a phupur gwyn
30g caws Gruyère, wedi'i gratio'n fân
1 cwpanaid o friwsion bara ffres
Dil neu bersli wedi'i falu'n fân a bara crystiog i'w weini

Cynheswch y menyn mewn ffrimpan, sleisio'r cregyn blychog yn ddwy neu dair tafell denau, coginiwch nhw am tua 40 eiliad bob ochr a'u tynnu o'r ffrimpan. Coginiwch y corgimychiaid yn yr un ffrimpan am funud neu ddwy a'u tynnu oddi ar y gwres.

Rhowch ddarnau gwyn y shibwns mewn sosban a'u coginio am tua 10 eiliad. Mewn gwirionedd, dim ond gadael iddyn nhw gynhesu sydd ei angen. Yna ychwanegwch y llaeth a mudferwi'r cyfan.

Cymysgwch y gwin, yr hufen, y mwstard a'r caws Gruyère i mewn a'u mudferwi. Ychwanegwch halen a phpur gwyn yn ôl yr angen (mae'n iawn defnyddio pupur du, ond bydd yn ymddangos fel smotiau du yn y saws).

I dewhau'r saws, ychwanegwch lond llwy fwrdd o flawd corn wedi'i gymysgu ag ychydig o laeth. Trowch y cymysgedd dros wres canolig hyd nes i'r saws dewhau a llyfnhau. Tynnwch y sosban oddi ar y gwres.

SCALLOPS AND PRAWN MORNAY

For a special occasion or for a real treat, serve delicious scallops in their very attractive shells

8 scallops, cleaned
8 giant prawns
300ml whole milk
4 spring onions, sliced
30g butter
½ tbsp cornflour
1½ tsp mustard
3 tbsp white wine
3 tbsp double cream
Salt and white pepper
30g Gruyère cheese, finely grated
1 cupful of fresh breadcrumbs
Chopped dill or parsley and crusty bread, to serve

Heat the butter in a frying pan, slice each scallop into two or three thin slices and cook on each side for about 40 seconds. Remove them from the pan. Cook the prawns in the same frying pan for a minute or two and take them off the heat.

In a saucepan, add the white ends of the spring onions and cook for about 10 seconds, just to let them warm, then add the milk to the pan, and bring to a gentle simmer.

Stir in the wine, cream, mustard and the Gruyère cheese and bring to a gentle simmer. Season with salt and white pepper (black pepper is fine too, but you will see the dark spots in the sauce).

Thicken the sauce by adding a tablespoon of cornflour mixed with a little milk. Stir over a medium heat until the sauce is thick and smooth. Remove the pan from the heat.

* **Bydd un neu ddwy gragen y pen yn iawn fel pryd, ac mae un gragen yn ddelfrydol fel cwrs cyntaf.**

* **One to two shells per person is fine as a meal, and one shell is ideal as a starter.**

* Os nad oes gennych chi gregyn wrth law, rhowch y saws mornay mewn llestri ramecin bach ar gyfer prydau unigol neu defnyddiwch un llestr mawr a'i weini o'r ford. Ychwanegwch fwy o gorgimychiaid i'w wneud yn fwy moethus a rhoi briwsion bara cawsiog neu datws stwnsh hufennog ar ei ben.

* If you don't have the shells to hand, simply serve in small ramekins for individual portions, or use one large dish and serve at the table. Add a few prawns for more luxury and top with cheesy breadcrumbs or creamy mashed potato.

> Rhowch nifer cyfartal o'r cregyn bylchog a'r corgimychiaid i mewn yn y cregyn gweigion, glân a'u gorchuddio â'r saws mornay.

Cymysgwch y briwsion bara ag ychydig mwy o gaws wedi'i gratio ac ychwanegu ychydig o halen a phupur. Taenwch y briwsion bara dros y cregyn bylchog neu fe allwch eu gorchuddio â thatws stwnsh. Pobwch mewn ffwrn dwym am 10 munud hyd nes eu bod yn lliw euraid ac yn ffrwtian.

Ysgeintiwch berlysiau, fel dil neu bersli wedi'u torri'n fân, dros y cyfan cyn ei weini.

Mae'r rysáit hwn mor hawdd gan fy mod i'n defnyddio blawd corn i dewhau'r saws – ffordd ddi-feth o wneud y béchamel, sef y saws gwyn, gaiff ei wneud fel arfer o roux gwyn gan ddefnyddio menyn a blawd ac sy'n medru achosi problemau.

> Place equal amounts of the scallops and the cooked prawns into the clean scallop shells and spoon the mornay sauce evenly into the shells to cover them.

Mix the breadcrumbs with a little more grated cheese and season with salt and pepper. Sprinkle the breadcrumbs over the scallop shells or cover with creamed mashed potato. Bake in the hot oven for 10 minutes until golden brown and bubbling.

Sprinkle over some finely chopped herbs such as dill or parsley before serving.

This recipe is so easy as I use cornflour to thicken the sauce – a foolproof way to make the béchamel, the white sauce, which is usually made from a white roux of butter and flour and can often cause a few problems.

BROWNIS SIOCLED GORAU'R BYD

Alla i ddim pwysleisio digon pa mor wych yw'r brownis yma – ar ôl i fi wneud cyflenwad o'r rhain yn ein tŷ ni, fi yw'r fam orau yn y byd, neu dyna mae 'mhlant yn ei ddweud.

185g siocled plaen, wedi'i dorri
185g menyn heb halen
3 wy
275g siwgwr
85g blawd plaen
40g powdwr coco
50g siocled gwyn, wedi'i dorri'n fân – neu ffrwythau sych, malws melys, ceirios – dewiswch chi

Cynheswch y ffwrn i 180°C / 350°F / Nwy 4

Leiniwch dun sgwâr o faint 20cm, 5cm o ddyfnder.

Toddwch y siocled gyda'r menyn a'i oeri.

Chwisgiwch yr wyau a'r siwgwr ynghyd mewn powlen arall. Arllwyswch y siocled wedi'i oeri mewn i'r cymysgedd wyau a phlygu'r cyfan ynghyd.

Hidlwch y blawd a'r powdwr coco i mewn i'r cymysgedd siocled a phlygwch y cyfan ynghyd. Cyn arllwys y cymysgedd i'r tun parod, ychwanegwch y darnau siocled gwyn, y ffrwythau sych, y malws melys, y ceirios neu beth bynnag oedd eich dewis chi, a'u cymysgu. Pobwch am 25 munud.

Mae'r brownis yn barod pan mae'r cymysgedd yn edrych yn sgleiniog ac yn dechrau crebachu oddi wrth ymylon y tun ychydig.

Torrwch yn chwarteri, ac yna torrwch bob chwarter yn bedwar sgwâr. Torrwch bob sgwâr yn ei hanner i greu dau driongl. Mae'r brownis yma mor foethus, mwynhewch, ond pwyll pia hi.

 Adeg y Nadolig mae'r Brownis Gorau yn y Byd yma'n edrych yn hyfryd gyda cheirios glacé coch, neu fe allwch ychwanegu malws melys bach, gwnewch y rysáit hwn yn eiddo i chi drwy arbrofi â chynhwysion ychwanegol.

BEST-EVER CHOCOLATE BROWNIES

I can't emphasise enough how fantastic these brownies are – once I've made a batch of these beauties in our house, I become the best mother in the world, or so my children tell me.

185g plain chocolate, chopped
185g unsalted butter
3 eggs
275g sugar
85g plain flour
40g cocoa powder
50g white chocolate, chopped – or dried fruit, marshmallows, cherries – you choose

Preheat the oven to 180°C / 350°F / Gas 4

Line a 20cm square, 5cm deep, tin.

Melt the chocolate with the butter and cool.

Whisk the eggs and the sugar together in another bowl.

Pour the cooled chocolate into the egg mixture and fold together.

Sift the flour and the cocoa powder into the chocolate mixture and fold. Before pouring the mixture into the prepared tin, add the white chocolate chips, the dried fruit, the marshmallows, the cherries or whatever ingredients you chose, and mix. Bake for 25 minutes.

The brownies are ready when the top is shiny and they pull away from the sides of the tin slightly.

Cut into quarters, then cut each quarter into four squares. Cut each square in half to make two triangles. These brownies are rich, so enjoy them, but don't overdo it.

 At Christmas time, these Best-ever Brownies look lovely with red glacé cherries, and you can even add some mini marshmallows. Make the recipe yours by experimenting with your additional ingredients.

FFONDANTS SIOCLED

Dyma bwdin hawdd i'w baratoi ond un sy'n cael ymateb brwd bob tro.

175g menyn
175g siocled tywyll (70%)
85g blawd codi
200g siwgwr mân euraid
50ml coffi
4 wy mawr

Cynheswch y ffwrn i 200°C / 400°F / Nwy 6

Paratowch 6 llestr pwdin yn dda gan eu brwsio â menyn, eu hoeri yn yr oergell ac ychwanegu haen arall o fenyn.

Toddwch y menyn a'r siocled mewn powlen dros sosban wedi'i llenwi hyd at yr hanner gyda dŵr sy'n mudferwi.

Curwch y siwgwr a'r wyau gyda'i gilydd mewn powlen ar wahân.

Plygwch y cymysgedd siocled a'r cymysgedd wyau ynghyd, ychwanegwch y coffi a'r blawd a'u plygu i mewn.

Rhannwch y cymysgedd rhwng y 6 llestr pwdin. Gosodwch ar hambwrdd coginio a'u pobi am 12 munud union. Dylai crwstyn ffurfio ar ben y ffondant ond bydd y canol yn feddal fel jeli.

Trowch y ffondants allan ar blatiau unigol a'u gweini gyda hufen neu hufen iâ.

Mae modd oeri'r cymysgedd neu ei rewi. Coginiwch am 15 munud os yw wedi'i rewi.

CHOCOLATE FONDANTS

This is an easy pudding to prepare but it's one that gets an enthusiastic response every time.

175g butter
175g dark chocolate (70%)
85g self-raising flour
200g golden caster sugar
50ml coffee
4 large eggs

Preheat oven to 200°C / 400°F / Gas 6

Prepare 6 pudding dishes well by brushing them with butter, cooling them in the fridge and adding another layer of butter.

Melt the butter and chocolate in a bowl over a saucepan half full of simmering water.

Beat the sugar and eggs together in a separate bowl.

Fold the chocolate mixture and egg mixture together, add the coffee and the flour and fold.

Divide the mixture between 6 pudding dishes, place on a tray and bake for exactly 12 minutes. A crust should have formed but the centre will be wobbly, like a jelly.

Turn out the fondants onto individual serving plates and serve with cream or ice cream.

This mixture can be chilled or frozen, until needed. Cook for 15 minutes from frozen.

SYNIAD SYDYN
QUICK IDEA

Mefus siocled

Mefus
Siocled tywyll
Siocled llaeth
Siocled gwyn
Sbrincls siâp calon

Golchwch y mefus yn lân a'u sychu.

Gosodwch y siocled gwyn, siocled tywyll a'r siocled llaeth mewn powlenni ar wahân. Toddwch y siocled i gyd drwy osod y powlenni dros sosbanaid o ddŵr yn mudferwi. Trowch nes bydd y siocled wedi toddi, ond gwnewch yn siŵr nad oes unrhyw ddŵr yn disgyn i'r cymysgedd neu fe fydd yn crisialu'n syth.

Dipiwch y mefus yn y siocled, gan ddefnyddio'r tri math gwahanol i greu mefus siocled o liwiau gwahanol, yna gosodwch nhw ar ddarn o silicon neu bapur gwrthsaim.

Wedi iddyn nhw oeri, diferwch siocled o liw gwahanol drostynt.

Ychwanegwch sbrincls at rai o'r mefus a'u gosod ar blât ar ben bisgeden frau ag ychydig o hufen dwbl wedi'i chwipio arni.

Chocolate Strawberries

Strawberries
Dark chocolate
Milk chocolate
White chocolate
Heart sprinkles

Wash the strawberries clean, and dry.

Place the white chocolate, the dark and the milk chocolate into separate bowls. Melt the chocolate by placing the bowls over a pan of simmering water. Stir until melted, but ensure that no water falls into the chocolate or it will crystallise instantly.

Dip the strawberries into the chocolate, using the three types to create different coloured chocolate strawberries, then place on a sheet of silicone or greaseproof paper.

Once cooled, drizzle over a different coloured chocolate.

Add sprinkles to some of the strawberries and arrange on a plate, or place on a home-made shortbread biscuit with a dollop of whipped double cream on it.

Yr union beth ar gyfer ychydig o ramant!
Does dim swm i'r cynhwysion fan hyn, defnyddiwch
faint bynnag sydd wrth fodd eich calon chi.

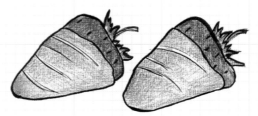

Just the thing for a little romance!
There are no amounts to the ingredients here,
use as much as your heart desires.

CREMPOG

Mae Chwefror yn dilyn Ionawr bob blwyddyn, a chyn i chi sylweddoli mae'n ddydd Mawrth Ynyd, neu ddydd Mawrth Crempog, ac ry'n ni oddeutu hanner ffordd drwy'r mis. Os nad ydych chi wedi gwneud crempogau cartref eto, gadewch i fi ddangos i chi sut mae gwneud.

Cyfunwch gwpanaid o flawd plaen â chwpanaid o laeth ac wy. Chwisgiwch yn dda ac arllwys y cymysgedd i ffrimpan ag olew neu fenyn poeth ynddi. Ffriwch ar y ddwy ochr, fflipiwch nhw os beiddiwch chi, a mwynhewch nhw gyda'ch hoff ychwanegiadau. Dyna ni, hawdd.

Rwy'n dwlu ar grempog, am eu bod nhw'n gwneud prydau mor amrywiol, yn ogystal â'r ffaith eu bod nhw jyst yn grempogau! Bwytewch nhw gyda siwgwr a lemwn, Nutella, neu lapiwch un o gwmpas banana. Plygwch nhw fel crempogau Ffrainc, neu rholiwch nhw yn y dull Cymreig. Am swper syml ond blasus, gwnewch nhw gyda chig moch, madarch wedi'u ffrio mewn ychydig o arlleg a hufen, caws wedi'i gratio a thomato, neu hyd yn oed samwn mwg a chaws hufennog â pherlysiau. Dylai crempog fod yn gyfaill i'r myfyriwr – mae'n rhad, yn flasus ac yn codi gwên.

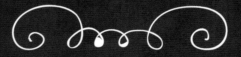

PANCAKES

February follows January every year, and before you know it, it's Shrove Tuesday or Pancake Tuesday, and we're around half way through the month. If you've yet to make some home-made pancakes – let me show you how.

Simply combine a cup of plain flour with a cup of milk and an egg. Whisk well and pour into a hot oiled or buttered pan. Fry on both sides, flip them if you dare, and enjoy with your favourite topping. That's it, easy.

I love pancakes for their versatility as well as for just being pancakes! Eat them with sugar, lemon, Nutella, or wrap a banana in one. Fold them the French way or roll them the Welsh way. For a simple but filling and delicious supper, serve them with bacon, mushrooms fried with a little garlic and cream, grated cheese and tomato, or even smoked salmon and a soft herby cream cheese. Pancakes should be a student's best friend – cheap, delicious and very cheerful.

Cam tua'r gwanwyn

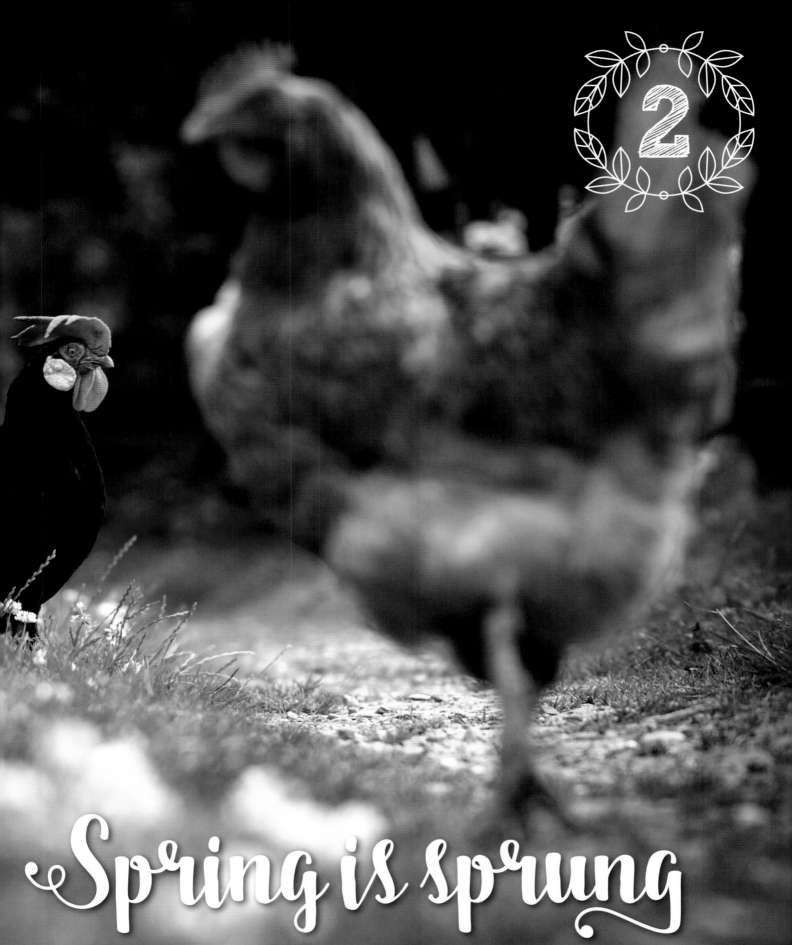

Spring is sprung

Daw gwanwyn a diwedd ein cyfnod o swatio yn y tŷ.

Yn sydyn, mae drysau'r gegin ar agor led y pen, ffenestri'n gadael awel wanwynol i glirio aer y gaeaf o'r tŷ. Gartref, ry'n ni'n plannu potiau'r gwanwyn ac yn mwynhau arogleuon a lliwiau eginflodau'r gwanwyn. P'un a ydych yn eu caru neu eu casáu, mae arogl cryf yr hiasinth yn llenwi'r awyr ac yn sydyn mae'n ymddangos fel petai popeth yn y tir ar ddeffro.

Ac yn sydyn mae digonedd o waith i'w wneud: torri'r lawnt, chwynnu, strimio, tocio a thorri 'nôl, ac o dipyn i beth mae'r ardd yn gorlifo ag egni. Caiff llonyddwch y gwanwyn a thrydar yr adar ei foddi gan sŵn aflafar y peiriannau … ond mae'n wych cael bod yn yr awyr agored. Ymlaen at yr haf, ond peidiwch ag anghofio mwynhau'r gwanwyn yn ei ogoniant yn y cyfamser.

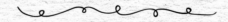

Spring is the end of our long hibernation.

Suddenly, kitchen doors are left open, windows allow the spring breeze to flush out the winter air. At home, we plant up the spring pots and enjoy the scent and colour of the spring bulbs. Love them or loathe them, the pungent scent of the hyacinth fills the air and it seems that suddenly everything wakes up.

Suddenly, there's an abundance of jobs to be done: mowing lawns, weeding, strimming, deadheading and cutting back, and gradually the garden is brimming with energy. The tranquil spring and chattering of birds is drowned out by the hum of machines … but it's still a delight to be outside. Bring on the summer, but don't forget to enjoy the glories of spring in the meantime.

Cennin Pedr

Os byddwch chi am gael arddangosfa brydferth o gennin Pedr ar eich bwrdd a chyflenwad yn barod i bawb eu gwisgo ar 1 Mawrth, peidiwch ag anghofio'u prynu nhw rai dyddiau cyn hynny, gan roi amser iddyn nhw agor.

Daffodils

If you want a pretty display of daffodils on the table and a supply ready for everyone to wear on 1 March, don't forget to buy them a few days before, giving them time to open.

DYDD GŴYL DEWI

⭐ Rwy'n dwlu ar fis Mawrth ac yn caru Dydd Gŵyl Dewi yn enwedig. O'r ieuengaf hyd yr hynaf, mae pawb yn mwynhau cymryd rhan yn y dathliad cenedlaethol hwn. Ry'n ni oll yn hynod frwd i wisgo cenhinen Bedr neu ddaffodil ar ein dillad a gorymdeithio yng ngorymdaith Gŵyl Ddewi'r dref. Bydd plant ym mhob cwr o Gymru'n gwisgo'u gwisg draddodiadol ac yn canu neu'n gorymdeithio; weithiau byddan nhw'n hawlio'r sylw ar lwyfan eisteddfod neu gyngerdd ysgol.

Yr adeg yma o'r flwyddyn bydd ein blodyn cenedlaethol yn gweddnewid y cloddiau gwlyb a llwm yn erddi bychain o wanwyn, a bydd lliaws o gennin Pedr balch yn ein cyfarch wrth i ni fynd ar ein taith a chodi'n calonnau. Mae'r tywydd cynhesach yma'n rhoi hwb i'r genedl gyfan ac yn addo bod dyddiau gwell i ddod, maes o law.

Mae cerdded drwy'r ardd neu drwy'r dref ar Ddydd Gŵyl Dewi yn rhoi teimlad braf o ddechrau newydd i fi bob tro. Mae'n deimlad da. Ac fel Dewi Sant ei hun, rwy'n hollol barod i fynd ati i wneud y pethau bychain mewn bywyd.

ST DAVID'S DAY

⭐ I love March and I love St David's Day especially. From the youngest to the oldest, everyone gets involved in this national celebration and we're all more than willing to pin a daffodil to our lapels and march in the town St David's Day Parade. Children all over the country dress up in traditional costume and do a bit of singing and parading; sometimes they're centre stage in eisteddfodau or concerts at school.

At this time of year our national flower converts our soaked and faintly threadbare hedgerows into spring gardens, swathes of bobbing daffodils greet us and lift our spirits as we go on our way. The arrival of a glimpse of warmer weather gives the whole nation more than a glimmer of hope that the days will surely become warmer.

Walking through the garden or through the town on St David's Day always gives me a sense of a new beginning, and I get a spring in my step. It's a very happy feeling. And like St David himself, I'm ready to attend to the small things in life.

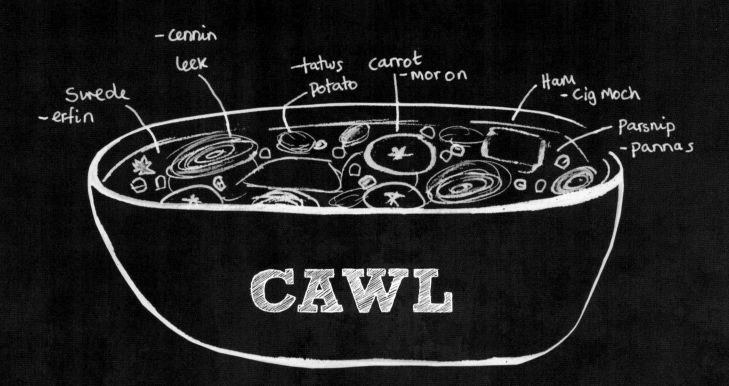

Swede
- erfin

- cennin
leek

- tatws
Potato

carrot
- mor on

Ham
- cig moch

Parsnip
- pannas

CAWL

Mae pawb yn gwneud cawl mewn ffordd ychydig yn wahanol i'w gilydd.

Ydych chi'n gwneud eich un chi gyda chig oen, cig eidion neu gyda ham?
Arferai fy mam-gu ferwi brisged a choes cig eidion i gael blas cyfoethog; byddai'n eu
stiwio dros nos ar y Rayburn cyn defnyddio'r stoc i ferwi'r llysiau y diwrnod canlynol.
Roedd Mam-gu'n dweud fod cawl yn well ar yr ail ddiwrnod, ond yr unig ffordd o
wybod hynny fyddai pe bai gennych chi gawl dros ben a doedd hynny ddim yn
digwydd yn aml.

Ond y newyddion da yw nad oes raid paratoi cawl ddiwrnod o flaen llaw; mae'n
bosib ei wneud a'i fwyta o fewn yr awr.

Everyone makes cawl slightly differently.

Do you have yours with lamb, beef or ham? Mam-gu used to boil some brisket
and shin of beef for a full flavour. She'd stew them overnight on the Rayburn before
using the stock to boil up the vegetables the following day. She'd always say that
cawl was better on the second day, but you'll only find out if you manage to have
some left and that didn't happen very often.

But, good news, cawl doesn't have to be prepared in advance – it is possible to make
and eat it within the hour.

CAWL CYFLYM

O ran ryseitiau Cymreig traddodiadol, does dim yn fwy Cymreig na chawl.

Dyma fersiwn cyflym y gellir ei wneud mewn awr a bydd yn barod i'w fwyta gan blant llwglyd ar ôl iddyn nhw dod adre o'r ysgol.

> Pecyn o gig moch di-fwg neu ddarn o ham wedi'i ferwi
> 1 winwnsyn
> 3 cenhinen
> Unrhyw gyfuniad o wreiddlysiau, e.e. tatws, moron, rwdins, pannas
> 1 ciwb stoc llysieuol
> Llond dwrn o bersli

Torrwch y winwnsyn a'r cennin yn ddarnau. Rhowch nhw i goginio mewn sosban fawr ag ychydig o olew a gadael iddyn nhw chwysu. Torrwch y llysiau'n ddarnau a'u taflu i mewn i'r sosban. Malwch giwb stoc mewn litr o ddŵr berw, ei gymysgu a'i arllwys dros y llysiau a gadael iddo fudferwi.

Torrwch y cig moch neu'r ham wedi'i ferwi yn ddarnau a'i ychwanegu i'r sosban. Gadewch i'r cymysgedd cyfan fudferwi ar wres canolig fel bod yr holl flasau'n cymysgu'n dda.

Peidiwch ag ychwanegu unrhyw halen yn ystod y coginio gan bod y cig moch yn ddigon hallt. Fe allwch ychwanegu halen wrth y bwrdd, os dymunwch. Os ydych chi'n dewis berwi ham i wneud cawl tebyg, rwy'n awgrymu eich bod yn berwi'r ham ac yn tynnu'r cig allan o'r sosban. Rhowch hanner y stoc mewn jwg ar wahân ac ychwanegu mwy o ddŵr ato a'i ddefnyddio i orchuddio'r llysiau i'w coginio. Byddai defnyddio'r stoc cyfan yn creu cawl hallt iawn. Cadwch weddill y stoc i'w ddefnyddio rhywbryd eto.

Am gawl gwahanol wedi'i wneud o gynhwysion y cwpwrdd bwyd a'r rhewgell, rhowch gynnig ar ddefnyddio tatws a moron, pys wedi'u rhewi a thun o India corn.

QUICK CAWL

As far as traditional Welsh recipes go, it doesn't get more Welsh than cawl.

This is a quick version that can be made in under an hour and is ready to eat by ravenous children when they come home from school.

> A pack of unsmoked bacon or a small joint of boiled ham
> 1 onion
> 3 leeks
> Any combination of root vegetables, e.g. potatoes, carrots, swedes, parsnips
> 1 vegetable stock cube
> A handful of parsley

Chop the onion and leeks. In a large pan, sweat them in some oil on a medium heat. Chop the root vegetables and throw into the pot. Crumble a stock cube into a litre of boiled water, stir and pour stock over the vegetables, allow to simmer.

Cut the bacon or boiled ham into pieces and add to the pan. Let the whole mixture simmer on a medium heat so that all the flavours mix well, enriching the cawl.

Remember not to add salt during the cooking as the bacon adds sufficient salt, and you can always season at the table if needed. If you choose to boil a small ham to make a similar cawl, I suggest that you boil the ham, and remove the meat from the pan. Pour half the stock into a separate jug to use for the cawl, add more water to it and use to cover the veg and cook. Using the whole stock can result in a very salty cawl. Reserve the remaining stock for another time.

For a store cupboard and freezer cawl alternative, try using potatoes and carrots, frozen peas and a tin of sweetcorn.

Peidiwch ag anghofio'r rholiau bara crystiog a chaws Cheddar Cymreig da.

Don't forget the crusty bread rolls
and a good Welsh Cheddar.

LL

BARA POT CYMREIG

Mae'r bara yma mor hawdd i'w wneud, dyma yw sail pob bara.

600g blawd bara cryf
1 ½ llwy de o halen
1 ½ llwy de o furum
1 llwy fwrdd o olew olewydd neu fenyn
350ml dŵr neu laeth llugoer

Cymysgwch y blawd, yr halen a'r burum mewn powlen.

Ychwanegwch yr olew a'r dŵr neu'r llaeth a'u cymysgu i greu toes. Tylinwch y toes ar arwyneb â blawd arno am tua 5–6 munud.

Gosodwch y toes mewn powlen, a'i orchuddio â haenen lynu neu liain llestri glân neu hyd yn oed â chap cawod glân! Rhowch y toes yn rhywle cynnes am tua 45 munud i godi, hyd nes y bydd wedi dyblu mewn maint.

Ar ôl awr, trowch y toes allan, a'i dylino'n ysgafn eto ar arwynebedd â blawd arno.

Rhannwch y toes yn ddarnau bach o feintiau tebyg a gosodwch nhw mewn potiau terracotta glân, neu mewn potiau silicon glân. Os byddwch chi am gael crwstyn euraid, brwsiwch ag ychydig o laeth ac wy wedi'u cymysgu a thaenu hadau neu geirch ar eu pennau.

Cynheswch y ffwrn i 180°C / 350°F / Nwy 4 a phobwch y potiau am tua 20–30 munud (yn dibynnu ar eu maint) hyd nes eu bod yn frown euraid. Gwnewch yn siŵr bod y gwaelod yn swnio'n wag wrth i chi roi cnoc i'r dorth a gadewch iddyn nhw oeri cyn bwrw iddi a bwyta.

V

WELSH POT BREAD

This bread is so easy to make – it's the basis of all breads.

600g strong bread flour
1 ½ tsp salt
1 ½ tsp yeast
1 tbsp olive oil or butter
350ml tepid water or milk

Mix the flour, salt and yeast in a bowl.

Add the oil and water, and mix to form a dough. Knead the dough on a floured table for about 5–6 minutes.

Place the kneaded dough into a bowl, cover with cling film or clean tea towel or even a clean shower cap! Put somewhere warm to rise for 45 minutes, until it has doubled in size.

After about an hour, tip the dough out, and lightly knead it again on a floured table.

Divide the dough into small pieces of equal size and place into well-lined clean terracotta pots, or silicone pots. For a golden crust, brush with a little milk mixed with egg, and top with seeds or oats.

Preheat the oven to 180°C / 350°F / Gas 4 and bake for about 20–30 minutes (depending on the size) until golden brown. Check that the bottom of the loaf sounds slightly hollow when tapped, and allow to cool before tucking in.

* **Defnyddiwch botiau glân a newydd. Peidiwch ag ailgylchu rhai o'r tŷ gwydr!**

* **Use new, clean pots. Don't recycle them from the greenhouse!**

PASTAI CYW IÂR A CHENNIN – TAIR FFORDD

Pastai cyw iâr yw un o fy hoff brydau i: mae'n faethlon ac yn flasus. Mae rhoi cennin yn gwmni iddo yn gwneud pastai berffaith.

1 cyw iâr wedi'i rhostio neu ddarnau
o gyw iâr dros ben
2 neu 3 cenhinen wedi'u torri
¾ litr o stoc cyw iâr
1 llwy fwrdd o fenyn ac olew
200ml llaeth neu hufen
Halen a phupur
1 llwy fwrdd o flawd corn

I wneud clawr y bastai, defnyddiwch
un o'r canlynol:
4 taten fawr ac 1 llwy fwrdd o semolina
Briwsion bara
Pecyn o does crwst pwff – wedi'i rolio

Cynheswch y ffwrn i 180°C / 350°F / Nwy 4

I wneud llenwad y bastai:

Rhowch y cennin wedi'u torri mewn ffrimpan fawr. Ychwanegwch ychydig o olew llysiau a thamaid o fenyn, a ffriwch ar dymheredd cymhedrol am tua 5 munud hyd nes eu bod wedi meddalu.

Ychwanegwch y darnau cyw iâr i'r ffrimpan gan sicrhau nad oes unrhyw esgyrn ar ôl gyda'r cig.

Ychwanegwch ¾ litr o stoc cyw iâr ac ychydig o halen a phupur i flasu.

Gadewch i'r cyfan fudferwi ac yna ychwanegwch tua 200ml o laeth neu hufen dwbl i greu saws hufennog. Gallwch dewhau'r saws â blawd corn os oes angen (gweler isod).

Dewisol: ychwanegwch 100ml o win gwyn i'r stoc cyw iâr.

I dewhau'r saws, rhowch lond llwy fwrdd o flawd corn mewn cwpan. Llenwch hyd at yr hanner â dŵr oer a chymysgwch yn dda. Gallwch ychwanegu hyn at unrhyw gymysgedd cawl neu sawsiau er mwyn eu tewhau.

CHICKEN AND LEEK PIE – THREE WAYS

Chicken pie is one of my favourite meals. It's nourishing and has a satisfying taste, and combining it with leeks make a perfect pie.

1 roast chicken or leftover chicken
2 or 3 leeks, chopped
¾ litre chicken stock
1 tbsp butter and oil
200ml milk or cream
Salt and pepper
1 tbsp cornflour

To top the pie, use on of the following:
4 large potatoes and 1 tbsp semolina
Breadcrumbs
Pack of puff pastry – rolled

Preheat the oven to 180°C / 350°F / Gas 4

To make the pie filling:

Place the chopped leeks into a large frying pan, add a little vegetable oil and a knob of butter and gently fry for about 5 minutes until softened.

Add the chicken pieces, ensuring that no bone remains with the meat.

Add about ¾ litre of chicken stock, and season with salt and pepper.

Allow to simmer and then, finally, add about 200ml of milk or double cream for a rich, creamy sauce. Thicken using cornflour if needed (see below).

Optional: add 100ml of white wine to the chicken stock.

To thicken using cornflour: place a tablespoon of cornflour into a cup, fill half full with cold water and mix well. You can add this mixture to any soup or sauce, to thicken it.

> Trowch yn gyson i sicrhau bod y saws yn tewhau ac nad oes yna unrhyw lympiau.

I wneud y bastai, arllwyswch y llenwad i un llestr mawr i'w roi yn y ffwrn, neu ddefnyddio sawl llestr llai.

Dewiswch un o'r isod fel topin:

• Pliciwch a sleisio'r tatws, gosodwch y darnau tatws ar ben y llenwad a'u hysgeintio â menyn rhewedig wedi'i gratio a semolina.

• Gorchuddiwch â brwision bara wedi'u cymysgu â phupur a halen a chaws wedi'i gratio.

• I wneud pastai draddodiadol, gorchuddiwch â haen o does crwst pwff.

Coginiwch am tua hanner awr hyd nes bod y topin wedi'i goginio ac o liw euraid.

> Stir continuously to ensure that the sauce thickens and that no lumps appear.

To make the pie, pour the pie filling into one large ovenproof dish or several small dishes.

Choose one of the toppings below:

• Peel and slice the potatoes, top the filling with several slices of potato and sprinkle with a little grated frozen butter and semolina.

• Cover with seasoned breadcrumbs and grated cheese.

• Cover with a layer of puff pastry for a traditional pie.

Cook for about half an hour until the topping is cooked and golden.

PICE AR Y MAEN OREN A LLUGAERON

Mae'r rysáit hon yn fersiwn ychydig bach yn wahanol i'r rysáit Cymreig draddodiadol – mae'n rhoi arlliw'r unfed ganrif ar hugain iddi.

225g blawd codi
Pinsiaid o halen
110g menyn
80g siwgwr
50g ffrwythau sych: llugaeron, cyrens neu rhowch gynnig ar sinsir
1 wy
Diferyn o laeth neu groen a sudd 1 oren
Menyn a siwgwr mân i weini

Hidlwch y blawd a rhwbio'r menyn a'r blawd i greu cymysgedd briwsionllyd.

Cymysgwch y siwgwr a'r ffrwythau sych neu'r sinsir. Chwisgiwch yr wy a'i ychwanegu at y cymysgedd. Ychwanegwch groen yr oren a'r sudd. Cymysgwch yn does cadarn gan ddefnyddio ychydig o laeth os oes angen.

Rholiwch allan i drwch o 5mm ar arwyneb sydd â blawd arno a thorri'r toes yn gylchoedd.

Gosodwch y pice ar radell boeth neu ffrimpan, trowch nhw unwaith a'u coginio hyd nes eu bod nhw o liw euraid.

* **Ychwanegwch ychydig o fenyn, ysgeintiwch â siwgwr mân a'u bwyta'n gynnes.**

CRANBERRY AND ORANGE WELSH CAKES

This recipe is a lovely twist on the traditional Welsh recipe – a little bit twenty-first century.

225g self-raising flour
A pinch of salt
110g butter
80g sugar
50g dried fruit: cranberries, currants, or try ginger
1 egg
A drop of milk or the zest and juice of 1 orange
Butter and caster sugar to serve

Sift the flour and rub in the butter to make crumbs.

Stir in the sugar and the fruit or ginger. Whisk the egg and add to the mixture. Add the orange zest and juice. Mix to a firm dough, using a little milk if needed.

Roll out to 5mm thickness on a floured surface and cut into circles.

Place Welsh cakes onto a hot griddle or frying pan, turn once and cook until golden.

* **Add a little butter, sprinkle with caster sugar and serve warm.**

Beth am rai syniadau o dramor ar gyfer brecwast? Dyma ambell un i chi.

Galettes a crêpes â chaws Cymreig

Rydym ni wedi mwynhau gwyliau draw yn Llydaw sawl gwaith fel teulu ac wedi cael blas ar y diwylliant, y tywydd a'r bwyd ac rwy'n argyhoeddedig nad ydym ni Gymry'n gwneud digon o'r grempogen ddi-nod.

Gelwir crempogau sy'n cael eu gwneud gan ddefnyddio 'blé noir' sef blawd du, o'r enw blawd gwenith yr hydd, yn galettes; mae'n grempogen sawrus ddiglwten flasus iawn. Gan fod blawd gwenith yr hydd yn hollol ddiglwten, ychwanegir ychydig o flawd plaen yn aml i helpu i gadw'r cytew at ei gilydd, er na fuasech am ddefnyddio blawd plaen os ydych chi am gadw pethau'n ddiglwten.

Er gwaetha'i enw, nid gwenith yw gwenith yr hydd, ond mae'n perthyn i deulu'r sorel, y clymog a rhiwbob. Dim ond dŵr, gwenith yr hydd diglwten a halen a ddefnyddir wrth wneud y cytew hwn yn draddodiadol, ond mae ychwanegu wy a blawd gwenith plaen yn ffordd o wneud y cytew yn llai tebygol o dorri ac yn haws ei daenu.

Rwy'n defnyddio mesuriadau mewn cwpanau yma er mwyn dangos nad oes angen offer pwyso arnoch hyd yn oed. Sdim ots beth yw maint y cwpan, ond cofiwch ddefnyddio cwpan o'r un maint yn ystod y broses.

> 2 lwy fwrdd o fenyn, wedi toddi
> 2½ cwpanaid o laeth
> ½ llwy de o halen
> 1 cwpanaid o flawd gwenith yr hydd
> ½ cwpanaid o flawd plaen – dewisol
> 2 wy buarth bach
> 2 lwy fwrdd o olew llysiau
> Dŵr – cymaint ag sydd ei angen
> Ar gyfer y llenwad: defnyddiwch ddarnau o ham, caws wedi'i gratio, madarch wedi'u sleisio ac wy – dewiswch chi.

Toddwch y menyn mewn sosban fach. Ychwanegwch y llaeth a'r halen, cymysgwch yn dda a diffodd y gwres.

Rhowch y ddau fath o flawd mewn powlen gymysgu. Gwnewch dwll yn y canol, arllwys yr olew llysiau iddo ac ychwanegu'r wyau. Cymysgwch yr wyau a'r olew gyda chwisg, gan dynnu'r blawd i mewn yn raddol o'r ochrau hyd nes bod y cymysgedd yn tewhau.

Ychwanegwch y cymysgedd fesul tipyn hyd nes bod y cyfan wedi'i ddefnyddio a'i gymysgu a bod y cytew yn llyfn. Yna, chwisgiwch ychydig o ddŵr iddo hyd nes bod y cytew yn edrych fel hufen trwchus.

Arllwyswch y cytew i jwg a'i roi yn yr oergell am ddwyawr o leia. Yn ystod yr amser hwn, mae'r cytew yn 'ymlacio' a'r blawd yn amsguno'r hylif yn llwyr. Gellid gwneud cytew crempog hyd at ddiwrnod ymlaen llaw a'i roi yn yr oergell.

I goginio, cynheswch ffrimpan 15–18cm o faint ac ychwanegu ychydig o olew. Pan fydd y ffrimpan yn boeth, arllwyswch ddigon o gytew i orchuddio'r gwaelod. Gadewch i'r cytew goginio am 1–2 munud ar un ochr, trowch y galette drosodd a'i choginio hyd nes bydd brychni euraid drosti.

Rhowch ar blât a'i chadw'n gynnes tra byddwch chi'n gwneud gweddill y galettes. Gallwch eu pentyrru ar ben ei gilydd a'u defnyddio yn nes ymlaen, ond maen nhw'n well o'u bwyta'n ffres o'r ffrimpan.

Ar gyfer y llenwad, rhowch eich galette yn ôl yn y ffrimpan, taenwch eich dewis o lenwad i ganol y galette a phlygu'r ymylon i mewn tua'r canol fel amlen fel ei fod yn cynhesu ac yn coginio'r llenwad ryw ychydig. Os ydych chi'n defnyddio wy, wedi i chi roi'ch llenwad yn y canol, torrwch wy heb ei goginio i ganol y galette, plygwch yr ochrau i mewn a gadewch i'r wy goginio yn y canol. Rhowch ar blât a'i gweini.

Galettes and crêpes with Welsh cheese

Having enjoyed several holidays under Breton skies as a family and savoured the culture, climate and cuisine out there, I'm convinced that we, the Welsh, don't make enough of a fuss of the humble pancake.

Pancakes made with 'blé noir' a black flour we know as buckwheat flour, become galettes, very tasty gluten-free savoury pancakes. As the buckwheat flour is totally gluten-free, a little plain flour is often added to help the batter hold together, though obviously you'd want to omit this if you wanted to keep things gluten free.

Despite the name, buckwheat is not related to wheat, as it is not a grass. Instead, buckwheat is related to sorrel, knotweed and rhubarb. A traditional buckwheat batter is made with only water, gluten-free buckwheat flour and salt, but the addition of an egg and plain wheat flour makes the batter less breakable and easier to spread.

I'm using measuring cups for the amounts here, just to show that you don't need weighing scales to make this recipe. It doesn't matter about the size of the cup, just use the same size cup in the process.

> 2 tbsp butter, melted
> 2½ cups milk
> ½ tsp salt
> 1 cup buckwheat flour
> ½ cup plain flour – optional
> 2 small free-range eggs
> 2 tbsp vegetable oil
> Water – as much as needed
> For the filling: use pieces of ham, grated cheese, sliced mushrooms and an egg – the choice is yours.

Melt the butter in a small pan. Add the milk and salt, stir well and turn off the heat.

Put both flours into a mixing bowl, make a well in the centre and pour in the vegetable oil and add the eggs. Mix the eggs and oil with a whisk, gradually bringing in flour from the sides until it begins to thicken.

Add the milk mixture little by little until all has been incorporated and the batter is smooth. Finally, whisk in some water until the batter resembles thick cream.

Pour the batter into a jug and refrigerate for at least two hours. The resting time allows the batter to relax and the flour to absorb the liquids fully. Pancake batter may be made up to a day ahead and refrigerated.

To cook, heat a 15–18cm frying pan. Add a little oil. When the frying pan is hot, pour in just enough batter to cover the base. Allow to cook on one side for 1–2 minutes, flip the galette over onto the other side and continue to cook until speckled and slightly golden.

Slide onto a plate and keep warm while you make the rest of the galettes. You can stack one on top of the other as they can be peeled apart later but are best eaten fresh from the pan.

For the fillings, place your galette back in the frying pan, sprinkle your choice of filling into the centre and fold the sides in like an envelope so that it heats up and cooks the filling slightly. If you're using an egg, once you've added your fillings, crack a raw egg onto the centre of the galette, fold in the sides and allow the egg to cook. Slide onto a plate and serve.

Bruschetta Cymreig â ham Caerfyrddin

Dyma frecwast moethus o dramor â dylanwad Cymreig. Rwy'n dwlu ar y dull o frecwasta dramor; tostadas o Sbaen wedi'u gwneud â thomatos melys o Sbaen a jòch o olew olewydd – uchafbwynt unrhyw wyliau yn Sbaen. Er bod y pryd hwn yn swnio'n egsotig, mae'n ffordd wych o ddefnyddio baguettes ddiwrnod oed neu fara cartref sydd wedi mynd yn galed.

Sleisiwch ddarn trwchus o fara cartref a'i dostio'n ysgafn. Sleisiwch neu torrwch rai tomatos sy'n oraeddfed a'u cynhesu mewn sosban fach; defnyddiwch domatos o dun os nad oes gennych chi rai ffres. Unwaith mae'r bara wedi'i dostio, rhwbiwch ewin garlleg arno i ychwanegu blas a thaenu ychydig o olew olewydd drosto. Rhowch y tomatos wedi'u cynhesu ar y bara sydd wedi'i dostio ac yna gosod tafell o ham Caerfyrddin ar ei ben a thaenu dail basil wedi'u torri dros y cyfan. Neu, fe allwch gymysgu'r tomatos wedi'u torri, yr olew olewydd a'r dail basil yn dda ac ychwanegu llwy de o finegr balsamig. Yna, rhowch y cymysgedd blasus hwn dros y bara sydd wedi'i dostio.

Welsh bruschetta with Carmarthen ham

This is a luxurious continental breakfast with a Welsh twist. I love the continental-style breakfasts. The Spanish tostadas made with sweet warmed Spanish plum tomatoes and a glug of olive oil is the highlight of any Spanish holiday. Despite sounding very exotic, it's a great way to use day-old baguettes or home-made bread which is often past its best by day two.

Slice a thick piece of home-made bread and toast it lightly. Slice or dice some overripe tomatoes and warm in a small saucepan. Use tinned tomatoes if you don't have fresh ones. Once it's toasted, rub the bread with a clove of garlic to add flavour and drizzle over a little olive oil. Finally, top the bread with the warmed tomatoes and lay on a slice of Carmarthen ham and sprinkle with torn basil leaves. Alternatively, mix the chopped tomatoes, the olive oil and the basil leaves, mix well and add just a teaspoon of balsamic vinegar. Then, top your toasted bread with the delicious mixture.

SYNIAD SYDYN
QUICK IDEA

LL

Caws pob Cymreig

Does dim i guro pryd o fwyd o gaws a bara. Dyma goginio syml a da ar ei orau.

- 200g caws caled Cymreig, wedi'i gratio
- 25g menyn Cymreig
- 3 llwy fwrdd o laeth neu hufen
- 3–4 diferyn o saws Caerwrangon
- 1 llwy de o fwstard
- Tafelli o fara cartref
- Dewsiol: diferyn o gwrw Cymreig da

Toddwch y menyn mewn sosban a chymysgu'r holl gynhwysion eraill ynddi hefyd.

Tostiwch y bara.

Arllwyswch y saws caws dros y bara wedi'i dostio.

Am flasau ychwanegol, ychwanegwch fadarch neu gynhwysion eraill i wneud caws ar dost Cymreig arbennig.

V

Welsh rarebit

There's nothing to beat a meal made of bread and cheese. This is good basic cooking at its best.

- 200g grated hard Welsh cheese
- 25g Welsh butter
- 3 tbsp milk or cream
- 3–4 drops of Worcestershire sauce
- 1 tsp mustard
- Slices of home-made bread
- Optional: a drop of good Welsh beer

Melt the butter in a saucepan and stir in all the other ingredients.

Toast the bread.

Pour the cheese sauce over the toasted bread.

For additional flavours, add mushrooms or other ingredients to make a super Welsh cheese toastie.

SYNIAD SYDYN
QUICK IDEA

Pice ar y maen a thopin crymbl pice ar y maen

Dau am bris un – rysáit draddodiadol pice ar y maen i chi rhag ofn, a chrymbl pice ar y maen i'w ddefnyddio ar gyfer pwdin arall.

225g blawd codi
Pinsiaid o halen
110g menyn
25g siwgwr
50g cyrens
1 wy
Llaeth, os oes angen
Menyn a siwgwr mân i weini

Hidlwch y blawd a rhwbiwch y menyn i mewn iddo i greu cymysgedd briwsionllyd. Cymysgwch y siwgwr a'r ffrwythau sych. Chwisgiwch yr wy a'i ychwanegu i'r cymysgedd.

Cymysgwch nes ei fod yn ffurfio toes solet gan ddefnyddio ychydig o laeth os bydd angen. Rholiwch i drwch o 5mm ar arwyneb â blawd arno a'i dorri'n gylchoedd 7.5cm.

Gosodwch ar radell neu ffrimpan boeth, trowch nhw unwaith, a'u coginio nes eu bod yn euraid. Taenwch fenyn arnyn nhw, ysgeintiwch â swigwr mân a'u bwyta.

I wneud y topin crymbl:

Gosodwch yr holl ddarnau sbâr o does ar hambwrdd pobi wedi'i leinio a'u pobi yn y ffwrn am 10–15 munud, hyd nes eu bod yn euraid. Gadewch iddyn nhw oeri, yna malwch nhw mewn prosesydd bwyd a defnyddio'r briwsion fel topin crymbl – pwdin â blas Cymreig.

Welsh cakes and Welsh cake crumble topping

Two for the price of one – here's the traditional Welsh cake recipe for good measure, and a Welsh cake topping idea to use on another pudding.

225g self-raising flour
Pinch of salt
110g butter
25g sugar
50g currants
1 egg
Milk, if needed
Butter and caster sugar to serve

Sift the flour and rub in the butter to make a crumbly mixture. Stir in the sugar and the fruit. Whisk the egg and add to the mixture.

Mix to a firm dough using a little milk, if needed. Roll out to 5mm thickness on a floured surface and cut out into 7.5cm circles.

Place onto a hot griddle or frying pan, turn once, and cook until golden brown. Add a little butter, sprinkle with caster sugar, and eat.

←

To make a crumble topping:

Place all the offcuts of dough on a lined baking tray and bake in the oven for 10–15 minutes, until golden. Allow to cool, then blitz in a food processor, and use as a crumble topping – Welsh leftover pudding.

Yn yr ardd

In the garden

Mae'r gwanwyn yn gyfle gwych i roi cychwyn go dda ar yr ardd.

Oddeutu'r adeg yma bydd y pys a'r ffa eisoes wedi'u plannu, ond gan fod y tir yn dal i fod yn oer, bydd yr hadu'n cymryd peth amser. Er gwaetha'r dechreuadau cyndyn, fe fydd y blagur gwyrdd yn ymddangos yn fuan, arwydd sicr y bydd gwledd i'w gael ar gyfer bwrdd bwyd yr haf.

Mae'r gwelyau llysiau'n llenwi'n gyflym, ond rydw i'n hoffi gadael rhywfaint o le ar gyfer yr hwyrddyfodiaid, beth bynnag fyddan nhw. Mae tatws Anya a Pink Fir Apple yn llenwi un o'r gwelyau llysiau â'u dail gwyrdd, ir, mae'r winwns wedi hen wreiddio a'r ffa hud (y ffa dringo porffor Ffrengig) wedi'u hen sefydlu ar eu wigwam bambŵ.

Os oes unrhyw un yn cychwyn ar y daith o dyfu llysiau am y tro cyntaf, rwy'n argymell tatws o fath Anya a'r Pink Fir Apple am eu blas a'u hansawdd hynod. Mae'r Pink Fir Apple yn groesiad rhwng yr Anya a'r daten Desiree ac yn cynnwys y gorau o'r ddau fath yma mewn un daten. Fe'i disgrifir fel taten salad ac mae'n aeddfedu ymhell o flaen y lleill, rwy'n dwlu ar ei blas, sy'n debyg i gnau. Rai blynyddoedd yn ôl, penderfynais beidio â gwastraffu lle prin ar datws cyffredin a chanolbwyntio ar y rhai bach pinc anarferol eu siâp – maen nhw'n edrych yn hynod o od. A dyw'r ffaith mai dyma yw enw un o fy merched yn ddim i'w wneud ag e! Mae gan ei chwaer hynaf, Alisa, winwnsyn wedi'i henwi ar ei hôl hithau yn yr ardd, sef yr Alisa Craig, winwnsyn a dyfir am ei faint. Newydd ddechrau tyfu'r rhain ydyn ni. Cawn weld a fyddan nhw'n ennill gwobrau ymhen amser, ond mae'n siŵr y byddan nhw'n hollol iawn mewn saws Bolognese.

The arrival of spring brings a wonderful opportunity to give the garden a kick-start.

The peas and broad beans will have already been planted. And in spite of the reticent start, sprouts of green will appear soon, a sure sign that we will have an abundance of food for the summer table.

The vegetable beds are now filling up fast, but I do like to leave a few gaps for some late entries, whatever they may be. Anya and Pink Fir Apple potatoes now fill a bed with lush green foliage, the onion sets are well rooted and putting on weight and the magic beans (the French purple climbing beans) are well established on their wigwams.

For anyone embarking on a journey of vegetable growing for the very first time, I truly recommend the Anya and Pink Fir Apple potatoes for their amazing flavour and texture. The Pink Fir Apple is a cross between the Anya and the Desiree potato, capturing the best of both. Classed as a salad potato, it's streets ahead of the competition and I adore its slightly nutty flavour. I decided a few years back not to waste valuable space on main crop varieties but to concentrate my efforts on these little pink knobbly ones – they really are strange looking. The fact that one of my daughters is called Anya has nothing to do with it! Ailsa, her older sister, has this year also got her namesake in the garden – the Ailsa Craig onion, which are usually grown for their size. Time will tell whether they win any competitions, but I'm sure they'll be fine in a Bolognese.

PASG AC WYAU

⭐ Mae'r Pasg yn amser da i ddechrau pobi teisennau a danteithfwyd. Mae'r ieir wrthi'n dodwy wyau, ac mae pobi'n ffordd wych o'u defnyddio nhw. Mae teisennau yn gwneud digwyddiad cymdeithasol yn un llawer gwell.

Ond mae cymaint mwy y gallwch ei wneud ag wyau wrth gwrs. O bwdinau i brydau sawrus, boed eich byd yn gwt ieir cynhyrchiol iawn!

EASTER AND EGGS

⭐ Easter is a good time to get baking cakes and treats. With an abundance of eggs from the chicken shed, it's a great way to use them. Cakes make for a great social gathering.

But there are so many more things you can do with eggs of course. From puddings to savouries, the world is your chicken coop!

LL

TORTILA SBAENAIDD

Dyma flas o dramor. Mae'r teulu cyfan yn mwynhau darn o tortila bob tro – mae'n fwyd syml ond blasus.

5 neu 6 o datws cwyrog bychain
(Charlotte neu Jersey Royal)
1 winwnsyn canolig (dewisol)
1 pupur coch (dewisol)
Olew olewydd
5 neu 6 wy buarth
Halen a phupur du wedi'i falu

Golchwch y tatws a'u torri'n ddarnau bach neu'n haenau tenau. Gosodwch y tatws wedi'u torri mewn llond sosban o ddŵr oer a'u codi i'r berw. Berwch y tatws am 5 munud yn unig – digon i'w feddalu, ond nid i'w goginio'n llwyr.

Ffriwch yr winwns mewn ychydig o olew olewydd hyd nes eu bod nhw'n eitha meddal. Ychwanegwch nhw at y tatws sydd wedi'u coginio a'u draenio. Curwch yr wyau ac ychwanegu halen a phupur yn ôl y galw.

Ychwangewch y tatws, yr winwns a'r pupur at y cymysgedd wy; bydd gwres y tatws yn dechrau coginio'r wyau. Gadewch am ychydig o funudau tra byddwch chi'n ychwanegu mwy o olew i'r ffrimpan.

Cyneuwch y gril i wres canolig, neu gynnau'r ffwrn i 180°C / 350°F / Nwy 4. Arllwyswch y cymysgedd wy a thatws i'r ffrimpan a gadewch iddo goginio'n araf am 6–8 munud heb ei droi. Dylai fod yn euraid oddi tano ac ychydig yn rhedegog ar yr wyneb.

Nawr gosodwch y tortila o dan y gril am ychydig funudau i'w galedu, neu rhowch ef ar ddysgl addas i'r ffwrn a'i bobi yn y ffwrn am tua 10 munud hyd nes ei fod wedi caledu.

Tynnwch y tortila o'r ffwrn a gadael iddo oeri. Mae tortila Sbaenaidd yn well o'i weini'n gynnes ond gellir ei oeri a'i gadw yn yr oergell hyd nes eich bod yn barod i'w fwyta. Torrwch yn ddarnau fel teisen a bwytewch gyda mayonnaise garlleg neu aioli.

V

SPANISH TORTILLA

A little taste of abroad. The whole family enjoys a piece of tortilla every time – it's simple food but delicious.

5 or 6 waxy small potatoes
(Charlotte or Jersey Royal)
1 medium onion (optional)
1 red pepper (optional)
Olive oil
5 or 6 free range eggs
Salt and ground black pepper

Wash the potatoes and cut into small pieces or thin slices. Place the cut potatoes into a saucepan full of cold water and bring to the boil. Only boil for about 5 minutes – just enough to soften, but not totally cook the potatoes.

Fry the onion and pepper in a little olive oil until fairly soft. Add to the cooked, drained potatoes. Beat the eggs and season with salt and ground black pepper.

Add the potatoes, onion and pepper to the egg mixture; the heat of the potatoes will begin to cook the egg. Allow to stand for a few minutes while you add more oil to the frying pan.

Turn on the grill to a medium heat or heat the oven to 180°C / 350°F / Gas 4. Pour the egg and potato mixture into the frying pan and let it cook gently for 6–8 minutes without turning; it should be golden underneath and slightly runny on top.

Now either place it under the grill for a few minutes to firm, or slide it onto an oven-proof dish and bake in the oven for about 10 minutes until set.

Remove from the oven and allow to cool. Spanish tortilla is best served warm but can be cooled and stored in the fridge until eaten. Cut into wedges and serve with garlic mayonnaise or aioli.

✳ Mwynhewch gyda salad neu gymryd darnau yn eich bocs bwyd neu'ch basged bicnic.

✳ Serve with a salad or take some wedges in your lunchbox or in your picnic basket.

LL

RUBANAU PASTA PERFFAITH

Pwy sy'n gwneud eu pasta eu hunain?
Fi, a nawr chi! Mae'n hawdd.

100g o flawd plaen '00' ar gyfer pob unigolyn
1 wy am bob 100g o flawd
Ychydig o semolina

Rhowch y blawd mewn pentwr ar arwyneb glân, yn union fel llosgfynydd.

Torrwch yr wy neu'r wyau mewn powlen fach i weld a yw'n ffres. Yna, arllwyswch yr wy neu'r wyau i mewn i bwll yng nghanol y blawd a chymysgu â fforc.

Unwaith mae'r wy wedi'i gymysgu, defnyddiwch eich dwylo i greu toes; gallwch ychwanegu ychydig mwy o flawd os yw'r toes yn rhy wlyb.

Tylinwch y toes am ychydig funudau: mae hyn yn golygu tynnu a gwthio a phlygu'r toes i'w wneud yn fwy elastig. Yna rhowch ef yn yr oergell am tua 20 munud.

Os oes gennych beiriant pasta, rhowch y toes drwy'r peiriant ar lefel 1. Yna daliwch i roi blawd ar y toes a'i roi drwy'r peiriant sawl gwaith gan symud y rholwyr yn agosach at ei gilydd yn raddol. Os nad oes gennych chi beiriant pasta, rholiwch y toes pasta gan ddefnyddio rholbren hyd nes bod y toes yn denau iawn.

Torrwch yr haenen o basta yn stribedi tua 2cm o led, ac yna'u torri'n ddarnau petryal bach, tua 3cm o hyd.

Pinsiwch y darnau pasta ynghyd yn y canol i greu siâp ruban a'u gosod i sychu ar hambwrdd. Mae semolina yn helpu sychu pasta heb ei wneud yn ludiog.

I goginio'r pasta, berwch am ychydig funudau hyd nes ei fod yn feddal.

Tip: gellir siapio'r pasta yn wahanol fathau, tagliatelle (rubanau hirion), lasagne (dalennau fflat) neu unrhyw siâp yr hoffwch.

Tip: i greu pasta pinc, ychwanegwch 1 llwy fwrdd o fetys wedi'i goginio a'i stwnsio yn lle un o'r wyau, neu, i greu pasta gwyrdd ychwanegwch un llwy fwrdd o sbigoglys wedi'i goginio a'i stwnsio.

V

PERFECT PASTA BOWS

Who makes their own pasta?
Me, and now you! It's easy.

100g of plain '00' flour per person
1 egg per 100g of flour
A dusting of semolina

Place the flour in a mound on a clean surface, so that it looks just like a volcano.

Break the egg or eggs into a small bowl to check freshness, then pour the egg or eggs into a hole in the centre of the flour and mix with a fork

Once the egg is mixed in, use your hands to make a dough; you can add a little flour if the dough is too wet and sticky.

Knead the dough for a few minutes; this means you need to pull and push and fold the dough to make it really stretchy. Then place it in the fridge for about 20 minutes.

If you have a pasta machine, pass the dough through the machine on setting 1 and then continue to flour the dough and keep passing it through the machine several times, making the rollers gradually closer. If you don't have a pasta machine, roll the pasta dough using a rolling pin until the dough is really thin.

Cut the sheet of pasta into strips about 2cm wide, then into small rectangles about 3cm long.

Pinch the pasta together in the middle and place to dry on a tray. Semolina helps to dry out the pasta without making it sticky.

To cook, boil for just a few minutes until soft.

Tip: pasta can be made into tagliatelle (long ribbons), lasagne (flat sheets) or any shape you like.

Tip: for pink pasta, add 1 tablespoon of cooked blended beetroot instead of one egg; for green pasta, add 1 tablespoon of cooked blended spinach instead of one egg.

BYNS Y GROG

Adeg y Pasg rwy'n gweld byns y Grog yn cael eu gwerthu mewn siopau ym mhob man. Maen nhw mor hawdd i'w gwneud ac yn rhoi cymaint o foddhad wrth eu pobi â'u croesau bach gwynion.

400g blawd bara gwyn cryf
1 llwy de o halen
1 llwy de o furum sych
3 llwy fwrdd o siwgwr mân
1 llwy fwrdd o fenyn
280ml dŵr cynnes/llaeth
1 cwpanaid o gyrens neu resins
Dŵr a siwgwr mân ar gyfer sglein

Cynheswch y ffwrn i 220°C / 425°F / Nwy 7

Rhwbiwch y menyn mewn i'r blawd, ychwanegwch yr halen, y siwgwr a'r burum. Ychwanegwch y dŵr a'r ffrwythau a chymysgu'r cyfan i ffurfio toes. Tylinwch y toes ar arwyneb â blawd arno am tua 7 munud.

Gosodwch y toes wedi'i dylino mewn powlen, gorchuddiwch â lliain llaith, glân neu haenen lynu a rhowch y bowlen yn rhywle cynnes.

Ar ôl tua awr, rhowch y toes ar arwyneb â blawd arno eto a'i dylino. Yna, rhannwch y toes yn oddeutu 8 darn o feintiau cyfartal.

Siapiwch bob darn yn fynen gron, a'u gosod ar hambwrdd pobi wedi'i iro'n dda. Gorchuddiwch y byns unwaith yn rhagor a'u rhoi nhw yn rhywle cynnes am 30 munud. Yn olaf, ychwanegwch y groes ar bob un â thoes wedi'i wneud o gymysgedd tenau o flawd gwyn plaen a dŵr.

Pan fydd y byns wedi dyblu yn eu maint, pobwch nhw am 15–20 munud hyd nes eu bod yn euraidd.

Sgleiniwch y byns â chymysgedd wedi'i gynhesu o siwgwr a dŵr, neu â jam bricyll wedi'i gynhesu ar gyfer byns sgleiniog, gludiog.

HOT CROSS BUNS

At Easter time, I see hot cross buns sold in shops everywhere. They're so easy to make, and so satisfying to bake with their little white crosses.

400g strong white bread flour
1 tsp salt
1 tsp dried yeast
3 tbsp caster sugar
1 tbsp butter
280ml warm water/milk
1 cup of currants or raisins
Water and caster sugar for glazing

Preheat the oven to 220°C / 425°F / Gas 7

Rub the butter into the flour, add the salt, sugar and yeast. Add the water and the fruit and mix to form a dough. Knead the dough on a floured table for about 7 minutes.

Place the kneaded dough into a bowl, cover with a damp clean tea towel or cling film and place the bowl somewhere warm.

After about an hour, tip out the dough and knead it again on a floured table. Divide the dough into about 8 pieces of equal size.

Shape each piece into a round bun, then place them on a well oiled baking tray. Cover them once again, and place them somewhere warm for 30 minutes. Finally, put a cross on each one with a thin mixture of plain white flour and water.

When the buns have doubled in size, bake them for 15–20 minutes, until golden brown.

Glaze the buns with a heated mixture of sugar and water or with melted apricot jam for sticky, shiny buns.

TEISEN YN Y TŶ

Mae wastad yn braf cael ychydig bach o felyster yn llechu yn y pantri ar gyfer te teuluol neu i roi croeso twymgalon i westeion. Sdim byd fel darn o deisen wedi'i gwneud gartref, oes e?

Ac fe hoffwn i ddweud yn y fan yma bod teisen yn dda i chi. O ydy mae. I ddechrau, mae'r broses o greu rhywbeth yn un eitha therapiwtig, mae dilyn rysáit ac yna cael rhywbeth i ddangos amdano ar y diwedd yn beth da i'r hunanbarch, does bosib.

Ac unwaith i chi wneud y deisen, wel, bydd angen ei bwyta ac os ydych chi am fwyta'r deisen, bydd angen cwmni arnoch chi, ac os oes gennych chi gwmni, yna mi fyddwch chi'n iawn! Mae unrhyw deisen yn dda ar gyfer agosatrwydd.

Maen nhw'n dweud bod ychydig o rywbeth ry'ch chi'n ei chwennych yn dda i chi, a dyna'n union yw teisen. Rwy'n teimlo 'mod i'n medru rhannu sawl peth dros baned o de a sleisen ddeche o deisen – rhannu jôc neu rannu gofidiau ac y mae problem, o'i rhannu, yn dueddol o fynd yn llai – mae'n ddarn bach hyfryd o hapusrwydd.

HOME-MADE CAKE

It's always lovely to have a little bit of sweetness skulking in the pantry ready for a family tea or to give guests a warm welcome. There's nothing like a piece of home-made cake, is there?

And I'd just like to say here that cake is good for you. Oh yes it is. To start with, the process of making something is quite theraputic, just following a recipe and then having something to show for it at the end is surely good for your self-esteem.

And once you've made your cake, well you'll need to eat it, and if you're going to eat the cake, then you'll need company, and if you've got company, then you're alright! Any cake is great for togetherness.

They say that a little of what you fancy does you good, and that's exactly what cake is. I always think I can share many things over a cup of tea and a nice slice of cake – sharing a laugh or sharing your worries and a problem shared is a problem halved – it's a little slice of wellbeing really.

TEISEN SIOCLED HOLLOL YSBLENNYDD

225g menyn heb halen, wedi'i feddalu
225g siwgwr mân
4 wy mawr, wedi'u curo
1 llwy de o rinflas fanila
200g blawd codi
½ llwy de o bowdwr codi
30g powdwr coco
100g siocled tywyll, wedi'i doddi

Ar gyfer y ganache
200g siocled tywyll
100g siocled llaeth
250ml hufen dwbl

Cynheswch y ffwrn i 180°C / 350°F / Nwy 4

Hufennwch y menyn a'r siwgwr gyda'i gilydd mewn powlen cymysgydd trydan hyd nes eu bod nhw'n lliw golau ac yn ysgafn (gallwch ddefnyddio cymysgydd llaw trydanol). Ychwanegwch yr wyau wedi'u curo a'r rhinflas fanila. Ychwanegwch y blawd, y powdwr codi a'r powdwr coco, a chymysgu'r cyfan yn drylwyr. Ychwanegwch y siocled toddedig a chymysgu eto hyd nes bod y cymysgedd yn llyfn.

Rhannwch y cymysgedd yn gyfartal rhwng dau dun teisen crwn a'i daenu i greu haenen wastad yn y tuniau. Pobwch ar silff ganol y ffwrn am tua 22–25 munud hyd nes eu bod yn euraid a bod cyllell neu sgiwer yn dod allan yn lân o ganol y teisennau. Trowch y teisennau allan o'r tuniau ar rhesel wifrau i oeri a gadewch nhw nes eu bod yn oer.

I wneud y ganache, torrwch y ddau fath o siocled yn fân a'u rhoi mewn sosban gyda'r hufen dwbl. Gosodwch y sosban ar dymheredd isel i doddi'r siocled, gan droi'r cymysgedd yn gyson hyd nes ei fod yn llyfn. Arllwyswch y ganache i lestr bas a'i oeri yn yr oergell.

I roi'r cyfan at ei gilydd, gosodwch un o'r teisennau ar blât a thaenwch hanner y ganache drosti gan ddefnyddio llwy. Gorchuddiwch yr ail deisen â gweddill y ganache, gan ei daenu'n llyfn â chyllell balet. Gwasgwch y ddwy deisen at ei gilydd a'u haddurno mewn dull addas ar gyfer y tymor neu ar gyfer y digwyddiad.

ABSOLUTELY LUSH CHOCOLATE CAKE

225g unsalted butter, softened
225g caster sugar
4 large eggs, beaten
1 tsp vanilla extract
200g self-raising flour
½ tsp baking powder
30g cocoa
100g dark chocolate, melted

For the ganache
200g dark chocolate
100g milk chocolate
250ml double cream

Preheat the oven to 180°C / 350°F / Gas 4

In the bowl of a free-standing mixer, cream the butter and sugar together until pale, light and fluffy (you can use a handheld mixer). Gradually add the beaten eggs and vanilla extract. Add the flour, baking powder, and cocoa, then mix until combined. Add the melted chocolate and mix again until smooth.

Divide equally between the prepared sandwich tins. Spread level and bake on the middle shelf of the preheated oven for about 22–25 minutes until golden and a knife or skewer comes away clean when inserted into the middle of the cakes. Turn the cakes out of the tins onto a wire cooling rack and leave until cold.

To make the ganache, finely chop the two kinds of chocolates and tip into a saucepan along with the double cream. Set the pan over a low heat to melt the chocolate, stirring constantly until smooth. Pour the ganache into a shallow dish to cool and then chill.

To assemble the cake, place one of the cakes on a cake or serving plate and spoon half of the ganache on the cake and spread. Cover the top of the second cake layer with the rest of the ganache, spreading it smoothly with a palette knife. Sandwich the two cakes together and decorate in a style suitable for the season or the event.

Mae'r deisen hon yn hawdd i'w gwneud bob tro.
Dwi wedi gwneud cymaint o ffrindiau drwy'r deisen hon.

This cake is fail-safe and foolproof.
I've made so many friends with this cake.

✳ Dyma deisen siocled hyfryd ar gyfer y Pasg, teisen ddelfrydol i fwynhau dathlu Santes Dwynwen neu San Ffolant mewn modd rhamantus neu desien ysgubol i nodi pen-blwydd mewn steil gyda hi.

✳ This makes a lovely Easter chocolate cake, romantic Valentine's cake or a celebration birthday cake.

Teisen ardd siocled

Mae'r deisen ei hun wedi'i gwneud gan ddefnyddio rysáit y deisen siocled fendigedig rwy'n ei defnyddio'n aml (gweler tudalen 72). Mae'n deisen siocledaidd, hyfryd. Os nad ydych chi'n hoffi teisen simnel, yna defnyddiwch y rysáit yma i greu teisen Basg hyfryd – un sy'n dathlu'r bywyd newydd yn yr ardd. Coginiwch y deisen mewn tun pobi sgwâr i edrych fel darn o'r ardd.

Yr addurno sy'n cyfleu elfen yr arddelfen yr ardd gyda phridd siocled bwytadwy a dail bach a hadau'n edrych fel hambwrdd hadau sy'n gyforiog o fywyd gwyllt. O'i haddurno'n daclus, bydd yn edrych yn rhy dda i'w bwyta, ond gyda mymryn bach o anogaeth, diflannodd y deisen yn ddidrafferth yn ein tŷ ni. Mae'n hwyl i'w gwneud ac mi fyddai'n ychwanegiad ardderchog i unrhyw barti gardd, am resymau amlwg.

I wneud y pridd, berwch 100g o siwgwr ag ychydig lwyeidiau te o ddŵr. Gadewch i'r syrop chwilboeth ferwi heb ei droi am ychydig funudau hyd nes ei fod yn drwchus a gludiog. Toddwch 100g o siocled tywyll mewn microdon neu mewn bain-marie. Yna, ychwanegwch y siocled wedi'i doddi at y syrop siwgwr a'i droelli hyd nes ei fod yn caledu'n bridd siocled. Byddwch yn ofalus gan fod y siwgwr yn hynod boeth; dydy'r cam hwn yn y broses ddim yn addas i blant roi help llaw ag ef.

Chocolate garden cake

The cake itself is the lovely and very chocolatey 'lush chocolate cake' that I use regularly (see page 72). It's so versatile and can be transformed into many different cakes. If you don't like a fruity simnel cake, then use this recipe to make a beautiful chocolate Easter cake – one that celebrates new life in the garden. Bake the cake in a square tin to make it look like a part of the garden.

The garden aspect is in the decoration, with edible chocolate soil decorated with tiny leaves and seeds to resemble a seed tray that's bursting with plant life. Done well, it looks too good to eat, but with a tiny bit of encouragement, my family soon devoured the lot. It's certainly fun to make and would make a great addition to any garden party, for obvious reasons.

To make the soil, boil up 100g or so of granulated sugar with a few teaspoons of water. Allow the very hot syrup to boil away without stirring for a few minutes until thick and gloopy. Melt 100g of dark chocolate in the microwave or in a bain-marie. Then add the melted chocolate into the sugar syrup and stir until it hardens into chocolate soil. Be careful as the sugar is very hot; this step is not suitable for children to help.

Rhowch y pridd o'r neilltu i oeri a gwnewch gyflenwad o eisin menyn gan ddefnyddio 200g o siwgwr eisin, llwy fwrdd o fenyn ar dymheredd ystafell a diferion o ddŵr cynnes i greu past. Neu gallwch wneud ganache siocled gan ddefnyddio 200g o siocled tywyll a 200ml o hufen dwbl, wedi'u cynhesu mewn sosban, eu cymysgu ac yna gadael iddyn nhw oeri.

Gorchuddiwch y deisen siocled sgwâr â'r eisin menyn siocled meddal neu'r ganache ac yna rhoi pridd ar ei ben. Ychwanegwch hadau fel hadau sesame, hadau pwmpen, hadau pabi neu sbrincls gwyrdd, pert a dail gwyrdd bach.

I wneud y dail gwyrdd

Defnyddiwch becyn o eisin ffondant gwyrdd. Rholiwch yr eisin i drwch o 2mm gan gofio ysgeintio'r bwrdd â siwgwr eisin. Torrwch gasgliad o ddail bach gan ddefnyddio torrwr siâp deilen (mae torrwr siâp dail celyn yn dda) a'u cyrlio nhw ryw ychydig i edrych fel dail ifanc. Cofiwch eu cyrlio cyn i'r eisin sychu.

Set the soil aside to cool and make a batch of chocolate butter icing by using 200g icing sugar, a tablespoon of butter at room temperature and a drizzle of warm water mixed to a paste. Or make some chocolate ganache using 200g dark chocolate and 200ml double cream, heated in a pan, mixed and allowed to cool.

Cover the finished chocolate tray bake with the soft chocolate butter icing or ganache before spreading the soil on top. Finally add seeds such as sesame, pumpkin, poppy seeds or even pretty green sprinkles and little green leaves.

To make the green leaves

Using a pack of green fondant icing, roll out the icing to a 2mm thickness on a dusting of icing sugar on the work surface. Cut out a collection of little leaves using a leaf cutter (a holly-leaf cutter is great) and curl them slightly to resemble young leaves. Remember to curl them before the icing dries out.

TEISEN SIOCLED GUINNESS A BAILEYS

Ar gyfer y deisen
250ml Guinness
250g menyn heb halen
80g powdwr coco
400g siwgwr mân
2 wy
140ml llaeth
280g blawd plaen
2 llwy de o soda pobi
½ llwy de o bowdwr codi

Ar gyfer yr eisin menyn
75g menyn
300g siwgwr eisin
2 llwy fwrdd o Baileys a diferyn o ddŵr
Tun pobi 23cm (9 modfedd)

Cynheswch y ffwrn i 170°C / 325°F / Nwy 3

Leiniwch waelod y tun â phapur pobi.

Cynheswch y Guinness a'r menyn yn raddol mewn sosban hyd nes bod y cyfan wedi toddi. Yna ychwanegwch y powdwr coco a'r siwgwr, a'u cymysgu.

Cymysgwch yr wyau a'r llaeth ynghyd mewn jwg ac yna ychwanegwch hwn at y cymysgedd yn y sosban.

Yn olaf, cymysgwch y blawd, y soda pobi a'r powdwr codi ynghyd mewn powlen fawr neu mewn powlen cymysgydd trydan, os oes gennych chi un. Arllwyswch gynnwys y sosban i'r bowlen a chymysgu'r cyfan yn dda.

Arllwyswch y cymysgedd i'r tun teisen a'i bobi am oddeutu 45 munud i awr, hyd nes ei fod wedi coginio. Gadewch i'r deisen oeri ychydig yn y tun, yna gosodwch hi ar resel wifrau hyd nes bydd wedi oeri. Pan fydd y deisen yn oer, gallwch ychwanegu'r eisin menyn Baileys.

I wneud yr eisin menyn Baileys

Cymysgwch y menyn a 2 lwy fwrdd o Baileys i mewn i'r siwgwr eisin, a chael gwared ar unrhyw lympiau. Ychwanegwch ddŵr os bydd rhaid, ddiferyn ar y tro, hyd nes bod modd taenu'r eisen. Yna, rhowch y deisen sydd wedi'i hoeri ar blât a'i harddurno gyda'r eisin Baileys.

GUINNESS AND BAILEYS CHOCOLATE CAKE

For the cake
250ml Guinness
250g unsalted butter
80g cocoa powder
400g caster sugar
2 eggs
140ml milk
280g plain flour
2 tsp bicarbonate of soda
½ tsp baking powder

For the butter icing
75g butter
300g icing sugar
2 tbsp Baileys and a drop of water
23cm (9 inch) cake tin

Preheat the oven to 170°C / 325°F / Gas 3

Line the base of the tin with baking parchment.

Gently heat the Guinness and the butter in a saucepan until it has all melted, then stir in the cocoa powder and the sugar.

Mix the eggs and milk together in a jug, and then add this to the mixture in the pan.

Finally, mix the flour and baking agents together in a large bowl or into the bowl of an electric mixer, if you have one. Pour the contents of the pan into the bowl and mix well.

Pour the cake mixture into the cake tin and bake for approximately 45 minutes to an hour, until cooked. Allow the cake to cool a little, then place on a wire rack until cold. Once the cake is cold you can add the Baileys butter icing.

To make the Baileys butter icing

Mix the butter and 2 tablespoons of Baileys into the icing sugar, until there are no lumps. Add water if needed, a drop at a time, until the icing is spreadable. Then place the cooled cake on a plate and top with the Baileys frosting.

* Tip: i wneud y dail meillion ffondant gwyrdd ar gyfer deisen, defnyddiwch dorrwr bach siâp calon ar gyfer pob sbrigyn. Gallwch wneud un a phedair deilen am lwc.

A cake with a touch of the Emerald Isle to it.
Happy St Patrick's Day!

* Tip: to make the green fondant clover leaves of the cake, use a small heart shaped cutter and cut out three leaves for each sprig. You could make one four leafed one for luck.

TEISEN SIMNEL Y PASG

3 chwpanaid o ffrwythau sych cymysg
1 cwpanaid o laeth
1 cwpanaid o siwgwr brown
170g menyn wedi toddi
2 gwpanaid o flawd codi
½ llwy de o sbeis cymysg
1 llw de o bowdr pobi
3 wy wedi'u curo'n dda
Ychydig o jam bricyll
Ar gyfer addurno – marsipán

Y noson cynt

Rhowch y ffrwythau cymysg mewn powlen gyda the ffrwythau a rhai peli o farsipán. Cymysgwch yn dda er mwyn toddi'r marispán, a gadewch i sefyll dros nos.

Y diwrnod canlynol

Cynheswch y ffwrn 180°C / 350°F / Nwy 4

Rhowch y ffrwythau, y llaeth, y siwgwr a'r menyn mewn sosban fawr. Berwch am 5 munud. Gadewch i'r cymysgedd oeri.

Ychwanegwch 2 gwpanaid o flawd codi, y sbeis cymysg a'r powdwr codi at y cymysgedd. Yna, ychwanegwch 3 wy wedi'u curo'n dda, a'u cymysgu.

Leiniwch dun teisen 9 modfedd (22cm) â phapur pobi neu leiniwr teisen tun parod. Llenwch y tun wedi'i leinio â'r cymysgedd a'i roi yn y ffwrn am 1½ awr hyd nes bydd wedi coginio. Mi fedrech chi lenwi sawl tun llai i wneud teisennau unigol i'w rhoi i aelodau o'r teulu neu ffrindiau fel rhoddion Pasg. Rhowch y teisennau llai yn y ffwrn am tua 20–30 munud hyd nes byddan nhw wedi coginio.

Wedi gadael iddyn nhw oeri, gorchuddiwch bob teisen â jam bricyll wedi'i doddi; bydd hyn yn sicrhau bod y marsipán yn glynu i'r deisen.

Rholiwch y marsipán allan yn gylch tua 4mm o drwch ddigon o faint i orchuddio'r deisen. Ychwanegwch 11 pelen farsipán ar ben y deisen – mae pob un yn cynrychioli un o'r disgyblion, ond nid Jiwdas, wrth gwrs.

Er mwyn cael wyneb euraid i'r deisen, rhowch hi o dan y gril am funud. Cadwch lygad arni gan fod marsipán yn medru llosgi'n hawdd oherwydd y siwgwr sydd ynddo. Gallwch ddefnyddio lamp losgi ar gyfer y gegin, os oes gennych chi un.

EASTER SIMNEL CAKE

3 cups of dried mixed fruit
1 cup of milk
1 cup of brown sugar
170g melted butter
2 cups of self-raising flour
½ tsp mixed spice
1 tsp baking powder
3 eggs, well beaten
Some apricot jam
For the decoration – marzipan

The night before

Place the mixed fruit in a bowl with some fruit tea and a few balls of marzipan. Stir well, to melt the marzipan, and leave to stand overnight.

The next day

Preheat the oven to 180°C / 350°F / Gas 4

Place the mixed fruit, milk, sugar and butter in a large saucepan. Boil for 5 minutes. Allow the mixture to cool.

Add 2 cups of self-raising flour, the mixed spice and baking powder to the mixture, then add 3 well beaten eggs, and mix.

Line a 9-inch (22cm) cake tin with kitchen parchment paper or a ready-made cake tin liner. Fill the lined cake tin with the mixture and place in the oven for 1½ hrs until cooked. You could fill several smaller tins with the mixture to make individual cakes to give to family and friends as Easter gifts. Place the smaller cakes in the oven for about 20–30 minutes until cooked.

Once cooled, cover each cake with melted apricot jam – this will help to secure the marzipan to the cake.

Roll out the marzipan to about 4mm thick to a size that will cover the cake and place on top of the cake. Finally, add 11 marzipan balls, each one represents one of the disciples, apart from Judas, of course.

To get a golden top, place the cake under the grill for 1 minute. Keep an eye on it as marzipan colours easily and can burn due to the high sugar content. You could use a kitchen blowtorch if you have one.

Does dim yn creu mwy o argraff
dros gyfnod y Pasg na theisen simnel.

For the Easter wow factor, simnel does it every time.

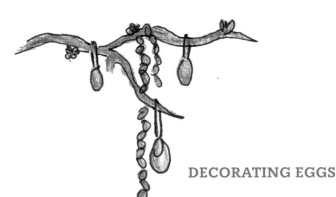

ADDURNO WYAU

Rwy'n hoffi dod â'r byd tu allan i'r tŷ dros y Pasg. Un o hoff weithgareddau'r plant yw ein pererindod adeg y Pasg i chwilio am blanhigion sy'n blaguro a blodeuo. Rwy'n addurno'r tŷ â brigau a changhennau i ffurfio siâp ein coeden Basg. Bydd yn cael ei gorchuddio â bisgedi'r Pasg, rhubanau ac wyau buarth wedi'u chwythu a'u peintio'n lliwgar. Yna'n sydyn, mae bwrdd y gegin wedi'i weddnewid ac yn troi tu mewn i'r tŷ yn lle sy'n llawn mor ffres a llawn bywyd â gardd y gwanwyn.

Fe gewch flas ar chwythu wyau yn ddi-os. Os nad ydych chi wedi gwneud hyn erioed, rhowch gynnig arni – mae'n llawer o hwyl ac yn dueddol o greu llanast. Mae addurno'r wyau'n sbri hefyd ac yn cadw bysedd bychain yn brysur am oriau. Mae'r plant wrth eu boddau'n cymryd rhan, ac mae'n amser gwych i fod yn greadigol, gan ddefnyddio sisyrnau, papur a glud i'r eithaf. Mae'n broses ddelicet, felly paratowch a chwythwch ddigon o wyau ar gyfer eich addurniadau Pasg chi – mi fyddwch yn siŵr o wastraffu rhai yn y broses.

Gan ddefnyddio pìn, crafwch ran fechan o ben a gwaelod yr wy yn ofalus hyd nes bod dau dwll bach yn ymddangos ar y ddau ben. Peidiwch â chael eich temtio i wthio'r pìn yn syth drwy'r plisgyn, gan y bydd yn torri'r wy cyfan. Gwnewch y twll yng ngwaelod yr wy ychydig yn fwy, tua 3mm ar draws. Yna, dros bowlen, chwythwch yn dyner drwy'r twll yn nhop yr wy. Yn raddol bydd y gwynnwy a'r melynwy yn ymddangos drwy'r twll yn y gwaelod ac yn llifo i'r bowlen. I hongian eich wy, tynnwch ddarn tenau o linyn neu edau cotwm drwy'r wy a'i glymu â glain bach neu ychydig o lud cryf.

Addurnwch â phaent, gleiniau neu ruban neu unrhyw beth hoffech chi, a'u rhoi nhw i hongian ar ganghennau neu frigau o'r ardd.

DECORATING EGGS

I like to bring the outdoors inside at Easter. I can never resist cutting just a few sprigs of blossom to cheer up the kitchen. One of the children's favourite activities is our little Easter pilgrimage to find some budding stems and blossom. I decorate the house with twigs and flowers from the garden and blossoming branches. The twigs and stems form the shape of our Easter tree, which is later covered with decorated Easter cookies, ribbons and painted free-range blown eggs from the chicken run. Then suddenly, the kitchen table is transformed, making the inside as fresh and airy as the spring garden.

Blowing eggs is great fun. If you've never tried, have a go – it's a blast, if a little messy. Decorating the eggs is great fun too and keeps little fingers busy for hours. The kids love to get involved, and it's a great time to get crafty, putting scissors, paper and glue to good use. It's a delicate process, so prepare and blow lots of eggs for your Easter decorations – you're sure to waste a few in the process.

Using a pin, carefully scratch a tiny part of the top and bottom of the egg until a small hole is formed at both ends. Don't be tempted to push the pin straight through the shell – it will crack the whole egg. Make the hole at the bottom of the egg slightly bigger, about 3mm across. Then, over a bowl, gently blow through the top pinhole. Gradually, the egg white and yolk will emerge through the hole at the bottom, and into the bowl. To hang your egg, pass a thin piece of string or cotton thread through the egg and secure with a small bead or a spot of superglue.

Decorate with paint, beads or ribbon or anything you like, and hang on some branches or twigs taken from the garden.

Hwyl yr haf

Summer fun

A ... yr haf ... dyna hyfryd ...

Y dyddiau difyr pan mae'r byd yn fôr o liw a natur ar ei odidocaf. Mae'r ardd yn gyfoeth o gynnyrch a bywyd gwyllt ac, mae'r dyddiau'n hirhau a'r tir yn gynnes. Mae bywyd cymdeithasol yn symud i'r tu allan a ninnau'n mwynhau cwmni ein gilydd yn yr awyr agored.

Dyma'r amser yr ydym ni'n ei gysylltu â gwyliau haf, nosweithiau cynnes yn ymlacio tu allan a digon i'w fwyta o'r ardd. Mae'r plant gartref o'r ysgol a dylai fod yn gyfnod hapus gyda'r teulu yn llygad yr haul. Galwch fi'n hen ramantydd, ond dyma rwy'n ei gofio wrth i fi feddwl am hafau fy mhlentyndod. Mae'r gwir ychydig yn wahanol, mae'n siŵr. Dydy'r nosweithiau ddim wastad yn gynnes ac mae glaw yr haf yn medru rhoi stop ar gynlluniau barbeciw teuluol, ond mae un peth yn sicr, bydd gwledd o lysiau yn y siopau ac i ddod o'r ardd hefyd.

Ah ... summer ... glorious ...

The lush, long days when the world is awash with colour and nature is at its most bountiful. The garden is full of riches and wildlife, the days get longer and the land warms up. The social life moves outside and we enjoy each other's company in the fresh air.

This is the time we associate with summer holidays, warm nights relaxing in the garden and plenty to eat from the garden. The children are home from school and it should be a happy time with the family in the sun. Call me an old romantic but this is how I remember the summers of my childhood. The truth is somewhat different probably. The nights aren't always so hot and the summer rain can put a stop to family barbeque plans, but one thing is certain, there'll be a glut of vegetables around, both in the shops and in the garden too.

AL FRESCO

⭐ Mae hwyl bwyta yn yr haf ynghlwm wrth fwyta al fresco i fi, nid dim ond cynnau golosg. P'run a ydych chi'n ei hoffi neu'n ei gasáu, mae'r barbeciw yn arwydd pendant fod yr haf wedi cyrraedd. Nid y cig sy'n bwysig; rwy'n dwlu ar y salad sy'n mynd gyda nhw – y rhuddygl, tomatos o'r ardd, ciwcymbers, tatws bach … mae'r rhestr yn ddiddiwedd. Rhowch lond powlen o ffa llydan, wedi'u masglu, eu berwi a'u gweini ag ychydig o fenyn, halen a phupur a bara crystiog – a dyna i chi bryd mewn ychydig funudau. Rwy'n hoff o gig, cofiwch – coesau cyw iâr wedi'u marinadu mewn iogwrt a mintys, neu mewn olew olewydd, tsili a sinsir, neu ddarn hyfryd o bysgodyn wedi'i goginio mewn parsel ffoil yng ngolosg y barbeciw … o, fe allwn sôn am hydoedd am fwyd hyfryd yr haf a bwyta'r tu allan.

Y ffordd symlaf o fwynhau bwyta yn haul cynnar diwedd dydd, yw coginio yn y gegin, gosod y bwyd ar blatiau ac yna symud tu allan i fwynhau. Os nad ydych chi'n rhai am farbeciws, gallwch goginio'ch cig yn llwyr yn y ffwrn i ddechrau, yna'i osod ar y barbeciw i orffen y broses.

⭐ For me, the joy of summer dining is not the delight of lighting the charcoal, but of eating al fresco. Love them or loathe them, barbecues are a sure sign that summer is upon us. It's not about the meat, I love the accompanying salads – the radish, homegrown tomatoes, cucumbers, salad potatoes … the list is endless. Give me a bowl of freshly picked broad beans, shelled and boiled, served with a little butter, salt and pepper with crusty bread – a meal in minutes. I do love meat, though. Succulent chicken drumsticks marinated in yoghurt and mint, or in olive oil, chilli and ginger, or a great piece of fish slowly cooked in a foil parcel in the barbecue charcoals … oh, I could go on about lovely summertime food, eaten outdoors.

The simplest way to enjoy eating in the early evening sun, is to cook in the kitchen, plate up and then move outdoors to enjoy. If you're not barbeque fans, you can always cook your meat thoroughly in the oven, before placing it on the barbecue to finish.

TARTENNI PICNIC

Dyma ddanteithion blasus i fynd gyda chi i'r awyr iach.

Ar gyfer y toes
225g blawd plaen neu 110g blawd plaen a 110g blawd codi
125g menyn
1 melynwy mawr

Ar gyfer y llenwad
60ml llaeth
60ml hufen dwbl
1 wy (wedi'i guro)
Halen a phupur
Darnau o gig moch wedi'u ffrio
Llysiau yn eu tymor – asbaragws, brocoli, puprau, tomatos bach

Ar gyfer y casyn crwst

Cynheswch y ffwrn i 200°C / 400°F / Nwy 6

Rhowch y blawd a phinsiaid o halen mewn powlen, ychwanegwch y menyn a'i rwbio mewn i'r blawd hyd nes ei fod yn edrych fel briwsion bara.

Ychwanegwch yr wy a chymysgwch i greu toes i'r crwst. Gwasgwch y toes yn bêl, gan adael y bowlen yn hollol lân.

Os oes gennych chi amser, rhowch y toes yn yr oergell am 20 munud. Os nad oes, rholiwch y toes allan ar arwyneb â blawd arno – dylai fod tua 3mm o drwch.

Defnyddiwch y toes i leinio tuniau bach ar gyfer quiche neu fflan. Neu fe allwch chi wneud fersiwn mwy gan ddefnyddio tun quiche mawr.

Leiniwch â chylch o papur gwrthsaim ac yna rholiwch y toes allan i'w ffitio. Gwnewch dyllau bach gyda fforc ar waelod y toes, ac yna rhoi ffa pobi neu reis ar ei waelod.

Pobwch y toes yn 'wag' yn y ffwrn am 10 munud. Tynnwch y ffa neu'r reis allan a phobwch am 5 munud arall. Yna, tynnwch y crwst o'r ffwrn a'i roi o'r neilltu hyd nes bydd y llenwad yn barod.

PICNIC TARTS

These are tasty morsels to take with you into the great outdoors.

For the pastry
225g plain flour or 110g plain and 110g self raising flour
125g butter
1 large egg yolk

For the filling
60ml milk
60ml double cream
1 egg (beaten)
Salt and pepper
Bacon pieces, fried
Seasonal vegetables – asparagus, broccoli, peppers, cherry tomatoes

For the pastry case

Preheat the oven to 200°C / 400°F / Gas 6

Place the flour and a pinch of salt into a bowl, add the butter and rub into the flour until it resembles breadcrumbs.

Add the egg, and mix to make pastry dough. Press the pastry into a ball, leaving the bowl totally clean.

If you have time, place the pastry in the fridge for 20 minutes. If not, roll out the pastry on a floured surface – it should be about 3mm thick.

Use the pastry to line some small quiche or flan tins with pastry. Or you could make a bigger version in a large quiche tin.

Prick the base of the pastry with a fork and then line with a circle of greaseproof paper, and fill with baking beans or rice.

Bake blind in the oven for 10 minutes. Remove the beans and paper, and bake for a further 5 minutes. Then remove and set aside until the filling is ready.

Ar gyfer y llenwad

Curwch yr wy, ychwanegwch y llaeth a'r hufen a rhoi halen a phupur yn ôl y galw.

Gosodwch y cig moch wedi'i ffrio ar waelod y toes sydd wedi'i goginio. Rhowch y cymysgedd wy ar ei ben, ac ychwanegu unrhyw lysiau tymhorol wedi hynny.

Pobwch yn y ffwrn am tua 15–20 munud hyd nes bydd y cyfan wedi caledu fymryn ac wedi troi'n euraid, tynnwch y tartenni o'r ffwrn a gadael iddyn nhw oeri cyn eu storio yn yr oergell hyd nes byddwch am eu bwyta.

For the filling

Beat the egg, add the milk and cream and season with salt and pepper.

Place some fried bacon at the bottom of the cooked pastry cases and add the egg mixture on top, followed by any seasonal vegetables, e.g. asparagus, purple sprouting broccoli, peppers or tomatoes.

Bake in the oven for about 15–20 minutes until they are set and golden, remove from the oven and allow to cool and store in the fridge until eaten.

BRECHDAN BICNIC

Y frechdan ddiymhongar, ond fel na welsoch chi hi erioed o'r blaen. Y bwyd perffaith i'w fwyta tu allan.

Torth fawr, gron, grystiog o fara
Olew olewydd
Finegr balsamig
Caws hufen meddal, plaen neu â blas
½ winwnsyn coch, wedi'i blicio a'i sleisio'n denau
Dail salad
Dail basil ffres
Olifau gwyrdd
Eich hoff gaws wedi'i gratio
3 tomato ffres wedi'u sleisio'n denau
2 dafell o ham wedi'i goginio
Ciwcymber wedi'i sleisio
Halen a phupur

Cyn i chi ddechrau llunio'ch brechdan, sleisiwch y tomatos a'u rhoi mewn powlen gyda diferyn o olew olewydd ac ychydig o finegr balsamig. Gadewch iddyn nhw fwydo yn y cymysgedd.

Torrwch haenen denau oddi ar ben y dorth a thynnu'r holl fara meddal allan ohoni. Ceisiwch adael cragen gadarn o grwst i'r dorth.

Brwsiwch tu mewn i'r gragen â'r olew olewydd neu'r caws hufen meddal er mwyn selio'r bara. Bydd hyn yn atal y dorth rhag mynd yn feddal.

PICNIC SANDWICH

The humble sandwich, but with knobs on. The perfect outdoor food.

A large crusty, round loaf of bread
Olive oil
Balsamic vinegar
Soft cream cheese, plain or flavoured
½ red onion, peeled and sliced thinly
Salad leaves
Fresh basil leaves
Green olives
Your favourite cheese, grated
3 fresh tomatoes, thinly sliced
2 slices of cooked ham
Cucumber, sliced
Salt and pepper

Before you start building your sandwich, slice the tomatoes and place them in a bowl with a drop of olive oil and a dash of balsamic vinegar. Allow them to soak.

Cut a thin slice off the top of the bread and pull out all the soft bread from inside the loaf; try to leave a firm crust shell.

Brush the inside of the bread shell with the olive oil or with a soft cream cheese to seal the bread. This stops it going too soft.

Dyma gychwyn yr hwyl ...
dechreuwch adeiladu haenau eich brechdan.

Yn gyntaf, gosodwch ddail amrywiol ar waelod y gragen, rhoi dail basil wedi'u torri ar ben y rheiny ac yna'r olifau. Nesa, gosodwch y caws ar eu pennau.

Nawr, ychwanegwch haenen o'r tomatos wedi'u mwydo mewn olew a finegr, ac ychydig o halen a phupur du drostynt. Rhowch ham ar ben y cyfan.

Gallwch ddefnyddio rhai o'r cynhwysion eto, gan ychwanegu mwy o haenau a mwy o'ch hoff flasau, hyd nes bydd y dorth yn llawn.

Yn olaf, gosodwch y clawr yn ôl ar y dorth. Lapiwch y cyfan mewn papur gwrthsaim a'i glymu â darn o gortyn.

Rhowch yn yr oergell i'w gadw'n oer hyd nes byddwch chi'n barod i'w fwyta neu i fynd am bicnic.

Sleisiwch drwy'r dorth â chyllell fara ar gyfer tafell bert o frechdan haenog.

 Tip: gallwch wneud torthau picnic bach unigol gan ddefnyddio rholiau bara crystiog – delfrydol ar gyfer tamaid o ginio iach.

Then the fun begins ...
start to layer your sandwich.

First, place some salad leaves at the bottom of the shell, then some torn basil leaves and then the olives. Next, place the cheese on top.

Now add a layer of the soaked sliced tomatoes, season them with salt and black pepper. Place some ham on top of this.

You can repeat some of the ingredients again, adding more and more of your favourite flavours, until the loaf is full.

Finally, place the top back on the loaf, wrap in greaseproof paper and tie with twine or string.

Place in the fridge to keep chilled until you are ready to eat or go on your picnic.

Slice through the loaf with a bread knife for a pretty layered sandwich slice.

 Tip: you can make small, individual picnic loaves using crusty bread rolls, perfect for a healthy lunch.

RHOLIAU SELSIG BACH HAWDD

Dyma gonglfeini picnics a phartïon. Does dim i beidio â'i hoffi am y byrbryd bendigedig hwn.

> 1 pecyn o grwst pwff
> 1 wy, wedi'i guro
> 1 pecyn o selsig plaen neu rai â pherlysiau ynddyn nhw
> Ychydig o saws tomato neu fwstard neu ddarnau o afal

Cynheswch y ffwrn i 190°C / 375°F / Nwy 5

Rholiwch y toes allan i wneud petryal mawr. Torrwch y petryal ar ei hyd er mwyn gwneud dau stribed hir. Yna, gallwch dorri pob stribed yn bedwar darn i'w gwneud yn llai ac yn haws i'w rholio.

Brwsiwch un pen i bob darn o does â'r wy wedi'i guro.

Gosodwch ddarn o selsig ar un pen i'r toes ac ychwanegu halen a phupur yn ôl y galw. Rholiwch y toes o amgylch y selsigen a gwnewch batrwm ar ben pob un.

Cyn rholio'r selsig, rhowch gynnig ar ychwanegu ychydig bach o saws llugaeron, saws tomato neu fwstard neu hyd yn oed rai perlysiau at y selsig. Gallwch hefyd ychwanegu stribedi o afal at y rholiau selsig cyn eu rholio. Gwnewch amrywiaeth o flasau i blesio pawb.

Brwsiwch bob rholyn selsig â gweddill yr wy a'u pobi yn y ffwrn am tua 25 munud.

EASY MINI SAUSAGE ROLLS

The mainstay of picnics and parties. What's not to like about this wondersnack?

> 1 pack of puff pastry
> 1 egg, beaten
> 1 pack of plain or herby sausages
> A little ketchup or mustard or slices of apple

Preheat the oven to 190°C / 375°F / Gas 5

Roll out the pastry to make a large rectangle, and cut the rectangle in two along its length to make two long strips. Then, you can cut each of the strips into four pieces, making them smaller and easier to roll.

Brush one end of each piece of pastry with the beaten egg.

Lay a piece of sausage on the other end and season with a little salt and pepper. Roll the pastry around the sausage and make a pattern on the top of each one.

Before rolling up the sausage add a small dollop of cranberry sauce, tomato ketchup or mustard or even some herbs to the sausage rolls. Or try baking them with strips of apple inside. Make an assortment to suit all tastes.

Brush the top of each sausage roll with the rest of the egg and bake in the oven for about 25 minutes.

MYFFINS AERON FFEIN

Cacennau bychain â ffrwythau ynddyn nhw – does dim yn cyfleu'r haf yn well, ac maen nhw mor hawdd i'w gwneud.

- 75g blawd codi
- 75g blawd codi cyflawn
- 1 llwy de o bowdwr codi
- 50g siwgwr mân
- 75ml olew llysiau
- 1 wy buarth mawr
- 75ml llaeth
- Llond llaw o aeron – mwyar, cyrens cochion neu fafon

Cynheswch y ffwrn i 200°C / 400°F / Nwy 6

Leiniwch y tun myffins â chasys myffin.

Mewn powlen fawr, cymysgwch y blawd a'r siwgwr.

Curwch yr wyau, y llaeth a'r olew gan ddefnyddio fforc.

Ychwanegwch y cynhwysion gwlyb at y cynhwysion sych a'u cymysgu.

Ychwanegwch y ffrwythau a'u cymysgu'n ofalus i mewn i'r cymysgedd myffin.

Rhowch lwyeidiau o'r cymysgedd i mewn yn y casys myffins, tua llond llwy fwrdd ym mhob un. Pobwch yn y ffwrn am tua 15 munud hyd nes eu bod yn euraid ac wedi codi'n dda. Tynnwch nhw o'r ffwrn a'u rhoi i oeri ar resel wifrau.

BERRY NICE MUFFINS

Small cakes with fruit in them – nothing says summer better, and they're so easy to make.

- 75g self raising flour
- 75g self raising wholemeal flour
- 1 teaspoon baking powder
- 50g caster sugar
- 75ml vegetable oil
- 1 large free-range egg
- 75ml milk
- A handful of fruit – blackberries, redcurrants or raspberries

Preheat the oven to 200°C / 400°F / Gas 6

Line the muffin tins with muffin cases.

In a large bowl, mix together the flour and sugar.

Beat the eggs, milk and oil together with a fork.

Add the liquid ingredients to the dry ingredients and mix.

Add the fruit and carefully mix into the muffin mixture.

Spoon the mixture into cake cases, about a dessert spoonful into each. Bake in the oven for about 15 minutes until golden and well risen. Remove from the oven and cool on a wire rack.

CEBABS FFRWYTHAU

Ffrwyth-tastig!

Afalau, gellyg, pinafal, ciwi, melon, mango,
ffrwythau sêr, grawnwin, mefus, melon dŵr
Ychydig o sudd lemwn
50g siocled
Sbrincls
Sudd oren neu sudd afal (ar gyfer gwneud
salad ffrwythau)

Paratowch y ffrwythau – golchwch, pliciwch a'u torri
nhw. Ceisiwch sicrhau bod pob darn oddeutu'r un
faint. Brwsiwch yr afalau a'r gellyg â sudd lemwn i'w
hatal rhag troi'n frown.

Bwydwch y ffrwythau'n ofalus ar sgiwer, gan geisio
amrywio'r lliwiau.

Toddwch y siocled mewn powlen dros sosban o ddŵr
berwedig, sef bain-marie.

Diferwch ychydig o'r siocled yn ofalus dros y
ffrwythau ac ychwanegwch sbrincls i'w haddurno.
Rhowch yn yr oergell hyd nes bydd eu hangen nhw.

 *Os nad oes gennych chi sgiwers, yna gwnewch
salad ffrwythau. Rhowch y darnau ffrwythau
mewn powlen ac ychwanegu ychydig o sudd oren
neu sudd afal.*

*Ychwanegwch lwyaid o hufen iâ neu iogwrt i gael
pwdin iachus.*

FRUIT KEBABS

Fruit-tastic!

Apples, pears, pineapples, kiwi, melon, mango,
star fruit, grapes, strawberries, watermelon
A little lemon juice
50g chocolate
Sprinkles
Orange or apple juice (to make fruit salad)

Prepare the fruit – wash, peel and chop. Try to ensure
that all the fruit are about the same size. Brush all apples
and pears with lemon juice to prevent them from turning
brown.

Carefully thread the fruit onto skewers, and try to balance
the colours, if possible.

Melt about 50g chocolate in a clean bowl over a
saucepan of boiling water, a bain-marie.

Carefully drizzle some of the chocolate over the fruit and
add some sprinkles to decorate.

Keep in the fridge until needed.

*If you have no skewers, then make fruit salad.
Place the chopped the fruit in a bowl and add a little
orange or apple juice.*

*Add a scoop of ice cream or yoghurt for a healthy
dessert.*

* Defnyddiwch unrhyw ffrwythau sy'n cymryd eich ffansi, ond ceisiwch ddefnyddio ffrwythau yn eu tymor, er enghraifft, mefus ym misoedd Mehefin a Gorffennaf neu afalau ym Medi a Hydref.

* Any fruit you like, but try to use fruit that's in season, for example, strawberries in June and July or apples in September and October.

DIODYDD A SUDD

Does dim i guro blas yr haf mewn potel. Pan fo'r gwres ar ei fwyaf gormesol, bydd pawb mor falch y penderfynoch chi greu elicsir gorwych i dorri'r syched. A bydd phobl yn synnu at eich gallu. Ond yr hyn nad oes yn rhaid i bawb ei wybod yw pa mor hawdd yw gwneud y diodydd hyn. Mwynhewch nhw gyda dŵr wedi'i oeri neu defnyddiwch nhw i roi blas i goctêls, pwdinau a phethau eraill.

Mae'r diodydd a'r sudd yma'n gymysgedd o ffrwythau (neu flodau), siwgwr, dŵr ac asid tartatig neu asid sitrig. Defnyddir yr asid tartarig neu asid citrig fel elfen sy'n cadw'r cynnyrch am ychydig yn hirach, does dim rhaid eu defnyddio, a gellir eu prynu o'ch siop gyfanfwyd leol. Felly, dim ond dewis eich hoff ffrwythau a rhoi cynnig arni sydd angen i chi wneud – eirin Mair, mafon, mefus, riwbob, cyrens duon a mwyar – beth bynnag sydd yn ei dymor.

O ran offer, yr unig beth sydd ei angen arnoch yw potel neu jar wedi'i sterileiddio, ffilter a lliain mwslin neu liain sychu llestri glân er mwyn straenio'r cymysgedd drwyddo. Rydych chi'n barod i gamu i fyd llesmeiriol gwneud sudd.

Bydd diodydd a sudd yn cadw'n iawn mewn lle oer a thywyll am hyd at fis, neu yn yr oergell am ychydig yn hwy. Gwnewch yn siŵr bod eich diod yn cael ei gadw'n gywir neu fe all ddechrau eplesu. Mae'n iawn i chi ei rewi hefyd os hoffech ei gadw am gyfnod hirach.

<hr>

CORDIALS AND DRINKS

There's nothing to beat the taste of summer in a bottle. At the height of a heatwave everybody will be so grateful that you decided to create some glorious elixir to quench the thirst. People will be astonished at your knowhow. But what they don't need to know is how easy cordial is to make. Enjoy just with chilled water or use them to flavour cocktails, desserts and other dishes.

Cordials are a mix of fruit (or florals), sugar, water and tartaric or citric acid. The tartaric or citric acid are used as a preservative, they're optional, they can be bought from your local health food shop. So, just choose your favourite fruit and get going – gooseberries, raspberries, strawberries, rhubarb, blackcurrants and blackberries – whatever's in season.

As far as equipment goes, all you need is a sterilised bottle or jar for your cordial, a filter and clean muslin cloth or tea towel to strain the mixture through. You're ready to enter the heady world of cordial making.

Cordials will keep in a cool, dark place for up to a month, or in the fridge for slightly longer. Make sure your cordial is stored correctly or it can start to ferment. It's also fine to freeze if you want to keep it for longer.

DIOD YSGAW

I wneud y gorau o arogl a blas cryf yr ysgawen, casglwch nhw yn llygad yr haul rai dyddiau ar ôl iddyn nhw ymddangos gyntaf.

Mae hyn yn sicrhau bod pob blodyn bychan yn y sbrigyn wedi agor ac yn rhoi cymaint â phosib o baill a blas. Unwaith bydd y paill wedi gollwng o'r blodau, bydd eu lliw yn llai hufennog a bydd y blas yn llai dwys hefyd. Yn ei hanfod, yr hyn sydd angen i wneud y ddiod yw rhoi blas ysgaw i'r dŵr, gan ychwanegu siwgwr ac asid tartarig neu asid citrig i'r ddiod. Peidiwch ag anghofio bod angen ychwanegu dŵr at y ddiod cyn ei hyfed.

> 20–25 sbrigyn o flodau'r ysgaw
> 2 lemwn
> 2 litr o ddŵr twym
> Hyd at 1.5 kilo o siwgwr
> 30g asid tartarig neu asid citrig
> Iâ

Gwaredwch unrhyw bryfed oddi ar yr ysgaw a'u rhoi mewn sosban fawr. Ychwanegwch sudd 2 lemwn.

Gorchuddiwch y blodau a'r sudd lemwn mewn tua 2 litr o ddŵr twym, ond nid dŵr berw, a gadael iddyn nhw fwydo am o leiaf 4 awr; dros nos fyddai'n ddelfrydol.

Straeniwch yr hylif drwy ridyll mân neu liain cotwm glân a mesurwch yr hylif sydd ar ôl.

Ychwanegwch 350g o siwgwr a llond llwy de o asid tartarig am bob 500ml o hylif sydd gennych. Dewch â'ch cymysgedd i'r berw'n raddol, gan ei droi er mwyn toddi'r siwgwr.

Gadewch i'r ddiod oeri ac yna arllwys i boteli glân – gall twndish fod yn ddefnyddiol.

Ychwanegwch ddŵr oer ati, tua 4:1 dŵr i ddiod. Arllwyswch i wydr gydag ychydig o iâ.

> *Tip: gallwch rewi'r cymysgedd i wneud lolis iâ, cofiwch ychwanegu'r dŵr cyn eu rhewi er mwyn cael blas gwannach.*

ELDERFLOWER CORDIAL

To make the most of the elderflower's strong aroma and flavour, pick them in full sun a few days after they first appear.

This ensures that every tiny flower in the spray is open and will give maximum pollen and flavour. Once the pollen drops from the flowers, their colour becomes less creamy and the intensity of the flavour also diminishes. Basically, to make the cordial, you simply want to flavour the water with the elderflowers. Adding sugar and tartaric or citric acid preserves the cordial. Don't forget that the cordial must be diluted before drinking.

> 20–25 elderflower heads
> 2 lemons
> 2 litres hot water
> Up to 1.5 kilos granulated sugar
> 30g tartaric or citric acid
> Ice

Shake any insects off the picked elderflowers and place them in a large saucepan. Add the juice of 2 lemons.

Cover the flowers and lemons with about 2 litres of hot but not boiling water, and allow to soak for at least 4 hours – overnight is ideal.

Strain the liquid using a fine strainer or a clean cotton cloth and measure the liquid you have left.

Add 350g of granulated sugar and a teaspoonful of tartaric acid for every 500ml of liquid.

Bring the mixture gradually to the boil, stirring to dissolve the sugar.

Allow the cordial to cool and then pour into clean bottles – a funnel is useful for this.

Dilute with cold water (about 4:1 water to cordial). Pour into a glass with ice.

> *Tip: try freezing some to make your own homemade lollies, but remember to add water to reduce the concentration first.*

LEMONÊD CWMWL HAF

Blas yr haf, heb os

4 lemwn
750ml dŵr berw
100g siwgwr mân
Iâ

Golchwch y lemwn i waredu unrhyw lwch neu fryntni.

Gan ddefnyddio pliciwr, pliciwch stribedi trwchus o groen y lemwn i'w defnyddio fel addurn yn nes ymlaen.

Torrwch bob lemwn yn ei hanner a gwasgu'r sudd allan ohonyn nhw.

Rhowch yr haneri lemwn wedi'u gwasgu a'r sudd mewn jygaid mawr o ddŵr berw a throi'r cyfan.

Ychwanegwch 100g o siwgwr mân a'i droelli hyd nes bydd wedi toddi.

Gadewch i oeri am ychydig oriau.

Pan fydd lemonêd yn oer, gallwch naill ai straenio'r hylif i gael gwared ar yr holl ddarnau lemwn neu ei arllwys o'r jwg gan ddal yr haneri lemwn yn ôl gan ddefnyddio llwy.

Cadwch y lemonêd yn yr oergell, a gallwch ychwanegu dŵr ato os dymunwch os gwelwch ei fod yn rhy gryf.

I'w weini, arllwyswch i wydr ac ychwanegu iâ a stribedyn o groen lemwn.

 Tip: gallwch rewi peth mewn mowldiau i wneud eich lolis iâ eich hun.

COOL CLOUDY LEMONADE

The taste of summer, without a doubt.

4 lemons
750ml boiling water
100g caster sugar
Ice

Wash the lemons to remove any dust or dirt.

Using a peeler, peel a few thick strips of zest off the lemons to use as decoration later.

Cut each lemon in half and squeeze the juice from them.

Place the squeezed lemons and the juice in a large jug with the boiling water and stir.

Add 100g of caster sugar to sweeten and stir until dissolved.

Allow to stand for a few hours to cool.

Once the lemonade is cool, either strain the liquid to remove all the lemon bits or simply pour from the jug holding back the lemon with a large spoon.

Store the lemonade in the fridge and dilute to taste if you find it too strong.

To serve, pour into a glass with ice and a strip of zest.

Tip: try freezing some in moulds to make your own home-made lollies.

JAM EIRIN MAIR AC YSGAW

Mae eirin Mair yn ddanteithion eraill sy'n barod i'w casglu yng ngardd y gegin yr adeg hon o'r flwyddyn. Maen nhw'n gweithio'n dda gydag ysgaw.

> 1kg eirin Mair
> 500ml dŵr
> 5 sbrigyn ysgaw neu 4 llwy fwrdd o syrop diod ysgaw
> 800g siwgwr
> Jariau jam glân

Tynnwch bennau a chynffonnau'r eirin Mair a'u rhoi mewn sosban fawr neu sosban gwneud jam, os oes gennych chi un.

Ychwanegwch y dŵr a'r blodau ysgaw neu'r syrop ysgaw, a'u cynhesu ar wres isel hyd nes bydd yr eirin Mair yn dechrau meddalu. Torrwch goesau'r ysgaw a'u taflu.

Ychwanegwch y siwgwr a throwch y cymysgedd hyd nes bydd wedi toddi, ond peidiwch â throi'n rhy egnïol neu fe gollwch chi siâp yr eirin Mair.

Dewch â'r jam i'r berw am 10 munud a gwiriwch i weld a yw wedi cyrraedd y pwynt setio. Gallwch wneud hyn drwy ollwng ychydig o jam ar blât sydd wedi'i oeri yn yr oergell; os yw'n setio ar ôl munud neu ddwy, mae'r jam yn barod. Os nad yw, berwch am ychydig mwy a gwiriwch eto.

Pan fydd y jam yn barod, gadewch iddo oeri ychydig, yna tynnu unrhyw lysnafedd sydd wedi casglu ar yr wyneb a defnyddio lletwad i roi'r jam mewn jariau glân. Gosodwch ddisgiau cwyr ar ben y jam a chaead ar y jar, ac yna labelwch eich cynnyrch.

GOOSEBERRY AND ELDERFLOWER JAM

Gooseberries are another treat to find in the kitchen garden this time of year; they work well with elderflower.

> 1kg gooseberries
> 500ml water
> 5 elderflower heads or 4 tablespoons elderflower cordial syrup
> 800g granulated sugar
> Sterilised jam jars

Top and tail the gooseberries and place them in a large pan or preserving pan, if you have one.

Add the water and the elderflower heads, or the cordial, and heat over a low heat until the gooseberries just begin to soften. Remove the elderflower stems.

Add the sugar and stir until dissolved, but don't stir too energetically or you will lose the shape of the gooseberries.

Bring the jam to a rolling boil for about 10 minutes and check for the setting point. You can check for this by dropping a small amount of jam on to a fridge-cold plate; if it sets after a minute or two, the jam is ready. If not, boil for a little longer and check again.

Once the jam is ready, allow it to cool slightly, skim off any scum, then ladle into warm, sterilised jars. Cover with a wax disc and lid, and label your produce.

Ewch â'r salad
hafaidd hwn i'r
gwaith neu ar bicnic.

Take this summery
salad to work
or on a picnic.

LL **DG**

Salad jar Kilner

Ar gyfer y dresin

Sudd un lemwn a'i groen wedi'i gratio'n fân, 3 llwy fwrdd o olew olewydd, ½ tsili coch heb hadau, wedi'i sleisio'n fân. Cymysgwch y cynhwysion ynghyd.

Dewiswch eich hoff ffrwythau a llysiau ar gyfer y salad hwn, e.e. betys, moron, ciwcymber, afocado, tomatos bach neu shibwns. Ychwanegwch eich hoff ddail salad a dail basil ag olifau gwyrdd (heb gerrig) ynghyd â hadau cymysg (hadau blodau'r haul, sesame neu bwmpen) a ffrwythau sych cymysg (llugaeron, bricyll, cyrens). Tynnwch y croen, torrwch, sleisiwch a gratiwch yr holl ffrwythau a'r llysiau. Peidiwch ag anghofio defnyddio ychydig o sudd lemwn i orchuddio'r ffrwythau sy'n medru troi'n 'frown'. Ffriwch ddarnau o gaws halloumi yn ysgafn hyd nes eu bod wedi brownio.

Rhowch y betys a'r dresin ar waelod jar Kilner fawr, yna gosodwch haenau o'r holl gynhwysion eraill ar eu pen. Seliwch y jar a'i rhoi yn yr oergell hyd nes byddwch yn barod i'w ddefnyddio.

V **GF**

Kilner jar Salad

For the dressing

The juice and finely grated zest of one lemon, 3 tbsp of olive oil, ½ red chilli, deseeded and finely sliced. Mix together.

Choose your favourite fruit and vegetables for this salad, e.g. beetroot, carrots, cucumber, avocado, cherry tomatoes or spring onions. Add your favourite salad leaves, basil leaves and pitted green olives along with mixed seeds (sunflower, sesame or pumpkin) and mixed dried fruit (cranberries, apricots, raisins). Peel, chop, slice and grate all the fruit and vegetables. Don't forget to dip all fruit that tend to 'brown' in a little lemon juice. Gently fry some chunks of halloumi cheese until browned.

Place the beetroot and the dressing in the bottom of a large Kilner jar and then layer all the other ingredients on top. Seal the jar and place in the fridge until ready to serve.

Yr hyn sy'n gwneud salad yn wahanol yw'r dresin, a dyma i chi ddewis o rai gwahanol. Mwynhewch yr amrywiaeth o flasau.

What makes salads different is the dressing, and here is a selection of different ones. Enjoy the plethora of different tastes.

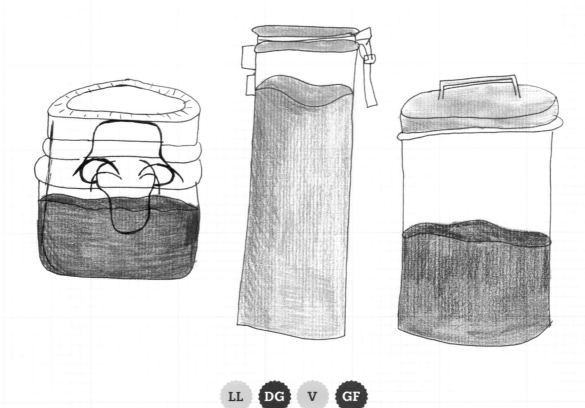

LL · DG · V · GF

DRESINS JAR JAM
JAM JAR DRESSINGS

Dewiswch eich dresin, rhowch eich cynhwysion
mewn jar jam glân, gwag ac ysgwydwch.
Hawdd i'w cysmygu a hawdd i'w storio.

Choose your dressing, add the ingredients
to a clean and empty jam jar and shake.
Easy to mix and easy to store.

Dresin Ffrengig

1 ewin garlleg
1 llwy de o fwstard Dijon
2 lwy de o finegr gwin gwyn neu goch
6 llwy fwrdd o olew olewydd
1 pinsiaid o halen môr
1 pinsiaid o bupur du, wedi'i falu

French dressing

1 clove garlic
1 teaspoon Dijon mustard
2 tablespoons white or red wine vinegar
6 tablespoons olive oil
1 pinch sea salt
1 pinch ground black pepper

Dresin iogwrt

1/3 cwpanaid o iogwrt naturiol
2 lwy fwrdd o finegr gwin gwyn
1 llwy fwrdd o olew olewydd
1 pinsiaid o halen môr
1 pinsiaid o bupur du, wedi'i falu

Yoghurt dressing

1/3 cup natural yoghurt
2 tablespoons white wine vinegar
1 tablespoon olive oil
1 pinch sea salt
1 pinch freshly ground black pepper

Dresin basil a lemwn

4–5 llwy de o sudd lemwn
150ml olew olewydd
1 ewin garlleg
Llond llaw o ddail basil, wedi'u torri
2 lwy de o gaprys

Basil and lemon dressing

4–5 tsp lemon juice
150ml olive oil
1 clove garlic
A handful of basil leaves, torn
2 tsp capers

Dresin Gwlad Thai

1 llwy de o finegr gwin gwyn
2 lwy fwrdd o sudd leim
6 llwy fwrdd o olew olewydd
1 llwy fwrdd o siwgwr mân
1 shibwnsyn
1 tsili coch

Thai dressing

1 tsp white wine vinegar
2 tbs lime juice
6 tbs olive oil
1 tbs caster sugar
1 spring onion
1 red chilli

Finegrét lemwn

1 sialotsyn
1 ewin garlleg
3 llwy fwrdd o olew olewydd
Sudd ½ lemwn

Lemon vinaigrette

1 shallot
1 garlic clove
3 tbs olive oil
½ lemon, juiced

O BEDWAR BAN Y BYD

⭐ Yn draddodiadol dyma'r adeg i fynd ar wyliau neu wneud pethau ychydig yn wahanol i'r arfer. Ond, wrth gwrs, does dim rhaid teithio i bob cwr o'r ddaear i gael profiadau a blasu bywyd gwahanol. Mae modd cael y byd i gyd yn grwn ar eich plât drwy goginio prydau o wledydd eraill. Barod am y daith?

FROM AROUND THE WORLD

⭐ Traditionally, this is the time of year for going on holiday or for doing things a little different from the usual. But of course, you don't need to travel to the four corners of the earth to experience new things and tastes. You can have the whole world on your plate by cooking meals from other countries. Are you ready for the trip?

DG

PAELLA

Ychydig bach o 'ta-raaa!' i'r bwrdd bwyd.

4 clun cyw iâr wedi'u torri'n 3 darn
450g cregyn gleision
200g ystifflog, wedi'i dorri'n ddarnau
6 corgimwch mawr neu langwstîn
200g selsig chorizo
200g reis paella neu reis Calasparra
(grawn byr Sbaenaidd)
Darnau o lemwn i weini

Hefyd, bydd angen
150ml gwin gwyn sych
1 winwnsyn mawr, wedi'i dorri'n fân
1 pupur coch wedi'i sleisio
2 llwy fwrdd o olew olewydd
2 ewin garlleg wedi'u torri
1 litr stoc cyw iâr
100g pys wedi'u rhewi ac wedi'u dadmer
2 llwy de o deim ffres, wedi'i dorri
Pinsiaid mawr o saffrwm
2 lwy de o baprica mwg

Yn gyntaf, gwnewch yn siŵr bod eich cregyn gleision yn iawn. Os nad yw'n cau pan fyddwch chi'n ei tharo'n sydyn, taflwch y gragen las. Bydd cragen las iach yn cau o gael ei tharo; mae'n ffordd o'i hamddiffyn ei hun.

Rhowch y gwin gwyn ac ychydig (75 ml) o'r stoc cyw iâr ynghyd â'r teim mewn sosban fawr a'u berwi. Ychwanegwch y cregyn gleision, rhoi clawr arnyn nhw, a gadael iddyn nhw stemio am rai munudau hyd nes bod y cregyn yn agor. Draeniwch yr hylif a'i gadw; gwaredwch unrhyw gregyn gleision sydd heb agor.

Rhowch y saffrwm mewn 100ml o stoc cyw iâr a gadael iddo fwydo. Rhowch y chorizo, yr winwns, y pupur a'r garlleg mewn ffrimpan fawr neu ban paella a ffriwch y cyfan am ychydig funudau hyd nes eu bod yn feddal. Ychwanegwch y reis Calasparra neu reis paella, a'i droi hyd nes bydd pob gronyn o reis wedi'i orchuddio ac yn sgleinio. Nawr ychwanegwch y paprica a sudd y cregyn

GF

PAELLA

A little bit of 'ta-raaa!' on the table.

4 chicken thighs, cut into 3 pieces
450g fresh mussels
200g squid, cut into pieces
6 raw king prawns or langoustines
200g chorizo sausage
200g paella rice or Calasparra rice
(Spanish shortgrain)
Lemon wedges to serve

You will also need
150ml dry white wine
1 large onion, finely chopped
1 red pepper, sliced
2 tbsp olive oil
2 garlic cloves, chopped
1 litre chicken stock
100g frozen peas, defrosted
2 tsp chopped fresh thyme
A large pinch of saffron
2 tsp smoked paprika

First check your mussels. If it refuses to close when given a sudden tap, discard the mussel. A healthy mussel will always close when tapped; it is a way of defending itself.

Place the white wine, a drop (75 ml) of the chicken stock, and thyme in a large pan and bring to the boil. Add the mussels, cover with a lid and allow to steam for a few minutes until the shells open. Drain, reserve the juices and discard any unopened mussels.

Put the saffron into 100ml of hot chicken stock and allow to soak. Add the chorizo, onion, pepper and garlic to a large frying pan or paella pan and fry for

> gleision, oedd wedi'i gadw a phan fydd yn byrlymu, arllwyswch y stoc cyw iâr a'r stoc â'r saffrwm ynddo ac ychwanegwch y darnau cyw iâr a'u coginio am 5–10 munud.

Ychwanegwch yr ystifflog, y corgimychiaid neu'r langwstîns ar ben y cyfan a mudferwch yn dyner am tua 15 munud. Ceisiwch beidio â'u cymysgu yn y munudau olaf.

Gosodwch y cregyn gleision wedi'u coginio ar ben y paella yn ogystal â'r pys ar gyfer y munudau olaf hyd nes bydd y cyfan wedi cynhesu drwyddo.

Bwytewch gyda'r darnau o lemwn a gwin coch o Sbaen.

> a few minutes until soft. Add the Calasparra or paella rice, and stir until all the grains of rice are coated and glossy. Now add the paprika and the reserved mussel juices and when the mixture is bubbling, pour in the hot chicken stock as well as the stock with the saffron. Add the chicken thighs and cook for 5–10 minutes.

Add the squid, prawns or langoustines on top and simmer gently for about 15 minutes until the rice is tender. Try not to stir for the final few minutes.

Place the cooked mussels on top and finally add the peas for the last few minutes until heated through.

Serve with the lemon wedges and Spanish red wine.

POISSON EN PAPILLOTE

Dyma ffordd ardderchog o goginio samwn, neu unrhyw bysgodyn hoffech chi – mae'n gyfrwng da i gyflwyno blasau cryfion hyfryd.

Ar gyfer pob parsel
1 ffiled pysgodyn o'ch dewis chi ar gyfer pob person
2 lwy fwrdd o olew olewydd
½ llwy de o sinsir ffres wedi'i blicio a'i sleisio
Tsili coch wedi'i ddadhadu a'i sleisio
1 shibwnsyn wedi'i sleisio'n denau
2 domato bach
1 llwy fwrdd o sudd oren ffres
Tafell o lemwn

Cynheswch y ffwrn i 190°C / 375°F / Nwy 5

Torrwch ddarn o bapur gwrthsaim yn mesur tua 25cm sgwâr – bydd angen torri un darn i bob person. Taenwch ddiferion olew olewydd dros y papur.

Rhowch y tsili, y sinsir, y shibwnsyn a'r tomatos ar bob darn o bapur a rhoi'r ffiled samwn ar ben y cyfan. Defnyddiwch ychydig o bupur a halen i flasu.

Lapiwch y papur i ffurfio parsel, a phlygwch yr ymylon i'w selio.

Gosodwch ar hambwrdd pobi a phobi am 10–15 munud.

Bwytewch gyda thatws bach wedi'u berwi ynghyd ag ychydig o bys melys, brocoli porffor, ffa gwyrdd a phys. Berwch y tatws hyd nes eu bod yn feddal. Paratowch a choginio'r ffa a'r pys, eu rhoi mewn powlen fawr a'u cymysgu'n dda ag ychydig o fenyn.

POISSON EN PAPILLOTE

This is a great way to cook salmon, or any fish you like. It's an intense infusion of flavour.

Per parcel
1 fish fillet of your choice per person
2 tablespoons olive oil
½ teaspoon fresh ginger, peeled and sliced
Sliced red chilli, deseeded
1 spring onion, thinly sliced
2 cherry tomatoes
1 tablespoon fresh orange juice
Slice of lemon

Preheat the oven to 190°C / 375°F / Gas 5

Cut a piece of greaseproof paper measuring about 25cm square. You'll need one per person. Drizzle paper with olive oil.

Put the chilli, ginger, spring onion and tomatoes on each sheet of paper, and place the salmon fillet on top. Season with salt and pepper.

Wrap up the paper to form parcels, folding the edges to seal.

Place on a baking sheet and bake for 10–15 minutes.

Serve with boiled salad potatoes and some sugar snap peas, purple sprouting broccoli, green beans and peas. Boil the potatoes until tender. Prepare and cook the beans and peas, then place them in a large bowl, mix well with a little butter.

CIG OEN MOROCO WEDI'I ROSTIO'N ARAF

2 lwy fwrdd o olew olewydd
2 lwy de o sbeis ras el hanout
3 neu 4 ewin garlleg
Sudd 1 lemwn
1 pinsiaid o halen
1 coes neu ysgwydd fawr cig oen
2 lwy fwrdd o ddŵr neu win coch

Cynheswch y ffwrn i 170ºC / 325ºF / Nwy 3

Gosodwch y cig oen ar ddarn mawr, dwbl o ffoil cegin.

Gan ddefnyddio cyllell finiog, gwnewch sawl toriad yn y cig oen.

Rhwbiwch y sbeis yn drylwyr i mewn i'r cig.

Arllwyswch y gwin coch a'r sudd lemwn dros y cig â llwy. Ychwanegwch y lemwn cyfan wedi'i haneru a gwthiwch y tri neu bedwar ewin garlleg i mewn i'r toriadau wnaethoch chi yn y cig oen.

Rhowch ddau ddarn arall o ffoil dros y cig oen a seliwch y pedair ochr yn dynn gan rolio'r ffoil sawl gwaith.

Gosodwch y cig oen, wedi'i lapio yn y ffoil mewn tun rhostio a'i rostio am 4 awr, hyd nes ei fod yn dyner iawn ac yn llaith.

Dewisol: gallwch ychwanegu llysiau eraill i'r tun rhostio am awr olaf y coginio i greu pryd cyflawn.

SLOW ROAST MOROCCAN LAMB

2 tbsps olive oil
2 tsps of ras el hanout spice
3 or 4 cloves of garlic
Juice 1 lemon
1 pinch salt
1 large lamb shoulder/leg
2 tbsp water or red wine

Preheat the oven to 170ºC / 325ºF / Gas 3

Place the lamb shoulder on a large double sheet of kitchen foil.

Using a sharp knife, cut several incisions into the lamb.

Rub the spice thoroughly into the meat.

Spoon over the red wine, the lemon juice, add the whole halved lemon and insert three or four cloves of garlic into the incisions made in the lamb.

Place two further sheets of foil over the lamb and tightly seal all four sides by rolling the foil several times.

Place the foil-wrapped lamb in a roasting tray and roast for 4 hours, until very tender and moist.

Optional: add additional vegetables to the roasting tray and roast for the last hour to make a complete meal.

RAS EL HANOUT: cymysgedd poblogaidd o sbeisiau o Foroco a ddefnyddir ar draws gogledd Affrica. Mae'r enw'n golygu 'pen y siop' mewn Arabeg. Does dim un cyfuniad diffiniol o sbeis yn gwneud ras el hanout. Byddai gan bawb ei gyfuniad cyfrinachol ei hun. Fel arfer fyddai'n cynnwys cardamom, clof, sinamon, puprau tsili wedi'u malu, coriander, cwmin, nytmeg, grawn pupur a thyrmerig. Gallwch ei brynu wedi'i baratoi'n barod yn y rhan fwyaf o archfarchnadoedd neu mewn siopau bwydydd iach.

RAS EL HANOUT: a popular Moroccan blend of spices that is used across north Africa. The name means 'head of the shop' in Arabic. There is no definitive set combination of spices that makes up ras el hanout. Each person would have their own secret combination of spices. Typically they would include cardamom, clove, cinnamon, ground chilli peppers, coriander, cumin, nutmeg, peppercorn and turmeric. You can buy it ready-made in most supermarkets and health food shops.

Dyma i chi flas amheuthun y Dwyrain i'ch hudo.

The heady taste of the East to enchant you.

TAGINE LLYSIEUOL MOROCO

Dyma gydymaith syml i'r cig oen, neu mae'n mynd yn berffaith gyda chwscws a sgiwers cyw iâr.

Llond llaw o sialóts
2 daten felys, wedi'u ciwbio
2 goesyn seleri wedi'u torri
2 ewin garlleg
10 bricyll parod i'w bwyta
Sudd 1 lemwn
2 lwy fwrdd o fêl
4 llwy fwrdd o almonau wedi'u fflawio
300ml stoc llysiau
3cm o wreiddyn sinsir wedi'i dorri
1 llwy de o cwmin, sinamon, tyrmerig
1 tun o ffacbys
Tsili (dewisol)
Halen a phupur du wedi'i falu

Cynheswch y ffwrn i 180°C / 350°F / Nwy 4

Defnyddiwch ddysgl tagine draddodiadol os oes gennych un. Mae'n hynod drawiadol os oes gennych chi westeion. Ond gallwch ddefnyddio sosban, pot caserol neu goginiwr araf hyd yn oed. Mae'r blas yr un pa ffordd bynnag y gwnewch chi'r coginio.

Cyfunwch yr holl gynhwysion uchod mewn tagine, sosban neu bot caserol â chlawr arno a'u coginio mewn ffrwn ar wres cymedrol am awr hyd nes bod y tatws wedi'u coginio.

Ychwanegwch halen a phupur i flasu a bwytewch gyda'r cig oen, bara fflat ac ychydig o iogwrt a dail mintys wedi'u torri ynddo.

MOROCCAN VEGETABLE TAGINE

A simple companion for the slow roast lamb or perfect with couscous and chicken skewers.

A handful of shallots
2 sweet potatoes, cubed
2 celery sticks, chopped
2 cloves garlic
10 ready-to-eat apricots
Juice of 1 lemon
2 tbsp honey
4 tbsp flaked almonds
300ml vegetable stock
3cm root ginger, chopped
1 tsp cumin, cinnamon, turmeric
1 tin chickpeas
Chilli (optional)
Salt and ground black pepper

Preheat the oven to 180°C / 350°F / Gas 4

Use a traditional tagine dish if you have one. This really does have a wow factor if you're entertaining guests. But you can use a saucepan, casserole dish or even a slow cooker. The taste is the same, whichever way you cook it.

Combine all the above ingredients in a tagine, saucepan or a lidded casserole dish and bake in a medium oven for an hour until the potatoes are cooked.

Season to taste and serve with slow roast lamb, flatbread and a dollop of minted yoghurt, using chopped mint leaves.

* **This is a lovely, fresh-tasting accompaniment to any meal.**

 LL

Cwscws Moroco

250g cwscws (gwenith bulgur)
Tomato mawr wedi'i ddeisio'n ddarnau mân
2 shibwnsyn, wedi'u torri'n fân
½ ciwcymber, wedi'i ddeisio'n fân
Pupur coch neu felyn, wedi'i ddeisio'n fân
200ml stoc twym cyw iâr neu lysiau
2 lwy fwrdd o olew olewydd
2 lwy fwrdd o sudd lemwn
Llond llaw o bersli, coriander neu fintys wedi'i dorri
Halen a phupur
Dewisol: India corn, pys, afal, cyrens, oren, cnau

Rhowch y cwscws mewn powlen fawr ac ychwanegu'r stoc twym.

Gadewch i'r cwscws amsguno'r dŵr am tua 10 munud tra byddwch chi'n paratoi'r llysiau.

Deisiwch neu dorrwch y shibwns, y tomato, y pupur, y ciwcymber a'r perlysiau.

Ychwanegwch y llysiau i'r cwscws sydd wedi oeri a'u troi'n ofalus.

Cymysgwch yr olew olewydd, y sudd lemwn, a'r halen a'r pupur; yna, ychwanegwch at y cwscws a throi'r cyfan.

Am gic ychwanegol, defnyddiwch ychydig o olew tsili neu tsili wedi'i dorri'n fân a'r hadau wedi'u tynnu.

Oerwch cyn ei weini.

* **Dyma gydymaith hyfryd, ffres ei flas, i fynd ag unrhyw bryd.**

 V

Moroccan couscous

250g couscous (bulgur wheat)
1 large tomato, diced into small pieces
2 spring onions, chopped
Cucumber, diced
Red or yellow pepper, diced
200ml hot chicken or vegetable stock
2 tablespoons olive oil
2 tablespoons lemon juice
A handful of chopped parsley, coriander or mint
Salt and pepper to taste
Optional: sweetcorn, peas, apple, currants, orange, nuts

Place the couscous in a large bowl and add the hot stock.

Leave the couscous to absorb the water for about 10 minutes whilst you prepare the vegetables.

Dice or chop the onions or spring onions, tomato, pepper, cucumber and herbs.

Add the vegetables to the cooled couscous and mix gently.

Mix the olive oil, lemon juice and salt and pepper; finally, add to the couscous and stir.

Add a dash of chilli oil or a chopped, deseeded chilli for a little extra kick.

Chill before serving.

CAWL HADOG A CHIG MOCH HUFENNOG

Pryd maethlon yn llawn blasau cyfoethog.

Ffiled hadog
25g menyn
1 winwnsyn wedi'i dorri'n fân
1 coesyn seleri, wedi'i drimio a'i sleisio
3 tafell o gig moch mwg heb y grofen, wedi'u sleisio
1 deilen lawryf
Sbrigyn o deim
300g tatws
300ml llaeth braster llawn
300ml stoc, wedi'i wneud gan ddefnyddio ciwb stoc
1 cenhinen ganolig, wedi'i sleisio'n fân
100ml hufen dwbwl
100ml gwin gwyn
Persli, wedi'i dorri'n fras
Darnau lemwn i addurno

Toddwch y menyn mewn sosban fawr neu mewn ffrimpan ddofn a ffriwch y winwnsyn, y seleri a'r cig moch gyda'r ddeilen lawryf a'r sbrigyn teim am 5 munud, neu hyd nes bod y winwnsyn bron wedi'i goginio, ond heb frownio.

Torrwch y tatws yn gwibiau bach a'u hychwanegu at gynnwys y sosban. Ychwanegwch y llaeth a'r stoc, a dewch â'r cyfan i'r berw ar wres isel. Coginiwch am 15 munud, neu hyd nes bydd y tatws yn meddalu.

Rhowch y pysgod yn y cawl, â'r croen tuag i fyny, gan sicrhau bod y pysgodyn o dan wyneb y llaeth, a photsio'r pysgodyn nes bydd wedi coginio. Dylai hyn gymryd tua 5 munud. Tynnwch y pysgodyn o'r cymysgedd a gadael iddo oeri ychydig. Ychwanegwch y genhinen, yr hufen a'r gwin a choginiwch ar wres isel am tua 3 munud, hyd nes bod y genhinen wedi meddalu.

Torrwch y pysgodyn yn haenau â'ch bysedd gan chwilio am esgyrn. Rhowch y pysgodyn yn ôl yn y cawl a throi'r cyfan yn ofalus. Ceisiwch gadw'r darnau mwy o bysgod yn gyfan. Bwytewch gyda bara ffres, persli wedi'i dorri a darnau o lemwn.

CREAMY HADDOCK AND BACON CHOWDER

A delicious meal, full of rich flavours.

Haddock fillet
25g butter
1 onion, finely chopped
1 celery stick, trimmed and sliced
3 rashers rindless smoked streaky bacon, sliced
1 bay leaf
Sprig of thyme
300g potatoes
300ml full-fat milk
300ml stock, made with stock cube
1 medium leek, finely sliced
100ml double cream
100ml white wine
Roughly chopped parsley
Lemon pieces to garnish

Melt the butter in a large saucepan or deep frying pan and gently fry the onion, celery and bacon with the bay leaf and the sprig of thyme for 5 minutes, or until the onion is almost cooked, but not browned.

Cut the potatoes into small cubes and add to the pan. Add the milk and stock, and bring to a gentle simmer. Cook for 15 minutes, or until the potatoes are tender.

Place the fish into the chowder, skin side up, ensuring that the fish is below the surface of the milk, and poach until cooked. This should only take about 5 minutes. Then, remove the fish and allow to cool slightly. Add the leek, cream and wine and return to a gentle simmer and cook for about three minutes, until the leek is softened.

Flake the fish with your fingers and check for bones. Place the fish back into the chowder, stir gently, and try to keep some larger pieces of fish intact. Serve with fresh bread, chopped parsley and a wedge of lemon.

* Tip: i dewhau'r cawl, defnyddiwch flawd corn. Rhowch lond llwy fwrdd o flawd corn mewn cwpan, llenwch hyd at ei hanner â dŵr oer neu laeth a chymysgwch yn dda. Ychwanegwch y cymysgedd hwn at y cawl. Trowch yn gyson i sicrhau bod y cawl yn tewhau ac nad oes unrhyw lympiau ynddo.

* Tip: to thicken using cornflour. Place a tablespoon of cornflour into a cup, half fill with cold water or milk and mix well. Add this mixture to the soup. Stir continuously to ensure that the soup thickens and that no lumps appear.

MOULES MARINIÈRE GYDA BARA CRYSTIOG

Blas o'r môr a gwyliau – mae'r rysáit hwn yn fy atgoffa i o haul a bod dramor.

500g cregyn gleision byw ffres
150ml gwin gwyn sych
1 winwnsyn mawr, wedi'i dorri'n fân
¼ pupur coch, wedi'i dorri'n fân iawn
2 lwy fwrdd o olew olewydd
2 ewin garlleg, wedi'u malu
2 lwy de o deim ffres, wedi'i falu
Llond llaw o bersli dail fflat
Pot bach (150g) o hufen dwbwl

Gwiriwch eich cregyn gleision – os ydyn nhw'n gwrthod agor wedi i chi roi tap ar eu pen, taflwch nhw. Bydd cragen las iach yn cau bob tro o'i thapio.

Rhowch yr olew olewydd mewn sosban fawr, drom, a ffriwch yr winwnsyn, y pupur a'r garlleg yn ysgafn, gan gadw'r tymheredd yn isel.

Ychwanegwch y gwin gwyn a'r teim i'r sosban, a mudferwi'r cyfan. Ychwanegwch y cregyn gleision, gorchuddiwch y sosban â chlawr a gadael iddyn nhw stemio am 4 i 5 munud. Gallwch edrych i weld a ydyn nhw wedi agor: codwch glawr y sosban, ac os yw'r cregyn gleision ar agor, maen nhw'n barod. Gwaredwch unrhyw gregyn gleision sydd heb agor. Mae hyn yn bwysig: y rheol yw y dylai'r gragen agor os yw wedi'i choginio.

Ychwanegwch yr hufen i'r sosban a chynheswch y cyfan drwyddo am funud arall. Yna arllwyswch i bowlen fawr agored. Taflwch ychydig o bersli wedi'i dorri'n fân drosto a bywtewch gyda bara crystiog hyfryd.

 Tip: defnyddiwch gragen fel llwy i gasglu'r sudd hyfryd ynghyd, mopiwch y sudd â'r bara.

MOULES MARINIÈRE WITH CRUSTY BREAD

A taste of the sea and holidays – this recipe always reminds me of sun and foreign climes.

500g fresh live mussels
150ml dry white wine
1 large onion, finely chopped
¼ red pepper, really finely chopped
2 tbsp olive oil
2 garlic cloves, chopped
2 tsp chopped fresh thyme
A handful of chopped flat leaf parsley
Small pot (150g) double cream

Check your mussels – if it refuses to close when given a sudden tap, discard the mussel. A healthy mussel will always close when tapped.

Place the olive oil in a large, heavy pan and gently fry the onion, pepper and garlic. Do not colour the onions – keep the temperature low.

Add the white wine and the thyme to the pan and then bring to a simmer. Add the mussels, cover with a lid and allow to steam for 4 to 5 minutes. You can check to see whether they are cooked: lift the pan lid and if the mussels are open, they're ready. Discard any unopened mussels. This is important, the rule is: the mussel should open if cooked.

Add the cream to the pan and warm through for a further minute. Then tip into a large open bowl, scatter with finely chopped parsley and serve with lovely crusty bread.

 Tip: use the mussel shell to scoop up all the lovely juices. Mop up leftover juices with the bread.

TARTE TATIN

Enw ffansi am darten afalau Ffrengig!

Pecyn o does crwst pwff
4 afal bwyta o unrhyw fath
Llond llaw o fwyar duon
50g siwgwr mân
50g menyn
Sudd un lemwn

Cynheswch y ffwrn i 200°C / 400°F / Nwy 6

Pliciwch yr afalau, a'u torri'n eu hanner. Tynnwch y craidd ac yna'u gorchuddio â sudd lemwn rhag iddyn nhw frownio.

Cynheswch y siwgwr a'r menyn mewn ffrimpan addas i'w roi mewn ffwrn, neu ddysgl tatin, hyd nes eu bod wedi toddi ac yn dwym.

Gosodwch y darnau afal, a'r ymylon crwn tuag i lawr, yn y ffrimpan, ac ychwanegwch y llond llaw o fwyar.

Rholiwch y toes crwst pwff i tua ½ cm o drwch. Torrwch gylch digon mawr i orchuddio'r ffrwythau a phlygu'r toes i mewn ar ymylon y badell. Gwnewch dyllau yn y toes â fforc.

Pobwch yn y ffrwn am tua ½ awr hyd nes ei fod yn euraid ac yn dwym.

Tynnwch o'r ffrwn a throwch y darten allan drwy osod plât dros y badell – yn gadarn ac yn hyderus, trowch y darten drosodd a'i thynnu'n ofalus o'r badell. Voilà!

Tip: os am deisen afal a mwyar wyneb i waered, peidiwch â gwneud y toes, gwnewch gymysgedd sbwng syml (gweler tudalen 166 am rysáit sbwng). Rhowch lwyeidiau o'r cymysgedd ar ben yr afal a'r mwyar mewn llestr sy'n addas i'w roi yn y ffwrn a phobwch am 20 munud hyd nes ei fod yn frown euraid. Trowch y deisen allan ar blât a bwytewch gyda hufen, crème fraîche neu gwstard.

Tip: rhowch gynnig ar y darten hon gan ddefnyddio cyfuniadau eraill o ffrwythau – afal a mafon, bricyll, eirin neu riwbob.

TARTE TATIN

A fancy name for a French apple tart!

Pack of puff pastry
4 eating apples of any kind
A handful of blackberries
50g caster sugar
50g butter
Juice of a lemon

Preheat the oven to 200°C / 400°F / Gas 6

Peel all the apples, and cut them all in half. Remove the cores, then cover with lemon juice.

Heat the sugar and butter in an ovenproof frying pan or tatin dish, until melted and hot.

Arrange the apple pieces, rounded side down, in the pan, and add the handful of blackberries.

Roll out the pastry to about ½ cm thick, and cut a circle large enough to cover the fruit. Place over the apples, and tuck in the edges. Prick the pastry with a fork.

Bake in the oven for about ½ hour until golden and hot.

Remove from the oven and turn out by placing a plate over the pan – firmly, and with confidence, turn over and carefully remove the pan. Voilà!

Tip: for an apple and blackberry upside down cake, don't make pastry, just make a simple sponge mixture (see page 166 for a sponge recipe). Spoon the mixture on top of the apple and blackberries placed in an ovenproof dish and bake in the oven for 20 minutes until golden brown. Turn out onto a large serving plate and serve with cream, crème fraîche or custard.

Tip: Try this with other fruit combinations – apple and raspberry, apricots, plum or rhubarb.

'Nôl i'r ysgol

Back to school

**Mae'r hydref yn amser arbennig, pan fod tymhorau
fel petaen nhw'n cyd-daro.**
Mor bell 'nôl ag y medra i gofio, byddai mis Medi yn cael ei nodi gan
ddechrau blwyddyn ysgol newydd, esgidiau newydd, dobsarth newydd a
boreau niwlog a phrynhawniau chwilboeth.

Roedden ni'n sylwi ar y gwres am fod ein gwisgoedd ysgol yn gynnes iawn.
Os oeddech chi'n ddisgybl yn yr ysgol uwchradd Gymraeg yng
Nghaerfyrddin yn yr wythdegau fe gofiwch y dillad ysgol streipiog du a
phinc trawiadol a wisgid ganddom ni'r merched. Roedd y ffrogiau gwlanen
yn goslyd a chynnes. Roedden ni'n iawn ar gyfer dyddiau oer, gaeafol, ond, ar
brynhawniau cynnes ym Medi, fe fyddem yn gybolfa chwyslyd, streipiog.

Mi fydda i'n aml yn agor y llenni ar fore o hydref a gweld blanced
drwchus o niwl yn llifo ar hyd dyffryn Tywi, a chaf fy atgoffa o'r boreau
Medi hynny ddegawdau yn ôl.

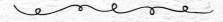

Autumn is a special time of year, when seasons collide.
As far back as I remember, September was marked by a new
school year, new school shoes, a new classroom and misty mornings
with bakingly hot afternoons.

We noticed the heat as our school uniforms were very warm. If you went to the
Welsh school in Carmarthen in the eighties, you will remember the distinctive
black and pink striped woollen tunics worn by us girls. These woollen
dresses were itchy and hot; we were well set for cold winter days, but on hot
September afternoons we'd be a steaming, stripy mess of sweat.

Often on an autumn morning, I open the curtains to see a thick blanket
of fog meandering down the Tywi valley, and I'm reminded of those
September mornings from decades ago.

BOCSYS BWYD
A BWYDYDD BACH

⭐ Ac felly, yn ôl i'r ysgol, a throi'n golygon at amserlen a gwersi a threfn wythnosol ddeddfol i fywyd. Hwrê medd y mamau! Wedi hamdden yr haf, mae'n beth eitha da dod yn ôl i ryw fath o drefn mewn gwirionedd. Yn aml byddwn yn dweud hwyl fawr wrth y plant yn y bore, â'u bocs bwyd yn eu bagiau ar gyfer amser cinio. Ond hyd yn oed os yw'ch angylion bach chi yn cael cinio ysgol, fe fyddan nhw'n cyrraedd adre ddiwedd y dydd ar eu cythlwng ac yn ysu am fwyd. Fe ddylen ni geisio llenwi eu boliau â bwydydd maethlon.

LUNCHBOXES AND
AFTERNOON SNACKS

⭐ And so, back to school, and we turn our attention towards a timetable and lessons and a weekly order to life. Hurrah, say all the mums! After the relaxation of summer, in fact it's good to get back to some sort of routine. We often say goodbye to the children in the morning, with a lunchbox tucked into their bags for lunch. But even if your little angels have school dinners, they will arrive back home at the end of the day starving and desperate for food. We should try and fill their bellies with nutritious food.

GOUJONS CYW IÂR CRIMP

Rydyn ni'n gwybod am y nygets cyw iâr dadleuol, dynion drwg y bwydydd cyflym ... wel, dyma'r dynion da. Cyw iâr iachus a blasus.

2 ffiled brest cyw iâr (i wneud 8 goujon)
2 wy buarth
2 gwpanaid o friwsion bara sych
1 cwpanaid o flawd plaen
1½ llwy de o baprica
½ llwy de o halen
½ llwy de o bupur
2 lwy fwrdd o olew blodau'r haul
1 lemwn, wedi'i dorri'n ddarnau
Dail salad neu roced o'ch dewis chi a thomatos bach i weini

Rhowch yr wyau mewn powlen fawr a chwisgiwch nhw'n dda i'w cyfuno.

Rhowch y blawd mewn powlen arall ac ychwanegwch yr halen a'r pupur. Yna, rhowch y ddau gwpanaid o friwsion bara mewn trydedd powlen ac ychwanegu'r paprica ato, i gael blas a lliw.

Sleisiwch y cyw iâr a throi'r darnau yn y blawd. Yna, rhowch nhw yn yr wy a'u gorchuddio'n dda. Tynnwch y darnau cyw iâr o'r cymysgedd wy ac yna'u gorchuddio â briwsion bara. Gadewch iddyn nhw sychu allan am ychydig.

Cynheswch yr olew mewn ffrimpan a ffriwch y cyw iâr am 3 munud. Trowch y darnau drosodd yn ofalus a'u coginio am 3 munud ar yr ochr arall. Rhaid coginio'r cyw iâr drwyddo, felly gwiriwch hynny gan ddefnyddio mesurydd gwres. Dylai'r tymheredd craidd gyrraedd 75°C yn rhan fwyaf trwchus y cyw iâr.

Tynnwch y cyw iâr o'r ffrimpan a bwytewch gyda thatws rhost a dail roced neu ddail salad amrywiol. Bydd tafell o lemwn yn ychwanegu blas munud olaf hyfryd i'r cyfan.

Tip: gellir pobi'r rhain yn y ffwrn am tua 10 munud ar 180°C / 350°F / Nwy 4. Cofiwch wneud yn siŵr bod tymheredd craidd y cig yn iawn cyn ei fwyta.

CRISPY CHICKEN GOUJONS

We all know about the contentious chicken nuggets, bad guys of fast food ... well, here are the good guys. Healthy, tasty chicken.

2 chicken breast fillets (makes 8 goujons)
2 free range eggs
2 cups dried breadcrumbs
1 cup of plain flour
1½ teaspoons paprika
½ tsp salt
½ tsp pepper
2 tbsps sunflower oil
1 lemons, cut into wedges
Rocket or salad leaves of your choice and cherry tomatoes to serve

Place the eggs in a large bowl and whisk them well to combine the egg white and the yolk.

Place the flour in another bowl and add the salt and pepper. Finally, place two cupfuls of breadcrumbs in a third bowl and add the paprika, for taste and colour.

Slice the chicken and turn in the flour. Then, place the pieces in the egg and coat them well. Remove the chicken pieces from the egg mixture and cover them in breadcrumbs. Allow to dry out for a few minutes.

Heat the oil in a frying pan and fry the chicken for 3 minutes. Turn the pieces over carefully, and cook for another 3 minutes on the other side. The chicken must be cooked through, so check using a temperature probe. It should reach 75°C in the thickest part of the chicken.

Remove the chicken pieces from the pan, and serve with roasted tomatoes and rocket or salad leaves of your choice. A slice of lemon adds a last-minute burst of loveliness.

Tip: these can be baked in the oven, about 10 minutes at 180°C / 350°F / Gas 4. Check the core temperature of the meat before eating.

✳ Tip: torrwch y goujons yn dafelli, ychwanegwch ddigonedd o ddail salad, tafell neu ddwy o domato a'u rhoi mewn bara tortila. Rholiwch yn dynn i greu pryd ar glud cyflym, iachus.

✳ Tip: slice the goujons, add lots of fresh salad leaves, a slice or two of tomato and place them in a tortilla wrap. Roll tightly for a quick healthy meal on the go.

TEISENNAU PYSGOD A THATWS MELYS

Dyma i chi fwydydd sylfaenol diguro – tatws a physgod – wedi'u cymysgu; maen nhw mor flasus a maethlon.

300g hadog mwg neu samwn
1 sialotsyn, wedi'i dorri'n fân
250ml llaeth
1 deilen lawryf
75g tatws melys
75g tatws gwyn
Pupur a halen
3 shibwnsyn, wedi'u torri'n fân
Llond llaw o bersli wedi'i dorri
Pinsiaid o ddarnau tsili
1 llwy fwrdd o fenyn
1 wy
Briwsion bara
Olew llysiau

Ffriwch y sialotsyn hyd nes bydd wedi coginio.

Rhowch yr hadog neu'r samwn mewn sosban gyda'r ddeilen lawryf a'r llaeth a'u codi i'r berw. Tynnwch oddi ar y gwres yn syth – bydd y pysgod yn dal i goginio yng ngwres y llaeth.

Berwch y tatws a'r tatws melys nes byddan nhw'n feddal. Yna, stwnsiwch nhw ag ychydig o laeth o'r pysgod. Ychwanegwch ychydig o fenyn, halen a digon o bupur.

Cyfunwch y sialotsyn, y tatws stwnsh, y shibwns a'r persli mewn powlen.

Malwch y pysgod yn fras gan chwilio am unrhyw esgyrn, ac yna'u hychwanegu at y cymysgedd. Defnyddiwch bupur a halen i roi blas ac ychwanegwch y tsili os ydych chi'n hoffi pethau'n boeth.

Rhowch y cymysgedd yn yr oergell am ychydig, gan ei fod yn haws ei siapio pan fydd wedi oeri. I'w siapio, rholiwch y cymysgedd yn beli bach. Yna, gwasgwch nhw ychydig i wneud 8 teisen bysgod, neu gallwch wneud sawl teisen bysgod lai, os hoffech.

SWEET POTATO FISHCAKES

Good, basic, unbeatable foods – potatoes and fish – mixed; so tasty, so nutritious.

300g smoked haddock or salmon
1 shallot, chopped
250ml milk
1 bay leaf
75g sweet potato
75g white potatoes
Salt and pepper
3 spring onions, chopped
A handful of chopped parsley
A pinch of chilli flakes
1 tbsp of butter
1 egg
Some breadcrumbs
Vegetable oil

Fry the chopped shallot until cooked.

Place the haddock or salmon in a pan with the bay leaf and milk and bring to the boil. Immediately remove from the heat and allow to stand – the fish will cook in the heat of the milk.

Boil the potatoes and sweet potatoes until tender, then mash them with a little of the milk from the fish. Add a little butter, salt and lots of pepper.

Combine the shallot, mashed potatoes, spring onion and parsley in a bowl.

Flake the fish and check for any bones, and then add the fish to the mixture. Be gentle and try to keep some of the flakes intact. Check the seasoning and add the chilli if you like a bit of heat.

> Unwaith y byddwch wedi'u siapio nhw, gallwch eu storio yn yr oergell hyd nes eich bod yn barod i'w coginio.

Dipiwch nhw fesul mewn wy wedi'i guro ac yna'u gorchuddio â briwsion bara. Ffriwch y teisennau pysgod mewn ychydig o olew hyd nes eu bod yn euraid.

Bwytewch nhw'n gynnes gyda jam tsili melys.

> Place the fishcake mixture in the fridge for a while, as it's easier to shape when chilled. To shape, roll the mixture into small balls, then flatten slightly to make 8 fishcakes, or make lots of little fishcake bites if you prefer. Once shaped, you can store them in the fridge until ready to cook.

Dip each one in beaten egg and then coat with breadcrumbs. Shallow fry the fishcakes in a little oil until golden.

Serve warm with a sweet chili jam.

LL

PIZZA HYNOD HAWDD

Mae'r cliw yn yr enw y tro hwn. Mae'r rhain mor hawdd i'w gwneud ac yn cadw yn yr oergell am ychydig – perffaith fel byrbryd ar ôl ysgol.

I wneud y toes
600g blawd cryf
1 llwy de o halen
1½ llwy de o furum sych
350ml dŵr cynnes
2 llwy fwrdd o olew

Ar gyfer y topin
Passata tomato
Caws Cheddar, wedi'i gratio
Caws mozzarella, wedi'i dorri'n ddarnau
Topins gwahanol – eich ffefrynnau, e.e. pupur, madarch, olewyddion, winwns, courgette

Cynheswch y ffwrn i 220°C / 425°F / Nwy 7

Rhowch y blawd, yr halen, y burum, yr olew a'r dŵr cynnes mewn powlen fawr a'u cymysgu i greu toes.

Tylinwch y toes gan ei dynnu a'i wthio am 2–3 munud, hyd nes bydd o ansawdd llyfn ac elastig. Yna, rhowch y toes yn ôl yn y bowlen a'i orchuddio â haenen lynu (neu gap cawod glân) a'i adael yn rhywle cynnes am tua 45 munud er mwyn i'r toes godi.

Yna, trowch y toes allan ar arwyneb â blawd arno. Rhannwch y toes yn 6 darn a rholiwch bob un allan i ffurfio siâp pizza. Wrth reswm, fe allwch wneud un neu ddau pizza mawr os hoffech, ond mae'n hwyl i bawb gael gwneud eu rhai eu hunain.

Gosodwch y toes ar hambwrdd pobi wedi'i iro, a thaenu'r passata tomato dros y crwst pizza. Ychwanegwch ychydig o gaws Cheddar, peth caws mozzarella a'ch hoff gynhwysion fel topins.

Pobwch am 10–15 munud hyd nes y byddan nhw'n euraid, tynnwch o'r ffwrn a mwynhewch.

V

EASY-PEASY PIZZA

The clue is in the name here. These are so easy to make and they keep in the fridge for a while, perfect for an after-school snack.

To make the dough
600g strong flour
1 tsp salt
1½ tsps dried yeast
350ml warm water
2 tbsps oil

For the topping
Tomato passata
Cheddar cheese, grated
Mozzarella cheese, sliced
Various toppings – your favourites, e.g. peppers, mushrooms, olives, onions, courgettes

Preheat oven to 220°C / 425°F / Gas 7

Place flour, salt, yeast, oil and warm water into a large bowl and mix to form a dough.

Knead the dough by pulling and pushing it for 2–3 minutes, until the texture becomes smooth and elastic. Then return the dough to the bowl, cover with cling film (or a clean shower cap) and place somewhere warm for about 45 minutes to prove.

Then, tip the dough out onto a floured surface, divide the dough into 6 pieces and roll each one to form a pizza shape. Obviously you can make one or two large pizza if you prefer, but it's fun for everyone to make their own.

Place the dough onto an oiled baking tray, and spread the tomato passata over the pizza base. Add a little grated Cheddar cheese, some mozzarella and your favourite toppings.

Bake for 10–15 minutes until golden, remove from oven and serve.

* Tip: peidiwch â gorlwytho'ch pizza – mae ychydig o gaws a rhai llysiau yn gwneud pizza iach.

* Tip: don't overdo the amount of toppings, a little cheese and some vegetables makes a healthy pizza.

FFLAPJACS FFANTASTIG

Byrbryd blasus sy'n gyforiog o egni da ar gyfer pobol ar eu prifiant.

175g menyn
275g ceirch uwd
125g siwgwr brown golau meddal
55g syrop euraid neu fêl
50g ffrwythau cymysg sych a chnau neu resin, bricyll, datys, hadau blodau haul neu hadau pwmpen

Cynheswch y ffwrn i 180°C / 350°F / Nwy 4

Rhowch y menyn, y syrop a'r siwgwr mewn sosban. Cynheswch dros wres isel am 2–3 munud a throwch y cyfan hyd nes bydd wedi toddi.

Ychwanegwch y ceirch uwd, y ffrwythau cymysg a'r cnau, a'u cymysgu'n dda.

Arllwyswch y cymysgedd i dun â gwaelod gwastad a gwasgwch y cyfan i lawr gan ddefnyddio sbatiwla.

Pobwch yn y ffwrn am 25 munud hyd nes bydd yn euraid ond yn feddal.

Tynnwch o'r ffwrn a'i oeri am ddeg munud. Yna, torrwch yn sgwariau a gadael iddyn nhw oeri yn y tun.

Tynnwch y fflapjacs yn ofalus o'r tun a'u storio mewn bocs aerglos.

 Tip: i greu fflapjacs moethus; wedi iddyn nhw oeri, diferwch siocled wedi toddi drostyn nhw.

Tip: i wneud y rysáit yn un heb wenith, defnyddiwch geirch diglwten.

FANTASTIC FLAPJACKS

A tasty snack bursting with good energy for those growing bodies.

175g butter
275g porridge oats
125g soft light brown sugar
55g golden syrup or honey
50g mixed dried fruit and nuts or raisins, apricots, dates, sunflower seeds or pumpkin seeds

Preheat the oven to 180°C / 350°F / Gas 4

Put the butter, syrup and sugar into a saucepan. Heat over a low heat for 2–3 minutes and stir until melted.

Add the porridge oats and mixed fruit and nuts, mix well.

Pour the mixture into a flat-bottomed tin and press down using a spatula.

Bake in the oven for 25 minutes until golden but still soft.

Remove from the oven and cool for ten minutes. Then cut into squares and allow to cool in the tin.

Carefully remove from the tin, and store in an airtight container.

 Tip: drizzle melted chocolate over the cooled flapjacks for a special treat.

Tip: use gluten free oats and this becomes a gluten free recipe.

SYNIAD SYDYN
QUICK IDEA

Peli egni ffrwythau a chnau

1 cwpan yn llawn datys, a'u cerrig wedi'u tynnu
¼ cwpanaid o fêl, syrop masarn neu agave
¼ cwpanaid o fenyn cnau mwnci, neu fenyn almon, neu unrhyw fenyn cnau
1 cwpanaid o almonau dihalen, wedi'u rhostio, a'u malu
½ cwpanaid o geirch wedi'u rholio
Dewisol: darnau bach o siocled, ffrwythau sych, cnau, darnau banana sych, fanila ayyb
¾ cwpanaid o gnau coco sych er mwyn rholio'r peli ynddo i orffen

Cynheswch y ffwrn i 180°C / 350F / Nwy 4

Rhowch y datys mewn prosesydd bwyd a'u malu hyd nes bod eu hansawdd yn debyg i does gludiog.

Tostiwch eich ceirch yn y ffwrn am tua 15 munud neu hyd nes eu bod ychydig yn euraid, ond gallwch eu gadael heb eu coginio.

Rhowch y ceirch, yr almonau a'r cymysgedd datys mewn powlen gymysgu fawr.

Cynheswch y mêl a'r menyn cnau mwnci mewn sosban hyd nes byddan nhw wedi toddi. Yna cymysgwch nhw a'u harllwys i mewn i'r cymysgedd sych a throi'r cyfan yn dda.

I wneud y peli egni, rholiwch ychydig bach o'r cymysgedd yn beli o faint cnau Ffrengig. Gall rhoi ychydig o flawd ar eich dwylo rhag i'ch dwylo helpu rhag iddyn nhw fynd yn rhy ludiog.

Rholiwch y peli mewn ychydig o gnau coco wedi'u sychu a'u storio mewn bocs aerglos. Gellir eu cadw am ychydig ddyddiau.

 Tip: defnyddiwch geirch diglwten i wneud y rysáit yn un heb wenith.

Fruit and nut energy balls

1 cup packed dates, pitted
¼ cup honey, maple syrup or agave
¼ cup salted peanut butter, or almond butter, or any nut butter
1 cup roasted unsalted almonds, chopped
½ cup rolled oats
Optional: chocolate chips, dried fruit, nuts, banana chips, vanilla, etc.
¾ cup of desiccated coconut for rolling the balls in to finish

Preheat the oven to 180°C / 350F / Gas 4

Blitz the dates in a food processor until the form a sticky doughlike consistency.

Toast your oats in oven for about 15 minutes or until slightly golden, but you can leave them uncooked.

Place the oats, almonds and the sticky date mixture in a large mixing bowl.

Heat the honey and the peanut butter in a saucepan until they are melted. Then stir and pour into the dry mixture and mix well.

To make the energy balls, roll small quantities of the mixture into walnut sized balls. It may help to flour your hands slightly to prevent you getting too sticky.

Roll the balls in a little desiccated coconut and store in an airtight container. They can be kept for up to a few days.

Tip: use gluten free oats and this becomes a gluten free recipe.

Tanwydd roced i blant. Tameidiau bach hawdd i'w gwneud gan ddefnyddio cynhwysion egni uchel.

Rocket fuel for children. Easy little morsels to make using high-energy ingredients.

BLAS Y CYNHAEAF

⭐ Does dim prinder ryseitiau i'w cael yr adeg hon o'r flwyddyn. Wrth i'r tymheredd oeri'n raddol a'r dyddiau fyrhau, caiff ein hoffter o salad a barbeciw ei newid i hoffter o gawl a phrydau cynhesach. Bydd llysiau wedi'u rhostio a stiwiau cysurlon yn ymddangos ar dudalennau'r cylchgronau bwyd, a chyn i ni droi rownd, mi fyddwn ni'n chwilio am ein menig a'n sgarff.

Gall yr hydref fod yn dymor byr, wedi'i wasgu rhwng yr haf hwyr a'r gaeaf. Weithiau, bydd yr haf yn aros yn hir ac yn para ymhell i mewn i fis Hydref, ond gan wybod am y dyddiau hir a thywyll sydd i ddod, rwy'n croesawu haf bach Mihangel. Mae pob prynhawn cynnes a heulog yn gyfle arall i baratoi ar gyfer y misoedd i ddod, i beintio a chywiro, i glirio tyfiant yr haf ymaith, i droi'r compost ac i baratoi'r ardd yn raddol am drwmgwsg.

A thra bo'r ardd yn gorffwys, bydd y gegin yn llawn bwrlwm, gyda digonedd o lysiau a ffrwythau i'w gweddnewid yn swperau, byrbrydau, jamiau a phiclau i'n cynnal dros y misoedd blin.

LATE SUMMER HARVEST

⭐ There's no shortage of recipes for this time of year. As the temperature gradually cools and daylight diminishes, our love of salads and barbecues is replaced by a sudden desire for soups and warmer dishes. Roasted vegetables and more comforting stews appear in food magazines and before we know it, we're looking for our scarves and gloves.

Autumn can be a short season, sandwiched somewhere between late summer and winter. Sometimes summer stays on and lasts well into October, but knowing of the long, dark winter days that lie ahead, I always welcome summer's late intrusion. Every warm and sunny afternoon is another chance to prepare for the months ahead, to paint and repair, to clear away the summer growth, turn the compost, and to gradually put the garden into hibernation.

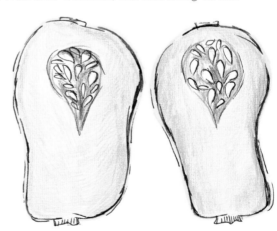

Whilst the garden rests, the kitchen will be bustling, with plenty of vegetables and fruit to transform into suppers, snacks and preserves to see us through the leaner months.

LL

PARSELI FFILO LLYSIAU
A CHAWS GAFR

*Dyma bryd brau yr olwg ond un sy'n
llawn blasau cadarn.*

> 1 pecyn toes ffilo
> 1 sgwash cnau menyn, wedi'i dorri'n giwbiau
> 1 sialotsyn, wedi'i bilio
> 1 pupur coch, wedi'i sleisio
> Llond llaw o ysbigoglys
> Halen a phupur wedi'i falu
> 150g caws gafr
> Llond llaw o ffrwythau cymysg a chnau
> 1 llwy de o sesnin Cajun
> 1 llwy de o hadau cymysg neu hadau pabi
> 25g menyn, wedi toddi

Piliwch, sleisiwch a thorrwch y dewis o lysiau a'u
gosod ar hambwrdd pobi gyda diferyn o olew
olewydd. Ychwanegwch ychydig o halen a phupur du
wedi'i falu.

Ychwanegwch lwy de o sesnin Cajun i'r sgwash yn
unig. Bydd hyn yn ychwanegu ychydig o flas poeth i'r
parsel terfynol.

Rhowch y llysiau yn y ffwrn i rostio am tua hanner
awr hyd nes byddan nhw wedi meddalu, ond heb eu
llosgi na'u crimpio.

Agorwch y pecyn o does ffilo a thynnu allan ddwy
haenen. Brwsiwch un haenen ag ychydig o fenyn
wedi toddi, ychwanegwch yr ail haenen a briwsio eto
â'r menyn wedi toddi.

Trefnwch y darnau sgwash wedi'u rostio yn un llinell
ar waelod yr haenau toes, gan adael ychydig o le ar
bob ochr iddyn nhw.

Gosodwch y pupur coch a'r sialotsyn ar ben y sgwash,
ac yna rhowch yr ysbigoglys heb ei goginio ar ben y
pentwr o lysiau rhost.

Defnyddiwch ychydig o halen a phupur a malwch
ychydig o gaws gafr i mewn i'r ysbigoglys cyn
plygu'r ddwy ochr i mewn a rholio'r toes i greu
'spring roll' anferth. Brwsiwch â'r menyn wedi toddi a
gwasgarwch ychydig o hadau dros ei ben.

Pobwch yn y ffwrn am tua 25 munud hyd nes bydd y
crwst yn frown euraid.

V

ROAST VEGETABLE
AND GOAT'S CHEESE
FILO PARCELS

*This is such a delicate-looking dish but
packs a mighty tasty punch.*

> 1 pack of filo pastry
> 1 butternut squash, diced
> 1 shallot, peeled
> 1 red pepper, sliced
> A handful of spinach
> Salt and pepper
> 150g goat's cheese
> A handful of mixed fruit and nuts
> 1 teaspoon Cajun seasoning
> 1 teaspoon mixed seeds or poppy seeds
> 25g melted butter

Peel, slice and dice the selection of vegetables and
place on a baking tray with a drizzle of olive oil.
Season with a little salt and black pepper.

Add a teaspoon of Cajun seasoning to the squash
only. This will add a touch of heat and flavour to the
final parcel.

Place the vegetables in the oven to roast for about
half an hour until softened, but not crisp nor charred.

Open the pack of filo pastry and remove two sheets.
Brush a whole sheet with a little melted butter, add a
second sheet and again, brush with melted butter.

Arrange the roast squash in one line along the bottom
of the pastry sheets, allowing a small gap at each side.

Place the red pepper and the shallots on top of the
squash. Then finally place the uncooked spinach on
top of the mound of roast vegetables.

Season with a little salt and pepper and sprinkle some
goat's cheese into the spinach before tucking in both
the sides and rolling up the pastry to form a giant
'spring roll'. Brush with melted butter and sprinkle
some seeds on top.

Bake in the oven for approximately 25 minutes until
the pastry is golden brown.

TARTENNI BROCOLI A WINWNS COCH

Ar gyfer y crwst
250g blawd plaen
150g menyn
1 melynwy mawr
Diferyn o laeth oer

Ar gyfer y llenwad
60ml llaeth cyflawn
60ml hufen dwbwl
1 wy canolig
8 sbrigyn o frocoli porffor
1 winwnsyn coch
Ychydig o domatos bach, wedi'u sleisio

Cynheswch y ffwrn i 200°C / 400°F / Nwy 6

Ar gyfer y casyn toes

Paratowch gyflenwad o does yn y prosesydd bwyd. Cymysgwch y cynhwysion ynghyd, oerwch nhw ac yna rholiwch y toes allan i leinio sawl tun bach (gallwch ddefnyddio un tun quiche mawr 28cm, os hoffech).

Pobwch y gragen does yn 'wag'. I wneud hyn, leiniwch waelod y tuniau â phapur pobi. Rholiwch y toes allan i ffitio'r tuniau a defnyddiwch fforc i dyllu'r casyn toes. Yna, pwyswch y toes i lawr gyda ffa pobi. Pobwch mewn ffwrn o wres canolig am tua 10 munud. Tynnwch o'r ffwrn a gwagio'r ffa. Brwsiwch y toes ag ychydig o wy wedi'i guro a'i bobi am 10 munud arall.

Ar gyfer y llenwad

Chwisgiwch y llaeth, yr hufen a'r wy ynghyd (efallai bydd angen dyblu'r cynhwysion os ydych chi'n gwneud quiche mawr).

Gosodwch y brocoli wedi'i stemio yn y casys toes. Ychwanegwch rywfaint o'r winwns coch wedi'u ffrio a rhai tomatos. Yna llenwch y tuniau â'r cymysgedd hufen a llaeth.

Pobwch yn y ffwrn am hyd at ½ awr hyd nes eu bod wedi setio ac yn euraid (efallai bydd angen ychydig mwy o amser yn y ffwrn arnoch i setio os ydych chi'n gwneud un quiche mawr).

BROCCOLI AND RED ONION TARTS

For the pastry
250g plain flour
150g butter
1 large egg yolk
A drop of cold milk

For the filling
60ml whole milk
60ml double cream
1 medium egg
8 sprigs of purple sprouting broccoli
1 red onion, chopped
A few cherry tomatoes, sliced

Preheat the oven to 200°C / 400°F / Gas 6

For the pastry case

Prepare a batch of pastry in a food processor. Mix the pastry ingredients together. Chill and then line several small tins with pastry (you can use a large 28cm quiche tin).

Bake the pastry shell blind. To do this, line the base of the tins with baking parchment, roll the pastry out to fit the tins, prick the base of the pastry case all over with a fork and weigh it down with baking beans. Bake in a medium oven for about 10 minutes. Remove from the oven and take out the beans. Brush the base with a little beaten egg and bake for a further 10 minutes.

For the filling

Whisk together the milk, cream and egg (you may need double quantity for making a large quiche).

Place the steamed broccoli in the pastry cases. Add some gently fried red onion and some tomatoes and then fill with the cream and milk mixture.

Bake in the oven for up to ½ hour until set and golden (if you're making one big quiche, you might need to bake for a little while longer in order to set).

Blaswch, rhyfeddwch a phlygwch ger eu bron.

Such lovely tarts - taste them and weep.

SALAD TATO BACH A FFA GWYRDD CYNNES

2–3 taten fach, wedi'u torri'n giwbiau a'u berwi,
i bob person
1 cwpan o ffa gwyrdd wedi'u trimio
1 cwpan o bys gardd
1 cwpan o ffa llydan
Olew olewydd
1 llwy fwrdd o fenyn
1 ewin garlleg
Halen môr a phupur du wedi'i falu'n ffres

Dewisol: darnau o gig moch neu selsigen
chorizo wedi'i thafellu (nid ar gyfer llysieuwyr)

Masglwch y ffa llydan, gan fod croen y ffa llydan yn
eitha gwydn.

Deisiwch a berwch y tatws, gwaredwch y dŵr a'u rhoi
nhw i oeri.

Coginiwch y ffa gwyrdd a'r ffa llydan yn rhannol gan
eu mudferwi mewn sosban o ddŵr berw am ddwy
funud yn unig. Tynnwch y ffa o'r dŵr a gadael iddyn
nhw oeri.

Rhowch peth olew a menyn mewn ffrimpan mawr.
Ychwanegwch ewin garlleg wedi'i falu ac ychydig
mwy o fenyn. Ffriwch y cig moch neu'r selsig chorizo,
os ydych yn defnyddio cig.

Ychwanegwch y pys gardd – mae pys wedi'u rhewi
yn syth o'r rhewgell yn iawn. Ychwanegwch y ffa
llydan wedi'u masglo a'r ffa gwyrdd i'r ffrimpan.

Rhowch y tatws wedi'u torri'n giwbiau a'u berwi yn y
gymysgedd a'u cynhesu drwyddynt.

Ychwanegwch ychydig o halen a digonedd o bupur.
Mwynhewch fel cydymaith llysieuol i'ch hoff bryd.

I'w wneud fel cwrs cyntaf neu fel pryd ysgafn,
gallwch ychwanegu mwy o gig moch neu selsig
chorizo, ond cofiwch ddefnyddio llai o halen gan fod
cig moch yn hallt.

*Tip: gallwch ychwanegu halen tsili i gael mwy
o flas.*

*Tip: gallwch ddefnyddio cyw iâr sydd dros ben
gyda'r cig moch neu ddefnyddio tatws sydd dos ben
yn hytrach na thatws bach wedi'u berwi'n ffres.*

WARM SALAD POTATO AND GREEN BEAN SALAD

2–3 salad potatoes, diced and boiled,
per person
1 cup green beans, top and tailed
1 cup garden peas
1 cup broad beans
Olive oil
1 tbsp butter
1 clove garlic
Sea salt and freshly ground black pepper

Optional: bacon pieces or sliced
chorizo sausage (not for vegetarian)

Shell the broad beans for the best results as the
broad bean skins are quite tough.

Dice and cook the potatoes, drain and leave aside
to cool.

Parboil the green beans and broad beans by
simmering them in a pan full of boiling hot water for
just two minutes. Remove the beans from the water
and allow to cool.

Place a little oil and butter in a large frying pan. Add
a clove of crushed garlic and a little more butter.
Fry the bacon or chorizo sausage, if using meat.

Add the garden peas – frozen peas straight from the
freezer are fine. Add the shelled broad beans and the
green beans to the pan.

Mix in the diced boiled potatoes and warm through.

Season with salt and plenty of pepper. Serve as a
vegetable side dish with your favourite meal.

To make this a starter or a light lunch, you can
add more bacon or chorizo sausage to the recipe,
but remember to cut back on the salt as bacon is
quite salty.

*Tip: chilli salt can be added for additional
flavour.*

*Tip: use up leftover chicken with the bacon or
use leftover boiled potatoes instead of freshly
boiled salad potatoes.*

Dyma blatiad o flas traddodiadol yr ardd yn wir, gan ddefnyddio cynhwysion ffres. Nefoedd!

This is truly the traditional taste of the garden on a plate using fresh ingredients. Heaven!

RATATOUILLE

Dwi'n dwlu ar flasau tomato suddog y pryd hwn. Po hiraf y medrwch chi ei adael i goginio, y cyfoethoca y bydd.

> 1 aubergine mawr
> 2 courgette mawr
> 2 winwnsyn canolig
> 1 pupur coch
> 4 tomato mawr neu dun o domatos
> 2 lwy fwrdd o olew olewydd
> Llond llaw o ddail basil ffres, wedi'u rhwygo
> Halen a phupur i flasu
> ½ llwy de yr un o bupur cayenne a siwgwr mân
> 1 ewin garlleg wedi'i falu

Pliciwch yr winwns, hanerwch y pupur a thynnu'r hadau. Torrwch ben a chwt yr aubergine a'r courgettes, ac yna torrwch nhw'n ddarnau sgwâr 2cm o faint.

Gosodwch yr winwns, y garlleg a'r pupur mewn sosban fawr gyda'r olew olewydd. Ychwanegwch un llwy de o halen, siwgwr a phupur cayenne. Gorchuddiwch a choginio ar wres isel am 10 munud. Ychwanegwch y tomatos a pharhau â'r coginio.

Gan ddefnyddio ychydig o olew llysieuol, ffriwch y darnau aubergine am tua 2 funud bob ochr hyd nes byddan nhw wedi brownio. Yna gwnewch yr un fath ar gyfer y courgette.

Ychwanegwch y darnau aubergine a'r courgette i'r cymysgedd. Gorchuddiwch y cyfan a'i fudferwi am 20 munud, neu'n hirach os medrwch chi.

Ychwanegwch halen a phupur os dymunwch.

Mae'r ratatouille'n flasus iawn gyda bara crystiog cynnes ar ddiwrnod oer.

RATATOUILLE

I love the tomatoey juiciness of this meal. The longer you can leave it to cook, the richer it becomes.

> 1 large aubergine
> 2 medium courgettes
> 2 medium onions
> 1 red pepper
> 4 large tomatoes or a can of tomatoes
> 2 tbsps of olive oil
> A handful of torn fresh basil
> Salt and pepper to taste
> ½ teaspoon each of cayenne pepper
> and caster sugar
> 1 clove of garlic, crushed

Peel the onions, halve and de-seed the pepper, and top and tail the aubergine and the courgettes. Then chop them all into 2cm chunks.

Place the onion, garlic and peppers into a large pan with the olive oil. Add 1 teaspoon of salt, sugar and cayenne pepper. Cover and cook gently for 10 minutes, add the tomatoes and continue cooking.

Using a little vegetable oil, fry the aubergine for about 2 minutes on each side until browned. Do exactly the same for the courgette.

Add both the aubergine and the courgette to the mixture, cover and simmer for 20 minutes, or longer if you can.

Add salt and pepper to season to your taste.

Delicious with hot, crusty bread on a cold day.

MYFFINS TEISEN FORON BRIWSIONOG

Mae pawb wedi arfer â theisen foron, a dyma fersiynau bach o'r clasur hwnnw. Cofiwch, does dim i'ch atal rhag defnyddio'r rysáit i wneud un teisen fawr.

150ml olew blodau'r haul
175g siwgwr brown meddal
250g blawd codi cyflawn
2 llwy de o bowdwr codi
60g cnau Ffrengig
Llond llaw o syltanas
150g moron, wedi'u gratio
3 wy mawr
Diferyn o laeth
Dewisol: ½ banana; sbeis cymysg;
croen a sudd un oren

Cynheswch y ffwrn i 180°C / 350°F / Nwy 4

Paratowch hambwrdd pobi teisennau bach gan osod casys papur myffins yn eu lle.

Cyfunwch holl gynhwysion y deisen mewn powlen fawr neu defnyddiwch gymysgydd trydanol ar stand.

Cymysgwch yn dda ac arllwyswch y cymysgedd i'r casys myffins. Pobwch am tua 20 munud (40 munud os ydych chi'n gwneud un deisen fawr).

Tynnwch o'r ffwrn a gadael i'r myffins oeri.

I wneud y topin

Cymysgwch 250g o gaws hufennog braster llawn (1 pot) â 75g o siwgwr eisin a 75g o fenyn. Peidiwch â gorgymysgu'r cyfan nes bydd yr eisin yn mynd yn llipa ac yn methu cynnal ei siâp. Rwy'n defnyddio bag peipio i roi'r eisin ar y cacennau. Yna, addurnwch â darnau o gnau Ffrengig, neu, os ydych chi'n teimlo'n greadigol, â moron bach wedi'u gwneud gan ddefnyddio eisin neu farsipán lliw oren.

CRUMBLY CARROT CAKE MUFFINS

Everybody's familiar with carrot cake, and here are little versions of that classic. Mind you, there's nothing stopping you from making one big cake using the same recipe.

150ml sunflower oil
175g soft brown sugar
250g wholemeal self-raising flour
2 tsp baking powder
60g walnuts
A handful of sultanas
150g grated carrot
3 large eggs
A drop of milk
Optional: ½ banana; mixed spice;
zest and juice of an orange

Preheat the oven to 180°C / 350°F / Gas 4

Prepare a muffin tray with muffin paper cases.

Combine all the cake ingredients in a large bowl or use a stand mixer.

Mix well and pour into muffin cases. Bake for about 20 minutes (or for 40 minutes if you're making one large cake).

Remove from the oven and allow the muffins to cool.

To make the topping

Mix together 250g full fat soft cream cheese (1 tub) with 75g of icing sugar and 75g of butter. Do not overmix as the frosting will collapse and fail to hold its shape. I use a piping bag to pipe the frosting onto the cakes. Finally, decorate with walnuts pieces or, if you're feeling creative, with small carrots made using orange icing or marzipan.

SYNIAD SYDYN
QUICK IDEA

Rhiwbob rhost melys

Ni ddylid diystyru blas riwbob o gwbl. Mae'n un o fy hoff gynnyrch gardd, ac er ein bod ni'n ei fwyta fel pwdin, llysieuyn yw e go iawn!

> 3–4 coesyn rhiwbob
> 2 lwy fwrdd o siwgwr brown golau
> 2 llwy fwrdd o sudd oren
> 2 lwy fwrdd o sudd grenadine
> 1 coden fanila neu 1 darn tua modfedd
> o hyd o sinsir ffres
> Crème fraîche neu iogwrt Groegaidd neu
> iogwrt naturiol wedi'i felysu â diferyn o fêl
> rhedegog a thopin granola i'w weini

Cynheswch y ffwrn i 180°C / 350°F / Nwy 4

Torrwch y rhiwbob yn ddarnau 5cm o hyd a'u rhoi mewn tun rhostio. Ysgeintiwch nhw â siwgwr a'r sudd oren.

Ychwanegwch hadau ½ hyd coden fanila, neu dafelli tenau o sinsir ffres. Rhowch y 2 lwy fwrdd o grenadine i ychwanegu melyster a lliw i'r rhiwbob.

Gwnewch yn siŵr fod pob dim wedi'i gymysgu a bod pob darn o riwbob wedi'i orchuddio'n dda â'r sudd a'r fanila neu'r sinsir.

Rhostiwch yn y ffwrn am tua 10–15 munud hyd nes bod y rhiwbob wedi meddalu ond ddim gormod, a gadewch iddo oeri.

 Tip: i'w weini, gallech ychwanegu'r topin crymbl pice ar y maen (o dud 58) ac ychydig o crème fraîche neu iogwrt Groegaidd wedi'i felysu â mêl i orffen.

Sweet roast rhubarb

The taste of rhubarb is not to be sniffed at – it's one of my favourite garden products, and even though we eat it as a pudding, it's really a vegetable!

> 3–4 lengths of rhubarb
> 2 tbsps light brown sugar
> 2 tbsps of orange juice
> 2 tbsps of grenadine
> 1 vanilla pod or 1 piece of stem ginger,
> about an inch in size
> Crème fraîche or natural or Greek yoghurt
> sweetened with a drizzle of runny honey
> and granola topping to serve

Preheat the oen to 180°C / 350°F / Gas 4

Cut the rhubarb into 5cm lengths and place in a roasting dish. Sprinkle with sugar and the orange juice.

Add the seeds of ½ a length of vanilla pod, or thin slices of stem ginger. Add the 2 tablespoons of grenadine to give sweetness and colour to the rhubarb.

Ensure that everything is well mixed and the rhubarb is well coated with juice and vanilla or the ginger.

Roast in the oven for about 10–15 minutes until tender but not soft, and allow cool.

 Tip: to serve, you could add the Welshcake crumble topping (from page 59) followed by a little honey sweetened crème fraîche or Greek yoghurt.

JAM A CHYFFAITH

⭐ Efallai fod yr ardd yn dechrau gwagio, ond mae'r perthi a'r caeau yn darparu digonedd o ffrwythau ar gyfer jamiau a jelis o hyd. Ac mae tomatos olaf y flwyddyn a phwmpenni a sgwashys a gynheswyd gan yr haul hefyd yn cynnig rhesymau da dros fwrw ati i biclo a storio'r cynhaeaf ymddangosiadol ddiddiwedd.

Mae bywyd yn dda ac yn brysur nawr, ac mae dyddiau hir o gymoni a pharatoi ar gyfer y gaeaf o'n blaenau, bron fel petai storm fawr ar y gorwel. Rwy'n cael blas ar y dasg o roi'r ardd i gysgu am y tro olaf yn y flwyddyn, am ychydig o leia. Mae'n debyg i ddiweddglo hapus i lyfr da.

Yn Fferm Allt y Gog, arwyddion sicr bod yr hydref wedi cyrraedd yw bwrlwm ffarwél ein cymdogion – y gwenoliaid – a'r niwloedd oer trwchus sy'n ein cyfarch bob bore. Hwyl fawr, wenoliaid; helo, hydref! Wrth i'r flwyddyn fwrw yn ei blaen, mae'r silffoedd yn llenwi gyda chyffeithiau yn barod ar gyfer y gaeaf sydd o'n blaen.

JAMS AND CHUTNEYS

⭐ The garden has started to empty, but the hedgerows are still providing us with ample fruit for jams and jellies. Late maturing tomatoes and sun-ripened pumpkins and squashes also give us good reasons to get pickling and storing the seemingly never-ending harvest.

Life is good and busy: there are long days of clearing away and preparing for the winter ahead almost as though a huge storm is imminent. The task of finally putting the garden into near hibernation for a few months is a task I relish. It's like a happy ending to a good book.

At Allt y Gog Farm, sure signs that autumn is finally upon us are the chattering farewells of our resident swallows and the thick, cold mists that greet us each morning. It's bye-bye, swallows; hello, autumn! As the year moves on, the shelves and cupboards gradually fill with preserves ready for the winter ahead.

Mae'r ffrwythau'n lluosog yr adeg hon o'r flwyddyn, o ddiwedd tymor y mefus i'r hydref a'i gynhaeaf toreithiog. Felly mae'n bryd estyn am y jariau jam a chostrelu blas y tymor mewn jariau.

Dyma rai ryseitiau yr ydw i wedi'u defnyddio dro ar ôl tro, ac maen nhw'n hawdd i'w gwneud. Fe gewch chi oddeutu 3 jar o jam suddog ar y diwedd, felly mae hynny'n ddigon i chi ac un ychwanegol yn anrheg i rywun, os ydych chi'n teimlo'n hael …

Berries are plentiful this time of year, from the end of the strawberry season to the seasons of mists and mellow fruitfulness. So it's time to dig out the jam jars and put the seasons in a jar.

Here are some tried and tested recipes – they're easy to do. You will get around 3 jars of juicy jam at the end, so that's enough for you, plus a present for someone, if you're feeling generous …

JAM AERON TRWY'R TRWCH

500g mwyar duon neu gymysgedd o aeron gwahanol: mefus, mafon, cyrens cochion neu gyrens duon
500g siwgwr jam
Sudd hanner lemwn

Oerwch blât neu soser yn y rhewgell.

Golchwch yr holl ffrwythau a gadewch iddyn nhw ddraenio.

Rhowch y sudd lemwn a'r aeron mewn sosban fawr, drom, neu mewn sosban gwneud jam a throwch y cyfan ychydig o weithiau.

Ychwanegwch y siwgwr a thoddwch dros wres isel. Dewch â'r cyfan i'r berw a berwch yn araf hyd nes bydd y jam yn cyrraedd y pwynt setio (gweler gyferbyn).

Rhowch y jam mewn potiau glân, cynnes, a'u selio.

JUMBLE-BERRY JAM

500g blackberries or a jumble of different berries: strawberries, raspberries, red or black currants
500g jam sugar
Juice of half a lemon

Chill a saucer or plate in the freezer.

Wash all the fruit and allow to drain.

Put the lemon juice and berries into a large, heavy saucepan or preserving pan and stir a couple of times.

Add the sugar and dissolve over a low heat. Bring to the boil and boil gently until the jam reaches setting point (see opposite).

Pot the jam in warm, clean pots and seal.

DG

JELI MWYAR

1kg mwyar duon
2–3 afalau coginio, wedi'u torri'n fras
Sudd 1 lemwn
Siwgwr jam, tua 450g am bob 600ml o sudd

Oerwch soser neu blât yn y rhewgell.

Golchwch y ffrwythau a gadewch iddynt draenio.
Rhowch y sudd lemwn, y mwyar a'r afalau mewn
sosban fawr, ychwanegwch 1.2 litr o ddŵr (1200ml) a
berwch y cyfan.

Mudferwch hyd nes bydd y ffrwythau'n feddal ac yna
gadewch iddo oeri ychydig.

Trosglwyddwch y ffrwythau i fag jeli neu ddarn o
liain mwslin a gadewch i'r sudd ddraenio am sawl
awr. Mae gwneud hyn dros nos yn syniad da. Yna,
mesurwch y sudd – dylai fod gennych oddeutu 1.2 litr.

Ychwanegwch 450g o siwgwr am bob 600ml o sudd.

Rhowch y sudd mewn sosban fawr a'i ferwi.
Ychwanegwch y siwgwr a dal i'w droi hyd nes bydd y
siwgwr wedi toddi.

Nawr berwch yr hylif yn ffyrnig am tua 10 munud, nes
cyrraedd y pwynt setio.

Potiwch a seliwch cyn gynted ag sy'n bosib.

GF

BRAMBLE JELLY

1kg blackberries
2–3 cooking apples, roughly chopped
Juice of 1 lemon
Jam sugar, about 450g for every 600ml of juice

Chill a saucer or plate in the freezer.

Wash all the fruit and allow to drain. Put the lemon
juice, blackberries and apples into a large saucepan.
Add 1.2 litres of water (1200ml) and bring to the boil.

Simmer until the fruit is soft and then allow to cool
slightly.

Transfer the fruit into a jelly bag or a piece of muslin
cloth and allow the juices to drain for several hours
(overnight is a good idea). Then, measure the juice – it
should be in the region of 1.2 litre.

Add 450g sugar for every 600 ml juice.

Place the juice into a large pan and bring to the boil.
Add the sugar and keep stirring until the sugar has
dissolved.

Now boil rapidly for about 10 minutes until setting
point is reached.

Pot and seal as soon as possible.

Profi am y pwynt setio:
Cymerwch lond llwy de o jam a'i roi ar y plât neu'r llestr oer.
Gadewch am funud, yna gwthiwch y jam â llwy de. Os yw'n crychu ar yr ywneb, yna mae'n barod.
Oerwch y jam neu'r jeli ryw gymaint cyn ei roi mewn jariau.
Yn ddelfrydol, dylai'r jariau fod yn gynnes wrth i chi roi'r jam neu'r jeli ynddyn nhw.
Seliwch y jariau'n dynn ac edrychwch ymlaen at fwynhau eich cynnyrch drwy gydol y misoedd tywyll.

To test for the setting point
Take a teaspoon of jam and place it on the chilled saucer.
Leave for a minute and then push it with a teaspoon.
If it creases on the surface, it's ready.
Cool the jam or jelly a little before putting into jars.
Ideally, the jars should be warm when the jam or jelly is added.
Seal tightly and look forward to enjoying your produce
throughout the dark days of the next few months.

PWT AM EIRIN TAGU

Yr adeg pan fydda i'n meddwl 'mod i wedi dirwyn fy chwilota hydrefol am ffrwythau'r perthi i ben, fe ddaw cynhaeaf ffrwythau helaeth arall i'r amlwg. Dyw'r eirinen dagu ddim yn flasus yn amrwd, ond mae'n hollol hyfryd wedi iddi gael ei thrawsnewid yn jam, yn jeli neu'n jin ac mae sôn am eirin tagu fel arfer yn gwneud i rywun feddwl am jin eirin tagu.

Mae'r Prunus spinosa, neu'r ddraenen ddu, ynghudd yn y perthi ac yn tyfu ar hap mewn llawer man, ac fe'i defnyddiwyd yn helaeth i greu ffiniau rhwng caeau ar draws y wlad.

Er gwaetha'r cyngor yw i hel eirin tagu wedi'r rhew cyntaf, fel bo strwythur mewnol y ffrwyth yn dirywio i fod o gymorth i ryddhau'r blas, 'Ewch allan a chasglwch'. Dyna fy nghyngor i, achos os na wnewch chi, mi fydd yr adar yn cael y blaen arnoch chi.

Jam, jeli neu jin eirin tagu – penderfynwch chi, ond da chi, gwnewch y gorau o'r cynnyrch gwych yma sydd ar gael yn rhad ac am ddim.

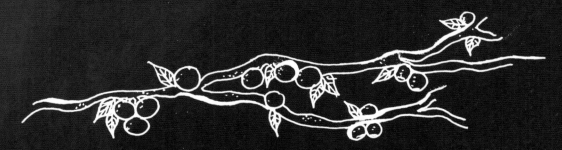

A BIT ABOUT SLOES

Just when I think I've finished my autumn foraging for the abundant free harvest offered by the fields and hedgerows, I discover another truly abundant harvest of fruit. Sloes are not the most delicious fruit in their raw state, but they're totally delightful when transformed into jams and jellies and gin, and the mention of sloes usually brings one thing to mind – sloe gin.

Hidden and dotted randomly in most hedgerows are the Prunus spinosa, commonly known as the blackthorn – one of the most popular hedgerow plants used to mark the boundaries of fields all around the country.

Despite advice to pick after the first frost, so that the internal structure is broken down to help the flavour escape, I say, 'Get out there and get picking'. If you don't, the birds will.

Sloe jam, sloe jelly or sloe gin – you decide, but do make the most of this wonderful freebie

JIN EIRIN TAGU

Nid anrheg rad yw hon, ond bydd y jin yn bendant yn bwnc trafod a chaiff ei werthfawrogi'n fawr.

>   450g eirin tagu
>   225g siwgwr mân
>   1 litr o jin

Gwnewch dwll yng nghroen gwydn yr eirin â nodwydd lân, neu rhowch yr eirin yn y rhewgell. Dylai'r broses rewi hollti'r crwyn. Yna, rhowch nhw mewn jar mawr wedi'i sterileiddio.

Arllwyswch y siwgwr a'r jin i mewn i'r jar a'i selio'n dynn. Ysgydwch yn dda.

Storiwch mewn cwpwrdd oer, tywyll a'i hysgwyd bob yn ail ddiwrnod am wythnos. Yna, ysgydwch hi unwaith yr wythnos am o leia ddau fis.

Straeniwch y jin eirin tagu drwy fwslin i mewn i botel (neu boteli) wedi'i sterileiddio.

* **Rhowch gynnig ar wneud jin neu focda o flasau gwahanol, gan ddefnyddio mwyar duon.**

SLOE GIN

It's not a cheap present but the gin will definitely be a talking point and very much appreciated.

>   450g sloes
>   225g caster sugar
>   1 litre gin

Prick the tough skin of the sloes all over with a clean needle, or place the sloes in the freezer, which should pop the skins as they freeze. Then put them in a large sterilised jar.

Pour in the sugar and the gin, seal tightly and shake well.

Store in a cool, dark cupboard and shake every other day for a week. Then shake once a week for at least two months.

Strain the sloe gin through muslin into a sterilised bottle (or bottles).

* **Try making an alternative flavoured gin or vodka, using blackberries.**

JELI AFAL AC EIRIN TAGU

Mae gwneud jam a jeli ar ôl treulio rhai oriau yn casglu ffrwythau yn ffordd arbennig o dda o ymlacio. Mae'r rysáit hwn yn gwneud jeli syml.

700g eirin tagu wedi'u golchi
700g afalau coginio
700g siwgwr jam am bob peint neu 750ml o sudd wedi'i straenio

Cyn decrau gwneud y jeli, rhowch ddau blât bach yn y rhewgell, yn barod i'w defnyddio yn nes ymlaen i brofi'r pwynt setio.

Golchwch yr afalau a'u torri'n fras. Nid oes angen tynnu croen na chraidd yr afalau chwaith.

Rhowch yr eirin tagu a'r afalau mewn sosban fawr, drom, neu mewn sosban gwneud jam.

Ychwanegwch ddŵr i orchuddio hanner y ffrwythau. Codwch y cyfan i'r berw'n raddol a mudferwch yn araf hyd nes bydd y ffrwythau'n feddal.

Arllwyswch y ffrwythau wedi'u coginio i bowlen drwy liain mwslin glân neu fag jeli y medrwch eu cael yn hawdd o siopau coginio. Yn aml cyfeirir at y mwslin fel bag jeli.

Gadewch y jeli yn y bag i ddiferu dros nos neu am tua 12 awr, ac yna mesurwch faint o hylif sydd gennych.

Arllwyswch yr hylif i sosban fawr, drom, ac ychwanegu 700g o siwgwr gwyn am bob peint neu 570ml o sudd sydd gennych.

Cynheswch y sudd ffrwythau a'r siwgwr yn araf. Gwnewch yn siŵr bod y siwgwr wedi toddi drwy droi'r cymysgedd o dro i dro, ac yna dewch â'r hylif i'r berw'n araf.

Berwch y jeli am tua 6–10 munud, ac yna profwch y jeli i weld a yw wedi cyrraedd y pwynt setio. Gollyngwch ychydig o jeli ar un o'r platiau oer i weld a yw'n setio wrth iddo oeri. Os nad yw, parhewch i ferwi am ddwy funud arall, yna profwch eto. Unwaith y bydd y jeli yn cyrraedd y pwynt setio, arllwyswch y cymysgedd i jariau cynnes, glân. Gorchuddiwch yn syth â disgiau cwyr a chau'r cloriau.

APPLE AND SLOE JELLY

Making jams and jellies after a few hours of fruit picking is a great way to unwind. This makes a simple jelly.

700g sloes, washed
700g of cooking apples
700g jam sugar to each pint or 750ml of strained juice

Before starting to make the jelly, place two small plates into the freezer, ready for using later to test for the setting point.

Wash the apples and chop roughly. There is no need to peel or core the apples.

Place sloes and apples in a large deep heavy-bottomed saucepan, or preserving pan.

Add water to cover half of the fruit. Bring slowly to the boil and simmer very gently until all the fruit is soft.

Pour the cooked fruit into a bowl through clean washed muslin cloth or a jelly bag that is easy to buy from any cook shop. The muslin is often referred to as a jelly bag.

Leave the jelly bag to drip overnight or for about 12 hours, and then measure the quantity of liquid that you have.

Pour the juice into a deep heavy-bottomed saucepan and add 700g of white granulated sugar for each pint or 570ml of juice.

Heat the fruit juice and sugar very gently. Make sure that all the sugar has dissolved by stirring from time to time, then bring the liquid slowly to the boil.

Boil the jelly for about 6–10 minutes, then test the jelly to see if it's reached the setting point. Drop a little of the jelly onto one of the cold plates to check that it sets as it cools. If not, continue to boil for two more minutes, then check again. Once the jelly has reached the setting point, pour into warm sterilised jars, cover immediately with waxed disks and close the tops.

Ychydig iawn o bleserau bywyd sydd cystal â gweld cwpwrdd bwyd yn llawn potiau sgleiniog o bicls a siytnis.

Mae prynu cyflenwad yn y farchnad ffermwyr leol yn gwneud i chi deimlo'n dda, ond bydd gwneud eich rhai eich hun yn gwneud i chi deimlo'n well eto. Mae'n nhw'n gwneud anrheg Nadolig wych i dadau a thadau-cu. Mae picls a siytnis yn curo sanau bob tro!

SIYTNI BETYS

2kg betys
700g afalau coginio, wedi'u pilio a'u craidd wedi'i dynnu
700g winwns
450g siwgwr
½ llwy de o bupur
1½ llwy de o halen
600ml finegr

I baratoi'r betys, berwch nhw yn eu crwyn am tua awr i'w meddalu. I osgoi 'gwaedu', peidiwch â thynnu'r gwreiddyn, ond trimiwch y dail hyd at 5cm. Wedi iddyn nhw goginio, tynnwch o'r dŵr a gadael iddyn nhw oeri, cyn tynnu'r croen, y gwraidd a'r dail a'u torri'n ddarnau bach.

Torrwch yr winwns a'r afalau yn ddarnau bach a'u rhoi ynghyd â'r betys mewn sosban fawr.

Ychwanegwch yr holl gynhwysion eraill: y siwgwr, yr halen a'r pupur a'r finegr.

Berwch y cyfan am 1 awr, gadewch i'r cymysgedd oeri ychydig cyn llenwi jariau parod â'r cymysgedd.

I baratoi'r jariau, gallwch eu golchi yn y peiriant golchi llestri ar dymheredd twym neu eu golchi'n dda yn y sinc a'u rhoi mewn ffwrn dwym am 5 munud i'w sterileiddio – llenwch y jariau tra'u bod nhw'n dwym.

Tip: mae siytnis yn ffordd ardderchog o gadw gormodedd o ffrwythau a llysiau i'w defnyddio dros fisoedd y gaeaf. Dyma flasau arbennig i gyd-fynd â chigoedd oer a saladau ac mewn brechdanau.

There are very few pleasures in the world commensurate with seeing a well-stocked cupboard full of gleaming pots of pickles and chutneys.

Buying at the local farmer's market makes you feel good, but making your own will make you feel better. They also make great gifts for dads and grandads at Christmas. Pickles and chutneys always beat socks!

BEETROOT CHUTNEY

2kg beetroot
700g cooking apples, peeled and cored
700g onions
450g sugar
½ tsp pepper
1½ tsp salt
600ml vinegar

To prepare the beetroot, simply boil them unpeeled for about an hour until soft. To prevent 'bleeding', do not remove the root; trim the stalks, leaving about 5cm. When they're cooked, take from the water and leave to cool before peeling and topping and tailing. Then chop the beetroot into small pieces.

Chop the onions and the peeled and cored apples into small pieces and place in a large pan.

Add all the other ingredients: the sugar, salt and pepper and vinegar.

Boil for about 1 hour, allow to cool a little before filling the prepared jars.

To prepare the jars, you can wash them in the dishwasher on a hot setting or wash well in the sink and place in a hot oven for 5 minutes to sterilise. Fill the jars whilst they're still hot.

Tip: chutneys are a great way to preserve surplus fruit and vegetables for use in the winter months. They are great with cold meats and salads and in sandwiches.

WINWNS PICL SBEISLYD

1kg winwns piclo
4–5 llwy de o sbeisys piclo o'r siop
1 litr o finegr brown
185g siwgwr
Halen

Y diwrnod cyn y byddwch chi'n gwneud y piclo, pliciwch eich winwns – gweler y dull isod.

Yna ysgeintiwch lond llwy fwrdd o halen cyffredin drostyn nhw a'u gadael dros nos. Mae hyn yn tynnu'r dŵr allan o'r winwns ac yn eu hatal rhag mynd yn feddal yn y finegr. Wedi dweud hyn, dwi'n hepgor y cam hwn yn aml, a dydw i ddim wedi cael y broblem yma, ond wedyn, rydyn ni'n bwyta'n picls acha rât yn ein tŷ ni!

Rhowch y sbeisys piclo, y finegr a'r siwgwr mewn sosban a'u cynhesu er mwyn toddi'r siwgwr.

Gosodwch y winwns wedi'u plicio mewn jariau glân, sydd wedi'u sterileiddio. Gwasgwch nhw mewn yn dynn – mae lle i un arall bob tro. Rwy'n hoffi rhoi deilen lawryf i mewn gyda nhw – mae'n edrych yn eitha pert wedi'i rhoi lawr ochr y jar. Os ydych chi'n hoffi picls 'poeth' ychydig o wres, ychwanegwch tsili i'r jar.

Arllwyswch y finegr a'r sbeis i'r jariau, gan geisio peidio ag anadlu'r nwyon wrth i chi wneud hyn, dyw e ddim yn gwneud lles i'r trwyn!

Llenwch bob jar i'r ymylon gan sicrhau bod pob winwnsyn wedi'u orchuddio mewn finegr. Seliwch y jar a gadael iddi oeri.

Bydd yr winwns yn barod i'w bwyta ar ôl tua mis, ond mi fyddan nhw'n blasu'n well fyth ar ôl tua dau fis. Rwy'n gwneud fy nghyflenwad i yn ystod gwyliau hanner tymor diwedd mis Hydref.

Tip: mae plicio'r winwns bach yn job drafferthus. I wneud pethau'n haws, tynnwch ben a chwt yr winwns a'u gosod mewn powlen fawr. Berwch y tegell ac arllwyswch ddŵr berw drostyn nhw ac yna gadewch i'r dŵr oeri. Draeniwch y dŵr wedi iddo oeri a dylai'r winwns fod yn gymaint haws i'w plicio.

✳ **Tip: i wneud eich sbeis piclo eich hunan, cymysgwch y canlynol a'i storio mewn jar glân: 1 llwy de yr un o hadau coriander, hadau mwstard, pupur du neu bupur cymysg, a darnau tsili.**

SPICY PICKLED ONIONS

1kg pickling onions
4–5 tsps pickling spices from the shop
1 litre of malt vinegar
185g granulated sugar
Salt

The day before you want to make your pickled onions, peel the onions – see the method below.

Next, sprinkle a tablespoonful of ordinary table salt over them and leave overnight. This draws excess water out of them and stops them getting soggy in the vinegar. However, I often leave this step out, and I've never had a problem, but then, we do eat our pickles rather quickly in our house!

Place the pickling spice blend, the vinegar and the sugar into pan, and heat to dissolve the sugar.

Place the onions into clean, sterilised jars. Pack them in tightly, there's always room for one more. I like to put a bay leaf in with them; it looks quite pretty placed down the side of the jar. If you like hot, spicy pickles, add a chilli to the jar.

Pour the vinegar and spices into the jars, trying not to breathe in the fumes as you do this – it's not good for the nose!

Fill each jar up to the top, ensuring that all the onions are submerged in vinegar. Seal the jars and leave to cool.

The onions will be ready to eat after about one month, but taste even better after about two months. I always make mine during the half-term holiday at the end of October.

Tip: peeling the tiny onions is a fiddly job. To make it easier, top and tail the onions and put them in a large bowl. Boil the kettle and pour boiling water over the onions; then allow the water to cool. Drain away the cooled water and now they should be much easier to peel.

✳ **Tip: to make your own pickling spice, mix the following and store in a clean jar: 1 teaspoon each of coriander seed, mustard seed, black or mixed peppercorns, chilli flakes.**

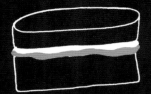

TEISEN FICTORIA

Er mwyn i chi wneud defnydd da o'ch jam cartref hyfryd chi, rwy'n meddwl bod teisen felen Fictoria draddodiadol yn ffordd ardderchog o arddangos eich sgiliau i'r dim. Dyma sut i wneud teisen syml, ond ew, mae'n blasu'n dda.

Mae'r cynhwysion yn hawdd i'w cofio bob tro: bydd angen 225g menyn ar dymheredd yr ystafell, 225g siwgwr mân, 225g blawd codi, 4 wy canolig, 2 lwy de o rinflas fanila a pheth llaeth i ryddhau'r cymysgedd.

Cynheswch y ffwrn i 180ºC / 350ºF / Nwy 4. Irwch a leinio dau dun teisen 18cm gyda phapur pobi. Hufennwch y menyn a'r sigwr gyda'i gilydd mewn powlen nes eu bod yn lliw golau yna curo'r wyau a'u hychwanegu ychydig ar y tro a chymysgu'r rhinflas fanila. Plygwch y blawd mewn gan ddefnyddio llwy fetel fawr, yna ychwanegu ychydig o laeth os oes angen i greu cymysgedd sy'n syrthio'n hawdd oddi ar y llwy.
Rhannwch y cymysgedd rhwng y tuniau teisen a'u taenu gyda sbatiwla. Pobwch am 20–25 munud, neu hyd nes eu bod yn frown euraid ar yr wyneb a bod sgiwer yn dod allan yn lân o'r canol.

Tynnwch o'r ffwrn a'i rhoi o'r neilltu am 5 munud. Tynnwch o'r tun a thynnu'r papur. Gosodwch ar resel wifrog yna gwasgu'r cacennau at ei gilydd gan ddefnyddio'ch jam cartref blasus a pheth hufen wedi'i chwipio.

VICTORIA SPONGE

So that you can make good use of your lovely homemade jam, I think that a good, old-fashioned Victoria sponge should show off your skills a treat. Here's how to make the simplest of cakes, but my, how good it tastes.

The ingredients always are easy to remember: you'll need 225g butter at room temperature, 225g caster sugar, 225g self raising flour, 4 medium eggs, 2 teaspoons vanilla extract and some milk, to loosen the mixture.

Preheat the oven to 180ºC / 350ºF / Gas 4. Grease and line two 18cm cake tins with baking paper. Cream the butter and the sugar together in a bowl until pale. Beat the eggs and add a little at a time, stir in the vanilla extract. Fold in the flour using a large metal spoon, adding a little milk, if necessary, to create a batter that falls easily off the spoon.
Divide the mixture between the cake tins and spread out with a spatula, bake for 20–25 minutes, or until golden-brown on top and a skewer inserted into the middle comes out clean.

Remove from the oven and set aside for 5 minutes, remove from the tin and peel off the paper. Place onto a wire rack before sandwiching the cakes together using your very own delicious homemade jam and some whipped cream.

Y nos yn cau amdanom

5

The nights drawing in

Dyma ni'n bendant yng nghanol yr hydref a hyd yn oed yn goglais bodiau traed y gaeaf.

Erbyn i ni ddathlu Calan Gaeaf a rhoi trefn ar Guto Ffowc am flwyddyn arall, bydd y clociau wedi mynd 'nôl a bydd hi'n anodd tynnu pobol allan o'u hetiau, eu sgarffiau a'u menyg.

Ond mi ydw i'n hoff o'r amser yma o'r flwyddyn ac wrth i'r dyddiau fyrhau ac oeri, fe gymerwn fwy o ofal dros fwydo ein cyrff a'n heneidiau. Bydd ychydig o fwyd da, goleuadau'n pefrio, tanllwyth o dân a chwmni da yn rhoi dechrau da i ni ar gyfer y tymor sydd i ddod.

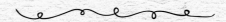

We are well and truly into autumn and even tickling the toes of winter.

By the time we've done Hallowe'en and sorted Guy Fawkes out for another year, the clocks will have gone back and it'll be hard to prise people out of their hats and scarves.

But I do like this time of year, and as the nights draw in and get colder we take more care to feed our bodies and our souls. Some good food, a few twinkling lights, roaring fires and good company will set us up for the season to come.

CALAN GAEA

⭐ Yr adeg hon o'r flwyddyn, er gwell neu er gwaeth, mae'r siopau'n llawn pwmpenni. O fewn wythnos neu ddwy mi fyddan nhw wedi diflannu, wedi'u cerfio i farwolaeth a'u taflu o'r neilltu, ar ôl iddyn nhw roi oriau o hwyl ac adloniant i blant ac oedolion ar draws y wlad. Ond mae gweld cymaint o bwmpenni hyfryd yn cael eu prynu, eu defnyddio a'u taflu heb eu bwyta yn fy ngwneud i'n drist.

Felly, eleni, wrth i chi gerfio'n llawen pam na wnewch chi gawl pwmpen cynhesol o'r 'gwastraff'? Efallai ei fod yn ymddangos yn rhyfedd ond gyda llond dyrnaid neu ddau o gnawd y bwmpen, cwpwl o foron, winwnsyn a thun o domatos, fe allwch chi wneud swper blasus i'r teulu ei fwynhau.

A phan fydd yr holl dwrw am bwmpenni wedi tawelu ac nad oes modd cael yr un bwmpen yn y siopau mwyach, gallwch gyfnewid y bwmpen am sgwash cnau menyn yn eich rysáit, er mwyn gwneud cawl sydd hyd yn oed yn well, yn fy marn i.

HALLOWEEN

⭐ At this time of year, love it or loathe it, the shelves are full of pumpkins in the shops. Within a week or two they will be gone, carved to death and discarded, having provided hours of fun and entertainment for children and adults across the land. But it does make me slightly sad to see so many beautiful pumpkins being bought, used, discarded and not eaten.

So, this year, as you carve away, why not make a warming pumpkin soup out of the 'waste'? It may sound odd, but with a handful or two of pumpkin flesh, a couple of carrots, an onion and a tin of tomatoes, you can make your family a great supper to enjoy.

When all the pumpkin mania has died down and pumpkins are no longer available, just substitute the pumpkin with a butternut squash in your recipe, for what I think is an even better soup.

CAWL PWMPEN SBEISLYD

Dyma un o fy hoff ryseitiau ar gyfer cawl, wrth gwrs! Mae'n cynhesu 'nghalon ac yn dod â lliw gwych i'r bwrdd.

1 bwmpen canolig neu sgwash
cnau menyn mawr
1 winwnsyn
2 foronen
1 ewin garlleg
5cm o wreiddyn sinsir
500ml o stoc llysiau
Tun tomato (dewisol)
20g menyn
1 llwy fwrdd o olew llysieuol
Halen a phupur du wedi'i falu
½ tsili, wedi'i dorri'n fân (dewisol)

Torrwch eich pwmpen yn chwarteri, a thynnu'r cnawd meddal o'r tu mewn ynghyd â hadau'r bwmpen (gallwch gadw'r rhain i'w bwyta'n nes ymlaen neu eu cadw ar gyfer yr adar). Tynnwch y croen a thorrwch y cnawd oren yn ddarnau bychain, sgwâr yn barod i'w coginio.

Tynnwch groen yr winwnsyn a thorrwch ef yn ddarnau bach. Gwnewch yr un fath â'r sinsir a'r garlleg, a'u ffrio mewn ychydig o fenyn ac olew ar waelod sosban fawr hyd nes bydd y cyfan yn feddal.

Pliciwch y moron a'u torri'n ddarnau bychain sgwâr. Rhowch nhw yn y sosban ynghyd â'r bwmpen sydd eisoes wedi'i pharatoi.

Ychwanegwch tua litr o stoc, digon i orchuddio'r llysiau, a'u codi i'r berw.

Os ydych chi'n hoffi cawl tenau, ychwanegwch dun o domatos.

Unwaith y mae'r cyfan yn berwi, trowch y gwres yn is a mudferwch am oddeutu 20 munud, hyd nes bydd yr holl lysiau wedi'u coginio ac yn feddal.

Gadewch i'r cymysgedd oeri ryw gymaint ac yna cymysgwch yn dda gan ddefnyddio cymysgydd trydan, neu stwnshwr tatws, hyd nes bydd yn llyfn.

SPICY PUMPKIN SOUP

This is one of my favourite soup recipes, of course! It warms the cockles of my heart and brings great colour to the table.

1 medium pumpkin or a large butternut squash
1 onion
2 carrots
1 clove of garlic
5cm of root ginger
500ml vegetable stock
Tin of tomatoes (optional)
20g butter
1 tbsp vegetable oil
Salt and ground black pepper
½ chilli, finely chopped (optional)

Cut your pumpkin into quarters, remove all the soft inside and the pumpkin seeds (you can keep these to eat later or keep them for the birds). Peel and chop the orange flesh into small cubes, ready for cooking.

Peel and chop the onion, the ginger and the garlic and fry in a little butter and oil in the bottom of a large saucepan until soft.

Peel the carrots, chop into small chunks and add to the saucepan together with your prepared pumpkin.

Add about a litre of stock, enough to cover the vegetables, and bring to the boil.

Add a tin of tomatoes if you like a thinner soup.

When the soup starts to boil, turn down the heat and simmer for about 20 minutes, until all the vegetables are cooked and soft.

Allow to cool a little and then blend using an electric blender, or a potato masher, until smooth.

Ychwanegwch halen a phupur, rhowch y cawl mewn bowlenni a throelli ychydig o hufen ar ei ben a'i weini gyda bara cynnes, blasus.

 Tip: ffordd hawdd o wahanu hadau pwmpen oddi wrth y cnawd yw rhoi'r cyfan mewn llond powlen o ddŵr oer. Bydd yr hadau'n arnofio i'r wyneb a gallwch eu codi'n hawdd. Peidiwch â'u taflu; naill ai sychwch nhw i'w defnyddio eich hun, neu bwydwch yr adar â nhw.

Tip: rhowch olwg mwy glam neu sbŵci i'ch cawl drwy ei weini mewn pwmpen. Ychwanegwch chwyrlïad o hufen neu crème fraîche, ychydig o hadau pwmpen a thafell o fara crystiog, ac mae gennych chi wledd. Mae'r rysáit hon mor hawdd, ond fe allwch ei haddasu: ychwanegwch lwy de o bowdwr cyrri am ychydig o gic, gallwch deneuo'r cawl ag ychydig o sudd oren i wneud cawl pwmpen ac oren.

Season with salt and pepper, ladle into bowls and swirl in a little cream before serving with warmed crusty bread.

Tip: an easy way to separate the pumpkin seeds from the remainder of the flesh is to place the whole lot into a bowl of cold water. The seeds will float to the top and you can just scoop them away. Don't throw them away, either dry them out for yourself or feed them to the birds.

Tip: give it an even more glam or spooky look by serving it in a pumpkin. Add a swirl of cream or crème fraîche, a few pumpkin seeds and a slice of crusty bread and you have a feast. This recipe is so easy, but play around with it: add a teaspoon of curry powder or a sprinkle of cayenne pepper for a bit of heat, and you can even thin it down with some orange juice to make a pumpkin and orange soup.

PELI SELSIG MEWN SAWS TOMATO SBEISLYD

Mae'r rysáit hon yn gwneud pryd harti, da. Bydd y peli selsig yn glynu wrth eich asennau, yr union beth sydd ei angen arnoch ar noson oer.

8 selsig sbeislyd o ansawdd da
1 afal
1 winwnsyn bach
1 pupur
1 tun o domatos wedi'u malu
Darn bach o sinsir
2 ewin garlleg
Halen a phupur du wedi'i falu
Olew i ffrio

Holltwch grwyn y selsig a thynnu'r cig selsig allan. Gan ddefnyddio bysedd â blawd arnyn nhw, siapiwch y cig selsig yn beli o faint cneuen Ffrengig.

Ffriwch y peli cig selsig, gan geisio peidio â'u torri. Pan fyddan nhw wedi'u coginio, draeniwch nhw ar bapur cegin.

Pliciwch yr winwnsyn a'r afal a'u torri'n ddarnau bach tebyg o ran maint. Gwnewch yr un fath â'r pupur.

Rhowch ychydig o olew mewn sosban fawr neu mewn ffrimpan ag ochrau uchel a ffrio'r winwnsyn, y pupur, y sinsir a'r garlleg hyd nes eu bod yn feddal. Yna, ychwanegwch weddill y cynhwysion, gan gynnwys y tun tomatos.

Cynheswch ar wres cymedrol, rhowch glawr ar y sosban neu'r ffrimpan a gadael i'r saws fudferwi am 15 munud.

Ychwanegwch y peli cig i'r saws a'u mudferwi am 15 munud arall, gan droi'r cymysgedd yn achlysurol i sicrhau bod y cyfan yn cael ei orchuddio gan y saws ac nad yw'n glynu wrth y sosban. Ychwanegwch halen a phupur du wedi'i falu yn ôl eich dymuniad.

Trosglwyddwch i lestr a mwynhewch gyda rholiau bara crystiog neu basta.

SAUSAGE MEATBALLS AND SPICY TOMATO SAUCE

This recipe makes such a good, hearty meal. It'll stick to your sides, which is exactly what you need on a cold evening.

8 good quality spicy sausages
1 apple
1 small onion
1 pepper
1 tin of chopped tomatoes
Small piece of ginger
2 cloves of garlic
Salt and ground black pepper
Oil for frying

Split the sausage skins and take the sausage meat out. Using floured fingers, shape the sausage meat into walnut-sized balls.

Gently fry the sausage meat balls, trying not to break them up. Once cooked, drain them on some kitchen roll.

Peel the onion and the apple, chop them into small, equally sized pieces. Do the same with the pepper.

Into a large pan or a deep sided frying pan, add a little oil and fry the onion, the pepper, the ginger and garlic until softened. Then add the remainder of the ingredients, including the tin of tomatoes.

Place over a medium heat, cover with a lid and allow to simmer for 15 minutes.

Add the meatballs into the sauce, and simmer for a further 15 minutes, stirring occasionally to ensure that they are covered in the sauce, and that the bottom doesn't stick to the pan. Season with salt and ground black pepper.

Transfer to a serving dish and serve with a crusty bread roll or pasta.

CACCIATORE CYW IÂR

Ystyr cacciatore mewn Eidaleg yw heliwr. Yn y byd coginio, mae alla cacciatora yn cyfeirio at bryd a baratowyd yn null yr heliwr – wedi'i wneud gan ddefnyddio tomatos, winwns, perlysiau, puprod a gwin fel arfer. Gellir gwneud cacciatore hefyd gan ddefnyddio cig cwningen.

1 cyw iâr, â'r cymalau wedi'u tynnu, neu defnyddiwch nifer cyfatebol o ddarnau cyw iâr – gallwch ddewis defnyddio cig brest cyw iâr neu gig coes
Halen a phupur du wedi'i falu'n ffres
2 ddeilen lawryf
2 sbrigyn o rosmari ffres neu deim, gallwch ddefnyddio'r ddau berlysieuyn
3 ewin garlleg wedi'u malu
½ potel o win coch neu beth bynnag sydd gennych dros ben
Blawd, i ysgeintio
Olew olewydd
Llond llaw o olifau gwyrdd neu ddu, heb eu cerrig
2 dun 400g o domatos, neu mae tomatos ffres yn ardderchog os oes gennych ormodedd ar ôl yn y tŷ gwydr >

CHICKEN CACCIATORE

Cacciatore means hunter in Italian. In cuisine, alla cacciatora refers to a meal prepared hunter-style – made with tomatoes, onions, herbs, peppers and usually wine. Cacciatore can also be made with rabbit meat.

1 chicken, jointed, or use the equivalent amount of chicken pieces – you can choose to use chicken breast or thigh/leg meat
Salt and freshly ground black pepper
2 bay leaves
2 sprigs of fresh rosemary or thyme, or you can use both herbs
3 cloves of garlic
½ bottle of red wine or whatever you have leftover
Flour, for dusting
Olive oil
A handful of green or black olives, stoned
2 tins 400g of plum tomatoes, or fresh tomatoes are great if you have a glut of them in the greenhouse >

> Cynheswch y ffwrn i 200C / 400F / Nwy 6

Gallwch hepgor y cam hwn: ond byddai'n dda petaech yn medru mwydo'r cyw iâr yn y gwin a'r perlysiau ac un ewin garlleg wedi'i falu am o leia awr cyn i chi ddechrau paratoi. Os ydych chi'n mwydo'r cyw iâr dros nos, peidiwch ag anghofio rhoi'r cyw iâr mewn bocs wedi'i selio yn yr oergell.

Tynnwch y cyw iâr o'r marinad, gan gadw'r marinad i'w ddefnyddio'n ddiweddarach. Patiwch y cig yn sych â phapur cegin. Ysgeintiwch y darnau cyw iar â blawd. Gellir gwneud hyn yn hawdd drwy roi'r cyw iâr a'r blawd mewn bag plastig mawr a'u hysgwyd gyda'i gilydd.

Rhowch rai llwyeidiau o olew olewydd mewn ffrimpan fawr a ffriwch y darnau cyw iâr hyd nes bod lliw da arnyn nhw. Rhowch nhw o'r neilltu.

Rhowch y ffrimpan yn ôl ar y gwres ac ychwanegu'r garlleg sy'n weddill. Ffriwch y garlleg ar wres isel, ac ychwanegwch yr olewydd, y tomatos ac yna'r darnau o gig cyw iâr.

Ychwanegwch y marinad gwin a'i gymysgu'n dda. Codwch y cyfan i'r berw a rhowch glawr ar y ffrimpan. Pobwch yn y ffwrn am 1½ awr. Os yw'ch sosbenni'n rhai â dolenni plastig, peidiwch ag anghofio trosglwyddo'r cymysgedd i lestr y medrir ei roi yn y ffwrn cyn pobi.

Wedi i'r cymysgedd goginio, sgimiwch unrhyw ormodedd olew oddi arno. Yna trowch y cymysgedd, blaswch ac ychwanegu ychydig o halen neu bupur os oes angen.

Tynnwch y dail llawryf a'r sbrigynnau rhosmari a bwytewch gyda salad.

> Preheat the oven to 200C / 400F / Gas 6

You can leave this stage out: but it's good if you can start this dish by marinating the chicken in the wine and the herbs and 1 crushed clove of garlic for at least an hour before you start. If you prepare the chicken marinade the night before, please don't forget to place the chicken in a sealed container in the fridge overnight.

Remove the chicken from the marinade, reserving the marinade until later, and pat the meat dry with kitchen paper. Now dust the chicken pieces with flour. This is easily done by placing the chicken and the flour into a large plastic bag and shaking them together.

Add a good few spoonfuls of olive oil to a large pan, then fry the chicken pieces until nicely tanned. Put to one side.

Place the pan back on the heat and add the remaining garlic. Gently fry the garlic, then add olives, tomatoes and the browned chicken pieces.

Add the wine marinade and mix well. Bring to the boil and cover with a lid. Bake in the oven for 1½ hours. If your pans have plastic handles don't forget to transfer to an ovenproof dish before baking.

When cooked, skim off any excess oil. Then stir, taste and add a little salt and pepper if necessary.

Remove the bay leaves and rosemary sprigs and serve with a salad.

SYNIAD SYDYN
QUICK IDEA

Tatws lond eu crwyn

Mae taten bob dda yn berffeithrwydd. Dyma ffordd gyflym o wneud perffeithrwydd yn fwy perffaith fyth, os yw hynny'n bosib.

> 1 daten bob i bob person
> 1 llwy de o fenyn i bob taten
> Halen a phupur du wedi'i falu
> Cawsiau sydd dros ben, wedi'u gratio
> Ham neu diwna (ond ddim ar gyfer fersiwn llysieuol), India corn, tomatos, winwns neu unrhyw lenwadau eraill ry'ch chi'n eu dewis

Cynheswch y ffwrn i 200°C / 400°F / Nwy 6

Golchwch y tatws, eu pricio â fforc a'u gosod ar hambwrdd pobi. Coginiwch nhw yn y ffwrn am tua awr nes byddan nhw'n feddal.

Tynnwch y tatws o'r ffwrn, torrwch bob taten yn ei hanner a tynnu'r darn meddal allan a'u roi mewn powlen.

Stwnsiwch y tatws â fforc, ac ychwanegwch y menyn a phinsiaid o halen a phupur.

Rhowch yr ham wedi'i dorri'n ddarnau neu'r tiwna yn y crwyn tatws, a'i orchuddio â'r cymysgedd tatws stwnsh. Ychwanegwch fwy o dopin, fel shibwns wedi'u torri, pupur, India corn neu bys, a thaenwch gaws wedi'i gratio ar ben y cyfan. Defnyddiwch gawsiau cryf er mwyn cael blas da.

Rhowch 'nôl yn y ffwrn am ychydig hyd nes bydd y caws yn euraid.

Bwytewch gydag ychydig o salad neu golslo.

Loaded potato skins

A good baked potato is perfection. Here's a quick way to make perfection even more perfect, if that's at all possible.

> 1 baking potato per person
> 1 tsp butter per potato
> Salt and ground black pepper
> Leftover grated cheeses
> Ham or tuna (but not for the vegetarian option), sweetcorn, tomatoes, onion or any other favourite fillings

Preheat the oven to 200°C / 400°F / Gas 6

Wash the potatoes, prick with a fork and place on a baking. Cook in the oven for about an hour until soft.

Remove from the oven and cut each potato in half. Carefully scoop out the soft potato and place in a bowl.

Mash the potato with a fork, add the butter and a pinch of salt and pepper.

Put the chopped ham or tuna into the potato skins, and cover with some mashed potato mixture. Add more toppings, such as chopped spring onions, peppers, sweetcorn or peas, and sprinkle with grated cheese; use a strong flavoured cheese for a great taste.

Place back in the oven until the cheese is golden.

Serve with a little salad or coleslaw.

Y PATSHYN PWMPEN

Cnydau hwyliog i'w tyfu yw pwmpenni a sgwashys, ond mae angen cryn dipyn o le arnyn nhw. Gall courgettes, ar y llaw arall, dyfu mewn plot llai o faint neu mewn pot mawr hyd yn oed. Wrth i bwmpenni dyfu, maen nhw'n dueddol o ymledu o gwmpas yr ardd am tua 5 metr. Felly, rhaid i chi ystyried go iawn lle yn union fyddwch chi am eu plannu.

Mae sgwashys haf yn hwyl i'w tyfu hefyd, mae'r rhain yn llawer llai a dylid eu cynaeafu a'u defnyddio fel courgette. Mae pwmpenni a sgwashys gaeaf yn aeddfedu'n hwyrach yn y tymor, ac mae angen amser arnyn nhw i ddod i'w llawn dwf ac i haul yr hydref wneud eu crwyn yn wydn.

Nid oren yw lliw un o fy hoff bwmpenni i, sef y Crown Prince; mae'n lliw llwyd ac yn fawr, ond ychydig yn fflat, neu o leia'n llai crwn na siâp pwmpen glasurol. Ffefrynnau eraill gen i yw Turk's Turban, ffrwyth streipiog tebyg i siâp twrban sydd bron yn rhy bert i'w fwyta, a'r Jack Be Little bychan, lliwgar; y bwmpen berffaith i'r plantos. Mae pwmpenni Jack Be Little yn bitw bach ac yn ffitio'n gyfforddus yng nghledr eich llaw. Os cadwch chi nhw allan o'r haul fe baran nhw am fisoedd – mae'r pwmpenni hyn yn addurno tu allan y tŷ a bwrdd ein cegin ni hyd at y Nadolig. Ac ar ben hynny, mae eu blas yn hyfryd os ydych chi'n barod i'w haberthu a'u bwyta.

Dyna ddigon am fy hoff ffrwyth, ie, *ffrwyth* … nid llysieuyn!

 Tip: er mwyn personoleiddio'ch pwmpen, torrwch eich enw, neu enw'ch plentyn, pan fydd y bwmpen yn fach ac wrth iddi dyfu, bydd yr enw'n tyfu hefyd.

THE PUMPKIN PATCH

Pumpkins and squashes are fun crops to grow, but they do need a fair amount of space. Courgettes, on the other hand, can be managed in a smaller plot or even a large pot. As pumpkin plants grow, they tend to meander around the garden for up to 5 metres, their amazingly large leaves cast shadows and shade over other plants so you really do need to give some thought to where exactly they should be planted.

Summer squashes are also fun to grow, are much smaller and should be picked and used just like a courgette. The winter pumpkins and squashes mature later in the season and need time to ripen and the autumn sun to mature and toughen the skins.

One of my favourite pumpkins, the Crown Prince, isn't orange at all; it's a large steel-grey coloured variety, slightly flat or at least less rounded than the classic-shaped pumpkin. Other favourites of mine are the Turk's Turban, a stripy turban shaped fruit that is almost too pretty to eat, and the brightly coloured Jack Be Little, the perfect toddler's pumpkin. Jack Be Little pumpkins are tiny and fit in the palm of your hand. When kept out of direct sunlight they will last for months. We have them decorating the kitchen deck and house right up till Christmas. They also have the added bonus of having a great flavour, if you can bring yourself to eat them.

Enough about my favourite fruit; yes, *fruit*, not vegetable!

 Tip: in order to personalise your pumpkin, cut your name, or your child's name, on the pumpkin when it's small and as it grows, the name will grow too.

PETHAU I'W GWNEUD YN YSTOD HANNER TYMOR YR HYDREF

- Gwnewch y mwyaf o'r pwmpenni a'r sgwashys pert sydd yn y siopau drwy eu defnyddio i addurno'r tŷ gyda nhw. Rhowch rai wrth ddrws y tŷ i ddod â lliwiau'r hydref i garreg y drws – does dim rhaid eu cerfio nhw.

- Defnyddiwch y sgwashys bach i wneud pethau i ddala canhwyllau bach ar gyfer bwrdd y gegin. Torrwch eu pennau a gwneud twll digon mawr i ddal cannwyll.

- Trefnwch arddangosfa o ddail hydrefol lliwgar wedi'u sychu, egroes a mes – lluniwch fwrdd natur teuluol.

THINGS TO DO DURING AUTUMN HALF TERM

- Make the most of the pumpkins and pretty squashes in the shops by decorating your home with them. Put some by the front door to add autumn colour – they don't have to be carved.

- Use the small squashes to make tea light holders for the kitchen table. Cut the top off and make a hole just large enough for a candle.

- Arrange a display out of colourful dried autumn leaves, rose-hips, and acorns – make a family autumn nature table.

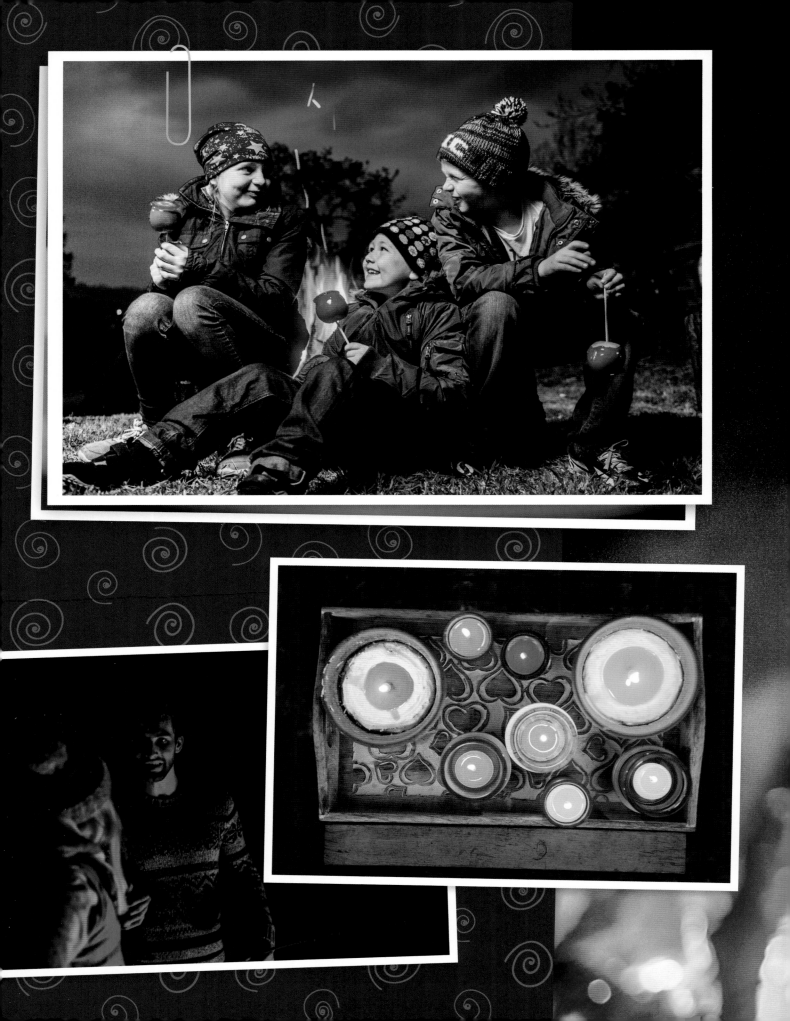

NOSON GUTO FFOWC

★ Rwy'n dwlu ar noson Guto Ffowc. Os ydw i'n hollol onest, hoffi coelcerth ar nosweithiau sych, llonydd ydw i. Mae rhywbeth hudolus and gamu allan i'r nos dywyll er mwyn cynnau coelcerth. Bydd troi'r clociau 'nôl wedi'n taflu i mewn i'r gaeaf. Y mae un awr yn gwneud llawer o wahaniaeth. Gall y plant fwynhau'r gwreichion a'r tân gwyllt, ac fe fyddan nhw'n cynhyrfu o fod yn yr awyr agored mewn tywyllwch, ac fe allan nhw fod yn ddiogel yn eu gwelyau erbyn wyth o'r gloch.

Mae'n hawdd anghofio weithiau am Guto Ffowc ei hun yng nghanol holl firi'r tân gwyllt, y coelcerthi a'r dod ynghyd i fwynhau cwmni'n gilydd ar noson serog, oer. Roedd yr hyn oedd ar ei feddwl e a'i gyfeillion, yn ddwfn yng nghrombil y Senedd, ymhell o fod yn debyg i'r rhialtwch llawen sy'n digwydd yn awr – dim llai na chwyldro!

Chafodd e mo'i ffordd, wrth gwrs, a dyma ni, dros bedwar can mlynedd yn ddiweddarach, yn cofio am yr ymgais aflwyddiannus honno i chwalu'r llywodraeth yn chwilfriw. Ry'n ni'n defnyddio'r digwyddiad dramatig hwn fel rheswm dros gymdeithasu, a pham lai? Ar nosweithiau tywyll, does dim yn well na bwyta'n dda a chael blas ar y cwmni ... gyda 'rhen Guto, neu hebddo!

BONFIRE NIGHT

★ I love bonfire night. Well, if I'm perfectly honest, I love a dry, still bonfire night. There's something quite magical about venturing out into the night's crisp air to light the bonfire. The turning back of the clock at the end of October and the end of British Summer Time really does catapult us into winter. One hour makes all the difference! Suddenly, late afternoon and early evening feels hours later than it it actually is, but this is great for bonfire night! Children can enjoy the sparklers and the fireworks, they can feel the excitement of being out in the dark, and still be tucked up in bed by 8pm.

It's easy to forget about Guy Fawkes himself, in the midst of all the hoop-la of fireworks and bonfires and the coming together to enjoy each other's company on cold, starry nights. What was on his mind and the minds of his friends, deep in the bowels of Parliament, is a far cry from the jollities and fun that happens today – nothing short of revolution!

He didn't get his way, of course, and here we are, over four hundred years later, remembering his unsuccessful attempt at shattering the government into a million pieces. We use this dramatic event as a reason to socialise, and why not? On these dark nights, there's nothing better than eating well and savouring the company ... with or without old Guy!

SELSIG ROCED Y GOELCERTH

*Does dim i guro selsigen dda!
Am hwyl, gwnewch 'selsig roced' i'r
plant eu mwynhau wrth y goelcerth.
Wshhh! Bang! Pop!*

Pecyn o'ch hoff selsig
1 llwy fwrdd o fêl rhedegog neu
1 llwy fwrdd o saws dipio blas tsili
1 llwy fwrdd o hadau sesame
1 pupur coch wedi'i dorri ar siâp trionglau

Coginiwch y selsig yn eich ffordd arferol – eu ffrio, eu grilio neu eu pobi yn y ffwrn.

Gosodwch y selsig mewn powlen ddwfn a gadael iddyn nhw oeri ryw gymaint. Yna, diferwch lond llwy fwrdd o fêl rhedegog neu saws dipio tsili dros y cyfan a'u cymysgu'n dda; ceisiwch peidio a thorri'r selsig. Taflwch yr hadau sesame drostynt a chymysgwch eto.

Torrwch siâp triongl o bupur coch a'i roi ar ffon cebab. Bwydwch y selsigen oddi tano ar ei hyd ar y ffon i wneud roced sesame ludiog.

BONFIRE ROCKET SAUSAGES

*There's nothing like a good sausage!
For a bit of fun, make some 'rocket
sausages' for the children to enjoy by
the bonfire. Whizz! Bang! Pop!*

A packet of your favourite sausages
1 tbsp of runny honey or
1 tbsp of chilli dipping sauce
1 tbsp of sesame seeds
1 red pepper, cut in triangular shapes

Cook the sausages in your usual way – fry, grill or bake in the oven.

Place the sausages in a deep bowl and allow to cool slightly. Then drizzle a tablespoon of runny honey or chilli dipping sauce over the top and mix well. Do this gently and try not to break the sausages. Sprinkle over the sesame seeds, then mix again.

Cut a triangle of red pepper and thread it onto a kebab stick, followed by the sausage lengthways to make a sesame rocket on a stick.

STIW SGWASH CNAU MENYN Â CHNAU COCO

Rwy'n dwlu ar y darnau sylweddol o lysiau sydd yn y rysáit hwn, mae'n gwneud i chi deimlo'n gynnes hyd at fêr eich esgyrn ar noson aeafol.

500g sialóts
1.5kg sgwash a'r hadau wedi'u tynnu ac wedi'i dorri'n ddarnau bras
2 lwy fwrdd o olew llysiau
3 pupur coch wedi tynnu'r hadau ac wedi'u torri'n fras
3 ewin garlleg, wedi'u malu
2 lwy fwrdd o sesnin Cajun
150ml stoc llysiau
Tun 400ml o laeth cnau coco
Tun 400g o domatos wedi'u malu
Olew i ffrio

Cynheswch yr olew mewn sosban fawr, ychwanegwch y pupurau a'r sialóts a ffrio'n ysgafn am 10 munud, gan eu troi'n gyson hyd nes eu bod wedi meddalu a brownio.

Ychwanegwch y sgwash, y garlleg a'r sesnin Cajun ynghyd â'r llaeth cnau coco, y tun o domatos a'r stoc.

Codwch y cyfan i'r berw ac yna trowch y gwres i lawr. Rhowch glawr ar y sosban a choginio'r cyfan ar wres isel am 45 munud, gan droi yn achlysurol hyd nes byddd y llysiau wedi meddalu.

Gadewch i'r cymysgedd oeri am 10 munud cyn ei weini.

BUTTERNUT SQUASH WITH COCONUT STEW

I love the chunkiness of this recipe. It really makes you feel warmed though on a wintry night.

500g shallots
1.5kg squash, deseeded and roughly chopped
2 tbsp vegetable oil
3 red peppers deseeded and roughly chopped
3 cloves of garlic, chopped
2 tbsp of Cajun seasoning
150ml veg stock
400ml can of coconut milk
400g can of chopped tomatoes
Oil for frying

Heat the vegetable oil in a large saucepan, add the peppers and shallots and fry gently for 10 minutes, stirring frequently until softened and browned.

Add the squash, garlic and Cajun seasoning with the coconut milk, tinned chopped tomatoes and the stock.

Bring to the boil, and then reduce the heat. Cover and cook gently for 45 minutes, stirring occasionally until the vegetables are tender.

Leave to cool for 10 minutes before serving.

LL

PWDIN SWYDD EFROG

Weithiau mae gwybod sut i wneud y pethau symlaf yn ymddangos yn fwy o dasg nag y mae rhywun yn ei feddwl. Felly dydw i ddim yn ymddiheuro am gynnwys y rysáit syml hwn ar gyfer y pwdin Swydd Efrog traddodiadol.

200ml blawd plaen
4 wy
200ml llaeth
Ychydig o olew blodau'r haul i goginio.

Cynheswch y ffwrn i 230°C / 450°F / Nwy 8

Arllwyswch ychydig ddiferion o olew llysiau yn weddol gyfartal i dun pwdin Swydd Efrog neu dun cacennau bach 12 twll a'i roi yn y ffwrn i gynhesu drwyddo.

I wneud y cytew, rhowch y llaeth mewn powlen fawr. Curwch y pedwar wy hyd nes eu bod yn llyfn.

Ychwanegwch y blawd yn raddol a daliwch i guro'r cymysgedd hyd nes ei fod yn ddi-lwmp. Defnyddiwch halen a phupur os dymunwch.

Arllwyswch y cytew i jwg. Yna, yn ofalus, tynnwch y tun poeth o'r ffwrn.

Arllwyswch y cytew i'r tun. Rhowch y tun yn ôl yn y ffwrn a'i adael yn llonydd am 20–25 munud hyd nes bod y pwdinau wedi chwyddo ac wedi brownio.

Bwytewch yn boeth neu gallwch adael iddyn nhw oeri a'u rhewi am gyfnod o hyd at fis.

V

YORKSHIRE PUDDING

It's with the basics that we get unstuck sometimes, so I make no apology for including a failsafe recipe for good old Yorkshire pud.

200ml plain flour
4 eggs
200ml milk
Some sunflower oil, for cooking

Heat the oven to 230°C / 450°F / Gas 8

Drizzle a little sunflower oil evenly into a Yorkshire pudding tin or a 12-hole non-stick muffin tin and place in the oven to heat through.

To make the batter, place the milk in a large bowl, and beat in four eggs until smooth.

Gradually add the flour and carry on beating until the mix is completely lump-free. Season with salt and pepper.

Pour the batter into a jug, then carefully remove the hot tin from the oven.

Pour the batter into the tin. Place the tin back in the oven and leave undisturbed for 20–25 minutes until the puddings have puffed up and browned.

Serve piping hot or you can cool them and freeze for up to 1 month.

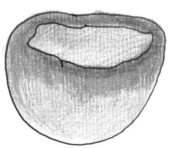

TEISEN AFAL TAFFI

Teisen ludiog, flasus: y math o deisen sy'n medru gwneud popeth yn eich byd yn iawn. Mae'n felys ac yn gwneud i chi deimlo'n dda.

1–2 afal, wedi'u sleisio
200g siwgwr
300g blawd codi
225g menyn
240ml llaeth
200g dêts
4 wy
1 llwy fwrdd o sbeis cymysg
¼ llwy de o bowdwr codi
¼ llwy de o fanila
Llond llaw o losin taffi

Cynheswch y ffwrn i 180°C / 350°F / Nwy 4

Rhowch y dêts a'r llaeth mewn sosban fach a'u berwi. Yna, tynnwch nhw oddi ar y gwres a'u gadael ar un ochr am 10 munud.

Gwnewch biwrê llyfn o gymysgedd y dêts gan ddefnyddio prosesydd neu gymysgydd tydan. Yna, rhowch y cymysgedd mewn powlen gymysgu fawr.

Ychwanegwch y menyn, y blawd, y siwgwr, y powdwr codi, yr wyau, y sbeis cymysg a'r fanila. Cymysgwch y cyfan ynghyd a'i arllwys mewn i dun pobi.

Sleisiwch yr afalau a'u gosod yn daclus ar ben y deisen. Pobwch yn y ffwrn am tua 40 munud hyd nes ei bod hi wedi'i choginio ac yn euraid.

I wneud y saws

Toddwch lond llaw o losin taffi mewn diferyn o laeth dros wres isel gan droi'r cymysgedd yn gyson. Arllwyswch y saws dros y deisen i wneud y topin taffi.

TOFFEE APPLE CAKE

A sticky, tasty cake: the kind of cake that can make everything alright in your world. It's sweet and makes you feel good.

1–2 apples, sliced
200g sugar
300g self-raising flour
225g butter
240ml milk
200g dates
4 eggs
1 tbsp mixed spice
¼ tsp baking powder
¼ tsp vanilla
A handful of toffee sweets

Preheat the oven to 180°C / 350°F / Gas 4

Put the dates and milk into a small pan and bring to the boil. Take off the heat and leave to one side for 10 minutes.

Whizz the date mixture into a smooth purée in a food processor or blender, then scrape into a large mixing bowl.

Add the butter, flour, sugar, baking powder, eggs, mixed spice and vanilla. Mix everything together and pour into a baking tray.

Slice the apples, and place them neatly on top of the cake. Bake in the oven for about 40 minutes until cooked and golden.

To make the sauce

Melt a handful of toffees in a drop of milk over a low heat, stirring continuously. Pour the sauce over the cooked cake to make a sticky toffee topping.

Afalau taffi

Mae afalau taffi yn un o fy hoff ryseitiau hydrefol ac un sy'n defnyddio cryn dipyn o afalau cartref. Maen nhw'n ddigon hawdd i'w paratoi ond mae'r rysáit yn un sy'n gofyn am ferwi siwgwr. Felly, byddwch yn ofalus gyda phlant awyddus, a gwnewch yn siŵr bod y taffi'n oeri'n llwyr cyn ei flasu.

Mae'r rhain yn flasus ar noson Guto Ffowc, neu unrhyw noson o'r flwyddyn o ran hynny. Lapiwch yn gynnes o flaen y goecerth neu mwynhewch danllwyth wrth wersylla ar noswaith iach yn yr haf.

> 4–6 afal bwyta
> 225g siwgwr brown neu siwgwr gwyn
> 1 llwy de o finegr brown
> 110ml dŵr
> Lliw bwyd coch (dewisol)

Rhowch y siwgwr mewn sosban â haenen wrthlud iddi ac ychwanegwch 100ml o ddŵr.

Cynheswch y siwgwr a'r dŵr ar wres cymedrol hyd nes bydd wedi toddi. Os hoffech chi afalau taffi coch, ychwanegwch liw bywd coch.

Pan fydd y siwgwr wedi toddi ychwanegwch y finegr a'i droi.

Gadewch i'r cymysgedd ferwi am 7–8 munud hyd nes ei fod yn debyg i syrop. Pan feddyliwch chi ei fod yn barod, rhowch ychydig bach mewn powlennaid o ddŵr oer. Bydd hyn yn oeri'r taffi'n gyflym ac yn eich galluogi i weld pa mor galed fydd y taffi wedi iddo oeri ar eich afal. Os yw'n caledu mae eich taffi'n barod. Tynnwch y sosban oddi ar y gwres fel nad yw'n llosgi.

I wneud yr afalau taffi, gwthiwch ffon bren i ganol pob afal a'u troi nhw, un ar y tro, yn y taffi hyd nes eu bod wedi'u gorchuddio'n gyfartal. Os oes genych afalau â chwyr arnyn nhw, bydd angen i chi rhwbio'r cwyr oddi arnyn nhw gan ddefnyddio papur cegin.

Os hoffech ychwanegu cnau neu sbrincls, gwnewch hynny'n syth.

Rhowch nhw i oeri ar hambwrdd pobi wedi'i leinio neu ar haenen silicon.

 Tip: i'w rhoi'n anrhegion, lapiwch nhw mewn seloffen a chlymu ruban pert o'u hamgylch.

Tip: os nad ydych chi am wneud taffi, toddwch siocled a gwnewch afalau siocled.

Toffee apples

This toffee apple recipe is one of my favourite autumn recipes and one that uses up a load of home-grown apples. They are quite easy to prepare, but the recipe involves boiling sugar. So, please be careful with eager children and always allow the toffee to cool completely before tasting.

These are delicious on bonfire night, or any other night of the year for that matter. Wrap up warm in front of the fire or even enjoy a campfire on a cool summer evening.

> 4–6 eating apples
> 225g brown or white sugar
> 1 tsp of malt vinegar
> 110ml water
> Red food colouring (optional)

Place the sugar in a non-stick saucepan and add 100ml of water.

Pace the saucepan over a medium heat until the sugar dissolves. If you'd like red toffee apples, add red food colouring.

When the sugar has dissolved, add the vinegar and stir.

Let the mixture boil for 7–8 minutes until it becomes very syrupy. When you think it's ready, drop a small amount into a bowl of cold water. This cools the toffee quickly and allows you to see how hard the toffee will become when it cools on your apple. If it turns solid, your toffee is ready. Remove from the heat immediately to prevent it from burning.

To make the toffee apples, push a lolly stick into each apple and, one at a time, turn them in the toffee until they are evenly coated. If you have waxed apples, you will need to rub the wax off using some kitchen roll.

If you wish to add nuts or sprinkles, add them straight away.

Place them to cool on a lined baking tray or on a silicone sheet.

 Tip: to give as a gift, wrap them in cellophane and tie a pretty ribbon around them.

Tip: if you don't want the hassle of making toffee, then melt some chocolate and make some chocolate-coated apples.

SYNIAD SYDYN
QUICK IDEA

Talpiau tatws paprica

Dydw i ddim yn berwi tatws yn aml. Na, wir nawr. Rwy'n hoffi eu torri'n ddarnau talpiog neu'n ddisgiau neu eu torri yn eu hanner hyd yn oed. Rhowch nhw ar hambwrdd pobi gyda diferyn o olew llysiau, dim ond diferyn – dydw i ddim yn eu boddi nhw mewn olew.

Taenwch lond llwy de neu binsiaid go lew o baprica neu sesnin Cajun dros y tatws, defnyddiwch eich bysedd i wneud yn siŵr eu bod nhw wedi'u gorchuddio'n dda a phobwch hyd nes eu bod yn frown euraid.

Os bydda i'n eu defnyddio gyda phryd rhost traddodiadol, dim ond halen a phupur fydda i'n eu hychwanegu i gael blas da.

Paprika potato wedges

I very rarely boil potatoes. No, really. I like to chop them into wedge shapes or into discs or even in half. Place them on a baking tray with a drizzle of vegetable oil, just a drop – I don't drown them in oil.

Sprinkle over a teaspoon or a good pinch of either Cajun seasoning or paprika. Use your fingers to make sure they're well covered and bake them until they are golden brown.

If I use them with a traditional roast, I just add salt and pepper, without the spice, for a good taste.

SYNIAD SYDYN
QUICK IDEA

Sgon ffon

Beth feddyliwch chi sydd ei angen arnoch i wneud sgon ffon? Wel, cymerwch un ffon a chymysgedd sgon, a dyna chi. Blasusfwyd al fresco diwedd dydd, gwell na malws melys.

> 25g blawd codi
> Pinsiaid o halen
> 55g menyn
> 25g siwgwr mân
> 150ml llaeth

Gwnewch gymysgedd sgon sylfaenol drwy gymysgu'r blawd a'r halen â'i gilydd a rhwbio'r menyn i mewn. Rhowch y cymysgedd ar arwyneb â blawd arno a thylinwch yn ysgafn.

Rholiwch ychydig bach o'r cymysgedd â'ch bys i wneud siâp selsigen. Lapiwch y cymysgedd yn ofalus o gwmpas ffon lân neu sgiwer, a'u coginio nhw yng ngwres y goelcerth neu'r barbeciw. Peidiwch â'u rhoi nhw yn y fflamau neu fe losgan nhw. Trowch nhw'n araf a'u gwylio nhw'n coginio.

Dipiwch nhw mewn jam mefus cyn eu bwyta.

Sticky scones

Sticky scones are not sticky! Or at least they shouldn't be if you've cooked them well – they are scones on a stick. A lovely al fresco end-of-evening treat, better than marshmallows.

> 25g self-raising flour
> A pinch of salt
> 55g butter
> 25g caster sugar
> 150ml milk

Make a basic scone mixture by mixing together the flour and salt and rubbing in the butter. Stir in the sugar and then the milk to get a soft dough. Turn onto a floured work surface and knead very lightly.

Roll a small amount of the mixture with your fingers to make a sausage shape. Wrap it carefully around a clean stick or skewer and cook in the heat of the bonfire or barbecue. Don't put then in the flames or they'll burn – just turn them slowly and watch then cook.

Dip them in some strawberry jam before eating.

Clo ar y flwyddyn

End of the year

6

Allwch chi gredu'r peth? Mae'r flwyddyn bron â darfod.
Fe hedfanodd y misoedd ac eisoes ry'n ni'n syllu i lygad
y flwyddyn newydd.

Pa fath o flwyddyn fuodd hi i chi? Sut bynnag wnaeth y
flwyddyn ein trin ni, mae'r cyfan y tu ôl i ni bellach. Felly, gadewch
i ni edrych ymlaen a dathlu bod gyda'n gilydd, atgoffa'n gilydd
pa mor lwcus ydyn ni go iawn, o ran ffrindiau a theulu a phob
dim. Mae'n adeg ardderchog i ddod ynghyd a mwynhau cwmni'n
gilydd. Rhowch broc i'r tân, cadwch yn gynnes a chwerthin
ar y cyfan â boliau llawn a llawen. Mae'r byd yn arafu rywsut;
ymlaciwch a mwynhewch yr eiliadau hyn.

Can you believe it? The year is nearly at its end.
The months have flown by and already we're staring
into the jaws of a new year.

What kind of year has it been for you? However the year's
treated us, it's all behind us now. So, let's look forward and celebrate
being together, reminding ourselves how lucky we are, what with
friends and family and all. It's a great time to come together, to enjoy
each other's company just because we can. Stoke the fire, keep
warm and laugh at it all with a full and happy stomach. The world
seems to slow down – relax and savour these moments.

NADOLIG
★ ☆ ☆ ★ ★
CHRISTMAS

⭐ Fy neges i'r byd a'r betws yr adeg hon o'r flwyddyn yw: cadwch bethau'n syml. Peidiwch ag anghofio y dylai'r ryseitiau Nadolig gorau fod yn rhwydd. Pam ddylech chi fod dan bwysau yn ceisio datrys ryseitiau gwallgo a chymhleth – a'r unig beth sy'n bwysig i'r plant a gweddill y teulu yw cael eich cwmni chi er mwyn chwarae gêm neu i gymryd amser i wylio ffilm Nadolig dda?

Rwy'n dwlu ar addurno'r gegin gyda goleuadau bychain a gwylio'u golau'n adlewyrchu ar y ffenestri wrth i'r nosweithiau dywyllu. Er nad ydw i'n gwrando ar gerddoriaeth yn y gegin fel arfer, wrth i'r Nadolig agosáu, rwy'n cael hyd i'r CDs Nadolig cyfarwydd ac yn gwrando ar yr hen ffefrynnau fel Bing Crosby a Nat King Cole, ac mae clywed llais melfedaidd Michael Bublé yn fy nghegin yn arwydd pendant bod y Nadolig ar ei ffordd.

Rwy'n breuddwydio am eira a boreuau barugog y cerdyn Nadolig traddodiadol. Bydd y byd tu allan o dan gysgod blanced y tywyllwch wrth i'r dyddiau ddirwyn i ben, ond bydd hi'n gynnes a diddos tu fewn, y tân ynghyn a'r ffwrn ymlaen.

⭐ My message to all and sundry at this time of year is: keep it simple. Don't forget that the best Christmas recipes should be easy. Why get stressed by trying to untangle crazy and complicated recipes when all the children and the rest of the family want is your company to play a game or to watch a good Christmas film?

I love to decorate the kitchen with fairy lights and watch their reflection bounce off the windows as night closes in. Although I don't usually listen to music in kitchen, as Christmas approaches, I dust off the familiar Christmas CDs and listen to old favourites like Bing Crosby and Nat King Cole, the smooth velvety voice of Michael Bublé in my kitchen means that Christmas is just around the corner.

I dream of snow and frosty mornings, the traditional Christmas card scene. The outside will be hidden under the blanket of darkness which descends each late afternoon, but inside will be warm and cosy, the fire lit and the oven on.

TERRINE NADOLIG

Dyma i chi holl flasau'r Nadolig mewn un greadigaeth hyfryd.

12 tafell o pancetta neu gig moch brith
2 neu 3 brest cyw iâr, wedi'u sleisio
1 ffiled porc (canol lwyn) wedi'i sleisio
½ jar o saws llugaeron cartref (gweler tud. 218)
½ pecyn o ysbigoglys
2 lond cwpan o'ch hoff stwffin Nadolig
Llond llaw o fricyll sych

Cynheswch y ffwrn i 180°C / 350°F / Nwy 4

Leiniwch dun terrine neu dun torth 9cm wrth 17cm (1 litr) â pancetta neu dafelli o gig moch brith. Gadewch ddigon yn hongian dros yr ochrau er mwyn gallu cau'r cyfan fel parsel.

Gosodwch haenen o'r ffiled borc ar hyd gwaelod y tun, ar ben y cig moch.

Ychwanegwch haenen o ysbigoglys gwyrdd a gwasgu'r cyfan lawr yn gadarn.

Gorchuddiwch yr ysbigoglys â'ch hoff stwffin, a'i wasgu i lawr yn gadarn.

Gorchuddiwch y stwffin â thafelli cyw iâr, gan sicrhau bod gennych haenen wastad o gig. Yn olaf, ychwanegwch y saws llugaeron dros ben y cyfan a gorffen â haenen arall o ysbigoglys.

Plygwch y stribedi cig moch dros y tun llawn. Ychwanegwch haenen arall o gig moch neu pancetta os bydd angen. Yna, gorchuddiwch y terrine â ffoil a'i osod ar dun rhostio. Pwyswch y terrine i lawr â phwysau trwm, neu fricsen, a phobwch am tua 45 munud.

Tynnwch y ffoil a phobwch am 10 munud arall neu hyd nes bydd y cig moch neu'r pancetta'n grimp ar yr wyneb.

Tynnwch y terrine o'r tun rhostio a'i oeri. Gellir ei weini'n boeth neu'n oer.

Ar ôl iddo goginio, trowch y terrine allan a'i addurno â rhesaid o fricyll i lawr y canol. Yna, gorchuddiwch â mwy o saws llugaeron. Rwy'n dwlu ar y pryd yma'n boeth, ond wrth iddo oeri mae'n caledu ac mae'n sleisio'n hyfryd i fynd â salad a chigoedd oer eraill.

CHRISTMAS TERRINE

Here are all the tastes of Christmas in one lovely creation.

12 slices of pancetta or streaky bacon
2 or 3 chicken breasts, sliced
1 pork fillet (tenderloin), sliced
½ jar of homemade cranberry sauce (see p 218)
½ packet of spinach
2 cupfuls of your favourite Christmas stuffing
A handful of dried apricots

Preheat the oven to 180°C / 350°F / Gas 4

Line a 9cm by 17cm (1 litre) terrine or loaf pan with pancetta or streaky bacon slices, leaving enough overhanging the sides to enclose the top like a parcel.

Place a layer of the pork tenderloin along the bottom of the loaf tin, on top of the bacon.

Add a layer of bright green spinach, and press down firmly.

Cover the spinach with your favourite stuffing, press down firmly.

Cover the stuffing with the chicken slices, ensuring that you have an even layer of meat and finally, add the cranberry sauce on top and finish with another layer of spinach.

Now, fold the bacon strips over the full tin. Add another slice of bacon or pancetta if needed. Cover terrine with foil, and place on a roasting tin. Weigh the terrine down with a heavy weight, or a brick, and bake for about 45 minutes.

Remove the foil, and bake for a further 10 minutes or until the bacon or pancetta is crisp on top.

Remove terrine from roasting pan and cool. Can be served hot or cold.

Once cooked, turn it out and decorate the top with a line of apricots down the centre. Top with more home-made chunky cranberry sauce. I love this hot, but as it cools it firms up and it can be sliced beautifully to accompany salads and other cold meats.

* **I originally made it with a combination of pork tenderloin, a favourite of mine, and chicken, but I've decided it's equally as tasty with a layer of good quality sausage meat.**

HAM SGLEIN MÊL

Rwy'n hoffi cael ham ar y bwrdd bwyd Nadolig, ac er mod i'n ffan o dwrci a gŵydd, rhaid cael darn o ham hefyd.

2kg o goesyn gamon heb asgwrn ynddo
Tua 20 clof

Y sglein mêl
200g siwgwr demerara
25ml sieri neu finegr gwin coch
100ml gwin Madeira
1 llwy de o baprica mwg
250g mêl

Rhowch y coesyn gamon mewn sosban fawr a'i orchuddio â dŵr oer.

Dewch ag ef i'r berw, yna trowch y gwres i lawr a'i fudferwi am tua 2½ awr, gan ychwanegu dŵr berw os oes angen. Tynnwch unrhyw amhureddau sy'n codi i wyneb y dŵr.

Arllwyswch yr hylif; rwy'n hoffi ei gadw ar gyfer gwneud cawl. Gadewch i'r ham oeri ychydig tra byddwch yn cynhesu'r ffwrn i 190ºC / 375ºF / Nwy 5.

Codwch yr ham i dun rhostio, a thorri'r croen i ffwrdd gan adael haenen denau o fraster.

Crafwch rychau dros y braster ar ffurf patrwm cris-groes, a gwthio'r clofs mewn i groen yr ham.

I wneud y sglein: rhowch y siwgwr, y sieri neu'r finegr a'r gwin Madeira mewn sosban a'u berwi.

Ychwanegwch y mêl, dewch â'r hylif i'r berw a'i dynnu oddi ar y gwres.

Arllwyswch hanner y sglein dros fraster yr ham, a'i rostio am 15 munud. Yna, arllwyswch y gweddill drosto a rhoi'r coesyn yn ôl yn y ffwrn am oddeutu 35 munud arall, gan arllwys ei hylifau dros y coesyn ham wrth iddo bobi.

Trowch y tun o gwmpas ychydig o weithiau yn ystod y broses goginio fel bod y braster yn troi'n lliw cyson drosto, a daliwch ati i godi ac arllwys yr hylifau.

Tynnwch o'r ffwrn a gadewch iddo orffwys am 15 munud cyn ei dorri'n haenau.

HONEY-GLAZED HAM

I always like some ham on the table at Christmas and even though I'm a fan of turkey and goose, the ham completes the table.

2kg boneless gammon joint
About 20 cloves

The honey glaze
200g demerara sugar
25ml sherry or red wine vinegar
100ml Madeira wine
1 tsp smoked paprika
250g honey

Put the gammon into a large pan and cover with cold water.

Bring to the boil, then turn down to simmer for around 2½ hours, topping up the water with boiling water if necessary. Scoop off any impurities that rise to the top.

Carefully pour the liquid away – I like to keep it for making soup. Let the ham cool a little while you heat the oven to 190ºC / 375ºF / Gas 5.

Lift the ham into a roasting tin, and cut away the skin, leaving behind a thin layer of fat.

Score the fat all over in a criss-cross pattern, and stud cloves all over the ham.

To make the glaze: put the sugar, sherry or vinegar and Madeira wine in a pan and bring to the boil.

Add the honey, bring to the boil and remove from the heat.

Pour half of the glaze over the fat of the ham, and roast for 15 minutes. Then pour over the rest and return to the oven for another 35 minutes, basting with the pan juices as it bakes.

Turn the pan around a few times during cooking so that the fat colours evenly, and keep basting.

Remove from the oven and allow to rest for 15 minutes before carving.

COLSLO NADOLIG

Mae colslo yn ychwanegiad iachus a lliwgar i'r bwrdd ar unrhyw adeg o'r flwyddyn. Bydd y cynnwys yn amrwyio yn ôl eich dewis chi, yn ôl y tymor ac yn ôl beth sydd gennych yn yr oergell.

Adeg y Nadolig, rwy'n defnyddio llysiau coch ac yn taflu llond llaw o lugaeron sych i'r cymysgedd i felysu'r cyfan ac ychwanegu lliw.

Ar gyfer colslo sylfaenol
2 foronen
½ bresychen goch neu wyn
½ winwnsyn, wedi'i blicio

Yr elfennau Nadoligaidd
1 bwlb ffenigl
1 betys heb ei choginio, wedi'i golchi
½ seleriac bach
3 neu 4 rhuddygl

Ar gyfer y dresin
Sudd ½ lemwn
1 llwy fwrdd o olew olewydd
1 llond llaw o berlysiau ffres, e.e. persli, ffenigl, dil neu goriander, wedi'u torri'n fân (dewisol)
300ml mayonnaise neu iogwrt, neu gymysgedd o'r ddau
2 lwy de o fwstard grawn cyflawn
Halen a phupur du wedi'i falu'n ffres

Gratiwch neu torrwch y moron ac unrhyw lysiau caled, fel y rhuddygl, y beyts neu'r seleriac. Gallwch ddefnyddio mandolin, neu defnyddiwch eich prosesydd bwyd i wneud y gwaith yn gynt.

Sleisiwch y bresych a'r winwnsyn coch yn fân a chymysgu'r llysiau'n dda â'i gilydd.

Cyfunwch gynhwysion y dresin mewn powlen, neu ysgydwch nhw â'i gilydd mewn jar neu botel fawr.

Arllwyswch y dresin dros y llysiau a'u cymysgu. Am fersiwn iachach, defnyddiwch iogwrt naturiol heb siwgwr, yn hytrach na mayonnaise.

CHRISTMAS COLESLAW

Coleslaw is a healthy, colourful addition to the table at any time of year. The ingredients will vary according to your taste, the season and what you have in the fridge.

At Christmas, I use red vegetables and throw in a handful of dried cranberries to sweeten the slaw and add a little glamour.

For a basic coleslaw
2 carrots
½ red or white cabbage
½ red onion, peeled

For the Christmassy twist
1 bulb fennel
1 raw, washed beetroot
½ small celeriac
3 or 4 radish

For the dressing
Juice of ½ lemon
1 tbsp of olive oil
1 handful fresh herbs, such as parsley, fennel, dill or coriander, finely chopped (optional)
300ml mayonnaise or yoghurt, or a mix of both
2 teaspoons wholegrain mustard
Salt and freshly ground black pepper

Grate or shred the carrots and any hard vegetables you choose, such as radish, beetroot or celeriac. You can use a mandolin, or use your food processor for a quicker job.

Thinly slice the cabbage and the red onion, and give all the vegetables a good mix together.

Combine all the dressing ingredients in a bowl or shake them all together in a large jar or bottle.

Pour the dressing over the vegetables and mix. For a healthier option, use natural unsweetened yoghurt instead of mayonnaise.

✴ Tip: ychwanegwch ffrwythau sych, llugaeron adeg y Nadolig. Mae bricyll yn gweithio'n dda hefyd, ac ambell gneuen Ffrengig wedi'i thorri i gael colslo mwy crensiog.

Tip: gallwch baratoi'r llysiau o flaen llaw a'u cadw yn yr oergell. Ychwanegwch y dresin ar y funud olaf ar gyfer colslo crensiog, ffres.

✴ Tip: add some dried fruit, cranberries at Christmas time. Apricots also work well, and even a few chopped walnuts for extra crunch.

Tip: you can prepare the vegetables in advance and keep them in the fridge. Add the dressing at the last minute for a fresh, crisp coleslaw.

TÝ SINSIR A BECHGYN A MERCHED SINSIR

Mae'r tŷ bara sinsir yn dod o fyd ffantasi, y tŷ bach twt yn y goedwig lle'r aeth Hansel a Gretel ar goll. Mae mor hawdd i chi greu eich ffantasi flasus eich hun a chael prynhawn wrth eich bodd yng nghwmni'r plant.

> 350g blawd plaen
> 1 llwy de o soda pobi
> 2 lwy de o sinsir, wedi'i falu
> 1 llwy de o sinamon, wedi'i falu
> 125g menyn
> 175g siwgwr muscovado golau neu siwgwr brown meddal
> 1 wy canolig
> 4 llwy fwrdd o syrop melyn
>
> Ar gyfer yr addurno: siwgwr eisin a gwynnwy, Smarties bach a sbrincls

Cynheswch y ffwrn i 180°C / 350°F / Nwy 4

Leiniwch dun pobi mawr â phapur pobi gwrthlud.

Rhidyllwch y blawd, y soda pobi, y sinsir a'r sinamon mewn i bowlen a'u cymysgu'n dda. Rhwbiwch y menyn i'r cymysgedd blawd hyd nes ei fod yn edrych fel briwsion bara, neu defnyddiwch brosesydd bwyd. Yna, ychwanegwch y siwgwr a a'i gymysgu.

Cymysgwch yr wy a'r syrop yn ysgafn â'i gilydd a'u hychwanegu at y cymysgedd i wneud toes.

Os oes gennych chi ddigon o amser, rhowch y toes yn yr oergell i oeri. Yna, rholiwch y toes ar arwyneb â blawd arno nes ei fod tua ½cm o drwch.

I wneud y tŷ sinsir

Defnyddiwch y templed sydd yng nghefn y gyfrol hon i greu'r waliau, y to a'r simdde (tud. 248). Dilynwch y cyfarwyddiadau yng ngweddill y rysáit. Ar ôl eu pobi, gludiwch y darnau ynghyd gan ddefnyddio eisin mewn bag eisio.

Defnyddiwch dorrwr toes i dorri siâp eich bechgyn a'ch merched sinsir a'u gosod ar hambwrdd pobi, gan adael bwlch rhwng pob bisgïen.

GINGERBREAD HOUSE AND BOYS AND GIRLS

The gingerbread house is the stuff of fantasy – the little house in the forest where Hansel and Gretel got lost. It's so easy to make your own tasty fantasy and to while away an afternoon with the children.

> 350g plain flour
> 1 tsp bicarbonate of soda
> 2 tsp ground ginger
> 1 tsp ground cinnamon
> 125g butter
> 175g unrefined light muscovado or soft brown sugar
> 1 medium egg
> 4 tbsp golden syrup
>
> For decoration: icing sugar and egg white, mini Smarties and sprinkles

Preheat the oven to 180°C / 350°F / Gas 4

Line a large baking tin with non-stick baking paper.

Sift the flour, bicarbonate of soda, ginger and cinnamon into a bowl and mix well. Rub the butter into the flour mixture until it looks like breadcrumbs, or use a food processor, then stir in the sugar.

Lightly mix the egg and syrup together and add to the mix to make a dough.

If you have time put the dough in the fridge to chill. Then roll out the dough on a floured surface to about ½cm thickness.

To make the gingerbread house

Use the template in the back of this book to make the walls, the roof and the chimney (p. 248). Follow the instructions in the rest of the recipe. After you've baked them, glue the components together using icing in a piping bag.

Use a pastry cutter to cut out the shape of your gingerbread boys and girls, and place on a baking tray, leaving a gap between each biscuit.

> Pobwch am tua 15 munud hyd nes eu bod yn euraid. Gadewch ar yr hambwrdd am 10 munud, yna trosglwyddwch nhw i resel wifrau i oeri. Addurnwch ag eisin, losin a sbrincls.

Mae toes sinsir yn does syml y medrwch ei dorri i unrhyw faint neu siâp i wneud bisgedi pert. Mae bisgedi botwm neu rai petryal ag eisin arnyn nhw i greu set o ddominos yn ffordd ardderchog o gyflwyno plant i hwyl coginio Nadolig. Gadewch i'ch dychmyg fynd yn rhydd. Peidiwch ag anghofio cadw'ch bisgedi mewn bocs wedi'i selio i'w cadw'n ffres, neu fe fyddan nhw'n mynd yn feddal ar ôl amser.

> *Tip: er mwyn arbed amser, gallech brynu cit tŷ sinsir o'r siop ac addurno'r tŷ eich hun i gael ychydig o hwyl yr ŵyl yn y gegin.*

> Bake for about 15 minutes until golden. Leave on the tray for 10 minutes, then transfer to a wire rack to finish cooling. Decorate with icing, sweets and sprinkles.

The gingerbread dough is a basic dough that can be cut to any shape and size to make pretty biscuits. Button-shaped biscuits or rectangles, iced, to form a set of dominoes, is a great way to introduce young children to the fun of Christmas cookery. Let your imagination run wild. Don't forget to store them in an airtight container to keep them crisp otherwise they'll become soft after a while.

> *Tip: to save time, buy a gingerbread house kit from the shops and decorate the house yourself for a bit of Christmas fun in the kitchen.*

213

BRIWGACS SEROG

Dyw hi byth yn rhy gynnar i ddechrau gwneud briwgacs (fel y'u gelwir nhw yn ardal Caerfyrddin), yn enwedig gan fod modd eu rhewi. Gwnewch gyflenwad er mwyn arbed amser yn ystod y dyddiau olaf cyn y Nadolig. Os cewch eich temtio i brynu rhai, dyma rybudd ... mae'r rhai cartref yn gymaint mwy blasus.

Ar gyfer y toes
250g blawd plaen
125g menyn
85g siwgwr eisin
1 wy cyfan ac 1 melynwy

Defnyddiwch friwfwyd o ansawdd da neu gwnewch beth eich hun.

I wneud y toes

Mewn powlen fawr, torrwch y menyn wedi'i oeri yn giwbiau bach ac ychwanegu'r blawd. Gan ddefnyddio blaenau eich bysedd, rhwbiwch y menyn i'r blawd hyd nes ei fod yn edrych fel briwsion bara.

Ychwanegwch yr wy at y cymysgedd, a dewch â'r cyfan at ei gilydd i ffurfio pelen does.

Ychwanegwch y melynwy neu ddiferyn o ddŵr oer os yw'r cymysgedd yn rhy sych a briwsionog.

Gorchuddiwch â haenen lynu a'i oeri am 20 munud. Bydd mwy nag 20 munud yn oeri'r menyn ormod a bydd yn anodd i'w rolio.

I wneud y briwgacs

Rholiwch y toes i drwch o 3mm. Gan ddefnyddio torrwyr toes crwn neu gwpan neu fwg wyneb i waered, torrwch gylchoedd toes allan a llenwi hambwrdd cacennau bach â'r toes.

Cyn i chi orffen â'r toes, torrwch siapiau sêr bach allan o'r toes sydd dros ben.

Llenwch bob pastai â llond llwy de o friwfwyd a gosodwch seren ar ben pob un. Brwsiwch y seren â llaeth a choginiwch y briwgacs am tua 20 munud ar 180°C / 350°F / Nwy 4 hyd nes eu bod yn euraid.

STARRY MINCE PIES

It's never too early to start making mince pies, especially as they can be frozen. Make a few batches to save yourself time and effort during the final days in the run up to Christmas. If you are tempted to buy some, be warned ... home-made is always nicer.

For the pastry
250g plain flour
125g butter
85g icing sugar
1 whole egg and 1 egg yolk

Use good quality mincemeat or make your own.

To make the pastry

Cut the chilled butter into small cubes and add to the flour in a large bowl. Using your fingertips, rub the butter into the flour until it resembles breadcrumbs.

Add an egg to the mixture and bring it all together to form a ball of dough.

Add an additional egg yolk or a drop of cold water if the mixture is too dry and crumbly.

Cover in cling film and chill for just 20 minutes. Any longer than 20 minutes will chill the butter too much and it will be very difficult to roll

To make the mince pies

Roll out the dough to 3mm thickness, and using round pastry cutters or an upside-down tumbler or mug, cut out pastry circles and use to fill a cupcake or muffin tray.

Before you finish with the pastry, cut out small star shapes in the leftover pieces.

Fill each pie with a teaspoonful of mincemeat and top with a star. Brush the star with milk and cook for 20 minutes at 180°C / 350°F / Gas 4 until golden.

Tip: os na fedrwch chi ddweud 'na' wrth y briwgacs ond yr hoffech chi leihau nifer y calorïau neu gadw trefn ar eich gwast tan y flwyddyn newydd, defnyddiwch does ffilo. Mae toes ffilo'n ardderchog os ydych chi'n ofalus o'ch pwysau y Nadolig hwn. Mae'n cynnwys llai na 2% o fraster, o'i gymharu â 50% o fraster mewn toes traddodiadol. Felly, mynnwch becyn o ffilo a phobwch.

Tip: gratiwch ychydig o afal i mewn i'r briwfwyd i wneud mwy ohono, neu ychwanegwch ddiferyn o frandi i ychwanegu at y blas.

Tip: if you can't resist a mince pie, but you still want to reduce calories or keep your waistline into the new year, use filo pastry. Filo pastry is great if you are watching your weight this Christmas – it contains less that 2% fat compared to a whopping 50% fat in traditional pastry. So, get yourself a pack of filo and get baking

Tip: grate a little apple into the mincemeat to bulk it up, or add a drop of brandy to up the flavour.

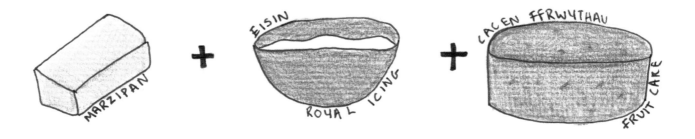

TEISEN NADOLIG

Fel arfer, rwy'n eitha hamddenol am ryseitiau, dydw i ddim yn poeni'n ormodol am fod yn rhy fanwl gyda chynhwysion. Gyda theisen Nadolig fodd bynnag, mae angen rhoi sylw i'r manylion. Os gadewch chi rai cynhwysion pwysig allan fe allwch gael teisen drom neu un ddi-flas. Rwy'n argymell eich bod chi'n pwyso pob dim o flaen llaw, ac felly wrth i chi weithio'ch ffordd drwy'r rysáit, does dim yn cael ei adael allan.

1kg ffrwythau sych cymysg
100g ceirios glacé
75g croen candi
50g cnau Ffrengig, wedi'u torri
2 lwy de o sbeis cymysg
300g menyn
300g siwgwr brown meddal
5 wy
300g blawd plaen
1 llwy fwrdd o driog du
1 croen oren a'r sudd
1 croen lemwn a'r sudd
Diferyn neu ddau o frandi

Y noson cynt

Mesurwch a chymysgu'r ffrwythau sych, y croen oren a lemwn a'r sudd oren. Ychwanegwch y brandi a'i adael i fwydo dros nos.

Cynheswch y ffwrn i 140°C / 275°F / Nwy 1

Irwch a leinio tun teisen 20cm.

Mesurwch y cynhwysion sych: y cnau, y sbeis, y siwgwr a'r blawd.

Rhowch y menyn wedi'i feddalu a'r wyau wedi'u curo mewn i beiriant cymysgu a'u cymysgu'n dda. Ychwangewch weddill y cynhwysion.

Cymysgwch y ffrwythau wedi'u mwydo yn y brandi â'r triog. Yn olaf, rhowch y cymysgedd fesul llwyaid yn y tun.

Coginiwch ar silff ganol neu silff isel am 3½–4 awr.

Edrychwch ar y deisen ar ôl 3½ awr yn enwedig os oes gennych chi ffwrn ffan. I wneud yn siŵr bod y deisen wedi'i choginio, gwthiwch sgiwer neu gyllell i ganol y deisen, dylai ddod allan yn lân.

Mwynhewch addurno'r deisen gyda marsipán, eisin a sbrincls Nadolig, celyn, peli bach arian a ruban.

 Tip: mae'n syniad da gwneud teisennau bychain i'w rhoi fel anrhegion. Mae'r cynhwysion yr un rhai, ond defnyddiwch duniau, fel tuniau ffa pob, wedi'u golchi a'u hailgylchu fel tuniau teisen. Tua 30–40 munud fydd yr amser coginio ar gyfer y teisennau bach.

Tip: os nad ydych chi am ddefnyddio brandi, mwydwch eich ffrwythau sych mewn te oer, fel petaech chi'n gwneud bara brith. Mae'n gweithio'n dda ac yn ychwanegu digon o wlybaniaeth at y ffrwythau sych, fydd yn gwneud y deisen yn un braf.

CHRISTMAS CAKE

Usually, I'm quite relaxed about recipes and don't worry too much about being exact with ingredients. With a Christmas cake however, a little attention to detail is needed. Leave out a few vital ingredients and your cake may become a door stop or just a tasteless one. I always recommend that you weigh everything out in advance, so as you work your way through the recipe, nothing is left out or forgotten.

> 1kg dried mixed fruit
> 100g glacé cherries
> 75g of mixed peel
> 50g chopped walnuts
> 2 tsp mixed spice
> 300g butter
> 300g soft brown sugar
> 5 eggs
> 300g plain flour
> 1 tbsp black treacle
> 1 orange rind and juice
> 1 lemon rind
> A drop or two of brandy

The night before

Measure out and mix the dried fruit, orange and lemon rind and orange juice. Add brandy and soak overnight.

Preheat the oven 140°C / 275°F / Gas 1

Grease and line a 20cm cake tin.

Measure out the dry ingredients: the nuts, spices, sugar and flour.

Place the softened butter, beaten eggs into a mixer, and mix well. Add the remainder of the ingredients.

Stir in the brandy soaked fruit and treacle and finally, spoon into the prepared tin.

Cook on the middle or low shelf for 3½–4 hours.

Check the cake after 3½ hours especially if using a fan oven. To make sure that the cake is cooked, insert a skewer or a knife into the centre of the cake, it should come out clean.

Have fun decorating with marzipan, icing and Christmas sprinkles, holly, silver balls and a ribbon.

Tip: it's great to make some mini cakes to give as gifts. The ingredients are exactly the same, but use washed, recycled tins, such as baked bean tins, as cake tins. Cooking time will be about 30–40 minutes for the small cakes.

Tip: if you don't want to use brandy, soak your dried fruit in some cold tea, just like when you make bara brith. It works well and adds plenty of moisture to the dried fruit, which in turn makes a lovely cake.

SYNIAD SYDYN
QUICK IDEA

Saws llugaeron

Mae saws llugaeron cartref yn gyfan gwbl nefolaidd ac yn haws na dim i'w wneud. Gwnewch y saws ychydig ddyddiau cyn y Nadolig.

> 300g llugaeron ffres
> Croen a sudd un oren mawr
> 1 afal coginio
> 200g siwgwr mân
> 100ml dŵr
> 2–3 llwy fwrdd o bort (dewisol)

Rhowch bopeth, heblaw'r port os ydych chi'n ei gynnwys, mewn sosban fawr a berwch y cyfan. Gadewch i'r cymysgedd ferwi am oddeutu 10 munud hyd nes bydd yr aeron yn popian.

Trowch y saws â llwy bren a gwasgu unrhyw aeron sy'n dal yn gyfan. Pan fydd y saws yn edrych yn iawn, mae'n barod.

Mae lefelau pectin yn uchel mewn llugaeron ac afalau coginio, felly mae'r saws yn siŵr o setio. Peidiwch â chael eich temtio i ferwi'r hylif nes bydd yn lleihau er mwyn tewhau'r saws.

Gadewch iddo oeri ychydig ac arllwyswch i jar wedi'i sterileiddio. Gorchuddiwch â disg cwyr a'i selio.

Rhowch label Nadoligaidd ar y jar a'i chadw yn yr oergell tan y diwrnod mawr.

Cranberry sauce

I think that home-made cranberry sauce is utterly divine and easier than anything to make. Make the sauce a few days before Christmas.

> 300g fresh cranberries
> Rind and juice of one large orange
> 1 cooking apple
> 200g caster sugar
> 100ml water
> 2–3 tablespoons of port (optional)

Place everything, except the port if you're using some, into a large saucepan and bring to the boil. Allow the mixture to boil for about 10 minutes until the berries begin to pop,.

Stir the sauce with a wooden spoon and pop any remaining berries. Once the sauce looks OK, it's ready.

Cranberries and bramley apples have an enormous amount of pectin, so the sauce is sure to set. Don't be tempted to boil away the liquid to thicken the sauce.

Allow to cool a little and pour into a sterilised jar. Cover with wax disk and seal.

Label the jar with a Christmassy sticky label and keep in the fridge until the big day.

SYNIAD SYDYN
QUICK IDEA

DG

Menyn brandi

Rwy'n dueddol o wneud fy menyn brandi sawl wythnos cyn y Nadolig – mae'n hawdd ac mae'n cadw.

> 150g menyn meddal
> 200g siwgwr eisin
> 3 llwy fwrdd o frandi neu wirod arall

Cyfunwch y siwgwr eisin a'r menyn a'u curo i sicrhau nad oes unrhyw lympiau. Gellid gwneud hyn gan ddefnyddio prosesydd bwyd bach – mae'n llawer haws.

Ychwanegwch y gwirod o'ch dewis chi, fesul llwyaid, hyd nes cewch y blas rydych chi'n ei hoffi. Gallai hyn fod yn fwy neu'n llai na'r 3 llond llwy fwrdd yn y rysáit hon.

Bydd y menyn yn cadw yn yr oergell am ryw bythefnos, ond gallwch ei rewi hefyd. Lapiwch y menyn mewn ffoil neu haenen lynu a'i storio yn y rhewgell am hyd at dri mis.

GF

Brandy butter

I tend to make my brandy butter several weeks before Christmas; it's easy and will keep.

> 150g soft butter
> 200g icing sugar
> 3 tbsp of brandy or another liqueur

Combine the icing sugar and the butter and beat to ensure that there are no lumps. This can be done in a small food processor – it's much easier.

Add the liqueur of your choice, a tablespoon at a time, until you reach the strength you like. This could well be more or less than the 3 tablespoons recommended in the recipe.

The butter will keep in the fridge for a couple of weeks, but it can also be frozen. Wrap the butter in foil or cling film and store in the freezer for up to three months.

219

SYNIAD SYDYN
QUICK IDEA

Rhisgl siocled

Dyma rywbeth gwahanol i'r wy Pasg arferol; gallwch ei lapio i wneud anrheg hyfryd.

> Chwistrellydd coginio olew llysiau
> Siocled llaeth, neu siocled gwyn wedi'i dorri, does dim ots faint
> Losin amrywiol i'w defnyddio fel addurn

Gosodwch ddarn mawr o bapur pobi neu silicon ar hambwrdd pobi mawr. Chwistrellwch ag olew llysiau.

Toddwch 2/3 o'r siocled mewn powlen sy'n gwrthsefyll gwres wedi'i gosod dros sosban gydag ychydig o ddŵr yn mudferwi ynddi, sef bain-marie. Cymysgwch y siocled nes ei fod wedi toddi, tynnwch y bowlen oddi ar y gwres ac yna ychwanegwch y darnau siocled sy'n weddill.

Arllwyswch y siocled toddedig ar y papur pobi a'i daenu i greu haenen wastad, ond peidwch â thaenu'n rhy denau. Gallwch doddi mwy o siocled o liw gwahanol (siocled tywyll, siocled llaeth neu siocled gwyn) er mwyn creu effaith marmor.

Gwasgarwch y losin ar ben yr haenen siocled yn syth, pethau fel botymau siocled, wyau bach siocled a losin jeli – i greu rhisgl siocled Pasg pert.

Oerwch yn yr oergell am tuag 1 awr, hyd nes ei fod yn solet. Tynnwch y papur pobi i ffwrdd a thorri'r rhisgl yn ddarnau.

Gallwch roi darnau o'r rhisgl mewn bagiau seloffên. Ychwanegwch ruban a thag anrheg lliwgar.

Chocolate bark

This is a great alternative to an Easter egg and can be easily wrapped to make a lovely present.

> Vegetable oil cooking spray
> Milk or white chocolate, chopped, doesn't matter what the amount is
> Various sweet toppings

Place a large piece of parchment paper or silicone on a large baking tray. Spray with vegetable cooking spray.

Melt 2/3 of the chocolate in a heatproof bowl set over a pan of simmering water; this is called a bain-marie. Stir the chocolate until it melts, remove the bowl from the heat, then add the remaining chocolate pieces.

Pour the melted chocolate onto the baking sheet, and spread in an even layer, but don't spread it too thinly. You can now melt and add more dark, milk or white chocolate, if you want to create a marbled effect.

Immediately sprinkle other chocolates on top, such as chocolate buttons, little chocolate eggs, and colourful jelly, to create a pretty Easter chocolate bark.

Refrigerate for about 1 hour, until firm. Peel off parchment, and break bark into pieces.

The bark can be bagged up in cellophane bags. Add a ribbon and a colourful gift tag.

DG

Seidr neu win poeth

Mae'r ddiod gynhesol hon yn cyrraedd y mannau dirgel!

    1 litr seidr
    neu
    1 potel o win coch a gwydraid o frandi
    6 chlof
    2 star anise
    ¼ nytmeg, wedi'i gratio'n fân i mewn
     i'r sosban
    1 coesyn sinamon
    2 afal
    1 oren neu glementin, wedi'i sleisio
    4–5 llwy fwrdd o siwgwr mân

Arllwyswch y seidr i sosban fawr a'i rhoi ar wres isel i gynhesu, ychwanegwch y sbeisys a dewch â'r cyfan yn agos at y berw. Yna, trowch y gwres i lawr a gadael i'r seidr fudferwi am 2–3 munud.

Torrwch yr afalau yn chwarteri, ac yna torrwch bob chwarter yn ei hanner.

Gwthiwch glof i groen y darnau afal a'u hychwanegu nhw i'r seidr. Mae gwneud hyn yn cadw'r clofs yn 'ddiogel', a fyddwch chi ddim yn eu llyncu nhw neu'n tagu arnyn nhw.

Sleisiwch yr oren neu'r clementin yn dafelli tenau a'u hychwanegu at y sosban sy'n mudferwi.

Yn olaf, ychwanegwch cyn gymaint o siwgwr ag y bydd ei angen arnoch – mae rhai mathau o seidr yn felysach na'i gilydd. Cadwch y seidr yn gynnes a defnyddiwch letwad i lenwi gwydrau sydd wedi'u cynhesu cyn ei weini.

GF

Mulled cider or wine

This warming drink reaches parts of you that you didn't know you had!

    1 litre cider
    or
    1 bottle of red wine and a glass of brandy
    6 cloves
    2 star anise
    ¼ nutmeg, finely grated into the pan
    1 cinnamon stick
    2 apples
    1 orange or clementine, sliced
    4–5 tbsp caster sugar

Pour the cider into a large pan and place over a low heat to warm. Add the spices and bring to near boiling, then turn down the heat and allow the cider to simmer for 2–3 minutes.

Chop the apples into quarters and then cut each quarter in half.

Stud the apple pieces with a clove and add to the cider. Doing this keeps the cloves 'safe' and you won't end up swallowing them, or choking on them.

Slice the orange or the clementine into thin slices, and add to the simmering pot.

Finally, add as much sugar as you need – some ciders are sweeter than others. Keep the cider warm and ladle into warmed glasses to serve.

ANRHEGION NADOLIG O'R GEGIN

HOMEMADE PRESENTS FROM THE KITCHEN

Adeg y Nadolig, yn anad yr un adeg arall o'r flwyddyn, mae'n ddefnyddiol cael syniadau a thips sut i wneud bywyd yn haws yn y gegin. Wrth gwrs, gallwch ddefnyddio'r tips yma drwy gydol y flwyddyn ond gydag ymwelwyr ychwanegol yn cyrraedd y tŷ yn ddiwahoddiad weithiau dros gyfnod y Nadolig, dyma'r adeg pan fydd pobl yn teimlo'r pwysau. Ac fe allwn ni wneud ag ychydig o help i'r cyfeiriad iawn ambell waith.

Yn aml bydd pobl yn chwilio am syniadau ar gyfer anrhegion a wnaed gartref, pethau wedi'u pobi gartref, er enghraifft. Ac mae anrhegion sydd wedi'u lapio'n ofalus â rubanau a thagiau anrheg cartref i'w rhoi i gyfeillion ac i deulu yn dangos ôl meddwl mawr y tu ôl i'w creu.

At Christmas, more that at any other time of the year, it's useful to get hints and tips on how to make things easier in and around the kitchen. Of course, these ideas can be applied at any time of year, but with extra guests and visitors turning up out of the blue at Christmas, this is when we tend to feel the pressure and need just a little help in the right direction.

People are always looking for ideas for home-made gifts, home baked and beautifully packaged with ribbons and home-made tags to give to family and friends. These lovingly packaged gifts show that great thought has been put into their creation. These can range from biscuits to simple home-made cakes, but your efforts won't go unnoticed.

HAMPERI

Mae hamper yn anrheg dda i'w rhoi i unrhyw un. Dydw i ddim yn sôn am fasged ddrudfawr yn llawn jariau a photeli o lefydd crand wedi'i hanfon i'ch drws am grocbris; rwy'n sôn am rai wedi'u casglu eich hun. Gallai'r fasged a'r bocs gael eu cyfnewid am fasged arddio, neu bowlen cogydd neu sosban hyd yn oed – dewiswch chi. Defnyddiwch eich dychymyg, meddyliwch am y person fydd yn derbyn yr anrheg a dewiswch eu 'hamper' gan feddwl amdanyn nhw. Gallwch addurno bocs â phapur pert a'i lenwi â danteithion addas.

Ar gyfer myfyrwyr, dewiswch bapur a ysgrifbinnau, llyfrau, losin a siocled, yn ogystal â bisgedi a jar o goffi – y pethau feddyliwch chi sydd eu hangen arnyn nhw a phethau y byddan nhw'n eu gwerthfawrogi. Ar gyfer rhywun sy'n hŷn, dewiswch bethau y byddan nhw'n debygol o'u cadw yn eu cwpwrdd bwyd ac ychwanegwch rai danteithion at y casgliad. Yn y modd hwn, byddwch yn gwario'ch arian ar bethau sydd eu hangen – ac nid ar anrhegion nad oes eu hangen ar neb ond afydd yn hongian o gwmpas y tŷ heb ddefnydd iddyn nhw – ac rydych chi'n gwneud anrheg hollol unigryw iddyn nhw.

Mae dynion yn aml yn bobl anodd iawn i brynu ar eu cyfer, yn fy mhrofiad i. Dy'n nhw byth eisiau unrhyw beth, ac mi fyddan nhw'n hapus iawn bob tro gyda hamper yn llawn bwydydd gwahanol. Yr unig beth fydd yn rhaid i chi ei wybod yw a oes ganddyn nhw ddant melys neu ydyn nhw'n hoff o bethau sawrus.

ANRHEGION JARIAU KILNER

Bydd y rhai hynny ohonoch chi sydd wedi bod yn fy nghegin i'n gwybod 'mod i'n ffan mawr o jariau Kilner, y jariau traddodiadol a ddefnyddir wrth wneud jam. Mae gen i silffoedd yn llawn ohonyn nhw a phob un yn dal pethau gwahanol – o siwgwr, perlysiau, pasta, hyd at rubanau a botymau.

I wneud anrheg sydd â thipyn o steil iddi ac sy'n ddefnyddiol hefyd, llenwch jar Kilner â'r holl gynhwysion sydd eu hangen i wneud cwcis siocled, brownis neu bice ar y maen. Ychwanegwch label parsel â chyfarwyddiadau ar sut i fynd ati i goginio, ac mae gennych anrheg ddefnyddiol a meddylgar i rywun. Gyda llaw, peidiwch â chynnwys y cynhwysion gwlyb yn eich jar; dim wyau na menyn, dim ond y cynhwysion sych!

HAMPERS

A hamper is a good present for anyone. I'm not talking about an expensive basket full of exclusive jars and bottles, delivered to your door at enormous cost, I'm talking home-made ones you've collected yourself. The basket, tray, box or crate could just as easily be a gardener's trug, a cook's mixing bowl or a saucepan – the choice is yours. Use your imagination, think of the person you have in mind for the gift and select accordingly. Alternatively, just decorate a box in pretty paper and load it up with appropriate goodies.

For students, choose paper and pens, books, sweets and chocolates, as well as some biscuits and a jar of coffee – the things you think they might need and appreciate. For an older person, choose all the store cupboard ingredients they are likely to use and need, and add a few extra treats they might like. This way, your budget, however large or small, will be well used and not wasted on unwanted gifts to clutter the home, and you produce a totally bespoke gift.

Men are often difficult to buy for, in my experience. They never want anything, and will always be delighted with a hamper full of different foods. You simply need to know whether they are the sweet or savoury type.

KILNER JAR GIFTS

Those of you who have been to my kitchen will know that I'm a huge fan of Kilner jars, the traditional preserving jars. I have shelves full of them, containing everything from sugar, spices, pasta, right through to ribbons and buttons.

To make a stylish and useful present, fill a Kilner jar with all the ingredients needed to make chocolate cookies, brownies or Welsh cakes. Add a little parcel label with the instructions how to make them, and you have another sweet and useful gift. The storage jar can be used again and again, whilst the contents offer an activity and a sweet treat, three pressies in one. By the way, just like the packet mixes in the shops, don't add the wet ingredients. Don't add eggs or butter, just the dry stuff.

SYNIAD SYDYN
QUICK IDEA

Troellwyr siocled

Rhywbeth bach i'r plant, ifanc a hen ...

> Siocled o'ch dewis chi
> Malws melys bach
> Sbrincls lliwgar i addurno
> Casynnau papur bach
> Ffyn lolipop pren neu lwyau pren bach

Torrwch eich siocled yn ddarnau a'u rhoi mewn powlen fetel fawr. Gosodwch y bowlen i orffwys ar sosban sy'n cynnwys dŵr sy'n mudferwi i greu bain-marie.

Pan fydd y siocled wedi toddi, arllwyswch ef i mewn i'r casynnau papur bach neu gallwch ddefnyddio mowldiau silicon.

Rhowch ffon lolipop bren neu lwy bren fechan i mewn ym mhob un. Yna, ychwanegwch ychydig o sbrincls a malws melys bach at y siocled cyn iddo galedu. Gellir addurno'r troellwyr yn lliwiau'r Pasg gan ddefnyddio lliwiau pastel, neu liwiau Nadoligaidd – coch a gwyrdd.

Gadewch iddyn nhw galedu. Defnyddiwch nhw i roi blas siocled ychwanegol i ddiod siocled boeth, hyfryd, neu dipiwch a llyfwch!

Rhowch nhw mewn bagiau seloffên bach, sydd ar gael o siopau crefft. Mae'r rhain yn anrhegion Nadolig bach gwych i ffrindiau ysgol ac maen nhw'n edrych yn dda yn hongian ar goeden Nadolig neu goeden Basg, ond DDIM os oes gennych chi gi!

Chocolate stirrers

A little something for the children, young and old ...

> Chocolate of your choice
> Small marshmallows
> Colourful sprinkles
> Small paper cases
> Lolly sticks or wooden spoons

Cut your chocolate into chunks and place in a large metal bowl. Place the bowl to rest over a saucepan containing simmering water to create a bain-marie.

Once the chocolate has melted, pour it into small paper cases or into silicone moulds.

Place a lolly stick or small wooden spoon into each one, then add a few sprinkles and tiny marshmallows to set in the chocolate. The stirrers can be decorated in Easter colours of pastel shades, or Christmassy colours of red and green.

Allow to set hard. Use to add extra chocolate flavour to a lovely hot-chocolate drink, or just dip and lick!

Place in small cellophane bags, available from most craft shops. These are great little Christmas gifts for school friends and they look great hanging on an Easter or Christmas tree, but NOT if you have a dog in house!

TIPS NADOLIG I'R COGYDD LLUDDEDIG

Felly, bydd wythnosau o baratoi a llawer o feddwl a threfnu yn dirwyn i ben mewn diwrnod neu ddau o ddathlu llawen gyda theulu a ffrindiau.

Wel, dyna'r ddamcaniaeth beth bynnag. Gall y realiti fod ychydig yn wahanol, a gall ein cynlluniau gofalus fynd i'r gwynt, ond na phoener, dyw hynny ddim yn golygu bod pethau wedi'u difetha.

Mae creu perffeithrwydd yn y gegin, a chadw'r plant, y rhieni, y rhieni yng nghyfraith, plant hŷn, eu partneriaid, ac weithiau wyrion yn ddiddig a hapus, yn dasg anferthol. Dim ond un ffwrn arferol sydd mewn cegin gyffredin â phedwar hob coginio; felly, mae coginio i'r lluoedd yn gallu bod yn her. Digonedd o blatiau a chyllyll a ffyrc? Gwydrau sy'n matsio? O ddifri! Bwrdd digon mawr? Digon o gadeiriau? A pheidiwch â dweud gair am fwytawyr ffyslyd â gofynion penodol.

Oes syndod bod y Nadolig yn heriol? Nerfau brau a photel o win unrhyw un?

Felly, beth allwn ni ei wneud i bob dim fod yn haws? Rydym ni wedi hen arfer â'n bywydau prysur nes ein bod ni'n anghofio sut mae ymlacio a mwynhau'r eiliad. Dylem geisio paratoi cymaint ag sy'n bosib o flaen llaw a gadael i'r diwrnod ei hun lifo heibio.

Cyn belled ag mae cinio Nadolig yn y cwestiwn, dyma rai tips syml iawn. Mewn rhai achosion, rwy'n dweud pethau amlwg iawn, ond weithiau mae'n dda atgoffa'n hunain. Daliwch i anadlu ...

- Paratowch gynifer o'r llysiau ag y medrwch ddiwrnod neu ddau ynghynt a'u storio mewn sosbenni o ddŵr oer, neu mewn bagiau rhewi yn yr oergell. Y peth pwysig yw eu cadw nhw'n llaith cyn i chi eu coginio nhw.

- Gwnewch lond jar neu ddwy o saws llugaeron yr wythnos cynt, bydd yn iawn tan ddydd Nadolig.

- Malwch a chwalwch y briwsion bara ar gyfer y stwffin ddiwrnod neu ddau ynghynt, storiwch nhw yn y rhewgell hyd nes byddwch chi'n barod i wneud y stwffin, neu gallwch wneud y stwffin ei hun o flaen llaw a'i rewi.

- Coginiwch lysiau fel rwdins, neu hyd yn oed y moron, o flaen llaw a'u cynhesu ar y diwrnod, bydd hyn yn rhyddhau lle ar yr hob.

- Cynhwyswch bawb. Mae gwaith i bob un, o hwylio'r bwrdd i gynnau canhwyllau, troi'r grefi i gynhesu'r llestri gweini.

- Os yw'r bwrdd yn eitha cyfyng, gosodwch y bwyd wedi'i goginio ar arwyneb arall (yn y gegin) a threfnwch bethau'n debyg i 'carvery' – gadewch i bawb helpu eu hunain.

- Pan fydd pawb wedi llenwi eu platiau, gosodwch y bwyd ychwanegol a'r grefi ar y bwrdd i bawb fedru estyn am fwy. Mae hyn yn arbed gwastraff hefyd.

- Peidiwch â bod yn rhy anhyblyg ynghylch cadw amser. Os yw cinio hanner awr yn hwyr, pwy fydd yn poeni?

- A phan fyddwch chi'n eistedd i lawr i fwyta'ch cinio, mwynhewch!

- Peidiwch ag anghofio bod gan bawb wrth y bwrdd ddwy droed! Gadewch iddyn nhw ymorol am bethau ychwanegol drostynt eu hunain ... eu halen a'u pupur ... eu cyllyll ... eu ffyrc ... eu llwyau ...

- Gellid gweini pwdin rai oriau yn hwyrach; peidiwch â rhuthro, mae digon o amser.

- Mynnwch help pawb gyda'r clirio.

- Gwnewch yn siŵr bod y peiriant golchi llestri – nid eich partner – yn wag cyn i chi ddechrau ar eich cinio. Gellir llwytho'r peiriant ac fe allwch chi eistedd i lawr am weddill y diwrnod. Os nad oes gennych beiriant golchi llestri, gwnewch yn siŵr fod y sinc yn wag ac yn barod i dderbyn llestri. Rhowch swyddi i bobl eu gwneud i sicrhau bod y llestri'n cael eu golchi, eu sychu a'u cadw.

Dyna ni. Nawr fe allwch chi gnoi cil ar dwrci a stwffin a'r holl bethau ychwanegol sydd yn yr oergell am y dyddiau nesaf yn hamddenol. Cymerwch Ddydd Gŵyl San Steffan bant a gadewch i bawb helpu eu hunain i'r bwffe oer.

CHRISTMAS TIPS FOR THE WEARY COOK

So, the weeks of preparation with much thought and organisation will culminate in a day or two of joyous celebration with family and friends.

Well, that's the theory anyway. Reality can be slightly different; our best-laid plans can be changed, but don't worry, the whole day needn't be ruined.

Creating culinary perfection, whilst keeping the young children, the parents, the in-laws, older children, their spouses and sometimes the grandchildren entertainied and happy, is a big ask. The normal domestic kitchen has one regular-sized oven and a standard four burners, so catering for the masses can be challenging. Plenty of plates and cutlery? Matching glasses? You are kidding! A sufficiently large table? Plenty of chairs? Don't get me started on fussy eaters and specific requirements.

Is it any wonder that Christmas can present a challenge? Raw nerves and bottle of wine anybody?

So what can we do to make things easier? We are so used to our busy lives that we can forget how to unwind and how to enjoy the moment. We should prepare as much as we can in advance and let the day itself flow.

As far as Christmas lunch goes, here are a few very simple tips. In some cases, I am stating the obvious, but sometimes it's good to remind ourselves! Keep breathing …

- Prepare as many of the vegetables a day or two before and store them in pans of cold water, or in freezer bags in the fridge; the important thing is to keep them them moist until you cook them.

- Make a jar or two of cranberry sauce the week before. It'll be fine till Christmas day.

- Blitz the breadcrumbs for the stuffing at least a day or two before, and store them in the freezer until you are ready to make the stuffing. You can also make the actual stuffing in advance and freeze it.

- Cook vegetables such as swede, or even the carrots, in advance and simply warm through on the day; it will free up cooker space.

- Get everyone involved. There can be a job for everyone, from laying the table to lighting candles, stirring the gravy to getting the serving dishes warmed.

- If the table is a little cramped, place all the cooked food on another surface (in the kitchen) and treat it like a 'carvery' – let everyone help themselves.

- When everyone has filled their plate, place the extras and the gravy on the table for everyone to top up. This also saves on a lot of waste.

- Don't be too rigid about the timekeeping. If lunch is half an hour late, who cares?

- And when you sit down for lunch, enjoy it!

- Don't forget that everyone else at the table also has a pair of feet! Let them get their own extras … salt and pepper … knife … fork … spoon …

- Pudding can be served a few hours later; don't rush, there's plenty of time.

- Get everyone to help with the clearing up.

- Make sure the dishwasher – the machine, not your partner – is empty before you start lunch, so the machine can be loaded and you can sit down for the rest of the afternoon. If you don't have a dishwasher, make sure the sink is empty and ready to accept dishes, and give people jobs to make sure that the dishes are washed, dried and put away.

That's it. Now you can graze on turkey and stuffing, salads and all the extras in the fridge for the next few days. Take Boxing Day off and let everybody help themselves to a cold buffet.

PROBLEMAU YN Y GEGIN

Yn gyntaf ac yn bennaf oll – na phanicier!

Lympiau yn y grefi? Rhowch eich grefi drwy ridyll i waredu'r lympiau. I osgoi'r lympiau yn y lle cyntaf, ceisiwch dewhau'r grefi â blawd corn. Cymysgwch ychydig lwyeidiau o flawd corn â ½ cwpanaid o ddŵr oer ac ychwanegu'r grefi poeth ato. Trowch yn gyson hyd bydd y grefi'n tewhau.

Grefi di-flas? Peidiwch â dal i ychwanegu halen, da chi, ond ychwanegwch lwyaid o saws llugaeron neu jeli cyrens cochion. Mae'n rhoi melyster hyfryd i'r grefi, a dyna ddatrys y broblem.

Tatws rhost wedi'u tangoginio a mynd yn slwtsh? Rhowch nhw mewn peiriant ffrio dwfn i'w gwneud yn fwy creisionllyd.

Ac os ewch i banig wrth feddwl am yr holl goginio Nadolig a'r ymwelwyr, ysgrifennwch restr o'ch hoff ryseitiau a'r rhai hawdd i'w gwneud. Mae fy rhai i yn y rhan hon o'r llyfr.

Tywydd gwael? Dyma weithgaredd hwyliog ar gyfer pob aelod o'ch teulu. Gwnewch restr o ddeg peth sy'n eich atgoffa chi o'r Nadolig, dyma fy un i:

1. Tanllwyth o dân (a chnau yn rhostio arno ... wrth gwrs)
2. Goleuadau bychain tylwyth teg
3. Gwneud stwffin
4. Briwgacs â sêr ar eu pennau
5. Nosweithiau tywyll
6. Dewis coeden Nadolig
7. Hetiau a sgarffiau
8. Cyngerdd Nadolig yr ysgol neu wasanaeth carolau
9. Cerddoriaeth Nadoligaidd
10. Cyfeillion a theulu
11. Model ein teulu ni o Ddrama'r Geni (ie, rwy'n gwybod, mae hynny'n gwneud un ar ddeg!)

PROBLEMS IN THE KITCHEN

Whatever happens – don't panic!

Lumpy gravy? Lumpy gravy? Simply pass it through a sieve to remove the lumps. To avoid lumps in the first place, try thickening the gravy with corn flour. Simply mix a few spoonfuls of cornflour with ½ cup of cold water and stir into the hot gravy, stir continually until the gravy thickens.

Tasteless gravy? Don't keep adding salt. Simply add a spoonful cranberry sauce or red currant jelly into the gravy. It adds a lovely sweetness. Problem solved.

Soggy, undercooked roast potatoes? Pop them in the deep fat fryer to crisp up.

If you get into a bit of a panic at the thought of Christmas cooking and visitors, write down a list of your foolproof and favourite recipes. Mine are in this section of the book.

The weather isn't great? Here's a jolly activity for children and adults:
Make list of ten things that remind you of Christmas; here's mine:

1. A log fire (nuts roasting on ... of course)
2. Sparkly fairy lights
3. Making stuffing
4. Mince pies with stars on top
5. Dark evenings
6. Choosing the Christmas tree
7. Hats and scarves
8. School Christmas concert or carol service
9. Christmas music
10. Friends and visitors
11. Our little Nativity scene (yes, OK, that's eleven)

DATHLU'R CALAN

⭐ Weithiau mae angen parti i godi'r hwyl, a does dim angen llawer o fwyd arnoch i lenwi twll. Mwynhewch y blasusfwydydd bychain hyn ynghyd â chwmni braf.

CELEBRATING NEW YEAR

⭐ Sometimes you need a party to lighten the mood, and you don't need much food to fill a hole. Enjoy these tasty morsels along with good company.

BLINIS GWENITH YR HYDD

Mae dweud y gair 'blini' yn gwneud i fi deimlo'n soffistigedig hyd yn oed! Rwy'n dwlu ar y pancos bach yma; maen nhw'n fwyd parti amlddefnydd gwych, llawn cystal fel llond cegaid melys neu sawrus.

> 1 cwpanaid o flawd codi
> ½ cwpanaid o flawd gwenith yr hydd
> ½ llwy de o bowdwr codi
> ½ cwpanaid o laeth
> ½ cwpanaid o crème fraîche
> 1 wy

Cymysgwch y cynhwysion ynghyd mewn powlen fawr. Cymysgwch yn dda gan sicrhau nad oes unrhyw lympiau yn y cymysgedd.

Pan fyddwch chi'n barod i wneud y blinis, brwsiwch ffrimpan fawr neu radell ag ychydig o fenyn wedi toddi a'i chadw ar dymheredd canolig.

Arllwyswch llond llwy fwrdd o'r cytew i'r ffrimpan ar y tro, gan adael digon o le rhwng pob un. Gadewch iddyn nhw goginio am tua 30 eiliad, yna'u troi drosodd a'u coginio am 30 eiliad arall.

Rhowch y blinis i oeri ar resel wifrau a daliwch ati i wneud mwy ohonynt, gan frwsio'r ffrimpan â menyn bob tro.

Rhowch gynhwysion o'ch dewis chi ar ben y blinis i wneud y bwyd parti perffaith. Dyma rai awgrymiadau:

- Taenwch gymysgedd o crème fraîche a llond llwy de o saws rhuddygl ynddo ar y blinis a rhoi samwn wedi'i gochi neu gafiar ar ei ben.
- Cymysgwch ychydig o gaws hufen â mecryll mwg, ychydig o sudd lemwn, halen a phupur i wneud pâté mecryll (gweler tudalen 234).
- Cymysgwch gaws mascarpone meddal ag ychydig bach o siwgwr eisin. Peipiwch ar y blini a rhoi ffrwyth ffres, fel cyrens cochion, llugaeron neu fefus ar ei ben.

Tip: i wneud fersiwn diglwten, defnyddiwch 1½ cwpanaid o flawd gwenith yr hydd a gwnewch yn siŵr bod eich powdwr codi chi'n ddiglwten hefyd.

BUCKWHEAT BLINIS

Just saying the word 'blini' makes me feel sophisticated! I love these tiny pancakes, such versatile party canapés. They're just as good for sweet and savoury bites.

> 1 cup self-raising flour
> ½ cup buckwheat flour
> ½ teaspoon baking powder
> ½ cup milk
> ½ cup crème fraîche
> 1 egg

Mix all the ingredients together in a large bowl. Mix well, ensuring that there are no lumps remaining.

When you're ready to make the blinis, brush a large frying pan or griddle with a little melted butter and place on a medium heat.

Add 1 tablespoon portions of batter to the pan, leaving a little room between each. Leave to cook for about 30 seconds, then flip over and cook for a further 30 seconds on the other side.

Transfer the cooked blinis to a wire cooling-rack and repeat the process to make more, brushing the pan with butter each time.

Top the blinis with your favourite toppings to make perfect party food. Here are some suggestions:

- Try crème fraîche mixed with a teaspoon of horseradish as a base, and top with smoked salmon or caviar.
- Blend a little soft cheese with smoked mackerel, a little lemon juice, salt and pepper, to make a mackerel pâté (see page 234).
- Mix soft mascarpone cheese with a small amount of icing sugar, pipe onto a blini and top with fresh fruit such as redcurrants, blueberries or strawberries.

Tip: to make a gluten free version, use 1½ cups of buckwheat flour instead of the self raising flour and make sure your baking powder is gluten free too.

PÂTÉ MECRYLL

*Mae tamaid o flas y pâté moethus hwn
yn mynd yn bell iawn.*

400g mecryll mwg
200g caws hufen braster isel
1 llwy fwrdd o iogwrt naturiol
Croen a sudd 1 lemwn
1 bocs o ferwr, wedi'i dorri

Tynnwch y croen oddi ar y mecryll mwg a'i daflu.
Rhowch y pysgod mewn prosesydd bwyd i'w malu,
neu fe allwch ddefnyddio fforc i wneud hyn. Os ydych
chi'n hoffi pâté llyfn, yna mae'n haws defnyddio
prosesydd bwyd.

Ychwanegwch y caws hufen, croen y lemwn a'r rhan
fwyaf o sudd ½ lemwn. Chwyrlïwch neu cymysgwch
y cyfan am tua 20 eiliad neu hyd nes y cewch chi
pâté hufennog hyfryd. Blaswch ac yna ychwanegwch
ychydig o halen a phupur, a mwy o sudd lemwn os
oes angen. Addurnwch ag ychydig o'r berwr.

I'w weini, torrwch lemwn yn ddarnau a'u gosod gyda'r
pâté a bara crystiog hyfryd.

MACKEREL PÂTÉ

*A little taste of this luxurious pâté
goes a long way.*

400g smoked mackerel
200g low-fat cream cheese
1 tbsp natural yogurt
Zest and juice of 1 lemon
1 punnet of cress, snipped

Peel the skin off the smoked mackerel and discard.
Put the fish in a food processor, or just break up the
fish using a fork. If you like a smooth pâté, it's easier to
use a food processor.

Add the cream cheese, the zest and most of the juice
of ½ lemon. Whizz or mix for about 20 seconds, or
until you get a nice creamy pâté. Check the taste,
add a little salt and pepper, and more lemon juice if
needed. Add some cress for decoration.

To serve, cut a lemon into wedges and place
alongside the pâté with lovely crusty bread.

PÂTÉ SGWASH CNAU MENYN

Mae'r pate hwn yn creu tipyn o argraff gyda'i flasau cyfoethog ardderchog.

½ sgwash cnau menyn, wedi'i dorri'n giwbiau
200g caws hufen braster isel
1 llwy fwrdd o iogwrt naturiol
1 llwy de o gymysgedd perlysiau Cajun
1 bocs o ferwr, wedi'i dorri
Olew olewydd
Pupur Cayenne neu baprica

Gosodwch y sgwash cnau menyn wedi'i dorri'n giwbiau ar hambwrdd pobi, taenwch olew olewydd drostynt ac ysgeintio'r cymysgedd perlysiau Cajun dros y cyfan. Rhostiwch y sgwash yn y ffwrn am tua 20 munud hyd nes ei fod yn feddal ond heb ei grimpio.

Gadewch i'r sgwash oeri, yna malwch gan ddefnyddio prosesydd bwyd i ffurfio past llyfn, neu stwnsiwch y sgwash gan ddefnyddio fforc. Os ydych chi'n hoffi pâté llyfn, yna mae'n haws defnyddio prosesydd bwyd.

Ychwanegwch y caws hufen at y sgwash cnau menyn a'u cymysgu. Chwyrlïwch neu cymysgwch yn dda am tua 20 eiliad, neu hyd nes cewch chi pâté hufennog braf. Blaswch ac ychwanegwch ychydig o halen a phupur os oes angen.

Ychwanegwch ychydig bach iawn o bupur cayenne, neu ddefnyddio paprica os nad ydych chi'n hoffi pupur poeth. Rhowch ychydig o ferwr ar ei ben cyn ei weini â bara crystiog, ffres.

BUTTERNUT SQUASH PÂTÉ

This pâté packs a punch – such fantastic rich flavours.

½ butternut squash, diced
200g low-fat cream cheese
1 tbsp natural yogurt
1 tsp Cajun seasoning
1 punnet of cress, snipped
Olive oil
Cayenne pepper or paprika

Place the diced butternut squash on a baking tray, drizzle over some olive oil and sprinkle with Cajun seasoning. Roast the squash in the oven for about 20 minutes until soft but not crispy.

Allow the roasted squash to cool, then blitz in a food processor to form a smooth paste, or just break it up using a fork. If you like a smooth pâté, it's easier to use a food processor.

Add the cream cheese to the butternut squash and mix well. Whizz or mix for 20 seconds or so, or until you get a nice creamy pâté. Check the taste, add a little salt and pepper if needed.

Sprinkle with a tiny amount of cayenne pepper to finish, or use paprika if you don't like too much heat. Snip some cress over the top before serving with fresh crusty bread.

LLOND CEG O DATWS BACH

Dyma fwyd maethlon, da, ac mae'n fwyd bys a bawd da i barti hefyd. Bargen!

Digonedd o datws salad canolig eu maint
1 llwy fwrdd o fenyn
Halen a phupur du wedi'i falu
Cawsiau cymysg sydd dros ben, wedi'u gratio neu wedi'u torri'n fân
Ham neu diwna (ond ddim ar gyfer fersiwn llysieuol), India corn, tomatos, winwns neu unrhyw lenwadau eraill o'ch dewis
Olew olewydd

Cynheswch y ffwrn i 200°C / 400°F / Nwy 6

Golchwch y tatws a'u gosod ar hambwrdd pobi. Taenwch olew olewydd drostynt a'u coginio yn y ffwrn am tua 30 munud, hyd nes eu byddan nhw'n feddal. Ysgydwch yr hambwrdd yn gyson er mwyn troi'r tatws i gael lliw braf drostynt.

Tynnwch nhw o'r ffwrn a gwneud croes ym mhob taten neu, gan ddefnyddio digreiddiwr, afalau, tynnwch ddarn bach o'r canol allan o bob taten.

Nawr, gallwch fynd i unrhyw gyfeiriad a gwneud eich llenwadau eich hun neu beth am dynnu rhywfaint o du mewn y daten a'i stwnsio â fforc. Ychwanegwch ychydig o fenyn, pinsiaid o halen a phupur, a chaws wedi'i gratio. Cymysgwch yn dda a llenwch y twll yn y daten â'r cymysgedd newydd. Gallech dynnu rhywfaint o du mewn y daten a'i gyfnewid am ham wedi'i dorri neu diwna. Gorchuddiwch ag ychydig o gaws wedi'i gratio – defnyddiwch gaws a blas cryf iddo ar gyfer blas da. Rhowch y tatws yn ôl yn y ffwrn i'w pobi hyd nes bod y caws yn euraid. Neu gan ddefnyddio llwy fach neu fag peipio, rhowch ychydig o'r pâté sgwash cnau menyn neu'r pâté mecryll (gweler tudalennau 234 a 235 am y ryseitiau) i mewn i'r tatws bach. Ychwanegwch ychydig o ddail mwstard neu ferwr fel addurn, neu sleisen denau o giwcymber.

MINI FILLED JACKET POTATOES

This is good, nutritious food but totally party at the same time! Bonus.

Lots of medium-sized salad potatoes
1 tbsp butter
Salt and ground black pepper
Leftover mixed cheeses, grated or finely chopped
Ham or tuna (but not for the vegetarian version), sweetcorn, tomatoes, onion or any other favourite fillings
Olive oil

Preheat the oven to 200°C / 400°F / Gas 6

Rinse the potatoes and place on a baking tray. Drizzle with olive oil and cook in the oven for about 30 minutes until soft. Shake the tray regularly to turn them for all an all-over tan.

Remove from the oven, and either cut a cross in each potato or, using an apple corer, carefully remove a small core of potato.

Now you can go off-piste and make up your own filling or mash the potato core with a fork, add a little butter, a pinch of salt and pepper and grated cheese. Mix well and fill the hole in the potato with the new mixture. Or how about replacing the potato with chopped ham or tuna, and cover with a sprinkling of grated cheese – use a strong-flavoured cheese for a great taste. Place the potatoes back in the oven to bake until the cheese is golden. Or why not use either a small spoon or a piping bag, place a small quantity of smooth butter nut squash pâté or mackerel pâté (see pages 234 and 235 for recipes) into the potatoes. Add a sprinkling of mustard leaves or cress to garnish or a thin sliver of cucumber.

SYNIAD SYDYN
QUICK IDEA

DG

Dêts wedi'u stwffio

Rwy'n dwlu ar y Nadolig ac rwy'n dwlu ar ddêts. Felly, ry'n ni'n gwneud y rhain bob Nadolig yn ddi-ffael. Maen nhw mor syml i'w gwneud: does dim angen rysáit, dim ond pecyn o ddêts, marsipán sydd dros ben a photyn o gnau Ffrengig.

Tynnwch y garreg o'r dêt a llenwch y twll â phelen fechan o farsipán a rhowch gneuen Ffrengig ar ei phen. Dyna ni, ac mae'n ddewis iachach na bocs o siocled.

Cofiwch, os oes gennych chi siocled dros ben, gallwch ei doddi a diferu ychydig ohono dros y marsipán cyn ychwanegu'r gneuen Ffrengig – am fersiwn mwy moethus.

GF

Stuffed dates

I love Christmas and I love dates! So, we make these every Christmas without fail.

They are so simple, you don't need a recipe: just a pack of dates, some leftover marzipan and a pot of walnuts.

Remove the stone from the dates and simply fill the cavity with a small ball of marzipan and top with a walnut. That's it, but a much healthier option than a box of chocolates.

Mind you, if you happen to have some leftover chocolate, melt it and drizzle the marzipan with just a small amount of chocolate before adding the walnut for a deluxe version.

PALMIERS

Mae'r palmiers bach hyn yn gegaid melys, ysgafn a chain – rydw i wedi dwlu'n deg arnyn nhw.

1 pecyn o does crwst pwff
Carton mawr o hufen dwbl neu hufen wedi'i chwipio
1 llwy fwrdd o siwgwr eisin
1 llwy de o rinflas fanila
Siwgwr eisin i ysgeintio
Llond llaw o fwyar (dewisol)

Cynheswch i ffwrn i 200°C / 400°F / Nwy 6

Rholiwch y toes, gan geisio cadw'r siâp petryal.

Rholiwch y toes yn dynn, fel Swiss roll, a stopiwch pan gyrhaeddwch y canol. Yna rholiwch o'r pen arall fel eu bod yn cwrdd yn y canol.

Torrwch y toes yn dafelli 1 cm o drwch a'u gosod yn ofalus ar hambwrdd pobi.

Rhowch ddigon o le rhyngddyn nhw i'r toes chwyddo. Pobwch yn y ffwrn am tua 20 munud, hyd nes eu bod yn euraid.

Ar gyfer y llenwad

Rhowch hufen mewn powlen a'i chwisgio hyd nes ei fod yn drwchus. Ychwanegwch y rhinflas fanila a llond llwy de o siwgwr eisin a chwisgiwch eto.

Gosodwch hanner y toes crwst pwff wedi'u coginio ar blât a rhowch lond llwy de o hufen ar ben bob un. Ychwanegwch ddwy neu dair mwyaren neu unrhyw aeron tymhorol, os dymunwch.

Rhowch ychydig bach iawn o hufen ar un o'r teisennau toes eraill, a'i gwasgu ar ben y gyntaf. Ysgeintiwch yn ysgafn â siwgwr eisin.

PALMIERS

These little palmiers are such light, dainty, sweet bites – I have a bit of a crush on them.

1 pack of puff pastry
Large carton of double or whipping cream
1 tbsp icing sugar
1 tsp vanilla essence
Icing sugar for dusting
A handful of blackberries (optional)

Preheat the oven to 200°C / 400°F / Gas 6

Roll out the pastry, trying to keep the rectangular shape.

Now roll the pastry tightly, like a Swiss roll, and stop when you reach the centre. Roll from the other side so that they meet at the middle.

Cut the rolled pastry into 1cm-thick slices and place them gently on a baking tray.

Give them enough room to puff up. Bake in the oven for about 20 minutes, until golden.

For the filling

Put the cream into a bowl and whisk until thickened. Add a teaspoon of vanilla essence and a teaspoon of icing sugar, and whisk again.

Place half the cooked pastry puffs on a plate and add a teaspoon of cream to each. Add two or three blackberries or any seasonal berries if you like.

Place a tiny amount of cream on another pastry and press on top of the first pastry puff, dust lightly with icing sugar.

LL

CORONBLETH O FARA

Dyma goron ar y flwyddyn. Rysáit bara sylfaenol sydd gen i, rwy'n newid y cynnwys yn ôl fy hwyliau ac yn ôl y tywydd. Gallwch ychwanegu unrhyw beth yr hoffech i roi blas.

> 500g blawd bara cryf
> 1 llwy de o halen
> 1 llwy de o siwgwr
> 1 llwy de o furum
> 1 llwy fwrdd o olew olewydd
> 300ml dŵr cynnes neu laeth
> Llond llaw o domatos bach
> Llond llaw o ddail basil

Cymysgwch y blawd, yr halen a'r burum mewn powlen ac ychwanegwch yr olew a'r dŵr. Cymysgwch y cyfan i greu toes.

Tylinwch y toes ar arwyneb â blawd arno am tua 6 munud.

Rhowch y toes mewn powlen, gorchuddiwch â haenen lynu neu liain llestri glân a'i roi am 45 munud yn rhywle cynnes i godi, hyd nes y bydd ddwywaith ei faint.

Ar ôl awr, rhowch y toes ar arwyneb â blawd arno a'i dylino yn ysgafn eto.

I gael siâp coron, gwasgwch y toes gan ddefnyddio'ch dwylo, neu defnyddiwch rolbren os yw'n anodd gwneud â'ch dwylo.

V

A CROWN OF BREAD

This is the year's crowning glory. I'm using a basic bread recipe and I change the ingredients according to my mood and the weather. You can add whatever you fancy to add to the taste.

> 500g strong bread flour
> 1 tsp salt
> 1 tsp sugar
> 1 tsp yeast
> 1 tbsp olive oil
> 300ml tepid water or milk
> A handful of cherry tomatoes
> A handful of basil leaves

Mix the flour, salt and yeast in a bowl. Add the oil and water, and mix to form a dough.

Knead the dough on a floured surface for about 6 minutes.

Place the kneaded dough into a bowl, cover with cling film or clean tea towel and place somewhere warm to rise for about 45 minutes, until it has doubled in size.

After about an hour, tip it out and lightly knead it again, on a floured surface.

To shape the dough into a crown, flatten the dough out using your hands, or use a rolling pin if it resists too much.

> Gorchuddiwch y toes wedi'i wasgu â thomatos bach wedi'u torri a dail basil wedi'u rhwygo ynghyd ag ychydig o halen a phupur.

Rholiwch y toes i fyny gan ddechrau ar yr ochr hiraf. Cydiwch ynddo'n gadarn er mwyn selio'r cynhwysion y tu mewn i'r rôl. Nawr, gan ddefnyddio siswrn mawr neu sgrafellwr bara, torrwch ar hyd canol y toes, ond gan adael y pen yn un darn. Bydd rhai o'r tomoatos yn disgyn allan ond peidiwch â phoeni am hynny.

Dewch â dau hanner y toes at ei gilydd a'u troi, un dros y llall, yn debyg i wneud plethen, ond yn symlach.

Ar y diwedd, dewch â'r ddau ben at ei gilydd a'u cysylltu. Rhowch unrhyw domatos neu ddail basil sydd dros ben yn ôl yn y blethen. Gosodwch hi ar hambwrdd pobi wedi'i iro a'i gorchuddio eto am 30 munud i godi.

Cynheswch y ffwrn i 180ºC / 350ºF / Nwy 4. Pan fydd y toes wedi dyblu ei faint, peintiwch â chymysgedd o felynwy a dŵr, a phobi'r goron am tua 35 munud hyd nes ei bod yn euraid.

 Tip: gwnewch y twll yng nghanol y goron mor fawr ag sy'n bosib, gan y bydd yn cau wrth i'r toes godi.

Tip: gallwch arbrofi â'r siâp a'r steil ac yna, yn olaf, gallwch fynd i'r afael â'r addurno – y sglein a phethau ychwanegol fel hadau a ffrwythau sychion.

Tip: mae menyn garlleg a shibwns yn gwneud llenwad da i'r canol hefyd.

> Cover the flattened dough with chopped cherry tomatoes and torn basil leaves; add a sprinkling of ground salt and pepper.

Roll the dough up, starting at the longest side, and handle firmly to seal the ingredients inside the roll. Now, using a large pair of scissors or a bread scraper, cut the dough right down the middle of the roll, but leave the very top attached. Some of the tomatoes may fall out, but don't worry.

Twist the two halves of the dough together. Just twist them, one side over the other, a little like making a plait, but simpler.

Finally, bring the two ends together and join. Place any tomatoes or basil leaves back into the twist, transfer to an oiled baking tray and cover again for 30 minutes.

Preheat the oven to 180ºC / 350ºF / Gas 4. When the dough has doubled in size, glaze with beaten egg yolk and water mix and bake for up 35 minutes, until golden brown.

 Tip: make the hole in the centre of the crown as large as possible, as it will close up as it proves.

Tip: you can play around with the shape and style of the bread, and you can really get to grips with decorating, using the glaze and adding bits like seeds and dried fruit.

Tip: spring onions and garlic butter make an alternative filling.

Cyngor yn y gegin

Efallai fod y gair darbodus yn swnio'n hen ffasiwn, ond mae bod yn ddarbodus yn golygu bod yn glyfar ac nid cyfaddawdu ar safonau neu ansawdd. Mae'n golygu eich bod chi'n cael mwy am eich arian.
Felly mae'n werth rhoi cynnig arni.

Gwnewch restr

Mae masnachwyr yn gwneud elw anferthol drwy ein harferion prynu mympwyol ni. Maen nhw am i ni brynu'r pethau hanfodol yn ogystal â llond trol o 'fargeinion' na allwn ni eu gadael yn y siop.

Gwiriwch beth sydd gennych yn yr oergell yn barod ...

... ac yn eich cypyrddau cyn i chi adael am y siopau. Os yw'n helpu, mae'n werth ysgrifennu rhestr o'r hyn sydd gennych chi eisoes yn ogystal â gwneud rhestr o'r hyn sydd ei angen arnoch, yna fe allwch fynd i'r afael go iawn â pheidio gor-stocio nwyddau. Mae hyn yn hynod wir am nwyddau darfodus, sydd â bywyd byr, fel ffrwythau meddal a salad, perlysiau a sudd. Pan welwch chi beth sydd gennych chi'n barod, dyna'r amser i feddwl am rysáit i ddefnyddio'r hyn sydd ar fin mynd heibio'i orau, gwnewch dorth fanana er enghraifft, neu darten ffrwythau neu salad i fwyd.

Bara

Peidiwch â thaflu gweddillion bara stêl, malwch nhw mewn prosesydd bwyd i wneud briwsion bara. Malwch fara Ffrengig, paninis neu fara focaccia i wneud briwsion bara o flasau gwahanol, gallwch wneud stwffin neu dopin pastai. Defnyddiwch y briwsion i'w rhoi dros bupur neu fadarch wedi'u stwffio. Gwnewch goujons cyw iâr neu croutons garlleg ar gyfer cawl neu stiw. Mi fyddan nhw'n ddefnyddiol, rwy'n addo.

Cadwch bethau'n dda

Bydd rhai llysiau a ffrwythau'n cadw'n well mewn lle tywyll, oer yn hytrach na mewn oergell. Peidiwch â rhoi bananas, afocado a basil yn yr oergell, fe fyddan nhw'n troi'n ddu a llaith yno. Gwell cadw gwreiddlysiau fel moron, pannas, rwdins a thatws y mewn lle oer a thywyll yn hytrach nag yn yr oergell.

Lemwn

Os oes gennych chi hanner lemwn yn yr oergell, peidiwch â'i adael yno hyd nes y bydd wedi sychu allan ac ffit i ddim byd heblaw am y bin compost. Sleisiwch y lemwn yn denau a'i rewi, yn barod ar gyfer diodydd. Defnyddiwch yr haenau lemwn yn syth o'r rhewgell – bydd y lemwn yn ffres ac yn oeri'ch diod ar yr un pryd.

Kitchen tips

Being thrifty may sound old fashioned, but being thrifty is also being clever. It doesn't mean compromising on standards or quality, it simply means you get more for your money. So it's well worth a try.

Make a list
Retailers make their vast profits on our impulse buys. They really want us to purchase the essentials as well as a load of additional 'bargains' and things we simply can't leave behind.

Check what you already have in the fridge ...
... and in the cupboards before you leave for the shops. If it helps, it's worth writing a list of what you have in addition to what you need, then you really can prevent overstocking. This is especially true for perishables, the things that have a short shelf life such as soft fruits and salads, herbs and juices. When you see what you have already, that's also the time to conjure up a recipe idea to use up what's about to go off, make a banana loaf for example or a mixed fruit pie or a salad for tea.

Bread
Don't just throw the stale loaf ends away, blitz them in a blender or food processor to make bread crumbs. Blitz French sticks, paninis, or a focaccia bread for tasty and different flavoured bread crumbs for making stuffing and pie toppings. Use them to top stuffed peppers and mushrooms. Make homemade chicken goujons or garlic croutons for soups and stews. They will come in handy, I promise.

Store things well
Root vegetables and certain fruit store better in a cool, dark place rather than in the fridge. Never put bananas, avocados and basil in the fridge, as they will turn black and soggy. Root vegetables such as carrots and parsnips, swede and potatoes are better stored out of the fridge, but somewhere cool and dark.

Lemons
If you have half a lemon in the fridge, don't leave it there till it's all dried out and ready for the compost bin. Slice it up thinly, and freeze, ready for drinks. Use the lemon straight from the freezer and this way the lemon stays fresh and it cools your drink at the same time.

Cyngor yn y gegin

Gwnewch fenyn perlysieuol

Dyma ffordd wych o arbed a chadw perlysiau'r haf fel basil a mintys o'r ardd at ddefnydd yn y gaeaf. Malwch y perlysiau a'u cymysgu'n dda mewn menyn meddal wedi'i adael ar dymheredd yr ystafell. Gosodwch y menyn meddal ar haenen lynu a'i rolio'n ofalus i wneud siâp selsigen. Trowch y ddau ben a'i roi yn yr oergell nes y bydd yn galed. Yna gallwch ei sleisio'n dafelli bach a'u cadw yn y rhegwell nes y byddwch yn barod i'w ddefnyddio. Cofiwch labeli'r pot oherwydd, unwaith eu bod wedi'u rhewi, fyddwch chi ddim yn medru'u hadnabod wrth eu haroglu.

Rhewi perlysiau

Yn hytrach na rhoi perlysiau yn yr oergell yn y gobaith y defnyddiwch chi nhw yn y pen draw, torrwch nhw'n fân a'u gosod mewn bagiau neu botiau bychain a'u rhoi yn syth yn y rhewgell. Defnyddiwch nhw ar gyfer cawl neu stiw.

Dwbwl y cynnyrch, hanner y gwaith

Mae'n llawn cymaint o waith i wneud un lasagne ag ydyw i wneud dau. Pan fyddwch chi'n gwneud teisen sgwâr neu stiw neu gawl, beth am ddefnyddio dwbwl y cynnyrch a gwneud dau ar y tro. Bwytewch un a chadw'r llall yn y rhegwell ar gyfer diwrnod arall. Efallai na fyddwch chi'n arbed llawer o arian ond fe fyddwch chi'n arbed amser ac egni. A does dim yn well na chladdu pryd blasus gan wybod na fuoch chi wrthi yn y gegin y diwrnod hwnnw yn ei wneud. Mae dod adref i'ch prydau parod eich hunan yn golygu nad oes rhaid i chi alw yn yr archfarchnad i brynu rhywbeth ar y ffordd adre. Does dim sosbenni a llestri paratoi i'w golchi chwaith.

Caws

Mae'r rhan fwyaf o gawsiau Cheddar a Stilton yn rhewi'n iawn. Prynwch ddigonedd ar y tro, ei dorri'n ddarnau a'i rewi nes bod ei angen arnoch. Gratiwch friwsion a manion cawsiau gwahanol ac yna'u rhannu nhw. Defnyddiwch nhw i'w hychwanegu at sawsiau neu pizzas.

Make a herby butter

A great way to save and preserve summer herbs such as basil and garden mint for use in the winter, is to make your own herby butter. Chop the herbs up and mix well into some soft butter, left at room temperature. Place the soft butter on a sheet of clingfilm and carefully roll to make a sausage shape. Twist the ends and refrigerate until firm, then slice into little patties and store in the freezer until needed. Don't forget to label the pot, once frozen you won't be able to smell the herb or identify one from any other.

Freezing herbs

Rather than putting herbs in the fridge in the hope that you may use them eventually, chop them up and place them into small bags or containers and pop them straight into the freezer. Use them in soups and stews.

Double up and save yourself some work

It's as much work to make one lasagne as it is to make two lasagnes. When you make a tray bake or a stew or a soup, try doubling up the ingredients and making two at a time. Eat one and put the other in the freezer for another day. This won't necessarily save you lots of money, but it will save time and energy. There is nothing better that tucking into a delicious meal that you didn't even make that day. Coming home to your very own ready meal, means you don't have to call in the supermarket to buy something on the way home. There are no pots and pans to wash either.

Cheese

Most Cheddar cheeses and Stilton freeze perfectly. Buy in bulk, cut up into chunks and freeze until you need it. Grate little odds and ends of different cheeses and them freeze them, use to add to sauces and pizza.

Nodiadau Notes

TABLAU TRAWSNEWID
CONVERSION TABLES

PWYSAU / WEIGHTS

IMPERIAL	METRIG / METRIC
½ oz	10 g
¾ oz	20 g
1 oz	25 g
1½ oz	40 g
2 oz	50 g
2½ oz	60 g
3 oz	75 g
4 oz	110 g
4½ oz	125 g
5 oz	150 g
6 oz	175 g
7 oz	200 g
8 oz	225 g
9 oz	250 g
10 oz	275 g
12 oz	350 g
1 lb	450 g
1 lb 8 oz	700 g
2 lb	900 g
3 lb	1.35 kg

HYLIF / LIQUID

IMPERIAL	METRIG / METRIC
2 fl oz	55 ml
3 fl oz	75 ml
5 fl oz (¼ peint / pint)	150 ml
10 fl oz (½ peint / pint)	275 ml
1 peint / pint	570 ml
1 ¼ peint / pint	725 ml
1 ¾ peint / pint	1 litr / litre
2 peint / pint	1.2 litr / litre
2½ peint / pint	1.5 litr / litre
4 peint / pint	2.25 litr / litres

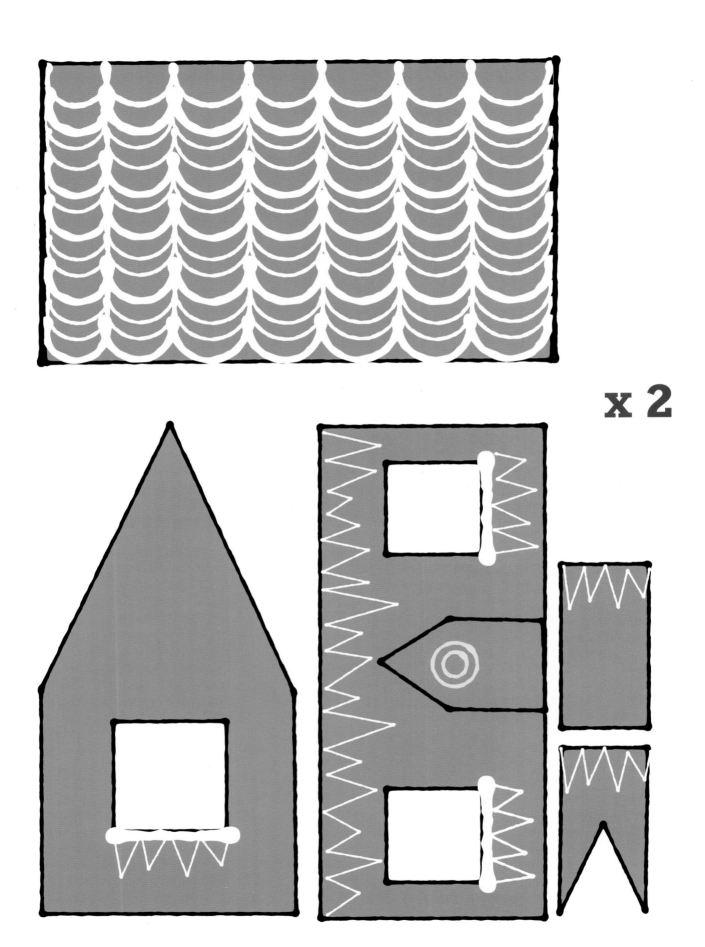

x 2

Rwy wedi mwynhau rhannu fy
nghegin a 'ngardd gyda chi mas
draw. Gadewch i ni wneud yr un
peth flwyddyn nesa!

....

I've really enjoyed sharing my
kitchen and garden with you.
Let's do it again next year!

TASCHEN's FAVOURITE
HOTELS

Hot Coffee

Cappuchino
Espresso
Chocolate
Latte
Mocca
Americano

Angelika Taschen

TASCHEN's FAVOURITE
HOTELS

1

TASCHEN

UK, The Bath Priory 26

CA, Wickaninnish Inn 292

CA, Hôtel de Glace 298

US, Sunset Beach 308

ES, Hotel Hurricane 118

PT, Pousada de Amares 122

US, Bedford Post 304

US, The Historic Hotel Congress 324

US, The Jane 314

US, Amangiri 330

MA, Hôtel Nord-Pinus Tanger 144

US, El Capitan Canyon 334

MA, Hôtel La Mamounia 152

US, Casa Malibu Inn on the Beach 338

318 El Cosmico, US

MA, Ksar Char-Bagh 158

US, Ace Hotel Palm Springs 342

MX, Verana 348

MX, Condesa DF 356

382 Golden Rock Estate, KN

MX, Distrito Capital 364

MX, La Purificadora 370

BZ, Blancaneaux Lodge 376

388 Uxua Casa Hotel, B

CL, Awasi 428

398 Hotel Fasano, BR

416 Yacutinga Lodge, AR

404 El Garzón, UY

AR, Tipiliuke 422

410 Casa Zinc Posada, UY

CL, Indigo 432

CL, Remota 438

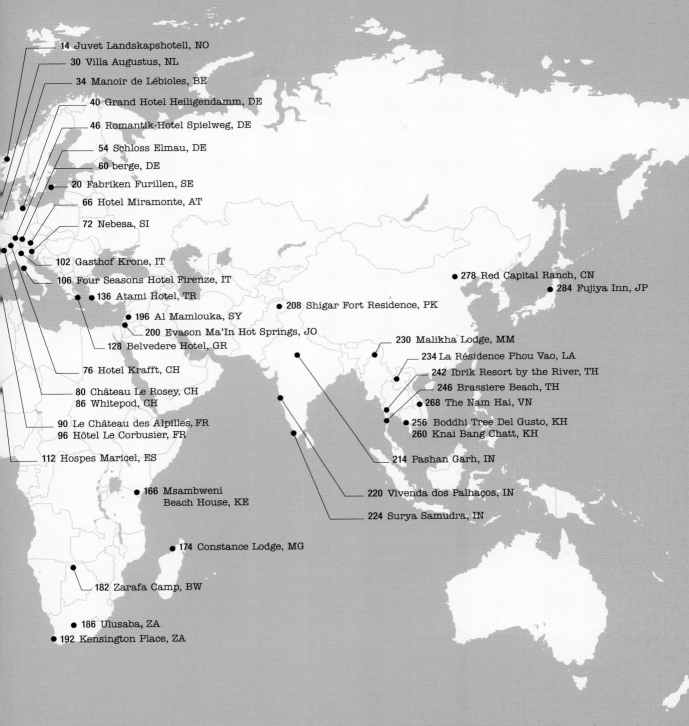

14 Juvet Landskapshotell, NO
30 Villa Augustus, NL
34 Manoir de Lébioles, BE
40 Grand Hotel Heiligendamm, DE
46 Romantik-Hotel Spielweg, DE
54 Schloss Elmau, DE
60 berge, DE
20 Fabriken Furillen, SE
66 Hotel Miramonte, AT
72 Nebesa, SI
102 Gasthof Krone, IT
106 Four Seasons Hotel Firenze, IT
136 Atami Hotel, TR
196 Al Mamlouka, SY
200 Evason Ma'In Hot Springs, JO
128 Belvedere Hotel, GR
76 Hotel Krafft, CH
80 Château Le Rosey, CH
86 Whitepod, CH
90 Le Château des Alpilles, FR
96 Hôtel Le Corbusier, FR
112 Hospes Maricel, ES
166 Msambweni Beach House, KE
174 Constance Lodge, MG
182 Zarafa Camp, BW
186 Ulusaba, ZA
192 Kensington Place, ZA
208 Shigar Fort Residence, PK
278 Red Capital Ranch, CN
284 Fujiya Inn, JP
230 Malikha Lodge, MM
234 La Résidence Phou Vao, LA
242 Ibrik Resort by the River, TH
246 Brassiere Beach, TH
268 The Nam Hai, VN
256 Boddhi Tree Del Gusto, KH
260 Knai Bang Chatt, KH
214 Pashan Garh, IN
220 Vivenda dos Palhaços, IN
224 Surya Samudra, IN

Now is Here

by Angelika Taschen

Living in the here and now is a great art that is much easier said than done in our information and stimulus-overloaded world. Billions of e-mails are sent every year along with innumerable text messages, tweets and Facebook news items. Instead of taking time for reflection, we are constantly drowning in this flood of multi-tasking.

Thank goodness there are still places where one can disconnect from the daily grind to concentrate on immersing ourselves in the beauty of the present. I would like to share just a few of these very special places with you in this book.

As you leaf through these pages, your journey begins with the most wonderful hotels in the most beautiful areas of the world. Some of the selected hotels are elegant and minimal; others are delightfully frivolous or tradition conscious. Regardless of whether your heart beats for a pulsing metropolis or for a secluded retreat surrounded by pristine nature, here you will find plenty of rooms and suites in which to pause for thought.

What all these hotels have in common are their distinctive character, their individuality and their stunning locations. In each of them you can dive right into a new atmosphere, switch off with a good book (a book to pack is recommended for each hotel) and truly arrive at your intended destination in a remarkably short space of time.

Happily, these wonderful moments are not tied to the price of the hotel room: you can lose yourself in another world just as easily by drinking a cup of tea on a colonial guesthouse terrace in Phnom Penh (rooms for under 40 dollars) as by watching the starry desert sky from architect Rick Joy's luxurious Amangiri in Utah, where guests pay up to 3,500 dollars per night.

This unusual mix of two- to five-star hotels ranges from the romantic hotel Spielweg in the Black Forest – where everyone should have the opportunity of spending at least one Christmas – to the Shigar Fort Residence, a four-hundred-year-old palace in north Pakistan, salvaged and restored by the Aga Khan Foundation.

Further insider tips include the Al Mamlouka in the middle of Damascus's fantastic souk, the Evason Ma'In spa hotel in Jordan fed by its own natural hot springs and the beach villas of the Knai Bang Chatt Resort that look as if they could have been built by the legendary architect Le Corbusier himself.

For those in search of "Splendid Isolation", I recommend the Bedford Post, owned by Richard Gere and his wife Carey Lowell, in the country north of New York, or the Golden Rock Estate on the Caribbean island of Nevis that belongs to the American artists Helen and Brice Marden. And finally, nobody who has visited Remota, amidst the mountains, lakes and glaciers of Chilean Patagonia, is ever likely to forget their stay there.

So dive into the here and now and enjoy the journey.

Jetzt im Hier

von Angelika Taschen

Im Hier und Jetzt zu sein, ist eine ganz große Kunst und viel einfacher gesagt als getan, in einer Welt der totalen Reiz- und Informationsüberflutung. Jährlich werden Milliarden E-Mails verschickt, hinzu kommen zahllose SMS, Tweets und Facebook-Nachrichten; statt zur Besinnung zu kommen, verlieren wir uns ständig im Multitasking.

Glücklicherweise gibt es ein paar Orte, an denen man, losgelöst vom Alltag, schneller und besser in die Gegenwart eintauchen kann. Und einige dieser besonderen Plätze habe ich für Sie in dem vorliegenden Buch zusammengestellt.

Bereits beim Durchblättern gehen Sie auf die Reise, in die wundervollsten Hotels in den schönsten Gegenden der Welt. Einige der ausgewählten Hotels sind edel und minimalistisch, andere herrlich plüschig oder traditionsbewusst mit der Region verbunden. Ganz gleich ob Sie pulsierende Metropolen bevorzugen oder ein einsames Refugium inmitten unberührter Natur suchen – hier finden Sie Zimmer oder Suiten, in denen Sie innehalten können.

Allen Häusern gemeinsam ist ihr Charakter, ihre Individualität und die ausgezeichnete Lage. Man taucht sofort ein in eine neue Atmosphäre, kann mit einem passenden Buch im Gepäck (zu jedem Hotel gibt es einen ausgewählten Buchtipp) abschalten und ist in kürzester Zeit im Hier angekommen.

Zum Glück sind diese wunderbaren Momente unabhängig vom Preis der Hotels. So kann man bei einer Tasse Tee auf der Terrasse des kolonialen Gästehauses in Phnom Penh – Zimmerpreis unter 30 Euro – ebenso leicht in eine andere Welt abtauchen wie beim Betrachten des Sternenhimmels über dem vom Wüstenarchitekten Rick Joy erbauten luxuriösen Amangiri in Utah, wo der Gast pro Nacht bis zu 2.850 Euro zahlt.

In der ausgefallenen Mischung von Zwei-Sterne- bis Fünf-Sterne-Hotels enthalten sind das romantische Hotel Spielweg im Schwarzwald, wo jeder mindestens einmal im Leben die Weihnachtszeit verbringen sollte; die Shigar Fort Residence, ein vierhundert Jahre alter Palast im Norden von Pakistan, der von der Aga Khan Foundation vor dem Verfall gerettet und restauriert wurde.

Weitere Geheimtipps sind das Al Mamlouka in Damaskus mit seinem fantastischen Souk; das von natürlichen heißen Quellen gespeiste Spa-Hotel Evason Ma'In in Jordanien und die Strandvillen des Knai Bang Chatt Resort in Kambodscha, die wirken, als hätte sie der legendäre Architekt Le Corbusier gebaut.

Wer »Splendid Isolation« sucht, dem empfehle ich auf dem Land das Bedford Post nördlich von New York, das Richard Gere und seine Frau Carey Lowell besitzen, oder das Golden Rock Estate auf der Karibikinsel Nevis, das den amerikanischen Künstlern Helen und Brice Marden gehört. Und niemand, der je im Remota im chilenischen Patagonien inmitten von Bergen, Seen und Gletschern gewohnt hat, wird seinen Aufenthalt jemals vergessen.

Tauchen Sie einfach ein ins Hier und Jetzt und genießen Sie die Reise.

Ici et maintenant

par Angelika Taschen

Rester ancré dans le moment présent, l'exercice est difficile – c'est en effet moins simple qu'il n'y paraît dans un monde inondé de stimuli et d'informations. Tous les ans, des milliards de courriels sont envoyés, sans compter les innombrables SMS, les tweets et les informations de Facebook – au lieu de nous recentrer, nous ne cessons de nous égarer dans le multitraitement.

Il existe par bonheur des lieux où l'on peut, détaché du quotidien, s'immerger plus rapidement et plus effectivement dans l'instant présent. Et vous pourrez découvrir certains de ces endroits particuliers au fil des pages qui suivent.

Feuilleter ce livre, c'est déjà partir en voyage, séjourner dans les hôtels les plus fantastiques des plus belles régions de la planète. Certains des établissements choisis marient l'élégance au minimalisme, d'autres sont divinement kitsch ou – tradition oblige – liés à la contrée où ils sont situés. Que vous ayez un faible pour les métropoles trépidantes ou que vous cherchiez un refuge à l'écart en pleine nature – vous trouverez ici des chambres ou des suites dans lesquelles vous pourrez faire une pause.

Tous ces hôtels ont en commun une personnalité originale et une situation excellente. L'arrivant baigne immédiatement dans une ambiance nouvelle, peut se changer les idées en lisant un ouvrage glissé dans ses bagages (une lecture appropriée est signalée dans chaque description d'hôtel) et toucher au terme de son voyage en un temps record.

Ces moments merveilleux ne dépendent heureusement pas des tarifs pratiqués. On peut s'évader aussi facilement en buvant une tasse de thé à la terrasse de la maison d'hôtes coloniale de Phnom Penh – la chambre y coûte moins de 30 euros – qu'en regardant le ciel étoilé au-dessus du luxueux Amangiri construit dans l'Utah par l'architecte du désert Rick Joy, où il faut débourser jusqu'à 2850 euros la nuitée.

Dans ce mélange insolite de deux, trois, quatre et cinq étoiles, on trouve le romantique hôtel Spielweg en Forêt Noire – il faudrait y passer Noël au moins une fois dans sa vie –, le Shigar Fort Residence, un palais édifié il y a quatre siècles dans le nord du Pakistan, que l'Aga Khan Foundation a sauvé de la ruine et restauré.

D'autres adresses confidentielles sont l'Al Mamlouka à Damas avec son souk fantastique, l'hôtel-spa jordanien Evason Ma'In, alimenté par des sources d'eau chaude naturelles, et les villas de plage du Knai Bang Chatt au Cambodge, dont on dirait qu'elles ont été construites par l'architecte légendaire Le Corbusier.

Si vous préférez la « Splendid Isolation », vous apprécierez le Bedford Post de Richard Gere et de sa femme, situé à la campagne, au nord de New York, ou le Golden Rock Estate sur l'île Niévès dans les Caraïbes, propriété des artistes américains Helen et Brice Marden. Enfin, le Remota, entouré de montagnes, de lacs et de glaciers en Patagonie chilienne, a laissé un souvenir impérissable à tous ceux qui y ont séjourné.

Vivez tout simplement ici et maintenant et jouissez de votre voyage.

Angelika Taschen

Europe

● 14 Juvet Landskapshotell, NO

SE, Fabriken Furillen 20 ●

● 40 Grand Hotel Heiligendamm, DE

● 30 Villa Augustus, NL

● 34 Manoir de Lébioles, BE

46 Romantik-Hotel Spielweg, DE

54 Schloss Elmau, DE

60 berge, DE

CH, Hotel Krafft 76

CH, Château Le Rosey 80 ●

● 66 Hotel Miramonte, AT

72 Nebesa, SI

CH, Whitepod 86

Le Château
● 90 des Alpilles, FR

102 Gasthof Krone, IT

● 106 Four Seasons Hotel Firenze, IT

96 Hôtel Le Corbusier, FR

● 112 Hospes Maricel, ES

GR, Belvedere Hotel 128 ●

TR, Atami Hotel 136

Juvet Landskapshotell

Valldal, Norddal, Norway

There is nothing here but forests of birch, aspen and pine, rocks worn smooth by river water and the Juvet. The architects Jensen & Skodvin have designed each room as a wooden cube with one or two walls made completely of glass. Here you can immerse yourself in the bosom of Mother Nature and allow yourself to be fascinated by her constantly changing colours, light and atmosphere.

Hier gibt es nur Wälder aus Birken, Espen und Kiefern; Felsen, die vom Flusswasser geschliffen sind – und das Juvet. Jedes Zimmer haben die Architekten Jensen & Skodvin als Holzkubus mit ein oder zwei Glaswänden konzipiert. Durch sie blickt man direkt in die Natur und lässt sich vom ständigen Wechsel ihrer Farben, des Lichts und der Stimmungen faszinieren.

Il n'y a ici que des forêts de bouleaux, de trembles et de pins, des rochers érodés par la rivière – et le Juvet. Les architectes Jensen & Skodvin ont conçu chaque chambre comme un cube en bois ayant une ou deux parois en verre. On a ainsi une vue imprenable sur la nature, fascinante avec les variations de ses couleurs, de la lumière et de l'atmosphère.

Juvet Landskapshotell
Alstad
6210 Valldal
Norway
Tel. +47 9503 2010
knut@juvet.com
www.juvet.com
Open from March to December

LOCATION
Situated near the Geiranger Fjord, 62 miles southeast of Ålesund airport and 310 miles northwest of Oslo.

RATES
Rooms from $420, breakfast included. Minimum stay is 2 nights.

ROOMS
7 rooms.

FOOD
Part of the hotel is what used to be one of the oldest farmhouses in the area. Rustic Norwegian fare is served in the former stables.

X-FACTOR
In summer there is hiking, in winter skiing, and all year round you can relax in the spa fed by St Olav's spring waters.

BOOK TO PACK
"Sophie's World" by Jostein Gaarder.

LAGE
Nahe des Geirangerfjords gelegen, 100 km südöstlich des Flughafens Ålesund, 500 km nordwestlich von Oslo.

PREISE
Zimmer ab 300 €, inklusive Frühstück. Mindestaufenthalt 2 Nächte.

ZIMMER
7 Zimmer.

KÜCHE
Zum Hotel gehört einer der ältesten Bauernhöfe der Gegend. Im ehemaligen Stall serviert das Restaurant rustikale norwegische Gerichte.

X-FAKTOR
Im Sommer kann man wandern, im Winter Ski laufen – und rund ums Jahr im von der St.-Olavs-Quelle gespeisten Spa entspannen.

BUCHTIPP
»Sofies Welt« von Jostein Gaarder.

SITUATION
Situé près du fjord de Geiranger, à 100 km au sud-est de l'aéroport Ålesund et à 500 km au nord-ouest d'Oslo.

PRIX
Chambre à partir de 300 €, petit-déjeuner compris. Séjour minimum : 2 nuits.

CHAMBRES
7 chambres.

RESTAURATION
L'une des plus vieilles fermes de la région fait partie de l'hôtel. Le restaurant propose des plats norvégiens rustiques dans l'ancienne étable.

LE « PETIT PLUS »
Randonnées en été, ski en hiver et spa toute l'année alimenté par les eaux de la source St Olav.

LIVRE À EMPORTER
« Le Monde de Sophie » de Jostein Gaarder.

Fabriken Furillen

Furillen, Gotland, Sweden

Anna-Karin and Johan Hellström opened this hotel, with its fascinating backdrop of a 1970s abandoned stone quarry, in 2000. The rooms in the former factory building combine an industrial atmosphere with classic Scandinavian design, and the tasteful, subdued colour scheme highlights the power and beauty of the landscape.

Vor der faszinierenden Kulisse eines in den 1970er Jahren stillgelegten Steinbruchs haben Anna-Karin und Johan Hellström im Jahr 2000 dieses Hotel eröffnet. Die Räume in den einstigen Fabrikbauten verbinden Industrieflair und klassisches skandinavisches Design in zurückhaltenden Farbnuancen – so sollen Stärke und Schönheit der Natur noch mehr betont werden.

En 2000, Anna-Karin et Johan Hellström ont ouvert cet hôtel devant une carrière désaffectée au cours des années 1970 et qui offrent un décor fascinant. Les salles de l'ancienne usine marient la touche industrielle et le design classique scandinave dans une palette toute en retenue, car rien ne doit troubler la force et la beauté de la nature.

Fabriken Furillen
62458 Lärbro
Gotland
Sweden
Tel. +46 498 223 040
Fax +46 498 223 041
fabriken@furillen.com
www.furillen.nu
Open in April & May for groups,
from June to September for
individual guests

LOCATION
Situated on Furillen Island on the
north coast of Gotland. The nearest
village is Lärbro, 25 miles northeast
of Visby airport.

RATES
Rooms from $270, breakfast included.

ROOMS
18 rooms.

FOOD
Delicious Swedish specialities made
from local, seasonal products.

X-FACTOR
If the hotel is not isolated enough for
you, there are also six wooden hermit
huts or an Airstream mobile home to
choose from.

BOOK TO PACK
"Sidetracked" by Henning Mankell.

LAGE
Auf der Insel Furillen an Gotlands
Nordostküste gelegen. Der nächste
Ort ist Lärbro, 40 km nordöstlich des
Flughafens Visby.

PREISE
Zimmer ab 200 €, inklusive Frühstück.

ZIMMER
18 Zimmer.

KÜCHE
Leckere schwedische Spezialitäten mit
saisonalen Produkten aus der Region.

X-FAKTOR
Wer nicht im Hotel wohnen möchte,
kann in eine von sechs einsam gelegenen
Eremiten-Holzhütten oder in einen
Airstream-Wohnwagen ziehen.

BUCHTIPP
»Die falsche Fährte« von Henning Mankell.

SITUATION
Situé sur l'île de Furillen au large de
la côte nord-est de Gotland. L'endroit
le plus proche est Lärbro, à 40 km au
nord-est de l'aéroport de Visby.

PRIX
Chambre à partir de 200 €, petit-
déjeuner compris.

CHAMBRES
18 chambres.

RESTAURATION
De savoureuses spécialités suédoises
préparées avec des produits de la
région.

LE « PETIT PLUS »
Celui qui ne désire pas séjourner à
l'hôtel peut s'installer dans l'une des
six cabanes situées à l'écart ou dans
une caravane Airstream.

LIVRE À EMPORTER
« Le Guerrier solitaire » de Henning
Mankell.

The Bath Priory

Bath, Somerset, England, United Kingdom

With its elegant terraced houses and Roman thermal springs, Bath is one of England's most picturesque cities – and The Bath Priory is its most stylish hotel. It was built in 1835 on land belonging to the city's Abbey. With its Victorian gardens and romantic, classic English interiors designed by Carole Roberts, this hotel is just perfect for a weekend getaway for two.

Mit seinen eleganten Häuserzeilen und römischen Thermen ist Bath eine der schönsten Städte Englands – und The Bath Priory ihr stilvollstes Hotel. Es wurde 1835 auf einem Grundstück der Abtei erbaut und ist mit seinem viktorianischen Park und seinen von Carole Roberts romantisch-britisch eingerichteten Zimmern wie geschaffen für ein Wochenende zu zweit.

Avec ses maisons élégantes et ses thermes romains, Bath est l'une des plus belles villes d'Angleterre – et The Bath Priory, son hôtel le plus chic. Construit en 1835 sur un terrain de l'abbaye, il est idéal pour un week-end en amoureux avec son parc victorien et ses chambres au romantisme très british, aménagées par Carole Roberts.

The Bath Priory Hotel,
Restaurant & Spa
Weston Road
Bath
BA1 2XT
United Kingdom
Tel. +44 1225 331 922
Fax +44 1225 448 276
mail@thebathpriory.co.uk
www.thebathpriory.co.uk

LOCATION
Bath is situated 12 miles southeast of Bristol and 102 miles west of London's Heathrow airport.

RATES
Rooms from $290 and suites from $520, breakfast included.

ROOMS
27 rooms and 4 suites. The "Heather" and "Lilac" rooms are particularly picturesque with private balconies overlooking the park.

FOOD
The award-winning restaurant is as excellent as it is elegant. It offers innovative dishes with local products from the southwest of England.

X-FACTOR
The "Garden Spa" with its delightful park views.

BOOK TO PACK
"Tess of the d'Urbervilles" by Thomas Hardy (the 1979 film version by Roman Polanski has Nastassja Kinski in the starring role).

LAGE
Bath liegt 20 km südöstlich von Bristol und 165 km westlich des Flughafens London Heathrow.

PREISE
Zimmer ab 215 €, Suite ab 380 €, inklusive Frühstück.

ZIMMER
27 Zimmer und 4 Suiten. Sehr malerisch sind die Räume »Heather« und »Lilac« mit privaten Balkonen zum Park.

KÜCHE
Das mehrfach ausgezeichnete Restaurant ist so elegant wie exzellent – es bietet innovative Menüs mit Produkten aus Englands Südwesten.

X-FAKTOR
Das »Garden Spa« mit Blick ins Grüne.

BUCHTIPP
»Tess« von Thomas Hardy (wurde 1979 von Roman Polanski mit Nastassja Kinski in der Hauptrolle verfilmt).

SITUATION
Bath se trouve à 20 km au sud-est de Bristol et à 165 km à l'ouest de l'aéroport de Londres Heathrow.

PRIX
Chambre à partir de 215 €, suite à partir de 380 €, petit-déjeuner compris.

CHAMBRES
27 chambres et 4 suites. Les chambres « Heather » et « Lilac » sont très pittoresques avec leur balcon donnant sur le parc.

RESTAURATION
Le restaurant plusieurs fois primé est aussi élégant qu'excellent. Il propose des menus innovateurs avec des produits du Sud-Ouest de l'Angleterre.

LE « PETIT PLUS »
Le « Garden Spa » avec vue sur la verdure.

LIVRE À EMPORTER
« Tess d'Urberville » de Thomas Hardy (le roman a été porté à l'écran en 1979 par Roman Polanski avec Nastassja Kinski dans le rôle principal).

Villa Augustus
Dordrecht, Holland, The Netherlands

In 2007, Dorine de Vos converted Dordrecht's 19th-century water tower, with its 360-degree view of the city and its canals, into what is now called the "Villa Augustus". The interior mixes antiques with modern design classics such as Eames and Mies van der Rohe chairs. Outside there is a delightful garden that serves as inspiration to the in-house chef.

Den Wasserturm von Dordrecht, der seit Ende des 19. Jahrhunderts über die Kanäle rings um die Stadt blickt, verwandelte Dorine de Vos 2007 in die Villa Augustus. Innen kombinierte sie Antiquitäten und Designklassiker wie Stühle von Eames und Mies van der Rohe; außen entstand ein herrlicher Garten, von dem sich der Küchenchef täglich neu inspirieren lässt.

C'est en 2007 que Dorine de Vos a transformé en Villa Augustus le château d'eau de Dordrecht, qui domine les canaux de la ville depuis la fin du 19ᵉ siècle. À l'intérieur, elle a marié des antiquités et des classiques du design comme les chaises d'Eames et de Mies van der Rohe ; à l'extérieur, elle a créé un merveilleux jardin qui est une source d'inspiration quotidienne pour le chef de cuisine.

Villa Augustus
Oranjelaan 7
3311 DH Dordrecht
The Netherlands
Tel. +31 78 639 3111
info@villa-augustus.nl
www.villa-augustus.nl

LOCATION
Dordrecht is located 19 miles southwest
of Rotterdam.

RATES
Rooms from $170, excluding breakfast.

ROOMS
37 rooms, 20 of which are situated in
the old tower. On a clear day, you can
see all the way to Rotterdam from the
top floor.

FOOD
The open-plan kitchen is centred around
a wood-fired oven. The vegetable dishes
as well as the ever-changing range of
pizzas on offer are delicious.

X-FACTOR
The villa owns two boats that are
available for excursions around
Dordrecht's waterways.

BOOK TO PACK
"The Discovery of Heaven" by Harry
Mulisch.

LAGE
Dordrecht liegt 30 km südöstlich von
Rotterdam.

PREISE
Zimmer ab 125 €, ohne Frühstück.

ZIMMER
37 Zimmer. 20 davon liegen im alten
Turm – aus der obersten Etage sieht
man an klaren Tagen bis nach
Rotterdam.

KÜCHE
Herzstück der offenen Küche ist ein
Holzofen; die Gemüsegerichte sowie
die immer wieder neu variierten Pizzen
schmecken ausgezeichnet.

X-FAKTOR
Die Villa besitzt zwei Boote für Rund-
fahrten über Dordrechts Wasserwege.

BUCHTIPP
»Die Entdeckung des Himmels« von
Harry Mulisch.

SITUATION
Dordrecht se trouve à 30 km au sud-est
de Rotterdam.

PRIX
Chambre à partir de 125 €, sans petit-
déjeuner.

CHAMBRES
37 chambres dont 20 dans la vieille
tour – quand le temps est dégagé, on
peut voir jusqu'à Rotterdam depuis le
dernier étage.

RESTAURATION
Le four au feu de bois est le cœur de
la cuisine ouverte. Les plats de légumes
et les pizzas aux saveurs toujours
renouvelées sont délicieux.

LE « PETIT PLUS »
La Villa possède deux bateaux pour des
excursions sur les canaux de Dordrecht.

LIVRE À EMPORTER
« La Découverte du ciel » de Harry
Mulisch.

Manoir de Lébioles

Spa, Ardennes, Belgium

This castle was built by an illegitimate son of King Leopold I as a "little Versailles in the Ardennes" (1905–1910). A merchant family later used it for their hunts and balls. In 2006, the residence became a hotel, where guests can now enjoy four-poster beds, fireplaces and a terrace with views across the park. Thanks to the discreet service, this is a perfect place to unwind.

Ein unehelicher Sohn König Leopolds I. ließ dieses Schlösschen als »kleines Versailles der Ardennen« erbauen (1905–1910); später lud eine Kaufmannsfamilie hier zu Bällen und Jagdveranstaltungen ein. Seit 2006 ist das Anwesen ein elegantes Hotel, in dem man Himmelbetten, offene Kamine und eine wunderschöne Terrasse mit herrlichem Blick über den Park sowie einen höchst diskreten Service genießt. Perfekt zum Abschalten.

Sur les hauteurs de Spa, « Le petit Versailles des Ardennes » a été construit par un fils naturel du roi Léopold Ier (1905–1910). Plus tard il a appartenu à une famille de commerçants qui donnait ici des bals et des parties de chasse. Depuis 2006 le domaine est un hôtel élégant qui abrite des lits à baldaquin, des cheminées et est doté d'une superbe terrasse avec vue sur le parc. Tout cela et le service discret invitent à la détente.

Manoir de Lébioles – Hotel, Spa,
Wellness & Restaurant
Domaine de Lébioles 1/5
4900 Spa (Creppe)
Belgium
Tel. +32 87 791 900
Fax +32 87 791 999
manoir@manoirdelebioles.com
www.manoirdelebioles.com

LOCATION
Idyllically situated in the hills surrounding Spa, 80 miles west of Cologne and 87 miles east of Brussels.

RATES
Rooms from $240, suites from $350, excluding breakfast.

ROOMS
16 rooms and suites.

FOOD
The gourmet restaurant serves excellent regional dishes with fresh ingredients from the market and has a well-appointed wine cellar.

X-FACTOR
The Asian-inspired spa.

BOOK TO PACK
"Maigret on Holiday" by Georges Simenon.

LAGE
Idyllisch in den Hügeln von Spa gelegen, 130 km westlich von Köln, 140 km östlich von Brüssel.

PREISE
Zimmer ab 179 €, Suite ab 259 €, ohne Frühstück.

ZIMMER
16 Zimmer und Suiten.

KÜCHE
Das Gourmetrestaurant serviert sehr feine regionale Menüs mit Zutaten frisch vom Markt und besitzt einen gut sortierten Weinkeller.

X-FAKTOR
Das asiatisch inspirierte Spa.

BUCHTIPP
»Maigret macht Ferien« von Georges Simenon.

SITUATION
Situé dans les collines idylliques de Spa, à 130 km à l'ouest de Cologne et à 140 km à l'est de Bruxelles.

PRIX
Chambres à partir de 179 €, suite à partir de 259 €, sans petit-déjeuner.

CHAMBRES
16 chambres et suites.

RESTAURATION
Le restaurant gastronomique propose des menus régionaux d'une grande finesse préparés avec des produits du marché et possède une cave à vins bien assortie.

LE « PETIT » PLUS
Le spa d'inspiration asiatique.

LIVRE À EMPORTER
« Les Vacances de Maigret » de Georges Simenon.

Grand Hotel Heiligendamm

Bad Doberan, Baltic Sea, Germany

During the 19th century, Heiligendamm was Germany's most elegant seaside resort. Today you can still experience the style of this era in the Grand Hotel. The "white city by the sea" comprises a wonderful Neoclassical complex of buildings whose sophisticated interiors by Anne Maria Jagdfeld reflect the colours of the nearby sea, sand dunes and beech forests.

Im 19. Jahrhundert war Heiligendamm das eleganteste Seebad Deutschlands. Heute lebt das Flair dieser Epoche im Grand Hotel wieder auf: Die »Weiße Stadt am Meer« ist ein wunderschönes klassizistisches Ensemble, dessen Inneneinrichtung Anne Maria Jagdfeld sehr sophisticated gestaltet hat – überall spiegelt das Interieur die Farben von Meer, Dünen und Buchenwäldern wider.

Le Heiligendamm était au 19e siècle la station balnéaire la plus élégante d'Allemagne. L'atmosphère de l'époque revit de nos jours au Grand Hotel : la « ville blanche du bord de mer » est un magnifique complexe de style classique dont les bâtiments ont été aménagés de façon très sophistiquée par Anne Maria Jagdfeld : les intérieurs reflètent les couleurs de la mer, des dunes et des forêts de hêtres.

Grand Hotel Heiligendamm
Prof.-Dr.-Vogel-Straße 6
18209 Bad Doberan –
Heiligendamm
Germany
Tel. +49 38203 740 0
Fax +49 38203 740 7474
info@grandhotel-heiligendamm.de
www.grandhotel-heiligendamm.de

LOCATION
Situated by the Baltic Sea, 112 miles northeast of Hamburg airport.

RATES
Single rooms from $255, double rooms from $310 and suites from $485, breakfast included.

ROOMS
136 rooms and 79 suites are located in 5 buildings clustered around the spa.

FOOD
There are three restaurants: The "Friedrich Franz" with its Michelin star, the elegant "Kurhaus Restaurant" and "Medini's" which serves Italian food by the beach.

X-FACTOR
The 9,800-square-foot spa is one of the best in Europe and an homage to traditional bathing.

BOOK TO PACK
"Effi Briest" by Theodor Fontane.

LAGE
An der Ostsee gelegen, 180 km nordöstlich des Flughafens Hamburg.

PREISE
Einzelzimmer ab 190 €, Doppelzimmer ab 230 €, Suite ab 360 €, inklusive Frühstück.

ZIMMER
136 Zimmer und 79 Suiten in 5 Gebäuden rund ums Kurhaus.

KÜCHE
Drei Restaurants: das »Friedrich Franz« mit einem Michelin-Stern, das elegante »Kurhaus Restaurant« und das italienische »Medini's« am Strand.

X-FAKTOR
Das 3.000 qm große Spa ist eines der besten Europas und eine Hommage an die Bädertradition.

BUCHTIPP
»Effi Briest« von Theodor Fontane.

SITUATION
Situé sur la mer Baltique, à 180 km au nord-est de l'aéroport de Hambourg.

PRIX
Chambre simple à partir de 190 €, chambre double à partir de 230 €, suite à partir de 360 €, petit-déjeuner compris.

CHAMBRES
136 chambres et 79 suites réparties dans 5 bâtiments autour de l'établissement thermal.

RESTAURATION
Trois restaurants : le « Friedrich Franz » avec une étoile au guide Michelin, l'élégant « Kurhaus Restaurant » et le « Medini's », restaurant italien sur la plage.

LE « PETIT PLUS »
Hommage à la tradition balnéaire, le spa de 3000 mètres carrés est l'un des meilleurs d'Europe.

LIVRE À EMPORTER
« Effi Briest » de Theodor Fontane.

Romantik-Hotel Spielweg

Münstertal, Black Forest, Germany

The Spielweg, located in the picturesque Münstertal Valley, has belonged to the Fuchs family since 1861. Over the years, they have transformed what was once a simple inn into a hotel with cosy rooms and delicious food. The regional Baden lifestyle – a combination of the down-to-earth and highly cultivated – can be found here in perfect balance, which means you just can't help but feel at home.

Seit 1861 gehört der Spielweg im malerischen Münstertal der Familie Fuchs. Sie hat den einst schlichten Gasthof im Lauf der Zeit in ein Hotel mit gemütlichen Zimmern und köstlicher Küche verwandelt. Überall wird der badische Lebensstil in bodenständiger und äußerst kultivierter Art gepflegt – man fühlt sich einfach rundum wohl.

Situé à Münstertal, une pittoresque commune de la Forêt Noire, l'hôtel Spielweg appartient depuis 1861 à la famille Fuchs. Au fil du temps, celle-ci a transformé l'auberge toute simple en un hôtel qui offre des chambres confortables et une cuisine délicieuse. Partout l'art de vivre badois est cultivé de manière à la fois rustique et très subtile – ici, on se sent bien, tout simplement.

Romantik-Hotel Spielweg
Spielweg 61
79244 Münstertal
Germany
Tel. +49 7636 709 0
Fax +49 7636 709 66
fuchs@spielweg.com
www.spielweg.com

LOCATION
Situated 19 miles south of Freiburg and 43 miles north of Basel airport.

RATES
Double rooms from $175, suites from $355 and apartments from $222, breakfast included.

ROOMS
33 rooms, 2 suites, 5 apartments and 2 holiday homes.

FOOD
Fine dining can be enjoyed in parlours with a tiled stove and panelled ceilings. All the ingredients are locally sourced.

X-FACTOR
The outdoor pool next to a bubbling mountain stream.

BOOK TO PACK
"Flat Stanley" by Jeff Brown (a children's book illustrated by Tomi Ungerer, who is a regular guest; examples of his work are to be found hanging on many of the hotel's walls).

LAGE
30 km südlich von Freiburg und 70 km nördlich des Flughafens Basel gelegen.

PREISE
Doppelzimmer ab 130 €, Suite ab 264 €, Apartment ab 166 €, inklusive Frühstück.

ZIMMER
33 Zimmer, 2 Suiten, 5 Apartments, 2 Ferienhäuser.

KÜCHE
Alle Zutaten für die feinen Menüs stammen aus der Umgebung. Serviert wird in Stuben mit Kachelofen und Kassettendecken.

X-FAKTOR
Das Natur-Freibad.

BUCHTIPP
»Erzählungen für Erwachsene« von Tomi Ungerer (er ist Stammgast – seine Illustrationen zieren viele Wände des Hotels).

SITUATION
Situé à 30 km au sud de Fribourg et à 70 km au nord de l'aéroport de Bâle.

PRIX
Chambre double à partir de 130 €, suite à partir de 264 €, appartement à partir de 166 €, petit-déjeuner compris.

CHAMBRES
33 chambres, 2 suites, 5 appartements, 2 maisons de vacances.

RESTAURATION
Une cuisine raffinée préparée avec des produits de la région. Les plats sont servis dans des salles agrémentées de poêle de faïence et de plafonds à cassettes.

LE « PETIT » PLUS
La piscine à ciel ouvert.

LIVRE À EMPORTER
« Les Grenouillades » de Tomi Ungerer (un habitué – on peut admirer ses illustrations sur de nombreux murs de l'hôtel).

Schloss Elmau

Elmau, Bavaria, Germany

One of the grandsons of the German theologian Johannes Müller has turned his ancestor's former rural retreat into an exceptional country palace hotel. Dietmar Müller-Elmau re-opened Schloss Elmau as a cultural retreat and luxury resort to guests in 2007. The Asian-inspired rooms give the hotel a calming Zen atmosphere.

Aus dem einstigen Refugium des Theologen Johannes Müller hat dessen Enkel ein außergewöhnliches Schlosshotel gemacht: 2007 hat Dietmar Müller-Elmau Schloss Elmau als einen kulturellen und luxuriösen Retreat wiedereröffnet. Asiatische Accessoires verleihen den Räumen eine Zen-Atmosphäre.

Dietmar Müller-Elmau a métamorphosé l'ancien refuge de son grand-père, le théologien Johannes Müller, en un hôtel exceptionnel. En 2007, Dietmar Müller-Elmau a rouvert le château Elmau devenu une retraite culturelle et luxueuse. Les accessoires asiatiques lui procurent une ambiance zen.

Schloss Elmau
Luxury Spa & Cultural
Hideaway
82493 Elmau
Germany
Tel. +49 8823 18 0
Fax +49 8823 18 177
schloss@elmau.de
www.schloss-elmau.de

LOCATION
Situated 12 miles outside Garmisch-Partenkirchen and 87 miles south of Munich airport.

RATES
Single rooms from $170, double rooms from $335, suites from $365, excluding breakfast.

ROOMS
110 rooms and 20 suites.

FOOD
There are six restaurants serving a range of regional, Mediterranean and Asian dishes.

X-FACTOR
Even the architecture of Schloss Elmau has stayed in the family: the buildings were renovated under the guidance of Christoph Sattler, whose grandfather Carlo Sattler built the castle from 1914 to 1916.

BOOK TO PACK
"The Story of the Trapp Family Singers" by Maria Augusta Trapp.

LAGE
20 km von Garmisch-Partenkirchen entfernt; 140 km südlich des Flughafens München.

PREISE
Einzelzimmer ab 125 €, Doppelzimmer ab 250 €, Suite ab 270 €, ohne Frühstück.

ZIMMER
110 Zimmer und 20 Suiten.

KÜCHE
Sechs Restaurants mit regionaler, mediterraner und asiatischer Küche.

X-FAKTOR
Auch die Architektur ist Familiensache geblieben: Die Renovierung leitete Christoph Sattler – sein Großvater Carlo Sattler hatte das Schloss 1914–1916 erbaut.

BUCHTIPP
»Das Frühstücksei« von Loriot (der Autor ist regelmäßiger Gast).

SITUATION
Situé à 20 km de Garmisch-Partenkirchen et à 140 km au sud de l'aéroport de Munich.

PRIX
Chambre simple à partir de 125 €, chambre double à partir de 250 €, suite à partir de 270 €, sans petit-déjeuner.

CHAMBRES
110 chambres et 20 suites.

RESTAURATION
Six restaurants proposant une cuisine régionale, méditerranéenne et asiatique.

LE « PETIT PLUS »
L'architecture a toujours une affaire de famille : Christoph Sattler s'est chargé des rénovations et c'est son grand-père, Carlo Sattler, qui avait construit le château en 1914–1916.

LIVRE À EMPORTER
« Louis II de Bavière ou le roi foudroyé » de Jean des Cars.

berge

Aschau im Chiemgau, Bavaria, Germany

Nils Holger Moormann is one of Germany's best-known furniture designers. His conversion of a former village bakery into a set of extraordinary holiday apartments is a clever combination of reduced contemporary and rustic historical styles. In this Bavarian hideaway, which has neither telephones nor televisions to distract from the local scenery, the raw stone walls and exposed beams provide a perfect backdrop for his furniture designs.

In einem Haus, das einst die Dorfbäckerei beherbergte, hat Nils Holger Moormann, einer der bekanntesten deutschen Möbeldesigner, Ferienapartments eingerichtet und dabei Historisch-Rustikales mit Modern-Reduziertem kombiniert: Vor unverputztem Mauerwerk und unter alten Balken setzt er selbst entworfenes Mobiliar sehr effektvoll in Szene.

Le célèbre créateur de meubles allemand, Nils Holger Moormann, a aménagé des appartements de vacances dans une ancienne boulangerie en mariant rusticité historique et sobriété moderne : devant les murs laissés à l'état brut et les poutres anciennes, un mobilier qu'il a conçu lui-même et qu'il sait mettre parfaitement en valeur.

berge
Kampenwandstraße 85
83229 Aschau im Chiemgau
Germany
Tel. +49 8052 904 517
Fax +49 8052 904 545
berge@moormann.de
www.moormann-berge.de

LOCATION
Located in Chiemgau, 50 miles southeast of Munich.

RATES
Apartments between $110 and $350 per night; excluding breakfast.

ROOMS
There are 13 apartments ranging from 82 to 460 square feet in size that can each house between 2 and 4 guests. The "Nordwand" and "K3" are particularly recommended.

FOOD
11 of the apartments have fully equipped kitchenettes. The hotel can prepare breakfast and meals by arrangement (for groups of 10 or more) in the "Große Stube" and there is also a communal kitchen.

X-FACTOR
berge is full of books and in every apartment you will find a well-selected library packed with classics.

BOOK TO PACK
"Walden" by Henry David Thoreau.

LAGE
Im Chiemgau 80 km südöstlich von München gelegen.

PREISE
Wohnung zwischen 80 und 260 € pro Nacht, ohne Frühstück.

ZIMMER
13 Quartiere (25–140 qm, 2–4 Gäste). Besonders sehens- und empfehlenswert sind die Apartments »Nordwand« und »K3«.

KÜCHE
11 Wohnungen haben Kitchenettes. Frühstück (ab 10 Personen) sowie Brotzeit kann man aber auch in der »Großen Stube« bekommen, und das Haus besitzt eine Gemeinschaftsküche.

X-FAKTOR
Die kleine Bibliothek mit Klassikern in jedem Apartment.

BUCHTIPP
»Lausbubengeschichten« von Ludwig Thoma.

SITUATION
Situé à Chiemgau, à 80 km au sud-est de Munich.

PRIX
Appartements entre 80 et 260 € la nuit, sans petit-déjeuner.

CHAMBRES
13 appartements (25–140 mètres carrés, 2–4 personnes). Les appartements « Nordwand » et « K3 » sont particulièrement beaux et confortables.

RESTAURATION
11 appartements ont des kitchenettes. Le petit-déjeuner (à partir de 10 personnes) et des repas légers peuvent être pris dans la « Große Stube ». La maison possède aussi une cuisine commune.

LE « PETIT PLUS »
La petite bibliothèque avec ses classiques dans chaque appartement.

LIVRE À EMPORTER
« Les quatre cents Coups » de Ludwig Thoma.

Hotel Miramonte

Bad Gastein, Gastein Valley, Austria

An ideal place for everyone who loves the Alps but not the usual Alpine kitsch. Ike Ikrath, Olaf Krohne and Albert Weinzierl have decorated their hotel, with its fantastic mountain backdrop, in an urban style that mixes 1960s retro-chic with design classics such as Bertoia chairs and modern lamps from Megumi Ito. This is a place where creative guests will find both relaxation and inspiration.

Eine Adresse für alle, die die Alpen lieben, aber nicht den Alpenkitsch: Ike Ikrath, Olaf Krohne und Albert Weinzierl haben das Hotel vor einer traumhaften Bergkulisse urban eingerichtet: Sie mischen Retroschick der 1960er mit Designklassikern wie Bertoia-Stühlen und modernen Lampen von Megumi Ito. Hier findet ein kreatives Publikum viel Entspannung und Inspiration.

Conseillé à tous ceux qui aiment les Alpes mais détestent le kitsch alpin ; Ike Ikrath, Olaf Krohne et Albert Weinzierl ont aménagé l'hôtel selon un nouveau concept, mariant le chic rétro des années 1960 à des classiques du design tels des chaises Bertoia et des lampes modernes de Megumi Ito. Un public créatif trouve ici à la fois la détente et l'inspiration.

Hotel Miramonte & Aveda Spa
Reitlpromenade 3
5640 Bad Gastein
Austria
Tel. +43 6434 25 770
Fax +43 6434 25 779
info@hotelmiramonte.com
www.hotelmiramonte.com

LOCATION
Situated 62 miles south of Salzburg airport.

RATES
Single rooms from $95, double rooms from $140, half board included.

ROOMS
36 rooms. Be sure to book one with a panoramic view!

FOOD
The restaurant serves delicious regional dishes. The bar serves Italian coffee during the day and cocktails in the evenings, often accompanied by music mixed by guest DJs.

X-FACTOR
The Aveda spa.

BOOKS TO PACK
"The Magic Mountain" by Thomas Mann (who visited Bad Gastein for health reasons in the mid-1950s) and "Frost" by Thomas Bernhard.

LAGE
100 km südlich des Flughafens Salzburg gelegen.

PREISE
Einzelzimmer ab 72 €, Doppelzimmer ab 104 €, inklusive Halbpension.

ZIMMER
36 Zimmer. Unbedingt eines mit Panoramablick buchen!

KÜCHE
Das Restaurant serviert leckere regionale Gerichte, die Bar tagsüber italienischen Kaffee und abends Cocktails – oft legen hier auch DJs auf.

X-FAKTOR
Das Aveda-Spa.

BUCHTIPPS
»Tagebücher 1951–1952« von Thomas Mann (der in dieser Zeit zur Kur nach Bad Gastein kam) und »Frost« von Thomas Bernhard.

SITUATION
Situé à 100 km au sud de l'aéroport de Salzbourg.

PRIX
Chambre simple à partir de 72 €, chambre double à partir de 104 €, demi-pension comprise.

CHAMBRES
36 chambres. En choisir une avec vue panoramique !

RESTAURATION
Le restaurant propose de délicieux plats régionaux ; le bar sert du café italien pendant la journée et des cocktails le soir – les DJs passent souvent des disques.

LE « PETIT PLUS »
Le spa Aveda.

LIVRES À EMPORTER
« Journal, 1940–1955 » de Thomas Mann (il a fait une cure à Bad Gastein en 1952) et « Gel » de Thomas Bernhard.

Nebesa

Kobarid, Soča Valley, Slovenia

Nebesa means "heaven" in Slovenian, and you feel pretty close to it up here. These four cottages have been puristically designed in wood, metal, glass and stone by architect Rok Klanjšcek. Nothing on the inside detracts from the breathtaking view across the Soča Valley to the mountains of the Triglav national park, seen through the floor-to-ceiling windows.

Nebesa bedeutet auf Slowenisch »Himmel« – und diesem fühlt man sich hier oben wirklich ganz nah. Die vier Cottages aus Holz, Stein, Metall und Glas wurden vom Architekten Rok Klanjšcek puristisch designt – nichts im Inneren lenkt vom atemberaubenden Blick ab, den die raumhohen Fensterfronten über das Soča-Tal sowie die Berge des Triglav-National-parks eröffnen.

Nebesa signifie « ciel » en slovène, et on se sent vraiment tout près de lui ici. Les quatre chalets de bois, pierre, métal et verre de l'architecte Rok Klanjšcek offrent un design puriste – rien à l'intérieur ne distrait de la vue à couper le souffle que les grandes baies vitrées offrent sur la vallée de la Soča et les montagnes du parc national de Triglav.

Nebesa
Livek 39
5222 Kobarid
Slovenia
Tel. +386 538 44 620
info@nebesa.si
www.nebesa.si

LOCATION
Located 3,000 feet above the border between Slovenia and Italy, 1 mile from the village of Livek and 74 miles west of Ljubljana.

RATES
$335 per night, per house, breakfast included (for 5 nights or more: $282 per night).

ROOMS
4 cottages (167 square feet; each sleeps 2).

FOOD
Guests share a communal kitchen and dining room. Local cold meats, cheese and wine are available as snacks for guests at no extra cost.

X-FACTOR
An ideal base for hiking, horseback riding and fishing enthusiasts.

BOOK TO PACK
"Martin Kačur. The Biography of an Idealist" by Ivan Cankar.

LAGE
900 m hoch, nahe der slowenisch-italienischen Grenze gelegen. 2 km vom Dorf Livek entfernt, 120 km westlich von Ljubljana.

PREISE
Haus 250 € pro Nacht, inklusive Frühstück (ab 5 Nächten: 210 €).

ZIMMER
4 Cottages (51 qm, für 2 Personen).

KÜCHE
Die Gäste teilen sich eine Gemein-schaftsküche und ein Esszimmer. Für Snacks stehen einheimische Wurstwaren, Käse und Wein kosten-frei bereit.

X-FAKTOR
Ein idealer Ausgangspunkt zum Wandern, Reiten und Fischen.

BUCHTIPP
»Am Hang« von Ivan Cankar.

SITUATION
Situé à 900 m d'altitude, près de la frontière italo-slovène. Le village de Livek est à 2 km, Ljubljana à 120 km à l'ouest.

PRIX
Maison 250 € la nuit, petit-déjeuner compris (210 € à partir de 5 nuits).

CHAMBRES
4 chalets (51 m², pour deux personnes).

RESTAURATION
Les clients ont à leur disposition une cuisine commune et une salle à manger. Pour les petites faims, charcuterie régionale, fromage et vin sont offerts gracieusement.

LE « PETIT PLUS »
Le point de départ idéal pour faire des randonnées, des promenades à cheval et aller à la pêche.

LIVRE À EMPORTER
« Cartes brouillées » de Francek Rudolf.

TOILETT
SCHNÖG
TERRAS
ZUM RH

Hotel Krafft

Basel, Switzerland

Behind its 1872 façade, the Krafft hotel combines style elements from the Wilhelminian period and the 1950s with classic Swiss modernist furniture. This prize-winning mix is so comfortable that it feels more like a private residence than a guesthouse. The personal service is outstanding even by Swiss hotel standards.

Hinter seiner Fassade aus dem Jahr 1872 verbindet das Krafft Elemente aus der Gründerzeit, Interieurs der 1950er und Schweizer Typenmöbel zu einem preisgekrönten und so wohnlichen Ensemble, dass man sich eher wie in einem Privat- denn wie in einem Gasthaus fühlt. Dazu trägt auch der persönliche Service bei, der selbst im Hotelland Schweiz noch Maßstäbe setzt.

Derrière sa façade qui date de 1872, l'hôtel Krafft combine des éléments de l'ère wilhelminienne, des intérieurs de 1950 et des meubles typiquement suisses. L'ensemble obtenu a été primé et on s'y sent tellement bien que l'on a l'impression de séjourner chez un particulier. Le service personnalisé, qui impose de nouveaux critères même dans un pays hôtelier comme la Suisse, contribue encore au bien-être.

Krafft Basel
Rheingasse 12
4058 Basel
Switzerland
Tel. +41 61 690 9130
Fax +41 61 690 9131
info@krafftbasel.ch
www.krafftbasel.ch

LOCATION
Situated in the Old Town, directly on the banks of the Rhine, just 5 miles south-east of the airport.

RATES
Single rooms from $160, double rooms from $250, suites from $260, breakfast included.

ROOMS
52 rooms and 8 suites in the hotel and annexe opposite.

FOOD
The restaurant, with its Rhine terrace, serves Basel-style fresh market food.

X-FACTOR
The original Art Nouveau floor in the bar came from the Grand Hôtel National in Montreux.

BOOK TO PACK
"Steppenwolf" by Hermann Hesse (the author lived here in 1924 and wrote parts of this, his most famous, novel in room 401).

LAGE
In der Altstadt direkt am Rhein gelegen, 8 km südöstlich des Flughafens.

PREISE
Einzelzimmer ab 115 €, Doppelzimmer ab 185 €, Suite ab 190 €, inklusive Frühstück.

ZIMMER
52 Zimmer und 8 Suiten im Hotel und der Dependance gegenüber.

KÜCHE
Das Restaurant mit Rheinterrasse serviert Basler Marktküche.

X-FAKTOR
Der originale Jugendstilboden der Bar stammt aus dem Grand Hôtel National in Montreux.

BUCHTIPP
»Der Steppenwolf« von Hermann Hesse (er wohnte hier 1924 und schrieb Teile des Romans im Zimmer 401).

SITUATION
Situé dans la vieille ville, sur la rive du Rhin, à 8 km au sud-est de l'aéroport.

PRIX
Chambre simple à partir de 115 €, chambre double à partir de 185 €, suite à partir de 190 €, petit-déjeuner compris.

CHAMBRES
52 chambres et 8 suites dans l'hôtel et l'annexe située en face.

RESTAURATION
Le restaurant doté d'une terrasse avec vue sur le Rhin sert une cuisine régionale de saison.

LE « PETIT PLUS »
Le sol art nouveau original du bar provient du Grand Hôtel National de Montreux.

LIVRE À EMPORTER
« Le Loup des steppes » de Hermann Hesse (il a séjourné ici en 1924 dans la chambre 401 alors qu'il écrivait son roman).

Château Le Rosey

Bursins, Vaud, Switzerland

This atmospheric vineyard has roots that go back to the Middle Ages. When he renovated the building in 2000–2005, the owner and architect Pierre Bouvier fused historical styles with contemporary design. The luxurious rooms afford wonderful views across the vine terraces and guests can enjoy the superb homegrown, organic wine with their meals.

Die Wurzeln dieses atmosphärischen Weinguts reichen bis ins Mittelalter zurück. Bei der Renovierung (2000–2005) hat der Besitzer und Architekt Pierre Bouvier historische Stile und modernes Design verbunden – seine Gäste blicken aus luxuriösen Zimmern über die Rebhänge und genießen zum Essen die edlen Weine, deren Trauben dort ökologisch angebaut werden.

L'histoire de ce domaine viticole remonte au Moyen Âge. En rénovant les lieux de 2000 à 2005, le propriétaire Pierre Bouvier – qui est architecte – a marié des styles historiques et le design moderne. Installés dans des chambres luxueuses, ses hôtes ont une vue sur les vignobles en pente et savourent durant les repas des vins produits selon des critères rigoureux de respect de l'environnement.

Château Le Rosey
Maisonforte SA
1183 Bursins
Switzerland
Tel. +41 21 824 1248
Fax +41 21 824 0901
info@lerosey.ch
www.lerosey.ch

LOCATION
In the heart of the Lake Geneva wine region, 19 miles north of Geneva airport.

RATES
Double rooms from $395, breakfast included.

ROOMS
4 rooms, each named after a house wine.

FOOD
Well-known international chefs are regularly invited to create evening meals, which are served in the atmospheric dining room with its Gothic fireplace.

X-FACTOR
Excellent massages.

BOOK TO PACK
"The Way of the World" by Nicolas Bouvier (the author is the owner's uncle).

LAGE
Im Herzen der Weinregion La Côte am Genfer See gelegen, 30 km nördlich des Flughafens Genf.

PREISE
Doppelzimmer ab 285 €, inklusive Frühstück.

ZIMMER
4 Zimmer; benannt nach hauseigenen Weinen.

KÜCHE
Im stimmungsvollen Speisesaal mit gotischem Kamin wird regelmäßig zu Abendessen international renommierter Gastköche geladen.

X-FAKTOR
Die ausgezeichneten Massagen.

BUCHTIPP
»Die Erfahrung der Welt« von Nicolas Bouvier (der Autor ist der Onkel des Besitzers).

SITUATION
Situé au cœur de la région vinicole de La Côte au-dessus du lac Léman, à 30 km au nord de l'aéroport de Genève.

PRIX
Chambre double à partir de 285 €, petit-déjeuner compris.

CHAMBRES
4 chambres qui portent le nom de vins produits au château.

RESTAURATION
Des dîners préparés par de grands chefs invités sont régulièrement organisés dans la noble salle à manger dotée d'une cheminée gothique.

LE « PETIT PLUS »
Les massages revigorants.

LIVRE À EMPORTER
« L'Usage du monde » de Nicolas Bouvier (il est l'oncle du propriétaire).

Whitepod

Les Giettes, Valais, Switzerland

These 15 pods with their high-tech skins and cosy interiors, which include beds, baths and wood-burning stoves, look like a cross between tents and igloos. From here guests get to know the mountains from a whole new perspective and support eco-tourism at the same time. The camp was conceived as a nature-friendly project and has been awarded environmental prizes as a result.

Sie sehen aus wie eine Kombination aus Zelt und Iglu – die 15 Pods mit Hightech-Hülle und heimeligem Interieur aus Bett, Bad sowie Holzofen. Ihre Bewohner lernen die Berge aus einer ganz neuen Perspektive kennen und unterstützen zugleich den Öko-Tourismus: Das Camp wurde als naturnahes Projekt konzipiert und dafür bereits mit einem Umweltpreis ausgezeichnet.

À mi-chemin entre l'igloo et la tente, les 15 pods à enveloppe high-tech abritent un espace confortable avec lit, salle de bains et poêle à bois. Ceux qui séjournent ici apprennent à voir les montagnes sous un autre jour et soutiennent l'écotourisme : le camp qui vise à rapprocher l'homme de la nature a déjà été récompensé par un prix de l'environnement.

Whitepod Concept SA
1871 Les Giettes
Switzerland
Tel. +41 24 471 3838
Fax +41 24 471 3955
reservations@whitepod.com
www.whitepod.com
Open from June to October
and from December to April

LOCATION
Located at an altitude of 5,600 feet in the Wallis Alps near the village of Cerniers, 78 miles east of Geneva airport.

RATES
Pods from $135 in summer and $315 in winter, excluding breakfast.

ROOMS
15 pods (each 85–130 square feet) and 72 beds in the "Alpage de Chindonne" lodge (2- and 4-person bedrooms as well as dormitories).

FOOD
Breakfast is served in the main, 18th-century chalet. The complex also houses two Swiss restaurants – one serving light, the other more hearty, meals.

X-FACTOR
The camp has its own little ski resort with 4 miles of slopes.

BOOKS TO PACK
"Snow Waste" by Michael E. Bemis and "Water Witches" by Chris Bohjalian.

LAGE
Auf 1.700 m Höhe in den Walliser Alpen gelegen, nahe des Dorfs Les Cerniers. 125 km östlich des Flughafens Genf.

PREISE
Pod ab 100 € im Sommer, ab 234 € im Winter, ohne Frühstück.

ZIMMER
15 Pods (26–40 qm) sowie 72 Schlafplätze in der Hütte »Alpage de Chindonne« (2- und 4-Bettzimmer sowie Schlafsäle).

KÜCHE
Im zentralen Chalet aus dem 18. Jahrhundert gibt es Frühstück. Zudem besitzt die Anlage zwei Schweizer Restaurants – eines mit leichten, eines mit deftigen Gerichten.

X-FAKTOR
Zum Camp gehört ein kleines Skigebiet mit 7 km Pisten.

BUCHTIPP
»Die Schneefalle« von Silvio Blatter.

SITUATION
Situé à 1700 m d'altitude dans les Alpes valaisannes, à proximité du village Les Cerniers. À 125 km à l'est de l'aéroport de Genève.

PRIX
Pod à partir de 100 € en été, de 234 € en hiver, sans petit-déjeuner.

CHAMBRES
15 pods (26–40 m²) ainsi que le chalet de l'Alpage de Chindonne (chambres de 2/4 lits et dortoirs) qui peut accueillir 72 personnes.

RESTAURATION
Le petit-déjeuner est servi dans le chalet central qui date du 18e siècle. On trouve aussi ici deux restaurants suisses, l'un proposant une cuisine légère, l'autre des plats du terroir.

LE « PETIT PLUS »
Un domaine skiable avec 7 km de pistes fait partie du camp.

LIVRE À EMPORTER
« L'Homme apparaît au quaternaire » de Max Frisch.

Le Château des Alpilles

Saint-Rémy-de-Provence, Provence, France

This country residence once belonged to the family of the author Amédée Pichot, whose guests included French political and literary luminaries. These days the owner, Françoise Bon, and her daughter Catherine still have "tout Paris" as their guests – as well as others who appreciate a 19th-century atmosphere, charming rooms and the park with its ancient trees.

Einst gehörte dieser Landsitz der Familie des Romanciers Amédée Pichot, der hier französische Politiker und Künstler zu Gast hatte. Heute empfangen Françoise Bon und ihre Tochter Catherine noch immer »tout Paris« – sowie alle anderen, die sich in gepflegten Zimmern und einem Park mit uralten Bäumen vom Flair des 19. Jahrhunderts verzaubern lassen möchten.

Cette propriété a appartenu autrefois à la famille du romancier Amédée Pichot qui accueillait ici des personnalités du monde politique et artistique. Aujourd'hui, Françoise Bon et sa fille Catherine reçoivent le Tout-Paris ainsi que tous ceux qui sont prêts à se laisser séduire par le charme du 19e siècle dans des chambres décorées avec goût et un parc aux arbres centenaires.

Le Château des Alpilles
Départementale 31
13210 Saint-Rémy-de-Provence
France
Tel. +33 4 9092 0333
Fax +33 4 9092 4517
chateau.alpilles@wanadoo.fr
www.chateaudesalpilles.com
Open from mid-March to early
January

LOCATION
The 17-acre estate lies on the edge of Saint-Rémy-de-Provence, 56 miles northwest of Marseilles airport.

RATES
Rooms from $255, suites from $355, excluding breakfast.

ROOMS
21 rooms and suites located both in the château itself and in the more modern interiors of the "Mas du Cyprès" farmhouse as well as 2 cottages on the park grounds.

FOOD
Fine Provençal specialities. There are also occasional cookery courses on offer.

X-FACTOR
The attractive outdoor pool.

BOOK TO PACK
"Mireille" by Frédéric Mistral.

LAGE
Das 7 Hektar große Grundstück liegt am Rand von Saint-Rémy-de-Provence, 90 km nordwestlich des Flughafens Marseille.

PREISE
Zimmer ab 185 €, Suite ab 260 €, ohne Frühstück.

ZIMMER
21 Zimmer und Suiten im Château und dem moderner gehaltenen Nebengebäude »Mas du Cyprès«, sowie 2 Häuschen im Park.

KÜCHE
Feine provenzalische Spezialitäten. Gelegentlich werden auch Kochkurse angeboten.

X-FAKTOR
Der schöne Außenpool.

BUCHTIPP
»Mireille und meine Welt« von Frédéric Mistral.

SITUATION
Le domaine de 7 hectares est situé en bordure de Saint-Rémy-de-Provence, à 90 km au nord-ouest de l'aéroport de Marseille.

PRIX
Chambre à partir de 185 €, suite à partir de 260 €, sans petit-déjeuner.

CHAMBRES
21 chambres et suites au château et dans l'annexe plus moderne, le « Mas du Cyprès », 2 maisonnettes dans le parc.

RESTAURATION
Spécialités provençales raffinées. Des cours de cuisine sont parfois proposés.

LE « PETIT PLUS »
La jolie piscine extérieure.

LIVRE À EMPORTER
« Mireille » de Frédéric Mistral.

Hôtel Le Corbusier

Marseilles, Provence, France

With his 1952 "Cité radieuse" (radiant city), Le Corbusier realised his vision of a "vertical city within a city". The huge, brutalist concrete building is still very much in use and the Hôtel Le Corbusier occupies several floors of it. The rooms retain the original proportions and colour palette of the architect and are furnished with classic modernist furniture such as his legendary chaise longue.

Mit der »Cité radieuse« realisierte Le Corbusier 1952 seine Vision einer »vertikalen Stadt in der Stadt«. Der mächtige Betonblock ist noch immer bewohnt – auf einigen Etagen beherbergt er auch das Hôtel Le Corbusier, dessen Zimmer originalgetreu nach der Proportions- sowie Farbenlehre des Architekten und mit Klassikern wie seiner Chaiselongue ausgestattet sind.

En construisant en 1952 la Cité radieuse, Le Corbusier a réalisé sa vision d'une « ville verticale ». L'imposante barre de béton est encore habitée et quelques étages abritent l'Hôtel Le Corbusier, dont les chambres respectent fidèlement la grille de proportions et la palette de couleurs de l'architecte et abritent des classiques comme sa chaise longue.

Hôtel Le Corbusier
280, Boulevard Michelet
13008 Marseilles
France
Tel. +33 4 9116 7800
Fax +33 4 9116 7828
contact@hotellecorbusier.com
www.hotellecorbusier.com

LOCATION
Located in east Marseilles, 19 miles southeast of the airport.

RATES
Rooms from $90, excluding breakfast.

ROOMS
21 rooms, some with a view of the Mediterranean.

FOOD
The restaurant "Le Ventre de l'Architecte" serves simple French dishes.

X-FACTOR
Le Corbusier's "chambres cabines", inspired by the cells of La Tourette monastery are furnished with pieces by Charlotte Perriand.

BOOK TO PACK
"My Father's Glory & My Mother's Castle" by Marcel Pagnol.

LAGE
Im Osten von Marseille gelegen; 30 km südöstlich des Flughafens.

PREISE
Zimmer ab 65 €, ohne Frühstück.

ZIMMER
21 Zimmer, einige mit Blick bis zum Mittelmeer.

KÜCHE
Im Restaurant »Le Ventre de l'Architecte« stehen schlichte französische Menüs auf der Karte.

X-FAKTOR
Die »chambres cabines«, die Le Corbusier nach dem Vorbild der Zellen im Kloster La Tourette entwarf und mit Mobiliar von Charlotte Perriand einrichtete.

BUCHTIPP
»Marius, Fanny, César. Szenen aus Marseille« von Marcel Pagnol.

SITUATION
Situé à l'est de Marseille ; à 30 km au sud-est de l'aéroport.

PRIX
Chambre à partir de 65 €, sans petit-déjeuner.

CHAMBRES
21 chambres, certaines avec vue sur la Méditerranée.

RESTAURATION
Au restaurant « Le Ventre de l'Architecte », des menus à la carte proposent une cuisine française inventive et savoureuse.

LE « PETIT PLUS »
Les « chambres cabines », conçues par Le Corbusier sur le modèle des cellules du monastère de La Tourette, et qu'il a meublées avec des créations de Charlotte Perriand.

LIVRES À EMPORTER
« Souvenirs d'enfance » (quatre volumes) de Marcel Pagnol.

Gasthof Krone

Aldino, Trentino-South Tyrol, Italy

The Krone has stood in the idyllic village square of Aldino since 1577 and the Franzelin family has run this travellers' inn full of South Tyrolean tradition, character and charm since 1720. The guest rooms are furnished with wonderful antique farmhouse furniture and classic South Tyrolean fare is served in the cosy, wood-panelled parlour. Simply marvellous!

Seit 1577 steht die Krone am idyllischen Dorfplatz von Aldein, und seit 1720 führt sie die Familie Franzelin, die hier die Tradition, den Charakter und Charme Südtirols pflegt. So sind die Gästezimmer mit wunderschönen antiken Bauernmöbeln eingerichtet, und in behaglichen holzgetäfelten Stuben wird klassische Südtiroler Küche serviert. Einfach herrlich.

Située depuis 1577 sur l'idyllique place du village d'Aldein, l'auberge est dirigée depuis 1720 par la famille Franzelin, qui allie tradition, charme et caractère du Tyrol du Sud. Les chambres sont meublées dans un style campagnard magnifique et une cuisine typique du Tyrol du Sud est servie dans de petites pièces rustiques lambrissées de bois.

Historischer Gasthof Krone
Dorfplatz / Piazza Principale 3
39040 Aldein / Aldino
Italy
Tel. +39 0471 886 825
Fax +39 0471 886 696
info@gasthof-krone.it
www.gasthof-krone.it

LOCATION
Aldino is situated at an altitude of 3,900 feet, 22 miles south of Bolzano airport.

RATES
Single rooms from $85, double rooms from $170, suites from $210, breakfast included.

ROOMS
12 rooms and 1 suite. The main building is ideal for a winter visit. In the summer, the rooms in the annexe, with balconies, are recommended.

FOOD
The kitchen uses traditional recipes with ingredients from their own farm and the value for money is exceptional.

X-FACTOR
The cheerful service.

BOOK TO PACK
"Cleaver" by Tim Parks.

LAGE
Aldein liegt auf 1.200 m Höhe, 35 km südlich des Flughafens Bozen.

PREISE
Einzelzimmer ab 61 €, Doppelzimmer ab 122 €, Suite ab 155 €, inklusive Frühstück.

ZIMMER
12 Zimmer und 1 Suite. Im Winter wohnt man sehr schön im Haupthaus, im Sommer sind die Räume mit Balkonen im Anbau zu empfehlen.

KÜCHE
Gekocht wird nach alten Rezepten und mit Zutaten vom eigenen Hof. Das Preis-Leistungs-Verhältnis ist erstklassig.

X-FAKTOR
Der herzliche Service.

BUCHTIPP
»Der Schmerz der Gewöhnung« von Joseph Zoderer.

SITUATION
Aldein se trouve à 1200 m d'altitude, à 35 km au sud de l'aéroport de Bozen.

PRIX
Chambre simple à partir de 61 €, chambre double à partir de 122 €, suite à partir de 155 €, petit-déjeuner compris.

CHAMBRES
12 chambres et 1 suite. On logera de préférence dans le bâtiment principal en hiver et dans l'annexe avec ses balcons en été.

RESTAURATION
Plats préparés d'après d'anciennes recettes et avec des ingrédients provenant de la ferme de l'auberge. Très bon rapport qualité/prix.

LE « PETIT PLUS »
L'excellent service.

LIVRE À EMPORTER
« L'Eau sous la glace » de Joseph Zoderer.

Four Seasons Hotel Firenze

Florence, Tuscany, Italy

In 2008, after seven years of restoration, the 15th-century Palazzo della Gherardesca and its neighbouring monastery were converted into a luxury hotel. In the fabulous rooms, where designer Pierre-Yves Rochon has retained all the original frescoes and reliefs, you are transported back to the glory days of the Renaissance and can live here like a Florentine lord.

Nach siebenjähriger Restaurierung wurden der Palazzo della Gherardesca aus dem 15. Jahrhundert und das benachbarte Kloster 2008 als Luxushotel eröffnet. In den wunderschönen Räumen, in denen Designer Pierre-Yves Rochon originale Fresken und Reliefs erhalten hat, reist man in die prachtvolle Epoche der Renaissance zurück und fühlt sich wie ein Florentiner Adliger.

Reconvertis en hôtel de luxe, le Palazzo della Gherardesca datant du 15e siècle et le cloître avoisinant ont ouvert leurs portes après sept ans de restauration. Dans ces pièces somptueuses qui ont gardé leurs fresques et leurs reliefs originaux grâce au designer Pierre-Yves Rochon, on se croirait revenu à l'époque des fastes de la Renaissance dans la peau d'un noble florentin.

Four Seasons Hotel Firenze
Borgo Pinti, 99
50121 Florence
Italy
Tel. +39 055 2626 1
Fax +39 055 2626 500
firenze@fourseasons.com
www.fourseasons.com

LOCATION
Situated in the middle of Florence's biggest private park (11 acres), 20 min from Amerigo Vespucci airport.

RATES
Rooms from $395, suites from $1,050, excluding breakfast.

ROOMS
72 rooms and 44 suites.

FOOD
"La Magnolia" serves breakfast, "Il Palagio" fine Tuscan dishes and wines and the "Atrium Bar" is perfect to see and be seen in.

X-FACTOR
Even the spa takes its history seriously and uses products from Officina Profumo-Farmaceutica Santa Maria Novella, one of the oldest apothecaries in the world (since 1612).

BOOK TO PACK
"The Agony and the Ecstasy" by Irving Stone.

LAGE
Inmitten des größten Privatparks im Zentrum von Florenz gelegen (4,5 Hektar), 20 Min. vom Flughafen Amerigo Vespucci entfernt.

PREISE
Zimmer ab 295 €, Suite ab 750 €, ohne Frühstück.

ZIMMER
72 Zimmer und 44 Suiten.

KÜCHE
»La Magnolia« serviert Frühstück, »Il Palagio« feinste toskanische Menüs und Weine. Die »Atrium Bar« ist perfekt zum Sehen und Gesehen werden.

X-FAKTOR
Selbst das Spa führt in die Geschichte zurück: Es verwendet Produkte von Officina Profumo-Farmaceutica Santa Maria Novella, einer der ältesten Apotheken der Welt (seit 1612).

BUCHTIPP
»Michelangelo« von Irving Stone.

SITUATION
Situé au milieu du plus grand parc privé dans le centre de Florence (4,5 hectares), à 20 min de l'aéroport Amerigo Vespucci.

PRIX
Chambre à partir de 295 €, suite à partir de 750 €, sans petit-déjeuner.

CHAMBRES
72 chambres et 44 suites.

RESTAURATION
« La Magnolia » sert le petit-déjeuner, « Il Palagio » propose les menus et les vins toscans les plus fins. L' « Atrium Bar » est idéal pour voir et être vu.

LE « PETIT PLUS »
Même le spa vous offre un voyage dans le passé en utilisant les produits de l'Officina Profumo-Farmaceutica Santa Maria Novella, l'une des plus anciennes pharmacies au monde (depuis 1612).

LIVRE À EMPORTER
« La Vie ardente de Michel-Ange » d'Irving Stone.

Hospes Maricel

Calvià, Mallorca, Spain

This 1940s palace used to host some of Mallorcan chicest parties. In 2002, Xavier Claramunt turned it into a hotel "between heaven and the sea" (hence the name "Maricel"). The most spectacular rooms are to be found in the annexe: their typical Mallorcan stone walls contrast well with the modern glass, wood and steel design.

In diesem Palast aus den 1940ern fanden einst die schicksten Partys Mallorcas statt – 2002 verwandelte ihn Xavier Claramunt in ein Hotel zwischen Himmel und Meer (daher der Name Maricel). Die spektakulärsten Zimmer liegen in den Anbauten: Sie besitzen typisch mallorquinische Steinwände, vor denen modernes Design aus Glas, Holz und Stahl zur Geltung kommt.

Ce palais construit à la fin des années 1940 a vu les fêtes les plus chics de Majorque. En 2002, Xavier Claramunt l'a transformé en un hôtel entre le ciel et la mer (d'où son nom Maricel). Les chambres les plus spectaculaires sont situées dans les annexes : elles possèdent des murs de pierres typiquement majorquins qui mettent en valeur le design modern de verre, de bois et d'acier.

Hospes Maricel
Carretera d'Andratx, 11
07184 Calvià (Cas Català)
Mallorca
Spain
Tel. +34 971 707 744
Fax +34 971 707 745
reservations.hospes.maricel@
fuenso.com
www.hospes.com
Open from February to
mid-December

LOCATION
Situated directly by the sea in Calvià, just west of Palma. The airport is 15 min away.

RATES
Rooms from $315, suites from $705, excluding breakfast. 3-night minimum stay during high season.

ROOMS
44 rooms and 7 suites. All rooms in the annexe have their own pools.

FOOD
The "Senzone" restaurant serves innovative Mallorcan meals; there is also a pool bar and a cocktail lounge.

X-FACTOR
The massages in the spa that was extended in 2009.

BOOK TO PACK
"Winter in Majorca" by George Sand.

LAGE
Direkt am Meer in Calvià gelegen, westlich von Palma. Der Flughafen ist 15 Min. entfernt.

PREISE
Zimmer ab 235 €, Suite ab 525 €, ohne Frühstück. 3 Nächte Mindestaufenthalt in der Hochsaison.

ZIMMER
44 Zimmer und 7 Suiten. Alle Räume in den Nebengebäuden haben eigene Pools.

KÜCHE
Das »Senzone« serviert innovative mallorquinische Menüs; zudem gibt es eine Poolbar und Cocktail-Lounge.

X-FAKTOR
Die Massagen im Spa, das 2009 erweitert wurde.

BUCHTIPP
»Ein Winter auf Mallorca« von George Sand.

SITUATION
Situé en bord de mer à Calvià, à l'ouest de Palma. L'aéroport est à 15 min.

PRIX
Chambre à partir de 235 €, suite à partir de 525 €, sans petit déjeuner. Séjour de 3 nuits minimum durant la pleine saison.

CHAMBRES
44 chambres et 7 suites. Toutes les pièces situées dans les annexes ont leur propre piscine.

RESTAURATION
Le « Senzone » propose des menus innovants de la cuisine majorquine et le pool-bar prépare de délicieux cocktails.

LE « PETIT PLUS »
Les massages au spa, agrandi en 2009.

LIVRE À EMPORTER
« Un hiver à Majorque » de George Sand.

Hotel Hurricane

Tarifa, Costa de la Luz, Spain

The Hotel Hurricane is located next to one of the most beautiful sandy beaches in the area around Tarifa, the European "surf capital". Here you can find ideal wind conditions and on clear days a view that stretches right across to the North African coast. Indeed the architecture of this hotel has distinct Moroccan influences in both colour and form, as well as in its relaxed, exotic ambience.

Das Hotel Hurricane liegt an einem der schönsten Sandstrände nahe der europäischen »Surf-Hauptstadt« Tarifa. Hier herrschen ideale Windverhältnisse, und an klaren Tagen reicht die Sicht bis zur Küste Nordafrikas. Diese hat Architektur sowie Design des Hauses beeinflusst: Marokkanische Formen und Farben sorgen für ein entspannt-exotisches Ambiente.

L'hôtel Hurricane est situé sur l'une des plus belles plages à proximité de Tarifa, la « capitale du surf » européenne. Le vent est idéal et les jours de temps clairs, on peut voir la côte de l'Afrique du Nord. Celle-ci a d'ailleurs influencé l'architecture et le design de la maison : les formes et les couleurs marocaines créent une ambiance détendue et exotique.

Hotel Hurricane Tarifa
Carretera Nacional 340, km 78
11380 Tarifa (Cádiz)
Spain
Tel. +34 956 684 919
Fax +34 956 680 329
info@hotelhurricane.com
www.hotelhurricane.com

LOCATION
The hotel lies 4 miles northwest of Tarifa. Gibraltar airport is 30 miles away.

RATES
Rooms from $115, apartments from $195, suites from $235, breakfast included.

ROOMS
28 rooms, 2 suites and 3 family apartments. Book a room with a sea view and balcony if you can.

FOOD
The hotel has its own, excellent Mediterranean restaurant that serves home-made dishes using local ingredients.

X-FACTOR
The enchanted garden with its palm trees and two pools.

BOOK TO PACK
"The Shadow of the Wind" by Carlos Ruiz Zafón.

LAGE
7 km nordwestlich von Tarifa gelegen. Der Flughafen Gibraltar ist 49 km entfernt.

PREISE
Zimmer ab 87 €, Apartment ab 145 €, Suite ab 175 €, inklusive Frühstück.

ZIMMER
28 Zimmer, 2 Suiten, 3 Familien-Apartments. Am besten einen Raum mit Meerblick und Balkon buchen!

KÜCHE
Zum Hotel gehört ein exzellentes mediterranes Restaurant – hier wird alles aus lokalen Zutaten hausgemacht.

X-FAKTOR
Der verwunschene Garten mit Palmen und zwei Pools.

BUCHTIPP
»Der Schatten des Windes« von Carlos Ruiz Zafón.

SITUATION
Situé à 7 km au nord-ouest de Tarifa. L'aéroport de Gibraltar se trouve à 49 km.

PRIX
Chambre à partir de 87 €, appartement à partir de 145 €, suite à partir de 175 €, petit-déjeuner compris.

CHAMBRES
28 chambres, 2 suites, 3 appartements familiaux. Réservez de préférence une pièce avec balcon et vue sur la mer !

RESTAURATION
Un excellent restaurant méditerranéen fait partie de l'hôtel. Tout est fait maison à partir de produits locaux.

LE « PETIT PLUS »
Le jardin enchanté avec ses palmiers et ses deux piscines.

LIVRE À EMPORTER
« L'Ombre du vent » de Carlos Ruiz Zafón.

Pousada de Amares

Santa Maria do Bouro, Amares, Portugal

A 12th-century, former Cistercian monastery is where the historic past meets the present and combines to create this very atmospheric pousada. The architect Eduardo Souto de Moura has had the old granite walls, the vaulted ceilings and the sacred statues painstakingly restored and has combined them with modern furnishings.

Aus einem Zisterzienserkloster, dessen Ursprünge bis ins 12. Jahrhundert zurückreichen, wurde eine sehr stimmungsvolle Pousada, in der Geschichte und Gegenwart zusammenfließen: Der Architekt Eduardo Souto de Moura hat alte Granitmauern, Gewölbedecken sowie Heiligenstatuen sorgsam restauriert und mit modernem, minimalem Mobiliar kombiniert.

Un monastère cistercien dont les origines remontent au 12e siècle est devenu une pousada pleine de charme dans laquelle cohabitent le passé et le présent : l'architecte Eduardo Souto de Moura a soigneusement restauré les vieux murs de granit, les voûtes et les statues des saints et les a combinés à des meubles modernes aux lignes sobres.

Pousada de Amares
Santa Maria do Bouro
4720-688 Amares
Portugal
Tel. +351 253 371 970
Fax +351 253 371 976
recepcao.bouro@pousadas.pt
www.pousadas.pt

LOCATION
Idyllically situated between the town of Braga and the Gerês Mountains, 42 miles northeast of Porto airport.

RATES
Single rooms from $160, double rooms from $175, breakfast included.

ROOMS
32 rooms.

FOOD
The restaurant, with its gigantic fireplaces, has excellent Portuguese specialities and wines on the menu.

X-FACTOR
Walking tours and boat trips arranged on request; afterwards you can relax in the pool in the park.

BOOK TO PACK
"The Gospel According to Jesus Christ" by José Saramago.

LAGE
Idyllisch zwischen der Stadt Braga und den Gerês-Bergen gelegen, 68 km nordöstlich des Flughafens Porto.

PREISE
Einzelzimmer ab 118 €, Doppelzimmer ab 130 €, inklusive Frühstück.

ZIMMER
32 Zimmer.

KÜCHE
Im Restaurant mit mächtigen offenen Kaminen stehen hervorragende portugiesische Spezialitäten und Weine auf der Karte.

X-FAKTOR
Auf Wunsch werden Wanderungen und Bootsausflüge arrangiert; anschließend entspannt man am Pool im Park.

BUCHTIPP
»Das Evangelium nach Jesus Christus« von José Saramago.

SITUATION
Dans un site idyllique entre la ville de Braga et les montagnes de Gerês, à 68 km au nord-est de l'aéroport de Porto.

PRIX
Chambre simple à partir de 118 €, chambre double à partir de 130 €, petit-déjeuner compris.

CHAMBRES
32 chambres.

RESTAURATION
La carte du restaurant doté d'une grande cheminée propose des spécialités et des vins portugais.

LE « PETIT PLUS »
Les randonnées et les excursions en bateau organisées à la demande ; suivies de détente dans la piscine du parc.

LIVRE À EMPORTER
« L'Évangile selon Jésus-Christ » de José Saramago.

Belvedere Hotel

Mykonos, Aegean Islands, Greece

The white buildings here look like a traditional Cyclades village, but the interiors are totally modern. In a highly successful makeover (2007–2009), the Rockwell Group architects have blended angular furniture and yacht-inspired details with rosewood screens reminiscent of the undulating Aegean waves.

Die weißen Häuser wirken wie ein traditionelles Kykladen-Dorf, doch ihr Inneres ist ganz modern: Bei einer rundum gelungenen Renovierung (2007–2009) haben die Architekten der Rockwell Group das Hotel mit gradlinigen Möbeln und vom Jachtdesign inspirierten Details ausgestattet. Die Trennwände aus Rosenholz erinnern an die Wellen der Ägäis.

Les maisons blanches évoquent le village traditionnel des Cyclades mais elles abritent des pièces très modernes : au cours de leur rénovation absolument réussie (2007–2009), les architectes du Rockwell Group ont agrémenté l'hôtel de meubles aux lignes pures, de détails inspirés du design nautique et de cloisons en palissandre dont les formes rappellent celles des vagues de la mer Égée.

Belvedere Hotel
School of Fine Arts District
84600 Mykonos
Greece
Tel. +30 22890 25 122
Fax +30 22890 25 126
contact@belvederehotel.com
www.belvederehotel.com

LOCATION
Situated above the town of Mykonos. The airport is 1 mile to the south.

RATES
Rooms from $221, suites from $375, breakfast included.

ROOMS
35 rooms and 8 suites; some with private terraces.

FOOD
The Japanese/South American "Matsuhisa Mykonos" restaurant is world-famous and the "Belvedere Club" serves innovative Greek cuisine.

X-FACTOR
The pool – surrounded by comfortable sun beds by day – becomes a restaurant and club area by night.

BOOK TO PACK
"The Colossus of Maroussi" by Henry Miller.

LAGE
Über Mykonos-Stadt gelegen. Der Flughafen befindet sich 2 km südöstlich.

PREISE
Zimmer ab 165 €, Suite ab 280 €, inklusive Frühstück.

ZIMMER
35 Zimmer und 8 Suiten, einige davon mit privaten Terrassen.

KÜCHE
Weltberühmt ist das japanisch-südamerikanische »Matsuhisa Mykonos«, »The Belvedere Club« serviert innovative griechische Menüs.

X-FAKTOR
Der Pool – tagsüber warten hier bequeme Sonnenbetten, abends wird er zum Restaurant- und Klubbereich.

BUCHTIPP
»Der Koloß von Maroussi« von Henry Miller.

SITUATION
Situé au-dessus de Mykonos. L'aéroport est à 2 km au sud-est.

PRIX
Chambre à partir de 165 €, suite à partir de 280 €, petit-déjeuner compris.

CHAMBRES
35 chambres et 8 suites, certaines avec terrasse privée.

RESTAURATION
Le restaurant japonais-sud-américain « Matsuhisa Mykonos » est célèbre dans le monde entier, « The Belvedere Club » propose une cuisine grecque inventive.

LE « PETIT PLUS »
La piscine, bordée de confortables lits de plage pendant la journée, accueille le soir le restaurant et le club.

LIVRE À EMPORTER
« Le Colosse de Maroussi » d'Henry Miller.

Atami Hotel

Gölköy, Bodrum, Turkey

Midori and Atakan Öztaylan built their charming hotel in 2005 by the peaceful "Cennet Koyu" (paradise bay). It combines the arts and cultures of both their native lands: modern and antique Turkish furniture in beautiful, well-kept rooms with delicious Japanese sushi delicacies and ikebana flower arrangements.

An der friedlichen »Cennet Koyu« (Paradiesbucht) eröffneten Midori und Atakan Öztaylan 2005 dieses Hotel, das sie selbst erbaut haben und das Kunst und Kultur ihrer Heimatländer verbindet: Aus der Türkei stammen die modernen und antiken Möbel der äußerst gepflegten Zimmer – aus Japan kommen das köstliche Sushi sowie die Ikebana-Blumenarrangements.

C'est sur la paisible « Cennet Koyu » (baie du Paradis) que Midori et Atakan Öztaylan ont ouvert, en 2005, cet hôtel qu'ils ont construit eux-mêmes et qui marie l'art et la culture de leur patrie respective : les meubles modernes et anciens des chambres proviennent de Turquie, tandis que les délicieux sushis et les arrangements floraux ikebana viennent du Japon.

Atami Hotel
Cennet Koyu No. 48
48400 Gölköy, Bodrum
Turkey
Tel. +90 252 357 7416
Fax +90 252 357 7421
info@atamihotel.com
www.atamihotel.com

LOCATION
Situated on the Bodrum Peninsula,
2 miles from Gölköy and 25 miles
southwest of Bodrum airport.

RATES
Single rooms from $110, double rooms
from $120, suites from $340, breakfast
included.

ROOMS
19 standard rooms, 10 deluxe rooms,
2 suites; all with a sea view.

FOOD
The restaurant with its own terrace has
both traditional Turkish and Japanese
dishes on the menu.

X-FACTOR
The pool and its wonderful panoramic
view of the bay.

BOOK TO PACK
"My Name is Red" by Orhan Pamuk.

LAGE
Auf der Halbinsel Bodrum gelegen,
3 km von Gölköy entfernt und 40 km
südwestlich des Flughafens Bodrum.

PREISE
Einzelzimmer ab 80 €, Doppelzimmer
ab 90 €, Suite ab 255 €, inklusive
Frühstück.

ZIMMER
19 Standardzimmer, 10 Deluxezimmer,
2 Suiten; alle mit Meerblick.

KÜCHE
Im Restaurant mit Terrasse stehen
traditionelle türkische und japanische
Spezialitäten auf der Karte.

X-FAKTOR
Der Pool mit herrlichem Panoramablick
über die Bucht.

BUCHTIPP
»Rot ist mein Name« von Orhan Pamuk.

SITUATION
Situé sur la presqu'île de Bodrum,
à 3 km de Gölköy et à 40 km au
sud-ouest de l'aéroport de Bodrum.

PRIX
Chambre simple à partir de 80 €,
chambre double à partir de 90 €,
suite à partir de 255 €, petit-déjeuner
compris.

CHAMBRES
19 chambres standard, 10 chambres
de luxe, 2 suites ; toutes avec vue sur
la mer.

RESTAURATION
Le restaurant avec terrasse propose
des spécialités turques et japonaises
traditionnelles.

LE « PETIT PLUS »
La piscine avec une vue magnifique sur
le baie.

LIVRE À EMPORTER
« Mon nom est rouge » d'Orhan Pamuk.

MOROCCO

WESTERN
SAHARA

MAURITANIA

SENEGAL

GAMBIA

GUINEA BISSAU

GUINEA

SIERRA
LEONE

IVORY
COAST

LIBERIA

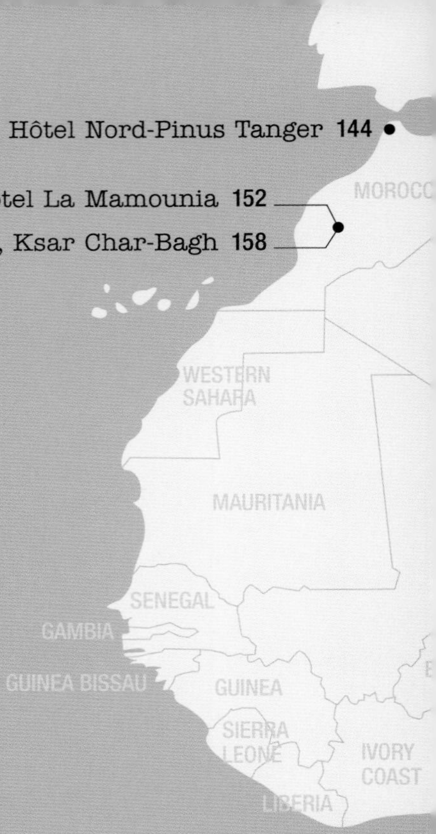

Africa
& the
Middle East

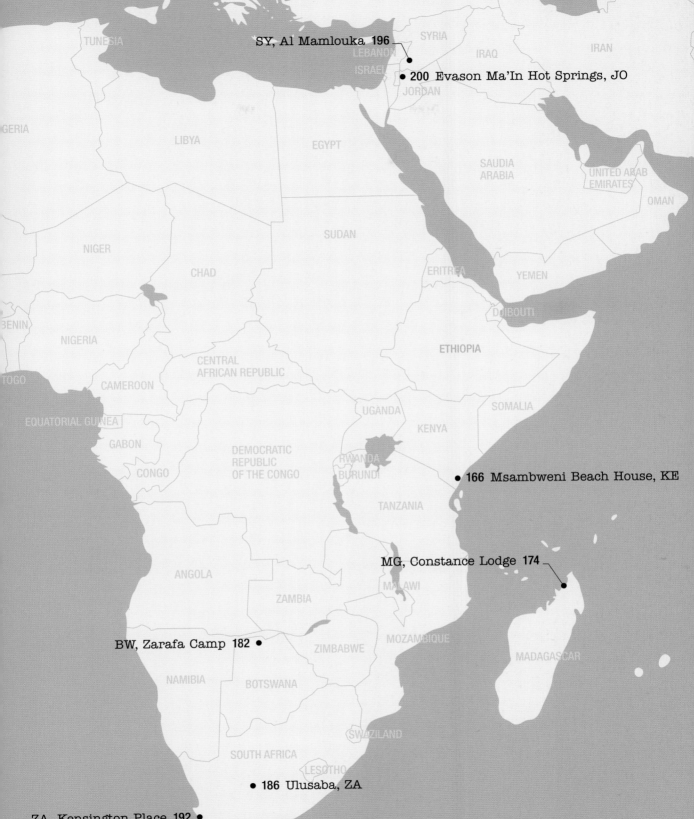

SY, Al Mamlouka 196

200 Evason Ma'In Hot Springs, JO

166 Msambweni Beach House, KE

MG, Constance Lodge 174

BW, Zarafa Camp 182

186 Ulusaba, ZA

ZA, Kensington Place 192

Hôtel Nord-Pinus Tanger

Tangier, Morocco

The terraces here offer a fantastic view of the heavens but the interior is also quite an eye-catcher. Anne Igou, who also owns the Grand Hôtel Nord-Pinus in Arles, has created an eclectic mix of antique and modern; Moroccan and Indian; coloured glass and black-and-white photos by Peter Lindbergh, reflecting the multicultural atmosphere of Tangier.

Die Terrassen eröffnen einen herrlichen Blick ins Blaue – doch auch das Interieur dieses Riads ist mehr als einen Blick wert. Anne Igou, der ebenfalls das Grand Hôtel Nord-Pinus in Arles gehört, mischt Antikes und Modernes, Marokkanisches und Indisches, buntes Glas und Schwarz-Weiß-Fotos von Peter Lindbergh – hier spiegelt sich das multikulturelle Flair Tangers wider.

Vue des terrasses, l'immensité bleue est magnifique, mais l'intérieur du riad n'a rien à lui envier. Anne Igou, qui possède également le Grand Hôtel Nord-Pinus en Arles, marie ici l'ancien et le moderne, le marocain et l'indien, le verre coloré et les photos en noir et blanc de Peter Lindbergh – l'hôtel est un miroir qui reflète les multiples facettes de Tanger.

Hôtel Nord-Pinus Tanger
11, Rue du Ryad Sultan Kasbah
Tangier
Morocco
Tel. +212 661 228 140
Fax +212 539 336 363
info@nord-pinus-tanger.com
www.hotel-nord-pinus-tanger.com

LOCATION
This former pasha's palace reigns from the highest point of the Old Town, 7 miles east of the airport.

RATES
Double rooms from $300, suites from $420, breakfast included.

ROOMS
1 room and 4 suites.

FOOD
The pergola-covered restaurant serves delicious Moroccan cuisine with seafood, vegetables and fruits, fresh from the kasbah.

X-FACTOR
The massages with oils from the Ourika Valley.

BOOKS TO PACK
"The Sheltering Sky" by Paul Bowles and "For Bread Alone" by Mohamed Choukri.

LAGE
Der ehemalige Pascha-Palast thront auf dem höchsten Punkt der Altstadt, 12 km östlich des Flughafens.

PREISE
Doppelzimmer ab 220 €, Suite ab 310 €, inklusive Frühstück.

ZIMMER
1 Zimmer und 4 Suiten.

KÜCHE
Im Restaurant mit Pergola stehen köstliche marokkanische Gerichte auf der Karte. Meeresfrüchte, Gemüse und Obst kommen frisch vom Stadtmarkt.

X-FAKTOR
Die Massagen mit Ölen aus dem Ourika-Tal.

BUCHTIPPS
»Himmel über der Wüste« von Paul Bowles und »Das nackte Brot« von Mohamed Choukri.

SITUATION
L'ancienne maison du pacha trône au-dessus de la casbah, à 12 km à l'est de l'aéroport.

PRIX
Chambre double à partir de 220 €, suite à partir de 310 €, petit-déjeuner compris.

CHAMBRES
1 chambre et 4 suites.

RESTAURANT
Le restaurant avec pergola propose de succulents plats marocains. Les fruits de mer, les légumes et les fruits viennent tout droit du marché de Tanger.

LE « PETIT PLUS »
Les massages aux huiles essentielles de la vallée de l'Ourika.

LIVRES À EMPORTER
« Un Thé au Sahara » de Paul Bowles et « Le Pain nu » de Mohamed Choukri.

Hôtel La Mamounia

Marrakech, Morocco

Since its opening in 1923, the Mamounia has been legendary. Thanks to a 2009 makeover by Jacques Garcia (who also redesigned the Hôtel Costes in Paris), it now shines once again in all its glory. Inspired by the Arabian-Andalusian style and Berber handcrafts, Garcia has created a masterpiece of opulent colours and filigree mosaic, metal and woodwork. A very sensual oriental spa adds the finishing touch to his composition.

Seit seiner Eröffnung 1923 gilt das Mamounia als Legende – 2009 hat es Jacques Garcia, der auch das Hôtel Costes in Paris gestaltet hat, neu belebt. Ganz vom arabisch-andalusischen Stil und der Handwerkskunst der Berber inspiriert, entwarf er ein Meisterwerk aus opulenten Farben, filigranen Mosaik-, Metall- sowie Holzarbeiten. Ein sehr sinnliches orientalisches Spa vervollständigt seine Komposition.

La Mamounia est un mythe depuis son ouverture en 1923. Jacques Garcia, qui a aussi décoré l'Hôtel Costes à Paris, l'a revisité avec talent en 2009. S'inspirant du style arabo-andalou et de l'artisanat berbère, il a créé un chef-d'œuvre de couleurs opulentes, de fines mosaïques, de travaux de métal et de bois. Un spa oriental très sensuel arrondit sa composition.

Hôtel La Mamounia
Avenue Bab Jdid
40040 Marrakech
Morocco
Tel. +212 524 388 600
Fax +212 524 444 044
informations@mamounia.com
www.mamounia.com

LOCATION
Situated in the medina, 15 min from Marrakech airport.

RATES
Rooms from $720, suites from $1,080, riads from $9,600, excluding breakfast.

ROOMS
136 rooms, 71 suites, 3 riads.

FOOD
Four restaurants serve Moroccan, French and Italian dishes.

X-FACTOR
The park with its 700 orange trees was once a wedding gift from a sultan to his son.

BOOK TO PACK
"The Voices of Marrakesh" by Elias Canetti.

LAGE
In der Medina gelegen, 15 Min. vom Flughafen Marrakesch entfernt.

PREISE
Zimmer ab 535 €, Suite ab 800 €, Riad ab 7.100 €, ohne Frühstück.

ZIMMER
136 Zimmer, 71 Suiten, 3 Riads.

KÜCHE
Vier Restaurants servieren marokkanische, französische und italienische Menüs.

X-FAKTOR
Der Park mit 700 Orangenbäumen – er war einst das Hochzeitsgeschenk eines Sultans an seinen Sohn.

BUCHTIPP
»Die Stimmen von Marrakesch« von Elias Canetti.

SITUATION
Situé dans la médina, à 15 min de l'aéroport de Marrakech.

PRIX
Chambres à partir de 535 €, suite à partir de 800 €, riad à partir de 7100 €, sans petit-déjeuner.

CHAMBRES
136 chambres, 71 suites, 3 riads.

RESTAURATION
Quatre restaurants proposent des plats de la cuisine marocaine, française et italienne.

LE « PETIT PLUS »
Le parc planté de 700 orangers – le cadeau d'un sultan à son fils au 18e siècle.

LIVRE À EMPORTER
« Les Voix de Marrakech » d'Elias Canetti.

Ksar Char-Bagh

Marrakech, Morocco

Nicole and Patrick Levillair were inspired by Moorish, Ottoman and Persian architecture when they built and decorated this Relais & Châteaux hotel in 2003. The soft sounds of water (a symbol of life) are heard everywhere and guests can relax under palms, in the hamam or in the "Harim" (Persian for: "little palace apartment") suites that truly do their name justice.

Nicole und Patrick Levillair haben sich bei dem 2003 gebauten Hotel (Relais & Châteaux) von maurischer, osmanischer und persischer Architektur inspirieren lassen. Überall rauscht als Symbol des Lebens leise Wasser, und man entspannt unter Palmen, im Hamam oder in den Suiten, die ihrem Namen alle Ehre machen: Das persische Wort »Harim« bedeutet »kleine Palastwohnung«.

En construisant l'hôtel Relais & Châteaux en 2003, Nicole et Patrick Levillair se sont inspirés de l'architecture maure, ottomane et perse. Partout on entend murmurer l'eau, symbole de vie, et l'on se détend sous les palmiers, au hammam ou dans les suites qui font honneur à leur nom – le mot perse « harim » ne signifie-t-il pas « petit appartement dans un palais » ?

Ksar Char-Bagh
Palmeraie de Marrakech
BP 2449
40000 Marrakech
Morocco
Tel. +212 524 329 244
Fax +212 524 329 214
info@ksarcharbagh.com
www.ksarcharbagh.com

LOCATION
9 miles west of the airport and 4 miles from the Marrakech medina.

RATES
Suites from $825, apartment $1,240, breakfast included.

ROOMS
1 apartment and 12 "Harim" suites (some with private pool).

FOOD
An homage to the intensive tastes of Morocco; meals are served by the beautifully lit pool or in the garden.

X-FACTOR
The boutique with furniture and accessories that the owners designed exclusively for the hotel.

BOOK TO PACK
"The Sand Child" by Tahar Ben Jelloun.

LAGE
15 km westlich des Flughafens, 6 km entfernt von Marrakeschs Medina.

PREISE
Suite ab 600 €, Apartment 900 €, inklusive Frühstück.

ZIMMER
1 Apartment und 12 »Harim«-Suiten (einige mit privatem Pool).

KÜCHE
Eine Hommage an die intensiven Aromen Marokkos. Serviert wird am wunderschön beleuchteten Pool oder im Garten.

X-FAKTOR
Die Boutique mit Möbeln und Accessoires, welche die Besitzer exklusiv für das Hotel entworfen haben.

BUCHTIPP
»Sohn ihres Vaters« von Tahar Ben Jelloun.

SITUATION
Situé à 15 km à l'ouest de l'aéroport, à 6 km de la médina de Marrakech.

PRIX
Suite à partir de 600 €, appartement à partir de 900 €, petit-déjeuner compris.

CHAMBRES
1 appartement et 12 suites « Harim » (certaines avec piscine privée).

RESTAURATION
Un hommage aux parfums intenses du Maroc. Les repas sont servis près du bassin magnifiquement éclairé ou au jardin.

LE « PETIT PLUS »
La boutique qui propose des meubles et des objets que les propriétaires ont créés exclusivement pour l'hôtel.

LIVRE À EMPORTER
« L'Enfant de sable » de Tahar Ben Jelloun.

Msambweni Beach House

Msambweni, Coast Province, Kenya

This luxurious, Lamu-style hideaway in Msambweni, the "land of the
sable antilope", was opened in 2007 by the brothers Frederik and Filip
Vanderhoeven. Arabian lamps and golden silk cushions accent the pre-
dominantly white suites and villas and outside one can enjoy unrestricted
views of the ocean from the pools and the private beach.

In Msambweni, dem »Land der Rappenantilope«, haben die Brüder
Frederik und Filip Vanderhoeven 2007 dieses luxuriöse, im Lamu-Stil er-
baute Hideaway eröffnet. In vornehmlich in Weiß gehaltenen Suiten und
Villen setzen arabische Lampen und goldene Seidenkissen Glanzpunkte
– draußen genießt man von den Pools sowie vom Privatstrand aus freien
Blick auf den Ozean.

C'est à Msambweni, le « pays de l'hippotrague noir », que les frères
Frederik et Filip Vanderhoeven ont ouvert en 2007 cette retraite luxueuse
construite en style Lamu. Dans les suites et les villas où le blanc domine,
des lampes arabes et des coussins de soie dorés posent des accents
lumineux. À l'extérieur, que l'on se trouve au bord des piscines ou sur la
plage privée, la vue sur l'océan Indien est imprenable.

Msambweni Beach House
P.O. Box 51
80404 Msambweni
Kenya
Tel. +254 20 357 7093
Fax +254 20 213 7599
msambwenihouse@yahoo.com
www.msambweni-house.com

LOCATION
Situated on Kenya's south coast near the Tanzanian border, 37 miles from Mombasa airport.

RATES
Suites from $580, villas from $780, full board inclusive.

ROOMS
3 suites in the main house, 1 tent suite and 3 villas with private pools.

FOOD
Belgian and French dishes are offered alongside Swahili specialities. For the absolutely exclusive experience, book a private dinner on one of the sandbanks.

X-FACTOR
The new spa right next to the Indian Ocean.

BOOK TO PACK
"Rules of the Wild: A Novel of Africa" by Francesca Marciano.

LAGE
An der Südküste Kenias nahe der Grenze zu Tansania gelegen, 60 km südlich des Flughafens Mombasa.

PREISE
Suite ab 430 €, Villa ab 580 €, inklusive Vollpension.

ZIMMER
3 Suiten im Haupthaus, 1 Zelt-Suite, 3 Villen mit Privatpools.

KÜCHE
Neben Swahili-Spezialitäten wird belgische und französische Küche serviert. Ganz exklusiv: ein privates Dinner auf einer Sandbank.

X-FAKTOR
Das neue Spa direkt am Indischen Ozean.

BUCHTIPP
»Himmel über Afrika« von Francesca Marciano.

SITUATION
Située sur la côte sud du Kenya près de la frontière tanzanienne, à 60 km au sud de l'aéroport de Mombasa.

PRIX
Suite à partir de 430 €, villa à partir de 580 €, avec pension complète.

CHAMBRES
3 suites dans la maison principale, 1 suite-tente, 3 villas avec piscine privée.

RESTAURATION
À côté de spécialités de la cuisine swahili, le restaurant propose des plats belges et français. La surprise : un dîner privé sur un banc de sable.

LE « PETIT PLUS »
Le nouveau spa au bord de l'océan Indien.

LIVRE À EMPORTER
« L'Africaine » de Francesca Marciano.

Constance Lodge

Tsarabanjina, Madagascar

The private island of Tsarabanjina is for the exclusive use of guests at this enchanting lodge. The bungalows have no telephones or televisions but instead offer other extras such as flippers for swimming in the crystal-clear sea waters. After your dip, you can relax on the powdery sands of the beach and watch the fishermen bringing in their day's catch.

Die Privatinsel Tsarabanjina gehört exklusiv den Gästen dieser zauber-haften Lodge. Ihre Bungalows bieten weder Telefon noch Fernseher – dafür aber Extras wie Schnorchelflossen, die im kristallklaren Meer zum Einsatz kommen. Anschließend entspannt man am Puderzuckerstrand und sieht den Fischern zu, die den Fang des Tages an Land bringen.

L'île privée de Tsarabanjina appartient aux hôtes de ce lodge en-chanteur. Les bungalows n'ont ni téléphone ni téléviseur – mais nombre d'extras, par exemple un tuba et des palmes pour plonger dans les eaux limpides. Ensuite, on se détend sur le sable blanc et fin et on observe les pêcheurs qui rapportent ce qu'ils ont capturé durant la journée passée en mer.

Constance Lodge Tsarabanjina
B.P. 380
207 Hellville, Nosy Be
Madagascar
Tel. +261 32 051 5229 (lodge)
Tel. +230 402 2774 (reservations)
Fax +230 402 2616
resa@tsarabanjina.com
www.tsarabanjina.com

LOCATION
Tsarabanjina lies 40 miles off the northwest coast of Madagascar. The boat transfer from Nosy Be takes 90 min.

RATES
Bungalows from $380 for single use and $580 for doubles, with full board.

ROOMS
25 straw-roofed, rosewood bungalows; each sleeps 2 and has its own ocean-facing veranda.

FOOD
The restaurant serves freshly caught fish and, on request, lobster on the beach under a star-studded sky – very romantic!

X-FACTOR
The massages on a natural rock plateau.

BOOK TO PACK
"The Aye-Aye and I" by Gerald Durrell.

LAGE
Tsarabanjina liegt 65 km vor der Nord-westküste Madagaskars. Der Boots-transfer ab Nosy Be dauert 90 Min.

PREISE
Bungalow ab 276 € bei Einzel-, ab 424 € bei Doppelbelegung, mit Vollpension.

ZIMMER
25 strohgedeckte Bungalows aus Rosenholz; alle für 2 Personen und mit Veranda zum Ozean.

KÜCHE
Im Restaurant steht fangfrischer Fisch auf der Karte. Auf Wunsch wird Hummer am Strand unterm Sternenhimmel serviert – sehr romantisch.

X-FAKTOR
Die Massagen auf einem Felsplateau.

BUCHTIPP
»Dadabé« von Michèle Rakotoson.

SITUATION
Tsarabanjina est située à 65 km au nord-ouest des côtes de Madagascar. Le transfert en bateau à partir de Nosy Be dure 90 min.

PRIX
Bungalow à partir de 276 € pour une personne, de 424 € pour deux personnes, avec pension complète.

CHAMBRES
25 bungalows en palissandre au toit de chaume ; tous pour 2 personnes, avec véranda ouverte sur l'océan.

RESTAURATION
Le restaurant propose des spécialités de poisson frais. Les romantiques apprécieront les fruits de mer servis le soir sur la plage à la demande.

LE « PETIT PLUS »
Les massages sur un plateau rocheux.

LIVRE À EMPORTER
« Dadabé » de Michèle Rakotoson.

Zarafa Camp

Zibadianja Lagoon, Selinda Reserve, Botswana

This camp, which opened in 2008, comprises four luxurious tents kitted out in classic safari style with handmade wood and leather furniture, fireplaces and copper bathtubs. From here you can watch the elephants as they pass a few yards from your tent flaps and the crocodiles and hippos lounging in the nearby lagoon.

Dieses im Juni 2008 eröffnete Camp umfasst vier luxuriöse Zelte, welche im klassischen Safaristil mit handgefertigten Holz- und Ledermöbeln, Kamin sowie Kupferbadewanne ausgestattet wurden. Von hier aus kann man in aller Ruhe die Elefanten beobachten, die nur wenige Meter entfernt vorbeiziehen, sowie die Krokodile und Nilpferde, die in der Lagune leben.

Ce camp ouvert en juin 2008 comprend quatre tentes luxueuses équipées dans le plus pur style safari avec ses meubles en bois et en cuir fabriqués à la main, ses cheminées et ses baignoires en cuivre. Un endroit bien tranquille pour observer les éléphants qui passent à quelques mètres de là, ainsi que les crocodiles et les hippopotames vivant dans les eaux du lagon.

Zarafa Camp
Selinda Reserve
P.O. Box 22
Kasane
Botswana
Tel. +267 62 50 505
Fax +27 11 807 2110
reservations@selindareserve.com
and enquiry@wilderness.co.za
www.selindareserve.com
and www.wilderness.co.za

LOCATION
Situated by the Zibadianja Lagoon in the Selinda Reserve (northeast of the Okavango Delta), 50 min flying time southwest of Kasane.

RATES
Tents from $1,550 per day for single use and $2,070 for doubles, including full board and safaris.

ROOMS
4 exclusive marquis-style tents – 300 square feet each with bath, outdoor shower and veranda with a plunge pool.

FOOD
Breakfast, brunch, afternoon tea and dinner are served in the main tent.

X-FACTOR
The nighttime safaris.

BOOK TO PACK
"Nisa: The Life and Words of a !Kung Woman" by Marjorie Shostak.

LAGE
An der Zibadianja Lagune im Selinda-Reservat gelegen (nordöstlich des Okavango-Deltas), 50 Flugminuten südwestlich von Kasane.

PREISE
Zelt pro Tag ab 1.135 € bei Einzel-, ab 1.515 € bei Doppelbelegung, mit Vollpension und Safaris.

ZIMMER
4 Zelte im exklusiven Marquis-Stil (93 qm, mit Bad, Außendusche und Veranda mit Tauchpool).

KÜCHE
Im Hauptzelt wird Frühstück, Brunch, Nachmittagstee und Abendessen serviert.

X-FAKTOR
Die Nachtsafaris.

BUCHTIPP
»Nisa erzählt« von Marjorie Shostak.

SITUATION
Situé sur le lagon Zibadianja dans la réserve Selinda (au nord-est du delta Okavango), à 50 min de vol au sud-ouest de Kasane.

PRIX
À partir de 1135 € par jour pour une tente d'une personne, à partir de 1515 € pour deux personnes, pension complète et safaris compris.

CHAMBRES
4 tentes dans le style marquis exclusif (93 m², salle de bains, douche en plein air et véranda avec piscine privative).

RESTAURATION
Le petit-déjeuner, le brunch, le thé de l'après-midi et le dîner sont servis dans la tente principale.

LE « PETIT PLUS »
Les safaris nocturnes.

LIVRE À EMPORTER
« Nisa, une vie de femme » de Marjorie Shostak.

Ulusaba

Sabi Sand Reserve, Mpumalanga Province, South Africa

Ulusaba – "place of little fear" – is what the Shangaan tribe once called this place, because it offers a good view of the surroundings and thus potential enemies. Today all that guests at Richard Branson's lodge need to keep a lookout for are the "Big Five" and they can take time to relax after first-rate safaris, in the luxurious suites and spa or together over an atmospheric evening dinner.

Ulusaba – »Platz der geringen Angst« – so nannte der Stamm der Shangaan diesen Ort einst, da er einen weiten Blick übers Land und auf mögliche Feinde bot. Heute erspähen die Gäste von Sir Richard Bransons Lodge von hier aus die »Big Five« und entspannen nach den ausgezeichneten Safaris in luxuriösen Suiten, im Spa und beim gemeinsamen Dinner.

La tribu des Shangaan nommait ce lieu Ulusaba – « la place de la petite peur » – car il offrait une large vue sur le pays et donc sur l'arrivée d'ennemis éventuels. Aujourd'hui, les clients du lodge de Sir Richard Branson sont plutôt à l'affût des « Big Five ». À l'issue de leurs excellents safaris, ils peuvent se détendre dans des suites luxueuses, au spa et lors d'un dîner plein d'ambiance pris en commun.

Ulusaba Private Game Reserve
P.O. Box 2220
Hazyview 1242
Mpumalanga Province
South Africa
Tel. +27 13 735 5460 (lodge)
Tel. +27 11 325 4405
(reservations)
enquiries@ulusaba.virgin.com
www.ulusaba.virgin.com

LOCATION
Situated in the west of the Sabi Sand
Reserve next to a private landing strip,
80 min flying time from Johannesburg.

RATES
Double rooms from $1,200 per day,
suites from $2,300, including full board
and safaris.

ROOMS
21 rooms and suites (10 in the Rock
Lodge on a hill and 11 in the Safari
Lodge in the bush).

FOOD
Outstanding Pan-African cuisine.

X-FACTOR
The lodge primarily employs locals and
supports nearby villages with charity
projects.

BOOK TO PACK
"Summertime" by J. M. Coetzee.

LAGE
Im Westen des Sabi-Sand-Reservats
gelegen, 80 Min. Flugzeit von Johannesburg entfernt (eigene Landebahn).

PREISE
Doppelzimmer pro Tag ab 900 €, Suite
ab 1.700 €, mit Vollpension und Safaris.

ZIMMER
21 Zimmer und Suiten (10 in der Rock
Lodge auf einem Hügel, 11 in der Safari
Lodge im Busch).

KÜCHE
Hervorragende panafrikanische
Spezialitäten.

X-FAKTOR
Die Lodge beschäftigt hauptsächlich
Einheimische und unterstützt die nahen
Dörfer mit Charity-Projekten.

BUCHTIPP
»Sommer des Lebens« von J. M.
Coetzee.

SITUATION
Situé à l'ouest de la réserve Sabi Sand,
à 80 min de vol de Johannesburg (piste
d'atterrissage privée).

PRIX
Chambre double à partir de 900 € par
jour, suite à partir de 1700 €, pension
complète et safaris compris.

CHAMBRES
21 chambres et suites (10 au Rock
Lodge sur une colline, 11 au Safari
Lodge dans la brousse).

RESTAURATION
Délicieuses spécialités panafricaines.

LE « PETIT PLUS »
Le lodge emploie essentiellement des
autochtones et soutient les villages
alentour par des projets d'assistance.

LIVRE À EMPORTER
« Disgrâce » de J. M. Coetzee.

Kensington Place
Cape Town, South Africa

Since Anton De Kock (architecture) and Chris Weir (interiors) gave this house a makeover in 2006, it has become the most desirable boutique hotel in Cape Town. Here, at the foot of Table Mountain, you can stay in first-class, glamorously designed rooms with an African touch. There are wonderful extras, ranging from a terrace with a view of the Atlantic to a laptop with an in-house Skype connection.

Seit Anton De Kock (Architektur) und Chris Weir (Interieurs) dieses Haus 2006 renoviert haben, ist es das begehrteste Boutiquehotel Kapstadts. Unterhalb des Tafelbergs wohnt man hier in edel und glamourös designten Zimmern mit afrikanischem Touch sowie wunderbaren Extras – von der Terrasse mit Atlantikblick bis zum Laptop mit Skype-Adresse.

Depuis qu'Anton De Kock (architecture) et Chris Weir (intérieurs) ont donné à cet établissement un nouveau visage en 2006, celui-ci est l'hôtel boutique le plus prisé du Cap. Niché au pied de la Montagne de la Table, il vous propose des chambres élégantes et glamour avec une touche africaine, ainsi que de merveilleux extras allant de la terrasse avec vue sur l'Atlantique à l'ordinateur portable avec adresse skype.

Kensington Place
38 Kensington Crescent
Higgovale
Cape Town 8001
South Africa
Tel. +27 21 424 4744
Fax +27 21 424 1810
kplace@mweb.co.za
www.kensingtonplace.co.za

LOCATION
Located in a cultivated residential area, 20 min from the airport. The hotel has its own pool and the beach is 10–15 min away by car.

RATES
Rooms from $250, breakfast included.

ROOMS
8 rooms. The "Garden Room" with its own little private garden is particularly lovely.

FOOD
The hotel has a chic restaurant with a terrace, lounge and bar.

X-FACTOR
The excellent service – the staff know Cape Town like the backs of their hands and give great sightseeing tips.

BOOK TO PACK
"Burger's Daughter" by Nadine Gordimer.

LAGE
In einem gepflegten Wohngebiet gelegen, 20 Min. vom Flughafen entfernt. Das Hotel hat einen Pool; zum Strand fährt man 10–15 Min.

PREISE
Zimmer ab 185 €, inklusive Frühstück.

ZIMMER
8 Zimmer. Besonders schön: der »Garden Room« mit privatem Gärtchen.

KÜCHE
Das Hotel besitzt ein schickes Restaurant mit Terrasse, eine Lounge und eine Bar.

X-FAKTOR
Der exzellente Service – die Mitarbeiter kennen sich in Kapstadt perfekt aus und geben ausgezeichnete Tipps.

BUCHTIPP
»Burgers Tochter« von Nadine Gordimer.

SITUATION
Situé dans un des beaux quartiers de la ville à 20 min de l'aéroport. L'hôtel a une piscine ; la plage est à 10–15 min en voiture.

PRIX
Chambre à partir de 185 €, petit-déjeuner compris.

CHAMBRES
8 chambres. La « Garden Room » avec son petit jardin privé est particulièrement belle.

RESTAURATION
L'hôtel possède un restaurant chic avec terrasse, lounge et bar.

LE « PETIT PLUS »
L'excellent service – les employés connaissent parfaitement Le Cap, ils vous donnent de bons tuyaux.

LIVRE À EMPORTER
« Fille de Burger » de Nadine Gordimer.

Al Mamlouka

Damascus, Syria

Whoever finds this hotel, hidden in a labyrinth of alleyways, discovers a jewel. The 18th-century residence has eight rooms, named by the
owner May Mamarbachi after Arabian philosophers and sultans. They are
all stuffed with opulent antiques, brocades and mosaics. The "Suleiman"
suite also has a rose-shaped fountain and 230-year-old frescoes.

Wer dieses Hotel im Labyrinth der Gassen findet, entdeckt ein Ju-
wel: Das Haus aus dem 17. Jahrhundert besitzt acht Zimmer, die May
Mamarbachi nach Sultanen und Philosophen benannt und mit Antiquitäten,
Brokat sowie Mosaiken opulent ausgestattet hat – die Suite »Suleiman«
besitzt sogar einen Brunnen in Form einer Rose und ein 230 Jahre altes
Fresko.

Celui qui finit par trouver cet hôtel dans le labyrinthe des ruelles,
découvre un petit joyau. La maison du 17e siècle possède huit chambres
que May Mamarbachi a baptisées d'après des sultans et des philosophes
d'Arabie et qui sont décorées avec une opulence d'antiquités, de brocarts
et de mosaïques. La suite « Suleiman » a même une fontaine en forme de
rose et une fresque vieille de 230 ans.

Beit Al Mamlouka
Bab Touma, in front of
Hammam Al Bakri
Damascus
Syria
Tel. +963 11 543 0445
Fax +963 11 541 7248
info@almamlouka.com
www.almamlouka.com

LOCATION
Situated in Bab Touma, the Christian quarter of Damascus, 35 min from the airport.

RATES
Single rooms from $130, double rooms from $150, suites from $275, breakfast included.

ROOMS
4 rooms and 4 suites, all individually decorated.

FOOD
The hotel serves Arabian and continental breakfasts and has a small bar. There are numerous restaurants within walking distance.

X-FACTOR
The patio with its sweet-smelling orange and lemon trees.

BOOK TO PACK
"Damascus Nights" by Rafik Schami.

LAGE
In Bab Touma, dem christlichen Viertel von Damaskus gelegen, 35 Min. vom Flughafen entfernt.

PREISE
Einzelzimmer ab 95 €, Doppelzimmer ab 110 €, Suite ab 205 €, inklusive Frühstück.

ZIMMER
4 Zimmer und 4 Suiten, alle individuell eingerichtet.

KÜCHE
Das Hotel serviert arabisches und kontinentales Frühstück und hat eine kleine Bar. In Gehweite befinden sich zahlreiche Restaurants.

X-FAKTOR
Der Patio mit duftenden Orangen- und Zitronenbäumen.

BUCHTIPP
»Erzähler der Nacht« von Rafik Schami.

SITUATION
Situé à Bab Touma, le quartier chrétien de Damas, à 35 min de l'aéroport.

PRIX
Chambre simple à partir de 95 €, chambre double à partir de 110 €, suite à partir de 205 €, petit-déjeuner compris.

CHAMBRES
4 chambres et 4 suites, toutes meublée individuellement.

RESTAURATION
L'hôtel sert un petit-déjeuner arabe et continental, il a aussi un petit bar. Plusieurs restaurants dans les alentours

LE « PETIT PLUS »
Le patio avec ses orangers et citronnier odorants.

LIVRE À EMPORTER
« Histoire de Milad qui partit pour mange à sa faim pendant vingt et un jours » de Rafik Schami.

Evason Ma'In Hot Springs

Madaba, Dead Sea, Jordan

The location of this oasis is fascinating: 870 feet below sea level and nestling close to a rough rockface streaming with the hot and healing waters of the Ma'In thermal springs. One of the waterfalls tumbles straight into the wonderful Six Senses Spa, where you can have treatments using salts from the nearby Dead Sea.

Die Lage dieser Oase ist faszinierend – 264 Meter unterhalb des Meeresspiegels und im Schatten schroffer Felsen, über welche die heißen und heilenden Quellen von Ma'In fließen. Einer der Wasserfälle rauscht direkt in den Pool des wunderbaren Six Senses Spa, in dem man auch mit Salz aus dem nahen Toten Meer gepflegt wird.

L'oasis se trouve dans un cadre fascinant, à 264 mètres en dessous du niveau de la mer et à l'ombre de rochers escarpés par-dessus lesquels coulent les sources chaudes de Ma'In. L'une de ses cascades dévale directement dans la piscine du merveilleux Six Senses Spa, qui propose aussi des soins au sel de la mer Morte toute proche.

Evason Ma'In Hot Springs & Six
Senses Spa
P.O. Box 801 Madaba
11117 Ma'In
Jordan
Tel. +962 5 324 5500
Fax +962 5 324 5550
reservations-main@sixsenses.com
www.sixsenses.com

LOCATION
19 miles southwest of the "mosaic city" Madaba. The drive from Amman airport takes 60 min, the Dead Sea is 30 min away and Petra 3 hours.

RATES
Rooms from $170, suites from $290, breakfast included.

ROOMS
78 rooms and 19 suites.

FOOD
Both Arabian and international cuisine – served in spectacular settings such as under a Bedouin tent or with a panoramic view of the Dead Sea.

X-FACTOR
This environmentally friendly resort was built using locally sourced materials.

BOOK TO PACK
"Cities of Salt" by Abdelrahman Munif.

LAGE
30 km südwestlich der »Mosaikstadt« Madaba gelegen. Die Fahrt vom Flughafen Amman dauert 60 Min., das Tote Meer ist 30 Min. entfernt, bis nach Petra fährt man 3 Std.

PREISE
Zimmer ab 125 €, Suite ab 215 €, inklusive Frühstück.

ZIMMER
78 Zimmer und 19 Suiten.

KÜCHE
Arabisch und international – serviert an spektakulären Plätzen wie unter dem Beduinenzelt oder mit Panoramablick über das Tote Meer.

X-FAKTOR
Das Resort wurde mit regionalen Materialien und umweltfreundlich erbaut.

BUCHTIPP
»Salzstädte« von Abdalrachman Munif.

SITUATION
Situé à 30 km au sud-ouest de Madaba, la « ville des mosaïques ». Le trajet depuis l'aéroport d'Amman dure 60 min, la mer Morte se trouve à 30 min et Petra à 3 h de voiture.

PRIX
Chambre à partir de 125 €, suite à partir de 215 €, petit-déjeuner compris.

CHAMBRES
78 chambres et 19 suites.

RESTAURATION
Cuisine arabe et internationale, servie dans des endroits spectaculaires, comme sous une tente bédouine ou avec vue panoramique sur la mer Morte.

LE « PETIT PLUS »
L'hôtel a été construit avec des matériaux de la région et en respectant l'environnement.

LIVRE À EMPORTER
« Une ville dans la mémoire : Amman » d'Abdul Rahman Mounif.

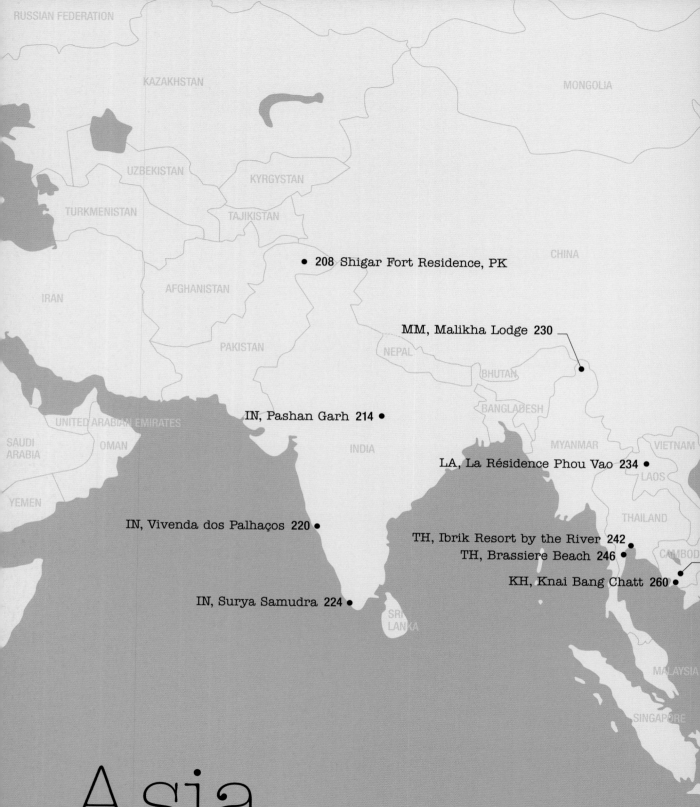

RUSSIAN FEDERATION

KAZAKHSTAN

MONGOLIA

UZBEKISTAN

KYRGYSTAN

TURKMENISTAN

TAJIKISTAN

CHINA

● 208 Shigar Fort Residence, PK

IRAN

AFGHANISTAN

MM, Malikha Lodge 230 ●

PAKISTAN

NEPAL

BHUTAN

BANGLADESH

UNITED ARABIAN EMIRATES

IN, Pashan Garh 214 ●

SAUDI
ARABIA

OMAN

INDIA

MYANMAR

VIETNAM

LA, La Résidence Phou Vao 234 ●

YEMEN

LAOS

THAILAND

IN, Vivenda dos Palhaços 220 ●

TH, Ibrik Resort by the River 242 ●
TH, Brassiere Beach 246 ●

CAMBOD

KH, Knai Bang Chatt 260 ●

IN, Surya Samudra 224 ●

SRI
LANKA

MALAYSIA

SINGAPORE

Asia

278 Red Capital Ranch, CN

284 Fujiya Inn, JP

268 The Nam Hai, VN

256 Boddhi Tree Del Gusto, KH

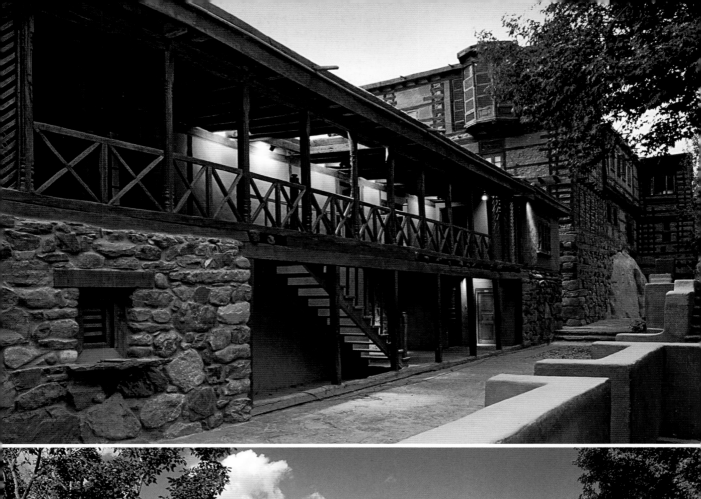

Shigar Fort Residence
Shigar Valley, Baltistan, Northern Areas, Pakistan

Shigar Fort is both hotel and museum: this 400-year-old Amacha dynasty palace was reopened in 2005 after a six-year restoration under the auspices of the Aga Khan Trust for Culture. Traditional buildings, antiques, carvings and weaving bear witness to the art and culture of Baltistan – the history of this region reaching back to early Tibetan Buddhist origins.

Shigar Fort ist Hotel und Museum zugleich: Der 400 Jahre alte Palast der Amacha-Dynastie wurde 2005 nach einer sechsjährigen Restaurierung unter Leitung des Aga Khan Trust for Culture wieder eröffnet. Traditionelle Bauten, Antiquitäten, Schnitz- und Webarbeiten sind Zeugen der Kunst und Kultur Baltistans – die Geschichte dieser Region reicht bis in frühe tibetische Zeiten zurück.

Shigar Fort est à la fois un hôtel et un musée : le palais vieux de 400 ans de la dynastie des Amacha a rouvert ses portes sous la direction de l'Aga Khan Trust for Culture après avoir été restauré pendant six ans. Bâtiments traditionnels, antiquités, ouvrages sculptés et tissés témoignent de l'art et de la culture du Baltistan. L'histoire de la région remonte aux origines du Tibet.

Shigar Fort Residence
Shigar
Baltistan, Northern Areas
Pakistan
Tel. +92 5831 66 107
Fax +92 5831 58 787
info@shigarfort.com
www.shigarfort.com

LOCATION
The hotel lies in the Shigar Valley, where the Karakorams meet the Himalayas. There are flights from Islamabad to Skardu and from there it is a 19-mile drive to the fort.

RATES
Single rooms from $91, double rooms from $130, breakfast included.

ROOMS
13 impressive rooms in the old palace and 7 in the new garden house.

FOOD
The restaurant serves local specialities made from organic produce.

X-FACTOR
The palace's own mosque.

BOOK TO PACK
"The Reluctant Fundamentalist" by Mohsin Hamid.

LAGE
Im Shigar-Tal gelegen, wo Karakorum und Himalaja zusammentreffen. Man fliegt von Islamabad nach Skardu und fährt von dort aus 30 km zum Fort.

PREISE
Einzelzimmer ab 70 €, Doppelzimmer ab 100 €, inklusive Frühstück.

ZIMMER
13 beeindruckende Räume im alten Palast, 7 im neu erbauten Gartenhaus.

KÜCHE
Das Restaurant serviert einheimische Spezialitäten mit Produkten aus organischem Anbau.

X-FAKTOR
Die palasteigene Moschee.

BUCHTIPP
»Der Fundamentalist, der keiner sein wollte« von Mohsin Hamid.

SITUATION
Situé dans la vallée de Shigar où se rencontrent le Karakoram et l'Himalaya. Liaison par avion d'Islamabad à Skardu, puis trajet de 30 km en voiture jusqu'au fort.

PRIX
Chambre simple à partir de 70 €, chambre double à partir de 100 €, petit-déjeuner compris.

CHAMBRES
13 chambres impressionnantes dans l'ancien palais, 7 chambres dans le nouveau pavillon.

RESTAURATION
Le restaurant sert des spécialités locales préparées avec des produits biologiques.

LE « PETIT PLUS »
La mosquée appartenant au palais.

LIVRE À EMPORTER
« L'Intégriste malgré lui » de Mohsin Hamid.

Pashan Garh

Panna, Madhya Pradesh, India

The cottages of this jungle lodge that opened at the end of 2008 are modelled on Indian dry-packed stone houses with tiled roofs. The interiors, designed by Nicholas Plewman Architects, with their white marble surfaces and modern ebony and leather furniture, provide a surprising contrast that lend the dwellings a certain urban feel.

Die Cottages dieser Ende 2008 eröffneten Dschungel-Lodge entstanden nach dem Vorbild der indischen Steinhäuser, die aus Trockenmauerwerk errichtet und mit einem Ziegeldach gedeckt sind. Überraschende Kontraste setzten die Designer des Architekturbüros Nicholas Plewman im Inneren: Weißer Marmor und moderne Möbel aus Leder und Ebenholz verleihen urbanes Flair.

Les cottages de ce lodge de la jungle ouvert fin 2008 ont pour modèle les maisons indiennes à toit de tuiles dont les murs sont faits de pierres et d'argile. À l'intérieur, les contrastes imaginés par les designers du bureau d'architecture Nicholas Plewman surprennent : le marbre blanc et les meubles modernes en cuir et ébène posent un accent élégant et moderne.

Pashan Garh
Panna National Park
Amanganj Road
Panna, Madhya Pradesh 488001
India
Tel. +91 22 6601 1825
Fax +91 22 6702 1825
pashangarh.panna@tajsafaris.com
www.tajhotels.com
Open from mid-October to June

LOCATION
Situated on a 185-acre private estate in the Vindhya hills. Visitors can fly from Delhi to Khajuraho (370 miles south) and then be picked up and driven to the lodge in 60 min.

RATES
Cottage from $840 per day (for 2 persons), full board included.

ROOMS
12 cottages.

FOOD
The restaurant serves fine Indian food and can arrange dinners in the bush on an old ox cart.

X-FACTOR
There are safaris twice daily through the bird-filled Panna National Park.

BOOK TO PACK
"Midnight's Children" by Salman Rushdie.

LAGE
Auf einem 75 Hektar großen Privatgelände im Vindhya-Gebirge gelegen. Man fliegt von Delhi nach Khajuraho (600 km südlich) und wird in 60 Min. zur Lodge gefahren.

PREISE
Cottage ab 610 € pro Tag (2 Personen), mit Vollpension.

ZIMMER
12 Cottages.

KÜCHE
Das Restaurant serviert feine indische Speisen und arrangiert auch ein Buschdinner auf einem alten Ochsenkarren.

X-FAKTOR
Zweimal täglich starten Safaris durch den vogelreichen Panna-Nationalpark.

BUCHTIPP
»Mitternachtskinder« von Salman Rushdie.

SITUATION
Situé dans un domaine privé de 75 hectares sur les collines de Vindhya. De Delhi, on prend l'avion à destination de Khajuraho (à 600 km au sud) ; le transfert au lodge dure 60 min.

PRIX
Cottage à partir de 610 € par jour (2 personnes), avec pension complète.

CHAMBRES
12 cottages.

RESTAURATION
Le restaurant propose des plats raffinés de la cuisine indienne et organise aussi un dîner dans la brousse sur un ancien char à bœufs.

LE « PETIT PLUS »
Les safaris organisés deux fois par jour dans le parc national de Panna, un paradis pour les oiseaux.

LIVRE À EMPORTER
« Les Enfants de minuit » de Salman Rushdie.

Vivenda dos Palhaços

Majorda, Goa, India

Brother and sister Charlotte and Simon Hayward have beautifully renovated a Hindu house and a Portuguese building from 1929 and named the rooms after their favourite Southeast Asian haunts. The rooms are decorated in the colours of Goa and furnished in part with antiques, such as a bathtub from the Royal Bombay Yacht Club.

Ein Hindu-Haus mit dicken Lehmmauern und ein portugiesisches Gebäude anno 1929 haben die Geschwister Charlotte und Simon Hayward wunderbar renoviert und die Zimmer nach ihren liebsten südasiatischen Orten benannt. Die Räume sind in den Farben Goas gehalten und zum Teil mit Antiquitäten ausgestattet – darunter eine Badewanne aus dem Royal Bombay Yacht Club.

Charlotte Hayward et son frère Simon ont merveilleusement restauré une maison hindoue aux épais murs de terre et une maison portugaise de 1929 avant de donner aux chambres le nom d'endroits qu'ils ont aimés en Asie du Sud. Les pièces sont peintes dans les couleurs de Goa et abritent en partie des antiquités, telles qu' une baignoire du Royal Bombay Yacht Club.

Vivenda dos Palhaços
Costa Vaddo
Majorda, Salcette
Goa 403713
India
Tel. +91 832 322 1119
Fax +91 832 288 1700
info@vivendagoa.com
www.vivendagoa.com

LOCATION
Located in Majorda village on the south coast of Goa, 30 min south of Dabolim airport. The nearest beach is half a mile away.

RATES
Rooms from $77, breakfast included.

ROOMS
6 rooms in the house and 1 tent room; all with their own bathrooms.

FOOD
Both Indian and international cuisine are served in the evenings and you can order a picnic basket for lunch by the pool or on the beach.

X-FACTOR
The charming owners.

BOOK TO PACK
"The White Tiger" by Aravind Adiga.

LAGE
Im Dorf Majorda an der Südküste Goas gelegen, 30 Min. südlich des Flughafens Dabolim. Der nächste Strand ist 1 km entfernt.

PREISE
Zimmer ab 57 €, inklusive Frühstück.

ZIMMER
6 Zimmer im Haus, 1 Zimmer im Zelt; alle mit eigenem Bad.

KÜCHE
Abends werden indische und internationale Menüs serviert. Auf Wunsch bekommt man einen Picknickkorb für den Lunch am Pool oder Strand.

X-FAKTOR
Der Charme der Besitzer.

BUCHTIPP
»Der weiße Tiger« von Aravind Adiga.

SITUATION
Située dans le village de Majorda sur la côte méridionale de Goa, à 30 min au sud de l'aéroport de Dabolim. La plage la plus proche est à 1 km.

PRIX
Chambre à partir de 57 €, petit-déjeuner compris.

CHAMBRES
6 chambres dans la maison, 1 chambre-tente ; toutes avec salle de bains.

RESTAURATION
Des plats de la cuisine indienne et internationale sont proposés le soir. On peut demander un panier de pique-nique pour déjeuner au bord de la piscine ou sur la plage.

LE « PETIT PLUS »
Le charme des propriétaires.

LIVRE À EMPORTER
« Le Tigre blanc » d'Aravind Adiga.

Surya Samudra
Kovalam, Kerala, India

This refuge celebrated its reopening in 2009 after a complete renovation. Here you can enjoy peace, privacy and Keralan culture far away from the tourist hordes. Each cottage is a carefully restored Tharavadu – a traditional Keralan house with terracotta roof tiles, wooden pillars, antiques and handcrafts.

Nach einer Renovierung feierte dieses Refugium Ende 2009 Neueröffnung. Fern des Touristentrubels genießt man hier höchste Privatsphäre und erlebt in aller Ruhe die Kultur Keralas ganz unmittelbar: Jedes Cottage ist ein sorgsam saniertes Tharavadu – ein traditionelles Haus der Region mit Ziegeldach, Holzsäulen, Antiquitäten sowie Kunsthandwerk.

Ce refuge a rouvert ses portes fin 2009 après avoir été rénové. Loin des centres touristiques, vous jouirez ici d'une sphère intime et découvrirez la culture de Kerala en toute tranquillité. Chaque cottage est un Tharavadu remis en état avec beaucoup de soin. Il s'agit de maisons traditionnelles avec toit en terre cuite, colonnes en bois, antiquités et art artisanal.

Surya Samudra Private Retreats,
Kovalam
Pulinkudi, Mullur P.O.
Thiruvananthapuram 695 521
Kerala
India
Tel. +91 471 226 7333
Fax +91 471 226 7124
reservations@suryasamudra.com
www.suryasamudra.com

LOCATION
Located in a tropical garden by the sea with two beaches, 14 miles south of the nearest airport at Thiruvananthapuram.

RATES
Cottages from $175 per night, breakfast included.

ROOMS
22 cottages situated on the cliffs above the sea or in the garden.

FOOD
Two restaurants offer Indian and Keralan dishes as well as international cuisine.

X-FACTOR
The "Spa Niraamaya" specialising in Ayurveda techniques.

BOOK TO PACK
"The God of Small Things" by Arundhati Roy.

LAGE
In einem tropischen Garten am Meer gelegen (zwei Strände); 22 km südlich von Thiruvananthapuram, wo sich der nächste Flughafen befindet.

PREISE
Cottage ab 130 € pro Nacht, inklusive Frühstück.

ZIMMER
22 Cottages; auf den Klippen über dem Meer oder im Garten gelegen.

KÜCHE
Zwei Restaurants bieten Gerichte aus Kerala und Indien sowie internationale Menüs.

X-FAKTOR
Das auf Ayurveda spezialisierte »Spa Niraamaya«.

BUCHTIPP
»Der Gott der kleinen Dinge« von Arundhati Roy.

SITUATION
Situé dans un jardin tropical en bord de mer (deux plages) ; à 22 km au sud de Thiruvananthapuram, où se trouve le prochain aéroport.

PRIX
Cottage à partir de 130 € la nuit, petit-déjeuner compris.

CHAMBRES
22 cottages sur les falaises au-dessus de la mer ou dans le jardin.

RESTAURATION
Deux restaurants proposent des plats de Kerala et de l'Inde ainsi que des menus internationaux.

LE « PETIT PLUS »
Le « Spa Niraamaya » spécialisé dans l'ayurvéda.

LIVRE À EMPORTER
« Le Dieu des petits riens » d'Arundhati Roy.

Malikha Lodge
Putao, Kachin State, Myanmar

This lodge is tucked away in isolated and breathtakingly beautiful northern Myanmar. Ten luxurious and puristic bungalows, designed in 2007 by
the Amanresort architect Jean-Michel Gathy, form a base for jungle treks.
At the centre of every house is a handcrafted teak bathtub that rises up on
an almost stage-like pedastal and can be enclosed in gauze curtains.

Diese Lodge verbirgt sich im einsamen, atemberaubend schönen
Norden Myanmars. Basis für Trekkings durch den Dschungel sind zehn
Bungalows, die der Amanresort-Architekt Jean-Michel Gathy 2007 puristisch und luxuriös designt hat. Herzstück jedes Hauses ist eine handge-
fertigte Teakwanne, die von zarten Vorhängen umgeben wird und eine fast
theatralische Wirkung erzielt.

Ce lodge établi au nord du Myanmar est dissimulé dans un paysage
d'une extraordinaire beauté. Dix bungalows à la fois sobres et luxueux
conçus en 2007 par l'architecte Jean-Michel Gathy, l'un des concepteurs
de la chaîne Amanresorts, servent de point de départ aux randonnées
dans la jungle. Dans chaque maison trône une baignoire en teck fabriquée
à la main et entourée de rideaux de gaze, dont l'effet est presque théâtral.

Malikha Lodge
Reservation Office
No. 41, Golden Valley
Bahan Township, Yangon
Myanmar
Tel. +95 1 513 300
Tel. +95 1 503 842
Fax +95 1 502 647
info@malikhalodge.com
www.malikhalodge.com
Open from October to April

LOCATION
Situated in Kachin State, the lodge can be reached only from Putao (3 flying hours north of Rangoon with stops in Mandalay and Myitkyina), the transfer from the airport takes 15 min.

RATES
Packages from 3 nights with rates from $3,800 per bungalow, full board and activities included.

ROOMS
10 bungalows; each sleeps 2.

FOOD
The chef serves refined, continental country-style dishes that change daily.

X-FACTOR
The spa massages with natural herb oils.

BOOKS TO PACK
"The Piano Tuner" by Daniel Mason and "Saving Fish from Drowning" by Amy Tan.

LAGE
Im Kachin-Staat gelegen. Nur von Putao aus zu erreichen (3 Flugstunden nördlich von Rangun, Stopps in Mandalay und Myitkyina), der Transfer dauert 15 Min.

PREISE
Packages ab 3 Nächten ab 2.800 € pro Bungalow, mit Vollpension und Aktivitäten.

ZIMMER
10 Bungalows für 2 Personen.

KÜCHE
Der Chefkoch stellt täglich wechselnde Menüs im verfeinerten kontinentalen Countrystil zusammen.

X-FAKTOR
Die Massagen mit natürlichen Kräuterölen im Spa.

BUCHTIPPS
»Der Klavierstimmer Ihrer Majestät« von Daniel Mason und »Der Geist der Madame Chen« von Amy Tan.

SITUATION
Situé dans l'État de Kachin, il n'est accessible qu'à partir de Putao (à 3 h d'avion de Rangoon, escales à Mandalay et Myitkyina), le transfert dure 15 min.

PRIX
Packages à partir de 3 nuits et de 2800 € par bungalow, pension complète et activités comprises.

CHAMBRES
10 bungalows pouvant abriter 2 personnes.

RESTAURATION
Variations raffinées du style country continental. Le chef propose chaque jour un menu différent.

LE « PETIT PLUS »
Les massages aux huiles essentielles que propose le spa.

LIVRES À EMPORTER
« L'Accordeur de piano » de Daniel Mason et « Noyade interdite » de Amy Tan.

La Résidence Phou Vao

Luang Prabang, Laos

A 1980s hotel situated in the heart of an exotic garden on top of the Hill of Kites, "Phou Vao", with a view of the holy mountain Phou Si. From 2000 to 2002, the architect François Greck completely revamped the interior with rosewood furniture and handwoven cotton fabrics from Laos. The spa is just as stylish as the rooms and uses traditional Laotian medicinal herbs.

Inmitten eines exotischen Gartens auf dem Drachenhügel »Phou Vao« gelegen, blickt dieses Hotel seit 1980 auf den Tempel und den heiligen Berg Phou Si. Der Architekt François Greck stattete es 2000–2002 ganz neu mit Rosenholzmöbeln und handgewebten Baumwollstoffen aus Laos aus – ebenso stilvoll wie die Zimmer ist das Spa, in dem traditionelle laotische Heilkräuter verwendet werden.

Construit au cœur d'un jardin exotique sur la Colline des Cerfs-volants « Phou Vao », cet hôtel offre depuis 1980 une vue imprenable sur le temple et la montagne sacrée Phou Si. L'architecte François Greck l'a redécoré entièrement en 2000–2002 avec des meubles en palissandre et des co-tonnades laotiennes tissées à la main. Le spa où l'on utilise des plantes traditionnelles laotiennes est aussi élégant que les chambres.

La Résidence Phou Vao
3 P.O. Box 50
Luang Prabang
Lao, 84330
Laos
Tel. +856 71 212 194
Tel. +856 71 212 530
Fax +856 71 212 534
reservations@
residencephouvao.com
www.residencephouvao.com

LOCATION
Located 2.5 miles east of Luang Prabang airport. The Old Town (a Unesco World Heritage Site) is just 1 mile away.

RATES
Rooms from $230, suites from $390, breakfast included.

ROOMS
32 rooms and 2 suites. Try to book a room with a mountain and pool view.

FOOD
The restaurant serves fine French cuisine with Laotian influences. There is also a lovely bar.

X-FACTOR
A private dinner in the garden – romantically lit with 500 candles.

BOOK TO PACK
"The Lover" by Marguerite Duras.

LAGE
4 km östlich des Flughafens Luang Prabang gelegen. Die Altstadt (Unesco-Weltkulturerbe) ist 2 km entfernt.

PREISE
Zimmer ab 170 €, Suite ab 290 €, inklusive Frühstück.

ZIMMER
32 Zimmer und 2 Suiten. Am besten einen Raum mit Berg- und Poolblick buchen.

KÜCHE
Das Restaurant serviert sehr feine französische Küche mit laotischen Einflüssen. Zudem gibt es eine schöne Bar.

X-FAKTOR
Ein privates Dinner im Garten – romantisch beleuchtet von 500 Kerzen.

BUCHTIPP
»Der Liebhaber« von Marguerite Duras.

SITUATION
Situé à 4 km à l'est de l'aéroport de Luang Prabang. L'ancienne capitale (classée par l'Unesco au patrimoine mondial de l'humanité) est à 2 km.

PRIX
Chambre à partir de 170 €, suite à partir de 290 €, petit-déjeuner compris.

CHAMBRES
32 chambres et 2 suites. Réserver une pièce avec vue sur la montagne et la piscine.

RESTAURATION
Le restaurant propose une cuisine française délicate, teintée d'influences laotiennes. Il y a aussi un très beau bar.

LE « PETIT PLUS »
Le dîner romantique au jardin, à la lueur de 500 bougies entourant la table.

LIVRE À EMPORTER
« L'Amant » de Marguerite Duras.

Ibrik Resort by the River

Bangkok, Thailand

In the heart of Bangkok, a seething metropolis and city of hotel palaces, Gobe Bunnag and Areerat Tantavichien created this charming bed and breakfast in 2004. There are just three rooms decked out in white with wooden floors, four-poster beds, balconies and Thai silk cushions. The loveliest is the "River" room, which has a view across the Chaophraya River.

Mitten in Bangkok, Millionenmetropole und Stadt der Hotelpaläste, haben Gobe Bunnag und Areerat Tantavichien 2004 diese charmante Pension mit nur drei Zimmern eröffnet. Alle sind vornehmlich in Weiß gehalten und besitzen Holzdielen, Himmelbetten mit Kissen aus Thai-Seide sowie Balkone – am schönsten liegt der Raum »River«, der auf den Chaophraya-Fluss blickt.

C'est en plein Bangkok, métropole de plusieurs millions d'habitants et ville des palaces, que Gobe Bunnag et Areerat Tantavichien ont ouvert, en 2004, cette charmante pension avec seulement trois chambres. Tout en blanc et élégantes, elles possèdent un parquet en bois, un lit à baldaquin avec des coussins en soie thaïlandaise et un balcon. La plus jolie est la chambre « River » qui donne sur le fleuve Chaophraya.

Ibrik Resort by the River
256 Soi Wat Rakang
Arunamarin Road, Bangkoknoi
Bangkok 10700
Thailand
Tel. +66 2848 9220
Fax +66 2866 2978
info@ibrikresort.com
www.ibrikresort.com

LOCATION
Situated in a quiet residential area right by the Chaophraya River. The journey from the airport, east of the city, takes 40–50 min.

RATES
Rooms from $120, breakfast included.

ROOMS
3 rooms: "River", "Sunshine" and "Moonlight"; each with its own bathroom.

FOOD
The hotel has its own café and there are many restaurants within walking distance.

X-FACTOR
There is a water taxi stand right by the hotel – an ideal means of transport in this traffic-jammed city.

BOOK TO PACK
"Nomad's Hotel: Travels in Time and Space" by Cees Nooteboom.

LAGE
Ruhig in einem Wohnviertel und direkt am Chaophraya-Fluss gelegen. Die Fahrt zum Flughafen (östlich der Stadt) dauert 40–50 Min.

PREISE
Zimmer ab 90 €, inklusive Frühstück.

ZIMMER
3 Zimmer: »River«, »Sunshine« und »Moonlight«; jedes mit eigenem Bad.

KÜCHE
Das Hotel besitzt ein Café, in Gehweite befinden sich zahlreiche Restaurants.

X-FAKTOR
In unmittelbarer Nähe legen Wassertaxis ab – ein ideales Verkehrsmittel im stau-geplagten Bangkok.

BUCHTIPP
»Der Buddha hinter dem Bretterzaun« von Cees Nooteboom.

SITUATION
Situé dans un quartier tranquille sur les bords du fleuve Chaophraya. Le trajet jusqu'à l'aéroport (à l'est de la ville) dure 40–50 min.

PRIX
Chambre à partir de 90 €, petit-déjeuner compris.

CHAMBRES
3 chambres: « River », « Sunshine » et « Moonlight » ; chacune avec salle de bains.

RESTAURATION
L'hôtel possède un salon de thé. Nombreux restaurants dans les alentours.

LE « PETIT PLUS »
Bateaux-taxis à proximité – un moyen de transport idéal pour éviter les embouteillages de Bangkok.

LIVRE À EMPORTER
« Le Bouddha derrière la palissade » de Cees Nooteboom.

Brassiere Beach
Prachuabkirikhan, Gulf of Thailand, Thailand

According to legend, the two rocks on the beach were once the naked breasts of a fisherman's daughter who came to a tragic end. Out of sympathy the locals collected bras ("brassieres") for her, which is how this hotel (which opened in 2005) came to its unusual name. The designer Yingluck Chareonying has created a charming and tongue-in-cheek décor with her bra-themed beach bungalows.

Der Sage nach sind die zwei Felsen vor dem Strand die nackten Brüste einer Fischerstochter, für die die Einheimischen aus Mitleid Büstenhalter (»brassieres«) sammelten – so kam dieses 2005 eröffnete Hotel zu seinem Namen. Mit einem Augenzwinkern lässt Designerin Yingluck Chareonying auch in den Bungalows überall BHs als Accessoires aufblitzen.

D'après la légende, les deux rochers devant la plage de cet hôtel (ouvert en 2005) seraient les seins nus d'une fille de pêcheur. Ayant eu pitié d'un tel dénuement, les habitants auraient collecté des soutiens-gorges (« brassieres »). C'est donc avec un petit clin d'œil à ce mythe, que la créatrice Yingluck Chareonying a placé un peu partout des accessoires en forme de soutien-gorge dans ses bungalows de plage.

Brassiere Beach
210 Moo 5
Tambol Samroiyod
Prachuabkirikhan 77220
Thailand
Tel. +66 2 511 1397
Tel. +66 32 630 555
brassierebeach@hotmail.com
www.brassierebeach.com

LOCATION
Situated south of Hua Hin in the Gulf of Thailand; 4 hours' drive from Bangkok airport.

RATES
Single rooms from $85, double rooms from $115, breakfast included.

ROOMS
9 rooms with mountain or sea views. Particularly recommended: the "No Bra" or "Pannee" rooms, with their own private pools.

FOOD
The restaurant serves simple, delicious Thai food.

X-FACTOR
The hotel hires out canoes and bicycles for exploring the coast by water or land.

BOOK TO PACK
"The Beach" by Alex Garland.

LAGE
Südlich von Hua Hin am Golf von Thailand gelegen; knapp 4 Fahrtstunden vom Flughafen Bangkok entfernt.

PREISE
Einzelzimmer ab 60 €, Doppelzimmer ab 85 €, inklusive Frühstück.

ZIMMER
9 Zimmer mit Berg- oder Meerblick. Herrlich: Die Räume »No Bra« und »Pannee« mit privaten Pools.

KÜCHE
Das Restaurant serviert einfache, leckere Thai-Gerichte.

X-FAKTOR
Für Ausflüge entlang der Küste – zu Wasser und an Land – verleiht das Hotel Kanus und Räder.

BUCHTIPP
»Der Strand« von Alex Garland.

SITUATION
Situé au sud de Hua Hin sur le golfe de Thaïlande à 4 h de voiture environ de l'aéroport de Bangkok.

PRIX
Chambre simple à partir de 60 €, chambre double à partir de 85 €, petit-déjeuner compris.

CHAMBRES
9 chambres avec vue sur la montagne ou sur la mer. Les chambres « No Bra » et « Pannee » ont une piscine privée.

RESTAURATION
Le restaurant propose des plats thaïlandais simples et délicieux.

LE « PETIT PLUS »
Location de canoës et de vélos pour vos promenades le long de la côte.

LIVRE À EMPORTER
« La Plage » d'Alex Garland.

Hot Coffee
Cappuchino
Espresso
Chocolate
Latte
Mocca
Americano

The Bikini

Boddhi Tree Del Gusto

Phnom Penh, Cambodia

This colonial residence from the 1930s, located in a jasmine-scented garden, was converted into a hotel in 2004 by Manuel J. Garcia. He has decorated the charming rooms with teak floors and handmade furniture, and offers his guests both individual service and excellent value for money.

Inmitten eines nach Jasmin duftenden Gartens steht dieses Kolonialhaus aus den 1930ern, das Manuel J. Garcia 2004 als Hotel eröffnete. Er hat die Räume mit Teakböden und handgefertigtem Mobiliar sehr charmant eingerichtet und bietet seinen Gästen neben persönlichem Service ein excellentes Preis-Leistungs-Verhältnis.

En 2004, Manuel J. Garcia a transformé en hôtel cette maison coloniale des années 1930 nichée dans un jardin embaumant le jasmin. À l'intérieur, il a fait poser des parquets en teck et choisi des meubles faits à la main. L'ensemble est charmant, le personnel assure un service individuel et le rapport qualité-prix est excellent.

Boddhi Tree Del Gusto
#43, Street 95, Beong Keng
Kong III
Phnom Penh
Cambodia
Tel. +855 23 211 396
(front desk)
Tel. +855 11 854 430
(reservations)
Fax +855 23 990 419
bookings@boddhitree.com
www.boddhitree.com

LOCATION
Located in a quiet neighbourhood in the centre of town, 6 miles from Phnom Penh international airport.

RATES
Single and double rooms excluding breakfast from $12 and 14, with breakfast from $36 and 42.

ROOMS
9 rooms (3 share a bathroom and have ventilators, 6 have air conditioning and their own bathrooms).

FOOD
The restaurant, renovated in 2009, serves delicious Cambodian meals and Mediterranean-inspired dishes.

X-FACTOR
Bread straight from the oven and cakes from the in-house patisserie.

BOOK TO PACK
"Lord Jim" by Joseph Conrad.

LAGE
In einem ruhigen Viertel im Stadtzentrum gelegen, 10 km vom internationalen Flughafen Phnom Penh entfernt.

PREISE
Einzel- und Doppelzimmer ohne Frühstück ab 9 und 10 €, mit Frühstück ab 27 und 31 €.

ZIMMER
9 Zimmer (3 teilen sich ein Bad und besitzen einen Ventilator, 6 verfügen über Klimaanlage und ein eigenes Bad).

KÜCHE
Das 2009 renovierte Restaurant serviert köstliche kambodschanische Speisen und mediterran inspirierte Menüs.

X-FAKTOR
Die ofenfrischen Brote und Kuchen aus der hauseigenen Patisserie.

BUCHTIPP
»Lord Jim« von Joseph Conrad.

SITUATION
Situé dans un quartier calme du centre-ville, à 10 km de l'aéroport international de Phnom Penh.

PRIX
Chambre simple et double sans petit-déjeuner à partir de 9 et 10 €, avec petit-déjeuner à partir de 27 et 31 €.

CHAMBRES
9 chambres (3 chambres ont une salle de bains commune et disposent d'un ventilateur, 6 sont climatisées et possèdent une salle de bains).

RESTAURATION
Le restaurant rénové en 2007 offre de délicieux plats de la cuisine cambod-gienne et des menus d'inspiration méditerranéenne.

LE « PETIT PLUS »
Le pain sortant du four et la pâtisserie maison.

LIVRE À EMPORTER
« Lord Jim » de Joseph Conrad.

Knai Bang Chatt

Kep, Cambodia

These three beach villas were built in the 1960s – when Kep was the most glamorous sea resort in the country – by Vann Molyvann, figurehead of New Khmer Architecture and pupil of Le Corbusier. In 2003, Axel Vervoordt's son Boris and Jef Moons bought the houses and stylishly combined their own modern design with traditional Cambodian interiors.

Als Kep in den 1960ern das glamouröseste Seebad des Landes war, wurden diese drei Strandvillen von Schützlingen des Neue-Khmer-Architekten und Le-Corbusier-Schülers Vann Molyvann entworfen. 2003 kauften Axel Vervoordts Sohn Boris und Jef Moons die Häuser und kombinierten ihr modernes Design sehr stilvoll und inspirierend mit traditionellen kambodschanischen Interieurs.

En 1960 – Kep était alors la station balnéaire la plus glamour du pays –, les trois villas modernistes ont été édifiées sur la plage par des protégés de l'architecte de la nouvelle architecture khmère, Vann Molyvann, un élève de Le Corbusier. En 2003, Boris Vervoordt, fils de l'antiquaire Axel Vervoordt, et Jef Moons les ont achetées et ont marié de manière élégante et inspirée leur design moderne avec la tradition cambodgienne.

Knai Bang Chatt Resort
Phum Thmey, Sangkat Prey Thom
Khan Kep
Kep City
Cambodia
Tel. +855 12 349 742
Tel. +855 11 823 552
info@knaibangchatt.com
www.knaibangchatt.com

LOCATION
Located on Cambodia's south coast, 112 miles southwest of Phnom Penh, near the Vietnam border.

RATES
Single rooms from $110, excluding breakfast.

ROOMS
11 rooms. The loveliest have terraces with a sea view.

FOOD
Two restaurants blend European flavours with Khmer cuisine. The local ingredients are all organic.

X-FACTOR
The spa offers very good Khmer massages, yoga and meditation courses.

BOOK TO PACK
"Lucky Child" by Loung Ung.

LAGE
An der Südostküste Kambodschas gelegen, 180 km südwestlich von Phnom Penh und nahe der Grenze zu Vietnam.

PREISE
Einzelzimmer ab 80 €, ohne Frühstück.

ZIMMER
11 Zimmer. Die schönsten haben Terrassen mit Meerblick.

KÜCHE
In zwei Restaurants verschmelzen europäische Aromen und Khmer-Küche; die lokalen Zutaten stammen aus biologischem Anbau.

X-FAKTOR
Das Spa bietet sehr gute Khmer-Massagen, Yoga- und Meditationskurse.

BUCHTIPP
»Der weite Weg der Hoffnung« von Loung Ung.

SITUATION
Situé sur la côte sud-est du Cambodge, à 180 km au sud-ouest de Phnom Penh et près de la frontière du Viêtnam.

PRIX
Chambre simple à partir de 80 €, sans petit-déjeuner.

CHAMBRES
11 chambres. Les plus belles ont une terrasse avec vue sur la mer.

RESTAURATION
Dans les deux restaurants, les saveurs de la cuisine européenne se mêlent à celles de la cuisine khmère ; à base de produits biologiques de la région.

LE « PETIT PLUS »
Le spa propose de très bons massages khmers, des cours de yoga et de méditation.

LIVRE À EMPORTER
« D'abord ils ont tué mon père » de Loung Ung.

The Nam Hai

China Beach, Hoi An, Vietnam

Architect Reda Amalou and designer Jaya Ibrahim created this resort on a dream beach in 2006, with palm gardens and wonderfully tiled pools. The private villas are elegantly decorated with dark woods and light fabrics. Artful lighting and details such as fresh flowers and golden bowls create a perfectly harmonious ambience.

An einem Traumstrand haben der Architekt Reda Amalou und der Designer Jaya Ibrahim 2006 diesen Resort gestaltet – mit Palmengärten, wunderschön gefliesten Pools sowie Privatvillen. Diese sind mit dunklem Holz und hellen Stoffen sehr edel eingerichtet – raffinierte Leuchten und Details wie frische Blüten oder goldene Schalen machen das harmonische Ambiente perfekt.

L'architecte Reda Amalou et le designer Jaya Ibrahim ont conçu en 2006 cet hôtel sur une plage de rêve – avec des palmeraies, des bassins décorés de superbes mosaïques ainsi que des villas privées. Celles-ci sont très élégamment aménagées avec des boiseries sombres et des étoffes claires – les luminaires raffinés et des détails comme les fleurs fraîches ou les coupes dorées parachèvent l'ensemble.

The Nam Hai
Hoi An
Hamlet 1, Dien Duong Village
Dien Ban District, Quang Nam
Province
Vietnam
Tel. +84 510 394 0000
Fax +84 510 394 0999
namhai@ghmhotels.com
and afomre@thenamhai.com
www.thenamhai.com

LOCATION
Situated on China Beach near Hoi An,
30 min south of Da Nang airport.

RATES
Villas from $750, excluding breakfast;
pool villas from $1,350, breakfast
included.

ROOMS
60 villas (260 square feet, 1 bedroom),
40 pool villas (820–2,100 square feet,
1–5 bedrooms).

FOOD
The main restaurant with its panoramic
terrace serves fine Vietnamese cuisine
and the beach restaurant specialises in
fish and seafood.

X-FACTOR
The holistically oriented spa is one of
the best in Asia.

BOOK TO PACK
"The Quiet American" by Graham
Greene.

LAGE
Am China Beach nahe von Hoi An
gelegen; 30 Min. südlich des Flughafens
Da Nang.

PREISE
Villa ab 550 €, ohne Frühstück; Poolvilla
ab 990 €, inklusive Frühstück.

ZIMMER
60 Villen (80 qm, 1 Schlafzimmer),
40 Poolvillen (250–660 qm, 1–5
Schlafzimmer).

KÜCHE
Das Hauptrestaurant mit Panorama-
terrasse serviert feine vietnamesische
Menüs, das Strandrestaurant Fisch und
Meeresfrüchte.

X-FAKTOR
Das ganzheitlich orientierte Spa gehört
zu den besten Asiens.

BUCHTIPP
»Der stille Amerikaner« von Graham
Greene.

SITUATION
Sur la China Beach à côté de Hoi An ;
à 30 min au sud de l'aéroport de
Da Nang.

PRIX
Villa à partir de 550 €, sans petit-
déjeuner ; villa avec piscine à partir de
990 €, petit-déjeuner compris.

CHAMBRES
60 villas (80 m², 1 chambre à coucher),
40 villas avec piscine (250–660 m²,
1–5 chambres).

RESTAURATION
Le restaurant principal avec terrasse
panoramique sert des menus vietna-
miens raffinés, le restaurant de la plage
propose du poisson et des fruits de mer.

LE « PETIT PLUS »
Avec son approche holistique, le spa
est l'un des meilleurs d'Asie.

LIVRE À EMPORTER
« Un Américain bien tranquille » de
Graham Greene.

Red Capital Ranch
Beijing, Great Wall of China, China

The guests staying at this Manchurian hunting lodge, which opened as a hotel in 2004, live right next to the Great Wall. Indeed this world wonder, built by China's first emperor, Qin Shi Huangdi, runs through the estate. Ten historic houses, meticulously furnished in Tibetan and Chinese style with many original Qing Dynasty details, are clustered around it.

Die Gäste dieses 2004 als Hotel eröffneten mandschurischen Jagd-anwesens wohnen direkt an der Chinesischen Mauer: Durch das Ge-lände verläuft der von Chinas erstem Kaiser Qin Shi Huangdi erbaute Mauerabschnitt. Ringsum stehen zehn historische Häuser, die sorgsam im chinesischen und tibetanischen Stil eingerichtet wurden – viele Accessoires sind Originale aus der Qing-Periode.

Les clients de cette résidence de chasse reconvertie en hôtel en 2004, habitent aux pieds de la Grande Muraille de Chine. En effet, la portion bâtie par le premier empereur Qin Shi Huangdi traverse la propriété. Tout autour se trouvent dix maisons historiques aménagées avec soin dans le style chinois et tibétain. Beaucoup d'objets sont des originaux datant de la période Qing.

Red Capital Ranch / Shambhala
at the Great Wall
No. 28 Xiaguandi Village
Yanxi Township, Huairou
District
101407 Beijing
China
Tel. +86 8961 7100
info@redcapitalclub.com.cn
www.redcapitalclub.com.cn
Open from mid-March to
mid-November

LOCATION
Situated a 1.5 hour drive northeast of central Beijing by one of the official access points to the Great Wall of China.

RATES
Houses (each sleeps 2) from $125, breakfast included.

ROOMS
10 houses.

FOOD
A gourmet restaurant serving Manchurian specialities is situated in the former stables.

X-FACTOR
Spoil yourself in the Tibetan spa with oils made from Himalayan herbs.

BOOKS TO PACK
"The Great Wall of China" by Franz Kafka and "The Last Empress" by Anchee Min.

LAGE
Nordöstlich des Zentrums von Peking an einem der offiziellen Aufgänge zur Chinesischen Mauer gelegen, 1,5 Std. Fahrt vom Flughafen Peking entfernt.

PREISE
Haus (2 Personen) ab 92 €, inklusive Frühstück.

ZIMMER
10 Häuser.

KÜCHE
Aus den ehemaligen Stallungen wurde ein Gourmetrestaurant, das mandschurische Spezialitäten serviert.

X-FAKTOR
Im tibetanischen Spa verwöhnen aus Himalaja-Kräutern hergestellte Öle.

BUCHTIPPS
»Beim Bau der Chinesischen Mauer« von Franz Kafka und »Die Kaiserin auf dem Drachenthron« von Anchee Min.

SITUATION
Situé au nord-est du centre de Pékin à l'une des entrées officielles de la Grande Muraille de Chine, à 1 h 30 min de voiture de l'aéroport de Pékin.

PRIX
Maison (2 personnes) à partir de 92 €, petit-déjeuner compris.

CHAMBRES
10 maisons.

RESTAURATION
Les anciennes écuries sont devenues un restaurant gastronomique proposant des spécialités mandchoues.

LE « PETIT PLUS »
Les huiles essentielles du spa, préparées à partir d'herbes aromatiques poussant sur les versants tibétains de l'Himalaya.

LIVRES À EMPORTER
« La Muraille de Chine » de Franz Kafka et « La Souveraine » de Anchee Min.

Fujiya Inn
Ginzan, Yamagata Prefecture, Japan

This centuries-old guesthouse was updated by Kengo Kuma in 2006. He introduced a range of different filters into the minimalist environment, from filigree wood dividers to bamboo screens ("sumushiko") and shimmering green glass walls that lend the rooms as well as the hot baths a fascinating ambience that lies somewhere between the opaque and floating transparency.

Dieses jahrhundertealte Gasthaus gestaltete Kengo Kuma im Jahr 2006 neu. In minimalistischem Ambiente setzte er verschiedene Filter ein – filigrane Holztrennwände, Bambusschirme (»sumushiko«) und grün schimmernde Glaswände schaffen in den Zimmern sowie heißen Bädern ein faszinierendes, zwischen undurchsichtig und transparent schwebendes Flair.

Ce ryokan multicentenaire a été restauré par Kengo Kuma en 2006. Dans une ambiance minimaliste, il a placé divers filtres – des claustras de bois laissant passer la lumière, des écrans de bambou incisé (« sumushiko ») et des parois de verre d'un vert laiteux créent dans les pièces et dans les bains chauds une atmosphère fascinante, qui joue avec l'opacité et la transparence.

Ginzan Hot Spring Fujiya Inn
443 Shinpata Oaza Ginzan
Obanazawa
Yamagata 999-4333
Japan
Tel. +81 237 28 2141
Fax +81 237 28 2140
info@fujiya-ginzan.com
www.fujiya-ginzan.com

LOCATION
Situated on the banks of the River
Ginzan, in a village of the same name,
21 miles north of Yamagata airport
(1 hour's flight from Tokyo).

RATES
Rooms from $630, breakfast and dinner
included.

ROOMS
8 rooms (2–3 beds).

FOOD
Delicious, traditional Japanese specialities made from very fresh ingredients.

X-FACTOR
The 5 hot baths (4 inside, 1 outside) are
fed by natural springs and are used to
treat fatigue and muscle aches.

BOOK TO PACK
"Memoirs of a Geisha" by Arthur Golden.

LAGE
Direkt am Fluss Ginzan im gleichnami-
gen Ort gelegen, 35 km nördlich des
Flughafens Yamagata (ab Tokio in
1 Flugstunde zu erreichen).

PREISE
Zimmer ab 470 €, inklusive Frühstück
und Abendessen.

ZIMMER
8 Zimmer (2–3 Betten).

KÜCHE
Köstliche, traditionelle japanische
Spezialitäten aus ganz frischen Zutaten.

X-FAKTOR
Die 5 heißen Bäder (4 innen, 1 draußen)
werden von natürlichen Quellen gespeist
und wirken wohltuend, z.B. bei Müdig-
keit und Muskelschmerzen.

BUCHTIPP
»Die Geisha« von Arthur Golden.

SITUATION
Sur la rivière Ginzan dans la station
thermale de même nom, à 35 km
au nord de l'aéroport de Yamagata
(à 1 h de vol de Tokyo).

PRIX
Chambre à partir de 470 €, petit-
déjeuner et dîner compris.

CHAMBRES
8 chambres (2–3 lits).

RESTAURATION
Savoureuses spécialités traditionnelles
japonaises à base de produits frais.

LE « PETIT PLUS »
Les 5 bains chauds (4 à l'intérieur, 1 à
l'extérieur) alimentés par des sources
naturelles, si bienfaisants en cas de
fatigue ou de douleurs musculaires.

LIVRE À EMPORTER
« Geisha » d'Arthur Golden.

WASHINGTON

OREGON

ID

NEVADA

CALIFORNIA

U N I T

North America

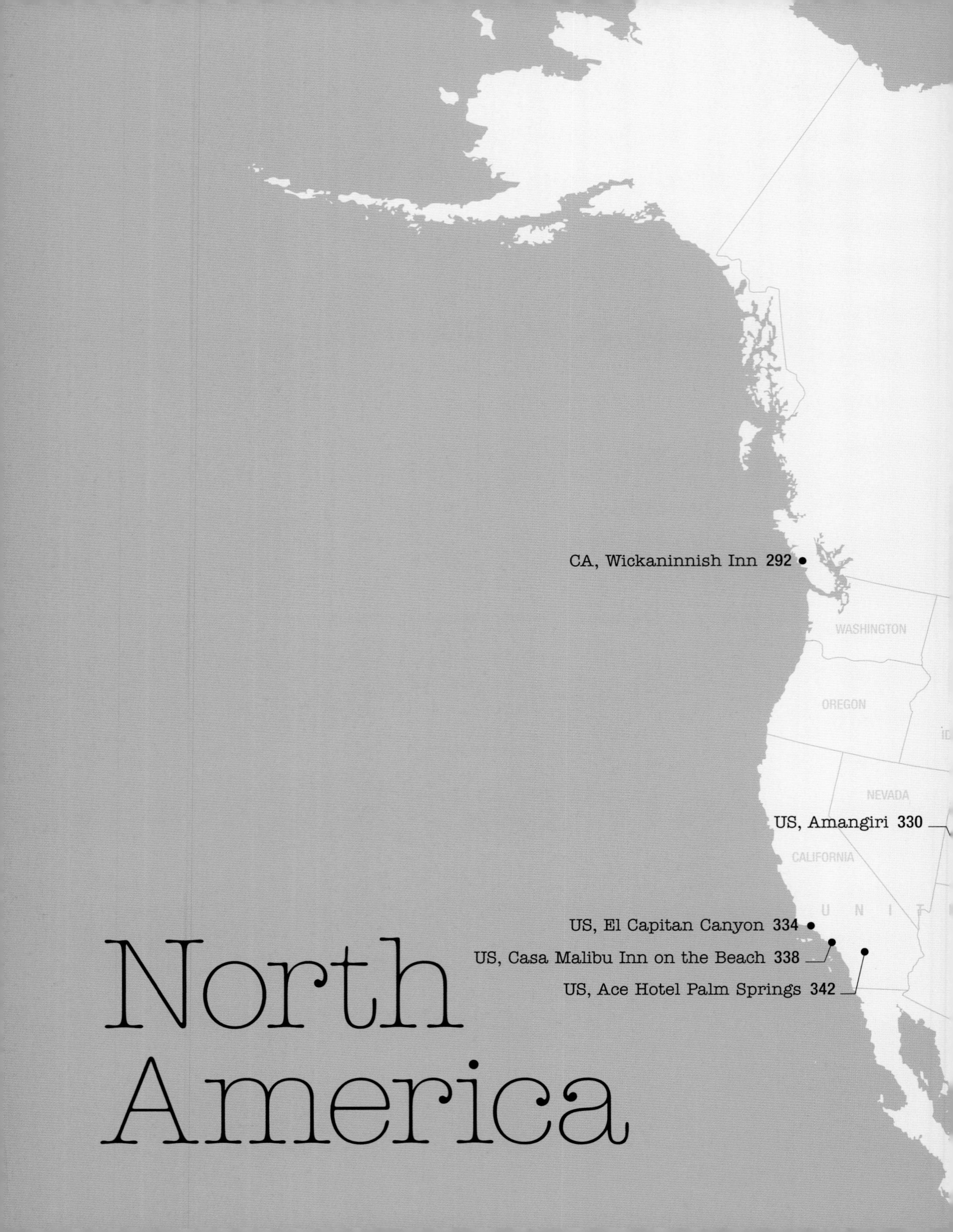

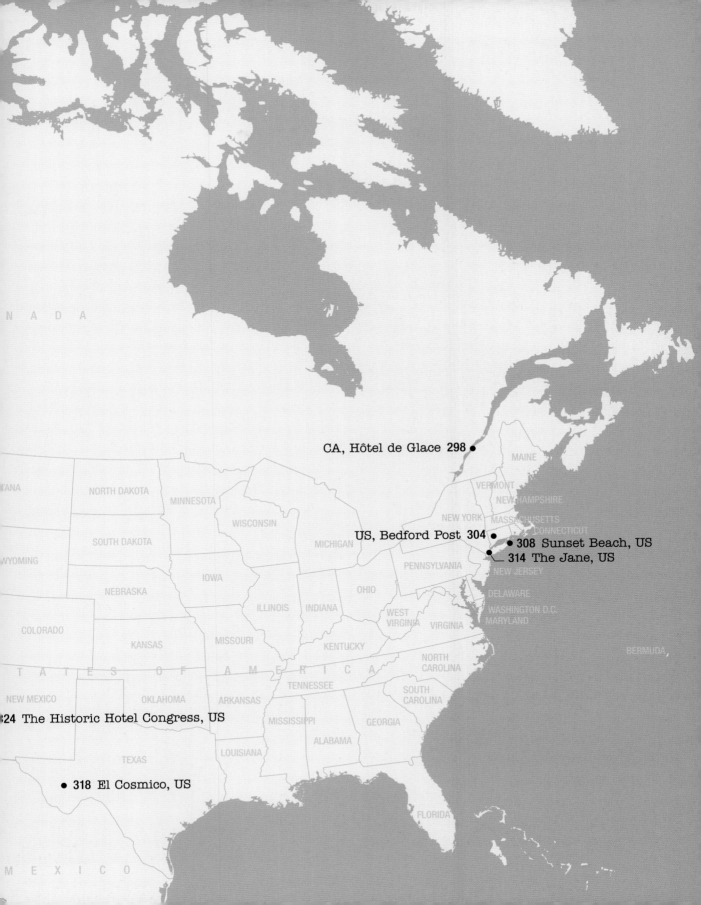

CA, Hôtel de Glace 298 •

US, Bedford Post 304 •
• 308 Sunset Beach, US
314 The Jane, US

24 The Historic Hotel Congress, US

• 318 El Cosmico, US

Wickaninnish Inn

Tofino, British Columbia, Canada

This Relais & Châteaux hotel was opened in 1996 by descendants of Dr Howard McDiarmid, who came to Tofino in the 1950s and co-founded the Pacific Rim National Park. Here they invented the pastime of "winter storm watching" – all the elegantly rustic rooms have panorama windows with views across the Pacific and its breathtaking natural spectacles.

Eröffnet wurde dieses Relais-&-Châteaux-Hotel 1996 von Nachfahren des Arztes Dr. Howard McDiarmid, der in den 1950ern nach Tofino kam und den Pacific-Rim-Nationalpark mitbegründete. Hier erfand man das »Winter Storm Watching« – alle rustikal-eleganten Zimmer blicken aus Panoramafenstern direkt auf den Pazifik und seine atemberaubenden Naturschauspiele.

Cet hôtel Relais & Châteaux a été ouvert en 1996 par des descendants du médecin Dr Howard McDiarmid, arrivé à Tofino au cours des années 1950 et qui est cofondateur du Pacific Rim Nationalpark. C'est ici que l'on inventé le « Winter Storm Watching » – toutes les chambres élégantes et rustiques bénéficient d'une vue splendide sur le Pacifique et les spectacles époustouflants qu'offre la nature.

Wickaninnish Inn
500 Osprey Lane
Box 250
Tofino, British Columbia V0R 2Z0
Canada
Tel. +1 250 725 3100
Fax +1 250 725 3110
info@wickinn.com
www.wickinn.com

LOCATION
Situated on Vancouver Island on Canada's west coast. Take a 2-hour ferry ride from Vancouver to Nanaimo and then it's a further 2.5–3-hour drive to Tofino.

RATES
Rooms from $315, suites from $430, excluding breakfast.

ROOMS
63 rooms and 12 suites in 2 buildings.

FOOD
The "Pointe Restaurant" with its 240-degree view serves northwest Canadian specialities.

X-FACTOR
At the spa, traditional techniques of the Nuu Chah Nulth Indians are used.

BOOK TO PACK
"Runaway" by Alice Munro.

LAGE
Auf Vancouver Island an der Westküste Kanadas gelegen. Von Vancouver setzt man mit der Fähre nach Nanaimo über (ca. 2 Std.) und fährt in weiteren 2,5 bis 3 Std. nach Tofino.

PREISE
Zimmer ab 230 €, Suite ab 320 €, ohne Frühstück.

ZIMMER
63 Zimmer und 12 Suiten in 2 Gebäuden.

KÜCHE
Das »Pointe Restaurant« mit 240-Grad-Blick serviert Spezialitäten aus Kanadas Nordwesten.

X-FAKTOR
Das Spa mit traditionellen Anwendungen der Nuu-Chah-Nulth-Indianer.

BUCHTIPP
»Der Traum meiner Mutter« von Alice Munro.

SITUATION
Situé sur l'île de Vancouver sur la côte ouest du Canada. De Vancouver on prend le ferry à destination de Nanaimo (env. 2 h) et on continue ensuite en voiture pendant 2 h 30 min à 3 h jusqu' Tofino.

PRIX
Chambre à partir de 230 €, suite à part. de 320 €, sans petit-déjeuner.

CHAMBRES
63 chambres et 12 suites dans deux bâtiments.

RESTAURATION
Le « Pointe Restaurant » avec panoram. de 240 degrés propose des spécialités du Nord-Ouest canadien.

LE « PETIT PLUS »
Le spa qui offre les soins traditionnels des Indiens Nuu Chah Nulth.

LIVRE À EMPORTER
« Du côté de Castle Rock » d'Alice Munro.

Hôtel de Glace

Sainte-Catherine-de-la-Jacques-Cartier, Québec, Canada

Inspired by the Swedish ice hotel in Jukkasjärvi, Jacques Desbois opened his Hôtel de Glace in Canada in 2001. The cathedral-like rooms are built anew every year from 15,500 tons of snow and ice – even the chandeliers are made of frozen water! Furs and polar sleeping bags keep you warm at night in temperatures between 23 and 37 degrees Fahrenheit.

Inspiriert vom schwedischen Eishotel in Jukkasjärvi hat Jacques Desbois 2001 das Hôtel de Glace in Kanada eröffnet. Die kathedralenartigen Räume werden jedes Jahr aus 14.000 Tonnen Schnee und Eis neu errichtet, selbst die Kronleuchter bestehen aus gefrorenem Wasser! Bei Temperaturen zwischen -3 und -5 Grad Celsius wärmen nachts Felle und Polarschlafsäcke.

S'inspirant de l'hôtel de glace de Jukkasjärvi en Suède, Jacques Desbois a ouvert en 2001 l'Hôtel de Glace au Canada. Les espaces qui évoquent l'intérieur d'une cathédrale sont recréés tous les ans avec 14 000 tonnes de neige et de glace, même les lustres sont de l'eau gelée ! La nuit, à une température ambiante située entre -3 et -5 Celsius, on se réchauffe dans des fourrures et des sacs de couchage polaires.

Hôtel de Glace
75, Montée de l'Auberge,
Pavillon Ukiuk
Station touristique Duchesnay
Sainte-Catherine-de-la-Jacques-
Cartier
Québec G3N 2Y5
Canada
Tel. +1 418 875 4522
Fax +1 418 875 2833
information@
hoteldeglace-canada.com
www.hoteldeglace-canada.com
Open from early January to
late March

LOCATION
The hotel is part of the "Station touristique Duchesnay", 30 min west of Québec city.

RATES
Overnight stays from $215 per person, breakfast included.

ROOMS
36 rooms and suites with shared bathrooms. The walls of the suites have carved ice reliefs and some have a fireplace.

FOOD
The hotel has a bar and a café. All meals are served in the neighbouring Auberge Duchesnay.

X-FACTOR
The ice chapel that can be booked for weddings.

BOOK TO PACK
"The Blind Assassin" by Margaret Atwood.

LAGE
Das Hotel ist Teil der Station touristique Duchesnay, 30 Min. westlich von Quebec.

PREISE
Übernachtung ab 155 € pro Person, inklusive Frühstück.

ZIMMER
36 Zimmer und Suiten mit Gemeinschaftsbad. Die Suiten besitzen mit Eisreliefs verzierte Wände und zum Teil einen Kamin.

KÜCHE
Das Hotel hat eine Bar und ein Café, alle Mahlzeiten werden in der benachbarten Auberge Duchesnay serviert.

X-FAKTOR
Die Eiskapelle, die für Hochzeiten gebucht werden kann.

BUCHTIPP
»Der blinde Mörder« von Margaret Atwood.

SITUATION
L'hôtel fait partie de la station touristique Duchesnay, située à 30 min à l'ouest de Québec.

PRIX
À partir de 155 € la nuit par personne, petit-déjeuner compris.

CHAMBRES
36 chambres et suites avec salle de bains commune. Les murs des suites sont décorés de reliefs sculptés dans la glace et certaines possèdent une cheminée.

RESTAURATION
L'hôtel a un bar et un café, tous les repas sont servis à l'Auberge Duchesnay toute proche.

LE « PETIT PLUS »
La chapelle de glace qui peut être louée pour les mariages.

LIVRE À EMPORTER
« Le Tueur aveugle » de Margaret Atwood.

Bedford Post

Bedford, Westchester, New York, USA

In 2008, Richard Gere's wife Carey Lowell and Tiffany Vassilakis converted this picturesque farm dating from 1762 into an elegant country hotel. Their guests reside in luxurious, romantic rooms, some with their own fireplaces and verandas. There are free yoga courses and excellent meals in a choice of two restaurants.

Diesen malerischen Hof aus dem Jahr 1762 haben Richard Geres Frau Carey Lowell und Tiffany Vassilakis 2008 als elegantes Landhotel eröffnet. Ihre Gäste wohnen in luxuriös-romantischen Zimmern, von denen einige einen Kamin und eine Veranda besitzen, und können an kostenfreien Yoga-Kursen teilnehmen sowie die ausgezeichnete Küche zweier Restaurants genießen.

Carey Lowell, la femme de Richard Gere, et Tiffany Vassilakis ont ouvert en 2008 cet hôtel de campagne élégant qui était à l'origine une ferme pittoresque datant de 1762. Leurs hôtes séjournent dans des chambres romantiques luxueuses – dont certaines possèdent une cheminée et une véranda –, peuvent participer aux cours de yoga gratuits et savourer les bons petits plats que leur proposent deux restaurants.

Bedford Post
954 Old Post Road
Bedford, NY 10506
USA
Tel. +1 914 234 7800
inn@bedfordpostinn.com
www.bedfordpostinn.com

LOCATION
Situated in the heart of Westchester, 43 miles northeast of Manhattan.

RATES
Rooms from $380, breakfast included.

ROOMS
8 rooms, each with its own marble bathroom.

FOOD
"The Barn" with its relaxed atmosphere and "The Farmhouse" with its more elegant ambience both serve seasonal delicacies made from organic ingredients.

X-FACTOR
The airy "Yoga Loft" under a pitched roof with original timber beams. There are lessons here every morning.

BOOK TO PACK
"American Pastoral" by Philip Roth.

LAGE
Im Herzen von Westchester gelegen, 70 km nordöstlich von Manhattan.

PREISE
Zimmer ab 270 €, inklusive Frühstück.

ZIMMER
8 Zimmer, alle mit eigenem Marmorbad.

KÜCHE
»The Barn« mit entspannter Atmosphäre und das gehobene »The Farmhouse« servieren saisonale Köstlichkeiten aus organisch angebauten Zutaten.

X-FAKTOR
Das weitläufige »Yoga Loft«, das unter einem Spitzdach mit alten Deckenbalken entstanden ist. Hier wird jeden Morgen unterrichtet.

BUCHTIPP
»Amerikanisches Idyll« von Philip Roth.

SITUATION
Situé au cœur du comté de Westchester, à 70 km au nord-est de Manhattan.

PRIX
Chambre à partir de 270 €, petit-déjeuner compris.

CHAMBRES
8 chambres, toutes dotées d'une salle de bains en marbre.

RESTAURATION
« The Barn » à l'ambiance relax et l'élégante « The Farmhouse » proposent des plats délicieux à base de produits de saison issus de l'agriculture biologique.

LE « PETIT PLUS »
Le vaste « Yoga Loft », construit sous un toit en pente à poutres anciennes. Les cours ont lieu ici chaque matin.

LIVRE À EMPORTER
« Pastorale américaine » de Philip Roth.

Sunset Beach

Shelter Island, Long Island, New York, USA

André Balazs has transformed a 1960s motel on Sunset Beach into a hotel that combines Hamptons chic with the charm of the French Riviera. The rooms are decorated in a retro style with design classics such as Hardoy Butterfly chairs, and the restaurant tempts guests with Provençal brasserie cuisine and a fabulous sunset view.

Unter Regie von André Balazs wurde aus einem Motel der 1960er das Sunset Beach, welches den Schick der Hamptons mit dem Charme der französischen Riviera verbindet. Die Zimmer sind im Retro-Stil sowie mit Klassikern wie Hardoys Butterfly Chair eingerichtet, das Restaurant lockt mit provenzalischer Brasserie-Küche und einem Traumblick in den Sonnenuntergang.

Sous la houlette d'André Balazs, un motel des années 1960 est devenu le Sunset Beach, alliant le chic des Hamptons au charme de la French Riviera. Les chambres sont de style rétro et meublées de classiques, tels que la Hardoy Butterfly Chair, le restaurant est renommé pour sa cuisine provençale et sa vue féerique sur le coucher de soleil.

Sunset Beach
35 Shore Road
Shelter Island
Long Island, NY 11965
USA
Tel. +1 631 749 2001
Fax +1 631 749 1843
reservations@sunsetbeachli.com
www.sunsetbeachli.com
Open from mid-May to mid-September

LOCATION
Situated in a delightful bay on Shelter Island, 100 miles east of New York City. The island can be reached by ferry from Greenport in 7 min.

RATES
Rooms from $220, excluding breakfast.

ROOMS
20 rooms, all with private sundecks and a sea view.

FOOD
André Balazs serves his home-produced rosé wine with Côte d'Azur classics such as Bouillabaisse and Salade Niçoise.

X-FACTOR
Mountain bikes are available for island excursions.

BOOK TO PACK
"Montauk" by Max Frisch.

LAGE
An einer herrlichen Bucht auf Shelter Island gelegen, 160 km östlich von New York City. Ab Greenport ist die Insel per Fähre erreichbar (7 Min.).

PREISE
Zimmer ab 165 €, ohne Frühstück.

ZIMMER
20 Zimmer, alle mit privatem Sonnendeck und Meerblick.

KÜCHE
Zu Klassikern von der Côte d'Azur, wie Bouillabaisse und Salade niçoise, lässt André Balazs Rosé-Wein aus eigener Herstellung ausschenken.

X-FAKTOR
Für Ausflüge über die Insel stehen Mountainbikes bereit.

BUCHTIPP
»Montauk« von Max Frisch.

SITUATION
Situé dans une baie magnifique à Shelte Island, à 160 km à l'est de New York. On peut joindre l'île par bac (7 min) à partir de Greenport.

PRIX
Chambre à partir de 165 €, sans petit-déjeuner.

CHAMBRES
20 chambres, toutes avec terrasse privée et vue sur la mer.

RESTAURATION
André Balazs accompagne les classiques de la Côte d'Azur, tels que la bouillabaisse et la salade niçoise, de vin rosé produit par ses soins.

LE « PETIT PLUS »
Les vélos tout terrain à la disposition des clients désireux de visiter l'île.

LIVRE À EMPORTER
« Montauk » de Max Frisch.

The Jane

New York City, New York, USA

This brick building was originally built as a hotel for sailors in 1908. Guests paid just 25 cents per night and in 1912 survivors of the "Titanic" were boarded here. The hotel's authentic maritime atmosphere has remained to this day: guests sleep in cabins with beds of polished wood, meet "tout New York" for a drink in the lounge and bar and enjoy purse-pleasing prices.

Dieser Backsteinbau wurde 1908 als Hotel für Seeleute errichtet, die pro Nacht nur 25 Cent zahlen mussten; 1912 beherbergte er die Über-lebenden der Titanic. Sein authentisches maritimes Flair blieb bis heute erhalten – hier schläft man in Kabinen mit Betten aus poliertem Holz, trifft in Lounge und Bar »tout New York« auf einen Drink und freut sich über budgetschonende Preise.

Construit en 1908, ce bâtiment en briques était un hôtel pour marins, qui ne payaient que 25 cents la nuit. En 1912, il accueillit les survivants du Titanic. Il a gardé son atmosphère maritime authentique puisqu'on dort dans des cabines aux lits en bois poli. On rencontrera au salon et au bar le « Tout-New-York » en prenant un verre et en se réjouissant des prix qui n'écornent pas trop notre budget.

The Jane
113 Jane Street
New York City, NY 10014
USA
Tel. +1 212 924 6700
Fax +1 212 924 6705
reservations@thejanenyc.com
www.thejanenyc.com

LOCATION
Situated in the West Village on the Hudson, 20 miles west of John F. Kennedy airport.

RATES
Rooms from $99, breakfast included.

ROOMS
208 rooms with shared bathrooms; only the rather more spacious "Captain's Cabins" have their own en suite facilities.

FOOD
The menu of "Café Gitane" features Moroccan and French-inspired dishes; the popular bar is wood panelled.

X-FACTOR
Bicycles are available free of charge for guests to explore Manhattan.

BOOK TO PACK
"Moby Dick" by Herman Melville.

LAGE
Im West Village am Hudson gelegen, 30 km westlich des Flughafens John F. Kennedy.

PREISE
Zimmer ab 73 €, inklusive Frühstück.

ZIMMER
208 Zimmer mit Gemeinschaftsbädern; nur die etwas geräumigeren »Captain's Cabins« haben ein eigenes Bad.

KÜCHE
Im »Café Gitane« stehen marokkanisch und französisch inspirierte Gerichte auf der Karte; die angesagte Bar ist holzgetäfelt.

X-FAKTOR
Für Ausflüge durch Manhattan stehen kostenfreie Fahrräder bereit.

BUCHTIPP
»Moby Dick« von Herman Melville.

SITUATION
Situé dans le West Village sur l'Hudson, à 30 km à l'ouest de l'aéroport John F. Kennedy.

PRIX
Chambre à partir de 73 €, petit-déjeuner compris.

CHAMBRES
208 chambres avec salles de bains communes ; un peu plus spacieuses, les « Captain's Cabins » sont les seules à avoir une salle de bains.

RESTAURATION
La carte du « Café Gitane » propose des plats d'inspiration marocaine et française ; ce bar branché est recouvert de boiseries.

LE « PETIT PLUS »
Des bicyclettes sont mises gratuitement à disposition pour des excursions dans Manhattan.

LIVRE À EMPORTER
« Moby Dick » de Herman Melville.

El Cosmico

Marfa, Texas, USA

With the help of Lake/Flato architects and Design Build Adventure in 2009, Liz Lambert created this retro lodge on a 17-acre piece of land in the Texan desert. Here you can travel back in time through American history and reside in wonderfully renovated 1950s trailers, yurts or a Sioux tepee.

Auf einem sieben Hektar großen Grundstück in der texanischen Wüste hat Liz Lambert mithilfe der Architekten von Lake/Flato sowie Design Build Adventure diese Retro-Lodge entworfen und 2009 eingeweiht. Hier reist man in die Geschichte Amerikas zurück und wohnt in wunderbar renovierten Wohnwagen der 1950er, Jurten oder einem Tipi der Sioux.

Liz Lambert a conçu ce lodge rétro avec l'aide des architectes de Lake/Flato et de Design Build Adventure sur un terrain de sept hectares dans le désert texan et l'a inauguré en 2009. On a ici l'occasion de faire un voyage dans le temps en habitant dans des caravanes des années 1950 superbement rénovées, dans des yourtes ou dans un tipi sioux.

El Cosmico
802 South Highland Avenue
Marfa, TX 79843
USA
Tel. +1 877 822 1950
info@elcosmico.com
www.elcosmico.com

LOCATION
Marfa is located in the west of Texas, 470 miles from Austin. El Cosmico is on Highway 67, south of the town centre.

RATES
Overnight stays in the trailers from $90, in the yurts from $60 and in a tepee from $75, excluding breakfast.

ROOMS
5 trailers (3 more are currently being renovated), 4 yurts, 1 teepee. There are also 3 safari tents available.

FOOD
Guests share a communal kitchen.

X-FACTOR
Recreational activities include cooking and painting courses as well as writing workshops.

BOOK TO PACK
"On the Road" by Jack Kerouac.

LAGE
Marfa liegt im Westen von Texas, 760 km von Austin entfernt. El Cosmico ist am Highway 67 zu finden, südlich des Zentrums.

PREISE
Übernachtung im Wohnwagen ab 66 €, in der Jurte 44 €, im Tipi 55 €, ohne Frühstück.

ZIMMER
5 Wohnwagen (3 weitere werden derzeit renoviert), 4 Jurten, 1 Tipi. Außerdem stehen 3 Safarizelte zur Verfügung.

KÜCHE
Die Gäste teilen sich eine Gemein-schaftsküche.

X-FAKTOR
Das Freizeitprogramm mit Koch- und Malkursen sowie Schreibwerkstätten.

BUCHTIPP
»Unterwegs« von Jack Kerouac.

SITUATION
Marfa est situé à l'ouest du Texas, à 760 km d'Austin. On trouve El Cosmico sur la Highway 67, au sud du centre.

PRIX
Nuit dans la caravane à partir de 66 €, sous la yourte 44 €, dans le tipi 55 €, sans petit-déjeuner.

CHAMBRES
5 caravanes (3 autres sont en cours de restauration), 4 yourtes, 1 tipi. 3 tentes de safari sont également disponibles.

RESTAURATION
Les hôtes ont une cuisine commune à leur disposition.

LE « PETIT PLUS »
Le programme de loisirs qui propose des cours de cuisine et de peinture, ain que des ateliers d'écriture.

LIVRE À EMPORTER
« Sur la route » de Jack Kerouac.

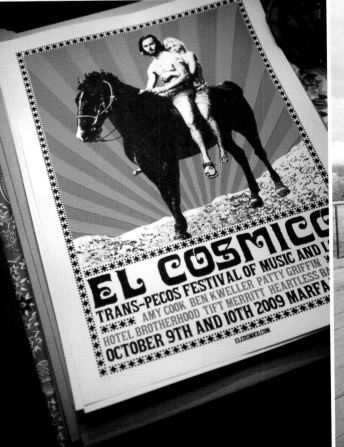

The Historic Hotel Congress

Tucson, Arizona, USA

This hotel was originally built for the railroad passengers of the Southern Pacific Line in 1919. History has it that when the bank robber John Dillinger was living here in 1934, he was captured by the FBI whilst fleeing from a fire. Today the rooms still contain the original iron bedsteads, cupboards and radios – even the 1930s telephone switchboard is still in operation.

1919 wurde dieses Hotel für die Passagiere der Southern Pacific Eisenbahnlinie erbaut. 1934 schrieb es Geschichte, als der Bankräuber John Dillinger hier wohnte, vor einem Feuer fliehen musste – und vom FBI verhaftet wurde. Bis heute stehen in den Räumen die originalen Eisenbetten, Kommoden und Radios; selbst das Telefonschaltbrett aus den 1930ern ist noch in Betrieb.

Cet hôtel a été construit en 1919 pour les passagers de la compagnie ferroviaire Southern Pacific Line. En 1934, il est entré dans l'histoire lorsque l'un de ses clients, le gangster John Dillinger, fut arrêté par le FBI en voulant échapper à un incendie. Dans les chambres, les lits de fer, les commodes et les radios sont d'origine. Le tableau de commande du téléphone, datant des années 1930, est même encore en service.

The Historic Hotel Congress
311 East Congress Street
Tucson, AZ 85701
USA
Tel. +1 520 622 8848
Fax +1 520 792 6366
reservations@hotelcongress.com
www.hotelcongress.com

LOCATION
Situated in the heart of Tucson, 8 miles north of the airport.

RATES
Rooms from $79, excluding breakfast.

ROOMS
40 rooms; all individually furnished with original vintage furniture – no televisions, but with en suite bathrooms.

FOOD
"The Cup Cafe" serves classic omelettes, sandwiches, salads and steaks.

X-FACTOR
The "Club Congress", which opened in 1985, is considered the best club in town.

BOOK TO PACK
"Winnetou: The Apache Knight" by Karl May.

LAGE
Im Zentrum von Tucson gelegen, 13 km nördlich des Flughafens.

PREISE
Zimmer ab 60 €, ohne Frühstück.

ZIMMER
40 Zimmer; alle individuell mit Vintage-Mobiliar aus der Anfangszeit des Hotels eingerichtet – ohne Fernseher, aber mit eigenem Bad.

KÜCHE
»The Cup Cafe« serviert klassische Omeletts, Sandwichs, Salate und Steaks.

X-FAKTOR
Der 1985 eröffnete »Club Congress« gilt als bester Nightclub der Stadt.

BUCHTIPP
»Im fernen Westen« von Karl May.

SITUATION
Situé dans le centre de Tucson, à 13 km au nord de l'aéroport.

PRIX
Chambre à partir de 60 €, sans petit-déjeuner.

CHAMBRES
40 chambres ; toutes personnalisées avec des meubles vintage datant de l'époque à laquelle l'hôtel a été constru[i] Pas de télévision, mais salle de bains individuelle.

RESTAURATION
« The Cup Cafe » sert des omelettes, des sandwichs, des salades et des steaks classiques.

LE « PETIT PLUS »
Ouvert en 1985, le « Club Congress » passe pour être l'un des meilleurs night-clubs de la ville.

LIVRE À EMPORTER
« Winnetou » de Karl May.

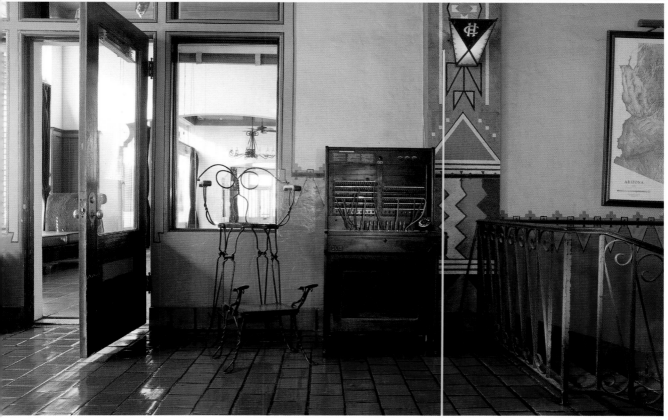

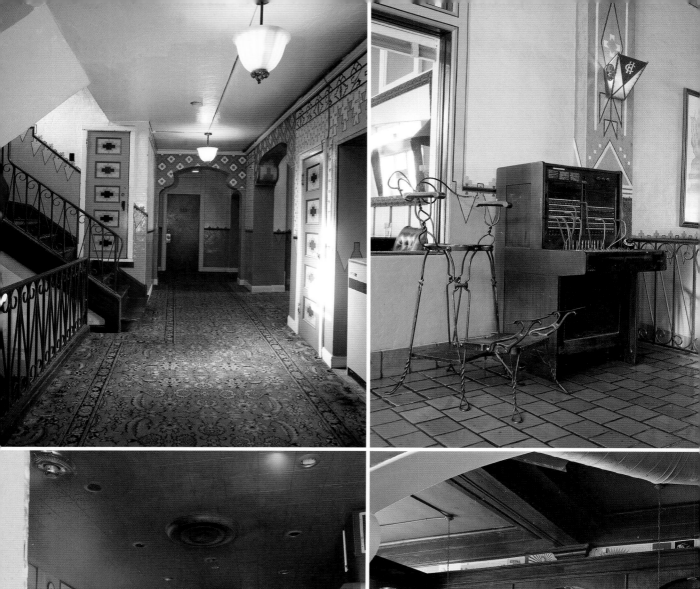

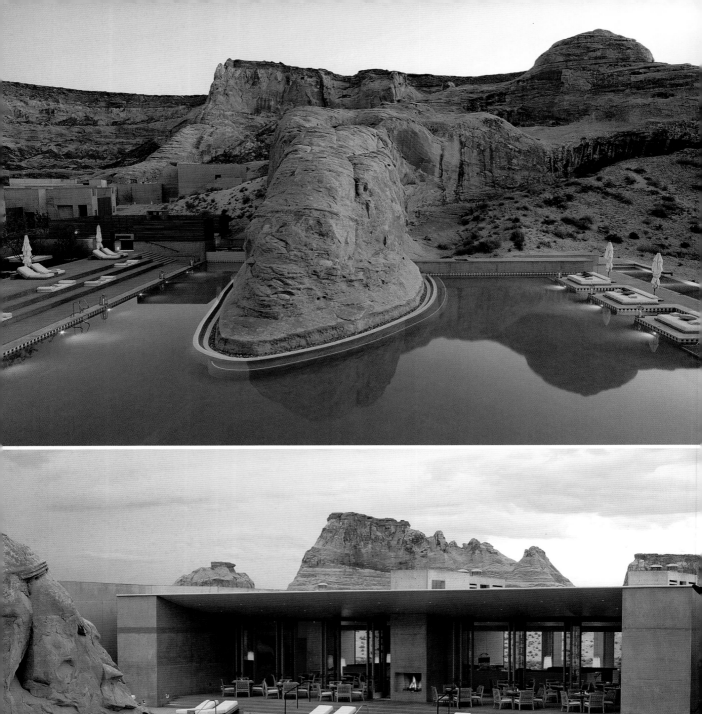

Amangiri
Canyon Point, Utah, USA

The Amangiri ("peaceful mountain"), which opened in 2009, nestles within the dramatic desertscape of southern Utah, surrounded by canyons and plateaus. The architects Marwan Al-Sayed, Wendell Burnette and Rick Joy have created buildings of concrete, stone and steel with room-height windows that merge with the natural landscape. The interiors have soft accents in wood and cream-coloured fabrics.

In der dramatischen Wüstenlandschaft Süd-Utahs wurde im Oktober 2009 das Amangiri (»friedlicher Berg«) eröffnet. Die Architekten Marwan Al-Sayed, Wendell Burnette und Rick Joy lassen die Bauten aus Beton, Stein und Stahl samt der raumhohen Fenster mit der Natur verschmelzen – innen setzen Holz sowie cremefarbene Stoffe weiche Akzente.

Entouré de canyons et de plateaux, l'Amangiri (« montagne paisible ») a ouvert ses portes en octobre 2009 dans le cadre spectaculaire du sud de l'Utah. Les architectes Marwan Al-Sayed, Wendell Burnette et Rick Joy laissent les constructions de béton, pierre et métal dotées de vastes baies vitrées fusionner avec le paysage environnant. À l'intérieur, le bois et des étoffes crème posent des accents délicats.

Amangiri
1 Kayenta Road
Canyon Point, UT 84741-285
USA
Tel. +1 435 675 3999
Fax +1 435 675 8999
reservations@amanresorts.com
and amangiri@amanresorts.com
www.amanresorts.com

LOCATION
Situated in the "Four Corners" region, where the states of Utah, Colorado, New Mexico and Arizona meet. The nearest airport is in Page, a 25-min drive south of the hotel.

RATES
Suites from $800, pool suites from $1,250, excluding breakfast.

ROOMS
34 suites, some with private pools.

FOOD
The centrepiece of the dining room is an open-plan kitchen with a wood-burning oven, where rustic, seasonal specialities are prepared.

X-FACTOR
The 7,500-square-foot spa with its walnut wood cubicles.

BOOK TO PACK
"The Border Trilogy" by Cormac McCarthy.

LAGE
Im Gebiet der »Four Corners« gelegen, wo Utah, Colorado, New Mexico und Arizona zusammentreffen. Der nächste Flughafen ist in Page, 25 Min. südlich des Hotels.

PREISE
Suite ab 590 €, Poolsuite ab 920 €, ohne Frühstück.

ZIMMER
34 Suiten, zum Teil mit privatem Pool.

KÜCHE
Herzstück des »Dining Room« ist die offene Küche mit Holzofen. Hier werden saisonale, rustikale Spezialitäten zubereitet.

X-FAKTOR
Das 2.300 qm große Spa mit Kabinen aus Walnussholz.

BUCHTIPP
»Die Border-Trilogie« von Cormac McCarthy.

SITUATION
Situé dans la région des « Four Corners », où l'Utah, le Colorado, le Nouveau-Mexique et l'Arizona se rejoignent. L'aéroport le plus proche est à Page, à 25 min au sud de l'hôtel.

PRIX
Suite à partir de 590 €, suite-piscine à partir de 920 €, sans petit-déjeuner.

CHAMBRES
34 suites, en partie avec piscine privée.

RESTAURATION
Le cœur de la salle à manger est la cuisine ouverte avec son poêle à bois. On y prépare des spécialités rustiques de saison.

LE « PETIT PLUS »
Le spa de 2300 m² équipé de cabines de noyer.

LIVRE À EMPORTER
« La Trilogie de la frontière » de Cormac McCarthy.

El Capitan Canyon

Santa Barbara, California, USA

This plot of land covered in oak and plane trees by El Capitan Creek is where the Chumash Indians once used to dance and celebrate. The camp first opened here in 1970 and was completely renovated in 2001. Guests live close to nature in comfortable wooden cabins or safari tents and can explore the Pacific coast on foot or horseback, with rafts or by bicycle.

Auf diesem von Eichenbäumen und Platanen bewachsenen Grundstück am El Capitan Creek tanzten und feierten einst die Chumash-Indianer. 1970 wurde hier dieses Camp eröffnet und 2001 rundum renoviert. Seine Gäste wohnen nahe an der Natur in komfortablen Holzhütten oder Safarizelten und erkunden die Pazifikküste beim Wandern, Radfahren, Reiten und Raften.

Jadis les indiens Chumash dansaient et célébraient leurs fêtes sur ce terrain planté de chênes et de platanes en bordure d'El Capitan Creek. Ouvert en 1970, le camp a été complètement rénové en 2001. Les clients habitent en harmonie avec la nature dans de confortables cabanes en bois ou dans des tentes safari. Randonnées à pied, à vélo, à cheval et en rafting permettent de découvrir la côte du Pacifique.

El Capitan Canyon
11560 Calle Real
Santa Barbara, CA 93117
USA
Tel. +1 805 685 3887
Fax +1 805 968 6772
info@elcapitancanyon.com
www.elcapitancanyon.com

LOCATION
Situated 20 min north of Santa Barbara
city centre and 10 min from the airport.

RATES
Tents from $135, cabins from $185
(for 2), excluding breakfast.

ROOMS
26 safari tents with double beds,
108 wood cabins (each sleeps 2–4).

FOOD
The "Canyon Market & Deli" serves
Californian-Mexican meals. The cabins
and tents have their own barbeque
areas and the cabins also have
kitchenettes.

X-FACTOR
Every Saturday from May to September
there are regular Jazz and Blues concerts.

BOOK TO PACK
"Tortilla Flat" by John Steinbeck.

LAGE
20 Min. nördlich des Zentrums von
Santa Barbara gelegen, 10 Min. vom
Flughafen der Stadt entfernt.

PREISE
Zelt ab 99 €, Hütte ab 135 € (jeweils für
2 Personen), ohne Frühstück.

ZIMMER
26 Safarizelte mit Doppelbett, 108 Holzhütten (2–4 Gäste).

KÜCHE
Der »Canyon Market & Deli« serviert
kalifornisch-mexikanische Speisen. Die
Hütten und Zelte besitzen Grillplätze, die
Hütten zudem Kitchenettes.

X-FAKTOR
Von Mai bis September finden jeden
Samstag Blues- und Jazzkonzerte statt.

BUCHTIPP
»Tortilla Flat« von John Steinbeck.

SITUATION
Situé à 20 min au nord du centre de
Santa Barbara et à 10 min de l'aéroport
de la ville.

PRIX
Tente à partir de 99 €, cabane à partir
de 135 € (chacune pour 2 personnes),
sans petit-déjeuner.

CHAMBRES
26 tentes safari avec lits pour deux
personnes, 108 cabanes en bois
(2–4 personnes).

RESTAURATION
Le « Canyon Market & Deli » sert des
plats mexicano-californiens. Les cabanes
et les tentes ont des coins-barbecue,
les cabanes possèdent en plus des
kitchenettes.

LE « PETIT PLUS »
Concerts de blues et de jazz tous les
samedis, de mai à septembre.

LIVRE À EMPORTER
« Tortilla Flat » de John Steinbeck.

Casa Malibu Inn on the Beach
Malibu, California, USA

There are only four hotels in Los Angeles that are located right on the beach – and only one hotel that owns a private beach: the Casa Malibu, whose Californian holiday atmosphere has been making guests happy since 1949. The best rooms have sundecks with a view of the Pacific, even more lovely is the "Catalina Suite", which was once Lana Turner's favourite room.

In Los Angeles gibt es nur vier Hotels, die direkt am Strand liegen – und nur ein Hotel, das einen privaten Strand besitzt: die Casa Malibu, deren kalifornisches Ferienflair schon seit 1949 Gäste glücklich macht. Die besten Räume haben Sonnendecks mit Pazifikblick – noch bezaubernder ist nur die »Catalina-Suite«, einst das Lieblingszimmer von Lana Turner.

À Los Angeles, il n'y a que quatre hôtels sur la plage et la Casa Malibu, dont la touche californienne enchantait déjà ses hôtes en 1949, est le seul à posséder une plage privée. Les meilleures chambres possèdent des terrasses avec vue sur le Pacifique – la « Suite Catalina », qui fut la chambre préférée de Lana Turner, est encore plus ravissante.

Casa Malibu Inn on the Beach
22752 Pacific Coast Highway
Malibu, CA 90265
USA
Tel. +1 310 456 2219
Fax +1 310 456 5418
casamalibu@earthlink.net
No website

LOCATION
28 miles northwest of Los Angeles airport.

RATES
Rooms from $170, breakfast included.

ROOMS
19 rooms and 2 suites. A beachfront room is a must!

FOOD
The hotel serves breakfast and offers room service midday and evenings in co-operation with a local restaurant. The staff are also happy to give tips about other local eateries.

X-FACTOR
Guests can take advantage of reduced rates at the nearby "Malibu Health & Spa".

BOOK TO PACK
"Bright Shiny Morning" by James Frey.

LAGE
45 km nordwestlich des Flughafens von Los Angeles gelegen.

PREISE
Zimmer ab 125 €, mit Frühstück.

ZIMMER
19 Zimmer und 2 Suiten. Unbedingt einen »beachfront room« buchen!

KÜCHE
Das Hotel serviert Frühstück und bietet in Kooperation mit einem nahen Restaurant mittags und abends Zimmerservice an. Zudem geben die Mitarbeiter gerne Tipps für weitere Lokale.

X-FAKTOR
Gäste profitieren von ermäßigten Tarifen im nahen »Malibu Health & Spa«.

BUCHTIPP
»Strahlend schöner Morgen« von James Frey.

SITUATION
Située à 45 km au nord-ouest de l'aéroport de Los Angeles.

PRIX
Chambre à partir de 125 €, avec petit-déjeuner.

CHAMBRES
19 chambres et 2 suites. Réserver absolument un « beachfront room » !

RESTAURATION
L'hôtel propose un petit-déjeuner et un service en chambre le midi et le soir en collaboration avec un restaurant tout proche. De plus, le personnel n'est pas avare de bonnes adresses.

LE « PETIT PLUS »
Les hôtes peuvent profiter de tarifs réduits au « Malibu Health & Spa » tout proche.

LIVRE À EMPORTER
« L. A. Story » de James Frey.

Ace Hotel Palm Springs

Palm Springs, California, USA

The designers from Atelier Ace and the studio Commune updated this 1965 Howard Johnson hotel in 2009. The atmosphere is a combination of relaxed urbanity and luxurious camping. The rooms contain vintage furniture and industrial details. Outside there are tarpaulin-shaded patios with fireplaces and hammocks.

Ein Howard-Johnson-Motel aus dem Jahr 1965 haben die Designer des Atelier Ace und des Studios Commune 2009 in dieses Hotel verwandelt, das lässig urbanes Flair und luxuriöses Camping-Ambiente verbindet. In den Zimmern findet man Vintage-Mobiliar und Industrie-Accessoires, draußen warten von Zeltplanen überspannte Patios mit Feuerstelle sowie Hängematten.

En 2009, les designers d'Atelier Ace et de Studio Commune ont métamorphosé un motel Howard Johnson de 1965 en un hôtel qui allie des accents urbains à une ambiance de camping haut de gamme. Les chambres abritent des meubles vintage et des objets industriels ; dehors, les patios recouverts de toile de tente sont dotés d'un foyer ouvert et équipés de hamacs.

Ace Hotel Palm Springs
701 East Palm Canyon Drive
Palm Springs, CA 92264
USA
Tel. +1 760 325 9900
Fax +1 760 325 7878
enquire.ps@acehotel.com
www.acehotel.com

LOCATION
Located just south of downtown Palm Springs and 110 miles from Los Angeles.

RATES
Rooms from $109, suites from $329, excluding breakfast.

ROOMS
165 rooms and 11 suites arranged around the pool area. The best rooms have private patios or gardens.

FOOD
"King's Highway" is an homage to the classic American roadside diner and the "Amigo Room" bar serves beer and cocktails.

X-FACTOR
Every Sunday there are DJs playing by the pool.

BOOK TO PACK
"The Grapes of Wrath" by John Steinbeck.

LAGE
Südlich von Downtown Palm Springs gelegen, 175 km von Los Angeles entfernt.

PREISE
Zimmer ab 80 €, Suite ab 245 €, ohne Frühstück.

ZIMMER
165 Zimmer und 11 Suiten rings um den Poolbereich. Die besten Räume haben private Patios oder Gärten.

KÜCHE
»King's Highway« ist eine Hommage ans klassische amerikanische Roadside-Diner, die »Amigo Room«-Bar serviert Bier und Cocktails.

X-FAKTOR
Jeden Sonntag legen am Pool DJs auf.

BUCHTIPP
»Früchte des Zorns« von John Steinbeck.

SITUATION
Situé au sud de Downtown Palm Springs, à 175 km de Los Angeles.

PRIX
Chambre à partir de 80 €, suite à partir de 245 €, sans petit-déjeuner.

CHAMBRES
165 chambres et 11 suites autour du bassin. Les plus belles chambres ont des patios ou des jardins privés.

RESTAURATION
« King's Highway » rend hommage aux classiques des restaurants routiers, le bar « Amigo Room » sert de la bière et des cocktails.

LE « PETIT PLUS »
Tous les dimanches, des DJ passent des disques au bord de la piscine.

LIVRE À EMPORTER
« Les Raisins de la colère » de John Steinbeck.

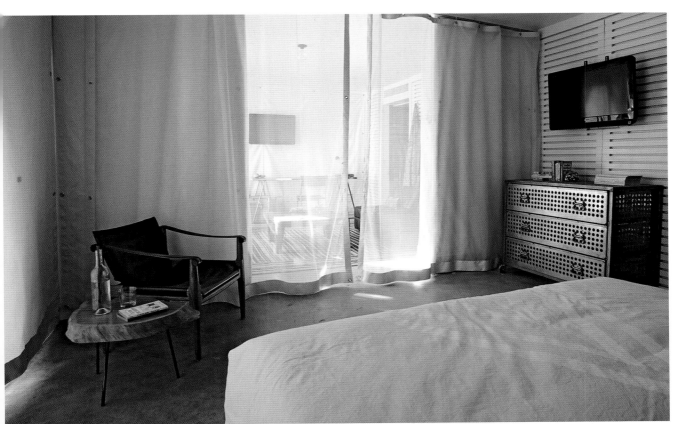

Latin America & the Caribbean

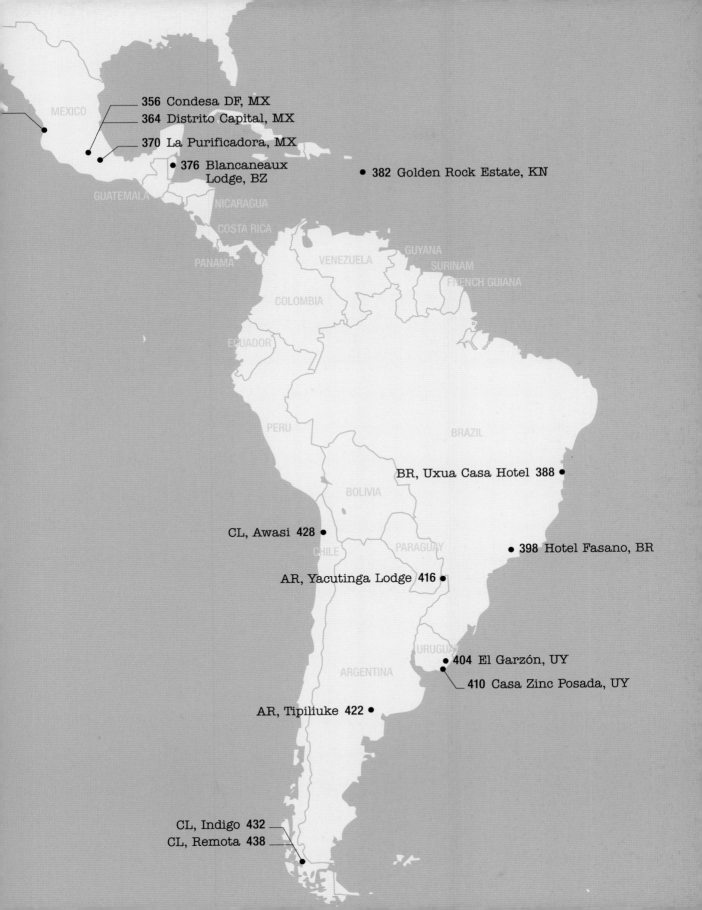

356 Condesa DF, MX
364 Distrito Capital, MX
370 La Purificadora, MX
376 Blancaneaux Lodge, BZ
382 Golden Rock Estate, KN
BR, Uxua Casa Hotel 388
CL, Awasi 428
398 Hotel Fasano, BR
AR, Yacutinga Lodge 416
404 El Garzón, UY
410 Casa Zinc Posada, UY
AR, Tipiliuke 422
CL, Indigo 432
CL, Remota 438

Verana

Puerto Vallarta, Bay of Banderas, Jalisco, Mexico

The photographer Heinz Legler and the stylist Veronique Lievre opened the Verana in the jungle above a stunning bay in 2000. Architecture and nature harmonise here perfectly. All the houses have private gardens, their interiors reflect the colours of their surroundings and they are furnished with vintage items as well as modernist classics such as George Nelson lamps.

Im Dschungel über der Bucht von Banderas haben der Fotograf Heinz Legler und die Stylistin Veronique Lievre Ende 2000 das Verana eröffnet. Natur und Architektur harmonieren hier wunderschön: Alle Häuser besitzen private Gärten; innen spiegeln sie die Farben der Umgebung wider und sind mit Vintage-Möbeln sowie modernen Lampen, z.B. von George Nelson, eingerichtet.

Le photographe Heinz Legler et la styliste Veronique Lievre ont fondé la Verana fin 2000 dans la jungle au-dessus de la baie de Banderas. Ici, la nature et l'architecture sont en harmonie : toutes les maisons possèdent des jardins privés. Reflétant à l'intérieur les couleurs de l'environnement, elles sont décorées avec des meubles vintage et des lampes modernes, comme celles créées par George Nelson.

Verana / Casa Sin Tiempo
Calle Zaragoza #449, Colonia Centro
48304 Puerto Vallarta, Jalisco Mexico
Tel. +52 322 222 0878
www.verana.com
Open from early November to early June

LOCATION
Situated 30 miles south of Puerto Vallarta and accessible only by boat from Boca de Tomatlán (30 min). From the beach you walk up through the jungle to the hotel whilst your baggage is transported by donkey.

RATES
Houses from $400, full board included. Minimum stay: 5 nights.

ROOMS
8 houses (each sleeps 2–4) and the "V House" (sleeps up to 6); no individual room bookings.

FOOD
Creative Mexican meals are served on the veranda and by the pool.

X-FACTOR
The natural cosmetics used at the spa papayas, avocados and bananas grow all around the hotel.

BOOK TO PACK
"Like Water for Chocolate" by Laura Esquivel.

LAGE
48 km südlich von Puerto Vallarta gelegen; ab Boca de Tomatlán nur per Boot erreichbar (30 Min.). Vom Strand aus wandert man ein Stück durch den Dschungel zum Hotel, das Gepäck transportieren Esel.

PREISE
Haus ab 295 €, mit Vollpension. Mindestaufenthalt 5 Nächte.

ZIMMER
8 Häuser (2–4 Gäste) und das »V House« (bis zu 6 Gäste), das als eigenständige Einheit vermietet wird.

KÜCHE
Kreative mexikanische Menüs; serviert auf der Veranda und am Pool.

X-FAKTOR
Im Spa pflegt Naturkosmetik – Papayas, Avocados und Bananen gedeihen rings ums Hotel.

BUCHTIPP
»Bittersüße Schokolade« von Laura Esquivel.

SITUATION
Situé à 48 km au sud de Puerto Vallarta ; à partir de Boca de Tomatlán, seulement accessible par bateau (30 min). Depuis la plage, il faut prévoir une petite marche à travers la jungle jusqu'à l'hôtel. Les bagages sont transportés par des ânes.

PRIX
Maison à partir de 295 €, pension complète. Séjour minimum de 5 nuits.

CHAMBRES
8 maisons (2–4 personnes) et la « V House » (jusqu'à 6 personnes), qui doit être louée entièrement.

RESTAURATION
Menus mexicains créatifs servis sur la véranda et au bord de la piscine.

LE « PETIT PLUS »
Soins naturels au spa – tout autour de l'hôtel poussent des papayes, des avocats et des bananes.

LIVRE À EMPORTER
« Chocolat amer » de Laura Esquivel.

Condesa DF

Colonia Condesa, Mexico City, Mexico

This triangular building was originally built in 1928 as an apartment block. Javier Sanchez and India Mahdavi converted it into a hotel in 2005. The distinctive building and its interior colour schemes of turquoise, brown and white bring a touch of Bohemian chic to the Condesa quarter and the hotel's roof terrace and patio are amongst the chicest hot spots in town.

1928 wurde dieses Gebäude mit triangelförmigem Grundriss als Apartmentblock entworfen – 2005 verwandelten es Javier Sanchez und India Mahdavi in ein Hotel. Die Interieurs in Türkis, Braun und Weiß bringen dabei ebenso viel Boheme und Schick ins Viertel Condesa wie das Exterieur: Patio sowie Dachterrasse zählen zu den stilvollsten Szenetreffs der Stadt.

Le bâtiment à plan triangulaire a été conçu en 1928 comme immeuble d'appartements. En 2005, Javier Sanchez et India Mahdavi l'ont transformé en hôtel bohème et chic, et ce aussi bien à l'intérieur avec des espaces dans des tonalités de turquoise, brun et blanc, qu'à l'extérieur : le patio et le toit-terrasse font partie des endroits les plus courus de la ville.

Condesa DF
Avenida Veracruz N. 102
Colonia Condesa
06700 Mexico City, D.F.
Mexico
Tel. +52 55 5241 2600
Fax + 52 55 5241 2601
contact@condesadf.com
www.condesadf.com

LOCATION
Situated in a pretty, tree-lined street full of historical buildings, 30 min from the airport.

RATES
Rooms from $175, suites from $245, excluding breakfast and taxes.

ROOMS
24 rooms and 16 suites with furniture from India Mahdavi, Patricia Urquiola and Norman Cherner. Be sure to book a room with a balcony.

FOOD
The patio restaurant serves innovative Mexican dishes, and the rooftop bar offers sushi.

X-FACTOR
The wellness area and hamam.

BOOK TO PACK
"The Labyrinth of Solitude" by Octavio Paz.

LAGE
In einer schönen baumgesäumten Straße mit historischen Bauten gelegen, 30 Min. vom Flughafen entfernt.

PREISE
Zimmer ab 130 €, Suite ab 180 €, ohne Frühstück (exkl. Steuern).

ZIMMER
24 Zimmer und 16 Suiten mit Möbeln von India Mahdavi, Patricia Urquiola und Norman Cherner. Unbedingt einen Raum mit Balkon buchen!

KÜCHE
Das Restaurant im Patio serviert innovative mexikanische Gerichte, die Bar auf dem Dach Sushi.

X-FAKTOR
Der Wellnessbereich mit Hamam.

BUCHTIPP
»Das Labyrinth der Einsamkeit« von Octavio Paz.

SITUATION
Situé dans une belle avenue bordée d'arbres et d'architectures historiques, à 30 min de l'aéroport.

PRIX
Chambre à partir de 130 €, suite à partir de 180 €, sans petit-déjeuner (taxes non comprises).

CHAMBRES
24 chambres et 16 suites avec des meubles signés India Mahdavi, Patricia Urquiola et Norman Cherner. La chambre avec balcon est un must !

RESTAURATION
Le restaurant du patio propose des plats mexicains innovants, le bar sur le toit des sushis.

LE « PETIT PLUS »
L'espace de remise en forme avec hammam.

LIVRE À EMPORTER
« Le Labyrinthe de la solitude » d'Octavio Paz.

Distrito Capital

Santa Fé, Mexico City, Mexico

The Distrito Capital hotel, which opened in 2009, is situated on eight floors of a skyscraper and affords perfect panorama views across Mexico City. The elegant black and white interior designed by Joseph Dirand are of particular note, so too the vintage furniture from designers such as Warren Platner, Eero Saarinen and Verner Panton.

Das 2009 eröffnete Hotel Distrito Capital ist auf acht Etagen eines Hochhauses untergebracht und bietet perfekte Panoramen über Mexiko-Stadt. Ebenso sehenswert ist das Interieur von Joseph Dirand – edel in Schwarz und Weiß gehalten sowie mit Vintage-Mobiliar nach Entwürfen großer Designer wie Warren Platner, Eero Saarinen und Verner Panton ausgestattet.

Ouvert en 2009, l'hôtel Distrito Capital qui occupe huit étages d'une tour, offre des vues imprenables sur la cité de Mexico. Le décor intérieur de Joseph Dirand est tout aussi remarquable – on apprécie l'élégance et la rigueur du noir et blanc et le mobilier vintage réalisé d'après des créations de grands designers tels Warren Platner, Eero Saarinen et Verner Panton.

Distrito Capital
Juan Salvador Agraz 37
Santa Fé
05300 Mexico City, D.F.
Mexico
Tel. +52 55 525 71300
Fax +52 55 525 71355
info@hoteldistritocapital.com
www.hoteldistritocapital.com

LOCATION
Located in the chic villa district of Santa Fé in the west of Mexico City. 1 hour's drive from Benito Juárez airport.

RATES
Rooms from $130, suites from $230, breakfast included.

ROOMS
17 rooms and 13 suites.

FOOD
The restaurant serves modern Mexican dishes and there is a marble bar.

X-FACTOR
The sophisticated lit pool with palm tree view and its own fireplace.

BOOK TO PACK
"The Savage Detectives" by Roberto Bolaño.

LAGE
Im schicken Viertel Santa Fé im Westen von Mexiko-Stadt gelegen. 1 Std. vom Flughafen Benito Juárez entfernt.

PREISE
Zimmer ab 95 €, Suite ab 170 €, inklusive Frühstück.

ZIMMER
17 Zimmer und 13 Suiten.

KÜCHE
Im Restaurant stehen moderne mexikanische Menüs auf der Karte; zudem gibt es eine Bar mit Marmortresen.

X-FAKTOR
Der raffiniert beleuchtete Pool mit Blick auf Palmen und einen offenen Kamin.

BUCHTIPP
»Mexikanische Novelle« von Bodo Kirchhoff.

SITUATION
Situé dans le quartier chic de Santa Fé à l'ouest de Mexico. À 1 h de route de l'aéroport Benito Juárez.

PRIX
Chambre à partir de 95 €, suite à partir de 170 €, petit-déjeuner compris.

CHAMBRES
17 chambres et 13 suites.

RESTAURATION
Le restaurant propose une cuisine mexicaine moderne ; il y a aussi un bar agrémenté d'un comptoir de marbre.

LE « PETIT PLUS »
La piscine subtilement éclairée avec vue sur des palmiers et dotée d'une cheminée.

LIVRE À EMPORTER
« Infanta » de Bodo Kirchhoff.

La Purificadora

Puebla, Mexico

In the 19th century, this was a water purification plant; in 2007, it became a hotel where purity and clarity still set the tone. The architects Ricardo and Victor Legorreta have combined the stone and wood from the original building with modern elements in glass, steel and onyx. Highly effective colour highlights are provided by purple sofas.

Im 19. Jahrhundert wurde in dieser Fabrik Wasser aufbereitet; seit 2007 ist sie ein Hotel, in dem Purismus und Klarheit noch immer alles bestimmen. Die Architekten Ricardo und Victor Legorreta haben Steine und Holz des originalen Baus wiederverwendet und mit Glas, Stahl sowie Onyx ergänzt. Die einzigen, sehr effektvollen Farbakzente setzen lila Sofas.

Au 19ᵉ siècle, le bâtiment abritait une usine d'épuration des eaux ; il a été reconverti en hôtel design tout de rigueur et de clarté en 2007. Les architectes Ricardo et Victor Legorreta ont réutilisé les pierres et le bois d'origine, complétant l'ensemble de verre, d'acier et d'onyx. La seule touche de couleur est celle des canapés violets, qui met en valeur les tonalités naturelles.

La Purificadora
Callejón de la 10 Norte 802
Paseo San Francisco, Barrio el Alto
72000 Puebla
Mexico
Tel. +52 222 309 1920
Fax +52 222 309 1949
info@lapurificadora.com
www.lapurificadora.com

LOCATION
Puebla is situated 80 miles southeast of Mexico City. The hotel in the centre of the Old Town is 20 min from Hermanos Serdán airport.

RATES
Rooms from $155, suites from $215, breakfast included.

ROOMS
23 rooms and 3 suites.

FOOD
The restaurant serves modern Mexican dishes. The hotel also has a rather chic bar.

X-FACTOR
Spectacular extras such as a glass-walled pool on the roof and log fires in the lobby.

BOOK TO PACK
"The Buried Mirror" by Carlos Fuentes.

LAGE
Puebla liegt 130 km südöstlich von Mexiko-Stadt. Das Hotel im historischen Zentrum ist 20 Min. vom Flughafen Hermanos Serdán entfernt.

PREISE
Zimmer ab 115 €, Suite ab 160 €, inklusive Frühstück.

ZIMMER
23 Zimmer und 3 Suiten.

KÜCHE
Das Restaurant serviert moderne mexikanische Menüs, zudem besitzt das Hotel eine schicke Bar.

X-FAKTOR
Spektakuläre Extras wie ein gläserner Pool auf dem Dach und offene Feuerstellen in der Lobby.

BUCHTIPP
»Die gläserne Grenze« von Carlos Fuentes.

SITUATION
Situé à 130 km au sud-est de Mexico. Édifié dans le centre historique, l'hôtel est à 20 min de l'aéroport Hermanos Serdán.

PRIX
Chambre à partir de 115 €, suite à partir de 160 €, petit-déjeuner compris.

CHAMBRES
23 chambres et 3 suites.

RESTAURATION
Le restaurant propose une version moderne de la cuisine mexicaine et l'hôtel abrite un bar chic.

LE « PETIT PLUS »
Des extras spectaculaires comme une piscine de verre sur le toit et des foyers ouverts dans le hall d'accueil.

LIVRE À EMPORTER
« La Frontière de verre » de Carlos Fuentes.

Blancaneaux Lodge

Mountain Pine Ridge Reserve, Cayo District, Belize

In the early 1980s, Francis Ford Coppola discovered an abandoned lodge in the rainforests of West Belize and converted it into a private refuge that was later to become a hotel. Since 1993, his guests have been coming to stay in the antique-furnished, straw-covered "cabañas" in the jungle and even in the famous owner's own elegant pool villa.

Im Regenwald von West-Belize entdeckte Francis Ford Coppola Anfang der 1980er eine verlassene Lodge und verwandelte sie erst in sein privates Refugium, dann in ein Hotel: Seit 1993 können seine Gäste in strohgedeckten und mit lokalen Antiquitäten eingerichteten »cabañas« im Dschungel wohnen und sogar in die elegante Poolvilla des prominenten Besitzers ziehen.

Au début des années 1980, Francis Ford Coppola a découvert dans la forêt tropicale de l'ouest du Belize un lodge abandonné qu'il a transformé en refuge privé, puis en hôtel. Depuis 1993, ses clients habitent en plein cœur de la jungle, dans des « cabañas » au toit de paille et décorées d'antiquités locales, ou dans l'élégante villa avec piscine du célèbre propriétaire.

Blancaneaux Lodge
Mountain Pine Ridge Reserve
P.O. Box B, Central Farm
Cayo District
Belize
Tel. +501 824 3878
info@coppolaresorts.com
www.coppolaresorts.com

LOCATION
Situated by Privassion Creek in the Maya Mountains; the nearest town is San Ignacio (70 miles southwest of Belize City).

RATES
Cabañas from $180 (single) and $230 (double), villa from $475, breakfast included.

ROOMS
20 cabañas and villas.

FOOD
Traditional Coppola Italian family recipes are cooked in the "Montagna Ristorante" and there is also a Guatamalan tavern.

X-FACTOR
The hikes and horseback rides to the sacred Mayan sites.

BOOK TO PACK
"Maya: Divine Kings of the Rainforest" by Nikolai Grube.

LAGE
Am Privassion Creek in den Maya Mountains gelegen; die nächste Stadt ist San Ignacio (115 km südwestlich von Belize City).

PREISE
Cabaña ab 130 € bzw. 170 € (Einzel- bzw. Doppelbelegung), Villa ab 350 €, inklusive Frühstück.

ZIMMER
20 Cabañas und Villen.

KÜCHE
Im »Montagna Ristorante« wird nach italienischen Rezepten der Coppolas gekocht, zudem gibt es ein guatemalte-kisches Lokal.

X-FAKTOR
Die Wanderungen und Ausritte zu heiligen Maya-Stätten.

BUCHTIPP
»Maya. Gottkönige im Regenwald« von Nikolai Grube.

SITUATION
Situé sur la crique de Privassion dans les montagnes mayas ; la ville la plus proche est San Ignacio (à 115 km au sud-ouest de Belize City).

PRIX
Cabaña à partir de 130 € ou 170 € (pour 1 ou 2 personnes), villa à partir de 350 €, petit-déjeuner compris.

CHAMBRES
20 cabañas et villas.

RESTAURATION
Le « Montagna Ristorante » qui prépare les plats d'après les recettes italiennes des Coppola et un restaurant guaté-maltèque.

LE « PETIT PLUS »
Les randonnées à pied et à cheval jusqu'aux sites sacrés des Mayas.

LIVRE À EMPORTER
« Mayas. Les dieux sacrés de la forêt tropicale » de Nikolai Grube.

Golden Rock Estate

Nevis, West Indies, Saint Kitts and Nevis

The Caribbean island of Nevis was once at the heart of the wealthy sugar cane industry and this plantation, built in 1801, belongs to those times. The co-owners – artist Brice Marden and his wife, Helen – have created charming guest rooms in the sugar mill tower and in the cottages. Furnishings include bamboo or mahogany beds as well as local handicrafts.

Der Karibikinsel Nevis verhalf einst die Zuckerproduktion zu Wohlstand. Aus dieser Zeit stammt diese 1801 erbaute Zuckerrohrplantage, deren Mitbesitzer der Künstler Brice Marden und seine Frau Helen sind. Sie haben im Turm einer Zuckermühle und in Cottages charmant-romantische Gästezimmer eingerichtet, die mit Bambus- oder Mahagonibetten sowie lokalem Kunsthandwerk ausgestattet sind.

L'île de Niévès a autrefois contribué à la prospérité des producteurs de sucre. C'est de cette époque (1801) que date la plantation de canne à sucre dont l'artiste Brice Marden et son épouse Helen sont les copropriétaires. Ils ont aménagé dans la tour d'un moulin à sucre et dans des cottages des chambres romantiques meublées de lits de bambou ou d'acajou et décorées d'objets artisanaux de la région.

Golden Rock Estate
P.O. Box 493
Charlestown
Nevis, West Indies
Tel. +1 869 469 3346
Fax +1 869 469 2113
goldenrockhotel@sisterisles.kn
www.golden-rock.com

LOCATION
Situated in the Nevis hills, 17 miles from the island's airport.

RATES
Cottages from $175 (single) and $200 (double), room in the tower from $235, excluding breakfast.

ROOMS
1 mill tower room and 7 garden cottages (each sleeps 1–5).

FOOD
Two restaurants serve Caribbean dishes prepared in the West Indian manner.

X-FACTOR
A drink at sunset with a view of the sun-drenched mountain that gave the hotel its name.

BOOK TO PACK
"Wide Sargasso Sea" by Jean Rhys.

LAGE
In den Hügeln von Nevis gelegen, 28 km südlich des Flughafens der Insel.

PREISE
Cottage ab 130 € bzw. 148 € (Einzel- bzw. Doppelzimmer), Übernachtung im Turm ab 173 €, ohne Frühstück.

ZIMMER
1 Zimmer im Mühlturm und 7 Garten- cottages (1–5 Gäste).

KÜCHE
In zwei Restaurants wird die karibische Küche der Westindischen Inseln serviert.

X-FAKTOR
Der Sundowner mit Blick auf den in goldenes Sonnenlicht getauchten Berg – er gab dem Hotel seinen Namen.

BUCHTIPP
»Sargassomeer« von Jean Rhys.

SITUATION
Situé dans les collines de Niévès, à 28 km au sud de l'aéroport de l'île.

PRIX
Cottage à partir de 130 € ou 148 € (chambre simple ou double), une nuit dans la tour à partir de 173 €, sans petit-déjeuner.

CHAMBRES
1 chambre dans la tour du moulin et 7 cottages (1–5 personnes) de jardin.

RESTAURATION
Deux restaurants proposent des plats de la cuisine antillaise.

LE « PETIT PLUS »
Le petit verre pris le soir en regardant la montagne dorée par la lumière du couchant – elle a donné son nom à l'hôtel.

LIVRE À EMPORTER
« La Prisonnière des Sargasses » de Jean Rhys.

Uxua Casa Hotel

Trancoso, Bahia, Brazil

The fashion designer Wilbert Das opened his own hotel in the heart of Trancoso in 2009. It comprises nine "casas" built together with indigenous craftsmen in cheerful Bahian style and decorated with a mix of Portuguese, Indian and African elements. The name "Uxua" describes this place perfectly; in the Pataxó Indian language, it means "marvellous".

Im Herzen von Trancoso hat Modedesigner Wilbert Das 2009 sein erstes eigenes Hotel eröffnet. Es umfasst neun »casas«, die in Zusammenarbeit mit einheimischen Handwerkern gebaut und im fröhlichen Stil Bahias mit portugiesischen, indianischen und afrikanischen Elementen eingerichtet wurden. Der Name des Hauses ist sein bestes Resümee: »Uxua« bedeutet in der Sprache der Pataxó-Indianer »wunderbar«.

Le designer de mode Wilbert Das a ouvert son premier hôtel en 2009 au cœur de Trancoso. Il comprend neuf « casas », construites avec l'aide des artisans locaux et décorées dans le style joyeux de Bahia avec des éléments portugais, indiens et africains. Le nom de la maison en dit long : dans la langue des Indiens Pataxó, « Uxua » signifie tout simplement « merveilleux ».

Uxua Casa Hotel
Quadrado
Trancoso, Bahia
Brazil
Tel. +55 73 3668 2277
info@uxua.com
www.uxua.com

LOCATION
Situated in Quadrado, Trancoso's main square, 15 miles south of Porto Seguro airport. The hotel also has a lounge on the beach, which is just 5 min. away.

RATES
Casa from $450 per night, breakfast included.

ROOMS
9 casas with 1–3 bedrooms.

FOOD
Fresh and delicious Bahian dishes with lots of fish and organically grown vegetables.

X-FACTOR
The pool lined with 40,000 pieces of aventurine quartz – a local stone reputed to have healing properties.

BOOK TO PACK
"Dona Flor and her Two Husbands" by Jorge Amado.

LAGE
Am Quadrado, dem Hauptplatz von Trancoso gelegen, 24 km südlich des Flughafens Porto Seguro. Am 5 Min. entfernten Strand besitzt das Hotel eine Beach Lounge.

PREISE
Casa ab 330 € pro Nacht, inklusive Frühstück.

ZIMMER
9 Casas mit 1–3 Schlafzimmern.

KÜCHE
Frische und köstliche Gerichte der regionalen Küche Bahias; mit viel Fisch und organisch angebautem Gemüse.

X-FAKTOR
Der mit 40.000 grünen Aventurin-Quarzen ausgelegte Pool – dieser lokale Stein soll heilende Kräfte haben.

BUCHTIPP
»Dona Flor und ihre zwei Ehemänner« von Jorge Amado.

SITUATION
Situé sur le Quadrado, la place principale de Trancoso, à 24 km au sud de l'aéroport de Porto Seguro. L'hôtel possède un beach lounge sur la plage qui est à 5 min.

PRIX
Une nuit dans la casa à partir de 330 €, petit-déjeuner compris.

CHAMBRES
9 casas comportant 1–3 chambres.

RESTAURATION
La cuisine de Bahia, fraîche et délicieuse beaucoup de poisson et de légumes biologiques.

LE « PETIT PLUS »
La piscine tapissée de 40 000 pierres d'aventurine verte, une variété de quartz locale censée posséder des propriétés thérapeutiques.

LIVRE À EMPORTER
« Dona Flor et ses deux maris » de Jorge Amado.

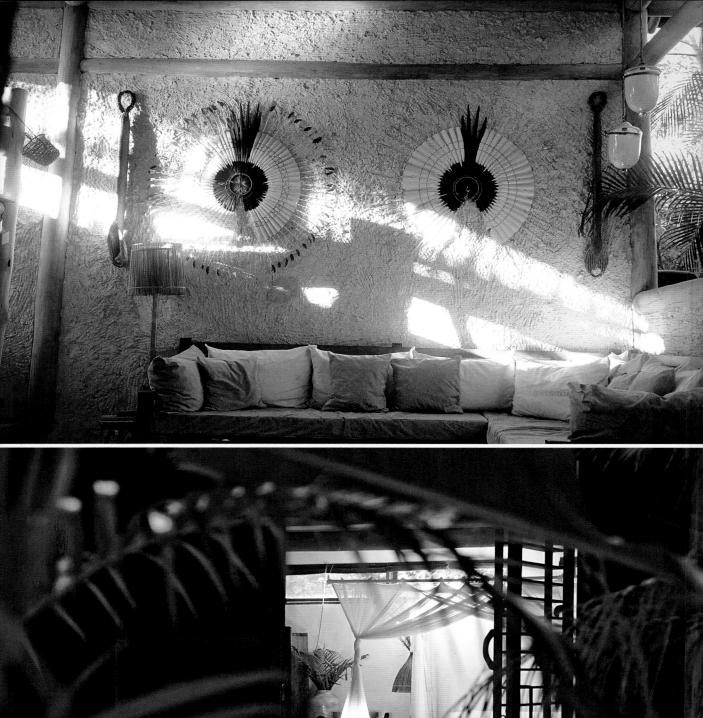

Hotel Fasano

São Paulo, Brazil

The hotelier and gastronome Fasano family built this hotel in 2003 with the spirit of 1930s and 1940s elegance combined with their own modern style. The design and sophisticated furnishings come from architects Isay Weinfeld and Marcio Kogan as well as Philippe Starck. Even the spa has designer furniture – here guests can relax on Hans Wegner loungers.

Seit 2003 lässt die Hoteliers- und Gastronomenfamilie Fasano hier den Geist der 1930er und 1940er wieder aufleben – und kombiniert ihn mit modernem Stil. Die Architekten Isay Weinfeld und Marcio Kogan sowie Philippe Starck haben den Backsteinbau und seine Zimmer sehr sophisticated ausgestattet. Selbst im Spa steht Designermobiliar – man entspannt auf Liegesesseln von Hans Wegner.

Depuis 2003, les Fasano, famille d'hôteliers et de gastronomes, font revivre ici l'esprit des années 1930 et 1940 tout en le combinant à un style moderne. Les architectes Isay Weinfeld et Marcio Kogan ainsi que Philippe Starck ont aménagé le bâtiment en briques et ses chambres avec beaucoup de sophistication. On trouve des meubles design jusque dans le spa, où l'on se détend sur des fauteuils de relaxation signés Hans Wegner.

Hotel Fasano São Paulo
Rua Vittorio Fasano 88
São Paulo-SP
01414-020
Brazil
Tel. +55 11 3896 4000
Fax +55 11 3896 4155
sp@fasano.com.br
www.fasano.com.br

LOCATION
Located in the chic Jardins quarter in the vicinity of elegant shopping streets. The nearest airports are Campo de Marte (7 miles) and Guarulhos (17 miles).

RATES
Rooms from $520, suites from $1,100, excluding breakfast.

ROOMS
81 rooms and 10 suites.

FOOD
The Fasanos originally came from Italy and their Italian restaurant is one of the best in town. There is also a jazz bar.

X-FACTOR
The lobby furnished with English and French antiques.

BOOK TO PACK
"Eleven Minutes" by Paulo Coelho.

LAGE
Im schicken Stadtteil Jardins gelegen und nahe eleganter Einkaufsstraßen. Die nächsten Flughäfen sind Campo de Marte (11 km) und Guarulhos (28 km).

PREISE
Zimmer ab 380 €, Suite ab 800 €, ohne Frühstück.

ZIMMER
81 Zimmer und 10 Suiten.

KÜCHE
Ursprünglich stammen die Fasanos aus Italien – das Restaurant ist eines der besten italienischen Lokale der Stadt. Zudem gibt es eine Jazzbar.

X-FAKTOR
Die mit Antiquitäten aus England und Frankreich eingerichtete Lobby.

BUCHTIPP
»Elf Minuten« von Paulo Coelho.

SITUATION
Situé dans le quartier chic Jardins et près d'élégantes rues commerçantes. Les aéroports les plus proches sont Campo de Marte (à 11 km) et Guarulhos (à 28 km).

PRIX
Chambre à partir de 380 €, suite à partir de 800 €, sans petit-déjeuner.

CHAMBRES
81 chambres et 10 suites.

RESTAURATION
Les Fasano venaient à l'origine d'Italie. Ceci explique pourquoi le restaurant italien est l'un des meilleurs de la ville. L'hôtel possède aussi un bar jazz.

LE « PETIT PLUS »
Le lobby décoré avec des antiquités venant d'Angleterre et de France.

LIVRE À EMPORTER
« Onze minutes » de Paulo Coelho.

El Garzón

Garzón, Maldonado, Uruguay

In 2004, the Argentinian star chef Francis Mallmann converted an old retail building in the idyllic, late 19th-century town of Garzón into this guesthouse. Guests wishing to pay repeat visits to his excellent restaurant can stay in one of the hotel rooms, which are decorated by Mallmann himself in a rustic style with a touch of the Bohemian.

In Garzón, einem Ende des 19. Jahrhunderts gegründeten idyllischen Städtchen, hat der argentinische Starkoch Francis Mallmann 2004 ein altes Ladengebäude in dieses Landhaus verwandelt. Wer das exzellente Restaurant mehrmals besuchen möchte, zieht in eines der Hotelzimmer, die Mallmann persönlich rustikal und mit einem Hauch Boheme eingerichtet hat.

À Garzón, une petite ville idyllique datant de la fin du 19e siècle, le cuisinier star argentin Francis Mallmann a transformé en 2004 un ancien magasin en maison de campagne. Celui qui apprécie la cuisine du chef peut s'installer dans une des chambres que celui-ci a décorées personnellement dans un style rustique et un peu bohème.

El Garzón Hotel & Restaurant
By Francis Mallmann & Finca
La Anita
Garzón
Uruguay
Tel. +598 410 2811
Tel. +598 410 2809
info@restaurantegarzon.com
www.restaurantegarzon.com

LOCATION
Garzón lies in the back country, northeast of Punta del Este, 25 miles from the beach resort of José Ignacio.

RATES
Rooms from $480, full board included.

ROOMS
5 rooms, all with elegant black bathrooms.

FOOD
Mallmann cooks using the old Andean "infiernillo" (little hell) technique. The dishes are brought to the table on iron grills and the accompanying wines come from the Finca La Anita in Mendoza.

X-FACTOR
The pool under the palms.

BOOK TO PACK
"A Brief Life" by Juan Carlos Onetti.

LAGE
Garzón liegt im Hinterland nordöstlich von Punta del Este, 40 km vom Badeort José Ignacio entfernt.

PREISE
Zimmer ab 355 €, inklusive Vollpension.

ZIMMER
5 Zimmer, alle mit eleganten Bädern in Schwarz.

KÜCHE
Mallmann kocht nach der alten Anden-Technik »infiernillo« (kleine Hölle) über Holzfeuer. Die Speisen werden auf heißen Eisengittern zum Tisch gebracht, die dazu servierten Weine kommen von der Finca La Anita in Mendoza.

X-FAKTOR
Der Pool unter Palmen.

BUCHTIPP
»Das kurze Leben« von Juan Carlos Onetti.

SITUATION
Garzón est situé dans l'arrière-pays, au nord-est de Punta del Este, à 40 km de la station balnéaire José Ignacio.

PRIX
Chambre à partir de 355 €, avec pension complète.

CHAMBRES
5 chambres, toutes pourvues d'une élégante salle de bain noire.

RESTAURATION
Mallmann prépare les repas sur un feu de bois selon l'ancienne technique andine dite « infiernillo » (petit enfer). Les plats sont apportés à table sur une grille chaude, les vins qui les accompagnent proviennent de la Finca La Anita à Mendoza.

LE « PETIT PLUS »
La piscine sous les palmiers.

LIVRE À EMPORTER
« La Vie brève » de Juan Carlos Onetti.

Casa Zinc Posada

La Barra, Punta del Este, Uruguay

Aaron Hojman's Trading Post shop has long enjoyed a reputation as Uruguay's best address for vintage design. At the end of 2008, Hojman opened his finest showroom yet, in the form of Casa Zinc. The family-run posada has been completely decorated with salvaged accessories from the 1890s to the 1940s, including windows from an old station in Montevideo and Art Deco furniture.

Aaron Hojmans Laden Trading Post gilt seit Jahren als Uruguays beste Adresse für Design im Vintage-Stil – Ende 2008 hat Hojman mit der Casa Zinc seinen schönsten Showroom eröffnet. Die familiär geführte Posada wurde mit Accessoires der 1890er bis 1940er ausgestattet, z.B. Fenstern von einem alten Bahnhof in Montevideo und Art-déco-Möbeln.

Trading Post, la boutique d'Aaron Hojman, est considérée depuis des années comme la meilleure adresse de l'Uruguay en ce qui concerne le design de style vintage. Hojman a inauguré Casa Zinc, son plus beau show-room, fin 2008. La posada, gérée par la famille, a été décorée avec des objets des années 1890 à 1940, tels que des fenêtres provenant d'une vieille gare de Montevideo et des meubles Art Déco.

Casa Zinc Posada
La Barra
Punta del Este
Uruguay
Tel. +598 9962 0066 (posada)
Tel. +598 42 773 003 (office)
posada@casazinc.com
www.casazinc.com

LOCATION
Located in the former fishing village of La Barra, 25 min away from Punta del Este airport.

RATES
Rooms from $130, breakfast included.

ROOMS
6 individual rooms – the "Estudio Arquitecto", reminiscent of a 1940s atelier, is particularly atmospheric.

FOOD
The breakfast is opulent and served until 4pm.

X-FACTOR
The idyllic patio with its 4-ton olive tree that came from an old estancia.

BOOK TO PACK
"Blood Pact: And Other Stories" by Mario Benedetti.

LAGE
Im ehemaligen Fischerdorf La Barra gelegen, 25 Min. vom Flughafen Punta del Este entfernt.

PREISE
Zimmer ab 95 €, inklusive Frühstück.

ZIMMER
6 individuelle Zimmer – sehr atmosphärisch ist das »Estudio Arquitecto«, das an ein Atelier der 1940er erinnert.

KÜCHE
Das Frühstück ist opulent und wird bis 4 Uhr nachmittags serviert.

X-FAKTOR
Der idyllische Patio mit seinem 4 Tonnen schweren Olivenbaum, welcher von einer alten Estancia stammt.

BUCHTIPP
»Die Gnadenfrist« von Mario Benedetti.

SITUATION
Située dans l'ancien village de pêcheurs La Barra, à 25 min de l'aéroport Punta del Este.

PRIX
Chambres à partir de 95 €, petit-déjeuner compris.

CHAMBRES
6 chambres individuelles – « l'Estudio Arquitecto » qui évoque un atelier des années 1940 a un charme fou.

RESTAURATION
Le copieux petit déjeuner est servi jusqu'à 16 heures.

LE « PETIT PLUS »
Le patio enchanteur avec son olivier de 4 tonnes qui provient d'une ancienne estancia.

LIVRE À EMPORTER
« La Trêve » de Mario Benedetti.

Yacutinga Lodge
Iguazú National Park, Argentina

The architect and expert on sustainable tourism Carlos Sandoval founded this unique eco-lodge in 2000 within a 1,400-acre private reserve in the middle of the jungle. The buildings are all made of native materials and guests play an active role in conservation by helping with activities such as tree planting and the classification of flora and fauna.

In einem 570 Hektar großen Privatreservat mitten im Dschungel gründete Carlos Sandoval, Architekt und Experte für nachhaltigen Tourismus, 2000 diese Öko-Lodge. Ihre Gebäude bestehen aus lokalen Materialien, und ihre Gäste betreiben aktiven Naturschutz – sie helfen z.B. bei Baumpflanzungen oder der Klassifizierung von Flora und Fauna.

Carlos Sandoval, architecte et expert en tourisme durable, a créé en 2000 ce lodge écologique unique en son genre dans une réserve privée de 570 hectares, située en pleine jungle. Les bâtiments ont été construits avec des matériaux locaux et les clients aident à préserver l'environnement, en plantant des arbres par exemple, ou en répertoriant la faune et la flore.

Yacutinga Lodge
Lote 7a
3371 Almirante Brown
Misiones
Argentina
Tel. +54 937 5166 4242
yacutinga@yacutinga.net
www.yacutinga.com

LOCATION
Situated in northeast Argentina, 50 miles from the Iguazú waterfalls. The lodge offers transfers from the Brazilian airport of Foz do Iguaçú and the Argentinian airport of Puerto Iguazú.

RATES
2-night packages from $473 (single room) and $1,000 (double room), full board and activities included.

ROOMS
20 rooms (2–3 beds) and 1 suite.

FOOD
Fresh local dishes made with organic products from neighbouring farmers.

X-FACTOR
The professional guides who accompany every excursion.

BOOK TO PACK
"The Aleph and Other Stories" by Jorge Luis Borges.

LAGE
Im Nordosten Argentiniens gelegen, 80 km entfernt von den Iguazú-Wasserfällen. Ab dem brasilianischen Flughafen Foz do Iguaçú sowie dem argentinischen Flughafen Puerto Iguazú bietet die Lodge Transfers an.

PREISE
Package mit 2 Nächten 545 € (Einzelzimmer) bzw. 735 € (Doppelzimmer), mit Vollpension und Aktivitäten.

ZIMMER
20 Zimmer (2–3 Betten) und 1 Suite.

KÜCHE
Frische lokale Gerichte mit organisch angebauten Produkten von umliegenden Bauernhöfen.

X-FAKTOR
Die professionellen Guides, die jede Exkursion begleiten.

BUCHTIPP
»Das Aleph« von Jorge Luis Borges.

SITUATION
Situé dans le Nord-Est de l'Argentine à 80 km des chutes d'Iguazú. L'hôtel propose le transfert depuis l'aéroport brésilien de Foz do Iguaçú et depuis l'aéroport argentin de Puerto Iguazú.

PRIX
Forfait de 2 nuits 545 € (chambre simple ou 735 € (chambre double), avec pension complète et activités.

CHAMBRES
20 chambres (2–3 lits) et 1 suite.

RESTAURATION
Plats locaux préparés avec des produits biologiques provenant des fermes voisines.

LE « PETIT PLUS »
Les guides professionnels qui se chargent de toutes les excursions.

LIVRE À EMPORTER
« L'Aleph » de Jorge Luis Borges.

Tipiliuke

San Martín de los Andes, Patagonia, Argentina

This congenial and professionally run lodge belongs to the Cerro de los Pinos estate, which was founded in 1909 by the ancestors of the current owners. It is an excellent location for fly fishing and horseback riding. Guests can also be introduced to the secrets of Argentinian animal husbandry: the estancia owns some 4,000 head of cattle.

Diese sehr herzlich und professionell geführte Lodge gehört zum Landgut Cerro de los Pinos, das die Vorfahren der heutigen Besitzer 1909 gegründet haben. Sie ist ein exzellentes Revier für Fliegenfischer und Reiter; zudem können sich Gäste in die Geheimnisse der argentinischen Tierzucht einweihen lassen – zum Viehbestand der Estancia zählen 4.000 Rinder.

Ce lodge dirigé avec beaucoup de chaleur et de professionnalisme fait partie de l'estancia Cerro de los Pinos, fondée en 1909 par les ancêtres des propriétaires actuels. Il est une adresse tout indiquée pour les pêcheurs à la mouche et les adeptes de l'équitation. Les clients peuvent par ailleurs s'initier aux secrets de l'élevage argentin puisque les troupeaux de l'estancia comptent 4000 bœufs.

Tipiliuke
San Martín de los Andes
Patagonia
Argentina
Tel. +54 2972 429 466 (lodge)
Tel. +54 11 4806 8877
(reservations)
info@tipiliuke.com
www.tipiliuke.com
Open from July to May

LOCATION
San Martín de los Andes is 2 flying hours southwest of Buenos Aires; the transfer to the lodge takes 10 min.

RATES
Single rooms from $460, double rooms from $740, full board and activities (except fishing) included.

ROOMS
9 modern yet rustic rooms in the lodge and 1 house with 5 rooms.

FOOD
Fine dining with traditional dishes and Argentinian wines.

X-FACTOR
The excursions to the old Mapuche sites.

BOOK TO PACK
"In Patagonia" by Bruce Chatwin.

LAGE
San Martín de los Andes liegt 2 Flugstunden südwestlich von Buenos Aires; der Transfer zur Lodge dauert 10 Min.

PREISE
Einzelzimmer ab 340 €, Doppelzimmer ab 545 €, mit Vollpension und Aktivitäten (ohne Fischen).

ZIMMER
9 modern-rustikale Zimmer in der Lodge, 1 Haus mit 5 Zimmern (nur als Einheit zu mieten).

KÜCHE
Hervorragend verfeinerte traditionelle Gerichte und argentinische Weine.

X-FAKTOR
Die Exkursionen zu historischen Stätten der Mapuche.

BUCHTIPP
»In Patagonien« von Bruce Chatwin.

SITUATION
San Martín de los Andes se trouve à 2 h de vol au sud-ouest de Buenos Aires ; le transfert jusqu'au lodge dure 10 min.

PRIX
Chambre simple à partir de 340 €, chambre double à partir de 545 €, avec pension complète et activités (sans la pêche).

CHAMBRES
9 chambres modernes et rustiques dans le lodge, 1 maison avec 5 chambres (à louer entièrement).

RESTAURATION
Plats traditionnels raffinés et vins argentins.

LE « PETIT PLUS »
Les excursions sur les anciens sites des Mapuches.

LIVRE À EMPORTER
« En Patagonie » de Bruce Chatwin.

Awasi

San Pedro de Atacama, Atacama Desert, Chile

There has been an oasis at San Pedro in the Atacama Desert since prehistoric times. Architect Gonzalo Domínguez and his family built the Awasi ("home") here in 2006. Inspired by traditional building techniques, they worked only with local stone, adobe and wood. The interior is regional, too: from the custom-made furniture to the handmade dolls.

In San Pedro, seit Urzeiten eine Oase in der Atacama-Wüste, gestalteten der Architekt Gonzalo Domínguez und seine Familie 2006 das Awasi (»Zuhause«). Inspiriert von traditionellen Bauweisen arbeiteten sie nur mit lokalem Stein, Lehm und Holz. Auch das Interieur stammt aus der Region – von den maßgefertigten Möbeln bis zu den handgemachten Püppchen.

C'est à San Pedro, une oasis du existant depuis des temps immémoriaux dans le désert d'Atacama, que l'architecte Gonzalo Domínguez et sa famille ont aménagé en 2006 l'Awasi « le chez-soi ». S'inspirant des constructions traditionnelles, ils ont utilisé de la pierre locale, de l'argile et du bois. Ce qui est à l'intérieur provient aussi de la région, des meubles sur mesure aux petites poupées faites à la main.

Awasi
Tocopilla 4
San Pedro de Atacama
Antofagasta
Chile
Tel. +56 55 851 460 (hotel)
Tel. +56 2 233 9641
(reservations)
info@awasi.cl
www.awasi.cl

LOCATION
San Pedro de Atacama lies at an altitude of 7,900 feet in the Atacama and 1,000 miles north of Santiago de Chile. The nearest airport is Calama and from there the hotel offers a 1-hour transfer.

RATES
Packages for 2 nights from $1,664 and $2,560 (single or double), full board and excursions included.

ROOMS
8 cottages, each sleeps 2.

FOOD
Delicious Chilean and international dishes; everything is homemade – even the bread.

X-FACTOR
The pool.

BOOK TO PACK
"Book of Questions" by Pablo Neruda.

LAGE
San Pedro de Atacama liegt 2.400 m hoch und 1.670 km nördlich von Santiago de Chile. Der nächste Flughafen ist Calama, von dort aus bietet das Hotel einen Transfer (1 Std.).

PREISE
Packages ab 2 Nächten ab 1.220 € bzw. 1.880 € (Einzel- bzw. Doppel-belegung), mit Vollpension und Ausflügen.

ZIMMER
8 Cottages für je 2 Personen.

KÜCHE
Köstliche chilenische und internationale Speisen. Alles ist hausgemacht, sogar das Brot wird selbst gebacken.

X-FAKTOR
Der Pool.

BUCHTIPP
»Der große Gesang« von Pablo Neruda.

SITUATION
San Pedro de Atacama est situé à 2400 m d'altitude et à 1670 km au nord de Santiago de Chile. L'aéroport le plus proche est Calama, un transfert est organisé jusqu'à l'hôtel (1 h de trajet).

PRIX
Forfait 2 nuits à partir de 1220 € ou 1880 € (simple ou double), avec pension complète et excursions.

CHAMBRES
8 cottages pouvant accueillir 2 personnes chacun.

RESTAURATION
Délicieux plats de la cuisine chilienne et internationale. Tout est préparé et fait sur place, même le pain.

LE « PETIT PLUS »
La piscine.

LIVRE À EMPORTER
« Chant général » de Pablo Neruda.

Indigo
Puerto Natales, Patagonia, Chile

Architect Sebastián Irarrazaval has laid out the Indigo (opened in 2006) in the symbolic form of a journey, with many stairs, ramps and bridges. The hotel is also an homage to Puerto Natales: typical local materials such as wood and steel have been used to develop a striking graphic design, and the signage on the façade, walls and doors is reminiscent of the shipping containers found in the harbour.

Mit vielen Treppen, Rampen und Brücken hat Architekt Sebastián Irarrazaval das Indigo (2006) als eine Art Reise angelegt – und zugleich als Hommage an Puerto Natales. So verwendete er ortstypische Materialien wie Holz sowie Stahl und entwickelte ein markantes Grafikdesign: Die Beschriftungen von Fassade, Wänden und Türen erinnern an die der Schiffscontainer im Hafen.

L'architecte Sebastián Irarrazaval a conçu l'Indigo (2006) comme un voyage, avec de nombreux escaliers, des rampes et des ponts, mais il a aussi rendu hommage à Puerto Natales. Il a ainsi utilisé des matériaux tels que le bois et l'acier et élaboré un design marquant : l'aspect de la façade, des murs et des portes évoque celui des conteneurs dans le port.

Indigo
Ladrilleros 105
Puerto Natales
Patagonia
Chile
Tel. +56 61 413 609
info@indigopatagonia.com
www.indigopatagonia.com

LOCATION
Puerto Natales lies by the "Fjord of Last Hope". There are direct flights from Santiago de Chile (the airport is 5 min away), or you can fly to Punta Arenas, 150 miles southwest, and the hotel will arrange to collect you.

RATES
Rooms from $196, suites from $257, breakfast included.

ROOMS
28 rooms and 1 suite.

FOOD
Patagonian fish, beef and lamb as well as fine French pastries.

X-FACTOR
The open-air jacuzzis on the roof.

BOOK TO PACK
"My Invented Country" by Isabel Allende.

LAGE
Puerto Natales liegt am »Fjord der letzten Hoffnung«. Von Santiago de Chile gibt es Direktflüge dorthin (der Flughafen ist 5 Min. vom Hotel entfernt), oder man fliegt ins 250 km südwestlich gelegene Punta Arenas und wird dort abgeholt.

PREISE
Zimmer ab 145 €, Suite ab 190 €, inklusive Frühstück.

ZIMMER
28 Zimmer und 1 Suite.

KÜCHE
Fisch, Rind und Lamm aus Patagonien sowie feine französische Backwaren.

X-FAKTOR
Die Open-Air-Jacuzzis auf dem Dach.

BUCHTIPP
»Mein erfundenes Land« von Isabel Allende.

SITUATION
Puerto Natales est situé dans le fjord « Ultima Esperanza ». Vols directs au départ de Santiago de Chile (l'aéroport est à 5 min de l'hôtel). Un transport à l'hôtel est organisé à l'aéroport de Punta Arenas, à 250 km au sud-ouest.

PRIX
Chambre à partir de 145 €, suite à partir de 190 €, petit-déjeuner compris.

CHAMBRES
28 chambres et 1 suite.

RESTAURATION
Du poisson, du bœuf et de l'agneau de Patagonie ainsi que des pâtisseries fines françaises.

LE « PETIT PLUS »
Les jacuzzis en extérieur sur le toit.

LIVRE À EMPORTER
« Mon Pays réinventé » d'Isabel Allende.

Remota

Puerto Natales, Patagonia, Chile

In his design for this hotel, which opened in 2005, architect Germán del Sol was inspired by how Patagionian stables offer protection from the elements. The fascinating façade and grass-covered roofs shelter light, airy rooms with geometric-style furniture made from local Lenga wood and fabrics in warm yellow tones.

Beim Entwurf für dieses 2005 eingeweihte Hotel ließ sich Architekt Germán del Sol von patagonischen Ställen inspirieren, die Schutz vor Wind und Wetter bieten. Hinter der faszinierenden Fassade und unter grasbewachsenen Dächern hat er helle Räume mit geometrisch wirkenden Möbeln aus lokalem Lenga-Holz sowie Stoffen in warmen Gelbtönen eingerichtet.

Pour concevoir cet hôtel ouvert en 2005, l'architecte Germán del Sol s'est inspiré des étables patagoniennes qui protègent du vent et des intempéries. Les façades captivantes et les toitures végétalisées dissimulent des espaces clairs abritant des meubles aux formes géométriques en bois de lenga local et des étoffes aux chaudes teintes jaunes.

Remota
Ruta 9 Norte, km 1.5
Huerto 279
Puerto Natales
Patagonia
Chile
Tel. +56 61 414 040 (hotel)
Tel. +56 2 387 1500
(reservations)
info@remota.cl
www.remota.cl

LOCATION
Situated by a fjord near Puerto Natales. There are direct flights from Santiago de Chile to either Puerto Natales or Punta Arenas, 150 miles to the southeast (on Wednesdays and Saturdays there is a free transfer from the airport to the hotel).

RATES
Packages for 2 nights from $1,480 (single) and $2,064 (double), full board and excursions included.

ROOMS
72 rooms.

FOOD
The ingredients of the hearty meals are supplied by local farms.

X-FACTOR
The hotel was built in a sustainable manner and saves both energy and water.

BOOK TO PACK
"Patagonia Express" by Luis Sepúlveda.

LAGE
Am Fjord bei Puerto Natales gelegen. Von Santiago de Chile aus fliegt man direkt nach Puerto Natales oder ins 250 km südöstlich gelegene Punta Arenas (mittwochs und samstags kostenloser Transfer vom Flughafen zum Hotel).

PREISE
Packages ab 2 Nächten ab 1.085 € bzw. 1.515 € (Einzel- bzw. Doppelbelegung), mit Vollpension und Ausflügen.

ZIMMER
72 Zimmer.

KÜCHE
Die Zutaten für die herzhaften Gerichte liefern Bauernhöfe der Region.

X-FAKTOR
Das Hotel wurde nachhaltig gebaut und spart Strom und Wasser.

BUCHTIPP
»Patagonien Express« von Luis Sepúlveda.

SITUATION
Situé dans le fjord de Puerto Natales. Vol direct au départ de Santiago de Chile ou vol pour Punta Arenas à 250 km au sud-est (mercredi et samedi, transfert gratuit à l'hôtel).

PRIX
Forfait 2 nuits à partir de 1085 € ou 1515 € (simple ou double), avec pension complète et excursions.

CHAMBRES
72 chambres.

RESTAURATION
Les produits utilisés pour préparer les plats savoureux proviennent des fermes de la région.

LE « PETIT PLUS »
L'hôtel répond aux critères du développement durable et économise l'eau et l'électricité.

LIVRE À EMPORTER
« Patagonia Express » de Luis Sepúlveda.

Photo Credits / Fotonachweis
Crédits photographiques

Europe

Juvet Landskapshotell
p. 14–19 supplied by the hotel (Knut Slinning &
Jan Olav Jensen, p. 17 bottom by Per Eide)

Fabriken Furillen
p. 20–25 Johan Hellström, supplied by the hotel

The Bath Priory
p. 26–29 supplied by the hotel

Villa Augustus
p. 30–33 supplied by the hotel

Manoir de Lébioles
p. 34–39 Eliophot, supplied by the hotel

Grand Hotel Heiligendamm
p. 40–45 supplied by the hotel

Romantik-Hotel Spielweg
p. 46–53 Daniel Schäfer/TASCHEN GmbH
www.danielschaeferphoto.com

Schloss Elmau
p. 54–59 supplied by the hotel

berge
p. 60–65 supplied by Nils Holger Moormann GmbH

Hotel Miramonte
p. 66–71 vyhnalek.com, supplied by the hotel

Nebesa
p. 72–75 supplied by the hotel

Hotel Krafft
p. 76–79 supplied by the hotel (p. 76–77, 79 by
Dirk Altenkirch, p. 78 by Dejan Jovanovic)

Château Le Rosey
p. 80–85 Pierre Bouvier, supplied by the hotel

Whitepod
p. 86–89 supplied by the hotel

Le Château des Alpilles
p. 90–95 supplied by the hotel (p. 90, 92–95 by Gilles
Martin-Raget, p. 91 by José Nicolas)

Hôtel Le Corbusier
p. 96–101 Daniel Schäfer/TASCHEN GmbH
www.danielschaeferphoto.com

Gasthof Krone
p. 102–105 supplied by the hotel

Four Seasons Hotel Firenze
p. 106–111 supplied by the hotel (p. 106–107,
110 top right, bottom left & right, 111 by Barbara Kraft,
p. 108, 109 bottom, 110 top left by Matthias Hamel,
p. 109 top by Francesco Bedin)

Hospes Maricel
p. 112–117 supplied by the hotel

Hotel Hurricane
p. 118–121 Photography Albert Font
Styling & Production Susana Ocaña
www.albertfont.com
www.susanaocanya.com

Pousada de Amares
p. 122–127 supplied by Pousadas de Portugal

Belvedere Hotel
p. 128–135 supplied by the hotel

Atami Hotel
p. 136–141 Daniel Schäfer/TASCHEN GmbH
www.danielschaeferphoto.com

Africa & the Middle East

Hôtel Nord-Pinus Tanger
p. 144–151 COTE SUD, Bernard Touillon, Cécile Vaiarelli

Hôtel La Mamounia
p. 152–157 supplied by the hotel

Ksar Char-Bagh
p. 158–165 supplied by the hotel (p. 158, 161 by Manuel
Zublena, p. 159, 162 bottom by J. S. Ramos, p. 160, 163
bottom by Nicole Grandsire-Levillair, p. 162 top by J. B.
Yaguiyan, p. 163 top, 164–165 by Patrice de Grandry)

Msambweni Beach House
p. 166–173 supplied by the hotel (p. 166–170, 171 top,
172 top, 173 by Eddy Van Gestel, p. 171 bottom by Frederik
Vanderhoeven, p. 172 bottom by Fabien Raes)

Constance Lodge
p. 174–181 supplied by the hotel

Zarafa Camp
p. 182–185 Dana Allen, supplied by Wilderness Safaris

Ulusaba
p. 186–191 supplied by Ulusaba/Virgin Limited Edition

Kensington Place
p. 192–195 Reto Guntli
www.zapaimages.com

Al Mamlouka
p. 196–199 Philip Lee Harvey
www.philipleeharvey.com

Evason Ma'In Hot Springs
p. 200–205 supplied by the hotel

Asia

North America

Latin America & the Caribbean

Imprint

To stay informed about upcoming TASCHEN titles, please request our magazine at www.taschen.com/magazine or write to TASCHEN, Hohenzollernring 53, D-50672 Cologne, Germany; contact@taschen.com; Fax: +49-221-254919. We will be happy to send you a free copy of our magazine, which is filled with information about all of our books.

Compiled, Edited & Layout
Angelika Taschen, Berlin

General Project Manager
Stephanie Paas, Cologne

Editorial Assistant
Nina Schumacher, Cologne

Texts
Christiane Reiter, Hamburg

English Translation
Sophie Lovell, Berlin

French Translation
Thérèse Chatelain-Südkamp, Cologne
Michèle Schreyer, Cologne

Design
Daniel Siciliano Bretas, Cologne

Lithograph Manager
Thomas Grell, Cologne

Front Endpaper
Hôtel Le Corbusier, Marseilles, France
Photo: Daniel Schäfer/TASCHEN GmbH
www.danielschaeferphoto.com

Back Endpaper
Brassiere Beach, Prachuabkirikhan, Thailand
Photo: Mirjam Bleeker
www.mirjambleeker.nl

Page 2
Brassiere Beach, Prachuabkirikhan, Thailand
Photo: Mirjam Bleeker
www.mirjambleeker.nl

Page 8
Belvedere Hotel, Mykonos, Greece
Photo: supplied by the hotel

Printed in Italy
ISBN 978-3-8365-1970-0